P9-DNU-681

American Constitutionalism
Heard Round the World,
1776–1989

American Constitutionalism Heard Round the World, 1776–1989

A Global Perspective

George Athan Billias

NEW YORK UNIVERSITY PRESS
New York and London

NEW YORK UNIVERSITY PRESS
New York and London
www.nyupress.org
© 2009 by George Athan Billias
All rights reserved

Library of Congress Cataloging-in-Publication Data
Billias, George Athan, 1919–
American constitutionalism heard round the world, 1776–1989 :
a global perspective / George Athan Billias.
p. cm.
Includes bibliographical references and index.
ISBN-13: 978-0-8147-9107-3 (cl : alk. paper)
ISBN-10: 0-8147-9107-7 (cl : alk. paper)
1. Constitutional history—United States. 2. Constitutional history.
3. Constitutional law—United States. 4. Constitutional law.
5. World politics—To 1900. 6. World politics—1900–1945.
7. World politics—1945–1989. 8. Civilization, Modern—
American influences. I. Title.
KF4541.B56   2009
346.7302'9—dc22   2009005946

New York University Press books are printed on acid-free paper,
and their binding materials are chosen for strength and durability.
We strive to use environmentally responsible suppliers and materials
to the greatest extent possible in publishing our books.

Manufactured in the United States of America

10 9 8 7 6 5 4 3 2 1

Contents

Acknowledgments

My vision of the republic of letters is broader than most. It acquired an international dimension when not only American colleagues but also foreign scholars came to my assistance. Time as well as space was involved as I became more aware of how much I relied on the findings of past scholars. The borders of my republic expanded further when individuals from other institutions of higher learning—universities, research centers, and foundations—contributed to the completion of this book. Finally, the boundaries of my republic were enlarged when I realized once again the tremendous importance of personal relationships—family, friends, and colleagues—as well as professional affiliations. They provide the emotional safety net without which no scholar can work. To these dedicated citizens in my republic of letters, I welcome this opportunity to express my heartfelt thanks.

Three friends and fellow historians in Worcester—Peter Onuf, Ronald Petrin, and Robert Kolesar—helped get the project under way in a brownbag seminar at Clark University. Peter continued to contribute handsomely after leaving Worcester Polytechnic Institute for the University of Virginia. A bold scholar and ebullient friend, he read the entire manuscript, critiqued chapters, and changed the parameters of the project as originally conceived.

Other gifted scholars contributed generously by reading the whole manuscript at various stages. Bernard Bailyn asked to see my first draft while working on his *To Begin the World Anew*. After performing the heroic task of plowing through fifteen hundred pages of raw manuscript, he offered useful suggestions and encouragement. Stanley Katz, whose grasp of American constitutionalism abroad is formidable among scholars worldwide, made searching criticisms and graciously shared his knowledge. Francis Couvares, a former Clark colleague, offered many astute insights, applied his exceptional editing skills, and suggested a major reorganization critical to the completion of the project. Herbert Bass, a former colleague at the University of Maine who had helped me many times before, made stylistic revisions and additions that allowed the narrative to emerge with greater clarity. Paul Lucas, a current Clark colleague, taught me much about comparative history, as befits a student of Robert R. Palmer, and corrected some of my misconceptions. Martin Ridge, the late director of research at the Huntington Library and the one-time editor of the *Journal of American History*, went over an early draft with his blue pencil. Mark Tushnet was kind enough to comb the text from his perspective of comparative legal history and to make an incisive critique. Robert Middlekauf was helpful by giving suggestions on where I might condense material. Alden Vaughan, a fellow Columbia PhD and longtime comrade, skillfully edited a late version with scrupulous care. Gerald Grob, my best friend and former Clark colleague with whom I have collaborated in the past, went over the final copy for glaring errors and responded with his usual dry and sly humor.

Besides those who read the entire manuscript, I am indebted to other scholars who went over portions of the work. Some of the greatest historians of early American history of this generation responded generously by reading parts of my manuscript dealing with their area of expertise. Among those who unselfishly took time from their own research were: Gordon Wood, Michael Kammen, Jack Greene, John Reid, Richard B. Bernstein, Richard D. Brown, Stanley Kutler, Herbert Johnson, Richard McCormick, and Stanley Elkins. I was fortunate to have America's most distinguished world historian, William McNeill, give me the benefit of his great store of learning. The late Milton Klein, whose friendship stretched for fifty-six years, deserves special mention for reading and editing much of what I wrote.

Another category of scholars contributed by commenting on countries or regions about which they had special knowledge: Alan Spitzer (France), Paul Cohen (modern Europe), Daniel Borg (Germany), John Dower (Japan), Lawrence Beer (Japan), Keith Rosenn (Latin America), Thomas Skidmore (Latin America), Pnina Lahav (Israel), Shlomo Slonim (Israel), John Iatrides (Greece), and Paul Ropp (China).

To Scott Gerber I am indebted for bringing my manuscript to the attention of New York University Press and for reading and editing several key chapters. I am obligated also to three members of the staff of the New York University Press, Deborah Gershenowitz, Gabrielle Begue, and Despina Papazoglou Gimbel for being so very helpful in textual editing and bringing the book to final form.

In completing the book, I am pleased to acknowledge the support of a number of institutions that enabled me to pursue research during the twenty-four years this work was in the making. In this regard, I am deeply indebted to the National Endowment for the Humanities for two fellowships and one from the Huntington Library. The Exxon Educational Foundation and Earhart Foundation also contributed grants.

Clark University has my great gratitude for funds provided by the Jacob and Frances Hiatt Chair in History which I held from 1983 to 1989. Financial support also was available from the Chester and Shirley Bland Research Fund. Administrators, particularly the current president, John Bassett, and his predecessors created a hospitable environment that encouraged research. Clark colleagues in the history department—Paul Lucas, Dan Borg, Doug Little, Drew McCoy, Paul Ropp, and Wim Klooster—whom I admire and whose friendship I treasure always were kind and responsive to my many queries. Graduate and undergraduate students in my research seminar on the U.S. Constitution provided skeptical listeners on whom I tried out ideas in the "elbow teaching" for which Clark is known. Other Clark colleagues helped by translating into English those foreign-language materials with which I was not familiar. The superb staff of the Goddard Library, including the magnanimous Mary Hartman, Irene Walch, Edward McDermott, Rachael Shea, Holly Howes, Anne Leroy, Gladys Bowker, and Helen Cohane, remained patient and gracious despite my repeated requests. Librarian Gwendolynne Arthur and archivist Mott Linn provided other assistance. Two departmental secretaries, Trudy Powers and Diane Fenner, treated me over the years with greater kindness and consideration than I deserved.

Although I have no formal affiliation with Harvard University, I am deeply indebted to that great institution for many courtesies, especially the encouragement offered by Oscar Handlin, one of its most outstanding scholars of American history. The holdings of Harvard's Widener Library and the International Legal Studies Library were crucial to my research, and their staffs were both cordial and competent. I benefited also from the holdings and staff of two other great research libraries, the American Antiquarian Society and the Huntington Library. The Richter Library and the Law Library of the University of Miami extended similar professional courtesies.

I believe firmly that family and friends profoundly affect a scholar's life and work in mysterious ways that are not always obvious to the eye. Anyone who has undertaken a long-term project knows that without the unstinting love, encouragement, and support provided by those with whom one lives most intimately, no work of this scope can be completed. I gratefully acknowledge the constant affection and attention members of my family have bestowed on me. Although listed last, they know that they come first in my heart.

To Margaret Rose Neussendorfer, this book is humbly dedicated for the love, joy, and beauty she brought into my life. Heine's lines, reflecting her German heritage, describe her sparkling presence better than can any words of mine:

You are like a flower
So beloved, beautiful, and pure.

Margaret's greatest gift, her love, made possible what Shakespeare called the "marriage of true minds." As a scholar, she challenged me in stimulating dialogues; as an editor, she honed my writing; and as a beloved, caring wife, she inspired me to soldier on when my spirits flagged. Without her, this book would never have been published.

My creative children—Stephen, grappling with the writer's craft as screenwriter, playwright, and novelist; Athan, producing state-of-the-art synthesizers used throughout the world; and Nancy, a philosophy professor and publishing scholar—prompted me by their example to follow Browning's exhortation that "man's reach should exceed his grasp." Their spouses, Stephen's Bela Breslau and Athan's Keiko Ikeda have been a warm source of support. As for my promising grandchildren—Scott Athan, Alisha Nancy, and Sophia Rachel—this book was really written for them, in the hope that they might live in a world with greater respect for democracy, the rule of law, human rights, and other humane values ingrained in American constitutionalism.

Preface

American constitutionalism represents this country's greatest gift to human freedom. This book demonstrates how its ideals, ideas, and institutions influenced different peoples, in different lands, and at different times for more than two hundred years. But the story of its influence abroad remains largely untold.[1]

This oversight is not for lack of scholars addressing the subject but for their narrow definition of two key terms: "American constitutionalism" and "influence." Most writers have equated American constitutionalism solely with the U.S. Constitution, one being viewed as the written expression of the other. To them, the measure of influence is the degree to which foreign constitutionalists copied this or that specific feature from the American charter. Not surprisingly, such scholars have concluded that the influence of American constitutionalism abroad is, in the words of one, "shallow and unstable."[2]

American constitutional influence is, however, more substantial and stable than critics have alleged. The complete expression of American constitutionalism derives not from a single document but rather from a collection of six texts written between 1776 and 1791. Besides the U.S. Constitution, these include the Declaration of Independence, the first state constitutions, the Articles of Confederation, *The Federalist*, and the Bill of Rights. All reflect the revolutionary republican constitutionalism of the founding era and articulate the principles of American constitutionalism. That decade and a half remains the greatest creative period of constitutional thought in all of American history: never again did the country's thinkers achieve such brilliance.

Nor has the meaning of the term *influence* been fully understood. *Influence* is as often indirect as direct and more subtle than obvious. The concepts of governance contained in the six seminal documents served not only as models for foreign constitutionalists and but also as *catalysts*, motivating them to reconsider their options. Carl J. Friedrich, a distinguished political scientist, described American influence best when he observed that "American constitutionalism's greatest impact occurred *not* by having American institutions taken over lock, stock, and barrel, but by stimulating men into thinking out the various alternatives confronting them."[3]

Evidence for tracing influence may be found in a wide range of sources: the transnational history of ideas, foreign translations of American constitutional documents, records of foreign constitutional conventions, writings of major thinkers abroad who publicized American ideas, and exchanges between American constitutionalists and their foreign counterparts. But such sources raise a recurring problem: how to distinguish the influence of American precedents from that of other constitutional practices. At what point, for example, does resemblance indicate not influence but a simple parallelism? Given the absence of written records in many instances, it is difficult to discover precisely how American ideas and institutions shaped directly or indirectly the constitutionalisms of other countries. Nonetheless, with careful analysis, it is possible to determine with a fair degree of accuracy where such influence occurred.

Viewing American constitutionalism from a perspective outside of American history and as an extension of European history is one way of overcoming the parochial and nationalistic tendencies of some American scholars.[4] To approach the study from this viewpoint, as William H. McNeill, the eminent world historian, reminds us, is not to diminish but to enrich it:

> Looking at the history of this nation as part of a larger process of European expansion may seem calculated to deprive the United States of its uniqueness. But appropriately moderated to recognize both differences and uniformities, it seems . . . this perspective provides a far more adequate and comprehensive vision of our past than anything older nationalistic histories of liberty and prosperity had to offer. It puts the United States back into the world as one of a family of peoples and nations similarly situated with respect to the old centers of European civilization.[5]

This call for a broader perspective may help prevent the provincialism that has sometimes led to an overemphasis on American exceptionalism: the idea that America is unique, distinctive, and fundamentally different from Europe and the rest of the world.

American constitutionalism has always been part of the much larger tradition called Western constitutionalism. Composed of a combination of Britain's long constitutional heritage, America's quasi-independent constitutionalism, and France's novel constitutionalism emerging from the French Revolution, this constitutional cohort held sway throughout much of the Western world for more than two centuries. Although modern Western constitutionalism developed during America's revolutionary era, it was an integral part of the history of the expansion of Europe, which some historians refer to as the "Europeanization of the world."[6] Although the three nations did not always maintain friendly relations, their constitutional values remained remarkably similar. They espoused liberal constitutional democracy, the rule of law, and recognition of individual rights. Within this constitutional constellation, however, the United States remained a subordinate partner until it became a superpower in the mid-twentieth century and assumed firm leadership.

The book is divided into two parts. Part 1 deals with the definitions of "constitution" and "constitutionalism." Employing a documentary history methodology, it introduces each of the six documents, demonstrating how they contributed separately and collectively to American constitutionalism. More than that of any other single document, the Declaration's egalitarian spirit touched the lives of American citizens at home, even if it initially excluded African Americans, Native Americans, women, and other socially disadvantaged groups. Abroad, the Declaration sometimes determined the actual wording of foreign constitutions, but even when it did not, it often inspired and informed the ideas of the men drafting them. The first American state constitutions were responsible for four remarkable political "inventions" that became norms for worldwide practices: the idea of a written constitution, the constituent constitutional convention, the process for ratifying a constitution, and the procedure for amending one. From the Articles of Confederation came the beginnings of constitutional federalism, a solution useful in countries with diverse regions, populations, and cultures. The Constitution itself contributed three monumental institutions to subsequent worldwide debates regarding governance: presidentialism, federalism, and judicial review. *The Federalist*, always more a commentary than a blueprint, taught foreign constitutionalists much about reconciling national power with social diversity and personal liberty. The bills of rights in the American state and federal constitutions, along with the bill of rights traditions in Britain and France, profoundly influenced constitution makers abroad.

Part 2, which forms the main body of this book, is organized by time and space. It traces the influence of American constitutionalism abroad

from the time of the Declaration to the disintegration of the Soviet empire in 1989. Emerson's memorable phrase about the opening shot of the
Revolution being "heard round the world" provides both a meaningful title and a way of dividing that long era into seven peak periods designated
as "echoes."

The first echo (1776–1800) launched a round of American-influenced
constitutions in northwestern Europe and its hinterlands. In the second
echo, beginning in 1811, Latin American and Caribbean revolutions produced a rash of constitutions in the newly independent republics in that
region. Europe's 1848 revolutions resulted in the appearance of similar
documents in the third echo, and America's acquisition of a colonial empire after the Spanish-American War led to the creation of new constitutions comprising the fourth echo. A series of new charters in the post–
World War I era made up the fifth echo. During the sixth echo—World
War II and its aftermath (1945 to 1974)—the global influence of American constitutionalism reached a crescendo. The seventh echo (1974–1989)
exceeded even that climax when more countries than ever before made
transitions from nondemocratic regimes to constitutional democracies.

Western constitutionalism was transformed during the seventh echo. It
had flourished after 1776 (along with its American component) as countries worldwide emulated the West and its constitutional democracy. Following the defeat of fascism in World War II, Western constitutionalism
underwent a significant change when the United States assumed leadership. The American model found itself facing a new challenge from the
socialist model based on Marxist–Leninist communism that dominated
large areas of the non-Western world. Throughout the cold war, the two
models battled for world supremacy, but in 1989, communist regimes in
Europe began collapsing as many countries became constitutional democracies. That year was a major turning point in global history, when the
forces of democracy exceeded those of autocracy for the first time. Two of
the world's great revolutions, the American in 1776 and the European in
1989, served as bookends to indicate the course that American constitutionalism had taken.

American Constitutionalism Heard Round the World concludes on a
note of caution rather than the celebratory tone adopted by triumphalist
scholars who trumpeted 1989 as the definitive victory for constitutional
democracy. They claimed that it would become universal and continue in
perpetuity. In contrast, this book argues that the influence of American
constitutionalism has always been limited despite its impressive spread

worldwide. Indeed, when democratizing countries sought guidance on constitutionalism, they often turned to the British or French models. Even when they resorted to the American model, the influence was frequently indirect, resulting in hybrid constitutions. Indigenous political traditions also sometimes strongly resisted assimilation. Nor has the story of American constitutionalism abroad been a validation of Whig history, which views progress as an engine of change moving inevitably on an onward and upward trajectory. In fact, the influence of American constitutionalism has both waxed and waned over time. Vast regions of the world, moreover, such as those where Confucian and Islamic cultures prevail, have resisted the simple adoption of the American constitutional model or European Enlightenment ideas. Although the late twentieth century witnessed an unprecedented growth of constitutional democracies, there is no way to predict whether American constitutional influence will continue to expand in the foreseeable future. Despite such caveats, there can be little doubt that the influence of American constitutionalism abroad was profound in the past and remains a remarkable contribution to humankind's search for freedom under a system of laws.[7]

PART I

Definitions

1

Of Constitutions and Constitutionalisms

On a chilly day in late November 1989, Zdeněk Janíček, dressed in grimy overalls, rose to address a rally of his fellow Prague brewery workers. Janíček and his listeners were among the several million in Czechoslovakia who had walked off their jobs in a two-hour general strike that had brought the country to a standstill. They were demanding not higher wages and improved working conditions but more democracy and an end to the Communist Party's monopoly on political power. In his speech, Janíček quoted from America's Declaration of Independence. There in Prague, thousands of miles away and more than two centuries after Thomas Jefferson asserted the unalienable rights of all men to life, liberty, and the pursuit of happiness, his words were once again called into service—as they had been by so many speakers in so many lands over so many years—to inspire, to instruct, and ultimately to empower. "Americans," Janíček observed, "understood these rights more than 200 years ago. We are only learning to believe that we are entitled to the same rights."[1]

What could more powerfully attest to the continuing appeal, relevance, and influence of one of the greatest documents of American and, for that matter, global history? What made the Declaration such a worldwide document was its inspiring statement of political principles and its status as a founding text. It proclaimed to the world the appearance of a new independent state taking its place "among the powers of the earth." Had American independence not been achieved, or the federal union not survived, the Declaration would not have had such global impact.

David Armitage, Harvard historian, voiced his conviction in his masterful study of the Declaration that the first paragraph emphasizing the "rights of states" under international law was of greater historical significance than the natural "rights of individuals" stressed in the second paragraph ("all men are created equal"). The Declaration thus provided a model, he pointed out, for other proclamations of independence by new states. Today more than half the countries in the world have followed America's lead by making such declarations of independence, thereby changing the course of global history from a world of empires in 1776 to the modern world of nation-states.[2]

Yet as important as it was and remains, the Declaration was only the first of six documents produced by America's founders in a fifteen-year burst of brilliance, never since equaled, that addressed the most relevant questions of governance of a free people: how to balance liberty and order and how to balance individual rights and freedoms with individual responsibilities. From these half dozen texts—the Declaration, the first state constitutions, the Articles of Confederation, the U.S. Constitution, *The Federalist*, and the American Bill of Rights—emerged a host of innovative ideas and practices. They included the new vogue of a written constitution; the principle that constitutions should be drawn up by constituent constitutional conventions; the practice of ratifying charters by the people or their representatives; the process of amending constitutions; and three important institutions incorporated in the U.S. Constitution: presidentialism, federalism, and judicial review. The six documents comprised the core of American constitutionalism, which gave birth to the new nation and, when combined with British and French constitutionalisms, gave rise to a new constitutional constellation, Western constitutionalism, to be discussed later.

Any study of constitutional influence must acknowledge at the outset that all constitutions are *autochthonous*; that is, they spring from native soil and are rooted in a country's indigenous traditions. Influences from other societies and cultures are only grafts on the main root. Constitutions are, to a greater or lesser degree, hybrid documents, since each new constitution is part of a larger process called *syncretism*, by which the traditions of one country incorporate the indigenous traditions of another country, resulting in a new creation to which both countries have contributed. When American constitutionalism moved abroad, it was transformed by this interactive, adaptive process. But as will be shown, indigenous traditions sometimes also resisted syncretism.

At the same time, it is clear that in no society do constitution makers operate in a historical, experiential, and intellectual vacuum, approaching such knotty problems as governance and individual rights *de novo*.

Inevitably there are borrowings and rejections, conscious and otherwise. Put another way, even though they may spring from native soil, all constitutions are syncretic and subject to outside influences.

The development of American constitutionalism itself is a case in point. The founding fathers inherited a constitutional tradition stretching back to ancient Greece and Rome. They were greatly influenced also by British constitutional history and the ideas of the European Enlightenment. Thomas Jefferson, Benjamin Franklin, John Adams, and others regularly exchanged ideas with their counterparts in England, France, Scotland, Switzerland, and elsewhere regarding natural law and natural rights. They engaged in public discourse about the role of reason in human affairs and the possibility that through its unfettered application humankind might create rational and just universal laws. Americans drew particularly heavily on British precedents, to be sure, but in the end, unique historical experiences led Americans in a direction of their own. Not having to cope with Europe's conservative institutions—monarchy, aristocracy, established churches, and large standing armies—they were in a better position to translate Enlightenment theories into living realities. Without Britain's ingrained traditions, Americans could forge a system of governance dividing and balancing the executive and legislative branches, create a federal rather than a centralized government, and institute judicial review to check the authority of the executive and the sovereignty of the legislature. These innovations alone marked American constitutionalism as more than a mere variant of British constitutionalism. They justified the motto of the Great Seal of the United States: *Novus ordo seclorum*: "A New Order of the Ages."

The worldwide influence of American constitutionalism, along with that of British and French constitutionalism, has long been recognized. What historian Robert R. Palmer wrote about the effects of the American Revolution overseas could be said as well about the influence of American constitutionalism abroad during the founding years:

> It inspired the sense of a new era. It added a new content to the conception of progress. It gave a whole new dimension to ideas of liberty and equality made familiar in the Enlightenment. It got people into the habit of thinking more concretely about political questions, and made them more readily critical of their own governments and society. It dethroned England and set up America as a model for those seeking a better world.[3]

Such influence continued well beyond the founding period. All through the nineteenth and twentieth centuries, those wanting to overthrow oppressive governments found both inspiration and validation in America's great Declaration. Foreign constitutionalists carefully studied the six seminal documents, mining them for insights, using them as catalysts, and sometimes copying their words and phrases in their newly minted charters.

Precisely to which features of American constitutionalism were other peoples attracted as they created their own frameworks of government? Which did they adopt, and why? And with what degree of change in wording, sense, or practice? Which did they reject, and why? What factors in their own histories, immediate circumstances, situations on the world scene, and intellectual currents of their age influenced their decisions, and in what direction? About these and similar questions our understanding has been less clear, and they are among the issues this book explores.

Since both *constitution* and *constitutionalism* are terms used frequently in this book, some definitions are in order. The term *constitution* has a long history. One might think of Aristotle and his famous classification of constitutions and of Plato, Cicero, and Tacitus, all of whom discussed constitutions, but their meanings have changed over the centuries. Something approximating the present-day definition was anticipated by the "charters of liberties" granted by monarchs to cities in medieval times and by the codification of customs, as in the Magna Carta. By the eighteenth century, certain countries had developed ideas, if not institutions, heading in the direction of a modern constitution. The British theorist and politician Viscount Bolingbroke offered one of the first modern definitions of a constitution: "that assemblage of laws, institutions, and customs, derived from certain fixed objects of public good, that compose the general system, according to which the community has agreed to be governed."[4]

Today, the term *constitution* generally refers to the fundamental system of principles and rules for governing a state and delimiting its power. Nowadays, with few exceptions, these principles and rules are incorporated in a single written document. At the most basic level, a constitution usually "constitutes" a government and outlines the framework under which it will operate. Thus, the American people constituted a government of limited power and "ordained" a constitution which is, according to one scholar, a written charter of government, representing "constitutionalism," and implying limited government and circumscribed political authority. Ordained by "We, the people," it stands for popular sovereignty. It is a blueprint for a federal government, the ancestor of all federal states. It prescribes a government of different branches, separate and independent, yet intermixed. Above all, it has come to stand for individual rights, protected even against the elected representatives of the people, and, in large measure, even when they act in good faith and in the public interest.[5]

It is true, of course, that not all modern constitutions share these attributes. Some constitutions have not been understood as social contracts between the people and their governments and have failed also to provide for any form of representative government. Others have failed to place effective limitations on government to protect individual rights. Still others have placed limitations on government but have qualified the protection they provided. Britain, for example, did not resort to a "higher law" concept and left the protection of individual rights subject to withdrawal by Parliament.[6] Then, of course, some modern constitutions are actually hostile to the philosophy embraced by the U.S. Constitution: they do not "constitute" a government; they do not limit governmental powers; and they do not protect the rights of individuals. Some serve as ideological manifestos, and others are simply "sham constitutions" whose purpose is to deceive the people about protecting rights; one thinks, for example, of the Soviet Constitution of 1936.

Constitutionalism, in contrast, is a more recent term, dating back to the early nineteenth century. It was used by proponents of written constitutions and constitutional governments to identify their underlying beliefs. Generally, *constitutionalism* refers to "the sum total of legal and political restraints that . . . safeguard the exercise of power and protect certain fundamental rights."[7] Historian Don Fehrenbacher further refined this compressed definition: "By 'constitutionalism' I mean a complex of ideas, attitudes, and patterns of behavior elaborating the principle that the authority of government derives from and is limited by a body of fundamental laws."[8]

From a global perspective, Western constitutionalism marked the culmination of three constitutional "moments" in world history, separated in time and place: Britain's Glorious Revolution of 1688; America's Revolution and its constitutional aftermath; and the French Revolution with its Declaration of the Rights of Man and the Citizen. The connection between these "moments," while important, is properly the subject for a different study.[9] What is more important to the purposes of this book is the origin of the concept of modern constitutionalism.

"The rise of [modern] constitutionalism may be dated from 1776," Walter Hamilton, an American scholar, asserted rightly in the 1930s.[10] But it was left to Horst Dippel, a noted German historian and constitutionalist, to make the most convincing case for that date by pointing out in a 2005 article that a single document—the Virginia Declaration of Rights of June 12, 1776—may be the source from which the idea of modern constitutionalism sprang. The document was written by "representatives of the . . . people . . . assembled in a full and free convention . . . [which declared] . . . rights do pertain to them, and their posterity, as the basis and foundation of government."[11] Dippel pointed out that the "inherent rights" of "all men" pertained to the people and their posterity and were not listed as derived from either the English constitution or referred to as ancient rights lost but to be restored—the two traditional arguments always used in the past. The revolutionary nature of the Virginia document was obvious from the statement that such rights would be the "basis and foundation of government," an interpretation of the English constitution unlike any ever offered before.[12]

What was the source of these inherent rights? It was nature and nature's law. Natural law conferred on the people "certain rights, of which when they enter into a state of society, they cannot by compact, deprive or divest their posterity." Natural law proved also "that all power is vested in, and consequently derived from, the people."[13] Thus the Virginia Declaration proclaimed to the world at large all the necessary elements of constitutionalism: sovereignty of the people, inherent individual rights, and universal principles developed in a written constitution as "the basis and foundation of government." It was, concluded Dippel, "the birth of what we understand today by modern constitutionalism."[14]

In this study, American constitutionalism is defined as "documentary constitutionalism" because its six documents both underlay and set forth the governmental order. Within the American governmental system, powers are distributed (rather than confined to the center), are subject to prescribed limitations, and have their source in the will of the majority of the people while at the same time protecting the rights of groups and individuals.[15]

The definition of American constitutionalism as documentary constitutionalism is justified, moreover, by the context that brought it into being.[16]

The founders lived in an era when the written word was increasingly prized and utilized as the populace became more literate. Their concept of communal government was based to a great extent on the models of colonial charters, religious covenants, and secular political compacts, all considered binding because of their written form and sometimes written signatures affixed to signify acceptance. It created a sense of not only permanence but also openness, transparency, and contractual agreement. This primacy of a written document represented a decisive departure from the British practice. It is a truism of modern constitutional history that the American founders were responsible for reviving the modern practice of incorporating a regime's governing principles and practices in a written document.[17]

There is a paradox inherent in the American founding, however, because its documentary constitutionalism did not emerge in a single step. The newly independent colonies did not yet constitute a unified, central regime, and the six written documents appeared in sequential stages over the span of fifteen years. The documents served as proxies for the principles involved, as the founding fathers struggled to embody their concepts of an ideal government in successive texts. In an oversimplified linear progression, we might summarize this process of development as follows: the Declaration (1776) asserted the colonists' intention to separate from Britain and to establish a new state; the first state constitutions (1776–1790) implemented the principle of humankind's right to self-government within the discrete new states by formulating written constitutions, each of which, however, presupposed a nascent unity with the other states; the Articles of Confederation (1781–1787) brought about the formation of that union based on the principle of federalism that allowed self-government simultaneously with shared government at both the state and national level; the Federal Constitution (1787), refining the quality of that federal union, consolidated national powers in a government characterized by limitations placed on all three branches through a sophisticated balance of powers; *The Federalist* (1787–1788), interpreting the system of government thus established, provided the rationale for its various provisions in a document intended for those to be governed; and the Bill of Rights (1791) completed the unfinished balance of powers between the people and the state by redressing the claim of individual rights against control by federal government.

But upon its completion, this linear development of the temporal stages of the documents should be viewed as a simultaneous whole. Although the six texts were written separately and at different times, when viewed together they constituted a kind of "supertext." Each document, by providing essential components and interrelating with the others, contributed to the formation of the completed American model. Sometimes that interrelationship was explicit and referred to, and sometimes one document even incorporated parts of other documents. At other times, however, the relationship was implicit, ambiguous, and subject to conflicting interpretations. Ideas introduced in earlier documents found their fulfillment in following texts. Nothing in this process, however, was foreordained or inevitable. Instead, it was driven by a sense of purpose to "get it right" as far as the form of government was concerned. Hence, the founding fathers continued to use the term *experiment*.

The phrase "one people" in the Declaration, for example, created a sense of identity of Americans as a separate entity, one capable of group action independent of the mother country.[18] This identity was crucial to the formation of American constitutionalism: no American people, no constitutionalism! The Constitution's subsequent preamble, "We the People," reinforced this sense of identity. Some of the Declaration's philosophy of rights formed the basis for principles enunciated in the Articles, then in the Constitution, and finally as particularized in the Bill of Rights.

The first state constitutions played a similar anticipatory role. Virginia's Declaration of Rights and Constitution of 1776, written before Jefferson's manifesto, introduced the body of charges brought against the king in the finished copy of the Declaration of Independence. Some key concepts in the first state constitutions—such as limitations on government—formed the basis for ideas and practices in the Articles and the U.S. Constitution. Furthermore, the constitutional documents that established legitimate government in the first state constitutions were complemented in the Articles and the U.S. Constitution. Though separate and territorially independent, the first state constitutions had to presuppose a "common cause" with the expectation that some sort of continental government would eventually be created. For its part, the Constitution not only accepted the validity of the state constitutions but also, in some respects, drew on their governing models.

The experiment in federalism begun in the Articles was refined and completed in the U.S. Constitution. In fact, the text of the Articles was largely absorbed in the Constitution. *The Federalist*, though less available for direct appropriation of principles-in-practice, was, of course, irrevocably linked to the Constitution as the commentary explicating both its philosophical underpinnings and pragmatic details. By such interactions—one document grounded on the other, leading to the generation of the other or completing the other—the documents formed a complex dynamic unity referred to in this study as *American documentary constitutionalism.*

In contemporary times, the American system of government as it evolved is usually identified as a *constitutional democracy.* The terms *democracy* and *constitutional government* are not synonymous, however, and operate on two different levels, though they sometimes intersect. Democracy, in fact, is theoretically the antithesis of mixed government and has no particular solicitude for property rights or the rule of law. Constitutionalism, in contrast, supports property rights, the rights of minorities, and the rule of law. Democracy and constitutionalism are blended in American constitutional democracy, though often with great instability because of the tension between the two.

Although it is focused on American constitutionalism, this book inevitably discusses democracy as well. As American constitutionalism moved chronologically away from the founding when democracy was an alien and even feared concept, the Jacksonian era brought a dramatic shift in the direction of representative democracy. This movement continued after the Civil War when the democratic ideal became more fully realized. Recognizing the historical tendency of American constitutionalism to overlap with democracy, the approach taken here is that of Klaus von Beyme, who emphasized that the influence of the American model abroad

> was to be found less in democracy in the modern sense of the term, with universal suffrage and the intensive involvement of all ordinary citizens, and more in the constitutional state and the liberal principles of constitutionalism such as the separation of powers, checks and balances . . . and the catalogue of guaranteed basic rights.[19]

The principles, in other words, contained in the six founding documents of the American model.

Foreign constitutionalists were well aware of the complexities of the American system. They recognized that their reception of the American model would necessarily be partial and subject to problems of translation and that autochthonous elements would be present on both sides. No country therefore, tried to adopt American constitutionalism *in toto.*

Foreign constitutionalists, moreover, sometimes resorted in jurisprudential terms to what amounted to a quasi-"originalist" mode of interpretation. That is, they went back to the original texts of the documents that they had lifted from their original context. They could do so because the texts were sufficiently "universal" and putatively timeless that they could address fundamental questions in political science and other disciplines. Thus, the documents could be translated, literally and metaphorically, into other academic idioms and circumstances.

Establishing American "influence" with anything resembling precision is, however, a daunting task. Ideas cross borders without the hindrance of passports or duties, mingle freely with others similarly circulating, and spawn offspring which then compete for place with the parent. Institutions modified by the traditions, cultures, and historical experiences of different peoples may have shared an outward appearance yet were fundamentally different. Parallelisms in the structure and even the wording of documents did not necessarily provide conclusive proof of the parentage of an earlier one. Palmer demonstrated this problem when he compared the Virginia Declaration of Rights of 1776 and the French Declaration of the Rights of Man and the Citizen of 1789.[20]

The situation becomes more complex when the influence is more indirect than direct. The Belgian Constitution of 1831, for example, borrowed certain features of American constitutionalism as well as elements from several other constitutional traditions. That constitution, in turn, became one of the most widely copied in nineteenth-century Europe, with even more syncretisms and adjustments. How can we assign a precise value to the influence of American constitutionalism in view of such a history of borrowings and adaptations?

On some occasions, foreign constitution makers, facing problems analogous to those dealt with by the American founders, considered an American solution but rejected it. That is, they used an American constitutional feature as an anti-model, in what has come to be called "aversive constitutionalism."[21] Granted that the consideration itself helped them clarify their thinking and broadened their awareness of alternatives, how far should we credit this rejection as an example of the "negative influence" of American constitutionalism?

Perhaps the most difficult problem is the case in which the formal written arrangement diverges greatly, often at the very outset, from the functioning constitution. Such a gap between the constitution-as-written and the constitution-in-action poses an enormous problem for measuring the influence of American constitutionalism. For example, if the Argentine Constitution of 1853 listed trial by jury as one of the rights of all citizens, but no trial by jury was conducted in Argentina for the next century and a half, how should we assess the influence of American constitutionalism?

Determining the influence of American constitutionalism abroad is complicated further by the fact that the U.S. Constitution itself changed over time, not only through amendments, but also through interpretation, even though the so-called originalists would have it otherwise.[22] While this book accepts to a certain degree the concept of a "living constitution"—a constitution that was developing and being reinterpreted by case law, statutory law, customs, and philosophical arguments—it relies on what is implied in both the form and spirit of the six documents. The founding texts established a framework that limited the scope of possible future developments in constitutional interpretation and amendment in much the same way the foundation of a house confines its structure. More particularly, the natural rights argument found in all the six seminal documents has served as the philosophical basis for change even as it has limited such changes.

American influence is constrained also by the difficulties encountered in transnational translations of the six documents. What was translated was often transformed. Sometimes the translators could not find adequate language to express precisely the concepts employed in American constitutionalism; at other times, they revised the rhetoric of the American documents to suit their own political purposes.[23]

America's constitutional influence abroad is circumscribed, moreover, by the fact that other constitutional models had enormous influence as well. For instance, many more countries relied on Britain's parliamentary model than on the U.S. model. Other countries looked for inspiration mainly to the French Revolution and subsequent French experiences in constitution making. Still other constitutions, such as the Belgian Constitution of 1831, Mexican Constitution of 1917, and Soviet Constitution of 1936, exercised widespread influence.

For all that, however, it is still possible to determine with a cautious degree of confidence the way and extent to which American constitutionalism has influenced others. That influence can be discovered by tracking down America's founding documents as translated or published in the original in the various countries. Evidence of such influence can be found also by studying the writings of important constitutional theorists who taught their compatriots about the American system. This is most obvious in the widespread adoption of certain features of American constitutionalism—written constitutions, judicial review, federalism, and written safeguards of individual rights—even if in modified form.

Influence is to be sought, too, in the subversive effect of republicanism—one of the most distinctive characteristics of American constitutionalism—on the monarchies that dominated eighteenth- and nineteenth-century Europe. If Gordon Wood is right, that it "was republicanism and republican principles that ultimately destroyed . . . monarchical society,"[24] then America's radical republican ideology and its success were crucial to that destruction and the emergence of modern constitutionalism.

The influence of American constitutionalism is to be found also in the decisions of millions and millions of ordinary folk abroad, immigrants who knew little about specific features of American constitutionalism but understood its essential spirit sufficiently to flock to the United States. It is to be sought further in the beliefs and behavior of those who remained behind and participated in the movements for freer constitutional governments in their own countries.

Finally, American constitutionalism's influence can be sought in the spread of democracy, the greatest political phenomenon in the world over the past two centuries. By 1990, almost half the countries in the world (45.4 percent of countries with a population greater than one million) were listed in one survey as being democratic.[25] To what extent can American constitutionalism be credited for this development? What influence can reasonably be assigned to the ideas of freedom and equality found in the Declaration, what to the formal and informal arrangements of government inscribed in the U.S. Constitution, and what to the protection of individual rights set out in the Bill of Rights? To what extent were the six seminal documents used by new democracies in their process of nation building? By pursuing such questions, this book seeks a better understanding of the long-term influence that American constitutionalism has had throughout the globe.

2

American Constitutionalism Defined

Six Seminal Documents

America's six founding documents were viewed from a global perspective right from the start. The Declaration was addressed, after all, to the whole world as well as to the American people. Jefferson's prescient claim in his famous deathbed letter in 1826 established its global import: "[The Declaration is] an instrument, pregnant with our own, and the fate of the world."[1] America's first state constitutions included concepts that entered immediately into the discourse of the transnational history of ideas. The Articles of Confederation were taken seriously by both French constitutional thinkers and members of the Opposition in the British Parliament. That the U.S. Constitution was crucial to any understanding of American constitutionalism goes without saying, but its complex system of checks and balances and its three key features were particularly subject to selective interpretation and application abroad. *The Federalist*, the Constitution's most enduring literary legacy, initiated a tradition of commentary that had a warm reception in France when first published. Finally, the Bill of Rights that completed the Constitution was viewed as linked to the French Declaration of 1789 and the English bills of rights. Although it is true that French constitutionalism exercised a greater influence worldwide after 1789, Carl J. Friedrich was correct when he concluded that from the beginning there was "almost universal enthusiasm for the American enterprise among forward-looking people."[2]

At the same time, the six documents were national texts whose primary purpose was to help create a new government for the new nation. Their Janus-faced orientation of being partly global and partly national was inherent in their makeup. To examine the contribution of each to the nation-building process is a necessary first step to understanding the American constitutionalism that, together, they comprised.

The Declaration of Independence: A Global and a National Document

The Declaration of Independence ranks as the single most important public paper ever published in the United States. Like many great historical documents, it may be interpreted in several ways. Although its message was global in part and aimed at the world at large, it also was a national document directed at the American people and rousing them to revolution.

The Declaration remains the most eloquent expression of America's core constitutional values. Its assertion that "all men are created equal" is surely the world's most famous utterance of that constitutional principle. Jefferson's deathbed letter predicted that now people everywhere were aware of the "rights of man" and that they would be convinced that all men were born not to be ruled by others but to rule themselves and therefore to "assume the blessings & security of self government."[3]

Although the Declaration is not a constitution, it has in the course of its history exercised the force of a near-constitutional text. According to the current school of legal realists—legal historians, law professors, and lawyers—a constitutional text must be based on a positivist view of the law, establish a government grounded on its principles, contain all necessary institutions, and include a proper codification of laws.[4] The Declaration met none of these requirements. Why, then, is it included as part of American constitutionalism? The answer lies in its status as a near-constitutional text: the Declaration functioned in a number of ways that approximate the role that a constitution would play.

The Declaration's statement that "these United Colonies are, and of Right ought to be FREE AND INDEPENDENT STATES," is by virtue of that phrase a document with strong constitutional implications. By emphasizing the "rights of states" under international law, the Declaration assumed a distinctive constitutional cast. The same was true of its principle that the natural "rights of individuals" formed the basis for a duly constituted government. The Declaration conveyed also the constitutional idea of a sovereign people possessing constituent power in the government. Its statement that "governments are instituted among Men deriving their just powers from the governed" is a constitutional assertion on its face. Although the founding fathers presumably intended this argument only for themselves, the idea assumed global proportions after the Revolution.

As David Armitage points out, the Declaration contains a declaration of the right to independent statehood as well as of the inalienable rights of individuals. Although Armitage does not consider the document a constitution, by focusing on these two issues, he is accentuating its near-constitutional status. By analyzing the Declaration's emphasis on statehood, Armitage also is bringing American independence more closely into the context of international law. He notes that the 1776 revolutionaries had emphasized their claims to sovereignty and the independence of free states. From the writings of Emer de Vattel, the Swiss jurist who published *The Law of Nations* in 1758, they were able to place the new American republic within the orbit of an emerging new global order.[5] Although this state system had yet to be formed, it was based on what we now call *international law*. Subsequent interpreters of the Declaration, however, stressed instead the natural-law theory on which the rights of individuals were based. That interpretation became the conventional wisdom among scholars to this day, as Armitage has noted.[6]

Armitage's insight enabled him to make a historiographical breakthrough and explain why the American Revolutionary era could be called the "first outbreak of a contagion of sovereignty." America's pronouncement regarding sovereignty was soon repeated throughout the globe, as the Declaration became a generic form for expressing this idea. This led to the Declaration's ultimately transforming the eighteenth-century conception of the world from one of empires to the modern view of the globe covered by free and independent states.[7] Armitage thus placed the Declaration in a new context, that of global history (the subtitle of his book), rather than the more nationalistic approach taken previously.[8]

In one sense, the Declaration of Independence also was a declaration of interdependence. Declaring independence meant that the American colonies were leaving the relative insularity imposed by their being a part of the British Empire. Independence amounted to a new status of interdependence: the United States was now a sovereign nation entitled to the privileges and responsibilities that came with that status. America thus became a member of the international community, which meant becoming a maker of treaties and alliances, a military ally in diplomacy, and a partner in foreign trade on a more equal basis.[9]

Apart from its global dimension, the Declaration functioned in its domestic sphere as a national document. The first paragraph proclaimed the document's main purpose, justifying the United States' separation from Britain. To most colonists, except the Loyalists, the document's proclamation marked the precise moment when the social contract between the king and people was broken. Since the British constitution presumably had been subverted by the king, the colonists, according to contract theory, were released from their "political bands" of obedience. Now it became necessary for them as "one people" to "assume among the powers of the earth, the separate and equal station to which the Laws of Nature and Nature's God entitle[d] them." The Declaration thus performed a constitutional function when it formally ended the colonies' relationship with the British regime.[10]

John Hancock, president of the Continental Congress, recognized the document's important constitutional implications when he wrote, while transmitting it to the states, that it was "the *Ground & Foundation* of a *Future Government.*" He went on to say that it was appropriate that the "People may be universally informed of it."[11] It was necessary to inform the people "universally," since they were presumably acting as "one people," and the consent of the governed could be achieved only if all persons had been informed of the choice facing them.

Who were the "one people" involved? The Declaration was very much a document of its time, and it defined the phrase "all men are created equal" in a limited way. The generic term "men" did not include women, black slaves, or Native Americans and other marginalized social groups such as indentured servants. Although the colonies had the broadest suffrage in the world, they still had property qualifications for voting, and officeholding was denied to certain ethnic and religious groups. The only "people" who mattered in public affairs were mainly male taxpayers, freeholders, and Christians of a particular Protestant persuasion.[12]

When Americans repudiated Britain's authority, they did so not as individuals but as organized groups. James Kettner's study of the idea of American citizenship indicates how this practice evolved:

> They withdrew their allegiance from George III and severed the connection with England in formal, public, and communal acts passed by representative bodies purporting to speak for a united people. The process began even before Congress approved the Declaration. By legislative resolves and constitutional provisions, some provincial governments had already cut themselves loose from royal authority and took steps tantamount to a general renunciation of allegiance.[13]

It was during the Revolutionary War that the American concept of volitional allegiance was first developed.

How widespread the colonists' support for the Declaration was may never be known because not enough contemporary sources are available. The response of the people in the ninety or so "other" declarations from state legislators, county conventions, and town resolutions indicated that there was broad public support for independence. These "other" declarations "offer the best opportunity to hear the voice of the people from the spring of 1776 that we are likely to get," concluded Pauline Maier.[14] One contemporary voice was heard distinctly, however, when Congress ordered the Declaration to be read to the troops in the Continental army. A soldier in western Pennsylvania recorded his reaction with joy: "The language of every man's countenance was, Now we are a people! We have a name among the states of this world!"[15]

The Declaration served also as the constitutional basis for establishing new social contracts between the people and their state governments. Because the first state constitutions established new governments based on the constituent power of the people, American revolutionaries viewed the Declaration as a kind of warrant on which to base their state governments.[16] With their commitment to natural rights philosophy and the social contract theory of government, the early paragraphs of the Declaration set forth principles close to the heart of America's documentary constitutionalism,[17] and parts of these paragraphs were embedded in the first state constitutions. No fewer than eight repeated entire phrases drawn from the Declaration, while in the case of New York, the entire document was reproduced in the 1777 constitution.[18]

Traces of the Declaration were evident as well in the Bill of Rights, which therefore should be interpreted in the context of the natural rights philosophy expressed in the 1776 text. The prohibition against quartering soldiers found its way into the Third Amendment. The Declaration's assertion of the right to "Life, Liberty and the pursuit of Happiness" was echoed in the Fifth Amendment, while the Fourteenth later reflected the document's expression of the principle of "equality."

Neither the natural rights philosophy nor the social contract theory in the Declaration was unfamiliar to the colonists. The beliefs that "the laws of Nature and of Nature's God" provided a standard against which the legitimacy of man-made laws could be measured; that all men possessed certain natural and unalienable rights by virtue of their being human; that the most important of those rights were "Life, Liberty and the pursuit of Happiness"; that the just purpose of government was to protect these rights; that government derived its just powers from the "consent of the governed"; and that whenever a government destroyed such rights, the people could alter or abolish it all were well-known ideas derived from the Enlightenment and were commonplace in European thought.

The theory of government that Americans embraced also bore the particular stamp of several English Whig revolutionary theorists, especially John Locke. His views were widely known and accepted in both Britain and America in the first half of the eighteenth century.[19] In America, they were made familiar through the writings of such coffeehouse pamphleteers as John Trenchard and Thomas Gordon. As Bernard Bailyn observed, "In pamphlet after pamphlet . . . American writers cited Locke on natural rights and on the social and governmental contract."[20]

Besides Lockeian liberalism, Jefferson drew on two other major sources of political theory in the broad sweep of Western culture. One, classical republicanism, was based on ancient Greek and Roman political thinkers like Aristotle and Tacitus. The other was Christianity, particularly the Reformed theology of John Calvin practiced in many colonial churches. Relying heavily on these three traditions, Jefferson produced his masterpiece with help from other members of the Continental Congress.[21]

Although Jefferson acknowledged that much of what he wrote was derivative, it nonetheless served his purpose. As he explained later to his friend Henry Lee in May 1825:

> Not to find out new principles, or new arguments, never before thought of, not merely to say things which had never been said before; but to place before mankind the common sense of the subject, in terms so plain and firm as to command their assent, and to justify ourselves in the independent stand we are compelled to take. Neither aiming at originality of principle or sentiment, nor yet copied from any particular and previous writing, it was intended to be an expression of the American mind, and to give to that expression the proper tone and spirit called for by the occasion.[22]

If the ideas in the Declaration had many precedents, the pathbreaking actions that followed it did not. In one of the first instances in modern world history, a people was actually embarking on the road to revolution as laid out in the contract theory: seeking to overthrow by force of arms a presumably abusive regime and to establish in its place a government of the people's own choosing. The constitutional implications of the new governments—the embrace of the natural rights philosophy, commitment to limited contractual government, and expression of republican values— were profound, even though many were backward-looking in the sense that their arguments were rooted in the past.

But the Declaration was also a forward-looking document. It was a century and three quarters ahead of its time in asserting that there should be a universal standard of human rights.[23] The American revolutionaries justified their claim to independence, moreover, *not* on their rights as Englishmen based on the British constitution (as British subjects had in the past when seeking concessions from their monarchs), but on a proposed new universal standard by which all governments in the world might be measured. Judged by this standard, Britain was considered guilty because of its alleged misrule of the colonies. The Declaration represented one of the first efforts in global history to establish this new standard. The line of descent from the 1776 document to the Universal Declaration of Human Rights proclaimed by the United Nations in 1948 calling for "equal rights of men and women" is quite clear.

The Declaration enjoyed a long and interesting afterlife in American history, as Maier has shown, and it eventually came to occupy a place of veneration with religious connotations as an "American scripture," or sacred text. Advocates of various social movements, such as blacks, women, and labor, appropriated its Enlightenment language and employed it in an instrumentalist way to advance their causes.[24]

The Declaration likewise continued its near-constitutional status during its afterlife in the courts. Throughout American history, the document was quoted, cited, or used as substantive law in more than 570 federal court cases. A survey reveals 234 federal cases before 1945 cited the Declaration in some way. Among them were some of the most famous cases in American history: *Chisholm v. Georgia*; *Fletcher v. Peck*; *Luther v. Borden*; *Gray v. Sanders*; and *Adkins v. Children's Hospital*. After 1945, 337 federal cases cited the Declaration, and these statistics do not even include a survey of state court opinions.[25]

The Declaration also made the United States "the first modern nation to achieve decolonization."[26] What began in the American colonies in 1776 grew into a massive decolonization movement during and after World War II. Stirred by the example of the American colonists, other colonial peoples launched wars of liberation against their masters.

As the first of the six founding documents that comprise American documentary constitutionalism, the Declaration has a unique status. It established the former colonies as sovereign states, made possible the emergence of the subsequent seminal documents, and, together with them, helped form the whole of what we call American constitutionalism.

The First State Constitutions

It was at the state, not the national, level that American revolutionaries first codified much of their constitutional thinking. In a single year, 1776, eight new state constitutions were written and adopted, and two others were modified, making that date and 1787 "the two most significant years in the history of modern constitution-making," according to one historian.[27] Another scholar ranked the first state constitutions alongside the Declaration and the Articles as seminal sources of American constitutionalism.[28]

Inevitably, many ideas that found their way into the state constitutions were influenced by Enlightenment thinkers, English Whig principles, and English political culture. But they were founded also on indigenous American experiences during the colonial period. Some early settlers, for example, had written communal covenants that were later secularized and transformed into political compacts resembling "constitution-like" documents. Well before Montesquieu and Locke, religious pioneers on the Piscataqua River (later Maine) drafted a document creating a government based on modern principles of both popular sovereignty and majority rule. Before constitutional thinkers in the Old World had formulated philosophical principles defining modern federalism, the New England Confederation of 1643 had already established a federal government that bore an implicit commitment to the dual sources of sovereignty and citizenship.[29]

More important, the state constitutions drew on American views formulated during the constitutional crisis just before the outbreak of the Revolutionary War. All in all, the novel formulations they introduced revolutionized Western constitutional thought. Americans could justly say of these new state constitutions what Pericles once said of Athens: "Our constitution does not copy the laws of neighboring states, we are rather a pattern to others than imitators ourselves."[30]

Four of the founding generation's constitutional "inventions" in the early state constitutions had an especially powerful influence on Western constitutionalism: the idea of a constituent constitutional convention, the practice of a written constitution, the principle of ratifying a constitution, and the procedure for amendment.

Of the four, the idea of a constituent constitutional convention was, without doubt, the most significant. "European thinkers," Robert R. Palmer wrote, "in all their discussions of the social contract, of government by consent, and of sovereignty of the people, had not imagined the people as actually contriving a constitution and creating the organs of government."[31] The idea of a constituent constitutional convention, of course, flowed logically—one might almost say inevitably—from the contract theory of government. The governed, that is, the sovereign people, would determine and declare exactly what power their government would and would not have and would do this through representatives elected to a convention established solely for that purpose.[32]

In the first hectic round of state constitution making, this theory was applied only partially and imperfectly. In some states, a constituent constitutional convention ostensibly said to mirror the body of the people was called. In other states, the sitting legislators, presuming to act for the people, drew up the constitution. In yet other states, revolutionary congresses were summoned, called by some "legally imperfect legislatures," but still representing the people, and wrote the charter.[33]

Not until 1779, three years after the earliest state constitutions, did the idea of the constituent constitutional convention receive its fullest application. In that year, the Massachusetts legislature summoned a convention, elected by manhood suffrage, for the sole purpose of writing a new constitution. That convention produced the Massachusetts Constitution of 1780, the oldest surviving written constitution in the Western world today.[34]

With the constituent constitutional convention, American revolutionaries had invented a mechanism for altering, abolishing, or remaking government by peaceful means. They had, in effect, legalized the process of revolution. France soon followed America's example. The word *convention* appeared for the first time on the Continent in France in the 1780s, by way of America's state constitutions.[35] In time, other countries in the world created constitutional conventions, although their constituencies varied widely. In the nineteenth century, the constitutions of Belgium in 1831, Switzerland in 1848, Denmark in 1849 and 1866, and France in 1875 all used this mechanism.[36] But in most instances, the constituencies were made up of elites or local notables rather than the people or their representatives.

Throughout the twentieth century, the practice was continued in many countries. Nearly all European constitutions after World War I were drafted by specially convened conventions of one kind or another. The same was true of the constitutions of some of Britain's self-governing dominions, like Canada and Australia, whose constitutions emanated from domestically called conventions, even though they were ultimately acts of law by the British Parliament. After World War II, the practice continued, and both the German Basic Law of 1949 and that of the Fifth French Republic of 1958 resulted from constituent assemblies.

The idea of a written constitution represented another important innovation. Since almost all charters in today's world are written documents, it is difficult to convey just how novel this notion was in 1776. Before that time, written constitutions were scarce. Although in Britain the practice of writing constitutions was on the wane by the eighteenth century, American revolutionaries revived it in the 1770s and 1780s. "The vogue of the written constitution may have brought all sorts of trouble in its train," wrote one historian, "but it also brought clarity and precision to forms of government to an extent not previously attained."[37] What the Americans did was "new and different," wrote another scholar:

> They made written constitutions a practical and everyday part of government life. They showed the world how written constitutions could be made truly fundamental and distinguishable from ordinary legislation and how such constitutions would be interpreted on a regular basis and altered when necessary. Further, they offered the world concrete and usable government institutions for carrying out these constitutional tasks.[38]

The British, however, defined a constitution in a different way. To them, a constitution did not mean a written document: it represented instead the already existing scheme of government, that is, the common law, customs, and institutions, along with principles such as those embodied in the Magna Carta. From the British perspective, therefore, a constitution was not a single written document but a compilation of oral and written precedents and ongoing practices.

Americans developed a different view. Over time, they had come to look on their colonial charters as protective barriers against British parliamentary authority. Their prerevolutionary debate with Britain made the colonists realize that the laws of Parliament were not necessarily constitutional from an American perspective. The American concept was different: it was a written document distinct from and superior to government, and the operations of government were separate and not considered part of the constitution.[39]

The precedent established by America's written constitutions changed not only this country's political culture but also that of much of the rest of the world. Charles McIlwain, a constitutional historian at Harvard, described how the idea expanded. The practice "first developed in North America, was naturalized in France and from there transmitted to the continent of Europe, from which it . . . spread."[40] With the writing of the first state constitutions, a new era in constitution making burst upon the world. An unprecedented epidemic of constitution writing was launched in both the New and Old Worlds. The two American national constitutions (the Articles of Confederation and U.S. Constitution), the fifteen European constitutions proclaimed between 1789 and 1799, and the charters of five Latin American countries from 1811 to 1824 all were written documents. By 1989, when this book ends, nearly all the more than 170 constitutions in the world were written.

Written constitutions were further legitimized by another American "invention," the requirement that the document be ratified by the people. Maryland and Pennsylvania were the first to do so in 1776. In 1780, Massachusetts required ratification by an extraordinary majority of two-thirds of the voters in all its towns. The requirement for ratification significantly broadened the concept of sovereignty of the people. Here again, France followed America's lead. Although the constitution of 1791 was not submitted for popular ratification, the constitution of 1793 was, and it received overwhelming endorsement.[41] In sending their 1793 constitution directly to the people for approval or rejection, however, the French surpassed the Americans, whose 1787 constitution was popularly ratified, but only indirectly by representatives in the states' ratifying conventions.

The fourth invention further extending the sovereignty of the people gave them the right to amend the constitution. Pennsylvania's constitution of 1776 was the first to institutionalize this process. It provided for a council of censors to determine whether the constitution had been violated or needed to be amended. If a certain number of censors agreed that the latter was the case, a constitutional convention with power to amend was to be called within two years. The idea of a council of censors had venerable predecessors going back to ancient Greece and Rome. But in America the amending process took place within the legislature itself. Here again the theory of amendment by the sovereign people was only imperfectly realized in practice. Only Vermont followed the Pennsylvania model, and by 1780 fewer than half the state constitutions included a procedure for amending. Nonetheless, the principle that the people had a right to amend their own constitution was established by the end of the revolutionary era.[42]

The American states also established republics that, except for a few small city-states in Europe, represented a form of government all but forgotten at the time.[43] In a world dominated by monarchies, the American revolutionaries based their new governments on the principle of popular sovereignty. This republican revolution, claims Gordon Wood,

> was the greatest utopian movement in American history. The revolutionaries aimed at nothing less than a reconstitution of American society. They hoped to destroy the bonds holding together the older monarchical society—kinship, patriarchy, and patronage—and put in their place new social bonds of love, respect, and consent. They sought to construct a society and government based on virtue and disinterested public leadership and to set in motion a moral government that would eventually be felt around the globe.[44]

Virginia's Declaration of Rights, appended to the 1776 Virginia state constitution, launched the republican revolution. It announced "that all power is invested in and consequently derived from the people" and that "magistrates are their trustees and servants, and at all times amenable to them."[45] One can hardly imagine a more clear and uncompromising statement of popular sovereignty. The first state constitutions also were well ahead of the rest of the world in regard to voting, the ultimate expression of popular sovereignty. Property qualifications and the exclusion of women, African Americans, Native Americans, and other segments of society notwithstanding, the voting public in America was much broader than that of any other nation on earth. Even Britain, generally considered the most liberal country in Europe, at that time was far behind the American republics in this regard.[46]

One important feature in all early state constitutions was the protection of individual rights against governmental authority. That "there was [also such a thing as] a public good," one authority observed, "and that legislatures and magistrates—properly curbed by one another and by a politically active citizenry—were obligated to pursue it," none doubted.[47] Yet against the all-too-fresh memories of the recent past, it was understandable that the writers of these constitutions would be consumed by the fear of arbitrary power and government tyranny, even at the hands of the people's own elected representatives. To guard against such abuses, they limited the powers of the new governments and dispersed even those through a separation of powers and bicameralism. They wrote bills of rights that guaranteed trial by jury, protection against search and seizure, no excessive bail, and due process of law. Further, as a direct reaction to the long-sitting Parliament in London, every state except South Carolina required annual legislative elections.[48] Many new state constitutions also prohibited the holding of more than one office and even deprived the governor of a veto power in some instances.

By creating state constitutions with such safeguards, the American revolutionaries restructured political life in the New World. The first state constitutions represented a major source of new political ideas and institutions, but more important, the charters exercised a profound influence on countries throughout the rest of the world.

The Articles of Confederation

The Articles of Confederation represented America's first federal constitution. Drawing on Benjamin Franklin's 1754 Albany Plan of Union and another of his plans in 1775 (neither of which was ever adopted), members of the Continental Congress in 1776 and 1777 drafted the new document. Adopted in 1781, the Articles remained in effect until replaced by the U.S. Constitution. They saw the country through its trying early years and, along with the actions of the Confederation government, contributed much to the development of American constitutionalism.

The Articles created a confederacy called the "United States of America" whose primary governing body was the Confederation congress, a unicameral legislature in which each of the thirteen states had only one vote. To enact laws of minor importance required a simple majority of seven states; those of greater importance (declaring war, making treaties, and coining or borrowing money), a majority of nine. Amending the Articles required the assent of all thirteen states. There was no single executive, leaving leadership to be provided by congressional committees.

It is clear that the Articles had serious flaws and, as many argue, fatal ones.[49] Perhaps it could not have been otherwise, given the drift of sentiment away from the strong feelings of nationalism in 1776. James Wilson, serving in the Congress in 1776 and 1777, described how close the revolutionaries had felt to one another at the time: "Virga. is no more . . . Masst.

is no more, Pa. is no more, &c. We are now one nation of brethren." But within a year, "the tables . . . began to turn. No sooner were the State Governments formed then their jealousy & ambition began to display themselves. Each endeavoured to cut a slice from the Common loaf . . . till at length the confederation became frittered down to the impotent condition it now stands."[50]

Two crucial powers, the power to tax and to regulate trade, were denied to the central government. Without the power to tax, no confederation in world history had ever succeeded. Even the locus of sovereignty itself was at best ambiguous. Article 2 said that each state retained its sovereignty, freedom, and independence; articles 3 and 4 declared that the states were entering "severally" into a "firm league of friendship."[51] The limitations on state power in article 6, moreover, raised questions about how absolute the power of the individual states was to be in foreign affairs.

Given the bitter experience of Americans with Britain's centralized government and their continuing state loyalties, the powers expressly granted to the new Confederation were, in fact, quite impressive. The Articles empowered Congress to conduct diplomatic relations, make war and peace, requisition the states for men and money, settle disputes between and among states, coin and borrow money, and regulate affairs with Native Americans: no mean list of powers. Gordon Wood highlighted the surprising achievement of the Articles:

> What is truly remarkable about the Confederation is the degree of union that was achieved. The equality of citizens of all states in privileges and immunities, the reciprocity of extradition and judicial proceedings among the states, and the substantial grant of powers to the Congress in Article 9 made a league of states as cohesive and strong as any sort of republican confederation in history—stronger in fact than some Americans had expected.[52]

Furthermore, the Articles introduced several extraordinary constitutional innovations. The Declaration, as noted, had already eliminated the possibility of monarchy, setting the new nation on the path of republicanism. Now the Articles eliminated as well any possibility of a hereditary aristocracy. In many societies, aristocrats had maintained their privileged positions for centuries based on a hierarchy of graded ranks and degrees. Through custom, kinship connections, patronage, and a system of dependency, they ruled alongside kings as a superior class. In colonial America there was no formal feudal aristocratic class, even though certain individuals with close connections to the British aristocracy—men like Thomas Hutchinson—achieved prominent positions and wealth through kinship ties, political patronage, and business connections. But for all that, America in the colonial era was said in Europe to be the "best poor man's country." Colonial society, though informally divided into superiors and inferiors, gentlemen and commoners, the leisured few and the laboring many, lacked a formal aristocracy.

As republican ideas swept the country, the feeling grew that the social distinctions of Europe's monarchical and hierarchical societies should no longer be tolerated. "Suddenly in the eyes of the revolutionaries, all fine calibrations of rank and degrees of unfreedom of the traditional monarchical society became absurd and degrading," observed Wood. "The Revolution became a full-fledged assault on dependency."[53] Reflecting this newfound spirit of equality, the Articles prohibited both the central and state governments from granting titles of nobility. Officeholders, moreover, were forbidden to accept "any . . . title of any kind whatever from any king, prince, or foreign state."[54] Some state constitutions had already denied the granting of titles, but this prohibition on the national level was unprecedented in world history. With a single stroke, American revolutionaries "destroyed aristocracy as it had been understood in the Western world for at least two millennia."[55]

The trend toward a more democratic constitutionalism was evident also in the Articles' requirement of ratification by the states. The same was true of the amending process, although it was more cumbersome in application. Here was the first national constitution in the Western world that was to be adhered to voluntarily rather than by imposition. Moreover, it could be altered only in the same consensual manner.

The continuity in democratic constitutionalism from the Articles to the U.S. Constitution was striking. One scholar pointed out that "from one-half to two-thirds of what appears in the Articles was retained in the Federal Constitution of 1787." He asserted, moreover, that far from the U.S. Constitution completely replacing the Articles, "it would be more accurate to say that the 1787 document, although providing for a fundamentally different kind of government, was generally constructed around an amended Articles of Confederation."[56]

A few examples should suffice. The "full faith and credit" clause of the U.S. Constitution is worded essentially the same as that clause in the Articles of Confederation. The underlying principles of the "privileges and immunities" clause also were borrowed from the Articles, although these privileges and immunities were spelled out in greater detail in the earlier document. The national court system established under the U.S. Constitution found a point of reference in the first federal appellate prize court established under the Articles.[57] The earlier suggested court system, moreover, anticipated the subsequent Judiciary Act of 1789.

Even the Tenth Amendment to the U.S. Constitution copied almost precisely the words of article 3 of the Articles of Confederation, changing only the phrase "expressly delegated" to simply "delegated." But this seemingly slight change made a huge difference. The words "expressly delegated" were crucial to distributing powers between the central and state governments. "The [single] word was no mere quibble," observed one scholar. "It embodied two quite different conceptions of the balance of power between the two sets of governments."[58]

The major problem facing the Confederation congress was how to administer the vast lands in the West as yet unsettled. Since the sale of public lands would be a major source of income, the various states with conflicting claims engaged in territorial controversies regarding boundaries that sometimes threatened to tear apart the Union. Maryland, for example, delayed adopting the Articles for nearly three years by refusing to sign until the issue of the western boundaries had been settled. Some kind of national land policy obviously was needed.

The lands out west between the Ohio and Mississippi rivers were of immediate importance, and a number of questions regarding them remained unanswered. How could Congress obtain cessions from the claimant states that would be acceptable to all parties? Then there was the question of the Native Americans, who would have to be induced to yield title to tribal claims. Congress had to determine also how the lands were to be distributed to prospective settlers. Finally, Congress had to prescribe how the new communities would be governed and what their relationship to the original states would be.

Many of these questions were addressed in the "ordinances" passed by the Confederation government. The ordinances constituted the greatest contribution to the American cause next to winning the war. They were not constitutional enactments, properly speaking, because they were acts of the Confederation congress, prescriptive in nature and below the standard required of constitutional measures. Nevertheless, they significantly advanced the aims of American constitutionalism. They were made possible by the ambiguous powers granted to the Confederation government, for it could legislate in matters only when it could reasonably expect the approval of the states or when state compliance was not required. Historian Richard P. McCormick Sr. concluded that in this matter, Congress was "bold," "daring," and "ingenious" in venturing beyond its enumerated powers.[59]

Three of the ordinances dealt with the survey and sale of lands in the public domain. The first, in 1784, divided the western regions from the Appalachians to the Mississippi into sixteen territories and provided that each would qualify for statehood when its population reached twenty thousand. In 1785, a second ordinance provided for systematic surveys and subdivisions of the public domain with clear-cut boundaries and titles. This approach remained the basis of public policy until the Homestead Act in the Civil War era.

The third, the Northwest Ordinance of 1787, was the Confederation's most significant act. It set the precedent, followed since, for admitting new states into the Union. It provided for a system of limited government until the states had reached a certain stage of population and other conditions, at which time the newly ordained states would be admitted as equal partners. Thus was introduced the federal principle that newly acquired territories would be accepted as parts of the country with equal status and responsibilities.

The states at first resisted giving up their claims and fought furiously over boundaries. Eventually, though, they realized that some central authority, like the Confederation government, was needed to act as a kind of referee to resolve competing claims. Peter Onuf's pathbreaking study shows that the struggle over land claims was less between the federal government and the states and more among states themselves as they defended their boundaries. The origins of the federal union that finally emerged in the Philadelphia Convention, Onuf concludes, are to be found in large part in the issue of competing land claims.[60]

Onuf's study of the Northwest Ordinance is equally provocative. He argues that the settlers in the territory struggled over exactly how they should interpret the act while living under its provisions. Ironically, the settlers were uncertain as to how they should respond to the ordinance. Different interest groups in the territory reacted differently on different issues: boundaries between the new states, timing of acceptance of statehood, and prohibition of slavery. Seeking solutions to such issues, the settlers invested the ordinance with near-constitutional authority to bring about some order.[61]

Contemporaries were well aware of the limitations of the Articles as a governing instrument. "It is the best Confederacy that Could be formed, especially when we consider the Number of States, their different Interests, Customs, &c &c," wrote Cornelius Hartnett of North Carolina in 1777.[62] Indeed, the Articles marked a considerable advance over earlier forms of contractual federalism and moved toward the beginnings of constitutional federalism.[63]

The U.S. Constitution

The U.S. Constitution remains one of the most remarkable charters throughout the globe. It was the first constitution to establish a republican government over a huge continent inhabited by a multiplicity of people of differing ethnic, racial, and religious backgrounds. It has proved to be the social "glue" holding together this diverse population over an astonishingly long time, despite a prolonged and bloody civil war. Domestically, it has maintained "a standard unmatched by any other national charter in the history of civilization," according to Michael Kammen.[64] Abroad, it ranks among the greatest and most influential constitutions in world history.

The Constitution achieved its unusual status for several reasons. One is its longevity as the oldest national written constitution in the world. Another is its durability, fulfilling Justice John Marshall's prescient declaration that it was "intended to endure for ages to come, and, consequently, to be adapted to the various crises of human affairs."[65] It has survived all manner of tests, including the Civil War, and achieved its adaptability through judicial reinterpretations of its words and with a minimum of amendments. It is also remarkably brief. Barely ten pages long with perhaps as many more for its twenty-seven amendments, it is short when compared with the charters that attempt to anticipate all contingencies and accordingly run on interminably: South Africa's constitution of 1993 for 150 pages, Brazil's of 1988 for 200, and India's of 1950 for a numbing 500 or more. Finally and most important, the Constitution created a new concept of a federal political order.

No frame of government, as observed earlier, is created *de novo*. Accordingly, although the Constitution is clearly an original creation, its framers drew inspiration, ideas, and institutions from a variety of sources: not only from the ideas and formulations in the Declaration, the state constitutions, and the Articles of Confederation, but also from certain long-standing traditions of Western moral and political thought. The tradition from ancient Greece provided the idea that human fulfillment is best achieved through active participation in the state. The Judeo-Christian tradition furnished two other important beliefs: the sanctity and worth of the individual and the denial of human perfectability. From the first of these beliefs, by way of Locke, came the American idea that government derives its just powers from the consent of the governed; from the second, that the power of government must be limited. The framers drew also on the ideas of men closer to their own time, most notably Montesquieu, Blackstone, and Locke.

More practically and unsurprisingly, the framers also borrowed freely from the British constitution under which they had achieved so much self-government. It was enough to lead one delegate at the Philadelphia Convention to grumble, "We are always following the British tradition."[66] That complaint missed the larger picture, however, for the Americans' idea of a constitution differed significantly from that of the British. As Oscar and Mary Handlin noted,

> In the New World the term, constitution, no longer referred to the actual organization of power developed through custom, prescription and precedent. Instead it had come to mean a written frame of government setting fixed limits on the use of power. The American view was, of course, closely related to the rejection of the old conception of authority descended from the Crown to its officials. In the newer view—that authority was derived from the consent of the governed—the written constitution became the instrument by which people entrusted power to their agents.[67]

The new conception was different enough to warrant regarding the U.S. Constitution as a hybrid creation, one conceived largely from a mix of British ideas and American experience.[68]

Framers of the document set themselves the task of protecting the country against the turbulent political cycles that had characterized earlier republics by striking a balance between a central government and subordinate governments and between liberty and order and, at the same time, by inspiring public virtue among citizens at home. All the while they were thinking too in visionary terms of setting an example for the rest of the world. This was, indeed, a tall order. In the process, they created three distinctive institutions that became essential components of American constitutionalism: presidentialism, federalism, and judicial review.

Presidentialism

Presidentialism was largely the invention of the framers.[69] They were aware, of course, of the writings of Montesquieu and others, but they were influenced perhaps less by theory than by the experiences of their own immediate past. The reason they assembled in Philadelphia was to remedy the deficiencies of the Articles of Confederation, one of the most glaring of which had been the virtual absence of executive power. At the same time, all of them could vividly recall the use of power by George III, which they had considered abusive. To create an executive with similar powers was unthinkable.[70]

Just what an executive should look like, just what powers—rather, *power*—it or he should have were therefore the subjects of spirited discussion in the Constitutional Convention. Delegates like James Wilson of Pennsylvania argued for a strong undivided executive who would be "the man of the people."[71] Others, like Roger Sherman of Connecticut, favored an executive who would be "an institution for carrying the will of the legislature into effect."[72] In other words, would the president be able to act on his own in large measure or be subject more to the will of the people or their representatives?

What the delegates created was an executive branch headed by an indirectly elected chief executive, the president, invested with considerable power.[73] All delegates assumed that George Washington would be the first occupant of the new office. This assumption in turn influenced them to grant the president more, rather than fewer, powers, exemplifying Max Weber's insight that "charismatic authority" may rest on faith in a leader "believed to be endowed with great personal worth."[74]

Although the delegates never wrote a job description of the presidency, Washington was the ideal man they had in mind. Aware that his every act was creating a precedent, Washington behaved accordingly, and his actions contributed more to the creation of the presidency than those of any other American chief executive. In that sense, his performance was almost the equivalent of a seventh seminal constitutional document.

The president was made commander in chief of the armed forces. He could conduct foreign relations and make treaties. He could appoint members to the Supreme Court with the advice and consent of the Senate, could appoint federal judges, heads of executive departments, and subordinate officials in his administration. He could recommend measures to Congress and was given a potential role in the legislative process by way of his power to veto legislation. His powers outlined in article 2 of the Constitution, moreover, suggest an undefined residual authority, in contrast to the carefully enumerated powers assigned to Congress.

Even so, the framers fenced in the presidential power in a variety of ways. The president could propose but he could not legislate; he could veto but his veto could be overridden. He could not spend as he wished, for Congress retained the all-important power of the purse. He could be impeached and, if convicted, removed from office.

The institution the framers thus fashioned has come to be known as "pure presidentialism." It is quite unlike any other chief executive existing in any nation at the time. Its essential features included an executive branch of government separate and distinct from the legislative branch, with a single executive at its head who is chosen either directly or indirectly by popular election. Both the executive's term of office and those of the members of the legislature are fixed and not contingent on mutual confidence. Functioning within a republican frame of government, the president directs the activities of the executive branch, names the heads of departments, and broadly establishes their policies. His other powers may be quite considerable, but they are by no means unlimited.

Although the term *presidentialism* might seem to imply that dominant power should reside in the chief executive rather than in the legislative body, that was clearly not the intent of the framers. Even Madison, who desired a more energetic government, conceded in *Federalist* 51 that "in republican government the legislative authority, necessarily, predominates."[75] In the end, the Constitution left unclear the question of whether the legislative or executive branch should dominate. Article 2 simply states that "the executive branch shall be vested in a President of the United States"; article 1, in contrast, stipulates that "all legislative powers herein granted shall be vested in the Congress of the United States" and does not compare or rank the two as to supremacy.

In actuality, over the generations it has sometimes been one, sometimes the other, of the two branches that has been ascendant. In the twentieth century, with its two world wars, Great Depression, and rise of the giant bureaucratic state, the presidency has almost steadily acquired increasing power.[76] In the nineteenth century, however, with the exception of the presidencies of Jackson, Polk, and especially Lincoln, the balance leaned heavily toward the legislative branch.

What was produced in the American presidency at first was what Carl J. Friedrich calls a dualistic system, which he properly termed "a presidential–congressional system of government." The designation "presidential system" did not come into its own until the twentieth century when the president (with some exceptions) became the strongest feature in the system.[77] Scholars for generations had defined various kinds of governing systems along lines derived from classical times, that is, monarchy, aristocracy, or democracy. When the need arose to distinguish among different kinds of democracy, scholars proposed categories to classify constitutions according to the most distinctive element in each system. Four different models of constitutional democracies emerged: (1) the "parliamentary system" to describe Britain, whose parliamentary cabinet system had become consolidated by 1810;[78] (2) the so-called presidential system in America; (3) the assembly system (the Third French Republic); and (4) the council system (Switzerland).[79] Although the American presidential system changed its dynamics between the nineteenth and twentieth centuries, it has nonetheless exercised far less influence in the world than Britain's parliamentary system.

Federalism

Unlike presidentialism, federalism—that form of government in which power is divided between a central authority and smaller or locally autonomous groups—is not an American invention.[80] Its history stretches back to ancient Greece, biblical times, and the Holy Roman Empire.[81] The beginnings of more modern ideas of federalism can be traced to the writings of Johannes Althusius in the seventeenth century and Montesquieu in the eighteenth. But the framers of the U.S. Constitution were the first nation builders to overcome the problems encountered in earlier attempts at federal unions.[82]

Andrew McLaughlin, a constitutional historian, long ago identified the experiential sources of American federalism in the country's past. Among the earliest was the federal theology of the Puritans, whose covenant theory posited a union between God and man in which each preserved a separate identity. The first British trading companies in America represented a federal system with their headquarters in England and branches in the New World. In the political realm, McLaughlin noted, agreements like the Mayflower Compact, the New England Confederation of 1643, and the Albany Plan of Union all assumed a federal form of one kind or another.[83] With the contractual federalism that the Articles of Confederation implemented, a different federal system was envisaged.

Historical precedents aside, the chief reason that Americans turned to a federal system may well have been the obvious but sometimes overlooked fact that the states existed before the Union. Short of the states maintaining all power and independence or giving up all power to a central government, there was little choice but to devise some sort of federal structure.[84] The Articles of Confederation, as noted earlier, made a significant start in initiating a new federalism, one that went beyond the earlier contractual federalism and moved in the direction of constitutional federalism. But the Articles did little to lessen state powers in favor of the central government, and the framers had to search for a more workable balance between the two. In Carl J. Friedrich's words, they were seeking "how to divide legislative powers between the states and federal government, how to balance the fields of governmental activity so as to produce a stable equilibrium between state and nation, and finally . . . how to arrange matters so as not to favor either the large or the small states."[85]

It was clear to the delegates that more governmental functions had to be shifted to the central government and, to most delegates, significantly more. Yet for many, doing so ran the risk of creating a too-powerful central government, which they feared most. They found the answer to that conundrum in the doctrine of separation of powers, by which they created a central government in which powers are distributed among the three branches of government, each branch separate from the others in a system of checks and balances preventing any one from riding roughshod over the others. Without agreement on this point, it is hard to imagine that many of the delegates would have assented to the extensive redistribution of functions from the state to the central level that was finally achieved.

Even as the founders wrestled with this question of the proper balance between the states and the nation, they took three crucial steps that came in large part to define American federalism. One was to provide in the Constitution that "the United States shall guarantee to every State in the Union a Republican Form of Government," thus binding federalism firmly to republicanism—and republicanism to federalism. One would prosper only as the other did.[86] The second had to do with creating the concept of dual citizenship of the people. Under the new Constitution, Americans were to be citizens of both the United States and the states in which they resided. Under the old theory of sovereignty an *imperium in imperio* was held to be an impossibility: two governments could not exist within the same geographical boundaries at the same time. The notion of dual citizenship, however, opened the door to exactly that.

Finally, the framers created a new definition of popular sovereignty. In the past, it is true, some theorists had argued that all government power was derived in a vague and general sense from the people. But according to Gordon Wood, the delegates claimed much more for the people as the ultimate sovereigns:

> Instead they were saying sovereignty remained always with the people and that the government was only a temporary and limited agency of the people—out to various government officials, so to speak, on a short term, always recallable loan. No longer would any parts of the state and federal governments, even popular houses of representatives, fully represent the people; instead all elected parts of governments—senators and governors and presidents—were now regarded in one way or another as simply partial representatives of the people.[87]

In these ways, the delegates to the Constitutional Convention created a distinctively American version of federalism.[88] It was one of the main features of American constitutionalism that, as we shall see, became a model for countries around the globe. Writing in the 1980s, Daniel Elazar pointed to the degree to which American federalism has affected the world:

> Today some 40 percent of the world's population lives within nineteen polities that have adopted constitutions at least purporting to be federal in character, while another 30 percent within eighteen political systems utilize federal principles to some degree within a formally unitary framework. While the variety of forms the federalist revolution has taken is great, the American federal system remains the single most influential standard against which others are measured, for better or for worse.[89]

Judicial Review

Although most scholars regard federalism as this country's most distinctive contribution to Western constitutionalism, some give priority to judicial review, the power of an independent judiciary to invalidate acts of a legislature held to contravene a constitution.[90] In the American context, this meant specifically the power of the federal courts to declare unconstitutional those acts of Congress as well as acts of state legislatures that the courts regarded as contraventions of the U.S. Constitution.

In light of its important place in the development of American constitutionalism, it may seem more than a little odd that judicial review is nowhere specifically mentioned in the Constitution. Were we to judge on the basis of that document solely, we could at most only infer that the framers intended for the federal judiciary to have this power. Yet it does seem clear that it was indeed their intention. In any case, judicial review soon became a firmly established feature of American constitutionalism.

The idea of judicial review first arose in England, where the Privy Council held the right to invalidate enactments of the colonial legislatures.[91] Colonial legislatures were therefore quite familiar with, if not happy about, the concept of judicial review. Later, on two separate occasions during the Confederation period, the highest court of a state exercised the right of judicial review, in one case specifically ruling that an act of the state legislature was unconstitutional.[92] However, during the first flush of republicanism in the founding years, the prevailing attitude was that the will of the people as expressed through their legislatures, not the courts, should determine the law. Over time, the framers discovered, however, that state legislators could be as oppressive as British ministers. Jefferson expressed the change in attitude that took place in the 1780s as uncontrolled legislators ran roughshod over laws they themselves had passed. "An elective despotism was not the government we fought for," he wrote in 1787.[93]

In Philadelphia the framers, who regarded the absence of federal courts to settle disputes between and among the states as one of the Articles' deficiencies, created an independent judiciary, the Supreme Court of the United States, and gave it jurisdiction in that and a number of other areas. They further authorized Congress to create other federal courts. Perhaps because of the continuing popular antipathy in some states toward an assertive judiciary, the framers were silent on whether the Court was to have the power to review the *constitutionality* of laws, that is, both the laws of state legislatures and the acts of Congress. In other words, whether it was intended that they pass on the validity of a statute in light of the Constitution was neither specifically affirmed nor denied.

Alexander Hamilton moved quickly into that opening. In *Federalist* 78, he argued that there was an ineluctable logic to judicial review, that the framers understood that logic very well, and that they intended the independent federal judiciary to have the power to review. A law was one thing, he wrote, a constitution—a "fundamental law"—was another. "Wherever a particular statute contravenes the constitution, it will be the duty of the judicial tribunals to adhere to the latter, and disregard the former." In other words, it would be the duty of the courts "to declare all acts contrary to the manifest tenor of the constitution void." There was no other way "than through the medium of the courts of justice" that specific limitations on the legislative branch could be preserved. To those who feared that this would make the judiciary the most powerful of the three branches, Hamilton pointed out that to the contrary, it would be the "weakest" and "least dangerous." The executive "holds the sword of the community," while "the legislature not only commands the purse, but prescribes the rules by which the duties and rights of every citizen are to be regulated."[94]

It was not until *Hylton v. United States*, 1796, and more especially *Marbury v. Madison* in 1803 that the Supreme Court asserted a claim to the power of judicial review.[95] Although another half century passed before the Court exercised that power again (in the *Dred Scott* decision in 1857), it seems clear that from the 1790s on, and more after *Marbury*, most lawyers, nearly all federal judges, and probably a substantial majority of the population accepted that the Court could invalidate an act of Congress on constitutional grounds.

On the question of whether federal courts could review the constitutionality of state laws, again the Constitution was not explicit. Nor did Hamilton address this question directly in his *Federalist* essays on the judiciary. Nonetheless, the supremacy clause lent weighty presumption in favor of such a doctrine: how could the Constitution be the supreme law of the land if the states could enact laws that contravened it? Most jurists of the time shared that view, and in the first decades of the new government, the federal courts developed a body of case law establishing that right of review, the resistance of states' rights champions notwithstanding. When Chief Justice John Marshall ruled in *McCulloch v. Maryland* (1819) that a state could not limit Congress in its exercise of a constitutionally authorized power, he completed fleshing out the Court's power of judicial review. That power now became a more fixed feature of American constitutionalism. Scholars abroad who studied the U.S. Constitution regarded judicial review as one of America's greatest contributions to Western constitutionalism, especially after World War II.

The Federalist

Writing about *The Federalist* to Alexander Hamilton in the summer of 1788, George Washington predicted that it would "merit the notice of posterity . . . in it are . . . ably discussed the principles of freedom and the topics of government—which will always be interesting to mankind as long as they are connected to Civil Society."[96] Washington was right. The unique collection of eighty-five essays by Hamilton, James Madison, and John Jay, originally published in newspapers to drum up support for ratification mainly in the New York convention, did indeed become the most authoritative and penetrating explication of the U.S. Constitution.

The Federalist differs from the other five documents because it serves another function and so is less available for any appropriation of its principles by foreign borrowers. Unlike the other texts, which offer specific principles of government for consideration, *The Federalist* offers a commentary, rationale, and interpretation of the U.S. Constitution itself, and in that function, it has provided the best exposition of the principles making up America's federal charter.

It is not too much to say that when scholars at home and abroad read the Constitution, they kept a copy of *The Federalist* at hand for an understanding of its provisions and its underlying philosophy. Time and again, *The Federalist* provided those abstract principles to which Supreme Court justices referred when analyzing the functions of American government. In England, John Stuart Mill, James Bryce, and Sir Henry Maine considered *The Federalist* crucial to an understanding of American constitutionalism.[97]

The reason for the canonical standing of *The Federalist* is that it began where most political treatises end. Ignoring the age-old problems in Western political thought—the origins of government, the nature of law and of sovereignty, the bases of citizen obligations to the state—*The Federalist* went straight to the theoretical premises for achieving political objectives in a republican state.[98] Indeed, one English scholar contended that on the basis of five of the essays alone, Madison deserved to be ranked "as one of the leading theorists of the dangers and opportunities . . . latent in the modern democratic state."[99]

All its brilliance as political theory notwithstanding, *The Federalist* must be viewed as a political document of its time. The publication of the heretofore secret Constitution on September 17, 1787, precipitated what Bernard Bailyn has called one of "the most extensive public debates on constitutionalism and on public principles ever recorded." In what is arguably the best analysis of the essays, Bailyn wrote that "literally thousands of people, in this nation of only approximately one million voters, participated in one way or another."[100] Hamilton, Madison, and Jay entered the fray with their essays written under the pseudonym "Publius."[101]

The intention of Publius was not only to explicate the proposed Constitution but also to answer specific criticisms leveled by its opponents, the Anti-federalists. There are many ways of viewing *The Federalist*, but perhaps one of the best is to see the essays as a continuation of the debates held in the Constitutional Convention between two sets of elitist leaders: the Federalists—Madison, Hamilton, and Jay—and the Anti-federalists— Elbridge Gerry, George Mason, and Edmund Randolph. A comparison of their views indicates that the term *Anti-federalist* with which the Federalists branded their opponents was not justified (even though it became the generally accepted designation of the group). All three Anti-federalists arrived at their anti-Constitution stance only at the end of the proceedings. Throughout the Convention it was difficult to distinguish between them and the Federalists because both groups voted the same on so many issues. Their anti-Constitution views, for the most part, arose from the same intellectual framework as that of the Federalists.[102]

Of the three Anti-federalists, Elbridge Gerry of Massachusetts was the most articulate and spoke more frequently in the convention than did the other two.[103] When he listed his reasons for refusing to sign the Constitution, Gerry charged that the central government had been given too much power under the elastic "necessary and proper" clause: Congress could raise armies and taxes without limit. The individual liberties of the people, moreover, lacked the protection of any bill of rights.[104] When he elaborated on his "Objections" in a Boston newspaper several weeks later, Gerry's piece became the most celebrated critique of the Constitution. His main argument was that the new government was dangerously unbalanced because of its centralizing and consolidating tendencies. "The Constitution proposed has few, if any *federal* features, but is rather a system of *national* government."[105]

Gerry expressed the fears of his fellow Anti-federalists: that a consolidated government would annihilate the sovereignty of the states and powers of the local governments. If the people adopted the proposed plan of government, they might lose their liberties, and if they rejected it, "Anarchy may ensue." Gerry's fear was that a civil war might break out.[106]

Mason, like Gerry, was deeply concerned about the absence of a bill of rights. Indeed, when Gerry introduced a motion to include a bill of rights near the end of the convention proceedings on September 12, Mason seconded it. Both men were shocked when it went down to a resounding defeat.[107] The two men had similar ideas about protecting trial by jury in civil cases as well as liberty of the press. Both feared the rise of an aristocracy in America, and Mason prophesied the government under the proposed constitution would "commence in a moderate Aristocracy" and might produce "a Monarchy or a corrupt oppressive Aristocracy [and] most probably vibrate some Years between the two, and then terminate in the one or the other."[108]

Randolph, too, feared a rapid ascent from president to king. To him, the presidency created in Philadelphia was but the "foetus of monarchy." "The fixt genius of the people of America," he declared, "required a different form of government."[109] He, too, supported the idea of a plural executive or an executive council. Randolph's other objections were similar in many ways to Gerry's. He thought the Senate might become a "countenance of an aristocracy" and the president, "a little monarch." Randolph, the first of the dissenting trio to voice objections to the proposed constitution, led the way. He introduced a motion calling for a second constitutional convention "to know more the sense of the people."[110] Supporting the motion, all three Anti-federalists became obstructionists threatening to undo the work of the Philadelphia Convention.

What the Anti-federalists feared, Bailyn notes, was that the proposed Constitution would be creating "a potentially powerful central government that would have armed force, that would enter into all the dangerous struggles of international conflicts, and that had the potential to sweep through the states and dominate the daily lives of the American people."[111] While Gerry, in particular, felt, as did Montesquieu, that a republic could succeed only in a geographically limited area and that what was being proposed—a republic spread over a vast portion of the North American continent—was in danger of failing.[112]

If *The Federalist* had done nothing more than provide a riposte for each Anti-federalist sally, it would have been only one more voice in the cacophonous debate leading up to the state ratifying conventions. But its three authors did far more: they expounded on and defended the proposed Constitution to their countrymen, not only its every provision— why the president must have the veto, the power to appoint, and the power to make treaties; why Congress required the "necessary and proper" clause—but also the fundamental governing philosophies in which it was grounded. They made a case for the supremacy clause and for the need to make citizens answerable to national laws: in that direction lay effective government, but in any other, only anarchy and its probable offsprings, war and despotism. They explained how the checks and balances prevented runaway power by any branch of government and would help make more secure the liberties of the people. They familiarized Americans with the novel idea of judicial review, explaining its logic a decade and a half before Chief Justice John Marshall did in *Marbury v. Madison.*

To answer the Anti-federalists' fears of a consolidated government rather than a loose federal system, Madison wrote his famous *Federalist* 10. Drawing on the ideas of David Hume, Madison argued that quite the reverse was true: a republican government would operate better in a large territory than in a small one. Madison believed that factions competing within society were inevitable and that it was better to control than to try to suppress them. The best way to do so was to establish a republican government and extend its jurisdiction over a larger area. "Extend the sphere, and you take in a greater variety of parties and interests, you make it less probable that a majority of the whole will have a common motive to invade the rights of other citizens."[113]

Because the Articles with their loose confederation of states had been so weak and ineffectual, the Federalists supported greater centralization in the proposed Constitution. In *Federalist* 15, Hamilton attacked what he called "this great and radical vice" in the Articles of Confederation. The result had been that resolutions passed under the Articles had been "mere recommendations" that the states could follow or disregard as they pleased.[114] In *Federalist* 16, Hamilton pushed his argument further by calling for national laws "to pass . . . upon citizens themselves." Failure to establish such a government would expose the United States to anarchy and chaos. The only way that the Union would be successful was to make individual citizens directly answerable to national laws.[115]

Responding to the Anti-federalists' fears that a standing army under the central government could be raised "without limit" and to their counterproposal that state militias would be safer, Hamilton attacked the idea. State militias serving as the first line of the nation's defense would not be effective. In *Federalist* 25, he noted that in Shays's Rebellion, when Massachusetts had to call up the state militia quickly, the Bay State had to get permission from the Confederation government. There would be occasions, he observed, when there would be no time for such bureaucratic steps.[116]

To counter Anti-federalist arguments that the central government would be able to raise taxes "without limit," Hamilton in his *Federalist* 30 pointed out that historically, no government without taxing power had lasted long. The system of money "quotas and requisitions" on the states simply had not worked. It thus was essential that the new central government be granted authority to raise revenues by traditional methods of taxation.[117]

In *Federalist* 39, Madison answered Gerry's charge that the Constitution had created what was a national government with few federal features. Madison countered that the Constitution was neither a national nor a federal constitution but a composition of both:

> In its foundation, it is federal, and not national; in the sources from which the ordinary powers of the Government are drawn, it is partly federal and partly national: in the operation of these powers, it is national, not federal: In the extent of them again, it is federal, not national: And finally, in the authoritative mode of introducing amendments, it is neither federal, nor wholly national.

In other words, the government had as many federal as national features. It was federal by virtue of the fact that the central government held only enumerated powers and left to the states "a residuary and inviolable sovereignty over all other objects." But at the same time it was national by virtue of its power to operate directly on individual citizens.[118]

When responding to the Anti-federalists' complaints about the violation of the separation of powers principle, Madison in *Federalist* 51 observed that this principle, among other things, protected the liberties of individuals. His argument was analogous to that he had employed in his *Federalist* 10. The civil rights of citizens would be protected better from conflicts arising from "the multiplicity of interests" in a free society. In the clash of differing interests, they would cancel out one another, and the inevitable result would be greater liberty.[119]

When the discussion turned to national institutions, Hamilton, who wanted a more energetic government, devoted several essays to the presidency. Although he tended to distrust both individuals and the masses with power, Hamilton considered the evils of the despot preferable to the anarchy of uncontrolled masses. He spent time defending the powers of the president—the veto, appointment powers, and treaty-making authority. For the Anti-federalists who argued for a plural presidency or an executive council out of fear of one-man rule, Hamilton in *Federalist 70* presented a strong brief for unity in the office.[120]

Hamilton introduced the rationale for another institutional innovation: the idea of judicial review. In *Federalist 78*, he provided the most memorable exposition for that doctrine: "Whenever a particular statute contravenes the constitution, it will be the duty of the judicial tribunals to adhere to the latter, and disregard the former."[121]

To Jay, the oft-neglected third author, was left the task of dealing with the Constitution with respect to foreign affairs. Although he wrote only five essays, Jay's role as minister to Spain during the war and as peace commissioner to England in the peace treaty of 1783 especially qualified him. Advocate of a strong central government, Jay's major worry was if the Union broke up into separate confederations, in which event a weakened America would fall prey to foreign powers. In his *Federalist 2, 3*, and *4*, he pointed out how much safer citizens would be if the Union stayed together.[122]

With their arguments in *The Federalist*, Madison, Hamilton, and Jay not only answered the Anti-federalists, but in the course of doing so they did something much more profound: they changed the whole conception of politics in the Western world. They transformed American political culture by proposing that sovereignty resided in the people rather than in any single branch of government. Every branch of government, therefore, represented the people. Madison observed in *Federalist 51* "that all the appointments for the supreme executive, legislative, and judiciary magistracies should be drawn from the same fountain of authority, the people."[123] This new way of thinking changed the relationship of government and society by dissolving the traditional idea of mixed government incorporating the elements of monarchy, aristocracy, and democracy that had been followed since time immemorial. It marked, as Gordon Wood observed, one of the most creative moments in the history of political thought.[124]

By making the people the locus of sovereignty, Federalists were able to think in new terms about the issue of divided sovereignty. "Only by making the people themselves, and not their representatives in the state legislatures or in the Congress, the one final supreme . . . law-making authority, could the Federalists explain the emerging idea of [American] federalism, that unusual division of legislative responsibilities in which neither is final and supreme."[125] This model of federalism not only was applied in America but also became the basis for similar divisions of legislative powers in governments throughout the globe.

The American Bill of Rights

The sixth and final seminal document of American constitutionalism is the Bill of Rights, the first ten amendments to the U.S. Constitution. Bills of rights have, of course, a long historical tradition. In England, the line of such documents runs from the Magna Carta in 1215 through the 1628 Petition of Right to the Bill of Rights of 1689. If those documents were not bills of rights in the modern sense, and the line connecting them not precisely direct, the documents had at least one underlying principle in common: certain rights—granted, in the case of the Magna Carta's belonging only to the nobility—were beyond the power of the Crown. By the late seventeenth century, these rights collectively came to be called "the rights of Englishmen," and the people of England gloried in them.[126]

So did the American colonists. From the earliest English settlements, the colonists claimed these rights equally for themselves. They, too, were Englishmen, they said. Their claim to such rights was not diminished by the fact that they were living in the New World. To make the point more emphatically, colonists wrote a number of charters and statutes to safeguard their personal freedoms from encroachment. There was a great difference, however, between the English and American texts. The English documents were acts of Parliament intended to protect the "rights of Englishmen" from abuse by the Crown, whereas the colonial documents were acts of colonial legislatures intended to protect those rights from abuses by Parliament as well as from abuses by the colonial assemblies themselves. These colonial texts were, if anything, even more expansive in their claims than their English models. James Logan of Pennsylvania at one point complained that they even sometimes claimed rights "unknown to others of the Queen's subjects."[127]

There was another important difference. After declaring independence, a number of states incorporated bills of rights into their new state constitutions. Virginia's Declaration of Rights of 1776 was embedded into the Virginia Constitution and served as a model for other states. The Virginia bill differed greatly from the English bills of rights, however. Being acts of Parliament, the English bills could easily be repealed by a succeeding Parliament, since that body was deemed supreme. But in the case of the Virginia bill, it could be repealed only by a constitutional amendment, a cumbersome, time-consuming, and difficult process.

Such was the situation when the delegates met in Philadelphia. The question before them was whether an enumeration of rights should be included in the proposed Constitution. They decided it should not be, and the Constitution was sent to the states for ratification without one.

It soon became clear that the Federalists supporting the Constitution had made a colossal mistake. In the debates leading up to ratification and in the state ratifying conventions themselves, the absence of a bill of rights became the subject of heated debates and a rallying point for the Anti-federalists. The Federalists were thrown on the defensive. Some sought to justify the decision not to include a bill of rights on the grounds that many state constitutions already contained declarations of rights. The inclusion of one in the new Constitution, they said, would be a breach in the principle of federalism.

James Wilson, an ardent nationalist from Pennsylvania, argued in the state's ratifying convention that it was impossible to enumerate and reserve all the powers of the people, since "a bill annexed to a constitution is an enumeration, everything that is not enumerated is presumed to be given. The consequence is, that an imperfect enumeration would throw all implied power into the scale of government; and the rights of the people would be rendered incomplete."[128]

In *Federalist* 84, Hamilton offered the feeble argument that a bill of rights was not needed because unlike England, where such bills originated as contracts between monarch and subjects, American constitutions were founded on the power of the people and executed by "their immediate representatives and servants." That, he said, rendered a bill of rights "unnecessary."[129]

On his part, Madison privately expressed opposition because he believed that a federal bill of rights would prove no better a shield against "overbearing majorities" than had the states' bills of rights. They would become only what he called "parchment barriers." In Virginia, Madison wrote, "I have seen the bill of rights violated in every instance where it has been opposed to a popular current."[130]

When Jefferson, serving as minister in France, received his copy of the Constitution, he immediately fixed on the absence of a bill of rights. His criticism had an electrifying effect, as it became the main basis of argument on which the Anti-federalists relied to oppose the document. More than a protest, Jefferson suggested a cunning strategy for getting a bill of rights added. If he were in America, he wrote: "I would advocate it [the Constitution] warmly until nine [states] should have adopted, and then as warmly the other side . . . to convince the remaining four that they ought not to come to it till the declaration of rights is annexed."[131] After he repeated his strategy to many friends, it became the tactic used by the Anti-federalists from New York to the Carolinas.[132]

Jefferson made a second significant contribution to the bill of rights cause. He persuaded Madison, who was unalterably opposed to any bill of rights, to change his mind. Madison did an about-face, pledging to propose rights-related amendments were he elected to serve in the first Congress. And he did exactly that on June 8, 1789. Madison's speech in support of adding a bill of rights to the Constitution was marked more by its generosity of spirit than by any deep conviction of a true need for one. Even if such a bill were unnecessary, he argued, it could do little harm to add one, as doing so would reassure those who still had doubts about the Constitution. Furthermore, even though the enumeration of rights might prove to be only "paper barriers," it would focus public attention on them and help compel the citizenry to abide by them.[133]

These promises of a bill of rights first in the state ratifying conventions and then by the Federalists in Congress won over even the three Anti-federalist elite leaders. Gerry had already announced his support for the Constitution before Madison's speech, after being convinced by Federalist promises that the demand of the Anti-federalists for a bill of rights would be addressed.[134] Mason was also appeased after the House passed the proposed amendments.[135] Randolph had already gone over to the enemy, so to speak, having accepted the position of attorney general in Washington's first administration.

The constitutional scholar Herbert Storing had it right when he observed, "While the Federalists gave us the Constitution, the legacy of the Anti-federalists was the Bill of Rights."[136] The Anti-federalist legacy has grown over the years. It has become stronger with the passage of time and is considered more relevant as a result of the human rights movement that developed in the late twentieth century.

The Bill of Rights is a document of both individual rights and restraints on federal power, the one being protected by the other. The most familiar of these rights and restraints, and no doubt the most important, are those in the First Amendment. It provides for freedom of speech and press, peaceable assembly and petition, and free exercise of religion, the last accompanied by a prohibition against the official establishment of any single religion. But the other nine amendments, such as those protecting against any unreasonable search and seizure (the Fourth), guaranteeing due process and fair trial (the Fifth, Sixth, and Seventh), and prohibiting excessive bail and cruel and unusual punishment (the Eighth), also deal with the fundamental rights of individuals. Their adoption in 1791 completed what proved to be the most creative constitutional period in American history.

The bill of rights concept is only one of several sources—English and French as well as American—that contributed to the formation of an all-inclusive bill of rights tradition. Each of the three had its partisans in the debate over whose contribution to the tradition was greatest. Since the strands of thought that have gone into the Western constitutional tradition are so intertwined, it is impossible to separate them. For that reason, references in this book are to the "*bill of rights tradition*" rather than to any one national tradition. But about the place of the first ten amendments in the American polity, there is no debate. The American Bill of Rights was the final building block that the founding generation erected in the edifice we call American constitutionalism.

There can be no doubt that American constitutionalism included much more than the U.S. Constitution, and earlier scholars have been remiss in applying such a narrow definition. At home, a systematic study of the six documents in America's domestic history can help us understand American constitutionalism and its workings in a new way. Abroad, it offers a fresh perspective not only in evaluating the influence of American constitutionalism on foreign constitutionalists but, more important, in understanding better the constitutional history of the modern world as a whole.

PART II

Seven Echoes of American Constitutionalism

A Global Perspective

Part 2 of this book is organized around seven "echoes," or peak periods, of American constitutional influence. Each occurred following a war, revolution, or similar upheaval. The first echo, 1776 to 1800, resounded after the American Revolution and set off a round of American-influenced constitutions in northwestern Europe and adjacent hinterlands. It was followed by six peak periods when American constitutionalism gradually spread around the rest of the globe.

This survey indicates how persistent, though unevenly, interest in the American model was in the world from 1776 to 1989. Although the model was never duplicated in its entirety in any one country, the example of America as a republic with a constitutional system guaranteeing self-government by a free people continued to inspire and instruct countries seeking new patterns of governance. There were other periods, called interludes, however, when interest in the American model flagged for various reasons. In Europe, the richness of the constitutional traditions often made it difficult for American constitutionalism to compete. For instance, the monarchical system showed great flexibility in meeting the challenges of aristocrats, the rising bourgeois class, and radical political movements of all sorts. These interludes were significant because they showed that the spread of American constitutionalism was not a series of uninterrupted triumphs, as portrayed in some accounts of Whig history. Rather, there were sporadic setbacks and periods of quiescence along the way when the American model did not advance.

3

First Echo

Europe, 1776–1800

"The 'shot heard round the world' sounded sharp and clear in the Gardens of the Tuileries," wrote one scholar.[1] The first echo of American constitutionalism abroad reverberated through countries bordering the northwest corner of the Atlantic basin and their central European hinterlands. Within the North Atlantic Basin, constitutional ties developed quickly between America and Europe as well as across the English Channel. A new awareness of this phenomenon is found in the current trend of reconceptualizing British and North Atlantic history inspired by Bernard Bailyn. Instead of a nationalistic perspective of events, a pan-Atlantic approach is taken. "We are all Atlanticists now," declared David Armitage. There developed an Atlantic community of shared ideas regarding natural rights, individual liberty, and sovereignty of the people, which fit the context of the new constitutional constellation called Western constitutionalism.[2]

The discourse over American constitutionalism on both sides of the Atlantic during the first echo marked the beginning also of "the age of the democratic revolution" that swept over Europe and North America from the 1760s to the 1840s, according to Robert R. Palmer.[3] He viewed the American Revolution as part of the process of democratization taking place throughout much of the Western world at that time. It resulted from the failure of monarchical regimes supported by conservative feudal and religious institutions to address pressing social, economic, and political problems. The outcome was a series of revolutionary repercussions—violent or nonviolent—arising among the popular elements in society. The American Revolution, French Revolution, and Britain's movements for parliamentary reform were responses to these challenges. In the last quarter of the eighteenth century, revolutionary upheavals occurred in other European countries, including Belgium, Poland, the Netherlands, Ireland, Switzerland, Hungary, and Italy.

One result of the democratic revolution was the concomitant development of Western constitutionalism—the constitutional tradition involving Britain, America, and France—whose influence lasted well beyond the 1840s. Although each country acted separately and spread its version of constitutional government into regions and colonies subject to its control, the combined impact was part of the process identified as the "Europeanization" of the developed world. To view American constitutionalism in its proper perspective, it is necessary to see it as part of this broader tradition of Western constitutionalism.

Much of American constitutionalism was derived from British constitutionalism, as is well known. Britain's constitutionalism itself had synthesized a collection of statutes, court judgments, customs, and key documents to which later generations granted constitutional status: the Magna Carta (1215), *Habeas Corpus* Act (1679), Petition of Right (1628), and English Bill of Rights (1689). Together they established what was called the "rights of Englishmen." This body of ideas, practices, and experience became the basis of the English constitutional system that we call *British constitutionalism*. It evolved over time, relied on precedent, and comprised the underlying principles by which Britain was governed.

Briefly put, the core of the British government in practice consisted of a set of three institutions: the Crown or monarch, the House of Lords, and the House of Commons, each of which served in theory to check the other two, along with the judiciary in order to protect liberty. The House of Lords and the House of Commons formed the Parliament, and the institutional framework for the British lawmaking process was known as the "King-in-Parliament" because legislation could become law only by consent of the king, Lords, and Commons. Although there existed a royal veto, not since the early eighteenth century had an English monarch exercised that power. In terms of the balance of power, however, the historical struggles between monarch and Parliament resulted ultimately in the sovereignty of Parliament as the defender of English liberty. Together with the principle of the rule of law, including the norm that every person was equal before the law, the sovereignty of Parliament formed the two pillars upholding English law.

While devoted to the rule of law principle, the American colonists ultimately took exception to the sovereignty of Parliament because in their eyes no person or institution could hold unchecked sovereignty, for that would lead to tyranny. To them, the only acceptable governmental system was one in which every component institution was subject to checks by the others. They were convinced that their view was vindicated when Parliament imposed a series of regulations and taxes that they felt violated their traditional rights as Englishmen, and not even a direct appeal to the monarch could resolve the resulting crisis. Their consequent decision to embrace independence and form a constitutional government based on the principles to which they subscribed led them also to reject the informal and precedent-laden form of British constitutionalism. To ensure that constitutional government would be clear to those who lived under it, it had to be a written constitution with the status of fundamental law. The people could exercise their constituent power to frame and adopt their constitution, and that exercise of power would be distilled into a written constitutional text.

As Carl J. Friedrich pointed out, American constitutionalism as represented in the U.S. Constitution was in many ways the very antithesis of British constitutionalism:

> Where the British constitution is a complex of laws, customs, and changing ways of behaving, the American Constitution is at the outset a formal document, carefully thought out in all its parts and seeking to construct a *rational* whole. Its rationalism strongly contrasts with British traditionalism—a second antithesis. Where the British constitution closely links executive and legislative authority, the American separates and balances them in its presidential system. Where the British constitution is strongly centralist, in spite of its tradition of local government, the American is distinguished by its federalism. Judicial guardianship, lest the legislative violate the basic law's provisions, is a third important feature of . . . [American] constitutionalism, whereas the British have maintained for many years the "sovereignty of parliament."[4]

The antitheses in Western constitutionalism created an ongoing debate between American and British principles while at the same time they held much in common in what was referred to as the *Anglo-American model*. The result was that while Americans retained the core of constitutional liberty that they had inherited from Britain, they moved beyond it to find a new way to protect that liberty. They devised a government system strong enough to cope with national needs and balanced enough to protect liberty and the ideals of clearly formulated constitutional government.

As regards French constitutionalism, historians have long recognized the direct influence of the American Revolution and its revolutionary

constitutionalism on the French Revolution and the subsequent constitutions it produced. But there is a tendency to downplay these connections
in light of the subsequent checkered course of French constitutional history. Moreover, France's emphasis on centralism and statism diverged radically from the Anglo-American model and became a third major source
of influence.

France thus took its place alongside Britain and the United States in
the Western constitutional constellation. In the decade of the 1790s,
France not only produced four constitutions but, in 1789, also the monumental Declaration of the Rights of Man and the Citizen. That document
affirmed the principles of the new French nation-state: the rule of law,
the equality of every citizen, and the collective sovereignty of the people.
These principles incorporated into the 1791 French Constitution not only
involved the people but also set limits on the power of the monarch and
gave France a kind of charter it had never had before.

The period from 1776 to 1800 represents, therefore, one of the most
revolutionary periods of constitutional change in global history. When
the three traditions—the British, American, and French—came together,
they formed Western constitutionalism, led by the United States and its
Virginia Declaration of Rights of 1776 which established the basis of modern constitutionalism (as noted previously). Subsequent developments in
the American Revolution, French Revolution, and British parliamentary
reforms strengthened Western constitutionalism to the point that it influenced much of northwestern Europe during the first echo.

The Role of Myths

The first echo also introduced an era of experiments in republicanism
that differed from the classical tradition. In America, two myths regarding American constitutionalism sprang up that were to influence European experiments in republicanism: the "cult of the constitution" and the
"American Dream." Although the two myths operated differently in different countries, they shared certain characteristics. One was the decades-
long influence they exercised on constitutional documents written on the
European continent.

The "cult of the constitution" arose from an idealistic vision that a republican utopia would eventually emerge out of the experiences of the
American and French revolutions.[5] This belief resulted from the romantic
notion reflected in the republican revolutionary movements affecting the

entire Western world at the time. As Justice Oliver Wendell Holmes put it, there was a search under way for absolute standards during a period of rapid change: "This demand [was] at the bottom of the philosopher's effort to prove that truth is absolute and of the jurist's search for criteria of universal validity which he collects under the head of natural law."[6]

This creed, derived from the Enlightenment, involved a faith that *rational* institutions, based on reason and justice, could be discovered that would have a universal appeal to peoples throughout the entire world. Motivated by an assumption of the unity of humankind, constitutionalists began to theorize about the perfectibility of man, the best forms of government, and the ideas related to the doctrine of natural rights. Documents written during the first echo, especially the American Declaration of Independence and the French Declaration of the Rights of Man, reflected this cult. The republican French Constitution of 1793 perhaps expressed its credo best. "Forgetfulness of, or contempt for, the natural rights of man," it read, "are the sole causes of the unhappiness of mankind."[7] By 1815, however, the cult had lost its luster, with the Napoleonic constitutions of the early 1800s signaling its decline.[8] Charters written after 1800 were characterized more by authoritarianism in search of order than by republican utopianism. The constitutions of the Restoration, with their bleak, pragmatic, and reactionary provisions, presented a completely different outlook.

In contrast, the American Dream was associated with the powerful appeal of American constitutionalism to Europe after 1776. This myth had a long tradition in the European imagination: it assumed that the New World would one day provide solutions for the ills of the Old.[9] The American Dream continued to fire the hopes of revolutionaries everywhere. Reformers, patriotic nationalists, and romantics from the rim of the Atlantic to the distant steppes of Russia and from Norway to the Italian peninsula became believers.

What was meant by the American Dream involved largely, though not exclusively, many of the constitutional innovations introduced by the six seminal documents. America was seen as a promised land—the wave of the future—one that would realize the dreams of the European Enlightenment. But when dealing with the American Dream in France, it is best to keep in mind the qualification implied in the title of Durand Echeverria's book *Mirage in the West*. Echeverria's study of French public opinion regarding the American Revolution showed that Frenchmen discovered in America's republican experiment exactly what they wanted to find. They attributed to America's revolutionary experience precisely those traits they felt were lacking in their own country: liberty, virtue, prosperity, and intellectual enlightenment. The *philosophes*, men of letters, and French visitors to America (including soldiers serving in the War of Independence) created an idealized image, a "mirage," which hardly resembled existing social realities. Distorted though it was, the American Dream nevertheless exerted a tremendous influence throughout France.[10]

The American Dream possessed a dynamic quality that allowed it to change Proteus-like over time and to assume a different shape from one country to another. From 1776 to 1800, the myth was most pronounced in France, but traces of it could be found elsewhere, even among British reformers in Parliament. As far as time was concerned, it kept cropping up whenever the American model exercised its appeal throughout the early nineteenth century.

Paine's Common Sense

These two myths were fused in the person of one man, Thomas Paine, one of the leading apostles of American constitutionalism abroad. Best known as a political pamphleteer and religious dissenter, Paine proved to be one of the most formidable constitutionalists during the first echo. He left his mark on not one but three countries, the United States, France, and Britain. If Lafayette deserves the title "hero of two worlds," Paine merits the sobriquet "hero of three worlds" for his international proselytizing.

Paine proclaimed his principles of American constitutionalism first in *Common Sense*, published in January 1776.[11] His message touched off a public discourse that led directly to the Declaration of Independence. Many Americans had hesitated about separating from Britain, but Paine's pamphlet finally galvanized them into action. Plunging into political writing soon after his arrival in America from England in 1774, his instantaneous success proved that there did, indeed, exist a kind of cosmopolitan mentality throughout the Atlantic world.[12] The fact that this English immigrant could communicate so quickly with the American people demonstrates the pervasiveness of many constitutional ideas.

The American Revolution, Paine declared, was more than a change of government; it was the beginning of a sweeping movement for republicanism throughout the world. He not only called for independence but also insisted that Americans abandon the British monarchy, establish a new republic, and protect their innate republican virtue as a people. Paine originated a new vocabulary to describe the colonists' quest for freedom. He was one of the first to change the definition of "revolution" from a scientific term applied primarily to the movement of planetary systems to one suggesting an irreversible social and political change. In America, that change was for the creation of a republican government committed to a universal standard of human rights.[13]

Common Sense opened with a spirited assault on the monarchy. Paine attacked the conventional view of the king-in-Parliament as the best basis for government and instead labeled the monarchy as the source of despotism. Unlike Benjamin Franklin, who had "gladly" offered George III the title of "King of Massachusetts" if he would govern in association with local officials, Paine shocked Americans by calling him a "Royal Brute,"[14] lumping the king with absolutist rulers governing Russia, Spain, and France.

Paine scoffed at the doctrine of the divine right of kings. He ridiculed the idea that the roots of monarchy could be traced to primitive Christianity and rejected the notion of hereditary succession.[15] To Paine, because all human beings were created equal in the sight of God, it was a despicable idea for one family to set itself up in perpetuity above all others. "Of more worth is one honest man in society and in the sight of God," declared Paine, "than all the crowned ruffians that ever lived."[16]

In America, Paine called for a revolution to sweep away all vestiges of the king and British aristocracy. "But where, some [would] say, is the King of America?" Paine's answer was clear: in "the charter" itself. Let a constitution be created and placed on "Divine Law," on the "Word of God," he wrote, reflecting the religious foundation of his political belief. "Let a crown be placed on it by which the world may know that, so far as we approve of monarchy, . . . in America *the law is King*."[17]

Paine made a crucial distinction between civil society and the state. To Paine, society meant civilized society functioning as a rational, self-regulating community that worked in harmony. It bound together people who held common social affections and believed in the same economic goals. One of Paine's great contributions was to popularize this Lockeian concept of a civil society. By doing so, he broadened the notion of individual rights, albeit within the framework of a society dedicated to the common good.

A government of our own is "our natural right," Paine told Americans. He distinguished between natural rights and man-made civil rights, making this difference the criterion for determining the proper sphere in which government should operate. "His ideal was a grand republic in which the pursuit of happiness should be possible for all men," wrote one scholar.[18] Paine's view, of course, was too utopian; he failed to take into account the social antagonisms, conflicting economic claims, and clashing political interests that usually divide societies and lead to less civilized behavior.

The state—by which in today's parlance Paine meant the government—would be based on popular sovereignty, a principle directly related to his sunny vision of civil society. Generally speaking, he posited a benign view of popular sovereignty and worried less about threats to liberty from below. Within this context, Paine provided "hints" to how governments in America, on both the national and state levels, could be created. First, a "national conference" should be called. His idea for a national constitutional convention was radical at the time. Remember, Paine pointed out, "Our strength is Continental, not Provincial," so the conference should be held on the national level. Once a national government had been formed, the constitutional convention—being a special constitution-making body only—should dissolve.[19]

Paine envisioned a federal system with a line of jurisdiction drawn between the national and state governments. State legislatures would be subject to the national congress, whose legislation would be the supreme law of the land. Paine's ideas of representative government reflected the standard republican tradition in many ways: a republic without a monarch, an executive separate from the legislature, and a congress balancing diverse interests in society. Annual elections were to be held to ensure rotation in office and to prevent continued political control. A huge representative congress, numbering some 390 members, was to be elected on the broadest suffrage possible.[20]

But one of Paine's major ideas—that of unicameralism on both the national and state levels—was out of step with the view held by most Americans. They were wedded to the idea of a bicameral legislature with upper houses serving as a check on unruly lower houses but also with lower houses representing the populace more directly. Along with his friend Benjamin Franklin, Paine emerged as the outstanding advocate for unicameralism. Their idea was derived, no doubt, from the experience of Pennsylvania (where they lived), which had only a one-house legislature in the colonial period.[21]

Paine's belief in the sanctity of private property was another major theme running through *Common Sense*. Securing freedom and property to all men, he believed, should be one of the main goals of all American governments. Only in this way could America achieve political stability. Under the British constitution, he concluded, "the property of no man is secure in the present unbraced system of things."[22]

A religious dissenter, Paine was committed also to religious liberty and freedom of conscience. "As to religion, I hold it . . . the indispensable duty of all governments, to protect all conscientious professors thereof, and know of no other business which government hath to do herewith."[23] The discriminatory laws against religious dissenters in England, Ireland, and Wales rankled the Quaker Paine, who had suffered a sense of deprivation at the hands of the Anglican establishment.[24]

Given the differences between Britain and America, Paine felt it imperative that the colonies break away to ensure America's economic well-being as well as its national security and republican virtue. Britain, like the rest of Europe, was corrupt. By separating from mercantilist Britain, America could develop a free-trade zone, enjoy greater prosperity, and be free from the wars plaguing Europe because of commercial rivalries. America had a golden opportunity to become a nation dedicated to freedom for people everywhere. Other countries had expelled freedom from their midst, but America could provide an asylum for all humankind. "We have every opportunity . . . to form the noblest, purest, constitution on the face of the earth. The birth-day of a new world is at hand," wrote Paine in a burst of exultation.[25]

The influence of *Common Sense* in America was enormous. Paine's pamphlet became a best seller, and its reception unprecedented. By the close of 1776, twenty-five separate editions had been printed, reaching hundreds of thousands of people.[26] Although its exact circulation is not known, the *Morning Post* in London reported in August 1776 that 46,000 copies had been printed in America alone.[27] British officials kept hoping that the popularity of the pamphlet in both America and Britain would fade. But such was not the case; the British were destined to hear more from Paine and his publications.

The Burke—Paine Controversy

In the early 1790s Paine became involved in what is arguably the greatest constitutional controversy ever conducted in the English language and which deeply influenced the British view of their own constitution as well as those of France and America. The controversy began in England in 1789 with the publication of a sermon, "Discourse on the Love of Our Country," by the radical nonconformist clergyman Richard Price. He was enthusiastic about events in France, where the Revolution was just getting under way.[28] Then, as the saying goes, "the French Revolution began in England." Price's pamphlet triggered a chain reaction. His "Discourse" was answered by Edmund Burke in his *Reflections on the Revolution in France*, published in 1790.[29] Burke's book in turn was challenged by Paine's *Rights of Man*, published in 1791/1792.

Paine was one of those in America best qualified to answer the British thinker. The crux of the argument between the two turned on what the nature of a constitution should be. Paine held that a constitution should be made from whole cloth, *de novo*, and he rejected the idea of prior experience or tradition being of much value. His statement "We have it in our power to begin the world over again" expressed his constitutional philosophy perfectly.[30]

Burke's *Reflections* presented an opposite point of view. His doctrine of prescription held that men's rights should depend more on historical tradition. To Burke, the British constitution was ideal, as it represented an accumulation of the wisdom of the past which deserved to be conserved, though certain allowances should be made for gradual change. Sensing the dangerous enthusiasm of antiestablishment men in Britain for the French Revolution, Burke attacked France's revolutionary ideas. The French, he wrote, relied blindly on theory, preferred abstract rights to established institutions, and held dependence on experience in contempt.[31]

Burke wanted to alert Britain to the threat posed by such subversive ideas. Observing the revolutionary changes in France, he feared a similar upheaval in Britain and aimed his pamphlet at Opposition members calling for parliamentary reforms. Unless these disaffected men were fought, Burke argued, they could bring down the three great pillars on which British society rested: the monarchy, the aristocracy, and the Church of England. In doing so, they would destroy the existing hierarchical social order, introduce chaos, and encourage the masses to attack the property of the rich.

Paine's impassioned response was *The Rights of Man*, in which he rejected the idea of appealing to past experience. Spurning any appeal to history, he insisted that the authority of one generation should not be considered binding on its successors. He stressed instead the natural rights of man, claiming that all men possessed such rights by virtue of their common humanity at birth.

With America in mind, Paine went on to define what a constitution should be:

> A constitution is not a thing in name only, but in fact. It has not an ideal but a real existence; and whenever it cannot be produced in a visible form, there is none. A constitution is a thing *antecedent* to government, and a government is only the creature of a constitution. The constitution of a country is not the acts of its government, but of the people constituting its government.[32]

In Paine's view, a constitution was ordained and established by the people as a contract with, and the condition of, the government they had established. Given his definition, Paine challenged Burke to produce the British constitution. Since it was not "visible," Paine argued, Britain had no constitution.[33]

Although his focus was on the French Revolution, Paine coupled his treatment of the events in France in 1789 with those in America in 1776, making America the model for reforming British government. After describing in detail the republican form of popular government, he concluded: "It is on this system that the American government is founded."[34] Paine went on to cite Pennsylvania's experience in 1776, showing how the people had gone about creating their own constitution, and urged the British to do the same.[35]

The purpose for discussing the Burke–Paine controversy is not to inquire into the complex arguments between the two men. Instead, the aim is to demonstrate how Paine's radical republicanism differed from Burke's views representing Britain's monarchical culture.

By this time, Paine had assumed the role of an international revolutionary, proselytizing republicanism wherever he went. In England, he attacked the British monarchy so vigorously that he was indicted for treason and forced to flee to France. Then, while Britain was waging war with France, he roused the radical movements in England, Scotland, and Ireland.[36] In France, he was made a French citizen, became a member of the National Convention in 1792, and helped Condorcet draft a constitution. When he joined the moderate faction and opposed the execution of the king, he was arrested on the charge that he was an enemy Englishman. After the Terror, he was released, but while in jail, he wrote *The Age of Reason* (1794–1796), an attack on sectarianism in religion that was misunderstood as being an irreligious tract.

Returning to America in 1802, Paine found himself rejected. Although one of the first to use the phrase "the United States of America," he ironically was denied citizenship. A prophet without honor in his adopted country, he kept up his attacks against monarchy, economic privilege, and religious superstition until he died in poverty in 1809.

While continuing his role as a leading international revolutionary, Paine had discussed the relative merits and defects of the U.S. Constitution with Jefferson and Lafayette. Although he wrote, "[I] could have voted for it myself had I been in America," he took strong exception to some provisions: the notion of a single executive, the elimination of the principle of rotation in office, and the lengthy senatorial terms as undemocratic.[37] But essentially he was in agreement with his two colleagues.

Paine's extraordinary reputation as a revolutionary had been demonstrated in France by a symbolic gesture involving his friend Lafayette. The Frenchman, appointed as commander of the National Guard, was ordered to destroy the Bastille. Handing the key of the notorious institution to Paine in 1790, Lafayette asked that he carry the sacred trophy to George Washington, then serving as president. Paine was selected for this symbolic mission because of his reputation as the leading apostle of American constitutionalism.

Although the Burke–Paine controversy had run its course by the early 1800s, the dispute about the two men from a broader historical perspective—that of Western political thought—survives to this day. According to conventional wisdom, Burke's ideas left the more lasting impression, with his *Reflections* still hailed as one of the world's great documents of conservative political thought. As the founder of modern philosophical conservatism, Burke ranks as one of Britain's foremost political thinkers, and his writings are still considered relevant.

In contrast, Paine's constitutional ideas have been viewed as being less original and more in the nature of propaganda than serious thought. As Carl Becker remarked: "Paine belongs to the history of opinion rather than to the history of thought; he is the propagandist through whom the ideas of great original thinkers are transmitted to the crowd."[38] That evaluation, while accurate, is not quite fair. Paine's contributions were historically significant, including his ideas about republicanism, the rights of man, and his radical ideology regarding the nature of American constitutionalism.[39] His democratic directness was effective, moreover, in reaching ordinary people and motivated many to take a step toward independence at the most critical time in American history.

Conventional wisdom notwithstanding, history has vindicated Paine in many respects. He could note with satisfaction his victory over Burke regarding hereditary monarchy, which is now considered a historical fossil in many parts of the globe. Even more significant was his successful proselytizing on behalf of American constitutionalism. Louis Henkin, a leading constitutional scholar, provided an assessment that is more on the mark:

> Thomas Paine had proclaimed constitutionalism as *the* right of man and as the foundation of all rights of man: today constitutionalism is accepted by virtually all, at least in principle. Paine argued hotly the sovereignty of the people; today popular sovereignty is accepted almost everywhere, at least in principle. For Paine, "representative" government is freedom; today suffrage is universal, and government is representative everywhere, at least in principle. For Paine, man's rights were natural, inherent in the equality of God's human creatures, and retained by them pursuant to their social contract. Today human rights—whether natural, contractual, psychological or political as positive law—are accepted by all, at least in principle.[40]

American Constitutionalism and European Constitutions, 1787–1800

Fifteen constitutions were written or promulgated in Europe between 1787 and 1800. All of them reflected some evidence of American constitutionalism, directly or indirectly. Although none lasted for more than four years, their influence lingered much longer.

When the Belgian revolution took place in the Austrian Netherlands in 1787, the leaders turned to the United States for their name, calling the region the United States of Belgium. Their constitution, created before the U.S. Constitution was written, represented "a conscious and avowed copy of the Articles of Confederation" then in force in America.[41] It was a protest, too, against centralizing government, just as the Articles had been against Britain's government. There was additional evidence of American inspiration. When each province announced its independence separately from the Hapsburg emperor, the declaration of independence in the Flanders province reproduced phrases from the American Declaration. Furthermore, several of America's state constitutions were cited by the Belgian democratic party as desirable examples of government. Then, when the new states named their central body, they called it a "congress." The

United States of Belgium, however, had a short life and soon disappeared from the scene.⁴²

In Poland, the abortive constitution of 1791 also reflected certain parallelisms with the U.S. Constitution. Both documents called for the separation of powers, bicameralism, and an independent judiciary. Each had property qualifications for participation in government, though they differed widely. Framers in both constitutions called for a respect for human rights, although a bill of rights in Poland was to be granted in separate legislation. In the final analysis, however, the Polish Constitution represented more of a check on the aristocracy than on the monarchy. It relied, moreover, more on British and French constitutionalism than on the American model. The Polish Constitution never went into effect and was renounced in 1792/1793. And when Poland was partitioned again by Russia and Prussia, it turned the dream of Polish reformers into a nightmare.⁴³

The French Constitution of 1791 followed the Polish Constitution by a few months and will be discussed later. The remaining twelve of the fifteen constitutions were the result of the French Revolution and the Napoleonic Wars. After the French Revolution, French constitutional ideas, especially the great French Declaration of 1789, exercised a more powerful influence throughout the world than did American constitutionalism.

France

More than any other European country, France was affected over the years by the six seminal American documents. The Declaration of Independence played a key role, particularly during the Revolutionary War and the early stages of the French Revolution. Paris, Europe's intellectual capital, served as a funnel through which news of the document passed to other urban centers. By August 20, the Russian envoy in Paris was reporting notice of it to Catherine the Great in St. Petersburg. That same month, the representative from one of the major principalities in Germany was calling the Declaration to the attention of his ruler. When Franklin returned to Paris a few months later, he discovered that copies of the Declaration had been distributed to most major cities and that "all Europe is on our side of the question."⁴⁴

The Declaration expressed the revolutionary idea that under certain circumstances, it was the right of the people to abolish their government. Such a comment taken literally could have been interpreted as a call to worldwide revolution and the overthrow of all monarchs. But was that really the case? At the time, "no one in his right mind dared suggest deposing of kings and replacing them with republican governments," concluded one scholar.[45] The document was viewed instead as America's specific response to British tyranny. Indeed, Americans could hardly have hoped to receive aid from King Louis XVI if they were seeking to unseat monarchs everywhere.[46]

Despite its subversive message, the Declaration was well received in French official circles. Although its rhetoric attacked the idea of monarchy and insisted on popular sovereignty, Silas Deane, the American emissary, reported that the document was met with favor. The United States, he was told, could count on some "succours and assistance."[47] This sympathetic response was motivated by the fact that France was seeking to destroy its hated enemy, Britain.

That the French government approved of the Declaration was evident also when it supported the document's wide dissemination. Vergennes, the French minister of foreign affairs, permitted its publication all over France. It was reprinted in a new journal called *Affaires de l'Angleterre et de l'Amérique* in 1777 and appeared a year before France officially recognized the United States.[48]

Any translations before the Franco-American alliance would have implied recognition of the legitimacy of the United States, so translations had to be published anonymously and outside France to escape censorship. The presses were located in the Netherlands, and the two men promoting this clandestine effort were the young French nobleman, Louis-Alexandre, duc de La Rochefoucauld–d'Enville, and the aging Benjamin Franklin.

Copies of the Declaration had circulated in London as early as August 1776. "It is not surprising that the Declaration was circulating within a month of its publication," writes Bailyn, "but it is surprising that it appeared simultaneously in a Dutch journal and then repeatedly in a series of French periodicals."[49] This earliest known translation on the continent was probably the one published in the Netherlands in the *Gazette de Leyde*. The next two translations were published in the *Affaires de l'Angleterre et de l'Amérique*, the underground journal advertised as though printed in Antwerp to escape censorship. Secretly subsidized by Vergennes, with whom Franklin had been in contact, it printed two different translations of the Declaration by Rochefoucauld.[50] In 1783, Rochefoucauld published under his own name his translation of several American founding documents under the title *Constitutions des treize États-Unis de l'Amérique.* It was this book, with Franklin's revisions, that apparently served as the major source of information for members of the French National Assembly.[51]

Within court circles and among radical intellectuals, the Declaration was greeted with wild enthusiasm. To *philosophes* who idealized America, the Declaration was a godsend. The American example was used by those hoping to reform and regenerate France. To them, the new nation represented a confirmation of their radical ideas and ideals. No longer did they have to speak in the abstract about an imagined state of nature: America had given them a living example.

Mirabeau, who became one of most brilliant figures in the Constituent Assembly, commented on the Declaration's reception later in 1778: "The sublime manifesto of the United States was very generally applauded."[52] To him and other American sympathizers, the document confirmed ideas long accepted but hitherto confined to books.[53]

Among Americans living in Paris, Franklin was the most active propagandist in getting the Declaration published. Besides helping Rochefoucauld translate the first copies circulated, Franklin collaborated with him on the *Constitutions des treize États-Unis de l'Amérique.* These copies "constituted the most important publications of American political documents in France during the war," according to one authority.[54]

Jefferson, serving as minister to France, was another avid propagandist. Approached by Jean Nicolas Démeunier, the French editor of *Encyclopédie méthodique,* Jefferson responded by publishing his *Notes on the State of Virginia.* Originally printed in 1784, this widely read work included a translation of the entire text of the Declaration.

The influence of the Declaration in France and other European countries was limited, however, by the complexities encountered in translation. The political discourse was hampered by the "distortions, transformations, and [different] insights" that crept into the process, resulting in omissions, misconceptions, and misunderstandings. Transnational translations demonstrated the serious difficulties of trying to convey the Declaration's message through the filter of different cultures.[55]

One example was the attempt by French constitutionalists to use the term *mankind* as employed in the American Declaration to frame one of France's constitutions as well as the French Declaration of 1789. They immediately encountered linguistic ambiguities that made the effort difficult, if not impossible. Although the Americans used *mankind* in a universal sense, they sometimes resorted also to certain particularisms or made specific national references such as "our British brethren" and "common kindred," usages that clearly violated any claim to universality.

In their deliberations during the 1789 National Assembly, the French also found they could not use *mankind* in the same way as the Americans. "French revolutionaries [were] paving the way for other European revolutions and for French expansion . . . [and] saw in their own actions and deliberations a *universal* message that was the bearer of profound changes in world history."[56] Members of the Assembly, moreover, viewed the French as a "regenerated people" with an ancient past, whereas they saw the Americans as a "new people," recently born, who came into being only after the break with Britain.[57]

As time went on, the French paid less and less attention to the American Declaration, and its language became increasingly irrelevant to their political culture. In the nineteenth and twentieth centuries, interest in the document in France died down except during periods of constitutional crisis or when historiographical battles were waged among academics about the relative importance of the American and French revolutions to world history. The changing character of translations over time, however, showed that the document could serve as a litmus test not only to measure America's contribution to ideas in the French Revolution but also to reveal what the French themselves thought of their own Revolution.

What was true of the Declaration applied as well to the other five documents. Great differences in meaning required that translations be treated with caution and, in some instances, were found nearly impossible because the proper word or term used in America could not be rendered with any accuracy in a foreign language or culture.

Between 1776 and 1786, other seminal documents were available in print in France. The state constitutions and bills of rights of Delaware, Maryland, New Jersey, New York, Pennsylvania, South Carolina, and Virginia all were published on at least five different occasions.[58] In 1777 these state documents were first printed in the *Affaires de l'Angleterre et de l' Amérique*. All the state constitutions, except that of New York, were reprinted extensively. In addition, the documents were reprinted in 1778 in the collection *Recuiel des lois constitutives des colonies anglaises*, attributed to Rochefoucauld. He declared that these documents were "the finest monuments of human wisdom. They constitute the purest democracy that ever existed; they already appear to be achieving the happiness of the people who have adopted them, and they will forever constitute the glory of the virtuous men who conceived them."[59] Five years later,

Rochefoucauld and Franklin published their *Constitutions des treize États-Unis de l'Amérique*, which included the bills of rights and state constitutions of all the states as well as some colonial charters.[60] These texts gave Frenchmen a clearer picture of America in the late 1770s and early 1780s.

The state constitutions appeared at precisely the right time: just before the beginning of the French Revolution when American political ideas exercised their greatest influence. France was still dealing in theories of government rather than coping with practical political problems, so the state constitutions were regarded as highly relevant.[61] Indeed, Franklin wrote from Paris that the French were reading the state constitutions "with Rapture."[62]

The Articles of Confederation, despite skepticism by some who questioned the ability of the United States to survive, were also of great interest, particularly to French thinkers interested in using them as a possible model. The first publication of the Articles in France (a preliminary and incomplete draft of the document that Congress eventually adopted in 1781) appeared in December 1776. Surprisingly, the Articles were published even more widely during the war years in France than either the Declaration or the first state constitutions.[63]

The Federalist also was recognized instantly as a classic. When the French Assembly took the extraordinary step of making Madison and Hamilton honorary citizens in 1792, the citation read: "Considering that men who, by their writing and courage, have served the cause of liberty and paved the way for the enfranchisement of man, cannot be regarded as strangers by a nation which was made free by their guiding light and courage."[64] American-style federalism was in favor in France at the time, and the second and third editions of the essays had just been published in Paris that year.[65] During the crucial debates in the Constituent Assembly, several speakers quoted from *The Federalist*.[66]

The climate of opinion suddenly changed the following year, however, and *The Federalist* fell into disfavor. France, fearing the country might break apart during its Revolution, now viewed federalism with suspicion. Saint-Just expressed skepticism whether the United States itself could remain united, and he predicted that a war among the states was inevitable.[67] In this changed environment, even reading the essays became dangerous. A report circulated that Brissot, one of the *philosophes*, had been condemned by a revolutionary tribunal because he admired the book. When he was found to have borrowed a copy, Brissot presumably was accused of advocating the dismemberment of France.[68]

Throughout the first echo, the Atlantic became an inland sea linking the two continents as men and ideas began traveling in both directions. Frenchmen like Lafayette, Brissot, and several other French revolutionaries came to America. Paine, Jefferson, John Adams, and Franklin meanwhile lived in France for a time, and the face-to-face exchanges between these and other constitutionalists marked a distinct change from the relative isolation that had existed before.

Up to the middle of the eighteenth century, American and French disciples of the Enlightenment had looked primarily to England for constitutional guidance. But with the removal of the French threat from Canada at the end of the French and Indian War, American animosity toward France declined. The prestige of French *philosophes* like Montesquieu and Rousseau soared as American thinkers entered into a discourse regarding their respective constitutional views. Out of these exchanges emerged on the part of the colonists a greater awareness of their own "Americanness" and a realization of the originality inherent in their constitutionalism.[69]

But such exchanges should be regarded with caution. Intellectuals on both sides were sometimes woefully misinformed and held serious misconceptions about each other. This was particularly true of the *philosophes* who believed in the myth of an "American Dream." Their idealized image of America as a land of virtuous, free farmers untouched by the vices of a commerce-oriented society was a fantasy. Such a distorted image showed that French constitutionalists sometimes saw in America what they wanted to see, so their observations often tell us more about the observers than what they were observing. The same was true of some American constitutionalists. John Adams, for example, predicted that France would never become a republic because from his parochial point of view they lacked the virtue to sustain a republican government.

Sheer ignorance of America and its system of government at times also resulted from reading outdated works or from careless analysis. Émile Boutmy, the well-known constitutional scholar, commented that as late as 1835 some serious French writers still thought of the Articles as the constitution operating in the United States![70] Boutmy went on to complain that some French lawyers treated the U.S. Constitution as though it could be compared easily with French constitutions by simplistic analogies. Such comparisons were "superficial," led to "fatal misconceptions," and gave rise to "mistaken interpretations."[71] Despite these limitations, the exchanges that took place proved valuable, especially when they involved the personal presence of important Frenchmen in America. Such was the case of Marie Joseph Paul Yves Roch Gilbert du Motier, marquis de Lafayette.

Lafayette

No other Frenchman was more important to the American cause of independence during the first echo than Lafayette, who understood and admired much about American constitutionalism. To most Frenchmen who identified with the United States, Lafayette personified the friendship between the two nations. His own countrymen, in fact, considered him practically an American citizen.[72]

Lafayette's most recent biographer called America "the definitive experience of his life." His command in the Continental army in his early twenties helped shape many constitutional views that Lafayette held until he died. He believed that the American Revolution was a pivotal event in world history and that America's independence was a turning point in the progress of all humankind. To him, the American view of natural rights in the Declaration was a major advance in the history of modern political thought. Moreover, the U.S. Constitution, he believed, could be a perfect model for the rest of the world.[73] Writing in 1777, he announced that the welfare of America was intimately connected with the happiness of all humankind. After the Revolutionary War ended, he wrote to John Adams: "As to my going to America, I first Went for the Revolution, and not for the war. Warfaring was truly a Secondary Incident, which in Support of the Rights of Mankind Had Become Necessary."[74] He took great satisfaction in what he had achieved and wrote eloquently that "America is assured her independence; mankind's cause is won and liberty is no longer homeless."[75]

The end of Lafayette's career in the Continental army marked the beginning of his important role in French politics. He plunged into political life immediately upon his return home. A member of the Assembly of Notables, he called for the formation of a National Assembly. Once the Estates General was convened in 1789, he emerged a leader among the liberal nobles who helped convert the Estates General into the National Assembly.

While France was coping with the coming of its Revolution, Lafayette kept in close touch with Jefferson, then serving as minister to France. After copies of the U.S. Constitution became available, the two men agreed it was wanting in four particulars: it lacked a bill of rights; it did not guarantee trial by jury in civil cases; it did not limit the reeligibility of the president; and the powers given to the executive were excessive.[76] Lafayette's advice proved crucial at this stage. He influenced Jefferson who in turn persuaded Madison to change his mind about incorporating a bill of rights. The Frenchman viewed himself, he said, as "a representative of American constitutional values and . . . an advocate of inalienable natural rights."[77]

The two men collaborated, moreover, in helping frame a draft for the French Declaration of Rights of 1789. Although Lafayette was by no means the sole author of the document, both his and Jefferson's contributions were highly significant.[78] Lafayette's admiration for the American Declaration of Independence and his hopes for a similar French Declaration was symbolized by a dramatic gesture. In his library in Paris, it was reported, he hung a copy of the American Declaration in a half-filled frame. To visitors, he explained that the empty part of the frame was reserved for the French Declaration of Rights that he hoped his country would adopt one day.[79]

Other Frenchmen also asked Jefferson for help in writing a constitution for France, but he declined. Given his official diplomatic position, his involvement would have been an embarrassment. France was in the throes of a constitutional crisis, and Jefferson could ill afford to take sides.[80] But he changed his mind once he received news that he had been relieved of his official duties. When Lafayette asked him to invite the warring French factions to a conference in Jefferson's home in August 1789, he agreed. During the meeting, Jefferson reported later, the U.S. Constitution was viewed as a veritable "model." When the Frenchmen quarreled among themselves, they always treated the American position on every constitutional issue with deference, "like . . . the bible, open to explanation, but not to question."[81] Jefferson claimed later that the conference had saved the proposed French constitution with a compromise, but such was hardly the case. What was more significant, perhaps, was the way that Lafayette was able to mediate American constitutional ideas with his fellow Frenchmen.[82]

Following the fall of the Bastille, Lafayette was named commander of the National Guard. From this important post, he wielded great power and influenced the course of the Revolution over the next two years. His goal, he said, was to insist on three conditions: the rule of law, the maintenance of peace and order, and the creation of an atmosphere in which the Assembly could frame a suitable constitution. His aims suggest he was seeking to achieve the same principles as those in the U.S. Constitution. Marie Antoinette, in fact, accused Lafayette in 1789 of seeking to "model everything in accordance with the ideas in Philadelphia."[83]

But it was difficult to maintain his political position on the slippery slope of the French revolutionary movement. In August 1790, Lafayette wrote Washington—whom he regarded as a father figure and role model—that he wanted to relinquish all political power. Like his mentor, he hoped to retire to his estate.[84] He identified with Washington, calling him "Generalissimo of Universal Liberty" and referring to himself as "your deputy . . . in this great cause."[85]

Instead of retiring, Lafayette soon found himself mired even more deeply in politics. After Louis XVI was made a constitutional monarch, the king attempted to flee France, was captured, and brought back to Paris a prisoner. Lafayette was made his jailer and guardian. From this time on, Lafayette tried to maintain a neutral stance among the various factions fighting for power. Once the French Constitution was promulgated in October 1791, a new Legislative Assembly was elected, and the Revolution appeared to be over. Lafayette quickly resigned his commission, relinquished his public duties, and retired to his birthplace in the Auvergne.

Lafayette's retirement, like that of Washington, was not destined to last long. France declared war on Austria in the spring of 1792, and Lafayette was recalled to command one of the armies. Writing to Washington, he explained that he had refused other calls to public service but accepted the military command because "I saw our liberties and Constitution seriously threatened and my services could be usefully emploid in fighting for *our old cause.*"[86]

When the Revolution entered its more radical phase in the summer of 1792, Lafayette found himself even more involved. His commitment to the constitutional principles of 1789, he said, was firm. He framed a fervent appeal to the contending factions on June 16, 1792, to preserve the constitutional monarchy and to maintain the Declaration of Rights.[87] Despite his lofty rhetoric, Lafayette tried to distinguish between members of the Legislative Assembly and the general will of the people.[88] He was damned by two groups of extremists: the radical republicans who saw him as a usurper and royalist, and the ultraroyalists who viewed him as a revolutionary republican. After the king was killed, Lafayette was impeached and forced to flee the country. He was imprisoned in Austria for five years but emerged with his reputation relatively intact, albeit somewhat tarnished.

Although Lafayette's first phase as a constitutionalist had come to an end, his faith in American constitutional principles remained firm. He believed in liberty in the abstract and in the universal rights of humankind. Whether in a constitutional monarchy or republic, his ideas called for a restrained executive, a two-house legislature with both houses elective, and a separation of powers. Many of these ideas were similar to those spelled out in the American constitutional documents at the time.

Turgot

Few French constitutionalists were more highly regarded than Anne-Robert-Jacques Turgot, a statesman, reformer, and economist who produced the most telling commentary on America's state constitutions. In 1778 he wrote to Richard Price, England's leading dissenting minister, listing those features to which he took exception. Six years later, after Turgot died, Price appended the Frenchman's letter to his famous pamphlet *Observations on the Importance of the American Revolution*.[89]

Turgot was particularly distressed by the concepts of divided sovereignty and separation of powers, which he considered useless. After throwing off British rule, Turgot complained, the Americans were still slavishly following the British constitution with its theory of balanced government. The separation of powers, representing among other things the hierarchy of ranks and social orders, had developed in England through the course of history, Turgot observed. The same was true of the Crown. In America, there no longer was any need to erect barriers against abuses by a hereditary monarch. "They [the Americans] think of balancing the different powers . . . as if the same equilibrium of forces, which was believed necessary to balance the great preponderance of royalty, could be any use in republics formed upon the equality of citizens."[90]

Turgot insisted that authority be concentrated instead in a single center, one and indivisible. What he was reacting to were his own experiences when he served as principal minister in France from 1774 to 1776. Like so many European constitutionalists, he interpreted American developments in light of the problems plaguing his own country. Turgot had encountered a fragmentation of political power among several constituted bodies in which aristocratic privilege, entrenched behind the *parlements*, had frustrated his reform efforts. Ultimately he had been driven from office. Certain corporate bodies with particular interests had made themselves "a body foreign to the State," he claimed, and operated against the best interests of the country. To overcome this problem, Turgot had suggested the enhancement of royal power, a solution hardly applicable to republican America.[91]

While favoring laissez-faire economic policies, Turgot also criticized the state constitutions on the grounds they made it possible to erect tariff barriers in domestic commerce. Governors and other state agencies in America, he observed, had the power to prohibit the movement of certain products across state lines. Turgot consequently wanted to restrict the role of government as much as possible in regulating commerce. "So far are [Americans] from realizing that the law of complete freedom of all commerce is a corollary of the right of property—so deep are they still immersed in the fog of European illusions."[92]

Turgot was as liberal in religion as he was in economic matters. He took exception to American state laws preventing clergymen from running for office. Such legislation, he warned, could create in the ministers a special group consciousness. By excluding them, Americans might make them into a separate entity, "a body foreign to the State." Indeed, Turgot believed that the clergy could become dangerous "as an organized body."[93]

In short, Turgot was critical of the state constitutions when they sought to balance any corporate bodies or resorted to a separation of powers. Any group of men singled out, he feared, would form a "body" with separate interests and thereby endanger the state's existence. He preferred a state constitution along the lines of the Pennsylvania model: a one-chamber legislature with no upper house and a restrained executive.

Turgot's criticism of the state constitutions aroused John Adams to fury. In response, he wrote his *A Defence of the Constitutions of Government of the United States* (1787–1788), a study rightly called "the most important work of political theory before the Federalist papers."[94] Adams's purpose was twofold: to analyze different theories of government and to study different periods of history that might disclose principles that could be applied in general terms. By studying the constitutional histories of more than fifty republican regimes in ancient, medieval, and modern times, Adams hoped to find the hidden springs of human nature and to seek universal laws that could be applied in all cases at all times. The first volume of his three-volume work was a rebuttal of Turgot and Condorcet.[95]

In his preface Adams placed America's state constitutions in a global setting. While earlier governments had been founded on the divine right of kings, those of the American states were "the finest example of governments erected on the simple principles of nature." They were "founded on the natural authority of the people alone. . . . The institutions now made in America, will never wear wholly out for thousands of years."[96]

The theme of his study of republican governments was that such regimes usually did not work because the few (the rich, well-born, and more able) inevitably would rise in society and acquire undue influence. The only way to achieve stability was to find a constitutional niche for such an aristocracy. Only by balancing the social orders with two houses in the legislature, one for the people (the democratic interest) and one for property (the aristocratic interest), with a powerful independent executive (the monarchical interest) to provide an equilibrium and complete the triad of forces, could a government stop the warring interests in society from tearing it apart. Such a counterpoise would maintain social stability. But by stubbornly staying with the classic doctrine of a mixed constitution of balanced social orders, Adams missed the most important intellectual breakthrough since the Revolution: the transformation of American political culture which located the principle of sovereignty in the people at large instead of in the specific institutions of government.[97]

What constitutional model could best achieve the balance? Adams asked. The British constitution, he answered. "What is the ingredient which in England has preserved the democratical authority? The balance and that only."[98] That balance in republican America would reside in the executive branch.[99] At the time, Adams was concerned mainly with the problems of state government and setting up what could be called "a regal republic" in which the monarchical impulse of the people could be satisfied by setting up strong governors, that is, the executive branch.[100]

Adams's *Defence* became a bone of contention between two French groups who advocated opposing points of view. The "Américanistes" favored using certain features resembling the American model. Briefly put, their program called for a reduction of special privileges for the aristocracy and the church, the inauguration of a constitutional monarchy, and the establishment of a unicameral popular assembly to express the general will. The "Anglomanes," however, looked to the British model, seeking to popularize English political institutions in their efforts to change France. Through the efforts of the Américanistes, the American state constitutions became an important political issue in France on the eve of the Revolution.

Turgot was critical also of the Articles of Confederation as a flawed document, because it had not created a strong enough union in America.

Commenting on a draft copy of the Articles printed in 1776—one differing substantially from the final version—Turgot wrote he could not "see . . . a coalition, a fusion of all parties . . . to make a body one and homogeneous." What Turgot wanted was a more centralized government to impose greater uniformity among the separate sections in America: "It is only an aggregation of parties, always too separated, and which will always maintain a tendency to separate, by diversity of laws, of their manners, of their actual forces, and still more by the inequality of their eventual progress."[101]

Although Adams agreed with Turgot that a closer union was desirable, he took exception to the ideas of centralization and uniformity. He defended the Articles and wrote that Turgot's approach would not work in America. One homogeneous body could never be formed out of the heterogeneous parts scattered throughout the immense American continent. "The parts are too distant," Adams noted, "as well as unlike."[102]

Turgot died in 1781, before the U.S. Constitution was written and before the constitutional debates in France reached their revolutionary phase. But the dialogue between the two men continued. On Adams's side, the exchange took two forms: the first was his *Defence*, and the second was the marginalia he scribbled in Turgot's books as he carried on an imaginary dialogue with the French *philosophe* long after he was dead.[103]

Condorcet

Many of Turgot's ideas were carried on by Condorcet, his biographer and protégé.[104] The marquis de Condorcet, political philosopher, mathematician, and statesman, and one of France's finest *philosophes*, expressed the reaction of many French intellectuals when he heaped high praise on the Declaration. "America has given us this example. The declaration by which she declared her independence is a simple and sublime statement of these sacred and long forgotten rights."[105] Condorcet also recognized instantly the historical importance of the constituent power of the people acting through a constitutional convention as representing an innovation of global significance:

> Then was observed for the first time, the example of a great people throwing off all their chains at once, and peaceably establishing a system of government which, it believed, would be most conducive to happiness. Their geographical situation and political history obliged Americans to

establish a federal republic; thirteen republican constitutions appeared, at about the same time, all based on the solemn recognition of the rights of man, the preservation of which was their chief object.[106]

When suggesting a government for France, Condorcet advocated a single-house legislature, thereby disagreeing with Adams's *Defence*. The state constitution that most attracted Condorcet was that of Pennsylvania in 1776. To him, this document was the height of political wisdom. He "doted" on it and declared that "it was distinguished from most other state constitutions by a greater equality, and from all of them in that the legislative power was confined to one house." Besides its unicameralism, he applauded two other features: Pennsylvania's popularly elected executive committee and the elected Council of Censors who possessed the power to inquire "whether the constitution had been preserved inviolate in every part."[107] Condorcet, like Adams, was seeking universal laws for free governments.

The reasons why the Pennsylvania Constitution caught the fancy of so many French intellectuals like Condorcet were obvious. It had most of the characteristics that many of them sought for their own government. A comparison of the Pennsylvania Constitution with the Jacobin Constitution of 1793 shows why. Both wanted to implement the principle of unrestricted popular sovereignty with an annually elected unicameral legislature as well as direct consultation of the people involved in lawmaking. Both desired a limited theoretical principle of separation of powers and a weak executive council dependent on a dominant legislature. To some degree, all these were present in both constitutions.[108] The unicameralism of the Pennsylvania Constitution, of course, was an exception to the general rule in bicameral America. Moreover, the principles of popular sovereignty and separation of powers were defined quite differently.

Condorcet's analysis of the Articles of Confederation contained the most brilliant argument advanced by the Américanistes. He became concerned in 1783 when interest in American ideas appeared to be waning and wrote his famous pamphlet *The Influence of the American Revolution on Europe*. His work argued that America provided France with a valuable object lesson. "It is not enough that the rights of man be written in books of philosophers and inscribed on the hearts of virtuous men, the weak and ignorant must be able to read them in the example of a great people. America has given us this example."[109]

In his pamphlet, Condorcet applauded the separation of church and state. This concept—one of the most radical features of American constitutionalism—intrigued him, and he predicted that America would become the pioneer in a worldwide movement for greater religious freedom. In Europe, he noted, enlightened statesmen adopted a policy of religious toleration but only on pragmatic grounds: to bring peace in countries torn by religious strife. Such religious toleration, however, invariably continued the privileged status of state churches and conceded liberty of worship only to certain dissenters. It did not go far enough. America, by contrast, regarded limited toleration an "outrage against human nature."[110] What Americans desired as an ideal was an outright separation of church and state. Condorcet failed to note, however, that the absence of a powerful established church in America created quite a different situation. With no national church to contend with, Americans found it easier to set up many different religious establishments. Condorcet was proved wrong on another score: most countries in the world failed to adopt the radical American feature.

Condorcet pointed also to America's superiority in freedom of the press. In France, he wrote sardonically, the absurdity of the laws against a free press were less obvious "because, unfortunately, habit has the fatal power of familiarizing our feeble human reason with what shocks it most." America, by contrast, experienced a more rapid diffusion of ideas throughout society precisely because of its freer press. Freedom of the press, he concluded, gave the American government a more powerful instrument "than the law itself."[111]

The Articles, Condorcet contended, would also make the United States a powerful force for world peace. Holding the views of a physiocrat, Condorcet believed that constitutions should deny governments the right to regulate commerce. He predicted that if they did so, European powers would no longer go to war over their Caribbean colonies. Furthermore, because of its location, America was bound to become the dominant power in that region. Being a peace-loving people interested more in commerce than in military adventures, Americans inevitably would follow the liberal ideas of their Revolution. Given their antimercantilist views, it was unlikely that they would ever embark on an imperialist policy. Only aggressive moves by European powers would force the United States to try to conquer the Caribbean islands or subdue subject peoples. Such a policy would be alien to a country that had just concluded a colonial rebellion. America's appearance in the Caribbean,

Condorcet observed, had created a peace zone in the New World, one which European powers would enter militarily only at their own risk. Condorcet's suggestion that America would respond militarily only if European powers intervened in the Caribbean anticipated in a way the Monroe Doctrine.[112]

Condorcet predicted as well that the Americans would become a pacifistic people. He argued Americans had no designs whatsoever for conquest in the Caribbean or for colonies anywhere. Throughout the Revolutionary War, they had opposed the European powers' expansionist mercantilist policies. Since militarism and mercantilism went hand in hand, the Articles contained no provisions for a standing army. In contrast, in mercantilist Europe, most countries had such armies. Monarchs used military force to expand their empires and compelled their citizens to perform military service. By having no standing army, however, the Americans would remain a peace-loving people. America would "help maintain peace in Europe by force of [its] example."[113]

Finally, Condorcet foresaw that the Articles would bring domestic peace and social harmony to America itself. When a people make their own laws, he wrote, they tend to obey them. In the United States, he observed: "We have . . . seen Americans submit peacefully to laws . . . they had violently criticized, and they have obeyed the representatives of public authority respectfully but without giving up their right to try to enlighten these representatives and to denounce to the nation their mistakes and errors."[114]

Written at around the time the Articles were about to be replaced, Condorcet's pamphlet had high praise for the document. Even Shays's Rebellion failed to dampen his optimistic outlook regarding the law-abiding nature of the American people. After comparing the Shays uprising to the serious upheavals in despotic European countries, he concluded that conditions in America were less violent.[115]

When the first copies of the U.S. Constitution arrived in France, however, Condorcet was shocked. Once he learned that the Americans had decided on a bicameral legislature, he thought the move to be a step backward. "I see with pain," he wrote Franklin, that "the aristocratic spirit seeks to introduce itself among you in spite of many wise precautions." At the time Condorcet was writing, France was in turmoil. In France, he pointed out, the aristocratic elements were united against the people. "Priests, magistrates, nobles, all unite against poor citizens who are of a very different character."[116]

Once the U.S. Constitution came into his hands, Condorcet translated it and appended comments after each article. His criticisms were particularly significant in view of his appointment as chairman of the committee to frame a constitution for France in 1793. Condorcet's reaction to the American document anticipated the draft of the French Constitution that he proposed later. Condorcet's main objection concerned the American Senate. The six-year term was much too long and would allow a consolidation of power. For that reason, he continued to favor a unicameral system. Being a strong advocate of proportional representation, he was opposed also to the idea of equal state representation in the Senate.[117]

Condorcet disapproved of the principle of separation of powers in general, and in the U.S. Constitution in particular. "Why . . . is the simplicity of these constitutions disfigured by [this] . . . system; and why is the identity of interests rather than equality of rights adopted as a principle?"[118] The separation of powers, he believed, would lead to a government in which the separated powers would be united to carry out corruption. To make the government operate more efficiently, politicians would be forced to use nonconstitutional mechanisms, like corruption, to integrate the separated parts. Although Condorcet did not predict the rise of political machines or political parties (in which corruption thrives as it unites and lubricates the separate parts of the governmental machinery), he appeared to be hinting at something of the sort.[119]

Condorcet was likewise critical of the American presidency. The chief executive had been granted too much power. His role as commander in chief of the army and navy with so few restraints raised the possibility of a military dictatorship. The absence of any limitation on presidential terms, moreover, could open the way to life tenure. Eventually such a move might lead to hereditary succession.[120]

When it came to the personal qualifications of the president, Condorcet believed that the method of election would favor men with demagogic traits rather than sound leaders of merit. He objected, moreover, to the age qualification of thirty-five years. He pointed to brilliant leaders achieving fame at a young age: Scipio Africanus at twenty-two had defeated Hannibal; William Pitt the Younger assumed the position of prime minister at twenty-four; and France's own Lafayette at nineteen had commanded American armies.[121]

Condorcet was distrustful also of the judiciary. Judges, he feared, might block important legislative measures. He was particularly concerned lest judges be given authority to suspend the right of *habeas corpus* and then use their power improperly. He disapproved, too, of the judicial power given the president to pardon criminals.[122]

But what Condorcet objected to most was the absence of a bill of rights. His passion for individual rights led him to argue for a wider and more inclusive method for protecting them. In his own proposed declaration of rights for France, he advocated even more rights than those adopted in America under the first ten amendments. He wanted the prohibition of slavery, equality under the law, and the right of citizens to a public education.[123] Condorcet concluded his criticisms of the U.S. Constitution by expressing the hope that the document might serve as a temporary stopgap until a second convention could be called.

Despite his reservations, Condorcet found one feature to praise, the provision for amending the Constitution. In the amendment process included in the first state constitutions, the Articles, and the 1787 Constitution, Condorcet saw the creation of an epoch-making mechanism for peaceful change. "Until now," he wrote in 1789, "several of the American States have been the only ones to realize the utility of providing, in advance, for methods to revise existing constitutions, and to submit these revisions . . . to the representatives of the nation, chosen for this special task."[124]

Besides being a critic of the Constitution, Condorcet was involved in the pamphlet warfare raging between the Américanistes and the Anglomanes. He attacked DeLolme's *Constitution de L'Angleterre*, which praised the British constitution; interpreted the *Examen*, the pamphlet of the American John Stevens, to suit his own polemical needs; and translated the writings of the revolutionary Philip Mazzei.[125] Unlike most Américanistes, who lost faith in the "American Dream" once the French became more involved with their own Revolution, Condorcet's enthusiasm for America's constitutional developments remained with him to the end of his days.[126]

His end, indeed, was tragic. Elected to the Legislative Assembly in 1791, he was nominated as president. When that body was succeeded by the National Convention, he was elected and eventually raised to the position of vice president. He had already proclaimed his support of the French Constitution of 1791, but his own plan for a constitution submitted in 1793 was rejected. His document—a geometrically perfect blueprint—proposed a balance among the separated powers of the legislative, executive, and judicial branches; the right to a referendum; and a general and nearly unlimited popular initiative. The document was impractical on its face, however, and would have turned France into a permanent debating society. When Condorcet protested against the Jacobin Constitution of 1793, his position was tantamount to signing his own death warrant. During the Terror he fled Paris and, while in hiding, wrote his final political and philosophical testament, the great *Esquisse*. Captured in 1794, he was thrown into prison and found dead in his cell at the age of fifty.[127]

John Adams took exception to Condorcet's *Esquisse*. Carrying on a posthumous dialogue with his notes in the margin of Condorcet's book, Adams railed against his ideas. He disagreed with the Frenchman's faith in genius, his presumed ignorance of the nature of free government, and his views regarding the social progress of humankind. Most of all, Adams took issue with Condorcet's attitude toward the American and French revolutions. The Frenchman had predicted that the French Revolution would become the great model for all humankind. Adams held, however, that the authority and order symbolized by the American Revolution would carry the day.[128]

Other French Constitutional Commentators

Brissot de Warville, Américaniste, *philosophe,* and colleague of Condorcet, took an unusual step: he actually traveled to the United States in 1788 to witness the "American Dream" firsthand. Brissot returned even more enthusiastic, and his writings were filled with pleas urging France to follow America's example. Any people seeking to recover their liberty, he concluded, would find America a true model.[129]

Brissot quickly understood the new doctrine of the American Revolution: the idea of the people as a constituent power. Through the device of a special constitution-making convention, the people possessed the power to create, grant, and delimit authority in all levels of government. After returning to France in 1788, Brissot published his "Plan of Conduct" for the deputies of the Estates General preparing to meet. Only a constitutional convention, he insisted, could draw up an instrument of government. What was the source of this idea? "We owe its discovery to the free Americans, and the convention which has just formed the plan for a federal system [in Philadelphia] has infinitely perfected it." This device, he went on, "can perhaps be very easily adapted to the circumstances in which France now finds itself."[130]

Brissot was taken also with the idea of a bill of rights. "A declaration of rights," he wrote, "is as necessary for a constitution as the foundation of a house. The constitution may change; [but] the declaration of rights ought never to change." He published this statement in the newspaper he founded, *Le patriote française*, in which he presented his republican theories.[131]

Brissot thought that the Americans were wise not to follow the British model too closely. To illustrate his argument, he compared the new Pennsylvania Constitution point by point with corresponding provisions in France, slanting his comparison in favor of the Americans.[132] He singled out the Pennsylvania Constitution because that state had a unicameral legislature, the arrangement that most Américanistes like himself favored.[133]

Arriving in America in July 1788, Brissot stayed only six months. But his visit was long enough to enable him to write a book about his travels. Its aim was to hold up the mirror of America to France. He extolled the virtues of the American character, the famous individuals he met, and the educational and philanthropic institutions he visited.[134]

More to the point, Brissot was on the scene precisely at the most critical constitutional moment in American history, the change from the Articles of Confederation to the Constitution. He saw much that he liked. In particular, he commended the system of checks and balances that followed the doctrine laid down by Montesquieu, whom he admired greatly. To Brissot the U.S. Constitution represented the embodiment of that liberty and equality he desired for France.[135]

But Brissot objected to one blot in the document, its recognition of slavery. Like many French liberals he was a fervent abolitionist and remained hopeful of change because of the agreement reached at the Philadelphia Convention to end the American slave trade within twenty years. The end of this trade and the growing sentiment against slavery at the time in both the North and South, he believed, would eventually result in the extinction of the institution.[136]

Although Brissot seriously contemplated settling in America, his visit came to an abrupt end with the dramatic developments erupting in France. He returned to play a key role in the Revolution and emerged as the leader of the Brissotins. But his American experience continued to exercise an important influence. Although he attempted to frame a constitution for France along lines similar to that of the United States, he failed to impress his fellow Frenchmen. The victory of the Jacobins resulted in his fall from high office, and he was guillotined in 1793.

Pierre-Samuel Du Pont de Nemours, another *philosophe*, was more utopian in his views about the U.S. Constitution. A protégé of Turgot, he was active in the Constituent Assembly and twice elected its president.

As a model for France, he favored the American charter over that of England.[137] But once the Revolution grew more violent and radical, he became disenchanted and was briefly imprisoned for his ideas. Du Pont believed it was possible to create a "perfect Government—one even better than that formed by the Americans." About the time the U.S. Constitution was being written, he informed Jefferson that nations would one day achieve such a *beau ideal* because of the innate perfectibility of the human spirit.[138] A perfectionist at heart, Du Pont believed that a great universal constitution would be written one day to serve all humankind.

The writings of these and other French constitutional theorists demonstrate that the United States on the eve of the French Revolution was viewed as a kind of laboratory of constitutional experiments, with the U.S. Constitution as the center of its focus.[139] That perspective had a profound influence on French constitutionalism at a critical stage. The French historian François Furet observed rightly that America served as an object lesson rather than a model to be imitated.[140]

America's state constitutions, in contrast, provided models to be either followed or rejected after the French Revolution began. Precedents from these documents were cited frequently by two opposing groups in the French National Assembly in 1789. One faction, headed by Jean-Joseph Mounier, argued for a bicameral legislature and an executive veto similar in many respects to the Massachusetts Constitution of 1780. The other faction, led by Abbé Sieyès, felt that such devices would frustrate the popular will. In the end, the Sieyès group prevailed. One result was greater emphasis on the doctrine of popular sovereignty in France than in America.[141]

With the calling of the Estates General in 1789, French constitutionalism underwent a profound transformation during which political theories suddenly were transformed into concrete proposals. When casting about for practical models, the French looked most to indigenous sources. The two great French theorists, Montesquieu and Rousseau, among others, provided the context for the French constitutional tradition that ultimately developed.

American constitutionalism lost its place of prominence in French thinking at precisely the moment the country was entering its greatest constitutional crisis. In the early stages of that crisis, the U.S. Constitution and the state constitutions had played an important role as points of reference. But both were quickly relegated to a secondary status. Although the French sometimes referred to the American documents in their deliberations late in the 1790s, they went very much their own way.

French Constitutions of the 1790s and American Constitutionalism

In early 1789, the French National Assembly elected a committee and charged it with drafting a constitution. The French Constitution of 1791 that emerged was the result *not* of a debate over what kind of a constitution should be written, or over which foreign constitutions might serve as models, but over two competing visions of what a constitution for France should be. Was there an old, originally good constitution to be restored? Or did ancient France really have no constitution at all and thus had to create one? After the deputies decided to draw up a declaration of rights, however, the grounds of the debate had shifted and a new question arose: Where did sovereignty lie? Did *all* sovereignty reside in the nation? Or did it lie partly with the king? This question had to be answered before the deputies could proceed. It raised a whole host of subsidiary questions regarding the principles of constitutionality, sovereignty, representation, and Rousseau's philosophy of the general will. Such questions occupied the Assembly from the fall of 1789 until the Revolution in August 1792.[142]

What was surprising about the initial discussions of a constitution in the early 1790s was the speed with which the French disposed of both the British and American models.[143] Jean-Joseph Mounier, a leading deputy and an author of the Tennis Court Oath, was astonished in September 1789 when the Assembly cast a "scornful eye on the Constitution of England, whereas a year ago we spoke enviously of English liberty."[144]

Something similar happened in the case of the U.S. Constitution. Despite Lafayette's support of a French constitution modeled somewhat along American lines—one with a bicameral legislature and strong executive who could command the armed forces, appoint ministers, and conduct foreign relations—the plan was voted down. Rabaut Saint-Étienne, commenting on the Pennsylvania Constitution, remarked, "French nation, you are not made to receive examples, but to set them."[145]

Although the French Constitution of 1791 was not modeled on the American document of 1787, the French did follow some of America's constitutional "inventions." First of all, the Assembly acted as a constituent constitutional convention somewhat along American lines. Moreover, the Assembly produced a written constitution. Finally, the 1791 constitution included a declaration of rights. The French declaration, however, appeared fifteen years after Virginia's Declaration of Rights in 1776.

But the 1791 constitution revealed far less American influence in the rest of its features. It called for a constitutional monarchy and granted the

king a suspensive veto: "a veto which could postpone everything, but settle nothing."[146] On the issue of suffrage, it was moderate and provided for
a unicameral legislature to be elected indirectly. The new system of local
government had nothing in common with the U.S. Constitution, and the
same could be said for its proposed new financial structure.[147]

The monarchical Constitution of 1791 was soon replaced by the Jacobin
Constitution of 1793. The Jacobins, the most radical group in the French
Assembly, favored the elimination of all remnants of monarchy and aristocracy. Their constitution was famous for its version of the Declaration
of Rights—a list much longer than in the French Constitution of 1791 and
the American Bill of Rights. The Jacobin model was never implemented,
but exercised a profound worldwide effect. It was constantly invoked by
reformers and revolutionaries in many countries because of its newly-
acknowledged "social and economic rights" of citizens.

The 1793 charter, however, did resort to one American "invention."
Ratification of a constitution had been introduced in America's first state
constitutions. Both of America's national constitutions underwent the
same process: the Articles of Confederation by the states in 1781, and the
1787 document by state ratifying conventions in 1787–88. The French went
a step further in 1793 when they offered the constitution for direct ratification by the people.

In terms of political representation, the Constitution of 1793 also followed the American pattern of broad suffrage. In fact, the French idea of
universal suffrage *in theory* went much further than the American. Taken
literally, the provisions for political representation in the 1793 charter were
based on universal manhood suffrage at a time when post-revolutionary
America still had suffrage qualifications.[148] "The Constitution of June 1793
was the work of the most determined partisans of universal suffrage,"
wrote one French historian.[149] But the victory proved empty when extreme
Jacobins seized control of the government and the Terror (1793–1794) prevented implementation of the constitution.

The democratic 1793 document was soon followed by the more conservative 1795 constitution prepared by the Thermidorean Convention.
This constitution bore only a slight resemblance to the American one.
The fourth and final French constitution of the 1790s—the charter of
1799—moved even further away from the American model. It proclaimed
a new form of republic (the Consulate) in which the idea of a free or constitutional government was abandoned. Although the Consulate ostensibly
retained a republican form, Bonaparte soon emerged as an authoritarian

leader. With such changes as the purge of the Tribunate, life consulship, and Napoleon's elevation to the rank of hereditary emperor, any resemblance to American constitutionalism disappeared.

The Bill of Rights Tradition: Origins

Around the turn of the twentieth century, two European scholars, Georg Jellinek and Emil Doumergue, started a controversy by focusing on the first American state constitutions and the bills of rights accompanying them. The question they raised was this: Was America or France the forerunner of the great rights tradition in Western constitutionalism? Was the natural-law concept the source of the rights of man? Or were these rights derived mainly from English common law, the tradition transplanted in the American colonies? Were the main sources of these statements of rights, in other words, European or American in origin?

Jellinek, a German jurist, wrote a widely read book in 1895 that argued that the French Declaration of 1789 was derived *not* from Rousseau's ideas of natural law but from the declarations of rights written in America. Jellinek stated further that the origins of the rights of man could be traced directly to the Anglo-American struggle for religious liberty. That struggle, he concluded, began with the Agreement of the People in England in 1647 and culminated in the American colonies.[150] Jellinek's book sparked a response in 1904 from the Frenchman Doumergue, who drew a line of descent from Calvin to the French Declaration and located the roots of the rights of man tradition in Europe, not America.[151]

The controversy was continued later in the twentieth century by two leading American scholars, Richard B. Morris and Robert R. Palmer. Morris was convinced that the French Declaration had been copied directly from the Virginia Declaration of Rights of 1776, which was largely written by Mason. "The Virginia statesman," Morris wrote in 1970, "might well have instituted an action of plagiarism." The resemblance of Mason's document to the French Declaration "was too close to be coincidental."[152] Palmer was more cautious in his conclusions. When he compared the Virginia Declaration with the French document, he conceded that there was a "remarkable parallelism." The parallelism, among other things, supported Palmer's thesis in his major work that a community of ideas existed on both sides of the Atlantic.[153]

Palmer went on to argue, however, that the ideas in the French Declaration were indigenous to France. They differed in several important respects from the Virginia Declaration. For example, they provided sharper definitions of such terms as *citizenship, individual liberty,* and *the source of rightful public authority.* To give one illustration, the French term for *citizenship* implied that rights, though natural, did not arise from some supposed state of nature, distant in time and place, as was presumed to be the case in America. Instead, rights in France, wrote Palmer, arose from conditions of an individual living in some properly organized civil community. Similarly, the term *citizen* did not appear in American usage until much later.[154] The evidence supported Palmer's position rather than Morris's.

Jacques Godechot, the distinguished French historian, agreed with Palmer. He, too, noted many striking resemblances between several American declarations of rights and the French Declaration of 1789. Although Godechot conceded that the American documents had influenced the French text, he went on to point out some significant differences.[155] The texts of the American declarations were very specific: each one was drafted with a particular American state in mind. The French Declaration, by comparison, was much more universal. It did not contain the word *France* (except once in the preamble) or the words *king* or *republic* (hence it could be applied to other regimes). The discussion of rights, in other words, was quite abstract. The American declarations, by contrast, were more concrete, as they were concerned more with procedures and less with rights. "There are perhaps more parallels than imitations," Godechot concluded, "between the American and French documents."[156]

Godechot observed also that succeeding French declarations grew increasingly distant from the American tradition. The French Declaration of 1793 (the Jacobin Constitution) listed the right to work and other "economic and social rights." These inclusions distinguished the Jacobin Declaration from the American emphasis on civil rights. With the rise of industrial capitalism and the recurring unemployment that accompanied it, the French model's emphasis on social and economic rights proved far more attractive to foreign constitutionalists. "This Jacobin declaration . . . casts a longer shadow into the nineteenth and twentieth centuries than perhaps any other clause from the constitutional documents of the first French Revolution," concluded one scholar.[157] The French Declaration of 1795 departed even further from the American tradition by going off in a different direction. Rather than specifying additional rights, the declaration of "Rights and Duties" laid down new obligations that French citizens owed the state.[158]

Pointing out their universality, Mirabeau concluded that the French deputies had prepared "declaration[s] applicable to all ages, all peoples, all moral and geographical latitudes."[159] This did not mean, however, that the Americans had failed to influence the French. As one French historian conceded, "The American model was on everyone's mind; it was also explicitly or implicitly in relation to it that the members of the Constituent Assembly staked out their positions." But then he went on to add, "The source gave rise not to imitation but to emulation."[160] This acute observation caught nicely the distinction between the two positions.

The relationship between the French 1789 Declaration and the American Bill of Rights gave rise to another historiographical controversy. Since the two documents were adopted or passed within a month of each other, it was assumed that the close connection in timing meant that there must have been a similarity in meaning. Such may not have been the case, however.

Whereas other historians—Gilbert Chinard, Robert R. Palmer, and Jacques Godechot—were concerned mainly with the question of how and to what degree the Americans influenced the French, Gordon Wood advanced another hypothesis, that the flow of ideas may have gone in the opposite direction as well. Wood was well aware that the French knew of the various American state bills of rights when they began debating the 1789 French Declaration in the National Assembly. French delegates, in fact, had cited these American models. He knew, too, that Jefferson had helped Lafayette prepare the original draft of the 1789 French Declaration.[161] But as Wood pointed out, such connections were not very meaningful. "The two documents were very different, their purposes were different, and their results were different," he concluded.[162]

First, the 1789 French Declaration played a different role than did the American Bill of Rights. The French document came at the beginning of the French Revolution and went on to influence the very heart of constitution making. The French, moreover, did not view their declaration as a list of civil rights directed against some preexisting government. Rather, they believed their document to be a declaration of universal natural rights inherent in all men *before* any government. The French declaration, moreover, articulated the aims of the French Revolution and specifically called on the world to follow suit by recognizing the universality of these natural rights.[163]

The same was not true of the American Bill of Rights. It came at the end of the Revolution and after the Constitution had been written. In fact, delegates had voted down the resolution calling for a bill of rights in the Constitutional Convention. Moreover, throughout the ratification debates, the Federalists kept arguing that a bill of rights was superfluous.

Jefferson was involved in the origins of both documents. He set down his thoughts for a declaration of rights for France as early as May 1788. In a perceptive letter entitled "SYMPTOMS OF RESISTANCE" written on the very eve of the French Revolution, Jefferson spelled out his ideas:

> that the rights of subjects are not less sacred than those of the sovereign; that the monarchy cannot be preserved except on the basis of immutable laws securing to the citizens the liberty of their persons and property; [and] that the nation has always guarded against the fatal effects of arbitrary power.[164]

By January 1789, Jefferson was cooperating with Lafayette on a draft for a "declaration of rights." The Frenchman stated the document would become "the catechism" for his country. On July 11 Lafayette proposed his "catechism" to the National Assembly, which adopted the Declaration of the Rights of Man on August 26, 1789.[165] Lafayette conceded, however, that the idea of a declaration of rights had been recognized for the first time in France at the "beginning of the American era."[166]

Even more important, Lafayette helped Jefferson recognize that "a bill of rights is what the people are entitled to against every government on earth, general or particular, and what no just government should refuse or rest on inference."[167] After Jefferson received his copy of the U.S. Constitution, as noted previously, his immediate response was to comment on the absence of a bill of rights and to persuade Madison to change his mind and begin supporting such a measure. It was on this basis that Wood hypothesized that the drafting of the French Declaration and Lafayette may have influenced the creation of the American Bill of Rights rather than the other way around.[168] Wood's hypothesis constituted a significant scholarly contribution to the controversy. His conclusion regarding the Lafayette–Jefferson relationship, moreover, was seconded by Godechot, who declared that the collaboration was crucial to the outcome of events.[169]

Disintegration of the American Dream in France

The declining influence of the U.S. Constitution may be dated from the Thermidorean counterrevolution of July 1794. Attitudes toward the United

States changed dramatically also with the return of the French émigrés. Many had fled France, arrived to reside in America temporarily, and then returned home disenchanted with what they had seen. Unable to adapt to conditions in the New World, they expressed their unhappiness to fellow Frenchmen. One effect was the loss of interest in American constitutionalism as a whole.[170]

An entirely new set of assumptions resulted from the émigré experience. A rediscovered sense of relativism arose that contrasted sharply with the earlier belief in the universalism of constitutions. The émigrés emphasized as well the differences between the French and American lifestyles. "The idea that circumstances were unique for each separate nation, and that the problems of one people were irrelevant to those of another people, contributed to this new nationalism."[171] The Enlightenment dream of a universal constitution suffered a shock and setback.

The idea of progress—one of the "givens" of the Enlightenment—suffered a similar fate. The theory that humankind was progressing toward perfection and that the "good" achieved in one area of human endeavor would inevitably result in a corresponding "good" in another was dashed. The United States presented a contradictory picture, as there appeared to be progress and retrogression at one and the same time. America's successful liberal government and its striking economic growth, for example, were accompanied by growing doubts about its materialism, moral corruption, and intellectual bankruptcy. The American Dream in its original form died in France for the time being.

American Constitutionalism and Other Regions of Europe

The influence of American constitutionalism was felt elsewhere in Europe in the 1780s and 1790s. Six sister republics were set up under the aegis of the French as their armies swept through the continent. Ten constitutions were written for these satellite states, stretching from the Netherlands to Italy, between 1796 and 1799. They were established in Belgium, the small bishoprics and principalities west of the Rhine, and, with the aid of local sympathizers, in a string of lesser revolutionary republics in the Dutch Netherlands, Switzerland, and much of Italy. As Lord Acton once remarked, the French Declaration of 1789 proved to be more powerful than the armies of Napoleon.[172]

Modeled on the French Constitution of 1795 or the regime of the French Directory, all these charters incorporated bills of rights.[173] These documents were influenced by American constitutionalism, but only indirectly. When they resorted to a written constitution, employed some form of popular sovereignty, or introduced a declaration of rights, moreover, these features of the American model were refracted through a French prism.

Even faraway Russia came to know about the American state constitutions. Aleksander Radishchev, a Russian reformer who greatly admired the American Revolution, wrote his stirring *Ode to Liberty* in 1782. In his poem he told the American people that their "example has set a goal for us. / We all wish for the same."[174] Likewise, in his celebrated travelogue *Journey from St. Petersburg to Moscow*, Radishchev lavished praise on the state constitutions and contrasted their protection of freedom of the press with the censorship imposed in France during the French Revolution.[175]

American Constitutionalism and the Netherlands

American constitutional documents exercised some influence also in the United Netherlands. Johan Derk van der Capellen, leader of the Dutch patriot movement against William V, the Stadtholder, had the Declaration of Independence translated into Dutch. One result was that the Dutch became more familiar with the language of representative government and soon began to identify the American Revolution with their own cause.[176]

The Massachusetts Constitution of 1780 proved particularly influential. John Adams was serving as minister to the Hague when the Dutch patriot movement got under way. As author of the document, Adams sent a copy to Johan Luzac, the editor of the *Gazette de Leyde*. "To tell you the truth, as I had some share in the Formation of this Constitution," Adams wrote with uncharacteristic modesty, "I am ambitious of seeing it translated by the Editor of the Leyden Gazette."[177] Luzac made the text and that of several other state constitutions available to his countrymen, and they were read widely.

In the mid-1770s, a brilliant young lawyer, Pieter Paulus, wrote a four-volume study of the Union of Utrecht. In his work he commented that the 1776 draft of the Articles of Confederation might provide a splendid model for a Dutch Union. After making a constitutional comparison, Paulus concluded that the American federation was much "neater" in form, stating, "I include their *Articles of Confederation and Perpetual Unity* in their entirety."[178] But Paulus's enthusiasm soon cooled. He decided that such a loose federal system would eventually lead to the collapse of the Dutch confederation, and that was exactly what happened.[179]

The reception of the U.S. Constitution was a different matter. When Johan Luzac published the entire text of the document in the *Gazette de Leyde* in November 1787, he apologized for the lack of any additional background information. Luzac later lauded the document but emphasized that the New World example could hardly be imitated in the Old.[180] Like many Dutchmen, Luzac realized that the U.S. Constitution served as a kind of litmus-paper test between two Dutch groups. The radicals who wished to follow the French example of drastic reform formed one group. The other was composed of moderate reformers or conservatives who had serious doubts about France's bloody revolution. They wanted to cast about for other models to follow. Luzac, an important opinion maker, sided with the latter group and supported the American document accordingly.

Gijsbert Karel van Hogendorp, another Dutch commentator, used the U.S. Constitution as an example, but in a different way. When he was twenty, Hogendorp came to America "to study how a state is born, so that I can help to reform my own country."[181] Arriving in late 1783, he stayed only a half year and returned home quite disillusioned. He thought that under the Articles, the American system was too decentralized and predicted that the country would soon fall apart. With the emergence of the new American Union in 1787, however, he changed his mind, praising the separation of powers in the U.S. Constitution and its system of checks and balances. Hogendorp, a conservative, noted the contrast between the American and French revolutions. In a long essay entitled *Equality*, he attacked abstract French ideas and compared them unfavorably with the more pragmatic American approach. But he went on to observe that what was possible in America under its Constitution could never be achieved in Europe because the gap between the rich and the poor in Europe was too great. The higher level of intellectual development in America (especially in the North, where he believed most people knew how to read and write), he said, had produced a more enlightened citizenry.[182]

The best-informed commentator on the U.S. Constitution in the region was Gerhard Dumbar, a scholar, philosopher, and administrator, who between 1793 and 1796 produced in Amsterdam a three-volume work entitled *The Old and New Constitutions of the United States*. Dumbar finished writing his third volume just before the French invasion ended the

Dutch Republic. Like Hogendorp, he viewed the separation of powers and checks and balances as the finest feature of the U.S. Constitution. Dumbar admired the American federal system, which did not centralize power as in France. The French, he wrote, "could even in a republic, cause all the horrors of despotism." Like so many Dutch observers, Dumbar favored American political moderation over French radicalism.[183]

It is difficult to determine how much influence Dumbar had on his colleagues. They were in process of framing a constitution just after his volumes were published. In the discussions in the Dutch Assembly in the mid-1790s, his work was sometimes quoted, especially by the Federalists or Moderates, who liked to appeal to the American example of balanced government and the federal system.[184] Dumbar was caught up in the political turmoil of the times as the Batavian Republic endured one coup d'état after another. Being a Moderate, he was seized during a radical coup in 1798 and jailed, but survived. Some time during this trying period, Dumbar drafted his own constitution which, though never published, was found later among his papers. His draft showed the distinct stamp of the U.S. Constitution. It included the separation of powers and proposed a federal system in which all powers not delegated to the central government were reserved to the provinces. The executive branch, however, was to be composed of a five-man directory.

In 1801 Dumbar had an opportunity at last to voice his views. A new conservative constitution was being implemented, one with a strong executive like the consular office in France. It was hardly the kind of constitution he wanted, but he defended it in a pamphlet published anonymously. Once again, he cited the U.S. Constitution. Why was it that so many constitutions in France and his homeland had been failures in recent years, he asked, while the American charter was in full vigor after twelve years?[185]

What effect Dumbar's writings might have had on his countrymen can never be known. Having suffered through six turbulent years under the French, the Dutch were so suspicious that they hardly troubled to go to the polls to vote on the Constitution of 1801. Those who did overwhelmingly rejected it. The government had the constitution adopted, nevertheless, by manipulating the results: those who abstained from voting were counted as being in favor of the document! The following year Dumbar was finally in a position to play an important role in the new Dutch government. He was appointed to the legislature and assumed his duties with great vigor. But in the summer of 1802, he died suddenly, and with his death, the last important Americanist in the Dutch provinces disappeared.

American Constitutionalism and Switzerland

The Swiss model of confederation government played a different role in the transatlantic constitutional dialogue, as it sometimes served as a negative example for the American framers. A year before the Constitutional Convention, James Madison wrote his essay "Notes on Ancient and Modern Confederacies," in which he generalized that one of the common "vices" of confederacies throughout history was the absence of power at the center. The Swiss Confederacy, he observed, did not "make one commonwealth . . . but are so many independent Commonwealths in strict alliance."[186] Madison underscored the weakness of the confederacy by pointing out that the government sometimes had been forced to call in outsiders to settle disputes between cantons.

In his comparative study of confederation governments, Madison made an implicit argument against the Articles of Confederation, then in force, and by inference suggested a stronger centralized government. History showed, Madison maintained, that absence of adequate authority at the center had brought about the collapse of confederacies in the past. It would certainly threaten to do so again in the modern era, he warned.[187]

During the Constitutional Convention, the Federalists and Anti-federalists debated the relative merits of the Swiss government model. The issue turned on the question of whether it had been a success or failure. The Anti-federalists argued that it had worked well, whereas the Federalists insisted it was a disaster. When Alexander Hamilton took the floor in June 1787, he protested: "The Swiss cantons have scarce any Union at all and have been more than once at war with one another. How then are these evils to be avoided?"[188] Madison followed by summarizing his essay and drew an analogy between the Swiss confederacy and the existing American confederation.[189]

Luther Martin, the shrewd Anti-federalist, responded by praising the Swiss. Each canton, irrespective of its size or population, had an equal vote, a proviso he and other Anti-federalists were trying to incorporate into the proposed U.S. Constitution. Berne alone, by virtue of its size and population, he predicted, could usurp "the whole power of the Helvetic confederacy, but she is contented still with being equal."[190]

The debates in the Constitutional Convention sometimes focused mainly on the relative merits of the Helvetic confederacy.[191] In the end, obviously the Federalists won out. The influence of the Swiss example on the American debates, nevertheless, was instructive. It showed Americans using

European models to decide what they themselves might do and indicated that the flow of ideas was east to west as well as the other way around.

The crisis created by the French Revolution caused many Swiss to reconsider the U.S. Constitution as a possible model. The Helvetic Republic, established after the French invasion in 1798, however, imposed a constitution that created a satellite state with a highly centralized government. The independence and sovereignty of individual cantons were destroyed, and all power was vested in the hands of a five-man directory. When the Helvetic Republic collapsed in 1803, few Swiss were sorry to see it go, and for the next four decades plans for revising the Swiss government seldom passed without some serious consideration given to the U.S. Constitution.[192]

American Constitutionalism and Germany

"The 'American Dream' existed in Germany as much as in France," wrote Robert R. Palmer.[193] But unlike the French, German public opinion of American matters was more diffuse because the region was made up of separate German principalities. The Hanoverian association with the British Crown, moreover, caused leading Germans to take a pro-British stance when discussing American affairs. The reaction of German society at large also was much slower in developing because information about the United States was not easily available. The political predisposition of the German middle class caused it to view the American Revolution as a triumph of philosophical ideals rather than a conflict over pragmatic objectives between clashing interest groups.

With the outbreak of the French Revolution, members of the German middle class suddenly began comparing the two revolutions. Frightened by the violence in France and the assault on property rights, with the French revolutionaries taking the offensive, Germans praised the American Revolution for its pragmatic, limited, and defensive nature. They began to view it as a "good" revolution, one of universal significance which had a helpful message for the rest of the world.[194] Not until the 1790s, however, was enough known about the U.S. Constitution to allow a meaningful dialogue to take place. Professors and publishers then proceeded to discuss its constitutional principles. Some showed great curiosity about American-style federalism, a subject destined later to attract the attention of important constitutional theorists. But the discussion at this early stage was neither detailed nor analytically astute.[195]

One commentator who held interesting views on the U.S. Constitution was Georg Forster, a German radical living in France during the Terror. Horrified by the bloody violence about him, Forster concluded that men were too evil by nature to live in a truly free society, at least as far as Europeans were concerned. But he held out hope for the Americans. The U.S. Constitution was completely aristocratic, he claimed, and its leaders wise and noble. Washington, as president, was actually more powerful than King George III, despite that monarch's hereditary rights. America's aristocracy, founded on property rather than inherited rights, gave Americans a better chance to succeed. Americans were also a more sober and pragmatic people than Europeans, Forster wrote, "for we [the German people] are, compared to Americans, hotheads and our principles are corrupted in the roots."[196]

In a brilliant essay in 1800 comparing the American and French revolutions, Friedrich von Gentz, a German publicist, made the most compelling argument about the differences between the two revolutionary movements. In his essay, Gentz popularized the idea that the American Revolution was conservative and marked by consensus, whereas the French Revolution was radical and characterized by chaos. After Gentz, European conservatives increasingly began to compare the two revolutions and saw the American Revolution more as an insurgent movement than as an outright rebellion.[197] Gentz's essay proved an important turning point not only in Germany but throughout Europe in emphasizing the conservatism of the American Revolution.

American Constitutionalism and Italy

Like Germany, Italy in 1800 was not yet a nation-state, and the region remained merely a "geographical expression," to use Metternich's phrase. Composed of separate sovereignties and dependencies relying on foreign powers for protection, the region was deeply divided, insecure, and unstable. A foundation for national unity was laid when Napoleon created some nominally independent kingdoms and established legal and administrative systems based on French ideas. But Italian theorists could rely on their strong indigenous constitutional traditions dating back to the days of ancient Rome and continued in the modern period with some thirty-five state constitutions written after 1797.

Before the American Revolution, Italians had relied mainly on French and British sources for information regarding the North American colonies. Direct contact between America and Italy was infrequent, but a major source was Abbé Raynal's popular book on North America translated into Italian in 1776. Through the eyes of this French freethinker, Italians were able to follow recent events, though to be sure, only a few people were literate, educated, or even interested in developments in distant America.[198] The "American Dream" existed in Italy, nevertheless, from the time the United States came into being as an independent nation.

Philip Mazzei, an Italian physician, merchant, and author, believed in the "American Dream." Arriving in America in 1773, he settled on a farm called "Colle" adjacent to Jefferson's "Monticello." The two men became close friends, and Mazzei soon was immersed in Virginia politics. A perceptive and original thinker on constitutional matters, Mazzei quickly took up the cause of American independence.

Mazzei was present at the creation of the new nation, so to speak. On the evening of July 3, 1776, when Jefferson was sitting alone in his room in Philadelphia, he made copies of his original draft of the Declaration of Independence and sent one to his friend and neighbor. Once the document was issued, excerpts from it appeared in Venice, no doubt through Mazzei's efforts.[199]

Mazzei shared the view held by many of his adopted countrymen that there existed a British conspiracy to rob the American people of their rights. In his eyes the Navigation Acts and restrictions on trade were sure signs of such a conspiracy.[200] His interpretation of the American Revolution, moreover, was that such moves freed the American colonists from any obligation under the social contract. Having identified the moral corruption in the British government and believing in a tyrannical plot to enslave the American people, Mazzei argued that the colonists were justified in refusing further obedience to King George.

He then plunged immediately into the fight over Virginia's state constitution. In his *Instructions of the Freeholders of Albemarle County to Their Delegates in Convention*, Mazzei took the position that rejection of British sovereignty presented Americans with a rare opportunity. They could change from the traditional practice of representation and adopt a more radical position. Virginians still adhered to the old British notion of mixed government in which local control remained in the hands of elites. What Mazzei proposed instead was a daring innovative step to restructure the relationship between the ruler and ruled. His plan called for political representatives to serve only as spokesmen and for their actions to be controlled by their constituents. Such a drastic reform would have revolutionized the existing power structure. It was, of course, rejected.[201]

The radical nature of Mazzei's ideas became even more obvious when he called for the Virginia Constitution of 1776 to be declared invalid. After he published his *Albemarle County Instructions Concerning the Virginia Constitution* in October 1776, Mazzei pointed out that the document had never been explicitly approved by the people. Years later, both Jefferson and Madison conceded that Mazzei's position was correct and that Mazzei proved to be more "American" than the two founding fathers.[202]

Mazzei's ability to enter so quickly into the constitutional dialogue demonstrated once again the degree to which Enlightenment ideas circulated throughout the Atlantic world.[203] The most penetrating analysis of America's state constitutions in Italy was Mazzei's multivolume work, *Recherches historique et politique sur les États-Unis de l'Amérique septentrionale*, published in Paris in 1788.[204] He saw the documents as evidence of the genius of the American people, a genius that gave rise to a unique form of representative democracy. According to Mazzei, the constitutions were social contracts resulting from two conditions: the return to a state of nature after the break with the British king, and the tradition of self-government in America that had developed during the colonial period. Mazzei believed that the American Revolution represented an exercise in republican virtue on the part of the American people.

Mazzei stressed also the modernity of the Americans and declared that they had created a completely new constitutional order. To him, the modernity of Americans was illustrated by their ability to behave according to reason. The Revolution demonstrated that they could profit from past political experience and, on the basis of what they learned, had established a new system of governance. On the one hand, they repudiated the supremacy of the king and existed "with no government, all equally free, as if in a state of nature, all equally interested in the public cause." On the other, they were "generally instructed about the [new] rights of man and the soundest principles of free government." In short, the Americans had broken and then renewed the social contract in Lockeian terms.[205]

Mazzei offered also some observations about America's state constitutions. He singled out for praise certain features in specific state constitutions, applauding the restriction in Georgia's state constitution requiring any legislator with a European title of nobility to renounce it before accepting public office. He noted with approval the indirect election of the executive and judicial branches of government in Georgia's constitution.

At the same time, he observed that in Connecticut—where the governor was popularly elected—the people had not been fickle or unpredictable.[206] Mazzei's study was one of the most insightful works on the American state constitutions written at the time.[207] He declared that they had produced state governments superior to any republican governments that ever existed. But Americans still had more to do. They had not reached that stage of perfection acceptable to a great political philosopher or lawgiver. There was, in other words, a strong utopian streak in Mazzei's thinking.

His enthusiasm cooled, however, when he received a copy of the U.S. Constitution. Mazzei thought the federal government would be beyond the control of the people and worried particularly about the excessive powers given to the president. He felt also that the Constitution granted too much power to the central government and did so at the expense of popular sovereignty and individual rights.

When Mazzei criticized the Constitution in a letter written to Madison from Paris in 1787, Madison admitted frankly he had backed the document on the grounds of expediency. Experience had shown, wrote Madison, that the "real danger to America & to liberty lies in the defect of *energy* & *stability* in the present establishments in the United States." Under the Articles, there had been too little exercise of power; the Confederation had drifted for lack of leadership and energy. Mazzei was writing from Paris, Madison noted, and would be more concerned "with the evils resulting from *too much Government all over Europe* . . . and it is natural for you to run into criticisms dictated by an extreme on that side." If Mazzei were living in America, Madison concluded, "I am sure [you] would think and feel as I do."[208] Although other Italian intellectuals wrote on American constitutionalism, none had the depth and penetration of Mazzei's work.[209]

Conclusion

The Madison–Mazzei exchange continued the constitutional discourse between America and Europe taking place during the first echo, a unique period in world history. The last quarter of the eighteenth century differed markedly from previous periods because of its extraordinary experiments in republicanism. The United States produced three different models of republican constitutions: the first state constitutions, the Articles, and the federal Constitution. France promulgated two more in the republican charters of 1793 and 1795. The ten constitutions for satellite states resulting from French conquests were republican at first until French generals changed them. In Britain, politicians in the Opposition were seeking republican changes in the British constitution.

But the other five seminal documents also were involved in the republican experiments during the first echo, and none more so than the Declaration of Independence. Thomas Jefferson best understood the profound global implications resulting from the promulgation of the document. Looking back a half century to the day it was proclaimed, he prophesied the role that the Declaration would play not only in American history but in all human history. Invited by Mayor Roger Weightman of Washington, D.C., to celebrate the fiftieth anniversary of the document, he was too ill to attend. Lying on his deathbed, he mustered one last burst of energy to write down his political testament for posterity. Richard B. Bernstein, a gifted Jefferson biographer, rightly ranks the letter written June 24, 1826, with the Virginian's "First Inaugural Address and [along] with Lincoln's Gettysburg Address and Second Inaugural Address as statements of the American experience and the central truths of the American experiment in government."[210] In soaring phrases approaching the eloquence of the original manifesto, Jefferson wrote:

> May it [the Declaration] be to the world what I believe it will be, (to some parts sooner, to others later, but finally to all,) the Signal of arousing men to burst the chains under which . . . ignorance and superstition had persuaded them to bind themselves, and to assume the blessings & security of self government. That form which we have substituted restores the free right to the unbounded exercise of reason and freedom of opinion. All eyes are opened, or opening to the rights of man. The general spread of the light of science has already laid open to every view the palpable truth, that the mass of mankind has not been born, with saddles on their backs, nor a favored few booted and spurred, ready to ride them legitimately, by the grace of god. These are grounds of hope for others. For ourselves let the annual return of this day, forever refresh our recollections of these rights, and an undiminished devotion to them.[211]

Jefferson's letter contains his personal beliefs, political principles, and constitutional views to which he was deeply committed: that the Declaration would shape not only the history of the United States but also the history of all future humankind; that the future belonged to the living and each succeeding generation should make its own choice regarding its form of government; that if any given generation was dissatisfied, it had the right of revolution to change its government. Jefferson's passionate devotion to the rights of man, his emphasis on reason derived from the Age of the Enlightenment, and his hope that the Declaration would gain larger significance in the future history of liberty were evident as well. Finally, it was his wish that the Fourth of July would become a national annual holiday so Americans could rededicate themselves by rituals to the ideals expressed in the Declaration. Like Lincoln's two masterpieces, Jefferson's letter was filled with striking metaphors that conveyed both truth and beauty.[212]

Ten days later, Jefferson died on July Fourth. His last letter was really a fulfillment of the first echo in calling for an annual rededication of the nation to the ideals of the Declaration and the American constitutionalism it inaugurated.

4

Second Echo

Latin America, 1811–1900

The second "echo" sounded in Latin America when Europe's revolutionary upheavals reached across the Atlantic and influenced Spanish American colonists who began their movement to independence with Venezuela's declaration in 1811. Inspired by the example of British American colonists to the North, they, too, threw off the control of European monarchs. The second echo was enormous in its original dimensions. In terms of space, Spanish America stretched from the San Francisco region to Buenos Aires and included some of the Caribbean islands. When Brazil, part of the Portuguese empire, became a republic in 1891, Latin America became the greatest laboratory for experimentation in republicanism in the world outside the United States.

No other region on the globe was so involved in nation building in the early nineteenth century, and few made greater use of North American constitutionalism. Although these countries borrowed heavily from the six seminal documents, Latin American constitution makers soon discovered that imitation was no simple matter. Time and again, they found that North American ideals, ideas, and institutions did not fit their situation. As one historian put it, paraphrasing a Latin American novelist: "It was like a lock ordered by catalogue from the United States that came with the wrong instructions and no keys."[1] "The limited transplantability of [North] American constitutional ideas is the main lesson of . . . Latin America," wrote another scholar.[2]

Despite the difficulties encountered, Latin American constitutionalists continued to emulate North American ideas and institutions. Huge sections of two constitutions—Argentina's in 1853 and Brazil's in 1891—were copied word for word from the U.S. Constitution. Venezuela's and Mexico's earliest constitutions also leaned heavily on the same source, and similar borrowings can be found in the charters of other countries to this day. But this is not to say that Latin American countries were on their way to becoming liberal constitutional democracies. On the contrary, "the record on the continent . . . is layered with constitutions tailored to please the ambitions of the powerful and marked by the utter inability to provide for the establishment of a vigorous constitutionalism," concluded one scholar.[3] "Unlike that of the United States, the Latin American experience with constitutionalism has generally been a failure," agreed another.[4]

Common Characteristics of Latin American Constitutionalism

Faced with a choice between monarchism or republicanism, almost all the former Spanish colonies declared themselves republics. They did so for several reasons: the break in monarchical continuity resulting from the Spanish king's detention by France, the influence of the American and French revolutions, the lengthy wars of independence, and the antimonarchical writings of North America's founding fathers and French *philosophes*. But the greatest motivation for emulation sprang from the startling success of the young republic to the North.

Latin America emerged as "the primary area of adoption" of presidentialism, according to one political scientist who conducted a worldwide comparative survey. "Upon their emancipation from the crown," he continued, "the Spanish colonies without exception adopted the presidential pattern of the American Constitution."[5] There were, of course, Spanish precedents for presidentialism: the colonial viceroys, captains general, and the king's role under the Cadiz Constitution of 1812. But the North American pattern of presidentialism proved to be a disaster, and what emerged was hardly recognizable compared with the original.

U.S.-style federalism also had great appeal. Arguments over the relative merits of federalism versus centralism broke out once independence was achieved. Domestic reasons for turning to federalism varied: reaction against the centralism of the Spanish colonial empire; fears of a presidential dictatorship; political divisions resulting from geographic, demographic, and economic differences; and the resistance of outlying provinces to control by large metropolitan cities. Once again, although federalism was adopted in many countries, its form differed considerably from that of the United States.

Judicial review likewise was transplanted. Although it failed to work as effectively as in the United States, the practice was incorporated into nearly all the Latin American constitutions. Indeed, the United States and the southern continent were the two greatest regions in the world for judicial review in the nineteenth century. Argentina, for example, first adopted the principle for provincial courts in its 1853 constitution. It was established on the national level when the Argentine Supreme Court cited *Marbury v. Madison*.[6] Brazil, for its part, went so far as to send a delegation to Washington to interview Supreme Court justices before writing judicial review into its 1891 constitution.

The main reasons why these North American constitutional traditions were so attractive are obvious. Confronted with the task of nation building, restraining the influence of the Catholic Church, and controlling the armies of liberation that turned on those whom they had liberated, elites began casting about for other constitutional models. Like the North American colonies, they too had resented restrictions on free trade, held an anti-European bias, and harbored hostility against the former mother country. Proximity to the United States and contacts through trade created other common bonds. Both regions, moreover, had been exposed to the same source of constitutional ideas: the European Enlightenment.

Many Creoles (whites of Spanish descent born in America) had been educated in Spain and France and were familiar with the writings of the French *philosophes*. French ideas, in fact, dominated in many parts of the continent, and Creole intellectuals tended to view North American constitutional documents as embodying European Enlightenment theories that could be put into practice. Even some *peninsulares* (those born in Spain and holding posts in the Spanish empire) were believers in the Enlightenment. But Enlightenment ideas should not be seen as the only motivation for emulating the North American model. Material motives—economic, political, and religious—proved even more powerful influences.[7]

Creole elites did not consider North American constitutional ideas to be unique, as they shared principles with many other constitutionalisms besides the American and French, including the Spanish and British. In Argentina, for example, some early constitutional drafts reflected the French model of a plural executive and unicameral legislature as well as the North American model of a single executive and bicameral legislature. In Mexico, Peru, and Chile, both North American constitutionalism and Spanish constitutionalism were clearly in evidence.[8]

The reason for such eclecticism was the desire of liberal elites to modernize Spanish America because they attributed their backwardness to Spain's outdated institutions. The success of the United States, they believed, resulted from its political and constitutional institutions and not necessarily from the character of its people. "Washington did so much good for mankind," José Miguel Infante told his fellow Chileans, "because the LAWS OF THE NORTH AMERICAN FEDERATION placed him in the happy position of being unable to do bad."[9]

The American Revolution, moreover, was regarded by many Spanish American elites as a better model than the French Revolution. When slaves revolted in the French colony of Saint-Domingue in 1791 and Toussaint L'Ouverture led a bloody uprising later in the decade, many liberal Spanish and Portuguese slaveholders who had held Enlightenment views became alarmed. The Terror of the French Revolution turned them away even more from that model. As Venezuela's Francisco de Miranda remarked, "We have before us two great examples, the American and French Revolutions. Let us prudently imitate the first and carefully shun the second."[10]

Transplantations Are Transformed

Applying North American constitutionalism, however, proved to be very complicated, as transplantation through the process of syncretism always results in different outcomes. Although indigenous conditions worked both for and against accepting the North American model, any comparison of political systems shows why it had such a profound influence.

The first attempts to transplant presidentialism took place shortly after independence. Beginning with Venezuela in 1811, almost all countries on the continent adopted the presidential pattern, though a few experimented with parliamentarianism.[11] But the presidential pattern quickly developed into a caricature of the North American model. U.S. framers had limited presidential authority through the separation of powers and a system of checks and balances. But in Spanish America such safeguards were usually not established, and an exaggerated form of presidentialism, known as *caudillismo*, emerged instead. *Caudillismo* was marked by certain characteristics: personal rule by a man with a charismatic personality, a repressive dictatorship, a resort to military force to gain political power, and the centralization of authority. The *caudillos* became so common early in the nineteenth century that the era became known as the "age of the *caudillos*." This phenomenon lasted well into the twentieth century.[12]

One important manifestation of *caudillismo* was modifying the separation of powers so that presidents could participate in drafting legislation. They sometimes were empowered to initiate laws and, more important, could legislate by decree under certain conditions.[13] An even more important feature was the president's right to declare "a state of emergency." Unlike the U.S. Constitution, Spanish American constitutions included provisions that distinguished between peacetime and emergency conditions. Whenever an emergency was declared, constitutional rights could be suspended. In that event, legislative power was usually delegated to the president, and the constitutional safeguards were either dropped or became vague. Such emergencies were declared with distressing frequency, and one of the most damaging results was the disappearance of safeguards for human rights.[14] Indeed, calling a state of emergency soon became a favorite way for *caudillos* to impose dictatorships.

Latin America was also one of the first regions outside the United States to try to adopt North American–style federalism. Throughout the nineteenth century, however, Latin American countries experienced difficulties in this regard because their colonial histories differed so much from those of the former British American colonies. Early English settlers had enjoyed a considerable degree of self-government. But Spain and Portugal, with their highly centralized governments, allowed colonists far less freedom. Federalism in Latin America, moreover, was sometimes viewed as a way of integrating previously autonomous regions into a single nation. Having lived under a unitary system for more than three centuries, former Spanish and Portuguese colonists often were skeptical about the fragmentation of authority. Despite this tendency, some new republics decided to throw off the old centralized system and experiment with federalism. Subordinate states or provinces were sometimes granted new powers under republican constitutions or even encouraged to exercise self-government.[15]

Such changes were not accepted without challenges. Competing claims arose between *federalistas* or decentralizers, on the one hand, and *unitarios* or centralizers, on the other. Federalism, according to the decentralizers, could better accommodate regional interests. It could also deal better with problems of transportation and communication encountered in large regions separated by jungles, mountains, or expansive rivers. In some instances, it could even bring a sense of greater cohesion, especially in those countries with huge alienated Indian populations. Finally, federalism could incorporate the long-standing tradition of municipal autonomy in Spanish America. The *unitarios* responded by arguing that centralization could handle the same problems more efficiently. It could combat regionalism and instill a sense of national cohesion in countries split by geographical, economic, or cultural differences. Given the illiteracy among most people at the time, a unitary constitution, many felt, might also encourage a stronger sense of nationalism.

Since federalism and a decentralized form of government authority had been operating successfully in the United States, it offered an attractive alternative model. Although some Latin American federalists were willing to consider the U.S. concept, the *unitarios* wanted to continue the old unitary system to maintain their political control. This clash of views resulted in violence, and bitter civil wars raged between the two groups.

Because federalism grants autonomy to subordinate units, it is particularly useful for governing large countries with a huge landmass. Hence, it is no coincidence that the five Latin American countries—Venezuela, Mexico, Chile, Argentina, and Brazil—that tried to adopt a federal system like the United States were among the largest on the continent.[16] Federalism, however, operated quite differently in each. In Venezuela, for example, the states were left with such limited powers that one authority labeled the country a "pseudo-federalist union."[17] In Mexico, a former president bluntly called Mexico's federalism "a great lie."[18]

A high degree of centralization was continued, nevertheless, even in these five countries. Two reasons explain the anomaly. The first was that all were civil-law countries, where most private law was set out in certain basic law codes. In Latin American countries (except for Mexico) the central government rather than the states or provinces exercised jurisdiction over these codes. The second was that the North American version of federalism has always been incompatible with any arbitrary abuse of executive power or form of dictatorship. In many Latin American countries, the central governments were allowed to intervene legally in the states during periods of emergency. Although the five Latin American countries were federal in theory, they did not always turn out to be that in practice.[19] Despite the similarity of wording drawn from the U.S. Constitution, Latin American countries fell far short of the northern model, and the influence of American-style federalism was accordingly limited.[20]

The American model of judicial review also was transplanted throughout much of Latin America early in the nineteenth century. This did not mean, however, that judicial review was actually practiced. It failed to work effectively in Latin America for several reasons. First, citizens were fearful of contesting federal government actions. That fear was rooted in the authoritarian rule practiced in the Spanish and Portuguese colonies, a situation that continued even after independence. Second, the courts were reluctant to challenge decisions made by other branches of government or by military authorities. Third, there existed a tradition of noncompliance with the law. Even when acts of the executive or legislature were declared unconstitutional, the custom of ignoring court rulings was widespread.[21]

Despite the bills of rights written into many Latin American constitutions, the courts often failed to protect individual rights by not making them judicially enforceable. Although Latin American courts usually were able to maintain their independence, judges often found their freedom of action hampered in other ways: their limited role in the civil-law tradition, the fragility of their tenure, the political nature of judicial appointments, and the autocratic actions of dictators.[22]

Latin American countries also differed markedly from the United States in their attitude toward the rule of law. From the beginning, the United States had operated with a strong commitment to this principle, but Latin American countries began with a lack of respect for the law. During the colonial period, patrimonial regimes were subject to widespread corruption, a penchant for huge bureaucracies, and highly personalized legal systems. This colonial legacy continued after independence, and disregard for law often degenerated into anarchy.[23]

Another important distinction was the tendency of Latin Americans to view the law as an optimistic hope rather than a constitutional reality. Latin American constitutions typically included aspirational, inspirational, or other utopian provisions difficult or impossible to achieve. It was relatively common, for example, for heavily Catholic countries to insist that divorce was unconstitutional, and such provisions were written into constitutions to protect the integrity of the family. Yet marriages broke up in Latin America at rates comparable to those in other countries. By including such obviously unenforceable mandates, constitutionalists encouraged citizens to regard their charters as aspirational texts rather than as documents designed for an enforceable system of governance.[24]

North American constitutionalism yielded different outcomes in Latin America for other reasons as well. The greater variety of races in Latin America resulted in different cultures and customs. The mixture of Indian, mestizo, black, and white European cultures presented difficult challenges to ruling elites. In many areas—mainly in the northern part of Latin America—a small number of elites ruled over great masses of Indian or partly Indian peoples who were usually excluded from political participation and whose presence loomed like a dark cloud over any democratic policies attempted. In regard to considerations of class, the land system of large estates (*latifundio*), the great inequalities in wealth, and the small size of the middle class created a much less democratic system than in the United States with its large middle class of landholding farmers. Regional differences—geographic, demographic, urban and rural, and various commercial, agricultural, and mining interests—also created volatile political situations. Such circumstances encouraged chronic coups d'état.

Why Latin American Constitutions Were Unstable

One prevalent condition characteristic of Latin American regimes was their political instability. Virtually every new regime that declared its independence enacted a new constitution that was soon followed by others. The statistics regarding the number of constitutions in each country are startling. It is estimated from the beginning of independence in 1811 to 1989, Latin American countries produced a total of 253 constitutions. This figure averages 12.6 per country, compared with three in the United States (including the Confederate Constitution) over the same period.[25] Constitutional comparisons of this sort, however, are misleading. For example, Latin American constitutions were notoriously easy to change. The changes were often cosmetic, and discontinued constitutions were sometimes revived or reinstated. As a result, a so-called new constitution was often a carbon copy of the old one with only minor changes.[26] Usually many North American features were retained.

The issue of North American influence aside, why did so many Latin American constitutions prove to be so short lived? The obvious answer lies in two conditions: the frequency of a legal "state of emergency" and the frequency of coups d'état. But even long periods without a coup did not necessarily mean that constitutionalism was in effect. Indeed, dictatorial regimes were able to stay in power through fraudulent elections, manipulation of the constitution, or a resort to military force. This phenomenon, known as *continuismo*, was quite common.

Other underlying conditions explain why constitutionalism was weaker in Latin America. Keith Rosenn, an American law professor, outlined the major causes in a perceptive essay.[27] First, few Latin American countries underwent as radical a social revolution as did the United States (except perhaps for Mexico). Indeed, the American Revolution may be considered a radical movement if viewed from the perspective of changes in the social order. North Americans had rejected their former colonial way of life, a society based on patriarchal dependence, a political system resting mainly on imperial patronage, and a worldview that divided the society into superiors and inferiors.[28] Latin American revolutions, however, rarely or never resulted in the kind of revolution that fundamentally restructured the system of wealth, political power, and social order.[29] Begun as rebellions by a loyal Creole elite in support of the Spanish king, these wars for independence were anything but a drive for democratic self-government. Instead, independence became "a *conservative* goal, a means of upholding traditional values and social goals."[30]

Lack of experience in self-government in both the Spanish and Portuguese colonies was another common characteristic. Compared with English colonists who had achieved a great deal of self-government under Britain's comparatively mild rule, the Iberian monarchs had been more paternalistic and absolutist. Once the Creoles gained independence, they were unprepared to govern themselves. As Simón Bolívar, the great Creole leader, complained, "We were left in a state of permanent childhood."[31]

Another distinction lay in the different attitude toward the rule of law. Unlike the English colonies, which had been governed largely by laws of their own legislatures and by English common law, and somewhat less by the Crown, Spanish and Portuguese colonists were ruled by laws proclaimed by monarchs. As a result, they began with a disrespect for the rule of law: imperial laws were often confusing, contradictory, and sometimes impossible to enforce. "I accept your authority, but will not execute this law" was a common response by colonial administrators.[32]

Latin American constitutions, moreover, often reflected an unresolved tension between the new liberal and more democratic constitutionalism found in the United States and the more authoritarian tradition inherited from Spain and Portugal. This tension remained unresolved and resulted in recurring cycles of liberty and despotism.[33] Latin American regimes often failed to achieve success because two crucial elements were lacking: a spirit of moderation in the conduct of political life and a willingness to compromise.

Traditions inherited from the former mother countries also created a distinct difference in the organizing controls on authority. Unlike North American constitutionalism, which established mechanisms to check arbitrary abuses of power by the executive branch, Latin American constitutionalism was much slower to develop such safeguards. English monarchs had had their power limited as early as Magna Carta and the constitutional settlement in the 1688 English revolution.

Militarism—the persistent intervention by army officers into the affairs of state—was another major cause for the weakness of Latin American constitutionalism. The wars for independence took a decade longer to fight than the struggle waged in the United States, thus giving rise to a more permanent military presence. In addition, the inability of civilians to manage political affairs allowed the military to gain control even before independence was achieved. Standing armies were subsequently justified on the grounds of national defense and domestic security, and so the military coup became a typical way to bypass the constitution.[34] A succession of military despots in the second quarter of the nineteenth century, for example, was broken only by brief periods of disorder, and the choice often was not "between constitutionalism and dictatorship, but between dictatorship and anarchy."[35]

In economic terms, while the United States enjoyed spectacular success, Latin America remained stagnant.[36] Divided as it was into disparate political units, the continent was unable to create a common market or to achieve economic integration.[37] Several efforts at an economic union involving some kind of league or confederation failed, and much of Latin American commerce was dominated by the British throughout most of the nineteenth century.[38]

In many Latin American countries, this century also turned out to be a period of accelerated monopolization of land by oligarchs.[39] Given the scarcity of arable land outside large estates, available labor was tied to these holdings under the *encomienda* system. Agricultural workers not only depended on large landholders for work but also provided the elites with a political power base in elections. Economic expansion was limited by the continuation of highly stratified rural societies with a small number of elites at the top, a slightly larger middle class, and huge masses in the lower classes.[40] Since economic success and constitutional success were inextricably linked, constitutional stability in Latin America was difficult to achieve precisely because it failed to address the economic needs of the lower classes.[41]

Rosenn's comparison of relative degrees of stability in the two regions would hardly be complete without reference to the power relationship between them. Simón Bolívar expressed the attitude held by many countrymen when he said he regarded the United States with fear and admiration. His experience during Venezuela's war for independence demonstrated what became a continuing problem. When two of his ships supplying the Spanish were intercepted, the United States retaliated by denying diplomatic recognition. Bolívar's warning in 1822 seemed to be a prescient forecast of the future when he described the United States as "a very rich and powerful nation, extremely warlike and capable of anything at the head of the continent."[42]

After the Colossus of the North annexed Texas, seized half of Mexico's territory in 1845, and posed additional threats later in the century, Bolívar's worst fears were realized. Such invasions were counter, of course, to the expressed constitutional principles of the United States, but they were justified in the minds of most North Americans as part of their "manifest destiny." Underlying this attitude was the assumption that "civilized" nations were justified in seizing territory from "uncivilized" ones because North Americans could improve the lives of the inhabitants under their "empire of liberty."

Dissemination of North American Constitutional Documents

One reason why North American constitutional influence nevertheless spread so quickly and widely in Latin America was the ready availability of the six seminal documents of North American constitutionalism. Latin American intellectuals circulated copies of these texts and soon were also reading the writings of Jefferson, Paine, and Washington. Although in 1808 and 1809, the Spanish government issued four edicts against the reprinting of such documents, they were generally disregarded.

The beginning of the struggle for independence sparked a great surge of interest in these documents.[43] In 1810 Manuel García de Sena, a native of Venezuela, published a volume containing translations of the most important texts: the Declaration of Independence, the Articles of Confederation, and the U.S. Constitution. But he also was interested in America's first state constitutions and published those of Massachusetts, Connecticut, New Jersey, Pennsylvania, and Virginia, as well as extracts of Thomas Paine's writings. The Venezuelan dedicated his work to Spanish Americans, hoping his translations might justify resistance against the Spanish government. His expectations were soon realized: in Venezuela his translations, including those of the state constitutions, were cited in the Venezuelan Congress and reprinted in the *Gazeta de Caracas*.[44]

In 1811 Miguel de Pomba in New Granada published Spanish translations of three documents—the Declaration, Articles of Confederation, and U.S. Constitution—in Bogota in a two hundred–page booklet. He prefaced his translation of the Constitution with his version of the Declaration. When describing the American Revolution, Pomba declared that the North Americans had broken the chains that bound them to England

and had assumed their rightful place among the nations of the world. He predicted that the "inevitable influence" of this "glorious Revolution" was "destined to exert upon the fate of the people of both the Old World and the New." The U.S. Constitution, he declared, had "promoted the happiness of our brothers of the North . . . [and] will promote our happiness also, if we imitate their virtues and adopt their principles."[45]

But it was Francisco de Miranda, the great leader in the independence movement, a founder of the Venezuelan Republic, and one of Latin America's original constitutional thinkers, who helped spread North American constitutional ideas most widely. He had fought on the side of the American colonists in the Revolutionary War, toured the United States in 1783 and 1784, and met with founding fathers like Samuel Adams and Alexander Hamilton. Miranda had studied English, read widely, and knew enough about the Massachusetts Constitution of 1780 to level some trenchant criticisms.

His comments were serious enough to give Samuel Adams pause. Miranda noted two contradictions he called "weighty solecisms." First, he observed that although presumably the Massachusetts Constitution was framed to establish a government based on virtue, there were no explicit provisions to encourage that ideal. Emphasis was placed instead on property qualifications for voting and officeholding rather than moral attributes. Miranda noted also an inherent contradiction with regard to religious toleration. The document listed freedom of religion as one of the rights of man, yet it prohibited by law the predominance of any religious sect. Moreover, it excluded from office any man who would not swear he was Christian! Adams responded that he would answer Miranda's objections after "he had chewed them well."[46]

The spread of North American constitutional ideas also was helped by the presses located in large urban centers like Buenos Aires, Santiago, and Mexico City. In Buenos Aires, the revolutionary Mariano Moreno in 1810 quoted in *La gazeta de Buenos Aires* from Jefferson's *Notes on Virginia*, describing the United States as a functioning federation of sovereign states united into a single nation. Although he felt that this form of government was the best that man had ever devised, he concluded it would be difficult to introduce this system in Spanish America.[47]

In Santiago, Camilio Henríquez, one of the founders of the Chilean press, likewise commented on constitutional ideas. The first issue of his newspaper, *La aurora de Chile*, came from a printing press imported from North America. A great admirer of the United States, he considered it "as a model, as an inspiration, as a hope—the Capital of Liberty."[48] A learned monk, Henríquez was steeped in American and French political philosophy and published translations of parts of Paine's *Common Sense*, Washington's Farewell Address, and Jefferson's First Inaugural.[49] In Mexico City, the *Diario de México*, despite strict censorship, serialized the U.S. Constitution.[50]

During the three years between Mexico's declaration of independence and the adoption of its 1824 constitution, large numbers of North American constitutional or near-constitutional documents were reprinted. They included the Declaration of Independence, Articles of Confederation, U.S. Constitution, and Paine's *Common Sense*, all of which appeared in an edition published in Puebla in 1823.[51] Copies of the U.S. Constitution translated into Spanish were offered for sale in Mexico City in 1823, and the entire document was reprinted in the *Seminario político y literario*.[52]

The importance of the Latin American press, however, must not be exaggerated. It did not play the same role as the newspapers up North did. The Latin American rate of literacy was much lower, and few leading intellectuals had mastered English.[53] Censorship in Spanish America, moreover, sometimes restricted freedom of expression as shown by Antonio Nariño's exile for treason when he published the French Declaration of the Rights of Man.[54] As far as Brazil was concerned, Portugal rigidly prohibited any printing presses in its American possessions.[55]

North American constitutional documents were not the only ones circulating throughout the continent. British and French documents were available, as was the Spanish charter, the great Constitution of Cadiz of 1812 which, when it was promulgated, served as the constitution for all overseas Spanish colonies and was familiar to the elites heading various independence movements.[56] The Cadiz Constitution, in turn, was greatly influenced by the French Constitution of 1791, which included some traces of American constitutionalism. Thus the process of syncretism and transnational communication of ideas came full circle.

Although the North American documents were disseminated primarily by Latin Americans themselves, proselytizers and propagandists from the United States also played an important role. When merchants put in at Spanish American ports, the ships carried these texts as well as goods before the wars for independence got under way. The *Lelia Byrd*, owned by two New England merchants, William Shaler and Richard Cleveland, spent nine weeks in Valparaiso in 1802, where they found Chileans debating independence. Shaler told them how much richer they would be if freed from Spanish mercantilist rules and regulations. The Americans were as much interested in a monopoly-free market as spreading the idea of freedom. "For better promotion of the embryo cause," wrote Cleveland, "we gave them a copy of our Federal Constitution, and a translation into Spanish of our Declaration of Independence."[57]

The two men then set sail for San Blas, Mexico, where they discovered discontented Creoles inciting Indians to rebellion. Once again, they left behind copies of the same two documents. Although most Spanish American leaders were not on the verge of rebellion and were interested more in greater home rule rather than outright independence, who knows what effect such revolutionary propaganda had on subsequent events.[58]

U.S. diplomats provided another source of such documents. The most energetic person in this regard was Joel Poinsett, who served as the American representative to Chile, Mexico, and Argentina. Wherever he went, Poinsett promoted the spread of republican doctrines and institutions. He believed firmly that the U.S. Constitution was the most perfect document of its kind and wanted to extend its influence throughout the continent.[59]

The first accredited agent of a foreign government to Chile in 1812, Poinsett urged local patriots to act on a symbolic date: the Fourth of July. General José Miguel Carrera, head of the junta, seriously entertained the idea. In his invitation to Carrera to the banquet and ball in honor of the occasion, Poinsett referred to the American Declaration of Independence:

> The special coincidence that on the same date of the separation of my country from Great Britain, you are going to assemble for the dedication of a national flag, places a curious significance on the reception tomorrow during which we shall see entwined the symbols of our two sister nations.[60]

Carrera, however, abandoned the idea at the last minute.

Poinsett, posted as minister to Mexico in 1825, vigorously continued his propaganda efforts. His instructions called for him to show "unobtrusive readiness" in explaining the advantages of joining the North American government. But Poinsett was anything but "unobtrusive." In Chile he backed one faction against another, went into battle with the troops, and constantly violated rules of diplomatic decorum. Because he backed the wrong side, the influence of North American constitutional ideas suffered a setback.[61] In Mexico in 1829 his behavior became so obnoxious that the Mexican government finally requested that he be recalled.[62]

Other American diplomats tampered with the constitutional affairs of Latin American countries. W. G. D. Worthington, U.S. agent to Chile, submitted a draft constitution in 1818 to Bernardo O'Higgins, the head of state. Worthington, indeed, went one step further by preparing a manifesto for O'Higgins to sign when submitting the proposed document to the people, something the Chilean leader refused to do. The constitution called for a "confederated Republic," which, Worthington wrote, the United States had given to the world as an "improved System of civil Polity."[63] Caesar Rodney, the minister to Buenos Aires, was told to promote "a Constitution emanating from the people" as part of his mission.[64] Three years later, John Forbes, U.S. chargé d'affaires in Buenos Aires, reported a proposed constitution that would "embrace most of the principles, and even the form of ours."[65]

The Federalist, which explained these principles, played an important role in such constitutional matters.[66] In 1819 Henry M. Brackenridge, an American lawyer and journalist, noted in his *A Voyage to South America*, "The writings of Franklin, the *Federalist*, and other American works are frequently quoted."[67] One of the earliest works written about federalism in the region made extensive use of Publius. Published in London in 1826, the unknown author took issue with Juan Egaña, a Chilean constitutionalist who was involved in efforts to establish federalism in his country, and quoted from the essays.[68]

Brazil's intense interest in the essays in the 1830s may have been tied to the *Ato adicional* of 1834 which emphasized federalism. Although Brazil was governed by a monarchy, there was a change after Dom Pedro I abdicated, and a triumvirate ruled the regency in his name. Fearful that Brazil might break up, the triumvirate gave the provinces a far greater measure of autonomy, and *The Federalist* might have played a part in that decision.[69]

The most important role of *The Federalist* in constitution making in the region, however, was dramatized by a well-known episode in Argentine history. When the constitution makers first met in Santa Fe, they were quite familiar with the writing of Publius. A contemporary historian described how distraught they became, however, when they discovered that their only copy of the book was missing. They considered the loss "irreparable" until they learned that the work of their leading constitutionalist, Juan Bautista Alberdi, was available. Alberdi had quoted copiously from *The Federalist* in his famous work *Bases y puntos de partida para la organización política de la República Argentina,* and his book "fixed the path . . . followed in drafting the constitution."[70]

The bill of rights tradition was also incorporated in Latin American constitutions written immediately after independence. In the early years, almost all the first constitutions of the newly independent countries included a list of unalienable rights such as freedom of the press and sometimes even trial by jury. "In all cases, the first Latin American constitutions incorporated . . . something ostensibly comparable to the U.S. Bill of Rights or (more likely) the French Revolutionary Declaration of the Rights of Man," wrote two scholars recently.[71] Almost all the first charters in Venezuela, New Granada, and Chile in 1811 and 1812 included a list of unalienable rights, although they differed from country to country.[72] Although the early bills of rights were short lived, the tradition nevertheless took root and established a practice that continued throughout the region for the rest of the nineteenth century. By the middle of the century, for example, the Mexican Constitution of 1857 contained a full bill of rights.[73]

The bill of rights tradition underwent a distinct change, however, with the appearance of a mechanism known as the writ of *amparo*. The *amparo* was a remedy, somewhat comparable to *habeas corpus* in common law, to protect a citizen's constitutional rights against any executive or legislative acts or even some court decisions. It could be invoked by any person who believed that his or her rights were being violated. It became popular because claimants could challenge whether the ordinary courts would protect them from government abuses. Although the practice originated in Spain, in the New World it started in Mexico and found its way eventually into virtually all Latin American constitutions. In fact, *amparo* became a global instrument when it was later included in the United Nations Declaration of Human Rights of 1948. Although *amparo* resembled in some ways the injunction in Anglo-Saxon jurisprudence, it fell short of the kind of judicial review practiced in the United States.[74]

The Influence of Certain North American Constitutional Documents

Tracing the specific influence of the six seminal documents is another way of demonstrating the connections among constitutionalisms. The sixteen republics on the South American mainland shared enough features to enable a few tentative generalizations. Most shared certain cultural characteristics: all were Catholic, followed the heritage of Roman law, and had lived under Iberian tutelage as colonies. Most important to this study, all Latin American countries borrowed ideals, ideas, and institutions from North American constitutionalism.

The Declaration of Independence was the most admired document of the six texts. Every country in Latin America except Brazil produced its own written declaration. Following the initial surge of such declarations in Europe after 1776, the Declaration's first great "moment" outside the United States (1790–1848) affected Spanish America especially during the 1810s and 1820s. Although they followed the form of the American Declaration and sometimes its phrases, the Spanish colonists did not always include a philosophy of revolution.[75]

The Venezuelans, for example, paraphrasing Jefferson's words, wrote that the provinces "ought to be in fact . . . free sovereign and independent states." Like their North American counterparts, Venezuelan patriots pledged "our lives, our fortunes, and sacred tie of national honor."[76] Venezuela went even further in behavioral terms, seeking to imitate the United States. Mindful of the symbolic significance of the Fourth of July, Venezuelan delegates in the constitutional convention tried to adopt their declaration on the same day. Failing to meet the deadline, they proclaimed their independence on July 5, 1811. But the Venezuelan document differed significantly from Jefferson's proclamation in two important respects: it failed to suggest any philosophy justifying its revolution, and it contained no bill of particulars against the mother country.[77]

Four months later, the members of a junta in the city of Cartagena in New Granada framed a declaration of independence that announced the motives for severing their bonds with the Spanish king. The declaration was directed to an "impartial world" and included other phrases drawn from Jefferson's document.[78]

At about the same time, Mexico issued its *Grito de dolores* on September 16, 1810. Although this anniversary is celebrated as the country's national independence day, the document can hardly be compared with the Jefferson Declaration because it was specifically Mexican and Catholic in outlook, with no universal appeal to humankind.[79] The subsequent Mexican Declaration of Independence—the Plan of Iguala of February 24, 1821—was issued by a military leader, Augustin de Iturbe, who declared: "At the head of a determined and valiant army, I have proclaimed the independence of Mexico."[80] But as one scholar pointed out, the Plan of Iguala differed from the North American document in two respects: it contained no indictment of the mother country and, more significantly, expressed no philosophy of revolution.[81]

The United Provinces of the Rio de la Plata (later a part of Argentina) took similar steps toward independence on July 9, 1816. Their declaration, however, repeated only a few suggestions from the Fourth of July document. Nevertheless, the constitution for these provinces proclaimed three years later revealed some direct and indirect influence of the U.S. Constitution.[82]

When Chile selected a symbolic date to announce its independence, it picked a secular date in the nation's history: February 12, 1818. That day was the first anniversary of the important battle of Chacabuco, in which a royalist army had been defeated. In Santiago, a huge stage was erected in the city square, and José de San Martín, the great liberator and victor in the battle, was there. In the midst of an enthusiastic crowd, the proclamation was read, and San Martín and others solemnly pledged their "lives, fortunes, and honor."[83]

In Ecuador, whose revolution occurred much later, the effect of the Declaration of Independence still was felt. Three of the leaders of the revolution of 1845—José Joaquin Olmedo, Vincente Ramón Roca, and Diego Noboa—all quoted verbatim from the document.[84]

The words and phrases in these declarations, however, did not always convey the same meaning in Latin American countries as in the United States. Terms such as *liberty, republic, people,* and *nation* sometimes carried subtle differences. They were identified more with traditional Spanish legal and political thought than Anglo-American theory, and even the use of the universal phrase "all men are created equal" was not necessarily reminiscent of Jefferson's Declaration. Nor was it a novel idea to Spanish Americans. In the sixteenth century, during debates about conquering native peoples in the New World, Thomist thinkers like Francisco Suárez supported the idea of equality of all men in the eyes of God.[85]

Many Latin American declarations of independence delivered a quite different message from Jefferson's manifesto. In Mexico, for example, the emphasis was on specific concrete goals, such as social reforms, political changes, and a proposed form of government. In the United States, these same goals were expressed in the lofty language of abstract principles.[86]

Throughout Latin America, local governing bodies at all levels—pueblos, municipal councils or committees, regional juntas, and provinces—issued their own declarations in the late 1810s and 1820s. Given the tradition of municipal autonomy, the number of such acts was not surprising. Most of them drew on the Spanish understanding of sovereignty as residing in the autonomy of specific towns and villages rather than in a particular state or nation. Nor was it always clear how free and independent these jurisdictions were in taking such steps. For example, in Lima, where the Peruvian declaration that more than 3,500 persons signed, it was said that the use of force, intimidation, and self-interest played a greater role than any desire for self-government.[87]

The first state constitutions likewise played a prominent role in the writing of Latin American constitutions. José Gervasio Artigas, leader of the independence movement in Uruguay, became familiar with the state constitutions through García de Sena's translations. Artigas used the Massachusetts Constitution of 1780 as a model for his "Constitución oriental," the proposed constitution of 1813 for *La banda oriental*. His "Instrucciones orientales" given to the delegates in the 1813 Constituent Assembly held in Buenos Aires were in large measure based on North American constitutional principles.[88] In Chile, General José de San Martín also made use of García de Sena's translations of the state constitutions and ordered them distributed throughout the territories to be liberated.[89] Certain intellectual leaders in Peru in 1833 also found the first state constitutions to their liking when they discussed the framing of their charter. In fact, they sometimes admired these documents more as a model than the U.S. Constitution itself.[90]

Juan Bautista Alberdi, like Artigas, was attracted by the Massachusetts Constitution of 1780. Well versed in the political thought of both North America and Europe, Alberdi in May 1852 published his famous *Bases*, which served as the blueprint for the subsequent Argentine constitution. Alberdi characterized the United States as a land of liberty and cited among his sources the Massachusetts Constitution of 1780, Articles of Confederation, U.S. Constitution, *Federalist Papers*, and Justice Story's *Commentaries*.[91]

In his second edition published a few months later, Alberdi acknowledged his indebtedness more specifically to the Massachusetts Constitution, calling it an "admirable model of good sense and clarity." What he found attractive was the way the document was divided into two main parts. The first focused on the principles, rights, and guarantees serving as the bases for political organization, and the second outlined the duties of those officials responsible for carrying these principles into practice. Alberdi resorted to a somewhat similar format in his *Bases*.[92]

Both Alberdi and Artigas cited the Articles of Confederation. In his "Instrucciones orientales" to the delegates in 1813, Artigas adapted some provisions of the Articles to fit the needs of his region. His instructions proposed that certain provinces of La Plata form an independent confederation and that the proposed state resemble the United States as it had operated under the Articles of Confederation.[93]

Interest in the Articles and state constitutions was also evident in Brazil during the Minas Gerais conspiracy of 1789. Minas Gerais was an important state containing 20 percent of Brazil's population and providing the main source of income to the Portuguese Crown. When the plot was discovered and the conspirators arrested, authorities found copies in French of the Articles as well as of certain state constitutions.[94]

Although the U.S. official government policy was to encourage the spread of constitutional ideas, several of the founding fathers privately expressed skepticism about whether Latin Americans had the virtue and values required to sustain a republican government. This patronizing attitude sometimes revealed an underlying feeling of racial superiority. In 1806 John Adams sarcastically compared the republican governments urged by Francisco de Miranda with attempts to establish democracies among "the birds, beasts, and fishes." Jefferson, for his part, wrote in 1821: "I feared from the beginning that these people were not sufficiently enlightened for self-government; and that after wading through blood and slaughter they would end in military tyrannies, more or less numerous." Neither the sage of Quincy or that of Monticello held out much hope for Latin American republicanism.[95]

On their part, many Latin American countries had a love/hate relationship with the United States. They admired North American constitutional principles, on the one hand, and tried to imitate them, on the other. At the same time they feared U.S. expansionist tendencies. When North American racist attitudes became more pronounced, Latin Americans became less inclined to follow the U.S. lead. In framing their constitution of 1824, for example, Mexicans had been influenced by the U.S. Constitution. But when John Randolph gave a speech in the U.S. Senate two years later, he insulted the Mexicans by claiming that his fellow Americans should not associate with them as equals because some were descendants of Africans. One major Mexican newspaper, angered by Randolph's remarks, called them "fanatical intolerance." Mexico's hostility grew even greater after the Texas revolution of 1836 and the Mexican War in 1845.[96]

The Influence of the U.S. Constitution

Tracing the influence of the U.S. Constitution offers another way of showing the connections between the two constitutionalisms. That relationship reached its peak during the first two decades of independence when the pioneers of independence—reformers, politicians, and men of learning—turned to the U.S. model for inspiration. After that time, *caudillos* interested in more personal power took over and North American influence declined.

The impact of the U.S. Constitution differed from country to country, however, because of the political context. Even during the colonial era, the imperial system had operated differently in different regions in response to the needs of the mother country. The wars for independence also affected countries differently in regard to physical destruction, loss of life, and enduring local hostilities. The importance of the Catholic Church varied also, as its powerful position in Mexico posed constitutional problems different from those in countries farther south where anticlericalism was more pronounced in early years. The role of the military differed as well: in Mexico and Peru it acted as a coherent interest group, while in Venezuela individual military leaders emerged. Landlocked countries produced a different set of elites from those with important seaports. When entering these different environments and operating in such different contexts, North American constitutionalism and the Constitution itself produced different results.

Because of the diversity in the region and the various contexts that American constitutionalism encountered during the nineteenth century, five countries have been selected as case studies—Venezuela, Chile, Mexico, Argentina, and Brazil—whose differences demonstrate why generalizations are so difficult to make.

Venezuela

Venezuela, the first republic proclaimed in Latin America, modeled its constitution of 1811 "unmistakably on that of the United States."[97] Its political organization—the division of powers between the central government and the provinces, the bicameral system, and the separation of powers—reflected this influence. The constitution, moreover, provided for a modified form of judicial review and an electoral college. In its full faith and credit clause and its amendment clause, it followed the example of its northern neighbor. Many clauses prohibiting actions by the Venezuelan executive also were obviously modeled on provisions in the U.S. Constitution.[98]

The outstanding feature of the 1811 charter was its federalism, derived largely from its history in the United States. As one delegate put it: "The advantages of the federal system . . . [were] well proved by the experience of the United States."[99] But prevailing regional geographic, economic, and ethnic differences also contributed to the movement for federalism, as did the developing opposition on the local level to the capital in Caracas. The constitution hardly suited the needs of the country at the time. Given the demands imposed by the war for independence, Venezuela's experiment in federalism was ill advised, and within one year the constitution was abandoned for an executive with dictatorial powers.

Two of Latin America's greatest military leaders and outstanding constitutionalists, Simón Bolívar and Francisco de Miranda, opposed the 1811 constitution. Bolívar, the liberator of Venezuela and other northern countries in Latin America, was the more accomplished constitutionalist of the two and developed an ambivalent attitude toward the U.S. Constitution. On the one hand, he called it "the most perfect of constitutions from the standpoint of the correctness of its principles and beneficent effects of its administration." On the other hand, as one historian observed, "Viewed in the historical perspective, his greatest political opponent was the United States Constitution of 1787."[100]

What accounted for this contradiction? It might be explained by Bolívar's skepticism regarding federalism in general and its application in Venezuela in particular. Bolivar acknowledged in theory that the federal system was "the most perfect and the most capable of providing human happiness in society." But in actual practice, he believed, it was contrary to the interests of any infant state seeking independence.[101] What was needed, Bolívar believed, was a centralized and unified government. "Division of power has never been established and perpetuated governments," he wrote. "Only concentration has infused respect." Bolívar drove home his point in 1813, when he wrote to the governor of one province: "I have not liberated Venezuela merely to realize this same [federal] system."[102]

Bolívar also objected to other principles drawn from the U.S. experience because he believed that local laws written for Spanish America should reflect local needs. Citing Montesquieu, Bolívar held that laws should conform to the climate, customs, and character of the people. "We should follow Montesquieu in drafting a constitution," Bolívar counseled, "not the code of Washington."[103] But Bolívar was inconsistent. He was willing to copy features of the U.S. Constitution when it served his purpose. He criticized the plural executive of the 1811 constitution, for example, and preferred instead a single executive. When he later submitted a draft constitution for Bolivia in 1826, he admitted that the president would enjoy "many of the powers of the [North] American chief executive."[104]

Bolívar's constitutional ideas were complicated and changed over time. He also was as much interested in the republican features of the British constitution as those of the United States. As he grew older, he became more pessimistic about the possibilities of democratic government for Spanish America. In 1826, the year he extolled George Washington as the "outstanding architect of political reform," he prepared the Bolivian Constitution, which masked a form of constitutional monarchy. Thus, Bolívar might be said to be an oxymoron, that is, an authoritarian republican.[105]

While Bolívar was opposing the 1811 constitution outside the congress, Francisco de Miranda as a delegate was fighting against it inside the assembly. The reasons for Miranda's opposition are not known because historical records are scanty. But as early as 1790, Miranda presented to William Pitt in England a grandiose constitutional plan reflecting many of his ideas. He proposed that a single independent government be established once Latin America had been liberated, stretching from the upper reaches of the Mississippi River to Cape Horn and from Brazil to San Francisco. His proposal for a South American empire incorporated many ideas and institutions drawn from the English constitution. Yet in two instances, he proposed features found in the U.S. Constitution. The first was the idea of judicial review. His 1790 plan included a clause calling for any laws conflicting with the constitution to be declared null and void. The doctrine of judicial review in the United States, though implied in the Constitution, was not strongly articulated until the *Marbury* decision in 1803. Whether Miranda's idea of judicial review was original, derived from a study of the debates in the Constitutional Convention of 1787, or resulted from contacts with his friends in North America is not known.[106] The second feature had to do with the clauses for amending Miranda's proposed constitution. The clauses, quite technical in nature, were to be applied to institutions of Latin American origin. But the principles on which they were based were patterned after those in the U.S. Constitution.[107]

Venezuela's ill-fated experiment with federalism, inspired by the U.S. Constitution, plagued the country off and on throughout the rest of its history. One result was that the number of constitutions adopted in Venezuela from independence in 1811 until the 1990s totaled twenty-five, the highest number among Latin American republics.[108]

Although federalism was not the single cause of Venezuela's problem, it contributed much to its chronically chaotic history. Throughout most of Venezuela's past, the country was subjected to long and tyrannical dictatorships, broken only by brief spells of quasi-democratic governments.

The federal system of 1811, the mixed centralized–federalized structure of 1830, and the constitution of 1864 all were rooted in regional sentiments based on economic, geographic, ethnic, and social differences. The struggle during these years was between local oligarchies determined to govern their localities and strong national rulers seeking power to organize the country as a private preserve. After five years of devastating war, Venezuela finally established a federal form of government in 1864, but given the powers exercised by strong military dictators, the political system was federal in name only. This pseudo-federalism was counteracted somewhat in the 1881 constitution when the number of states was reduced. But even after that date, the problem with federalism persisted, and the country continued to pay lip service to federalism while in reality functioning as a centralized republic.[109]

Chile

Chile also was vitally affected by the U.S. Constitution in the early period of its national history. During the years of the *patria vieja*, or "old fatherland," extending from 1810 to 1814, Chile produced five constitutional documents that reflected English, French, Spanish, and U.S. sources. One draft constitution was written by Joel Poinsett, who worked on his own draft while a member of a committee writing the 1812 constitution. His proposal reflected the influence of the U.S. Constitution in two ways: its federal form of government and the suggestion of popular sovereignty. He copied parts of the 1787 Constitution by incorporating the principle of participation by the provinces (i.e., states) in both the executive and legislative powers of the government of the central union, and he called for "all matters not expressly delegated by this constitution [to be] reserved to the sovereign people." Poinsett's constitution was rejected, however, except for certain sections concerning individual rights and a judicial system.[110]

During the 1820s, the federalist movement gained popular support because Chileans believed that the main reason for America's success was its federal form of government. Federalism and liberalism soon were considered practically synonymous, whereas centralism and conservatism were viewed as great evils. Liberal leaders like José Miguel Infante, a fanatic on federalism, were opposed to any idea of a strong national executive who would back centralization.

In 1826 Infante, as a member of the constitutional committee, proposed a federal government. By this time, Chile had experimented with several types of political organization, and Infante argued that it was time to give federalism a chance and referred to the U.S. example.[111] According to his biographer, his proposed document "plagiarized with little shame and no discretion from the Constitution of the United States."[112]

Through a series of government decrees, Chile was finally declared a federal republic in 1826. The period of federal rule proved to be short lived. Chile's constitution of 1828 was somewhat less federal than that of 1826 in its distribution of powers, but in 1829 a conservative reaction set in, resulting in chaos, disorder, and ultimately civil war. Its aim was to eliminate both federalism and liberalism. Federalism was criticized on the grounds that it had destroyed the unity of the country, while liberalism was accused of denying the country strong leadership and creating the 1820s debacle. Because of its close identification with both ideas, the U.S. Constitution consequently lost favor.

When the conservative constitution of 1833 was written, it called for a system of cabinet government more closely resembling that of England. As one political observer noted, Chile's "politics changed direction completely in 1833. It left the path of American democracy . . . to move closer to the model of Constitutional Europe."[113] The 1833 constitution, nevertheless, provided relative stability to the country for almost sixty years, making Chile something of an anomaly in the tortured history of Latin American constitutionalism.

Mexico

"Mexico—so far from God and so close to the United States," the old saying goes—was influenced much more by the U.S. Constitution than was Chile. Proximity to the United States obviously played an important part in its emulation, but before Mexico's independence in 1821, other influences were at work as well. There were slight traces of North American constitutional influence in the Constitution of Apatzingán of 1814 written in Chilpancingo by the first political assembly convened in the country. Although this constitution reflected mostly the influence of the Cadiz Constitution of 1812, among the names listed as contributing ideas were Jefferson and Paine.[114] The inspiration derived from two other North American sources—the U.S. Constitution and the Massachusetts

Constitution of 1780—also was acknowledged.[115] Proclaimed in October 1814, the constitution, however, was never implemented.[116]

The influence of the U.S. Constitution became much greater once Mexico achieved independence and wrote its 1824 charter. Stephen Austin, a citizen of Texas, then part of Mexico, submitted several plans for a charter. In writing his proposal in 1823, Austin frankly admitted, "I condensed the principles of the Constitution of the United States" and pointed out that a comparison of his plan with the *Acta constitutiva* of 1824 "shows a striking similarity." His biographer agrees.[117]

More evidence that Mexicans borrowed from the U.S. Constitution in 1824 came from other contemporaries. In the constitutional congress, an enthusiastic young delegate from Yucatan (who exaggerated) declared: "What we are offering for the deliberation of the congress [in the draft constitution] is taken from . . . [the U.S. document] with a few reforms to fit the circumstances of our people." José Luis Mora, who was the leader of the liberals and influenced much more by British and French constitutionalism, did not believe that the North American experience provided a proper model for Mexico. But even he was forced to concede that the 1824 constitution was "very similar" to the 1787 North American document. Henry Ward, the English chargé d'affaires, likewise concluded that Mexico had modeled some of its institutions after those of the United States.[118]

The best evidence of borrowing, however, comes from comparing the two constitutions, which reveals numerous parallelisms. Mexico established a federal form of government, a president elected for a fixed term, a bicameral legislature, and a judicial branch with a supreme court and justices appointed for life. As in the United States, lower house members were chosen for two-year terms according to population. The upper house was elected by the state legislatures, as was the case in North America at the time. Within the executive branch, the borrowing was even more obvious: the president and vice president had to be native-born citizens and thirty-five or more years of age and were elected to four-year terms. Bills vetoed by the president could be overridden only if passed by two-thirds of both houses. Certain powers specifically granted to the congress, such as the power to regulate commerce, also were quite similar to those granted to the Congress of the United States.[119]

The degree to which the U.S. Constitution affected the 1824 document was limited by other major influences. Hispanic and European influences such as the Cadiz Constitution of 1812, Mexican colonial practices, and Benjamin Constant's French constitutional liberalism were woven into the text as well. Mexico's federalism, moreover, was derived from indigenous conditions: the latent regionalism of Mexico resulting from geographic, demographic, and economic differences; the impetus to federalism from the colonial institution of the provincial deputation provided by the Cadiz Constitution of 1812; and the existing distrust of Mexico City in the provinces.[120] The 1824 constitution was, indeed, very much a hybrid document.

Following the constitution of 1824, the pendulum of power swung between the centralists and the federalists, the two groups contending for control. Generally speaking, the centralists favored a strong central government, a paid national army, and Catholicism as the exclusive religion. Opposed were the federalists, who desired a limited central government with nearly autonomous states and were anticlerical and antimilitary. But the labels *centralist* and *federalist* frequently masked factions based on personalist loyalties. López de Santa Anna, for example, who was in power off and on in the 1830s and 1840s, although allied with the federalists, seemed to have few fixed ideological convictions except to stay in power. This was a familiar phenomenon, but it should not be taken to mean that federalism had no substantive meaning in Latin America. Rather, it often was latent, as in Mexico's case.[121]

The goal of the federalists in Mexico thereafter became far-reaching and aimed at freeing citizens from entrenched corporatist entities in society, that is, the church, army, guilds, and Indian communities. After Mexico's disastrous defeat in 1845, a new generation of liberal reformers sprang up who believed the country's survival required fundamental changes. They created a liberal program from the mid-1850s to mid-1860s called La Reforma which aimed at abolishing remnants of colonialism and attaining greater justice for citizens. When writing the constitution in 1857, the reformers sought traditional liberal goals: individual liberty, abolition of slavery, greater separation of church and state, and diminution of military privileges.

The 1857 constitution reflected the influence of the U.S. Constitution largely through the goals it sought: a federal form of government, universal male suffrage, freedom of speech, and other civil liberties embodied in the bill of rights tradition. It eventually brought to power the great Indian leader Benito Juárez, whose democratic ideas enabled him to institute a series of liberal reforms, including a reduction of the power of the Catholic Church. The resulting republic consisted of states and territories bound together in a federal union much like that of the United States.

Certain sections of the constitution, furthermore, used almost the exact words of the U.S. Constitution, and much of the North American influence was exercised through provisions repeated from its predecessor, the 1824 constitution.[122] The 1824 and 1857 charters remained the twin peaks of North American influence in Mexico's constitutional history throughout the rest of the nineteenth century.

In the constitution of 1857, the principle of judicial review also was implicitly adopted.[123] Despite being federal in a limited sense only, Mexico succeeded in establishing a dual system of federal and state courts,[124] and the Mexican judiciary, although often subservient to the executive, was not as supine as the legislature.

Mexico's constitutional history remained unstable. Although the country was ostensibly liberated from foreign domination by its wars for independence, it continued to be invaded periodically by U.S. and European armies, especially in the Mexican-American War of 1845 and the ill-fated empire of Maximilian of Austria during the mid-1860s. Economically, the country was controlled to a great degree by foreign investors from Britain, the United States, and France.[125] Domestically, governments came and went, often at gunpoint. By the mid-nineteenth century, the country appeared to be heading toward a liberal form of government under La Reforma, but those hopes were dashed in 1876 by the dictatorship of Porfirio Díaz, who controlled Mexico's political life for more than thirty-five years.

Argentina

The influence of the U.S. Constitution was far greater in Argentina than in any other Latin American country. In the La Plata region—divided subsequently into Argentina, Uruguay, and Paraguay—the North American document was known to Artigas in Uruguay and to Fernando de la Mora, a member of the Paraguayan junta during the early years of independence. But French rather than North American ideas were dominant when the liberal inhabitants of Buenos Aires (the *porteños*) tried to impose a unitary government over the *provincianos* in outlying areas who favored federalism.

Although French constitutionalism was evident in the polity-making experiments of 1811, 1815, and 1817, the influence of the U.S. Constitution became more noticeable in the constitutions of 1819 and 1826. Both proposed a single executive, bicameral legislature, and independent judiciary system. The 1819 constitution became a landmark in Argentine history, however, because it was a finished and not a fragmentary document. Framers of the document admitted their use of the United States and England as models. Besides a bicameral legislature, the constitution resorted to two arrangements drawn from the United States: a lower house based on population, and an upper one drawn from individual states. The powers of the executive also followed those of the president of the United States in many particulars. Although the 1819 constitution never went into effect, many of its provisions entered the mainstream of Argentina's constitutional tradition.[126]

The constitution of 1826 also reflected the direct influence of the U.S. Constitution not only in certain provisions but also in the constitutional convention debates. Fifty references were made to North American political institutions during these deliberations. As in the U.S. Constitution, the Argentine congress was granted enumerated powers; executive power was vested in the president to be elected by an electoral college; and judicial power was granted to a high court whose members were to be appointed by the president with the advice and consent of the Senate. This North American–influenced document also affected subsequent constitutions.[127] But when the 1826 constitution was rejected by the provinces, it marked the last attempt at constitutional government for an entire generation.

Juan Manuel de Rosas, the greatest *caudillo* of his day, imposed a dictatorship after 1829. Only after Justo José de Urquiza, a rival *caudillo*, overthrew Rosas did exiles return to renew their constitutional debates. Despite the revival of old jealousies between the Buenos Aires metropolis and the other provinces, Urquiza called a constitutional convention in 1852 in Santa Fe. It proved to be the turning point in Argentina's constitutional history when delegates produced the constitution of 1853, the first truly effective Argentine constitution. This document relied more heavily on the U.S. Constitution than did any other Latin American charter of the nineteenth century.[128] Indigenous traditions, nevertheless, played a far greater role, so it too became a hybrid document.

By this time, North American constitutional ideas had become part of the Argentine constitutional tradition, as evidenced in the writings of Alberdi, the country's leading political theorist. Although his command of English was shaky, Alberdi had read, in French, the *Federalist Papers* and Joseph Story's *Commentaries on the Constitution of the United States*. In his famous book, *Bases*, he cited the U.S. Constitution, Articles of Confederation, and Massachusetts Constitution of 1780.[129] Comparing Argentina's situation in 1852 with that of the United States in 1781, Alberdi advocated the federal system as the most appropriate model for Argentina. "In that country as in ours," he noted, "the unitarian and federal tendencies fought for control of the national government, and the necessity to consolidate them in a mixed system suggested to them the idea of creating a mechanism which may be applied in similar situations."[130]

Alberdi's draft constitution bore a distinct resemblance to the U.S. charter, particularly because of its emphasis on federalism. The confederation would be composed of provinces with all the sovereignty not delegated to the central government. Public acts of one province were to be given full faith in other provinces. One section concerning the rights of Argentine citizens stated that the exercise of such rights would be regulated by congress but that congress could not enact any law diminishing, restricting, or altering these guarantees. This section, Alberdi explained, was based on the First, Second, and Fourth Amendments of the U.S. Constitution.

The precise influence of Alberdi's proposals regarding the constitution of 1853, however, has been a matter of some dispute among scholars.[131] If he was not the James Madison of the Argentine Constitution, his remarkable little book provided a valuable guide. The incident in which his *Bases* served as a substitute for *The Federalist* has already been related. Without the *Bases*, it is unlikely the constitution would have been written.[132] When the draft constitution was submitted in April 1853, the delegates readily acknowledged the influence of the U.S. Constitution. One committee member framing the draft said that it was "cast in the mold of the Constitution of the United States, the only model of true federation that exists in the world."[133] Another delegate concurred: "The Constitution is modeled on that of the United States."[134]

But Buenos Aires, the most important province in size and wealth, sent no members to the Santa Fe proceedings. Instead, it held its own convention later in 1860 to consider accepting the 1853 constitution. To an even greater degree than the Santa Fe delegates, those in Buenos Aires were influenced by the U.S. Constitution. More than 168 references were made to the document and its political and economic history. More important, the main purpose of some reforms proposed in the 1860 convention was to incorporate into the Argentine Constitution those provisions of the U.S. charter that had not been considered in Santa Fe. Eighteen of the additional thirty-four reforms were drawn from the North American document. Some delegates believed their political and economic situation was so similar to that of the United States that they suggested Buenos

Aires base its decision to join the Argentine federation on the principles of the U.S. Constitution, "the only authoritative constitution in the world whose essence cannot be altered without violating the basic principles of federalism."[135]

Although there can be no denying that there was considerable North American influence on the 1853 constitution, controversy continues as to its degree.[136] In this regard, the conclusions of Santos Amadeos, a learned Argentine scholar, are critical. After listing other foreign sources—the Chilean Constitution of 1833, Swiss Constitution of 1848, German Confederation, and French Constitution of 1791—he concluded, "The United States exercised a greater influence . . . than any others mentioned."[137]

Despite the many similarities, the Argentine Constitution of 1853 was no carbon copy of the U.S. Constitution. Federalism is generally acknowledged to be the most distinctive feature of the Argentine Constitution, and many, if not most, scholars concede that this feature borrowed extensively from the North American model. But indigenous factors played an important role as well. The scant population, the separation of different centers of population by open spaces dominated by hostile Indians, the late emergence of Buenos Aires as the political capital, and the ambition of that city to dominate outlying provinces resisting such control all weighed heavily in favor of a federal structure.[138]

Even though the constitutional provisions for establishing a federal system were nearly identical in the two countries, the differences were evident. Argentina's affinity for centralized authority, for example, resulted in numerous interventions into the affairs of the provinces. Whenever the national government did intervene (some 143 times by the middle of the twentieth century), it converted Argentina—nominally a federal state—into a unitary one.[139]

Another difference between the two federal systems was the power given to the Argentine congress to enact certain national codes based on the French Napoleonic civil codes. The sweeping power of these codes—civil, commercial, penal, and mining—increased the central authority.[140] An Argentine scholar perceptively observed that in Argentina, the nation had preceded the formation of its provinces and the approval of its federal constitution, whereas the North American states had existed before the formation of the national entity. Despite these caveats, the influence of the U.S. Constitution on the Argentine Constitution was undeniable.[141]

Nowhere was the influence of the U.S. Constitution more pronounced than in the Argentine judiciary with its two judicial systems, the national and the provincial. As the committee for organizing the federal judiciary reported: "For this we found only one model in the judicial history of all nations and that is the judicial history of the United States."[142] In particular, the Argentine federal judiciary—generally regarded as the most respected, strongest, and most independent judiciary in all of Latin America in the last half of the nineteenth century—showed clear evidence of North American influence. To set up the jurisdiction of the federal courts, the legislators specifically cited the U.S. Judiciary Act of 1789. The hierarchy of federal courts in Argentina was headed by a supreme court with the three powers presumably interconnected by a system of checks and balances.[143]

In regard to the idea of judicial review, the Argentine Constitution, like the U.S. Constitution, did not explicitly authorize the doctrine. But there was strong evidence in Argentina that the framers of the 1853 constitution intended the supreme court to rule on laws passed by the congress. First, the Argentine framers had consciously modeled their constitutional system on that of the United States, and since judicial review had already been established in North America, it may be assumed that they adopted this principle along with all the others. Second, in neither the Santa Fe or Buenos Aires convention was the issue of judicial review ever raised for consideration. Finally, in the Buenos Aires convention, the power of judicial review was recognized, since it was explicitly stated that the jurisdiction of the Argentine Supreme Court was modeled on that of the U.S. Supreme Court, and it was explained how and under what circumstances the power would be exercised.[144]

Evidence that Argentina closely followed the North American model also was clear when the Argentine courts began interpreting their constitution in the light of decisions made by the U.S. Supreme Court. In the first case in which the Argentine Supreme Court declared an act of congress unconstitutional, it cited not only *Marbury v. Madison* but also the constitutional commentaries of James Kent and Joseph Story.[145]

Brazil

Next to Argentina's 1853 constitution, Brazil's constitution of 1891 was the document most influenced by North American constitutionalism. Because of Brazil's Portuguese past, however, the country's constitutional history differed substantially from that of Spanish-speaking Latin America. Brazil adopted a constitutional monarchy from the start, under which the country enjoyed an eighty-one-year career of greater stability, comparatively speaking, than almost any other Iberian colony in the New World. Except for a series of regional revolts in the 1890s that appeared to threaten the unity of the empire, Brazil underwent less turmoil than did the Spanish colonies during their wars for independence.[146]

Brazil experienced a relatively peaceful transition in the legitimization of its power, largely because the *mazambo* elite (comparable to Creoles in Spanish America) supported the idea of a monarchical government, thus avoiding the acrimonious clashes between monarchists and republicans in the Spanish colonies. Certain common bonds, moreover—the Portuguese language, fear of slave uprisings, and a strong patriarchal family system among plantation owners—helped prevent the fragmentation into separate states so characteristic of Spanish America.

Brazil's constitutional history took its most dramatic turn during the Napoleonic Wars. When the prince regent of Portugal, Dom John, took refuge in 1808 in Brazil, the role was reversed, and the colony suddenly became the seat of government for the mother country. Brazil's status changed again in 1815 when the Portuguese dominions were made co-equals with Portugal in a united kingdom, and in 1816 Dom John succeeded to the Portuguese throne as John VI. But his presence was imperative in Portugal, and he sailed to Lisbon in 1821 after appointing his son, Dom Pedro, regent in Brazil. The Portuguese home government meanwhile favored the restoration of Brazil to its former status as a colony. When the Portuguese in Lisbon proceeded to undo most of the reforms that John VI had introduced in Brazil, the country declared its independence in 1822. Brazil's constitutional evolution thereafter was largely freed from the distracting influence of a distant imperial government.[147]

Brazil's first national document, the constitution of 1824, was monarchical and owed little to U.S. constitutionalism. The constitution turned out to be extremely durable. It lasted for sixty-five years until the monarchy fell in 1889 and was one of Latin America's longest-lived constitutions.[148]

During the years of constitutional monarchy, relatively little attention was paid to North American constitutional ideas. Rather, Brazil's political system followed Britain's parliamentary system. But beginning in the 1870s a dramatic political change caused many Brazilians to yearn for a U.S.-style federal republic. The Federal Republican Party that emerged in 1870 issued a manifesto denouncing the monarchy and calling for a federal republic. Reformers proposed a number of major structural changes, most notably the substitution of federalism for centralism, the abolition of slavery, and an expansion of the political base of power. These reforms weakened the monarchy and created a more favorable climate for North American republican ideas.

The fall of the monarchy in 1889 was not brought about by any high-minded debate of ideas, however, but for pragmatic reasons. It came about because of the restlessness of certain interest groups in society—an unruly military, a disgruntled landed aristocracy, and a resentful clergy—all of whom harbored ill will against Dom Pedro II. Equally important was the growing gulf between the reform-minded middle class in the cities and the traditional-minded agrarians in the countryside. Reformers felt that a republic better suited the goal of modernization that presumably lay ahead for a "new Brazil." The military suddenly overthrew the monarchy in a bloodless revolution and sent the aging emperor into exile.

The new constitution, characterized as presidential, federal, democratic, and republican, was proclaimed on February 24, 1891. Under this constitution, the country was transformed from a unitary state under a monarchy to a republican federation of twenty states. Its chief architect was Ruy Barbosa, whose draft constitution played the same role as Alberdi's in Argentina. A brilliant intellectual, Barbosa was trained in American constitutional law, which he studied in its original English, and had served as editor of the important newspaper *Diário de notícias*. A late convert to the republican cause, his main aim was to transplant the North American charter in Brazilian soil. "The Constitution of the United States," he affirmed, "is the only model for us."[149]

Barbosa drew a sharp distinction between French constitutional ideas that still lingered in many parts of Latin America and those of the United States: "The federalist Constitution of Brazil has not the remotest lineage from the banks of the Seine. Its origins are exclusively and notoriously American."[150] The United States, he noted, had enjoyed years of peace under its Constitution, while France had entered a period of tumultuous revolutions. Well before the French Rights of Man of 1789 appeared, the U.S. Constitution had been written and ratified. As Barbosa observed, "The United States was several years ahead in the regime of written constitutions and in the declaration of human liberties."[151]

Barbosa's grasp of the U.S. Constitution was evident when he noted that its framers "were entirely at one with the authors of the Brazilian Constitution in establishing a document of limited government that would not only check the power of the executive branch but also take action as necessary . . . against the assemblies." Citing Madison and Jefferson, Barbosa warned against the "reckless ambitions of representative bodies" and advocated "incessant vigilance" against "that menace."

In its transition from monarchism to republicanism, Barbosa realized, Brazil would experience difficulties.[152] For that reason, he revised the proposals for the draft document to incorporate stronger presidential powers. The constituent assembly made few changes in the completed draft, but one leading authority concluded, "Directly or indirectly . . . the example of the United States . . . was the most potent influence."[153]

The 1891 Brazilian constitution, like the North American charter, divided the federal government into the usual three branches. The popularly elected president had to be native-born and at least thirty-five years of age and would serve a four-year term. A comparison of his constitutional powers with those of the president of the United States shows that the Brazilian president had most powers of his North American counterpart and, in some respects, even more.

Constitutional provisions for the vice presidency and the bicameral legislature in the Brazilian Constitution also resembled those of the United States, as did the organization of the Brazilian judiciary. Brazil established a dual system of courts with a separate judicial organization for the federal government paralleling the judicial organization of the states. In defining the jurisdiction of the federal courts, the Brazilian Constitution assigned to them cases that by their nature should properly be tried by national tribunals. It expressly granted them, however, the right to review decisions of the state courts by a procedure quite similar to that of the North American Federal Judiciary Act of 1789.

Although the judicial power of the federal courts was closely modeled on article 3 of the U.S. Constitution, the Brazilian charter even included specific provisions to accommodate subsequent developments that had taken place in North America as the result of constitutional amendments, legislation, and judicial decisions. Guarantees regarding the independence of the judiciary, such as life tenure and protection from any diminution of salary, were also drawn from article 3. Although the Brazilian judiciary experienced some difficult times, the courts, especially the federal supreme court, achieved an enviable reputation as one of the best in Latin America.[154]

Brazil established judicial review from the time it became a republic.[155] In working out the doctrine, Brazil's courts frequently cited decisions of the U.S. Supreme Court and certain constitutional authorities. As one leading scholar concluded: "It is clear that our American constitutional practice, firmly established and recognized since . . . *Marbury v. Madison,* . . . and thoroughly familiar to Brazilian publicists, was intended to be incorporated into the Brazilian system."[156] Because civil-law countries had not developed a doctrine of *stare decisis,* however, the Brazilian system of judicial review evolved very differently.

Brazil later developed a different system for the protection of individual rights in both state and federal courts. A summary remedy called *mandado de segurança,* somewhat comparable to Mexico's *amparo,* was used to protect constitutional rights left unguarded by *habeas corpus.* Brazil also had other procedural devices to protect constitutional rights.[157]

When it came to the issue of federalism, Brazil's central government, like that of the United States, had enumerated powers. Strongly federalist, the 1891 constitution was explicitly modeled on the United States in this regard.[158] But in some respects, Brazil's brand of federalism differed from that of the United States because the Brazilian Constitution gave the states far more political and economic authority. The balance of power in Brazil's federalism was tempered by the powers delegated to the president. He could proclaim a state of siege (the *estado de sitio,* which allowed him to suspend civil rights), intervene in the internal affairs of a state, and replace any elected governor. Brazil's executive branch, therefore, clearly dominated the legislative and judicial branches.[159]

Other major differences demonstrate that the 1891 Brazilian Constitution was no mere imitation of the U.S. Constitution. Brazil's national government, for example, was given important powers that the U.S. federal government lacked or had not been expressly granted. The central government could enact legislation on civil, commercial, and criminal law, determine state boundaries, establish institutions of secondary and higher education, and even own and operate certain means of communication and transportation. In contrast, the Brazilian national government was more limited in certain areas in which its U.S. counterpart enjoyed larger powers. The U.S. government had greater control over the taxing power, owned public lands, and had stronger constitutional power to declare war. What is clear from this contrast is that in the matter of the constitutional distribution of powers between states and nation, Brazil did not resort to a mere paraphrase of the U.S. Constitution, as was sometimes asserted.[160]

Conclusion

The criticism that Latin American constitutions were unrealistic in borrowing institutions from the United States (and Europe) has considerable merit. Latin America has always been conflicted by two constitutional traditions that created an inherent tension. The liberal democratic tradition copied from the United States and France was superimposed on the region without enough thought given to its suitability for the environment. The authoritarian, corporatist, and elitist tradition inherited from Spain and Portugal and retained from the colonial past was hardly a context ready to receive sudden new freedoms and the responsibility of self-government. "Built into almost all Latin American constitutions," therefore, "are provisions that permit democracy and dictatorship. The cycle of democracy and dictatorship that most Latin American countries have experienced reflects the still unresolved tension between Latin America's conflicting political traditions."[161]

Military constitutionalism was an equally important factor, as it involved the legal status and role of military institutions in the practice of constitutional government. In most of Latin America, the armed forces identified themselves as the ultimate guardians of national interests. Military constitutionalism thus established the armed forces as a kind of fourth branch of government, assigning them functions alongside the executive, legislative, and judiciary. "In the nineteenth century, over eighty percent of the 103 national constitutions defined the constitutional functions of the armed forces as permanent institutions of the state."[162] North American constitutionalism, therefore, encountered many military barriers in the effort to establish republican forms of government.

Despite these conditions that limited the influence of North American constitutionalism in the region during the nineteenth century, the exposure to and partial assimilation of democratic institutions left Latin America in a much better position to make transitions to democracy in the late twentieth century. Without this earlier exposure to concepts of an egalitarian society with individual rights and popular sovereignty, the wealth, power, and privilege of aristocracy that have persisted in Latin American society since independence would have been even more pronounced. Without the adoption, however imperfect, of North American constitutional ideas and institutions, it is unlikely that the region would have made the strides that it did at a later date.

5

European Interlude

1800–1848

A long interlude separated the two echoes of the shot heard round the world: the era of the American and French revolutions and the European revolutions of 1848. Though continuing, the influence of American constitutionalism did not have as much effect as before. Three distinctive periods of Western constitutionalism mark this interlude. The first was the period when Napoleon ended the French Revolution with his coup d'état, created a new constitution that established a facade of parliamentary institutions at home, and introduced modernizing administrative decrees throughout much of western Europe. The second was the age of Metternich, which sought to restore stability and order in Europe with its legitimist constitutions after a quarter century of revolutions and warfare. The third was the period just before the outbreak of the 1848 revolutions.

Western constitutionalism appears to have followed the curve of industrialization after the early 1800s. The Industrial Revolution in England, France, the Netherlands, and Belgium gave rise to the bourgeoisie. In Germany, Austria, and Italy, however, industrialization did not penetrate as deeply; these countries remained agrarian and were politically more backward. From a constitutional viewpoint, these two regions presented a stark contrast, and their reactions to American constitutionalism differed accordingly.

One important constitutional change, however, modified the image of America in Europe. The Jacksonian movement in the United States in the 1830s, more than half a century after the American Revolution, gave the lie to the old assumption that a democratic country would inevitably degenerate into mob rule. Hence, many Europeans began to change their minds about the United States, viewing America in a quite different light than before.

American Constitutional Influence: General Considerations, 1800–1848

From 1800 to 1815, the greatest obstacle with which American constitutionalism had to contend was Napoleon and his revolutionary constitutional model. Surrounding France there emerged six satellite states, most of them ruled by Napoleon's relatives or favorites. Besides these so-called sister republics, Napoleon's authority stretched into Spain (where his brother was monarch) as well as into some newly created German principalities. Save for Russia in the east and Britain in the west, Napoleon dominated nearly all of western Europe.

The Napoleonic period was followed by an era of restored legitimist constitutions. These charters represented a rough compromise between a return to the practices of the *ancien régime* and Napoleon's revolutionary regime. The compromise in many European countries resulted in written constitutions, an American idea introduced in European nations for the first time. But as one scholar observed, the written constitutions were "conceded and revocable, the condescension of a prince to his subjects and not the freely adopted instrument of a sovereign people."[1]

Many constitutions underwent other changes during the 1830s. The French Charter of 1814, the archetype of all the legitimist constitutions, was revised as the result of the French revolution of 1830. Bourbon kings who had been restored to power violated the terms under which the Restoration had operated. Although sovereignty of the people was not recognized in the revised charter of 1830, the strict legitimist position became unacceptable, and "1830 [became] the half-way house to 1848."[2]

A new trend, constitutional monarchy, appeared after 1830 as the sovereignty of the people became better recognized and the power of kings more limited. This change, coupled with the important development of Jacksonian democracy in America, resulted in a more receptive attitude toward American constitutionalism. Constitutionalists all over Europe—in Norway, Belgium, France, Germany, Switzerland, Poland, Russia, Hungary, Italy and Greece—began to examine the American model more carefully as a catalyst, example, and source of inspiration.[3]

American Constitutionalism and Norway's Constitution of 1814

In Norway in the early 1800s, the people had become discontent with their centuries-long union with Denmark. Meeting in Eidsvold, the Norwegian estates declared their independence, invited a Danish prince to be their king, and promulgated their constitution in 1814. Within six months, however, they had to abandon the king of their choice and accept a Swedish king. Although the constitution of 1814 remained mostly the same and reflected mainly indigenous sources, in some respects it emulated the U.S. Constitution.

From the time it achieved independence, America had fired the imagination of Norwegians, to whom George Washington was a great hero. One important leader of the Norwegian revolution of 1814 was Judge Christian Magnus Falsen, often called the "father of the Norwegian Constitution." When his son was born that year, Falsen named him George Benjamin after his two favorite heroes, Washington and Franklin. The American Dream was obviously alive in Norway.[4]

Norway's constitution makers also were quite familiar with many of the six seminal documents, including, of course, of the Declaration of Independence. When the constituent assembly met at Eidsvold, moreover, one delegate brought along a copy of the French translation of the first state constitutions. The men at Eidsvold were aware too of the work of the framers at the Constitutional Convention in 1787 and of *The Federalist*.[5]

That these American models inspired Norway's constitution makers is clear: a draft of the Eidsvold Constitution actually incorporated a word-for-word translation of article 30 of the Massachusetts Constitution of 1780, which articulated the principle of the separation of powers.[6]

Other Norwegian provisions showed parallels to the U.S. Constitution, including the listing of the Storthing's legislative powers and its method of compensating lawmakers. The resemblance between the Norwegian constitutional rule of parliamentary immunity from arrest and the first article in the U.S. Constitution was striking. The same was true of the rules for impeaching members of the royal cabinet. Furthermore, the election of representatives was to be indirect, through a system in which they were chosen by primary electors, as was nominally done in the American presidential elections.[7] The Norwegian Constitution of 1814—after America's 1787 document, the world's second oldest surviving written national constitution—thus revealed some direct borrowing from and parallelisms with its predecessor.

American Constitutionalism and French Constitutionalists, 1800–1830s

In France, the political discourse regarding American constitutionalism during the first third of the nineteenth century was carried on primarily by three important commentators: Lafayette, Destutt de Tracy, and Alexis de Tocqueville.

Lafayette

Lafayette, entering his second phase as an Americanist, continued to be more a political activist than an original constitutional thinker. Although he presumably had retired in 1800 after returning to France from his Austrian prison, he actually played an important role in French affairs. He served as a mediator between contending factions, remained the principal figure in French–American relations, and continued to be an outspoken advocate for the U.S. Constitution. Through his correspondence with the leading constitutional theorists of the day—Destutt de Tracy, Benjamin Constant, and Jeremy Bentham—he became part of an important international intellectual network.[8]

While ruling France, Napoleon tried to co-opt Lafayette, but he failed. Although Lafayette claimed he was in retirement in his LaGrange estate, working as a "gentleman farmer," he actually was writing to Jefferson and John Adams about constitutional matters. Hostile to Napoleon's regime because of its authoritarian policies, Lafayette insisted on the Corsican's abdication after Waterloo.

Once back in public life, Lafayette emerged as an important leader in the Chamber of Deputies, to which he was elected in 1814. He became the leading promoter of liberal institutions, many of which had American models. An advocate of nineteenth-century liberalism, Lafayette tried to steer a middle course between conflicting factions, insisting that the *ancien régime* could never be reestablished in France. The majority of Frenchmen, he maintained, had come to appreciate the advantages of liberty and were now more restrained in their demands for individualism. For that reason, he supported the charter of 1814 and the restoration of the Bourbon monarchy.

Neither a strict royalist nor a radical, Lafayette remained a constitutional monarchist with strong republican tendencies. He hoped that France would establish a state based on French constitutional traditions, and at the same time he borrowed ideas about political institutions from America and Britain. During his six years in the Chamber of Deputies, he opposed the constitutional principles proposed by the restored Bourbon kings.

In regard to America, Lafayette kept reiterating the principles he felt had shaped the U.S. Constitution and other American institutions. During his tour of the United States in 1824/1825, he observed that the American people "have founded their constitutions upon . . . [a] clear definition of their natural and social rights." To Lafayette, this idea was important to world history and had inspired "immense majorities" in other countries. Despite the "combinations made . . . by despotism and aristocracy against those sacred rights of mankind," he believed that in the end the American position would prevail.[9]

Throughout his U.S. tour, Lafayette kept repeating the same theme: that America's commitment to the "sacred rights of mankind" in its Constitution was superior to the ideas held by European aristocrats. American children reared amid "liberty and equal rights," he observed, would learn to love their "republican institutions" once they understood more about "those parts of the world where aristocracy and despotism still retain their baneful influence."[10]

At the end of his tour, at a gathering at the White House where President John Quincy Adams was present, Lafayette reaffirmed his belief in the superiority of American institutions. He attributed it all to the U.S. Constitution:

> [It was]. . . a result of the republican principles for which we fought . . . a glorious demonstration to the most timid minds . . . of the superiority, over degrading aristocracy and despotism, of popular institutions founded on the plain rights of man, and where the local rights of every section are preserved under a constitutional bond of union.[11]

Upon returning to France, the aging hero was destined to play a key role in the revolution of 1830. While serving in the Chamber of Deputies, he was called again to head the National Guard, a symbolic post that gave him an unusual opportunity to regain some of the influence he had lost following his actions during the early 1790s. Although privately offered an opportunity to become president of the French republic, Lafayette declined, instead publicly embracing Louis-Philippe and helping make him the monarch. A limited constitutional monarchy, he felt, was France's best guarantee for liberty.[12] He told Louis-Philippe that the U.S. Constitution was the most perfect document ever to come from the hands of man and that the American republic represented the ideal form of government.[13]

Lafayette was doomed to be disappointed, as Louis-Philippe's policies soon drove him into the opposition. When Lafayette died in 1834, he was still struggling to achieve what he had consistently sought throughout his long career: liberty under law along republican lines.

In that quest, Lafayette retained his status as a "hero of two worlds." He helped confirm the belief of many Americans in their uniqueness and the rightness of their constitutional accomplishments. Insecure in their new nationalism, Americans benefited from the reinforcement of imposing public figures abroad. Lafayette strengthened the image Americans had of themselves as a republican people who had engaged in a revolution unique in world history and who had written a constitution worthy of imitation.

Destutt de Tracy

One of Lafayette's closest friends and fellow constitutionalists was Destutt de Tracy, a *philosophe* and economic theorist. Along with Benjamin Constant, they formed an important triumvirate and remained in constant communication.[14] Tracy was the first to coin the word *idéologie* and was partly responsible for the rise of the *idéologues*, members of a philosophical movement based largely on a rationalist, sensationalist theory of knowledge.[15] Tracy believed, for example, that an ideal political revolution should be based on reason and reform, and he viewed the American Revolution as a model.

Victims of self-deception, some *idéologues* had regarded Napoleon's seizure of power as a timely rescue of liberty from the deadly hands of the Directory.[16] Tracy himself served willingly as a senator during the Consulate and Empire periods but became disillusioned and eventually called for Napoleon's abdication. Tracy's friend Thomas Jefferson also had succumbed briefly to Napoleon's charm and in 1801 accepted a nomination to the Class of Moral and Political Science of the French National Institute. Like Tracy, Jefferson saw eye to eye with Napoleon for a time and then became disenchanted.

More important intellectually was Tracy's and Jefferson's disagreement with the ideas of Montesquieu. Tracy wrote a critique of Montesquieu entitled *Commentaire sur l'esprit des lois de Montesquieu* and asked Lafayette to send a copy to Jefferson, then president. He thought Lafayette could render the *idéologues* a great service by placing their works in the hands of an enlightened national leader.[17] Jefferson's response was highly enthusiastic: he praised the work, translated it himself, and promised to use it to educate American youth. He wrote to Tracy in 1811, declaring that the Frenchman had produced a "great desideratum . . . a radical correction of Montesquieu . . . [which] I consider . . . the most precious gift the present age has received."[18] Stating that he hoped to see the work "in the hands of every American student," Jefferson was as good as his word. He recommended to the College of William and Mary that Tracy's book be assigned as required reading in 1813.[19]

It is not hard to see why Jefferson thought so highly of Tracy's "gospel," as the *Commentaire* coincided with many of his own constitutional views. Like Jefferson, Tracy feared tyranny and supported popular sovereignty and representative government in theory. The Frenchman claimed that representative democracy, which he called "a new invention," was unknown in Montesquieu's time. Both Tracy and Jefferson disagreed, moreover, with Montesquieu's hypothesis that the republican form of government was practical only in small countries. And on other major issues, such as the need for a written constitution, distrust of executive power, fear of government interference, separation of church and state, and condemnation of colonialism, the two friends held similar positions.[20]

But they disagreed on several important points. Tracy's formula provided a liberal's justification for the support of monarchism or republicanism, depending on the historical context, whereas Jefferson would never agree to a monarchy under any conditions.[21] The same was true of the idea of a dual executive. Jefferson took exception to the notion, citing examples of pluralism in the executive branch in both American and French history that had failed.[22]

The two men were deeply divided as well over the concept of American federalism. Tracy thought it was impossible for France to apply the concept.[23] Surrounded by powerful enemies on the European Continent, lacking the ocean barriers that protected America, and needing a strong central government for military reasons, France could ill afford to consider any form of federalism that might diminish the power of the central government.

Despite their disagreements, Jefferson continued to hold Tracy's tract in high esteem. Five years before his death, Jefferson wrote to a family member that the Frenchman's work was the "best elementary book on government ever published." He planned to make it "the textbook of the Political lectures of the University [of Virginia]" which he was helping establish,[24] and when Lafayette visited the Virginia campus in 1825, he found the *Commentary* being used in the politics department.[25]

Tocqueville

Alexis Charles Henri Maurice Clérel de Tocqueville was the Frenchman most responsible for spreading ideas of American constitutionalism. His brilliant two-volume book, *Democracy in America*, published in France in 1835 and 1840, was translated quickly and read throughout the Western world. A genuine classic, the work remains the single most important study of the United States and its institutions ever written by a foreign observer, with the possible exception of Bryce's *American Commonwealth*.

Tocqueville's main thesis was the threat of tyranny by a majority within a democracy, in other words, dictatorship by public opinion. He feared that the untutored masses might destroy liberty and equality within the United States. Although he believed the spread of democracy throughout the world was inevitable and irreversible, he was aware of both its promise and its possible dangers.

To Tocqueville the ideas of freedom and democracy were inseparable, if not synonymous. To him, freedom meant individual independence, for liberalism was still in its individualistic phase when he was writing. Democracy, however, was seen as a social state in which greater equality could be achieved. Although successfully integrating freedom and democracy was the mark of a free society, the democracy that Tocqueville advocated posed certain problems.

Tocqueville agreed that democracy equalized social classes and fostered broad political participation. At the same time, however, it tended to destroy those local institutions that traditionally protected individuals from the despotic power of the state. Tocqueville warned, therefore, that safeguards should be erected against the overwhelming power of any majority in a democracy that might erode the freedom and liberty of the individual.[26]

Tocqueville was an ardent admirer of two American constitutional documents in particular, the Constitution and *The Federalist*. To him America's most original contribution was not the Declaration of Independence but the Constitution. He called the 1787 charter "a veritable work of art" and "the best of all known federal constitutions." It was, he said in a striking elaboration, "like one of those creations of human diligence which gives inventors glory and riches but remains sterile in other hands."[27] In the first edition of his *Democracy in America*, Tocqueville reproduced the entire text of the document.

In the chapter of *Democracy in America* devoted to the Constitution, Tocqueville addressed the question: "What Distinguishes the Federal Constitution . . . of America from All Other Federal Constitutions?" His answer? The American government was not a federal government but an incomplete national government. In previous confederations, peoples who allied for a common purpose had "agreed to obey the injunctions of the federal government, but they kept the right to direct and supervise the execution of the [U]nion's laws in their territories."[28] In 1787, however, the Americans agreed not only that the federal government should dictate the laws but also that it should itself see to their execution.

Previously a federal government had had to appeal to subordinate governments to provide its needs. In America, however, the subjects of the Union were private citizens. When the Union wanted to levy a tax, for example, it did not turn to the government of Massachusetts but to each Massachusetts inhabitant. In other words, the Union could act directly on private citizens without going through the states.[29]

There was always, of course, the danger of too much centralization on the part of the federal government. Such a situation could create a problematic relationship and lead to tension between the democratic polity and the centralization allowed the federal government. Tocqueville thereby addressed "certain peculiar and accidental causes" that might bring about such a crisis and, in doing so, discussed the concept of federalism to show how such problems might be resolved.[30]

In arguing the theory of American federalism, Tocqueville weighed whether the tendencies toward consolidation or disintegration of the Union were greater. After evaluating the forces that united Americans and those in the confederated states that might motivate them to break away, he concluded: "The Anglo-American Union is in reality a more united society than some European nations living under the same laws and the same prince."[31] Tocqueville recognized, however, that there were certain weaknesses in his argument and listed the limitations of American federalism.[32]

In this connection, Tocqueville discussed what might be called "the informal constitution" compared with the formal written document. He noted, for example, that the New England township provided one of those local institutions that established a sense of communal freedom as well as a social connection. It served as the basis of the principle of popular sovereignty operating within American society. The township succeeded in winning the affection of its inhabitants and created a strong local municipal spirit that formed those ties to the nation at large. Within the township, the theory and practice of popular sovereignty were developed to the highest degree. Local governments served as the safeguards and mediating agencies against the passions of the democratic masses, on the one hand, and the policies of the central government, on the other.[33] Tocqueville believed that townships also provided an essential forum for the exercise of democratic liberties, and he envisioned a progression from the smallest political unit (the town) through the states and up to the federal government.[34]

When he turned to the institutional character of the Constitution, Tocqueville dealt with the idea of presidentialism, his position being that the executive power in the United States was "limited and exceptional." Compared with the constitutional monarch in France, the American president was a feeble leader, indeed. He was elected subject to the will of the people which introduced an element of instability and was dependent on the national legislature in many situations. By contrast, a monarch had a much freer hand to exercise his authority.[35]

Tocqueville believed, however, that the weakness of the American presidency was the result of historical circumstances rather than the written laws. With this idea in mind, he predicted (presciently) that if the security of the United States were threatened in the future, the power of the presidency would grow accordingly.[36]

Along with federalism and presidentialism, Tocqueville considered judicial review one of the most interesting features of the Constitution. Almost all his information regarding the idea was drawn from *The Federalist*. He believed that an independent judiciary, armed with the power to declare laws unconstitutional, would help maintain balance in the federal system, check the legislative branch, and preserve the liberties of the people.

Judicial review would also act as a counterweight to the sovereignty of the people on which all of America's political institutions rested. Unlike the judges in France and England, American judges could declare laws to be unconstitutional and thus serve as guardians against any democratic excesses by the legislature.[37] Tocqueville stressed, too, the importance of preserving the independence of the judiciary. This was especially true for the Supreme Court, which had been given the highest standing among the great institutions in the state. "No other nation [has] ever constituted so powerful a judiciary as the Americans," Tocqueville concluded.[38] Yet like other branches of the federal government, the judiciary itself had to be kept in check. The legislature had to take precautions lest the right of the courts to declare laws unconstitutional be abused and the president, by his power of appointment, could affect the composition of the Supreme Court.[39]

The Federalist was a second major source for Tocqueville's ideas. He first read the essays while stuck on a sand bar in the Mississippi in the early 1830s and decided that the book "should be familiar to statesmen of all countries."[40] But the essays he used in his work were often not acknowledged because Tocqueville failed to indicate what he had borrowed.[41]

Tocqueville understood instantly the significance of the difference between the Articles of Confederation and the new Constitution as expressed in *The Federalist*. "The old Union," he wrote,

> governed *the States*, not the individuals. . . . The new federal government is . . . the government of the Union in all things within its competence; it addresses, not the *States*, but *individuals*; its orders are addressed to each of the American citizens, whether he be born in Massachusetts or Georgia, and not to Massachusetts or to Georgia.[42]

Madison's famous *Federalist* 39, as one might imagine, was another favorite source for Tocqueville, and he based his description of the Union in large part on Madison's language. Madison wrote about the Constitution's being, strictly speaking, "neither wholly national nor wholly federal, but a composition of both," whereas Tocqueville described the American government as "neither precisely national nor federal."[43] Clearly he plagiarized Madison without acknowledging it.

The Federalist also was the source for Tocqueville's discussion of many institutional barriers in the U.S. Constitution as having been erected by the framers against popular despotism. These included various sections addressing such problems as the nature of American federalism, bicameralism, the system of indirect elections, the local jury system, legal and judicial establishments, the press, political parties, and the important function of voluntary associations in American society. Tocqueville's discussion of these features revealed his grasp of the U.S. Constitution and its merits.[44] But it also demonstrated his insight into the significance of *The Federalist*, his interpretation of which did more at the time than any other commentator to spread the fame of Publius abroad.

In regard to the bill of rights tradition, Tocqueville was equally perceptive. His philosophy in this regard was set forth in his general statement that "up to now no one in the United States has dared to profess the maxim that everything is allowed in the interests of society, an impious maxim apparently invented in an age of freedom in order to legitimatize every future tyrant."[45]

Tocqueville also compared the freedom of the press in America and France, noting that the absence of an intellectual center like Paris, the decentralized press in America, and the coarseness of the nation's newspapers all made the press far less powerful in the United States. Freedom of the press, he observed, was a necessary concomitant of the sovereignty of the people as it was understood in America: no person would dare to suggest, therefore, restricting this freedom.[46]

Tocqueville believed that freedom of religion was particularly important to democratic societies like America because of the urgent need to instill morality in the people. The dangers of materialism inherent in all men, he felt, could be countered mainly by religion. Tocqueville was struck by the spirit of religion prevailing in the United States and believed that religion was a powerful contributor to the maintenance of America's civil society.[47]

Finally, Tocqueville took up the freedom of association characteristic of American society, demonstrating how Americans continually resorted to this freedom to create a civil society. The voluntary associations that had sprung up paved the way for political ones, which strengthened democracy. Although the freedom of political association could lead to instability, he noted that in America, the reverse was true.[48]

Tocqueville did not discuss at great length the remaining three of the six seminal documents. He barely mentioned the Declaration of Independence and used the Articles of Confederation as a negative example to show the weaknesses of that government.[49] But in the preface to the twelfth edition of *Democracy in America*, Tocqueville took note of the tremendous importance of America's first state constitutions. They rested, he observed, on the "principles of order, balance of powers, true liberty, and sincere and deep respect for law . . . indispensable for all republics." He concluded, moreover, that it was safe to prophesy "that where they are not found the republic will soon have ceased to exist."[50]

Tocqueville warned his fellow Frenchmen, however, not to copy American institutions slavishly. "Let us look there for instructions rather than models; let us adopt the principles rather than the details of her laws." The laws of the French republic, he maintained, would and, in many cases should, differ from those of the United States.[51] With this commentary, Tocqueville emerged as a classic example of Friedrich's contention that the American model should serve as a catalyst for foreign constitutionalists to rethink their ways of governance.

American Constitutionalism and French Royalist Constitutionalists

A bitter struggle took place between 1815 and 1830 regarding the restoration of the monarchy between the ultraroyalists (*ultras*) who wanted to roll back the achievements of the Revolution, and the liberals and their allies who hoped to retain the reforms achieved up to 1814.[52] The charter of 1814 incorporated some gains made in the Revolution: it guaranteed the principle of equality before the law, preserved the principle of religious toleration, and confirmed land titles acquired in the Revolution. It did not, however, reflect any influence of American constitutionalism.

The next charter, the French Constitution of 1831, though based primarily on indigenous traditions, reflected more British than American influence. An unstable compromise, the 1831 document took sovereignty from the Crown without expressly giving it to the people, and it created a parliamentary regime without guaranteeing government protection against monarchical manipulation. From the Restoration to 1831, a debate raged: should the settlement after the divisive French Revolution of 1789 be broadened, narrowed, or rejected altogether?

The French nobility, the *ultras*, were mostly hostile to the republicanism inherent in the U.S. Constitution. The killing of the French king, the slaughter of his family and friends, and the forced emigration of many aristocrats left the *ultras* fearful of republics in any shape or form. A few noblemen like Lafayette, to be sure, fought as officers in the American Revolution, became lifelong liberals, and retained friendships in the United States. But the vast majority of nobles were fearful of the symbol that a democratic republican America presented to the discontented elements in France.[53]

Some nobles, however, such as the comte de Ségur and the marquis de Barbé-Marbois, believed that France had something to learn by studying the United States and its Constitution. Both had been in America during the revolutionary era, Ségur as the French consul general in New York and Barbé-Marbois as a young officer in Virginia. Both remained faithful friends of the United States and held a highly idealized view of the new nation. Their romantic vision was largely inspired by the *philosophes* and uncritical, and they and men like them continued to believe in the American Dream throughout the Bourbon Restoration. Ségur described America as a "political Eldorado" and considered the U.S. Constitution one of history's most remarkable creations. Although both he and Barbé-Marbois agreed that the American form of government was not suited to the Old World, their admiration of it in the New World was boundless.[54]

Barbé-Marbois and Ségur were hardly typical of those who held royalist views. A better example was François-René, vicomte de Chateaubriand, a French poet and statesman. Chateaubriand visited the United States in 1791 and toured for almost five months. As a twenty-three-year-old youth, he became disenchanted by what he saw: America's materialism, ill treatment of the Indians, and ruination of the environment. His writings presented a hostile picture of America.

A true-blue royalist, Chateaubriand resisted both the French Revolution and Napoleon but welcomed the return of the exiled Bourbons and the charter of 1814. But his political views were complex and contradictory: although known as an *ultra*, he was not always in the king's favor. He warned the king and ministers against what he considered their liberal policies and claimed they were leading the monarchy down the road to ruin. One of the founders of the theoretical and practical conservatism in his country, Chateaubriand kept insisting that America's indigenous conditions made it impossible for either France or Europe to achieve its kind of constitution.[55] Intermittently shifting his views, in his posthumous *Mémoires d'outre tombe* he gave a favorable view of republican America based on political realism rather than ideology.[56]

Belgian Constitution of 1831

The greatest triumph of constitutional monarchy during the mid-nineteenth century was achieved in the Belgian revolution of 1831. Once the Belgians won their independence from the Dutch, they repudiated the king and his legitimist constitution and declared that members of the Dutch royal family were ineligible to hold public office. They proclaimed the sovereignty of the people, wrote a constitution recognizing it, and installed a king whose powers were limited to those specified in the new document. When the Belgians promulgated their new constitution of 1831, it became the most liberal governing document in Europe. The king was chosen by representatives of the people; the parliament became an organ of popular will; and the monarch had to take an oath to follow the constitution.

The section of the constitution labeled "Of Belgians and Their Rights" incorporated features from France, America, and Britain, as well as indigenous customs. The Belgian Constitution drew most heavily on the French Declaration of 1789 when expressing theoretical arguments regarding the basis for civil rights, but at the same time, it protected these rights from a more practical American point of view.[57] The extensive catalog of enumerated civil liberties also reflected some American influence.[58]

Hailed as one of the world's great democratic charters, the 1831 constitution upheld certain principles that were paralleled in the U.S. Constitution: limited powers in the executive branch, separation of powers, protection of civil liberties and private property, and, most important, the radical separation of church and state. The Belgians, however, depended more on indigenous than on foreign sources, so according to one commentary, half the constitution of 1831 was drawn from the 1815 Belgian Constitution and one-third from the 1830 French Constitution, leaving little room for the influence of the Americans and British.[59]

That the U.S. Constitution was much on the minds of the framers of the 1831 constitution, however, was evident from the comments of one of its framers, Désiré Pierre Antoine de Haerne. Speaking to the national parliament almost half a century later, Haerne remembered how deeply American principles had influenced Belgian constitutionalists: "We found a great people worthy of entire imitation, and it is the institutions of that people we have chiefly inscribed upon our organic charter. We have followed their example in all that regards public liberty, the distribution of power, the election of representatives and decentralization of rule."[60]

American principles refracted through the Belgian prism, therefore, indirectly affected much of the rest of Europe throughout the nineteenth century. The Belgian Constitution of 1831 served as a model for several other charters: the Spanish Constitution of 1833, the Greek Constitutions of 1844 and 1864, the Luxembourg Constitution of 1848, the Prussian Constitution of 1850, and the Bulgarian Constitution of 1864.[61] It was a classic example of the idea of world syncretisms at work.

Jacksonian Democracy and European Constitutionalism

The romantic image of America as a republic—"a TransAtlantic Arcadia" peopled in theory by virtuous farmer-citizens who loved liberty—started to change when the Jacksonian movement for greater democracy developed. America became increasingly identified as a representative democracy rather than as a republic, particularly in France. Although Alexander Hamilton had used the term *representative democracy* during the founding era, this characterization of the American system was not generally accepted by European intellectuals until the 1830s.[62] The idealization of America gave way to a more realistic picture as additional European travelers visited, early observers like Lafayette died, and political party differences became more obvious.[63]

European conservatives then began to view American constitutionalism in a new light after the rise of the 1830s Jacksonian liberalism. Although critical of Jacksonian democracy as a whole, they were attracted by the conservative nature of American constitutionalism which demonstrated that in the tension between republicanism and democracy, democracy did not necessarily have to degenerate into mobocracy.

At this time, the American system was being interpreted by European conservatives as a variation of the British, one that aimed to eliminate some of the presumed degeneration in the Westminster model, such as the cabinet system and role of political parties. What this approach overlooked was that the British themselves had long ago rejected elements of the Westminster model, like the executive right to veto. In a surprising contradiction, therefore, despite their fear of Jacksonian democracy, some European conservatives found attractive certain elements of the American liberal movement under Jackson.

As party strife in America became more pronounced, however, European constitutionalists began criticizing the United States for fostering political parties that encouraged conflict. The divisive slavery question in particular was seen as contradicting the emphasis on consensus stressed by French constitutionalists who still held to the concept of "the nation one and indivisible." America was also seen as being more depraved in economic terms as the society was increasingly judged to be materialistic, profit driven, and greedy.

Ironically, these criticisms came at a time when important constitutionalists were taking note of the spread of democracy as a worldwide phenomenon. Tocqueville wrote that it was evident to all that a great democratic revolution was rising everywhere. John Stuart Mill in England shared that vision, and Chateaubriand, though often hostile to it, was forced to admit democracy was spreading with the United States as its leading exemplar.

Liberals in France whose influence increased after 1830 were among the first to acknowledge the changing American image. They seemed more willing to accept American institutions and the ideas of Jacksonian liberalism, although not necessarily the social structure of the United States as a whole or belief in an outright egalitarian society.[64] Despite these qualifications, America began to enjoy a reputation as an important model among French liberals. Without this change in attitude, it is unlikely that American constitutionalism could have played the important part it did in France and elsewhere during the European revolutions of 1848.

American Constitutionalism and German Constitutionalists, 1800–1848

For Germany, the first three decades of the nineteenth century were only a period of preparation in regard to American constitutionalism. Then when German constitutionalists, jurists, and political thinkers gradually acquired a more realistic picture of the United States, they better understood the possibilities of applying American solutions to Germany's constitutional problems.[65]

There is no evidence that American constitutionalism had any influence on the 1815 Constitution of the German Confederation, despite its experiment with federalism. Once established, however, comparisons between it and the U.S. Constitution became inevitable, even though such analogies were usually inaccurate because the American model was so frequently misunderstood.[66]

One major exception to such inaccuracies was the work of Robert von Mohl, a giant in the field of German constitutional history. Mohl, a liberal, helped shape much of the thinking in Germany about the U.S. Constitution, not only in his day, but for a long time to come. Regarded by many as the greatest German political scientist of his time, Mohl produced a stunning pioneering work as a young man. No systematic study of the U.S. Constitution had been available in Europe before his monumental *Das Bundes-Staatsrecht der Vereinigten Staaten von Nord-*

Amerika was published in 1824. Although dubbed "Germany's de Tocqueville," Mohl actually anticipated his French counterpart by more than a decade.[67]

Mohl's masterpiece was divided into six chapters, each dealing with a separate subject: the member states in the American Union, the Constitution, the separation of powers, the relations between the states, the relationship between the states and the federal government, and the rights of American citizens. American constitutionalism, he concluded, was the "miracle of our time."[68]

Mohl was interested particularly in federalism, democracy, and judicial review, and his ideas about American federalism were best expressed in a subsequent publication. For example, he questioned the conventional wisdom that America's success was derived mainly from the country's favorable circumstances. Instead, it was the federal form of government, Mohl concluded, that enabled America to make the most of its advantages. The Constitution had satisfactorily resolved two of the most pressing problems of democratic government: how to establish a republic in a large territory and how to reconcile the participation of all citizens in public affairs with the then current notion of freedom, which called for the least possible government interference with the individual.[69]

Mohl considered federalism and popular sovereignty the most important contributions of the American governmental system. When studying the Constitution, he grasped instantly the distinction between the Staatenbund and the rarer and more complicated form of federal union, the Bundestaat. The Bundstaat, he observed, was formally a state and not just a treaty among states that remain independent or, at best, form a defensive alliance. A Bundestaat possessed all the attributes of an ordinary state, with its own legislation and laws binding directly on individuals and a government having all the means necessary to execute its laws by establishing federal courts. The Bundestaat was distinguished from an ordinary state only insofar as it was divided into different and separate "provinces" that were free to handle their own internal affairs. While meeting the criteria as a Staatenbund, Mohl asserted, the United States as a federal union was also fully qualified as a Bundestaat. To support his conclusion, Mohl enumerated the constitutional limitations on the states besides the different aspects of national sovereignty.[70]

On the issue of democracy, Mohl articulated his views best in the reviews he wrote later of Tocqueville's work, as well as in his own commentary on the California and Massachusetts constitutional conventions of

1849 and 1853. Like Tocqueville, he was aware that democracy was on the march worldwide. Democratic ideas were penetrating aristocratic circles everywhere. While casting about for a model democracy, he chose the United States and analyzed the democratic ideas at work in America, discussing their relative advantages and drawbacks.[71]

Mohl's high regard for the U.S. Constitution led him to predict that it would play an important part in Europe's future development. America was the best "prototype" to evaluate the workings of democracy under modern conditions, he wrote, because of the peaceful environment under which its ideas had developed.[72]

But along with his praise, Mohl pointed out some serious problems. Like Tocqueville after him, Mohl warned about the tyranny of the majority and its consequences for the freedom of individuals. Representative democracies like America tended to become more and more democratic over time, he observed. But by their very nature they failed to provide sufficient protection against the abuses of power: large majorities were often guilty of being unfair to minorities. There could be no freedom of the mind under majority rule because it was difficult for individuals to fight against the way of thinking held by a majority. Although there would be no accusations or punishments, resistance against majority public opinion would be resented deeply, and the social status of those individuals involved would suffer.

As a result, popular despotism had the effect of suppressing any serious discussion on intellectual matters. On this basis Mohl determined that intellectual life in America was more oppressed than even in the most absolutist of European countries. The natural outcome was a provincialism, a narrow-mindedness, and a passionate clinging to accepted values. This condition inevitably led to intellectual mediocrity, which was evident in America's low level of education, lack of talented writers, and scarcity of creative artists.[73]

Mohl sensed also a decline in the quality of America's political leadership. From the founding fathers to the presidencies of Andrew Jackson and Franklin Pierce, there had been a discernable downward trend. The "relatively aristocratic" founding fathers had been able to devise a government independent of public opinion because of their secret deliberations in the Philadelphia Convention. But as time went on, "the whole spirit of the people in all strata has changed slowly, step by step, but inevitably, as [if] it were sliding on a slanted plane, toward more democratic beliefs and institutions."[74]

The broadening of the suffrage, Mohl believed, resulted as well in the destruction of any aristocracy based on merit. It promoted the election of mediocre candidates to public office, men who simply flattered and pandered to the masses. This trend, he implied, did not bode well for the future of American democracy.[75]

A number of institutions that the founding fathers had considered indispensable to the protection of lawful liberty had already fallen victim to what Mohl called the "neodemocratic spirit." For example, Ohio, as well as some newer states entering the Union, was electing judges directly. Democratic demands that a short time ago would have been branded as "completely senseless" were gradually being taken for granted.[76]

One feature of the U.S. Constitution that most fascinated Mohl was the idea of judicial review. In fact, he considered this concept "one of the boldest and most interesting experiments in modern public law." But great as his admiration was for this feature, he doubted judges had the right to decide whether legislation was unconstitutional under the separation of powers.[77]

Mohl's perception was that the Constitution had been freely adopted by the American people as a whole and that national power rested naturally on the will of the people rather than on any concessions made by the states. National power, he wrote, was necessary to prevent any petty adherence to states' rights, and any determined resort to states' rights would result in the destruction of the federal government, general anarchy, and a civil war.[78]

After discussing the Constitution, Mohl turned to the other seminal documents, including the Declaration of Independence. His treatment of that text was insightful because his primary emphasis was on the freedom of the individual. On those grounds, he made an interesting observation by contrasting the Declaration and Constitution. The Declaration, on the one hand, cherished the idea of equality and made no distinction concerning individuals. The Constitution, on the other hand, divided the population into different classes, including slaves, and made other social distinctions.[79]

Mohl held America's first state constitutions in high esteem because they made wider use of the idea of popular sovereignty than did the U.S. Constitution. He then commented on the purity of the first state constitutions and on their decline once subsequent state charters grew more detailed. The later state constitutions reflected a "neodemocratic spirit" evident in such features as the election of judges and other local political officials. Persons could now vote who had "no pertinent ties whatsoever to the State, and often had not even been residents."[80]

Mohl had a great regard for *The Federalist*, recognizing its value to the science of government everywhere. "It would be difficult," he wrote, "to render a more careful and more brilliant account of the principles and essential institutions of the American Constitution."[81] But Mohl went even further, claiming that the work was "one of the best publications in the general field of politics and public law."[82]

Finally, Mohl took up the bill of rights tradition. Although his main concern again was freedom of the individual, he was not prepared to allow liberty to degenerate into license. He was opposed, for example, to the unlimited freedom of the press. Newspapers, he wrote, appealed to the baser human passions, as they encouraged people to accept superficialities and discouraged serious political discussions.[83]

Mohl's magnum opus and other writings had a tremendous impact throughout Germany and marked the beginning of serious interest in American constitutionalism. Although he admired the country, he was sufficiently detached to criticize its deficiencies as well: "The United States is by no means a paradise inhabited by angels, and her institutions are not of utopian excellence."[84] Mohl's honesty gave his work an aura of objectivity, and his writings set the stage for the 1848/1849 constitutional dialogue in Germany in which he took part.

From an institutional point of view, one German development in the 1830s of special interest to constitutionalists everywhere was the creation of the German Customs Union, or Zollverein. It highlighted the role of American constitutionalism by extending the concept of federalism beyond the political realm into the economic.[85] The Zollverein established a free-trade zone throughout much of the country and was seen as a significant step toward the ultimate unification of Germany. Some intellectuals viewed this system as a nonrevolutionary way to bring about great change in both the economic and political spheres.

To some reformers like George Friedrich List, a German economist who briefly migrated to the United States, the use of high tariffs among nation-states was anathema. Commercial warfare meant that the states remained separate entities and economically divided from one another. But if the states could get together and form a federal union, they could carry on free trade with one another over a larger area, an idea that explains why American-type federalism attracted foreign theorists like List.

The German political economy began to prosper after 1818 when List persuaded German governments run by petty princes to drop their high tariffs and create a Zollverein. List gave a speech in 1827 in the United States urging it to practice free trade. At the time, however, Henry Clay was calling for the opposite position, establishing an "American System" to protect young American industries against foreign competition. As a result, List's idea was never accepted.

List was a man well ahead of his time. He viewed the United States as a perfect model of a free-trade zone not only for Germany but for the entire world. "If the globe were united by a union like the twenty-four states of North America," he wrote, "free trade would be quite as natural and beneficial as it is for the union."[86] List was, indeed, a predecessor of the European Union and other integrated economies of modern times that anticipated globalization.

American Constitutionalism and Switzerland: "The Swiss Contagion," 1798–1848

Switzerland was greatly influenced by the U.S. Constitution during the first half of the nineteenth century, by what one scholar called the case of American–Swiss "constitutional contagion" between 1798, the year the unpopular Helvetic Constitution was imposed by the French, and the famous 1848 Swiss Constitution.[87]

With the collapse of the Helvetic Confederation in 1803, a controversy ensued regarding the future direction of the Swiss government. Under the Helvetic Confederation, the sovereignty and independence of the cantons were abolished, and power was centralized under a five-man directorate. Two opposing views dominated this debate. One favored the increased centralization under the republic, and the other supported the stronger cantonal powers, which had a long-standing tradition. Over the next half century, these two views—those of the "Unitarians" who wanted a more centralized government and those of the "Federalists" who desired stronger cantonal rights—could not be reconciled. But in either case, both invariably discussed the American model.

Besides federalism, bicameralism was another significant feature of American constitutionalism that attracted the Swiss. The idea of a two-house legislature, however, had become tarnished during the first half century because domination by the French had resulted in a wave of xenophobia against any foreign influences. Those favoring the U.S.

Constitution as a model were hesitant, therefore, about introducing yet another foreign example.

The French revolution of 1830 brought about some sudden changes. Swiss liberals, influenced by events in France, removed aristocrats from government in a series of cantonal coups d'état and promptly set up new establishments based on popular sovereignty. Thus began the so-called period of regeneration (1830–1848), during which the cantons shifted sides on issues according to changes in the domestic political scene.

Switzerland now reflected a patchwork of conflicting subcultures: ethnic (German, French, Italian), religious (Catholic and Protestant), economic (industrial and agricultural), and occupational (lawyers, farmers, and merchants, among others). Such competing groups made any kind of consensus on constitutional matters almost impossible. But in 1832 the liberals, many of whom were antidemocratic and antitraditionalist rather than true democratic radicals, persuaded the federal Diet to consider making changes in the central government. By doing so, they paved the way for further discussions by proponents of American-style federalism.[88]

Even before this move, certain groups and individuals had advocated changes based on the U.S. Constitution. The Helvetic Society, a private organization composed of public-spirited citizens from all parts of Switzerland and founded in 1761, had long suggested constitutional reform. Heinrich Zschokke, president of the organization, historian, and admirer of the United States, urged that the American model be followed. During the dark days of repression, he had written an article in 1818 entitled "Europa's Niedergang, Amerika's Aufgang" (Europe's Fall, America's Rise), which closed with this peroration: "From now on America shall be the home of human culture and the lighthouse of the globe, towards which the individual sages in all countries will look back with yearnings and grateful blessings."[89] In 1829 Zschokke was still singing the praises of the American federal state as the "lighthouse of the globe."[90]

An even more important publicist was Ignaz Paul Troxler, a learned doctor turned philosopher from Lucerne and a member of the Helvetic Society. Troxler was probably more responsible for the adoption of the American-style bicameral system than any other single individual.[91] More cosmopolitan and less provincial than his compatriots, he argued against the proposed draft constitution in 1833 and claimed that a federal state would serve Switzerland's needs best. At the same time, he urged the adoption of the American bicameral system and remained faithful to this concept throughout his life. In 1848 he published a political pamphlet appropriately entitled "The Constitution of the United States of America as a Model for the Swiss Federal Reform."[92] Troxler, like Zschokke, believed the Americans had created a constitution that had universal significance. "Through their federal constitution," he wrote, "they have translated into life an ideal of social organization which from now on in the history of the world must be looked upon as the authoritative pattern of all federal republics."[93] Troxler's writings ultimately helped overcome the xenophobic prejudice against the U.S. Constitution.

One of the reformers influenced most by Troxler was Karl Kasthofer, an elderly forester from Berne. Kasthofer helped popularize the "American system." To counter the nationalistic prejudice against foreign ideas, Kasthofer produced a widely circulated didactic pamphlet in which he propounded the doctrines of American federalism and bicameralism and demonstrated how they might be adapted to Switzerland despite the great differences.[94]

Thomas Bornhauser, another influential reformer, was a political pastor from Thurgau whose famous pro-American sermon in 1834 became one of the most popular writings of the time. Published in a pamphlet, it took the form of a make-believe dialogue. The principal exchanges were between two fictional characters, Treuherz (Trueheart), who advocated the American system, and his opponent, Schweitzerbart (Swissbeard). Under the guise of a give-and-take discussion, Treuherz concluded that not all American institutions should be copied in Switzerland: "We should, however, base our new federal constitution on the fundamental principles which experience has so gloriously consecrated beyond the Atlantic."[95]

All three men were German-Swiss, hailed from German-speaking cantons, and had attended German-speaking universities that offered courses on American civilization and U.S. constitutional law.[96] Their writings, therefore, reflected their upbringing and educational background.

In contrast, James Fazy, a fervent supporter of "the American system," was a leader of the French-Swiss point of view. Born in Geneva, Fazy spent some time in France, returned to Switzerland, and began publishing in the liberal *Journal de Genève*. He produced a draft constitution in 1837 which, one scholar claims, resembled the American model more closely than any other proposal before or after. Among its features were a bicameral legislature, a single executive somewhat similar to the American president, a separation of powers, and a bill of rights guaranteeing religious tolerance, equality before the law, and rights of assembly, speech, and free press.[97] Fazy, like Troxler, had been deeply influenced by *The Federalist*.[98]

Although the U.S. Constitution received a sympathetic hearing in the 1830s, no important constitutional changes were made. Faced with a deadlock, political opponents became mired in fierce fights that went nowhere. These clashes moved to the battlefield when a civil war erupted in 1847, which finally broke the existing gridlock and led to constitutional reforms in 1848.

American Constitutionalism and Poland: An Object Lesson

Poland, which promulgated the world's second national written constitution in 1791, was well aware of American constitutionalism. Because Poland had been broken up between the 1770s and the 1790s, it was the usual practice among intellectuals to contrast America's "success" with Poland's "failure." Poland lost its statehood when European powers partitioned Poland in 1772, 1793, and 1795, until it disappeared altogether as an independent country. But Charles Francis Adams, writing in the mid-nineteenth century, shrewdly observed that America might have had equally serious disorders had the positions of the two countries been reversed. Much of the success or failure of any given form of government, he suggested, could be traced to circumstances that had no connection whatsoever to the intrinsic value of the constitution involved. In Poland's case, the lack of natural protective boundaries created a virtually insurmountable problem. If the United States had suffered Poland's geographical disadvantages, Adams observed, "it is at least open to question" whether its constitution would have survived intact.[99]

Americans themselves had experienced partition fears of their own when on the verge of declaring independence, but on different grounds. The founding fathers had worried about a possible partition of North America by England, France, or Spain, and Philadelphia newspapers kept mentioning the European powers' "partition spirit" during the spring of 1776. With the Polish partitions on their minds, members of Congress were driven to adopt the Declaration of Independence immediately. Among those who specifically referred to such a partition was Richard Henry Lee, who proposed the resolution for the Declaration.[100]

The American Dream, though dimly perceived in the distant reaches of Poland, sometimes became quite visible. Thaddeus Kościuszko, a Polish patriot who fought with the Continental army, was inspired for the rest of his life by his American experience. Returning to his homeland, he led Polish troops against the Russian armies that invaded his country to suppress the reformist Constitution of 1791. When the Russians completed their occupation and forced the Polish king to renounce the constitution, Kościuszko fled into exile. After an underground movement was formed in Poland in 1793, he was asked to lead it. Standing before an immense crowd in Krakow in 1794, he solemnly vowed to regain Poland's independence.

During the ensuing Polish revolt, Kościuszko exercised virtual dictatorial powers as a political and military leader. At the same time, however, he tried to introduce policies similar to those in America. For instance, to promote greater equality in the conservative Polish society, he issued a proclamation in May 1794 freeing the serfs. A Kościuszko-inspired pamphlet, *Can the Poles Fight Their Way to Independence?* made specific references to the United States and even envisaged an institution patterned after the American Congress.[101]

Late in 1794, Russian troops put down the Polish uprising, and Kościuszko was wounded, captured, and imprisoned in Russia until 1796. After his release the following year, he traveled to the United States where he formed a lasting friendship with Jefferson. Rushing back to Europe in 1798, he was encouraged by Napoleon's rise to power to believe that the French leader might advance Poland's cause. But Kościuszko was to be disappointed. His subsequent proposal to the Russian czar in 1814 to establish a large Polish state with a liberal social order was likewise ignored, and his dreams remained unfulfilled.

American Constitutionalism and Russia in the 1820s

The one-day drama of the Decembrists in Russia was a sharp contrast with the decades-long Polish struggle for independence. Generally speaking, the goals of those involved in this well-known Russian conspiracy were quite varied. As one scholar put it: "It was possible, in Poland, to be a patriot without becoming a revolutionary, whereas in Tsarist Russia, any sincere liberal was bound to become a revolutionary, at least from the moment when granting a constitution to Russia proved a dream."[102] Such was the case of the Decembrist conspirators in 1825.

In 1815, Russian army officers battling Napoleon had occupied Paris. They were soon exposed to Western liberal ideas, including those of France and indirectly those from America. Secret societies were formed in the Russian officer corps and other elements of society, but members of these underground groups held contradictory views about the changes they desired: some sought a constitutional czardom; others demanded a republic; and a few even dreamed of emancipating the serfs.[103]

Although quickly put down, the Decembrist revolt was highly significant. It was the first modern revolutionary movement in Russia—an effort inspired by an ideological program—and therefore different from the earlier mass upheavals. The revolt provided the basis for a legendary past that inspired Russian dissidents for decades. Both the "radical" Decembrists like Pavel Ivanovich Pestel, who advocated a republic, and Nikita Murav'ev, who favored a limited monarchy, had been influenced by the U.S. Constitution. In the first version (1823) of his *Russkaia Pravda*, Pestel called for a republican system with full democracy and a popular vote. Murav'ev's draft constitution, which provided for a constitutional monarchy and a federal organization of the Russian empire, was patterned in certain ways after the American document. Remnants of these ideas survived in the writings of Alexander Herzen, a liberal socialist, and exercised considerable influence later.[104]

American Constitutionalism and Hungary

Hungary, like Poland and Russia, also was touched by the wave of revolutionary upheavals that affected Europe intermittently throughout the first three decades of the nineteenth century. Opposition movements in all these countries were led mainly by noblemen, some of them impoverished.

Hungary, then part of the multiethnic empire of the Hapsburg monarchy, had a long history of discontented noblemen. The Magyars, the local aristocracy, had been restless under Austrian rule during the early 1800s. Well before the Hungarian revolution in 1848, a generation of reformers—Stephen Széchenyi, Nicholas Wesselényi, Louis Kossuth, Francis Deák, and Sándor Farkas—were singing the praises of America. They showed a deep interest in the U.S. Constitution and had been inspired by the American Dream.

Stephen Széchenyi, called "the greatest of the Magyars" by Louis Kossuth, leader of the Hungarian revolution of 1848, was not only a member of the nobility but also a cosmopolitan citizen of the world.[105] After living most of his life abroad until he was thirty, he returned to his homeland and began spreading liberal Western ideas. So enamored was he of American thought, he was dubbed "der Americane" by the ladies in Viennese society.[106]

Széchenyi's view of America was highly idealized, however. It was part of the high esteem in which he held the achievements of the Anglo-Saxon world as a whole, which he considered to be civilized compared with the barbarity elsewhere. His enthusiasm for America—"the Land of the Future," in his words—was boundless. He dreamed of visiting the country one day, though a dream never realized.[107] In his writings in 1819, he compared America with the ancient Roman republic. Just as the torch of civilization had passed from Asia to Europe to Rome, so too culture and perfection had moved from the Old to the New World, but with one important difference: the Roman republic had remained a small city-state, whereas everything in the United States was on a grand scale.

Széchenyi also made an important distinction in the Anglo-American world between Britain and America. Impressed with America's strong sense of independence, he felt the new nation would find it impossible to imitate the mother country or to copy its political institutions. To support his argument, he pointed to the differences in behavior and physical appearance of the two peoples as well as their dissimilarities in manufacturing.[108]

These comparisons, drawn from Széchenyi's 1829 "Code of Conduct," were significant for several reasons. They indicated that America appealed to liberals and reformers in central Europe well before the publication of the Hungarian edition of Tocqueville's work. And they revealed the breadth of Széchenyi's political perspective and demonstrated his interest in comparative government. He intended to visit England one day to study the parliamentary reform movement and to compare it with the workings of American democracy.[109] Despondent over his failure to realize his goals, Széchenyi became mentally unbalanced and later took his own life in 1860.

Sándor Bölöni Farkas, a Hungarian writer who traveled to the United States in the early 1830s, had a different purpose in mind. This middle-aged nobleman set out to publish a primer on democracy for feudal Hungary and succeeded in producing a work that became a best seller: *Journey in North America, 1831*. Farkas analyzed American democracy and used its model of government to argue against Metternich's despotic regime.[110] The book's success was unprecedented in nineteenth-century Hungary, a society in which book reading was relatively rare.

While in America, Farkas met Tocqueville, who was in the midst of writing his *Democracy in America*. A comparison of Farkas's *Journey* and Tocqueville's *Democracy* is instructive. Unlike Tocqueville, Farkas made more concrete references to the U.S. Constitution and other documents, whereas Tocqueville's approach was more abstract.[111]

Farkas associated the genius of American politics with its two founding documents, the Declaration and the Constitution. "To me," he wrote, "the declaration of the rights of mankind . . . is the most significant, and the rest is just the frame around it." Aware that slavery violated the "principle of natural law," Farkas boldly prophesied that the United States would one day end the institution and achieve the ideals expressed in the Declaration. He was under no illusions that emancipation would be easy and was quite skeptical about the organizations already in existence for that purpose. Nor did Farkas believe that freeing the slaves would usher in any kind of American golden age.[112]

His brilliant insight, however, caught the true meaning of the Declaration, which he reprinted almost entirely in the first edition of *Journey in North America*. Farkas eloquently insisted that the document's uniqueness derived from its radical departure from European charters of freedom, which were royal grants subject to the ruler's discretion. The Declaration, in contrast, "declares that just power derives from the consent of the people who entrust some rights to the government. The language of the Declaration is not the language of diplomacy but the language of natural law."[113]

Farkas likewise grasped the essence of the U.S. Constitution when he compared how a European king exercised power with how an American president would do so. Europeans were used to the notion of a godlike ruler as "the elect of heaven" and familiar with the spectacle of "his halo" creating officials who surrounded him with "glitter and splendor" in order to be "obeyed and feared by subjects." As a result, they were unable to comprehend the "direct simplicity" of American presidents. This experience had instilled the belief that "fear teaches obedience," but the Americans nonetheless rejected this centuries-old European tradition.[114]

Farkas captured also the historical significance of the first state constitutions. Even though they differed in form, the documents "shared some fundamental principles." After drawing up their constitutions, the states entered the "Articles of Union" on their own volition and jointly created the Congress. Farkas reprinted the text of the New Hampshire Constitution as an example, identifying it as the first of the new state constitutions.[115]

Farkas's depiction of the U.S. Constitution as a model that could fulfill the moral and rational nature of the individual reflected the civic humanism in which he believed deeply.[116] The importance of his *Journey in North America* to the intellectual life of Hungary is difficult to overestimate;[117] its ideals carried his influence to the revolutions of 1848.

American Constitutionalism and Italy from 1800 to the 1830s

Italian constitutional thinkers, as noted, had indigenous traditions stretching back to ancient Roman times; nevertheless, their discussions of the U.S. Constitution played a small, though significant, role in developments after 1800. This contribution was made possible by a few educated Italians who kept abreast of constitutional changes in America through the writings of their own countrymen and foreign authors.[118]

The American Dream thus remained alive in the region. It was revived early in the 1800s by the remarkable four-volume history of the American Revolution published by Carlo Giuseppe Botta in 1809. A physician and historian from Piedmont, Botta had been inspired in his youth by the French Revolution and became a Jacobin. But in 1792 when he attempted to emulate his French friends in his native land, he was thrown into prison. After escaping to France, he served as a doctor in the army and then settled in Paris where he met and became friends with Lafayette.

Botta's book, translated into English in 1820, instantly became a best seller in both Italy and the United States, going through twenty-two printings in Italian and sixteen in America during its first forty years. So thorough was its coverage that Harvard University adopted it in 1839 as the textbook for its course on the American Revolution.[119]

Botta's history had severe shortcomings, however. He overlooked much of the civil war between the loyalists and patriots, put speeches into the mouths of persons who may or may not have uttered them, and was uncritically pro-American. His work focused too much on military affairs (as was the style of the time) and gave short shrift to social and economic history.

In regard to constitutional matters, however, Botta was very perceptive, singling out developments that had worldwide consequences and demonstrating his sound grasp of American constitutionalism in three ways. First, he underscored the importance of covenants, such as the Mayflower Compact, which had served as constitutional precedents. Second, he highlighted the importance of constitutional conventions—"conventions extraordinary," in his words—to produce "a system" in order "to satisfy the world that Americans could govern themselves by their own laws." He believed the same was true of the first state constitutions. Third, he wrote extensively about the Declaration of Independence, calling it a "manifesto" for "all mankind."[120] Botta's work, together with that of Tocqueville translated into Italian in the 1830s, served as the major sources for Italians reading about American constitutionalism.

Botta's success soon led to imitators, and in 1812/1813 Carlo Giuseppe Londonio published an exhaustive survey of the American colonies from settlement through independence. Whereas Botta had concentrated mainly on military history, Londonio stressed social and economic developments. In his survey, he analyzed the Declaration, reproduced the complete text of the U.S. Constitution, and included a copy of the federal Bill of Rights. Londonio also introduced two themes that appeared time and again in subsequent Italian histories: the by-now standard critique of the weakness of the Articles of Confederation, as compared with the strength of the U.S. Constitution, and an attack on slavery as the fundamental flaw in American society. In addition, he dwelled on the fate of the Native Americans and their condition in what had been their land before the European settlements.[121]

In the 1820s Giuseppe Compagnoni wrote a two-volume work on the United States which, like Londonio's, began in the colonial period and ended in his own time. Compagnoni praised the U.S. Constitution and "considered [it] to be the best among all constitutions until now." His account included a detailed discussion of every single article in the document. "America today," he wrote, "appears on the way to an orderly [development] which to . . . old and corrupt Europe should be [a source of] shame and a lesson."[122]

Not all the histories by Italian writers had a positive outlook. In 1818 Giovanni Grassi, a Jesuit who came to America to head a new Catholic school in Georgetown near Washington, D.C., published a short history which went through three editions in Italy.[123] He was skeptical about America's future success as a republic. France, Grassi noted, had gone from the blindest fanaticism for liberty to abject slavery and feared America might suffer the same fate.[124]

Another critical view came from a more radical source. The Jacobin sculptor Giuseppe Cerrachi visited the United States twice in the 1790s and was deeply disappointed in the results of both the Revolution and Constitution. In his eyes, neither was radical enough. Cerrachi came to his conclusion from the perspective of an extreme revolutionary. On his first visit in 1790, he stayed for two years, was welcomed warmly, and was admitted to the small select circle around Washington, Hamilton, and

Jefferson. But on his second trip, from 1794 to 1795, Cerrachi's pro-Jacobin sympathies, outspoken criticism, and friendship with a French diplomat in Philadelphia during the period of America's neutrality made him *persona non grata*. After returning to Europe, he was involved in radical movements in both France and Italy and died on the guillotine in 1800 for plotting to assassinate Napoleon.[125]

Italian observers from the American Revolution through numerous European revolutions were kept well-enough informed about the new republic to allow educated readers to sustain the American Dream. The U.S. Constitution, however, became much more meaningful as Italians approached the revolutionary period of 1848 and began thinking more about the kind of government they would establish once they gained independence.

American Constitutionalism and Greece, 1820s

Although during the early decades of the nineteenth century, most European revolutionaries were inspired by the French Revolution, the Greek revolution against the Turks in the 1820s was an exception. Adamantios Korais, a Greek patriot, grew disenchanted with French Enlightenment thinkers and turned instead to Jefferson and other American founders.

Korais met Jefferson when both were in Paris in the 1780s and interested him in the Greek cause, later seeking Jefferson's help when shaping a constitution for the new Greek republic.[126] Although many leaders of the Greek independence movement were cosmopolitan merchants living in Paris and influenced by French thought, others like Korais were affected more by American ideas.[127]

The American public likewise had a great affection for the Greeks. Many founding fathers, like Jefferson, considered themselves heirs of the cultural and constitutional traditions of ancient Greece, and discussions in the Constitutional Convention were filled with references to Greek republic city-states and ancient Greek philosophers like Aristotle.

Indeed, enthusiasm for the Greek independence movement was so great in the 1820s that it was dubbed the "Greek fever." President James Monroe wanted to support the Greek cause and at times seemed ready to challenge conservative European powers in contradiction to the doctrine that bears his name. The Greek independence movement, in fact, nearly succeeded in making America change its policy toward intervening in European affairs.[128]

During their war for independence, the Greeks turned to the U.S. Constitution as their model when considering their new government. The structure of the Constitution of Epidauros of 1822, for example, was based on French, British, and American models. The Greek executive council was headed by a president who held many of the same powers as did the American president. The Greek judicial system likewise bore a slight resemblance to the American model: it had an appellate court system, was headed by a supreme court, and enjoyed relative independence from the other two branches of government.[129] Such parallelisms showed that the Greeks were well aware of the American model.

When Korais wrote to Jefferson seeking advice on constitutional matters in 1823, he received an interesting response. Jefferson urged Korais to look instead at the state constitutions, warning that the principles of government in ancient Athens and other city-states could no longer be applied to "doctrines of the present age." Given the size of Greece, Jefferson recommended a unitary rather than a federal state. Expounding on federalism, states' rights, the system of checks and balances, bicameralism, and the differences between a collegiate as compared with a single executive, Jefferson instructed his friend. He strongly advocated, for example, the American idea of amendments and the incorporation of a bill of rights.[130]

Jefferson's ideas fit well with Korais's. He believed also that the decline of ancient Greece had been caused by the dissension among the city-states. Korais denounced the idea of direct participation of citizens in the government and agreed with Jefferson's reservations regarding American-style federalism for Greece.[131]

After the Greeks declared their independence, the Constitution of Troezen was adopted in 1827. Essentially indigenous in character, the document borrowed also some elements from both the U.S. and French constitutions. It explicitly affirmed, for example, the principle of popular sovereignty. The document also recognized the distinction between the legislative and constituent process in constitution making. Any thought of a constituent constitutional convention based on popular participation, however, was impossible under existing political circumstances. The Greek bill of rights embodied the ideal of the rule of law and reflected respect for the rights of citizens. It guaranteed equality before the law, security of life, liberty, and property, as well as freedom of speech and the press. Although many details of the Troezen Constitution did reflect Jefferson's advice, any application of his views resulted as much from the political situation in Greece as from conscious borrowing.[132] Although the constitution was stillborn, those parallelisms helped provide some basis for the Greek democratic state that eventually emerged.

Conclusion

That American constitutionalism was much on the minds of many European constitutionalists from 1800 to 1848 is quite clear, though not as much as during the first echo. Time and again, however, constitutionalists considered ideas from America's six seminal documents in their role as catalysts, examples, or inspirational models.

Nevertheless, the main constitutional issue dividing liberals and conservatives in Europe until 1830 was still the French Revolution. Even in those countries interested in American constitutionalism, the focus remained on France. Only with the advent of Jacksonian democracy was America considered seriously as a subject in its own right. The idea began to be recognized that for the first time since ancient days there now existed a country based on popular sovereignty by its citizens. Yet even many European liberals who acknowledged this development still viewed America as a "fledgling."[133] The primary political role of American constitutionalism appears to have been as an alternative model used mainly by opponents to attack the established regime.

The interlude years were, however, highly significant as a preparatory stage for the European revolutions of 1848. Without the changed attitude toward the United States, the continued spread of the six documents throughout western Europe, and the appearance of constitutionalists like Tocqueville and Mohl, the revolutions would have lacked their significant American dimension.

Constitutionalists aside, much evidence shows that the common people of Europe were increasingly influenced by American constitutionalism. In the year before the 1848 revolutions broke out, the United States had clearly been established as the primary destination for Old World immigrants coming to the New World. About 1.3 million people, or 79 percent of the total, came from the British Isles.[134] Obviously, many came because of their grasp of the English language. But how many were motivated also to cross the Atlantic because they learned by word of mouth about the land where, it was said, "all men are created equal," we shall never know.

6

Third Echo
European Revolutions of 1848

Writing from Europe where he was serving as minister to England in early March 1848, George Bancroft, the historian-diplomat, observed, "Our republic is teaching Europe to do the same. Of the six great civilised States, two now are republics: and more will follow."[1] Two weeks later, on the eve of the European revolutions of 1848, he wrote: "Has the echo of American Democracy which you now hear from France, and Austria, and Prussia and all Old Germany, no power to stir up the hearts of the American people to new achievements?"[2] The third "echo" of American constitutionalism abroad, the European revolutions of 1848, turned out to be loud, indeed.

The causes of these spontaneous upheavals in so many parts of central and eastern Europe, occurring within so brief a period of time and covering so vast an area, have long mystified scholars. One revolution began in Sicily on January 12 and spread to Naples where the king, under pressure, granted a constitution. A month and a half later, France drove King Louis-Philippe from his throne, to be followed by an uprising in Vienna eleven days later that sent Metternich into exile. Two other revolutions followed in quick succession: in Berlin on March 18 and in Madrid on March 24. The Romans rebelled against the papal government in November. Eastern Europe experienced serious disorders when nationalist movements broke out in Bohemia and Moravia and threatened to fragment the Austrian empire. Only Russia and England seemed immune, although Chartists held mass demonstrations in London during the spring of 1848. In all, almost fifty constitutional crises occurred during the first four months of 1848 alone.

Initially, the movements showed great promise for the widespread expansion of civil rights, and most had substantially similar goals. They clamored for more constitutional government, some limited form of representation, the unification and independence of ethnic groups, and an end to serfdom in many regions. Their aims, it seems, rose almost totally out of indigenous circumstances.

American constitutional ideas, nevertheless, were discussed almost everywhere, indicating that the American Dream persisted. The U.S. Constitution sometimes served as a model of government for regions aspiring to nationhood or desiring republican governments with more liberalism and individual rights. At other times, America provided an example for constitutionalists seeking to redress authoritarianism and to find solutions to specific problems of governance. In many instances, however, America was a major source of suggestions for "functional equivalents," that is, republican institutions that might perform functions similar to those already in use in a monarchical setting but being considered for replacement. The ruler, for example, might be a republican replacement with an image as close to a constitutional monarch as possible.[3]

Most historians agree that the revolutions of 1848 reflected three familiar "isms": industrialism, liberalism, and nationalism. By 1848 industrialism had become increasingly important in western Europe and had turned into a cause of discontent among workers who suffered from poor conditions or unemployment. Liberalism in the nineteenth century placed a high value on individual liberty, and parliamentary government sometimes offered constitutional monarchy as the best way of attaining it. Generally speaking, European liberals opposed universal suffrage, however, fearing the excesses of mob rule or revolutionary behavior. Nationalism also played a powerful role as various ethnic groups sought self-determination within existing multiethnic empires. This situation was particularly true in the far-flung Austro-Hungarian Empire.

The 1848 revolutions also followed some similar political patterns. They often began as uprisings led by artisans, professional people, students, or liberal groups rather than seasoned politicians. They usually promised bills of rights, some form of limited government, or outright constitutional reforms. But as the revolutions progressed, they sometimes pressured existing regimes into more radical changes. In the final stage, however, the conservative prerevolutionary regimes succeeded in pacifying the revolutionaries by exploiting their internal differences. They did so by playing on the fears of the middle class regarding future social disorders by the lower classes. Eventually the conservative forces managed to put down the revolutionaries with a series of strong military counterrevolutionary movements. By the end of 1848, the revolutionaries were in full retreat everywhere, and conservative forces had reasserted most of their previous control.[4]

The revolutionaries emerged disillusioned from their unsuccessful attempts and felt that nothing of consequence had been accomplished. In fact, in many countries the political situation seemed even worse than before. Constitutions that had been granted were repealed, suspended, or rendered ineffectual. Revolutionary leaders were killed, imprisoned, or exiled. Conservative forces seemed even more firmly in control than before.

Nonetheless, despite the so-called failure of the revolutions, they succeeded in achieving some gains and establishing constitutional goals that remained long after the movements were put down. In France, universal manhood suffrage became a permanent feature. In central Europe, the manorial system was largely abolished, even though the change was granted by conservative regimes under duress rather than by direct action by the revolutionaries. In Prussia, the king established a parliament, but with very limited power. In central and western Europe, the revolutions brought to an end the long period during which conservatives had been rigid, and liberals and middle-class reformers, passive.

For those Americans living in Europe during the revolutions, expectations remained high. To them, the United States still represented the spearhead of a worldwide republican movement. As George Bancroft wrote in the spring of 1848: "Revolutions succeed each other rapidly in Europe. The American Republic is an inspiring example of which the influence has long been preparing radical changes in every government."[5]

American constitutionalism played several key roles in these new constitutions. One was to offer models for American constitutional institutions that were adopted or to serve as catalysts for constitutional changes.[6] A second was to provide functional equivalents to replace already existing institutions under the monarchies. And a third was to serve as an inspiration for European constitutional reformers.

Most European constitutions differed greatly, however, from the U.S. Constitution in one important respect. In the Old World, most constitutions were *octroyed*; that is, the constitution was conceded from above. It was considered a condescension or grant of power by the king or prince to his subjects. The U.S. Constitution, by contrast, had been written, ratified, and recognized as an instrument of government by a sovereign people. It was this radical position—that the right of government was inherent in the people—that most forcibly inspired the hopes of 1848 revolutionaries.

The fact that the 1848 revolutions were composed of mostly common people—ordinary individuals from "the bottom up"—as well as constitutionalists could be seen in a significant episode in the life of a German immigrant, Carl Schurz. He recalled when he was a boy in the 1840s how the United States was described in his small village as a "young republic" in which people were "free" in a land "without kings, . . . without military service," and "without taxes." This glowing image, though not always accurate in its details, was essentially constitutional in nature. Schurz became a leader in the revolutionary movement, was compelled to flee the region, and migrated to the United States where he rose to become member of President Rutherford B. Hayes's cabinet. Millions of lowly European immigrants were motivated to move to the United States by the same rosy but somewhat unrealistic picture of America.[7]

France

In France, American constitutionalism exerted some influence on the constitution of 1848 largely through the efforts of Tocqueville. With his reputation established, he was in a position to put his grasp of American constitutionalism to good use. After being elected to the Chamber of Deputies, he became a member of the Constitutional Commission and suggested changes based on American examples.

An astute observer, Tocqueville summed up the sources of economic discontent in a perceptive speech he gave in the Chamber of Deputies on the eve of the uprising in Paris in January 1848:

See what is passing in the breasts of the working classes—who, I grant, are at present quiet. No doubt, they are not disturbed by political passion . . . to the same extent they have been, but can you not see their passions, instead of political, have become social? Do you not see that there are gradually forming in their breasts opinions and ideas that are destined to upset not only this or that ministry law or form of government, but society itself, until it totters upon the foundations on which it rests today? Do you not hear them repeating unceasingly that all that is above them is unworthy and uncapable[*sic*]; that the present distribution of goods throughout the world is unjust; that property rests on a foundation that is not equitable? And do you not realize that when such opinions take root, when they spread in an almost universal manner, when they sink deeply into the masses, they are bound to bring sooner or later, I know not how or when, a most formidable revolution?[8]

The establishment—King Louis-Philippe, his chief minister François Guizot, and the entrenched bourgeois bureaucracy—failed to see what Tocqueville saw or hear what he heard. As he predicted, France commenced its revolution the very next month. During the "Bloody June Days," class warfare raged in Paris. Louis-Philippe abdicated, fled to England, and a provisional government was formed. The new government called for a general election, universal manhood suffrage, and a republican constitution to replace the monarchy.

One of the first acts of the constituent assembly was to adopt universal male suffrage. Although proclaimed earlier in French history in 1793, it was in 1848 that it was actually put into effect. For the first time in French history, there was an election of a sovereign constituent assembly. There can be no doubt that the living example of the United States had had a profound effect.

The same constituent assembly framed the Constitution of 1848 of the Second Republic. Although its life was brief, the Second Republic ended Louis-Philippe's reign. Moderate political reforms were adopted, but the government's obligation to provide work for the unemployed was repudiated. A separate declaration of the rights and duties of the citizen was proposed but eventually voted down. Frightened by the demands of the working-class movement and their national workshops, the conservative constituent assembly fell far short of the declaration of rights contained in the Jacobin Constitution of 1793.[9] Instead, a short preamble declared that the general principles of the new constitution and the document itself provided a basic list of rights guaranteed to citizens.

In the National Assembly, Tocqueville proposed important changes based on the examples in his book. The two features of the U.S. Constitution that appealed to him most were the idea of a two-house legislature and the indirect election of the president.[10] His task was difficult, however, because delegates in the Assembly were deeply divided.

Tocqueville fought hard for a bicameral legislature, basing his arguments on America's prior experience. The United States, he noted, had started out with a unicameral legislature under the Articles of Confederation, and in 1787, the Americans then turned to the practice of bicameralism. "There is doubtless a host of institutions there which could not be transported to France, but as for the two chambers, the arguments are the same in the two countries."[11]

Tocqueville's suggestion gained some support: of the fourteen members who gave speeches, six referred to the U.S. situation. But the majority still opposed Tocqueville's proposal, suspicious that a second chamber might become a refuge for an aristocracy. Despite his efforts to demonstrate that the Americans had successfully established an upper house without its becoming an aristocratic institution, Tocqueville's idea was dropped.[12]

The most significant borrowing from the U.S. Constitution involved the French presidency.[13] In the 1848 French Constitution, executive power was to be largely concentrated in the president's hands. His powers, according to one scholar, were often "described in terms strongly reminiscent of the words of the U.S. Constitution."[14] He was to serve a four-year term and be native-born, like the American president. He could appoint and dismiss his cabinet, hold a suspensive veto over legislation, and be commander in chief of the armed forces. Some of these features presumably were derived from the American example, but in the end the French Constitution turned instead into a hybrid, semipresidential system.[15]

Once again Tocqueville played an important role in bringing American ideas into the deliberations. When the issue of electing the president came up, several members of the Constitutional Commission proposed elections by universal male suffrage. Tocqueville introduced instead a counterproposal: an electoral college created somewhat along American lines. Warning about the possible dangers of a president chosen by a minority and the inadequacy of the current system in France (i.e., nomination by the assembly of several candidates for popular election), he proposed instead an American remedy.

> I would like something analogous to what takes place in America. There every state names a certain number of delegates, who, to avoid intrigues, plots, and violence, do not meet together. There are as many electoral colleges as states. Each of these states meets the same day to name the President.[16]

The device was not new, he confessed. "I had borrowed [it] from the American Constitution."[17]

The reason why Tocqueville wanted an electoral college rather than election by the parliament seems clear. To him, the choice in a republican form of government was between "government by convention" (i.e., the assembly exercising the powers of the executive through delegates) or "presidential government." At the time, the term *parliamentary republic* still was equated with the convention. To Tocqueville, because of the separation of powers, a republican government meant the same as an executive elected by the people. But despite his advocacy for the idea, Tocqueville's proposal was not accepted.[18]

Another idea Tocqueville admitted borrowing from the U.S. Constitution was the procedure for picking a president if there was no absolute majority. If no candidate had a sufficient number of votes, the choice was to be among the leading five candidates proposed by the National Assembly.[19] This time the Assembly went along with his suggestion, and it was incorporated in the 1848 constitution.

Tocqueville felt strongly also that the French president should not be eligible for immediate reelection. The main goal of most American presidents, Tocqueville noted, was to get themselves reelected.[20] When he proposed that the French president be ineligible for reelection, therefore, it was a clear case of negative influence based on his reaction to the U.S. Constitution.[21] When Tocqueville's proposal was made part of the 1848 constitution, however, he failed to realize he had unwittingly contributed to the collapse of the Second Republic by not foreseeing that Louis-Napoléon Bonaparte would be elected, overthrow the republic in 1851, and secure his reelection despite the specific constitutional prohibition. Admitting his mistake later, Tocqueville confessed that his part in proposing the noneligibility of the president for immediate reelection had been an error.[22]

In the French constituent constitutional assembly of 1848 the American presidential idea never did become very popular. Whenever the French discussed constitutional possibilities, they tended to focus on their own experiences, particularly on the various charters drawn up during the French revolutionary era. In this regard, the Gironde Constitution had the greatest influence.[23] During the proceedings in the Assembly, moreover, practical politics sometimes played a greater role than ideology did. When the chairman of the constitutional committee of the Assembly outlined the various alternatives for a republican executive, he was not thinking primarily of the American example. After the decision had been made to elect a president, he decided to advocate direct election to the office. He did so not on the grounds of ideology but to achieve a compromise between two leading political factions.[24]

Just how great, then, was the direct influence of the U.S. Constitution on the framing of the 1848 French Constitution? Although the scholar who made the most intensive study of the subject deemed the influence "slight," he also described the constitution as an "American-Anglo-French piece of work."[25] A comparison of the two documents suggests many parallels between the eighteen French articles and the corresponding provisions in the American document.[26] A review of the work of the Constitutional Commission and the debates in the National Assembly shows that the U.S. Constitution remained high as a source of inspiration. One feature, its republicanism, drew special praise. One member of the Assembly said about the proposed preamble to the French Constitution: "The constitution of the Americans is more modern, it is perfectly republican . . . made by a people which has very republican manners, which has lasted over sixty years, and which has to its account long duration and a very great prosperity."[27] Quite obviously, the speaker was still speaking of America as a republic, whereas most of his colleagues viewed it as a representative democracy.

The influence of American constitutionalism as a whole was evident in other ways. The election of a constitutional assembly to write the constitution, for example, followed the American practice. Universal male suffrage also followed the American example, though France had developed its own tradition. And the effort to frame a bill of rights reflected the British–American as well as the French tradition.

Richard Rush, the American minister, believing that American-style federalism would fulfill French needs, took it upon himself to circulate *The Federalist Papers*. The copy he sent to the French economist Michel Chevalier was promptly publicized in the French press.[28] The Assembly, however, favored a highly centralized government, and the document had no great effect on their deliberations.

The Constitution of the Second Republic drew a mixed reaction from American diplomats living in Europe. Some were enthusiastic about the rhetoric regarding republican ideals that both countries espoused. In his position as minister to Paris, Richard Rush recognized the government of the Second Republic even before receiving official authorization from Washington. Later, during the February Revolution, he addressed the provisional government while crowds outside chanted, "Vive la République des États-Unis!" His bold moves were subsequently approved by President James Polk.[29] George Bancroft, however, was cool to the idea of the French emulating the U.S. Constitution: "A constitution should be the representation of national character," he observed in the spring of 1848, "To translate ours into French is not enough."[30] The French apparently felt much as Bancroft did.

Germany

In Germany, too, republicanism began gaining more support among the people. During the peasant revolts in southwest Germany in 1847/1848, a leaflet appeared calling for a change in government: "[We want a] state whose business is conducted by a parliament elected by us and by its president; we want *a republic like that in America.*" The author of the leaflet went on: "To those who say in a republic all laws and all order cease to exist, we will say: just stretch your nose in the direction of America; there a republic has existed for almost one hundred years with no disorder. *We want a republic and nothing else.*"[31]

In the Prussian capital of Berlin, the most important city in the Germanies after Vienna, antiestablishment forces erected barricades in the streets in protest. Every state of any consequence in the German Confederation experienced a revolution or some drastic political change in the spring of 1848. The ominous rumblings of revolution created a new urgency for leaders to face the task of unification and political change.

During this time of pending change, Germany seemed influenced more by American constitutionalism than even France. German unification appeared a distinct possibility, and America's earlier experience seemed useful. Copies of the U.S. Constitution were available not only to politicians but also to the man in the street. For example, a German professor from Frankfurt writing to a congressman in Washington reported: "The American name . . . never stood higher, everywhere are works and pamphlets in bookstores and on center tables in our Institutions, and almost every orator points to them as a glorious example."[32]

There even were official requests from Germany for help in coping with constitutional problems. Andrew Donelson, the American minister in Berlin, received letters from two government bureaucrats asking for copies of the Constitution. In Washington, the minister from Prussia wrote to John C. Calhoun, author of the idea of concurrent majorities, for suggestions regarding the proposed constitution for a united Germany.[33] Once the 1848 constitution had been formulated, Calhoun, a formidable constitutional theorist, criticized it, commenting especially on the far-reaching powers given to the central authorities. The proposed plan would result in one of two outcomes, he predicted. The central government might eventually absorb all the powers originally given to the member states, or a civil war might break out when subordinate member states resisted the trend toward greater centralization.

Calhoun's perspective, it should be remembered, was predicated on the strong states' rights position he adopted in the sectional controversy in the United States.[34] American influence was present, therefore, both before and after as well as during the discussions of the proposed new German constitution.

Responding to the growing demands of the populace, a Constitutional Assembly seeking a unified German state met in Frankfurt in the Church of St. Paul in May. The first order of business was deciding which territories should be included in the proposed future Germany, and the question sharply divided the delegates. Some wanted to exclude delegates from the larger states, particularly Prussia, because they would dominate. National sentiment prevailed, however, and the large states were admitted.

The second issue was federalism: how to divide power between the proposed central government and the states. Although it was at this point that American constitutionalism played its most important role in the discussions, the American model could not be adopted, for reasons discussed later. The Constitution Assembly, however, did adopt other key features of the U.S. Constitution. The new bicameral federal legislature was to consist of a lower house elected by universal male suffrage and an upper house chosen by the legislatures of the constituent states. Strong powers granted to the central government drew heavily on unitary features of the U.S. document. Although the federal structure of government did not strictly follow the American model, its influence was unmistakable, one example being the principle of reserved powers retained by the German states.[35] While the matter of individual rights was being considered, the U.S. Constitution again served as a point of reference. The proposed constitution listed fifty articles of fundamental rights, all very liberal. Among its provisions were equality before the law, abrogation of class privileges, freedom of religion, and freedom from censorship and arbitrary arrest.[36] These rights, however, were not to become effective until individual German states chose to accept them as law.

Another issue was the method of choosing an executive. Although delegates traveled to Berlin to offer the imperial crown to the king of Prussia, he refused them. In a private letter, he explained that the 1848 constitution had incorporated too much popular sovereignty, and he would not put on "the dog collar," making him "a serf of the revolution of 1848."[37] In the process of drawing up their plans for a federalized central government, members of the Assembly then considered the merits of the American presidency.

Although political discourse in the Frankfurt Assembly featured the U.S. Constitution, the delegates often used it to argue by analogy. "They defended an article by saying it resembled the American model and attacked it by saying it resembled the confederation of the Empire," according to one authority. Two leading studies agree, nevertheless, that the American influence was much greater than either the British or French traditions.[38]

German constitutionalists had earlier been attracted more by the British model of government. But in Frankfurt scarcely a day went by without some reference being made to American constitutionalism. One reason was the familiarity of the delegates with American ideas after reading Mohl, Tocqueville, and American jurists like Joseph Story and James Kent. As one recent German scholar put it, "Most of the leaders of the moderate liberal majority of the Frankfurt Parliament took it for granted that the transformation of Germany into a national state under a federal constitution would more or less have to follow along the lines of the American model."[39]

Mohl, who played a significant part in the proceedings of the St. Paul Assembly, had prepared much of the groundwork with his writings. In his great pioneering work, *Das Bundes-Staatsrecht der Vereinigten Staaten von Nord Amerika* (1824), Mohl had accurately described the relationship of the American federal government and the states.[40] The *Bundestaat*— the American form of union—he pointed out, was not just a treaty or defensive alliance among states that remained independent but was formally a union and fully a single state. Although he drew attention to the widespread distrust of a too-powerful central government in America in 1787, he favored the establishment of a unitary government for Germany. Indeed, his position was quite close to that advocated by Alexander Hamilton. Mohl portrayed the government under the U.S. Constitution as a representative democracy but at the same time expressed his fears of mob rule.[41] Nevertheless, his admiration of the American federal system was great. In a critique of Joseph Story's *Commentaries* in 1837, he had credited the Constitution's federalism with enabling America to achieve its great success.[42] According to his analysis of the nature of the American federal union, Mohl enabled his compatriots to see what distinguished the situation in Germany's independent monarchical principalities from America's government.

Karl Theodor Welcker, one of the leaders in the Baden Diet, was another important member of the Assembly. In a motion in the Diet in 1831, he had called for a national representative body to be established at the federal level, believing that the main criterion for any federal union was that it should represent *all* the German people. His proposal at the time seemed too radical, but after his idea had been voiced publicly, it became so popular that it was debated in the German parliament. In the St. Paul Assembly, therefore, it could not be ignored. Welcker argued also that the federal form of government was most appropriate for large countries, and that of all the federal constitutions in the world, he regarded the American to be the best.[43]

Welcker, along with his Baden colleague Karl von Rotteck, published a famous political dictionary, *Das Staats Lexikon*, about this time.[44] It contained essays on the U.S. Constitution that were widely read and discussed. One, by Friedrich Murhard of Hess, characterized the document as being both federal and national, in much the same way as James Madison described it, but although Murhard emphasized the democratic tendencies inherent in America, he despaired of ever transplanting the American model to Germany. The U.S. Constitution, he observed, had been framed under particularly favorable circumstances. Germany, for example, had not had the long tradition of self-government that America had had. The powerful position of entrenched princes, moreover, made the creation of a national government like America's highly unlikely.[45]

Friedrich von Raumer, a liberal Berlin historian, had high praise for America in his two-volume work published in 1845. He wrote that one had to look "not only to Europe" to learn "the probable future of humanity" but also to the workings of the national, state, and local governments in America. "In no other country in the world," he concluded, "is there so little rule from above and so much left to the people to determine." Raumer was particularly attracted to the American federal system as a check against the centralizing tendencies of democracy and as the kind of government in which the separate states of Germany could be unified.[46]

One of the key speeches leading to the calling of the Frankfurt Assembly was by Friedrich Daniel Bassermann. He reintroduced in the Baden Diet the motion originally proposed by Welcker. Tracing the process by which the Articles of Confederation had been replaced by the Constitution, Bassermann pointed to the analogies between the two countries:

> Are there not many points of comparison with our own conditions and needs to be found in the history of that country? There are almost as many states united in America as the states of a united Germany would

number and the purpose of federation is in both cases identical, namely, the upholding of the interests and the dignity of a great nation.

Bassermann's motion, one member cried out, would mark "an epoch in German history."[47]

Despite numerous references to the U.S. Constitution, understanding of the document was sometimes inaccurate. The Germans often failed to see the close interrelationship of the federal, republican, and democratic principles at work in America. By altering one set of principles, they failed to realize what impact it would have on the others. Generally speaking, the German constitutionalists tended to overemphasize the role of national authority in the American situation. They often underestimated also the impact of America's democratic way of life on its internal political processes. Some delegates mistakenly believed the American model could easily be transplanted in Germany by merely making a few substantive changes in the text, without realizing that significant structural changes were called for.[48]

Most delegates found the U.S. Constitution too radical for their taste. Early in the proceedings of the Frankfurt Assembly, Gustav von Struve, a radical, attempted to introduce a revolutionary program. He demanded the abolition of a hereditary monarch and proposed instead the establishment of an elected president. At the same time, he called for a federal constitution "after the model of the North American republics." His proposal fell on deaf ears.[49]

Although they rejected this call for an elected president, the members of the Assembly did discuss the American presidential model. Presidentialism, of course, had to be considered within the framework of a federation of monarchies rather than a republican form of government. The idea, nevertheless, enjoyed some support. The plan to establish a possible directory of three princes, which was also discussed, would have been only partly republican in nature, at best, and would have employed only certain specific features of the American presidential system. Moreover, it would have destroyed the unity of the executive branch, which was considered one of the strongest characteristics of the American system.[50] One rare amendment favoring an American-style executive, introduced toward the end of the proceedings, called for a president and vice president to be elected for a four-year term. The amendment would also have allowed any German citizen to stand for election for both offices. But the proposal was too radical to be seriously entertained, and the idea of a hereditary emperor was finally adopted instead.[51] The outcome was that the American presidential system as a whole was not accepted in Germany, and the framers of the 1848 draft constitution settled instead on a semipresidential hybrid solution.

As might be expected, the U.S. Constitution played its most important part in the proceedings when federalism was discussed. American-style federalism obviously appealed to the members because they faced problems similar to the Americans in 1787. They, too, were trying to frame a constitution to govern a region with different variables: a heterogeneous population, diverse cultural groups, different religions, and areas with conflicting political, economic, and geographic interests.

The recording secretary of the constitutional committee observed that "he who is concerned with the true form of a federal state will gladly look at the United States." His reason was that America had best solved the problem of "how to harmonize the power of the central government with the fullest beneficial development of the several states." Referring to the writings of Jefferson, Story, Kent, and other American constitutionalists, he noted how admirably they had described the U.S. Constitution.[52] But he ended on a note of caution. Blind admiration, he wrote, should not lead to simple imitation. Outright emulation would prove dangerous because existing circumstances were so different.[53]

One great difference was Germany's location in the middle of the European heartland surrounded by potentially hostile neighbors. National security was therefore of the greatest concern among those favoring a highly centralized government:

> We regard a strong, rigid, and indivisible union as being absolutely necessary. We find the essential reason for this not only in the fact that Germany is surrounded by powerful neighbors with unitary constitutions with whom it is in close contact and with whom it could find itself involved in large-scale conflicts at virtually any time. . . . [T]his would . . . require the unification of all its forces in a single hand—a consideration which is of much less moment in the case of the United States . . . on account of that federal state's more isolated position.[54]

A second problem was equally crucial: Germany was a federation of monarchies, whereas America's federated states were republican. Federalism functioned better in a liberal republic in which there was greater equality among member states. By its very nature, republicanism was more hospitable to the political give-and-take inherent in federalism.[55] Obviously, American-style federalism could not be transplanted unchanged. Therefore, despite numerous references to the U.S. model, the Frankfurt constitution failed to incorporate many of these features.

The Frankfurt constitution provided also for a supreme court, the Reichsgericht, modeled somewhat along the lines of the U.S. Supreme Court and providing for judicial review. The American style of judicial review was entertained seriously. During the discussions, one authority reported, "In no other single question was the USA so frequently brought into the debate."[56] Despite disagreements arising from the fear that the princes in a federated Germany might change the institution into a device to protect their own positions, proponents kept pressing for a supreme court with powers of judicial review. The most persuasive speech was given by Professor C. J. A. Mittermaier of Heidelberg, who was convinced that the court was the cornerstone without which the constitution could not stand or continue to function. "What is considered the finest ornament of the American Constitution?" he asked rhetorically then answered, "The Supreme Court." "The Constitution owes its life, its strength, the certainty of its provisions in detail to the Supreme Court." Concluding his remarks, Mittermaier urged: "Let us follow the example of the United States and we'll earn the most marvelous fruit. Give us this keystone for our constitution . . . a keystone which guarantees freedom, and one that gives every individual citizen the possibility of securing justice . . . and which will make possible the German unity."[57]

What emerged from the discussions instead was the Imperial Constitutional Court (Reichsgericht), the first specialized constitutional court in Europe. A genuinely special court, it possessed the right to challenge the constitutionality of laws and to provide enforcement of rights. The rights listed were indebted in large part to the Belgian Constitution of 1831, which, in turn, was based mainly on French, American, and British precedents. There was, however, one crucial difference: the French and Americans had referred to the rights of humankind, whereas the German document focused just on the rights of the German people.

The powers of the Imperial Court were broad, indeed, because all other imperial institutions were subject to its jurisdiction. American observers were most impressed by it. George Bancroft, the American historian now serving as envoy in London, was reported to have said: "It is a great improvement on our own [Supreme Court], the best thing in the world."[58]

Two key articles in the Frankfurt constitution were actually borrowed almost word for word from the U.S. Constitution. One gave the monopoly on foreign relations to the proposed German union. Given the power of Prussia, this issue was of paramount importance. It also indicated the desire of Assembly members to create a new Germany that would not permanently exclude fellow Germans living in Austria and other parts of the Hapsburg empire.[59] The other article provided for direct election of members to the Reichstag.

The Frankfurt Constitution also borrowed one of the most radical ideas in the U.S. Constitution, the separation of church and state. There is little doubt that this feature, of which America was the world's leading exemplar, influenced German constitution makers. The 1848 constitution specifically guaranteed the freedom of religion as in the United States, but it could do so because there was no national church in either country.[60]

The attempt to establish a new German federal state failed, however, and the Frankfurt Constitution was stillborn. Although the delegates waved the banner of popular sovereignty to arouse favorable sentiment among the people for purposes of national unity, they remained loyal to the monarchical principle. A new imperial constitution was promulgated instead. Nevertheless, the strengths and weaknesses of the Frankfurt Constitution are still debated by scholars. According to one, "It remains the most impressive to political scientists, the most disappointing to political idealists, and the most ludicrous to political opportunists of all still-born constitutions."[61]

The ideas entertained in the Frankfurt Assembly in 1848 marked a significant advance in the "fundamental rights" of the German people as they sought protection from abuses by princes and bureaucrats. The right of *habeas corpus* was asserted, as was equality before the law. Certain freedoms familiar to Americans were openly discussed, such as freedom of association, assembly, the press, scholarly teaching, and publication. With the dissolution of the Frankfurt Assembly, however, such ideas went by the board for the time being.[62]

Even though it was not adopted, the document was destined to have a great effect on Germany's subsequent constitutional history. Its ideas on federalism and judicial review came up later in the discussions of the 1871 constitution, the 1919 Weimar Constitution, and the 1949 Basic Law. Like many other so-called failures of the 1848 revolutions, Germany's was to have great influence in the subsequent history of Europe.

Switzerland

The powerful forces of particularism in Switzerland proved too strong to overcome, and a civil war erupted in 1847 called the Sonderbundskrieg. The brief conflict was between several hostile factions: Catholics and Protestants, Unitarians and Federalists, and liberals and conservatives. One result was the breakdown of resistance to constitutional reform. While preparing for war, the federal Diet actually voted to appoint a committee to revise the constitution.

The Swiss Constitution, which went into effect on September 12, 1848, was quite consciously patterned after the U.S. Constitution in two important respects. It adapted American-style federalism to Switzerland's needs, and it adopted a bicameral government. One of the most derivative constitutions in Europe, the Swiss Constitution also borrowed ideas from Belgium and France.[63] Switzerland thereby went from being a confederated to a federal state, just as the United States had done in 1787. The country, of course, had developed a federal tradition of its own over a long period of time. When making its transition, the Swiss operated under the assumption that the Americans had invented federalism.[64] Acting on that basis, supreme power was granted to the central government in certain areas, while the cantonal governments retained power in others.

There were significant differences, however, in the way the Swiss adapted the American idea. The express powers of the central authority in Switzerland were listed with watchlike precision, leaving little room for America's practice of implied powers. All the residual powers not expressly granted to the central government remained in the hands of the cantonal authorities and were based on the democratic authority of local assemblies.[65] Yet the central government was given more power to intervene in cantonal matters than was ever the case in America. In the event of internal disturbances or a threat of foreign intervention, the federal government could step in at any time without any request from cantonal authorities. There was, moreover, no supreme court to check the federal government if it did exceed its authority.

Switzerland, nevertheless, did adopt a two-house legislature, emulating the American model, a solution that preserved the rights of the cantons while at the same time provided for national unity.[66] For the second time in Swiss history, the idea of unicameralism was dropped. In the Council of States—comparable to the U.S. Senate—each canton had two votes.

A National Council—resembling the U.S. House of Representatives—was elected by the people at large. Once again, however, there was a significant difference: the Council of States never acquired the authority exercised by the American Senate.

Despite many seeming similarities between the two constitutions, there were other differences. The executive branch, for example, consisted of a completely new creation, the federal executive council, which differed considerably from both the American presidential system and Britain's parliamentary executive. Distrustful of centralized executive power that might be manipulated by a strong individual or group, the Swiss instead created a federal executive council.[67] They also deliberately rejected the American idea of presidentialism with the comment that "the institution [was] contrary to the ideas and habits of Switzerland. It might appear to be a step on the road to monarchy or dictatorship."[68] Despite these significant differences, two leading authorities on Swiss constitutional history agreed: the connection between the Swiss and American constitutions was quite close.[69]

To what degree can one prove that American constitutionalism was responsible for such changes? The answer is less clear than one might expect, as the specific role played by American precedents is difficult to determine. The committee writing the constitution met in private and adopted a rule that names of individuals would not be entered in the minutes. The anonymous nature of the records thereby makes it difficult to attribute provisions to specific persons. American examples, moreover, were rarely identified. At one point, mention was made that the United States had used the bicameral system successfully for more than sixty years. The committee members recorded drily that this example "allows us *a fortiori* to hope that it will also prove suitable to our country."[70]

One great obstacle that the American idea of bicameralism had to overcome was xenophobia. While the constitution was being written, the renowned Dr. Johann Jakob Rüttimann published a series of articles in the *Neue Zürcher Zeitung* supporting bicameralism. Other newspapers charged that bicameralism was being copied from the U.S. Constitution and was therefore a "foreign product to be scorned."[71] But practical politics rather than ideological considerations carried the day. The Swiss adopted bicameral federalism as a political compromise, thus satisfying enough cantons to make the reform possible.

The historian William Rappard described the political reaction to xenophobia in a homely analogy:

The Swiss people did not welcome the American gift with the enthusiastic alacrity with which a child snatches an attractive toy from the hands of its parents. Their attitude was rather that of an infant most reluctantly swallowing a strange and unsavory medicine . . . to find relief . . . in familiar household remedies.[72]

One other consideration motivated the Swiss to move quickly in making their constitutional reforms. In 1848 the great powers of Europe were temporarily distracted by the ongoing revolutionary movements, but who was to say that they might not intervene again if a constitutional compromise in Switzerland were not reached immediately?[73]

The most striking development once the constitution was ratified was the rapidity with which it was institutionalized. Having adapted some American principles of federalism and bicameralism, the Swiss never looked back to earlier constitutional formulations. Switzerland's conversion to the so-called American system was complete, and it remains one of the best examples of institutional borrowing from American constitutionalism in the entire nineteenth century.

Decades later, the Swiss repaid their debt to the "American system" with the so-called Swiss example. During the 1880s and 1890s, American reformers, casting about for ways to fight for a more democratic government against the interests of political bosses and big business, learned of the Swiss use of two government mechanisms, the initiative and the referendum. Scholars were sent to Switzerland to study these constitutional stratagems that permitted a more direct expression of the popular will. By 1912, eighteen state governments had adopted one or both of these devices and incorporated them into their constitutions.[74] Constitutional ideas continued their two-way flow across the Atlantic as they had done since 1787.

Hungary

The Hungarian revolution in 1848 is linked in the minds of most Americans with the name of Louis Kossuth. A revolutionary passionate about the cause of Hungarian independence, Kossuth, after a brief career as a lawyer and journalist, was elected to the Diet in 1847. A spell-binding orator, he assumed the leadership of the radical faction, arguing that political and social reforms were immediately necessary. News of the February revolution in France gave Kossuth his opening, which he exploited brilliantly.

In a dazzling speech on March 3, which one scholar called "the inaugural address of the Revolution," Kossuth demanded an end to Austria's absolutism and the restoration of Hungary's ancient constitution. This was the only way to safeguard the liberties of Hungary and the freedom of its people from monarchy. When helping draft Hungary's Declaration of Independence, Kossuth modeled it in part on the American document and submitted it to the National Assembly on April 19.[75] In the document, Hungary declared itself a free and sovereign state, citing the "unalienable rights" of its people.[76] Kossuth sought to show the relevance of the revolutionary upheavals of 1848 to the American Revolution of 1776.[77] Kossuth's speeches referred to the Declaration of Independence as "that noblest, happiest page of mankind."[78]

Like its American counterpart, Hungary's declaration was aimed mainly at the European powers in hopes of securing military aid or gaining recognition. Unlike the American document, however, the Hungarian declaration lacked any theoretical justification for revolution. It simply listed Hungary's assumed rights and its grievances against Austria. Written by lawyer-politicians for fellow professionals, the document had little broad appeal to the common people. It was less liberal in tone and in keeping with the backward nature of Hungary's political and economic institutions.[79]

When the new government was formed, Kossuth was named minister of finance, and in July 1848 he called on the Hungarian nation, with the Croatian army, to take up arms against the Austrians. In the spring of 1849, Kossuth was named governor-president and became the virtual dictator of the newly declared Hungarian republic. He seems to have visualized his role to be that of an American president and gradually assumed many similar presidential prerogatives.[80]

When Russian armies entered the savage civil war waged by several factions, Kossuth clearly faced defeat. Although he kept fighting, despite overwhelming odds, in the summer of 1849 he was forced to flee into exile in Turkey. Efforts by the American government to rescue him by extradition from Turkey made Kossuth world famous as a symbol of the struggle of liberty against tyranny. He came to the United States and traveled throughout the country for a year and a half in 1851 and 1852. Barnstorming in a tumultuous tour dubbed the "Kossuth craze," he raised hysteria, but few funds, for his cause.[81]

Disappointed, Kossuth returned to Europe empty-handed and brokenhearted. Over the next decade and a half, he spent time plotting a second revolution, but his hopes were blasted by the compromise of 1867, which made Hungary a separate kingdom and raised it to equal status with Austria. Kossuth remained in exile for the rest of his days, his name linked forever to two lost causes: Hungarian independence and civil rights.[82]

Hungary's revolution provides a good example of the way that the United States promoted American constitutionalism by encouraging movements for republicanism. America's enthusiasm for European republicanism was shown unofficially in the mass demonstrations held on Kossuth's behalf. A popular "Young America" movement sprang up in the United States, identifying itself with all European revolutions in 1848. Most of its members were Democrats, led by George Sanders of Kentucky, who formulated a vague program in 1852 to aid republican movements throughout the continent.[83] The program was clearly in violation of the Monroe Doctrine.

In regard to the official government response, the Hungarian revolution led to a near rupture in diplomatic relations between Austria and the United States. When Kossuth proclaimed the new Hungarian regime, he requested recognition from the United States. In June 1849, Ambrose Dudley Mann was sent as a "special and confidential agent" on a secret mission to give the Hungarian leader discreet assurances of American recognition. Mann, however, never reached Budapest because by mid-August the Hungarians had laid down their arms in defeat.

Both the Mann mission and the Kossuth asylum were, at bottom, constitutional issues. To the American government, the Hungarian revolution was part of the worldwide fight between republicanism and monarchy. Charles McCurdy, an American diplomat in Vienna, summed up the situation: "There must be a great struggle between force and opinion [i.e., between absolutism and constitutionalism], and even indirect influence of our country may not be a matter of indifference."[84]

The Austrian government, however, was firmly on the side of absolutism. It lodged a protest against America's partisan involvement, and through its chargé d'affaires, Georg Hulsemann, complained to three successive secretaries of state about America's diplomatic "improprieties." First there had been the Mann mission. Then had come the popular enthusiasm shown to Kossuth at American rallies. The crowning blow came when Daniel Webster, the current secretary of state, gave a speech at a public banquet in honor of Kossuth. Webster raised his glass and gave a ringing toast to "Hungarian independence." Webster's conduct, Hulsemann complained, violated the "most common international courtesy."[85]

Webster was arrogant in his response. One historian called his reply "one of the most sensational documents ever authored by an American secretary of state."[86] First, Webster defended America's right to take an interest in the revolutions in Europe, which he said "appeared to have their origins in those great ideas of responsible and popular governments, on which the American Constitutions themselves were wholly founded . . . [and] could not but command the warm sympathy of the People of this country."[87] Then, in a burst of nationalism, he heaped scorn on Austria by making an invidious comparison: "The power of this Republic, at the present time spread over a region, one of the richest and most fertile of the Globe, and of an extent in comparison with which the possessions of the House of Hapsburg are a patch on the earth's surface."[88] For Hulsemann, this blast was too much. He informed Webster he would never meet with him again, and normal relations between the State Department and the Austrian legation were not restored until after Webster's death in October 1852.

In other parts of the Hapsburg empire, Bohemia and Moravia, there also were revolutions and upheavals in 1848. The influence of American constitutionalism, however, was much less in evidence. One reason was absolutist rule by men like Metternich, who kept these regions largely isolated from Western ideas by tight censorship.[89]

Members of the Czech nationalist movement, nevertheless, were able to discuss the meaning of such words as *constitution*. When news arrived of Metternich's downfall on March 15, 1848, there was a burst of enthusiasm in urban areas. Suddenly the word *constitution* was on everyone's lips in Prague. Businessmen rushed to produce goods tailored to fit the mood of the moment. "Constitutional hats" were blocked, "constitutional parasols" were made, and "constitutional rolls" baked.[90] But the Czech revolution of 1848 was quickly crushed, as quickly as the uprising more than a century later against communist oppressors.

Italy

The revolution in Sicily in January 1848 anticipated the February revolution in France by about a month. Most of the Italian peninsula was in turmoil as people rose in revolt in different regions against the Hapsburg rule. A strong undercurrent of frustration that had been growing for decades finally reached a climax. What happened can only be described as a nationalist uprising in a region not yet a nation-state.

In Italy there was widespread dissatisfaction against the despotism of Austria and its Hapsburg rulers. Patriots in the numerous small states longed for a nation-state that might resurrect the greatness of ancient Rome, as the dream of an Italian *risorgimento* lingered despite the many political divisions. Giuseppi Mazzini established a secret society that favored a republic; the religious-minded agitated for a federation under the pope; while monarchists looked to the more open-minded Charles of Sardinia to lead a *risorgimento*.

Aside from the disagreements among Italians themselves, the two main obstacles to unification were the Hapsburg monarchy and the Papal States. The Hapsburgs tried desperately to control the various nationalities in their empire, and the liberal Pope Pius IX sometimes expressed himself in favor of Italy's nationalist hopes but at other times reacted negatively to revolutionary movements. Nevertheless Italian nationalists like Mazzini persevered.

Born in Genoa, Mazzini had been initiated as a young man into the Carbonari, a secret society dedicated to the overthrow of the Hapsburg rule. An enemy of absolute monarchy, he supported American ideas of republicanism all his life. After being arrested in 1830, he conceived of a new movement called "Young Italy" to replace the decaying Carbonari.[91] Although the movement failed as a nationalist organization, its spirit survived along international lines. Mazzini also founded the "Young Europe" movement, based on his faith in the universal standard of human rights and hopes for a worldwide republican federation. Sister organizations soon sprang up in other countries: "Young Germany," "Young Switzerland," and "Young Poland."[92]

Mazzini lived in England for the better part of the 1840s where he continued working on ideas for an international revolution. In 1848, however, he returned to Italy when the Milanese drove out the Austrians and Piedmont began its war to expel the Hapsburgs. Milan welcomed Mazzini warmly at first, but he soon became unpopular when he tried to make Lombardy a republic. After the Piedmontese armies withdrew from the field and the Austrians reentered Milan, Mazzini fled back to England.

Mazzini returned to Italy again in 1849, the high point of his career. He was elected one of the leaders of the new Roman republic that had been proclaimed, but his new role was short lived. When the pope, who had been driven out, appealed for help, a French army landed in Italy, crushed the Roman republic, and forced Mazzini to flee again.

Before he left, however, the Roman Republic under his leadership called a constitutional convention, a move in keeping with Mazzini's idea of following American models. The popularly elected Assembly appointed a commission to write a constitution, which was submitted in mid-June 1848. While French cannon were actually bombarding Rome, Assembly members bravely debated the issues. The Roman Constitution of 1849 proclaimed a republic on the Fourth of July, the very day the French entered the city. Mazzini did not enjoy his triumph, however, because the Assembly had voted against him on June 30 and he had resigned.[93]

Although its life was brief—only a single day—the Roman Constitution was symbolically significant. It was the only constitution promulgated in Italy at that time that originated with the people and their representatives.[94] This idea lay dormant until after World War II, but in this respect, the influence of American constitutionalism in Italy in the mid-nineteenth century helped pave the way for a democratic Italy that finally emerged a century later.

Conclusion

In concluding this account of the European revolutions of 1848, it is useful to recall the message of hope in desperate times voiced by Seamus Heaney, the modern Irish poet: although history may admonish us not to have hope this side of the grave, it happens "once in a lifetime" that justice, like a "tidal wave," may rise up.[95] So it was in 1848. A "tidal wave" rose up, and many individuals throughout Europe, believing in the goodness of human nature and the universality of human rights, launched a series of revolutions hoping for radical change. That change sometimes took the form of new constitutions, and wherever such documents were written, American constitutionalism usually played an important role either as a model or catalyst. In the case of France, Germany, and Switzerland, American constitutionalism, indeed, had proved quite significant.

What became clear in the 1848 revolutions is that the United States was actively proselytizing the idea of republicanism and representative democracy. Americans viewed the world in stark terms as a worldwide struggle of republicanism versus monarchy. In American eyes, the 1848 revolutions were "efforts by oppressed peoples to become like them, all species of the same revolutionary genus, *Americanus*."[96]

Despite the limited adaptations of American constitutional institutions, European life was never the same. Profoundly influenced by American ideals and ideas of governance, the worldview of European peoples after 1848 was changed forever. A new spirit of liberalism arose despite the defeat of the revolutions. From that time on, European rulers faced calls for more constitutional democracy, representative assemblies, and guarantees of personal liberties, all hallmarks of American constitutionalism. The "failed" 1848 revolutions succeeded in setting democratic agenda which, although not achieved at the time, became objectives for a distant future.

7

European Interlude

1850–1900 and the American Civil War

European history from 1850 to 1900 may be divided arbitrarily into two periods concerning the influence of American constitutionalism. During the first period, 1848 to 1865, Europe was coping with the effects of two momentous events: the 1848 revolutions and the American Civil War. In the second period, from about 1860 to 1900 (with some overlap), Europe witnessed a great burst of nationalism.[1] Nationalist movements precipitated by the French Revolution, Napoleon's domination of Europe, Metternich's regimes, and the 1848 European revolutions in the first half of the century resulted in the rise of new nation-states in the second half. Various forms of nation building took place in Italy, Germany, and the Dual Monarchy of Austria-Hungary, while in America the national authority refashioned the country after the defeat of the Confederacy.

Democracy and federalism, two major principles of American constitutionalism, were involved directly or indirectly in these developments. At home, democracy was challenged as never before when the Confederate states seceded from the Union and sought to establish a new nation-state based on slavery. Federalism suffered a great setback when the United States, the world's greatest exemplar of that principle, faced its most serious threat with the South's secession.

Throughout the antebellum period, America's image abroad as a democracy had been damaged by the South's insistence on slavery. Slavery in many other parts of the world had already been abolished, most notably in British and French colonies in 1833 and 1848, respectively, and in many Spanish-American republics during the first half of the nineteenth century. Steps also had been taken to abolish serfdom in the Hapsburg possessions in 1848 and in Russia in 1861. The American image thus suffered when compared with these democratic movements for greater human freedom.

Despite Tocqueville's prediction that democracy was the wave of the future, the Civil War between the democratic North and less democratic South showed that the issue was still in doubt. America's role in the world-wide trend toward democracy, therefore, was of the utmost significance. Throughout the first half of the nineteenth century, the United States was viewed as the spearhead in supporting prodemocratic revolutions. "In all the European insurrections of the century—the Greek revolt in 1821, the French constitutional transformation of 1830, [and] the general European insurrections in 1848 . . . the United States was always the first to extend diplomatic recognition to the new revolutionary regimes."[2]

Well aware that democracy was on the rise globally, European rulers made serious concessions in the second half of the nineteenth century. Britain broadened the right to vote in the Second Reform Bill in 1882. France maintained the principle of male suffrage in the Third Republic. Germany in 1867 allowed voting on the basis of universal male suffrage (although Bismarck weakened the practice by disregarding parliament). Universal male suffrage was extended elsewhere: Switzerland, Belgium, the Netherlands, and Italy all broadened their suffrage before 1900. Right after the turn of the century, Spain, Greece, Bulgaria, and Serbia also introduced universal male suffrage. The dilemma that European rulers faced was how to give in to democratic demands, like the right to vote, but not allow enough to the masses so they could gain political control.

Both European liberals and conservatives believed that the future of democracy hung in the balance during the Civil War. Despite slavery in the South during the antebellum period, America had still been identified with the cause of democracy abroad. "The need for a model republic during the nineteenth century had become so pressing that it almost seemed as if the United States would have to be invented if it had not existed," declared one scholar.[3] If the Union were shattered, the results would be devastating at home and abroad.

Federalism faced similar problems. In Germany, the Frankfurt parliament had found the idea attractive but unsuited to its situation. Although Switzerland had adopted certain features of American-type federalism, the borrowings were far from complete. In Italy, efforts to establish a federal government after 1848 were abandoned. The Austro-Hungarian Empire with its multiple ethnic groups, moreover, refused to even consider federalism as a possible solution in 1849.[4] "The period of the Civil War was the nadir of federalism both within and without the United States."[5]

In Europe during the Civil War, conservatives and liberals were divided on three main issues. Conservatives rejoiced when the republican experiment in America seemed about to collapse and hoped that the United States would break up, remove a challenge to their privileged status, and deal a deathblow to the idea of democracy. Liberals, however, were ecstatic: slaves would be freed; the stain of slavery would be removed from American democracy; and the United States would resume its position of leadership among the forces for freedom. On the second issue, Europe's response to the Constitution of the Confederate States showed conservatives and liberals split over the issue of secession. They debated whether secession was legal, could be applied to their own situations, and whether it presented a viable option for minorities facing abuses by large majorities.

The third issue concerned the future of American-style federalism. From after the Civil War to the turn of the century, the world witnessed an era of nation building never seen before. All the new nation-states required constitutions, and many faced the question of whether or not to adopt American-style federalism.

The rise of new nation-states in Europe and other parts of the world represented a global sea change. Before 1860, there were only three large nation-states in Europe: Britain, France, and Spain. Within a dozen years from 1859 to 1871, three more sprang up: the new German empire, the kingdom of Italy, and the multiethnic Russian empire, while the monarchy of Austria-Hungary worked out a compromise. By the early 1870s, the nation-state system prevailed everywhere in Europe when ethnic groups began yearning for a common flag, parliament, economy, and identity. The consolidation of larger countries provided a model for the smaller ones in southern Europe—Greece, Serbia, Bulgaria, and Romania—that emerged from the breakup of the Ottoman Empire. In other parts of the world, moreover, the same process was taking place: the Dominion of Canada was created, and modern Japan appeared on the scene.

From a diplomatic and economic point of view, certain groups in the British and French governments saw in the possible collapse of the United States the same potential as in the breakup of the former weak Spanish empire. Britain could look to the U.S. South as a producer of raw materials for its factories without paying the tariffs imposed by the North. France saw an opportunity to challenge the Monroe Doctrine by invading Mexico and establishing a puppet regime there.

The Constitution of the Confederate States of America

The appearance of the Confederate States of America directly challenged the U.S. Constitution. The Confederates claimed that their constitution represented a fundamental improvement over the 1787 constitution, but their charter never purported to extend its jurisdiction over the nonslaveholding states. Rather, they were content simply to proclaim secession from the Union, hoping only to offer an alternative to the existing U.S. government.

When the Confederates wrote their constitution, they took the classic position that revolutionaries often assume: claiming that *they* represented a restoration of the old order. This argument had been advanced by the revolutionaries of 1776, who insisted that they, not the British, were the true heirs of Britain's constitutional tradition. As one Southerner declared, "We are not revolutionaries; we are resisting revolution. We are upholding the true doctrines of the Federal Constitution. We are conservative."[6]

To support this position Southerners pointed out that the Confederate Constitution actually copied the U.S. Constitution. When the Confederates drafted their government blueprint in February 1861 in Montgomery, Alabama, they incorporated not only many principles of 1776 but also the very language of the 1787 document. All twelve amendments of the U.S. Constitution, for example, were worked into the Confederate charter. The Confederate Constitution also followed the U.S. Constitution closely in other particulars. Its structure had the same features: a president, Senate, House of Representatives, and Supreme Court. Whenever any section or clause of the U.S. Constitution did not have a provision to which the South took exception, it was repeated word for word. This imitation of the U.S. Constitution was deliberate: the Confederates really believed they were correcting errors in the document and improving it.

With their innovations, the Southerners assumed also that they were returning to the eighteenth-century spirit of the Articles of Confederation. "The . . . [1787] Constitution had been made an engine of power to crush out liberty, that of the Confederate States to preserve it," wrote Alexander Stephens, vice president of the Confederacy and the South's most articulate constitutionalist.[7] Stephens argued that the Articles of Confederation had created only a compact between the states and that the Constitutional Convention of 1787 had no legal basis for revising the Articles because that document declared the American Union to be "perpetual."[8] The Southern states based both their revisions of the federal Constitution and ultimately their right to secede on this interpretation.

In revising the 1787 document, the Southern states handled most differences by making a Southern adaptation or an outright rejection. The central government, for example, was denied authority to interfere with slavery in the states and, indeed, was required to pass laws instead to protect the institution. Revenue tariffs and internal improvements were reduced to diminish the financial power of the Confederate government. Most important, the revision recognized the sovereignty of the individual states.[9]

The Confederates insisted on expressing their own philosophy of states' rights, so the preamble to their Constitution began as follows: "We the people of the Confederate States, each state acting in its sovereign and independent character." State legislatures, for example, could impeach Confederate government officials. But state officials were not bound by any oath to the Confederate government.[10]

The balance between the president and the congress was changed by granting the executive far greater powers against the legislature. He was allowed to veto particular appropriations in a money bill (a line-item veto) while approving others in the same bill. A two-thirds majority was required for any congressional appropriation not first proposed by the executive. The president's hand was strengthened against the legislature by not allowing any bill to refer to more than one subject. Therefore, any omnibus bill in which legislators could tack on favorite projects was impossible. Although these measures made the executive the strongest branch *in theory*, the states' rights philosophy operating in the congress and the state legislatures themselves actually limited the power of the Confederate executive.

The enumerated powers of the Confederate Congress were essentially the same as those granted to the U.S. Congress in the U.S. Constitution. Certain significant amendments, however, reflected ideological differences. A Confederate protective tariff was forbidden, reflecting the South's reaction to what it perceived as the North's manipulation of tariff bills in its favor. The importation of blacks from any foreign country other than from slaveholding states or from territories of the United States was not allowed. Any laws denying or impairing the right to hold property in slaves was forbidden.[11]

Although a supreme court was to be established, it existed only on paper, as attempts to set up such a court along the lines of the Supreme Court of the United States failed to pass several times. Such measures were defeated on the grounds that they might be used to centralize the power of the Confederate government.

Stephens, a great admirer of the British constitution, was also the chief proponent of the "cabinet-in-congress" idea. This practice would allow cabinet members to sit in the congress when measures affecting their respective departments were discussed. No doubt, he felt the same as did Walter Bagehot, the leading authority on Britain's parliamentary government, who wrote later that in Britain, "the fusion of the executive power with legislative power . . . [was of] cardinal importance."[12] For Stephens, the admission of cabinet members to congress to explain a program of the administration represented the nonpartisan spirit he advocated. As he told a Savannah audience one month after the Confederate Constitution was written: "Our heads of department can speak for themselves and the administration . . . without resorting to the . . . highly objectionable medium of a newspaper. It is to be hoped that under our system we shall never have what is known as a Government organ."[13] As a matter of practice rather than theory, however, the Confederate Congress never exercised the option of inviting cabinet members to sit in its body.[14]

Stephens was deeply influenced also by the republican ideology of the American Revolution, as evidenced by the innovations he introduced into the Confederate document. He had strongly opposed the highly factional behavior in the state legislatures during the pre–Civil War period, a time when political fights had been fierce. Stephens was hoping to return to the pre-Revolutionary period when he believed politics had not been so deeply immersed in policymaking. But his philosophy reflected an effort to turn the clock back to a golden age that never was. He thus only imagined that there had once been greater concern for the public good and less self-interestedness than in the antebellum period.

The same philosophy was behind the expanded powers granted to the Confederate president. His six-year term, broad budget authority, and power to have cabinet members explain presidential policies on the floor of congress presumably would free him from the clutches of partisanship. What Stephens and his colleagues had in mind was the model of a "patriot president," a leader like Washington who would be above party. As one historian explained, in earlier days the image of such an ideal political leader had been an integral part of America's constitutional tradition.[15]

In the final analysis, the defeat of the South represented the death of the idea that the Union was a confederation from which members could withdraw at will, an issue that was decided on the battlefield. Never again has the United States faced a serious threat of withdrawal by any of the states.

The Civil War was, at bottom, a constitutional crisis over the nation's identity. It demonstrated that in the future the United States would be not a loose confederation of sovereign states but one nation indivisible. The Union was redefined as a single entity, a nation-state in which the separate states were ultimately subordinate, even while they still maintained considerable authority and retained residual powers. In this redefinition, power shifted to the national government, and what emerged was a nation-state more liberal and democratic in its political principles.

The war was fraught with serious constitutional consequences. Through the Thirteenth Amendment, it ended slavery, the most politically divisive institution in antebellum America. The Fourteenth Amendment declared that all Americans were to be citizens not of their separate and several states but of the United States. The states were forbidden to "deprive any person of life, liberty, or property without due process of law," thus nationalizing the Bill of Rights to apply to the states as well as to the federal government. From an economic perspective, seizing "property" (i.e., slaves) from the Southerners without any compensation resulted in what Charles Beard and Mary Beard called the "greatest sequestration of private property in the history of Anglo-Saxon jurisprudence."[16]

France and the American Civil War

France was the European country on the Continent most affected by the Civil War. Besides the unsuccessful invasion of Mexico that caused a diplomatic crisis with the United States, the horrifying loss of life in both the North and South had a sobering effect. The reputation of American constitutionalism, moreover, suffered by what was perceived as a failure of federalism. For this and other reasons, the American model failed to have much influence on the framing of the Constitution for France's Third Republic.[17]

The constitutional problem that most preoccupied the French was the legality of secession. French liberals viewed France as a unitary state by history and tradition and argued that secession was illegal. They asserted that sovereignty without question lay with the central government. To them, Lincoln's dictum "that a federation cannot be broken without the consent of all federated states" was gospel.[18] French liberals, therefore, favored the North for this reason, as well as the desire of many to abolish slavery.

Conservative supporters of Napoleon III, however, were less consistent. Most began by being friendly to the North. But as the war wore on, they openly began siding with the South, and the *Constitutionnel*, an administration-controlled organ, reflected this shift in opinion. By the summer of 1861, the newspaper hoisted the Union on its own petard: "The American faith had for its credo: governments depend only upon the consent of the governed. By what right, today, does the North desire to impose its government upon the South, which does not desire it?"[19] In the end, France, facing several royalist movements in its midst, never really resolved the issue of secession. The Third Republic continued its consolidated government for almost two-thirds of a century, and the secession question went unanswered.

The American Civil War and Italy

Italy's interest in the Civil War was not as intense as that of France. At the outbreak of the war, the Italian states had enough problems at home trying to create a unified nation-state. With the sole exception of the kingdom of Sardinia, which openly favored the North, rulers in the various Italian states remained neutral.[20]

Although the average Italian showed little interest in foreign affairs, the same could not be said of the intellectuals. As was true in France, opinion about the war and the legality of the Confederacy divided along liberal and conservative lines, and the level of writing was as incisive as any found in Europe. The liberal Giuseppe Mazzini, for example, described how the cause of Italian independence had benefited from the North's victory. "You have done more for us," he cried, "in four years than fifty years of teaching, preaching, and writing from all your European brothers have been able to do."[21] Among liberals like Mazzini, the war was seen primarily as an internal struggle, an effort by a progressive, humanitarian North to free the slaves from a reactionary and repressive South.[22]

An essay by Vincenzo Botta, an Italian intellectual living in New York City, was perhaps the best piece written from a liberal point of view. Publishing in the authoritative *Rivista contemporánea* in 1861/1862, Botta declared that the South's revolt was unjustified on four counts. First, it was seeking to destroy an American nation built on certain irrefutable forces: the physical geography of the land, the homogeneous character of the inhabitants, and its national identity based on the English language. Second, the South was violating the very principles of constitutional liberty that had made the United States great. Southern leaders had seized control of the majority vote and used it to strip their fellow citizens of the rights guaranteed them under the U.S. Constitution. Third, the South was flouting the laws of political economy by basing its unsound economic system on slavery. Finally, the Confederacy was offending "the sacred principles of justice and progress" not only in the present but for the future. The stagnating nature of the slave economy required a continual expansion by the South, as it needed fresh lands to keep the region alive. The leaders of the Confederacy, in short, were traitors to their fatherland. America had long ago passed from the status of a confederation to a Union. The theory of state sovereignty was an outmoded doctrine by which Confederate leaders hoped to confuse the issue. Their cries of oppression were demonstrably false: only one Northerner had been elected as president in eight of the preceding seventy-two years (Botta noted incorrectly). The North, moreover, had never dominated the Congress. Indeed, the desire for peace had made the Northerners involuntary accomplices to Southern oligarchs who supported slavery. No matter how protracted the war might be, Botta was confident that the North would win: justice, ethnographic considerations, and the stain of slavery made such an outcome a sacred necessity.[23]

Abbé Louis Rossi presented the best case for the Italian conservatives. A Catholic priest and monarchist, Rossi ascribed the immediate cause of the war to Douglas's theory of popular sovereignty. He concluded that Northern conservatives had placed the major blame for the war squarely on Lincoln and the radical Republicans, to whom the president had pandered by using force instead of resorting to conciliatory persuasion. Radical Republicans thus were guilty of insisting on a violent course of action, and these political fanatics had turned Lincoln into a despot willing to flout the will of the majority.[24]

During a period when many European governments favored the South, the Italians remained firm in their resolve not to become involved in the war. Accordingly, despite the involvement of individual intellectuals, on the official government level almost all the states remained neutral. Familiar from bitter experiences in their own recent civil wars, most Italians had no wish to favor one side or the other.[25]

The American Civil War and Other European Countries

In Austria the monarchy, as might be expected, took a pro-South position. Franz Josef, the emperor, backed the French move (1864–1867) to set up his brother, Archduke Ferdinand Joseph, as emperor of Mexico. He hoped such an enterprise would reclaim for the royal family a small portion of the huge Spanish domain once held by the Hapsburgs. Protests by the American government against the invasion went unheeded until the war was over. Then, in 1866, Secretary of State William Seward sent a stiff note demanding that the French withdraw. When they did, Maximilian was deprived of French support, and the affair ended with his capture and execution.

Prussia, in contrast, opposed the South on constitutional grounds. Its foreign minister informed the United States that his government "in principle consistently opposed . . . revolutionary movements." Prussia, he declared, would be the "last to recognize any governments *de facto* of the Secessionist States of the American Union."[26] Bismarck, engaged in a constitutional struggle to consolidate Germany, was not about to countenance any secession movements.

In Belgium, reaction was mixed: the monarchy held one view, and some members of the press another. Leopold, king of the Belgians, was distressed when he learned that two of his nephews had joined the Union army in 1861. He feared that they had a chance of "being shot for Abraham Lincoln and the most rank Radicalism," he wrote his niece, Queen Victoria of England. But a Belgian newspaper correspondent in New York that same year wrote that he could not understand why South Carolina took such an extreme constitutional position as secession. "I have the most violent hatred of slavery. But why, because the chimney is smoking, is it necessary to burn the house?"[27]

Europe's most reactionary response to the Civil War came from autocratic Spain. An editorial in the conservative *Pensamiento español* in the fall of 1862, reflected the extreme pro-Southern position:

> The history of the [American] model can be summed up in a few words. It came into being by rebellion. It was founded on atheism. It was populated by the dregs of all the nations in the world. It has lived without the laws of God or men. Within a hundred years, greed has ruined it. Now it is fighting like a cannibal, and it will die in a flood of blood and mire. . . . The example is too horrible to stir any desire for imitation in Europe.[28]

This image of a materialistic and atheist America was increasingly held by conservative intellectuals throughout Europe.

Laboulaye: France's Leading Americanist

Édouard de Laboulaye was to the second half of the nineteenth century in France what Tocqueville had been to the first. Remembered today mainly as the man who suggested France's gift of the Statue of Liberty to the United States, he was, in fact, the preeminent French authority on American constitutionalism. From 1850 to 1875, he labored to demonstrate through his writings, teachings, and political career that American democracy could serve as a useful model for France. "All his life he was the ardent defender of the United States and its institutions," wrote one French political historian, "publishing book after book and numerous articles and studies."[29]

Laboulaye began life as a reclusive scholar, supporter of the Orléans monarchy, and ardent advocate of the conservative 1814 charter. The revolution of 1848, however, overturned all his earlier ideas, transformed him into an activist, and propelled him into politics. His conversion resulted from his reading of American history. As he wrote later during the revolution of 1848, the United States, where "custom upheld the laws," was a "revelation" to him during a time of crisis and danger.[30]

The French Constitution of 1848 was an abstract and flawed document, Laboulaye argued in his book written that year. Although he had served on the commission that drafted it, he felt the framers had made a mistake by disregarding America's experience. The French had created a single-house legislature that did not provide many safeguards against tyranny. Unicameralism, Laboulaye concluded, was the "capital error" in the 1848 charter.[31] The executive branch was a confusing arrangement, as it combined the prerogatives of a constitutional monarch with the powers of the head of a republic.[32] He was inspired instead by the U.S. Constitution, a document that he viewed as the capstone of a long historical development that had brought religious and political liberty to the United States.[33] For this reason, he explicitly urged France to follow America's lead. To do so, he had to argue against a majority of French Catholics, most of whom were constitutional monarchists and considered republicanism and Catholicism to be incompatible.

Before the 1848 constitution was framed, Laboulaye had written to advise Louis-Eugène Cavaignac, the general who put down the June insurrection and then had been granted executive powers during the crisis. Laboulaye urged Cavaignac to imitate the U.S. Constitution. France, he pointed out, was facing in 1848 problems similar to those that America's founding fathers had confronted in 1787. Both countries struggled with the same issues: to achieve independence for the executive branch, to limit legislative power in order to prevent legislative tyranny, and to produce a bill of rights to protect liberty. Laboulaye feared despotism on the part of the legislature and warned Cavaignac there existed no countervailing forces to contain it.[34] His advice was ignored.

After being appointed to the Collège de France in 1848, Laboulaye announced that his inaugural lectures would deal with American history. His introductory lecture, entitled "De la constitution américaine et de l'utilité de son étude," later became the first chapter of his masterpiece, the magisterial three-volume *Histoire des États-Unis*.[35] At about the same time, Laboulaye emerged as the leader of the political opposition to Napoleon III just as the ruler was entering his authoritarian phase.

The first volume of the *Histoire* was published in 1855 and the last in 1866, the reason for the long-delayed publication being the political oppression during the first decade of the Second Empire. Laboulaye worked on his text in a series of lectures in 1849. But with the coup d'état in December 1851 and the proclamation of the Second Empire the following year, he suspended his lectures because he felt the political climate was too dangerous to proceed.[36]

In his first lecture, Laboulaye announced that his purpose would be to analyze the U.S. Constitution and to argue that its provisions could be useful for future French constitutionalists. He did not mean that the French should copy the document uncritically but should follow what he called its "spirit": "Let us not copy the Constitution of the United States, but let us profit from the lessons it contains, and while remaining French, let us not be embarrassed to follow the example or listen to the advice given by a Washington."[37] The French, he added, tended to be too theoretical and demanded too much from their constitutions, and even more from their law codes. Americans, in contrast, were more practical, relied on experience, and were consistently pragmatic. What was the result? Since 1789 the Americans had had one constitution, whereas by 1849 the French had had ten, according to his count.[38]

What began as a study of comparative constitutional law was soon transformed into a course on American history.[39] Laboulaye's first seven lectures were devoted to the theory of law, in keeping with the historical school of thought led by the jurist Savigny. A leading exponent of the historical and comparative school of law, Savigny held that each country's laws and constitutions were the result of a lengthy historical evolutionary process reflecting each nation's unique genius. Enlightenment thinkers, however, thought in more universal terms, theorizing that an eternally true constitution might be written to fit the needs of all nations. Laboulaye complicated the picture further by trying to reconcile these two contradictory points of view.[40]

Laboulaye's interpretation of the American colonial period rested on two main premises. The first was that the origins of America's concept of liberty could be traced to British roots in customs and charters like the Magna Carta. One major precondition for democracy was political liberty, an idea that had been introduced in America by the Puritans, who had transported the Old World tradition to the New World. "The United States is a new empire," Laboulaye observed perceptively, "but it is an ancient people; it is a European nation whose civilization is counted not in years but in centuries."[41] His second premise was that at bottom, religious ideas were the bases of all societies: a people's religious faith formed and determined their political institutions. He considered religious liberty a counterpart to political liberty; the two went hand in hand. Although the United States enjoyed both religious and political liberty, its traditions were essentially Puritan and republican in nature.[42]

Laboulaye turned to history to explain how the Puritan tradition had evolved into political liberty. Although the Puritans had left behind their privileges in the mother country, they had brought with them the idea of political equality in their religious organizations. The main foundations of American liberty rested on such organizations.[43] To Laboulaye the Mayflower Compact was, therefore, of prime importance, as it was the first document in American history to establish absolute political equality among its members. The Puritans went on to establish self-government in the form of the New England town meeting, which reflected "both the spirit of order and the spirit of liberty, independence and respect."[44]

Laboulaye's Comparative History

Laboulaye was especially astute when analyzing in his comparative history the cultural differences between France and America. He did so by taking up at great length three constitutional concepts: liberty, power, and sovereignty. Unlike France, he believed, America understood liberty, and its foundation was essentially English liberty. Because the United States did not have an aristocracy or gothic forms with which to contend, the outlines of American liberty in all its simplicity and splendor could be more easily discerned.

France, however, had known only the liberty that existed in its 1814 charter. Furthermore, many Frenchmen seriously underestimated the complexities of their own constitutional situation. To them, the only thing necessary to achieve liberty was to make a few minor changes: an electoral law, the abolition of censorship, or the establishment of a two-house legislature. The Left in France had never recognized, Laboulaye claimed, the great difference between the 1814 charter and the highly centralized government and huge bureaucracy that sprang up after the Restoration. Laboulaye thus put his finger squarely on one of the major problems of the French government. "Where precisely to situate the ubiquitous bureaucracy in a political system whose essence was popular sovereignty remained a dilemma of republican theory and practice throughout, and beyond, the nineteenth century," wrote Alan Spitzer, a perceptive American scholar of French history.[45]

Laboulaye was aware that a democratic regime based on the absolutist abstractions expressed by French theorists could never be established, as there was too much diversity among different peoples to allow such a regime. All peoples did not follow the same mores, Laboulaye concluded, and conditions of social life were not the same everywhere. Hence, it was unwise to assume that the same legislation or constitution could be applied to all nations.[46] Science had to take into account differences among people and their mores, as well as the variables of time and place. Thus, Laboulaye concluded, one could better understand and appreciate the "Anglo-American genius," a practical genius that excluded no theory but verified and modified instead the structure of governance according to the needs of the people and the necessities of the time.[47]

Could the U.S. Constitution be exported to other lands? Laboulaye asked. One should never forget the American people's specific role in and contribution to the making of their Constitution. To do otherwise, he wrote, resorting to a homely metaphor, would be like taking a suit of clothes from one person to dress another: one must know first whether the two individuals had the same measurements.[48] Laboulaye used the U.S. Constitution as his guide, not so much because he considered it an authoritative model for all governmental questions, but because it embodied wise reasoning.[49]

In the course of his studies, Laboulaye turned to *The Federalist*, calling it "a manual on liberty" and one of the best commentaries on the U.S.

Constitution. In doing so, he echoed the assessment of François Guizot, a fellow historian and statesman, who claimed that *The Federalist* was the world's greatest work regarding the application of elementary principles of government to practical administration.[50] In this context, Laboulaye discussed constitutional issues such as the concept of the separation of powers—the powers granted to the executive, legislative, and judicial branches—and bicameralism. But he studied these concepts from the perspective of comparative constitutionalism. Whenever he put forward an American example, he invariably discussed French and British solutions as well. If he suggested an American idea for use by France, he emphasized its British heritage and described it in terms of "Anglo-American genius."[51] Finally, he noted the transformations that occurred when these concepts moved from the Old World to the New.

Despite his acute observations, Laboulaye's views of American society, customs, and mores in the *Histoire* were often naïve. And unlike the two other leading Americanists in France, Lafayette and Tocqueville, he never visited the United States. Laboulaye's views were often overly idealistic, misinformed, and inaccurate. But despite such limitations, his *Histoire* marked Laboulaye as the outstanding Americanist during the Second Empire.

Laboulaye and the French Constitutional Settlement of 1875

Laboulaye ended his teaching career at the Collège de France in 1871 after a particularly stormy session and was elected the next year to the National Assembly. He was at this time a strong supporter of Adolphe Thiers and an advocate for a French republic. France was undergoing tumultuous times—the Franco-Prussian War, the Paris Commune, and proclamation of the Third Republic—all of which created deep-seated divisions. Laboulaye, a moderate liberal, was midway between the extreme Right (the Legitimists who dreamed of restoring France as it had been under the king in 1789) and the extreme Left (who drew their inspiration from the Jacobin Constitution of 1793, the Second Republic of 1848, and the Commune). Reacting to the violence of the Commune, Laboulaye wrote several articles urging constitution makers to stop the recurring cycle of liberty-to-authoritarianism-to-liberty that had given France so many constitutions since its Revolution. What was needed, he declared, was a workable, written document along the lines of the U.S. Constitution.[52]

Laboulaye plunged into the parliamentary debates with great enthusiasm. In 1873 he was elected to the Committee of Thirty entrusted with the task of drafting a new charter. But when he insisted that France was a "republic," he aroused the fury of the monarchist Right, who hated the term. It eventually was accepted, however, in an amendment framed by one of Laboulaye's colleagues and indirectly established the Third Republic. Although the word *republic* left France still deeply divided, it resonated in America, which viewed France as a sister republic.[53]

The new constitutional arrangement provided for a stronger president, a two-house parliament, and a council of ministers or cabinet, headed by a premier. The governmental system could hardly be described as a strong imitation of the American model, an accusation once leveled at Laboulaye. The role of the premier in the French parliamentary system—who owed his office to a parliamentary majority—bore only a slight resemblance to the powerful American presidency. The two-house legislature operated quite differently, moreover, in the French context of a parliamentary system.[54]

Laboulaye and his colleagues never produced a single written charter in 1875. Instead, the new system remained a series of constitutive laws rather than one document. Given the existing political divisions, only such a compromise was possible. Nevertheless, France moved in the direction of democracy. The Chamber of Deputies was elected directly by universal male suffrage, and the Senate, by a complicated indirect system of voting. No doubt, the U.S. example of universal male suffrage helped persuade France to preserve this important feature that the two countries shared.

American Constitutional Influence in Italy during Unification

The seeds of Italian nationalism sown during the first half of the nineteenth century flowered during the second: American constitutional ideas came to the fore again as the country struggled to be born. During the *risorgimento* many intellectuals looked to the United States for inspiration.[55]

Italy's problem was twofold: to achieve independence from Austria, whose petty princes controlled the principalities in northern Italy; and to gain hegemony over the region despite periodic opposition from the Catholic Church. In the complicated history of the *risorgiamento*, three giant figures stand out: Count Camillo Benso di Cavour, Italy's first prime minister and one of Europe's shrewdest politicians; Giuseppe Garibaldi, the rebel chieftain and master of guerrilla warfare; and Giuseppe Mazzini, the constitutional theorist, dynamic leader, and ideologue of revolutionary movements. Two of these men, Cavour and Mazzini, were deeply influenced by American constitutionalism.

Cavour, a liberal and constitutional monarchist, was the prime minister of Piedmont under King Victor Emmanuel II. He wanted to establish an Italian state with constitutional and parliamentary practices and without any socialist and populist institutions. A tough-minded realist, he was the opposite of the romantic nationalist and populist Garibaldi. Cavour found much to praise about the United States. He admired, above all, the principle of separation of church and state and fought for a free church in a free state. But his efforts to negotiate with the Vatican on that basis failed.[56]

Garibaldi, a Piedmont republican, was more a man of action. Called a "hero of two worlds," he had fought for the independence of Uruguay, lived in the United States for a time, and held an office in the Roman Republic of 1849. A charismatic leader, he headed a bold group of nationalists, the "Red Shirts," and formed an alliance with King Victor Emmanuel to establish Italy as a nation-state.

Mazzini, an uncompromising republican, was the one among the three men most impressed by America, as noted earlier. To him, the United States offered an example of the kind of government that he admired most and tried to follow in the 1849 Roman Republic. But Mazzini had an even grander vision for the future United States: he believed America had a God-given world mission. "You are called upon by God to enter a new career." Up to the end of the Civil War, America's mission had been "to constitute" itself and achieve those republican principles that served as the basis of its life. While achieving this goal, Mazzini noted, the United States had been isolationist and had carefully refrained from interfering in European affairs or from joining the general march of humankind. With the first phase of its history over, he urged America to embark on its second phase.[57]

The life of a great people, Mazzini pointed out, always worked both "inward" and "outward." By holding itself together during the Civil War, the United States had displayed great heroism and strength. More was required of a great nation, however, than mere existence. "It is an implement," he wrote, "given by God for the good of all." The abolition of slavery now bound America more closely to the rest of humankind, and the admiration of Europe demanded that America play a leading role in that "outward" march:

Above American life, above European life, there is mankind's life. . . .
That is the common aim in which we are all brothers and combatants.
There is our great battle—to which all local battles are episodes—fought
on both continents and everywhere between liberty and tyranny, equality and privilege, right and might, justice and arbitrary rule, good and
evil. . . . By these four years of noble deeds and self-sacrifice, you have
been enlisted to take a share in it wherever it is fought.[58]

There existed no better statement of America's role as standard bearer
of human rights by a foreign observer. Mazzini praised America's system
of local self-government in particular. Popular participation, he believed,
was the most important element in holding together the existence of all
nation-states. Mazzini hoped that once this unity had been achieved, the
Italian people would follow America's lead.[59] Despite his admiration for
the American model, however, Mazzini rejected one of its most important
principles: federalism. In an article written early in his career, he acknowledged that federalism had served the United States well but would not do
for Italy, which faced powerful neighbors.

Besides federalism, Mazzini had other reservations about the U.S.
Constitution and American society. He opposed the idea of separation of
church and state, and he was unhappy with the American way of life, particularly its emphasis on materialism and individualism. To Mazzini, the
good of the community should come before that of the individual.[60] Despite these qualms, Mazzini held a positive view of America. With America's power came responsibility, he stressed, and the country had a mission
to participate in the worldwide conflict taking place between "republican
faith and monarchical interest."[61]

The Italian nation was cobbled together through the efforts of the three
men: the cool-headed Cavour, the firebrand Garibaldi, and the high-
minded Mazzini. By 1859, all of Italy was unified except the city of Rome,
which was annexed in 1870. But American constitutionalism had contributed only indirectly, by serving mainly as an source of inspiration.

American Constitutional Influence in Germany

The unification of Germany, one of the most important political developments in European history in the nineteenth century, dramatically
changed the balance of power on the Continent. Following the failure
of the Frankfurt Assembly, both Prussia and Austria presented plans for

some kind of German union. Then Prussia backed down, though only temporarily, because Wilhelm I was determined that neither Austria nor France should frustrate Prussia's ambitions. He and his chief minister, Otto von Bismarck, decided that Prussia must become invulnerable first. Bismarck, a Prussian Junker with a shrewd mind and deep loyalty to the Crown, set about waging three wars and succeeded in gaining his goal. Wilhelm I was proclaimed German emperor in 1871.

The background to the German Constitution formed in 1871 recalls the steps taken towards German unification during the 1860s, when the U.S. Constitution did not play as important a role as it had in the Frankfurt Assembly.[62] Until 1866 Germany was divided into thirty-eight states, with Prussia being the strongest, largest, and most dominant. In that year, Bismarck took three steps that ultimately resulted in national unification. First, he waged war against Austria to remove that country as an obstacle. Then in 1867 he brought Mecklenberg, Saxony, Darmstadt, and other areas into the Prussian-dominated North German Confederation. By 1870/1871 Bismarck had absorbed Bavaria, Baden, Wurtemberg, and several other southern states as well as seizing Alsace and Lorraine from France. In 1871, he excluded Austria from the German Reich, thereby establishing Germany's borders as they remained until World War I.

German political thinkers meanwhile had been exposed to Tocqueville's writings on American federalism as well as to the analysis of federal states by their countryman, Robert von Mohl. The possibility of forming a German federation renewed interest in *The Federalist*. Georg Waitz, a political theorist, had reacted to the failure of the Frankfurt National Assembly to achieve a federated Germany by writing a treatise, "Das Wesen des Bundesstaates," in 1853.[63] Although Waitz's work addressed the doctrine of divided sovereignty, his interpretation was really based on the concept of a federal state introduced originally by Publius. Waitz's doctrine became a powerful influence in determining the kind of federalism the Germans kept considering for their federal union. Even after a younger generation of jurists replaced Waitz's doctrine, however, *The Federalist* continued to be regarded as a classic in Germany. Albert Haenel, one of the first Germans to take issue with the idea of divided sovereignty, called the essays a superb example of juristic-political thinking and, in his work published in 1870, credited *The Federalist* with creating the concept of the modern federal state.[64]

Faced with the constitutional problem of creating a union whose states were connected only by a loose confederation in 1867, German constitutionalists prepared drafts incorporating parts of various foreign models, particularly the American and Swiss. But in the final analysis, it was Otto von Bismarck who was mainly responsible for the outline of the constitution.[65] In forming the German Confederation of 1867, Bismarck resorted to an older tradition of confederation that had long existed under the Holy Roman Empire. Although war with Austria destroyed the old German Confederation, Bismarck re-formed a new one, the North German Confederation, which was composed of the twenty-two states north of the Main River.

The 1867 constitution differed substantially from the ideas of American constitutionalism because it was monarchical rather than republican in form. Its structure, however, was federal and much stronger than the old German Confederation. The king of Prussia was its hereditary head, and its ministers were directly responsible to him. There was a bicameral legislature, whose upper house, like the U.S. Senate, represented the states, although not equally. The lower house, the Reichstag, presumably represented the people, and ostensibly there was universal male suffrage, as in the United States. This was a bold step, considering that on the Continent, only France had universal manhood suffrage at the time. In these and other respects, Bismarck's North German Confederation resembled an adaptation of the American model.[66]

In reality, however, the Bismarckian German Constitution of 1871 represented more an application of the 1867 constitution to all of Germany. The king of Prussia and his chancellor headed the new federal organization now called the German Reich. At its head was the powerful hereditary president, the king of Prussia, which among the member states continued to be the largest and most important because it controlled the emperor's army and foreign policy.

In theory, the rights of the smaller states were preserved, as in American-style federalism. The Reichsrat, or Imperial Council, was a powerful body, and Prussia presumably could be voted down by a majority in ordinary legislation. In practice, however, the solid phalanx of Prussian delegates, whom the smaller states usually followed, enabled Prussia to have its way in most legislation. Prussia, moreover, held a permanent veto on all constitutional matters because constitutional amendments could be vetoed by fourteen votes, the number that Prussia possessed in the Reichsrat.

On the surface, the Reichstag appeared democratic because it was elected by universal male suffrage and consisted of a large number of members, 397. In practice, however, its power was limited: imperial officials attended Reichstag meetings; army quotas were fixed for each state; and there was little parliamentary control over foreign policy. The power of the parliament was impaired further by the fact that the Reichstag was invariably split into numerous political parties.

What American constitutional influence there was, was mostly indirect. Two concepts considered during the German deliberations in 1867 and 1871 referred to American debates that had been held earlier over similar issues. First, German constitutionalists remarked on the distinction between a confederacy and a federal state after the American model (Mohl's Staatenbund and Bundestaat), an issue that had been discussed in the 1848 Frankfurt proceedings. Second, German theorists accepted the idea that a federal state was characterized by a direct relationship between the central government and individual citizens, and they recognized also the status of member states as real states. But the 1871 constitution failed to follow the American pattern very closely, for obvious reasons: the former document was written for a federation of monarchical regimes dominated by the hegemonial position of the Prussian state.[67]

After 1867 and 1871, German constitutionalists began again focusing their attention on the U.S. Constitution and the idea of American-style federalism. Such a move from Staatenbund to Bundestaat, however, raised as many questions as it answered. Was the new German Reich a confederation of sovereign princes, or was it a national union? Was the jurisdiction of the new national government confined to the states, or was it meant to apply to the individual citizen as well?[68] These questions were discussed frequently in the context of the American experience. As one German American scholar concluded: "The American precedent contributed materially in causing the national interpretation of the Bismarckian constitution to be almost universally accepted. One might say that the American Constitution helped to overcome the traditions of the Holy Roman Empire."[69]

Conclusion

From the perspective of American constitutionalism abroad, the Civil War addressed two major issues that had troubled the United States since its founding: federalism and democracy. In American federalism before the war, the balance of power between the federal government and the states had teetered uneasily from 1787 to 1861. The supremacy of the nation over the states was assured, however, by the North's victory. The doctrine of divided sovereignty was dealt a severe blow, and the idea of secession and nullification was defeated on the battlefield. But because the force of arms was used to resolve the issue, American federalism in many foreign quarters was seen as having failed. From the viewpoint of some foreign constitutionalists, the Civil War had been caused by granting the states too much sovereignty. Many countries throughout the world were determined, therefore, to limit the power of the states or provinces in their nation-building process, and federalism briefly proved less attractive abroad. But the new forms of federalism that emerged seemed better suited to the needs of the coming new age. "Its adaptation to Bismarck's North German Confederation and attempts to apply it to the perennial Hapsburg problem" showed that the new face of American constitutionalism soon began to look better in Europe.[70]

In regard to democracy, the emancipation of the slaves made the American model more appealing to European liberals. Although the war had been fought at first to preserve the Union, as the conflict wore on, the abolition of slavery became the North's primary war aim. That move eliminated one of the self-contradictory features of the United States as a democratic and liberal nation-state.

Democracy not only in America but worldwide was on the march after 1900, a major turning point in global history. The progress of democracy from the end of the nineteenth through most of the twentieth century was absolutely "breathtaking" according to Larry Diamond, a scholar who compared the two:

> In 1900 most of the current states of the world were part of one or another colonial empire, or at least lacked SOVEREIGNTY in their current form. Few peoples living under imperial or colonial rule, or within the political system of a protectorate enjoyed the RIGHTS OF CITIZENSHIP that are today widely acknowledged and codified in international covenants and charters. Neither did the more than one-third of the world's population living under absolute monarchical rule. Not a single political system in the world "enjoyed competitive multiparty politics with universal suffrage." . . . Everywhere women were denied the right to vote and typically so were racial minorities and the poor.[71]

After 1900, however, much of the world's population lived in a new democratic universe—one in which each of these conditions underwent a radical change to allow greater freedom for humankind.[72]

8

Fourth Echo
American Empire

The fourth "echo" of American constitutionalism resounded with the Spanish-American War in 1898, after which the United States strode like a colossus across the world stage to become an imperial power. Winning the war meant acquiring the Philippines and Puerto Rico and ultimately the Hawaiian Islands and the Samoan archipelago, thus becoming a major presence in both the Atlantic and the Pacific. Never before in world history had an imperialist nation risen so far so fast as the United States did between 1776 and 1900.[1] With these possessions, America burst its continental bonds and emerged as a truly global power.

America's break with its presumed anti-imperialist past came at a cost, however, because American constitutionalism abroad was changed forever. Before the acquisition of an overseas empire, territories added to the Union were expected to become states. All the people along the Western frontier wished to become American citizens, or so it was assumed (except for the Native Americans whose dispossession of their lands presents a very different story of American imperialism). White settlers spoke the same languages, followed the same customs, and hoped to become a part of the United States. They joined the Union of their own volition. Acquisition of an overseas empire, however, changed all that. After the 1890s, the spread of American constitutionalism abroad often resulted more from imposition than volition. The United States resorted to force to compel peoples in its colonies, protectorates, and conquered lands to follow its constitutional lead.

The Constitution had no provisions for acquiring overseas possessions or adding non-American peoples to the body politic. Indeed, America's tradition of republicanism contradicted the idea of ruling over peoples in foreign lands. Having adopted the republican idea that all governments derive their just powers from the consent of the governed, Americans suddenly faced a dilemma after the Spanish-American War: could non-Americans abroad be incorporated into the body politic against their will? If so, what was their constitutional position? And what about the tradition of volition? Was it to disappear completely? Nonetheless, the American model remained attractive to many non-Americans, such as the white settlers in Hawaii who petitioned for statehood for more than six decades. Cubans, in contrast, wanted independence immediately and fought for it for a long time. The two policies, volition and imposition, continued to exist side by side and influenced different people, in different regions, at different times.

The motives behind imperialism were mixed, and Americans were ambivalent about their country's new role. Many feared that America's democratic institutions and the country's republican ethos were incompatible with imperialism, and they had no wish to acquire an empire. Others wanted to expand the empire for economic reasons, such as new markets for American products and outlets for American capital. Still others wanted an empire for national security: to protect the homeland, guard the approaches to the Panama Canal, or shield against foreign ideologies that might infect America. Others believed in imperialism as an ideological crusade, a sense of mission to spread America's democratic institutions and values and bring the blessings of the American model to foreign lands.

Most Americans traditionally saw themselves as an anti-imperialistic nation. Having been born in a revolution against an imperial power, they believed that their tradition of anti-imperialism could continue as long as they stayed away from European affairs. They considered themselves exemplars of democracy, and in expanding into the Western frontier, they were extending the empire of liberty rather than acting as imperialists. Even when Americans robbed the Native Americans of their lands, seized territory from Mexico, and wrested regions from Canada, they invoked the myth of "Manifest Destiny," a God-given right to stretch across the continent from the Atlantic to the Pacific. Before the Civil War, Americans also rationalized their expansion as a desire of an agrarian people seeking new lands, arguing that as Americans they were better prepared to civilize regions in the West than were the people living in them.[2] And in regard to the Native Americans, most whites assumed they would either fade away or eventually be absorbed into America's white civilization.[3]

American Imperialism

The reasons why the United States became involved in the wave of imperialism that had motivated other great world powers became the subject of an intense national debate.[4] It will suffice here to say only that America's motives were mixed, ambivalent, and overlapping. One thing is certain, however: ideas regarding America's mission abroad as a world power underwent a dramatic transformation after 1898.

Numerous domestic developments also affected America's new role as an imperial power. The country had become an economic titan because of its rapid industrial growth, and publicists accordingly began calling on the United States to act like one. The disappearance of the frontier after 1890 resulted in the growing conviction that America would have to find new markets for its ever-expanding industrial and agricultural goods. Captain Alfred T. Mahan claimed that the nation's greatness and national security would depend ultimately on a large navy supported by far-flung naval bases. Social Darwinists argued that international rivalries were inevitable. The world, they claimed, was a jungle in which only the fittest nations would survive, and to do so, the United States would have to become stronger by acquiring an empire. But idealists and religious leaders urged the country to take up the "white man's burden," that is, to bring the blessings of American constitutionalism, democracy, and Christianity to peoples considered "less civilized."[5]

The postwar period after 1898 reflected many of these motives. Americans were convinced that Spain was no longer morally fit to govern its former colonies—Cuba, Puerto Rico, the Philippines, Guam, and the Marianas—given the atrocities committed during the war. With America's occupation of former Spanish possessions, it suddenly confronted a crucial question: What should be done with them? The options were granting the colonies their independence, annexing them, or allowing foreign powers to take them over. The outcomes were mixed. Cuba was eventually granted independence. Puerto Rico was annexed to prevent any further European penetration into the Western Hemisphere. And the Philippines and Guam were annexed for fear that Spain's weakness would allow more powerful states—Germany or Japan—to seize them.[6]

Once America became an imperial power, one move almost inevitably led to others. Hawaii, which had already petitioned for annexation, was incorporated in 1893. Wake Island was annexed in 1899 to serve as a communication link between Hawaii and Guam. Parts of the Samoan archipelago were annexed in 1900 to resolve a quarrel between Germany and the United States. In this way, within the short space of two years, the United States acquired a huge empire ranging from the Pacific to the Caribbean.

At about the same time, a number of dependencies in the Caribbean basin came under the sway of the United States, presumably for reasons of national security. These newly acquired territories further stimulated the imperialist impulse. A direct sea route from the Atlantic to the Pacific seemed imperative if America's modernized two-ocean navy was to operate successfully. The United States thus helped the Panamanians engineer a revolt against Colombia to gain their independence. Once a new puppet state had been established, the United States quickly signed a treaty in 1904 to allow the construction of a canal across the isthmus.

Stability in Caribbean waters was now considered critical to the nation's safety. In 1904, President Theodore Roosevelt added a corollary to the Monroe Doctrine by announcing that any instability in the region "which results in the general loosening of the ties of civilized society may . . . require intervention by some civilized nation," that is, the United States.[7] Since instability was chronic in the Caribbean basin, several countries soon became subject to America's control under the Roosevelt Corollary. Treaties guaranteeing the United States the right of military occupation or control over local public finances were signed: Cuba in 1903, Nicaragua in 1911 and 1916, and Haiti in 1915. Under the Roosevelt Corollary, the United States occupied and governed Haiti and the Dominican Republic for short periods, and the finances of several countries were placed in the hands of American bankers under the policy of dollar diplomacy. To complete its control over the Caribbean basin, the United States also purchased Denmark's Virgin Islands. American constitutionalism thus was imposed as a matter of course whenever the United States intervened in or occupied these regions, and American imperialism overrode the needs of native populations for civil rights and liberties.[8]

Compared with British imperialism, which exercised direct control over foreign countries through formal institutions like the British Colonial Office, American imperialism was more fitful and informal. From the beginning, the United States applied only an informal kind of imperialism in the Philippines, Puerto Rico, and Samoa. The best indication that the United States expected its empire to be transitory was its refusal to create a bureaucracy like the British Colonial Office. "The various territories were allocated [by turns] to the Department of State, of the Interior, the Navy, and War."[9]

The Roosevelt Corollary proved so unpopular, however, that the United States eventually was forced to repudiate it. In 1933 another Roosevelt, Franklin Delano, inaugurated his "Good Neighbor" policy in its place. Nonetheless, military interventions continued, though less frequently, in the Caribbean basin: in Guatemala in 1954, the Dominican Republic in 1965, Grenada in 1983, and Panama in 1989.

From a constitutional point of view, America's policies in governing its colonies proved embarrassing. No one offered a theoretical framework into which the colonies might fit logically. The improvised nature of American imperialism resulted in a hodgepodge of conflicting policies. The only thing that set apart America's empire, as one scholar put it, was an "attempt to fit colonial possessions into the Procrustean bed of republicanism."[10]

There is much truth in this remark. One overarching theme in American constitutionalism was the deep-seated desire to try to export core constitutional values with which American republicanism had always identified itself: liberty and equality. If these republican values could be transplanted successfully, it was believed, then America's possessions would resemble the mother country; that is, "they" would become like "us." Although economic motives and national security concerns were behind American imperialism, so too was American idealism. America's mixed motives soon divided the country.

Does the Constitution Follow the Flag?

The decision to take the Spanish possessions erupted in an acrimonious debate in Congress. Critics asked whether the Constitution mentioned any power to acquire new territories or to incorporate them. The issue was framed by two questions. Did the Constitution stop at the water's edge, or did the Constitution follow the American flag wherever it flew overseas? Were the rights and responsibilities of the Constitution applicable to colonial peoples living outside the limits of the contiguous United States? Or were colonial peoples to be required instead to live under regulations issued by either Congress or its government agencies? What was to be done if imperialism demanded decisions contrary to the values implied or expressed in the Declaration of Independence? These questions went to the heart of American constitutionalism.

The result was a fierce constitutional crisis between imperialists and anti-imperialists. The imperialists, believing in progress, argued that it was the responsibility of Americans to bring such democratic values to so-called backward peoples. Theories of social Darwinism held that different races progressed at different rates according to their place on the evolutionary scale. Their failure to move forward meant that some races would fall behind, become victims to natural selection, and fail to survive. Underlying this theory, of course, was an implied belief in human inequality and the notion of superior and inferior races.

The anti-imperialists, by contrast, believed they were fighting to preserve the traditional principles of constitutional democracy expressed in the Declaration. They took the position that imperialism violated the fundamental principles on which American constitutionalism was based: liberty, democracy, and self-government.[11] Congressman George Vest of Missouri argued that the United States could not annex territories abroad against the will of the subject peoples without violating the principle of government by the consent of the governed.[12]

These opposing positions were expressed in letters written by two men responsible for framing America's colonial policy in the Philippines. Theodore Roosevelt, then vice president, wrote in 1900: "I wish to see the United States the dominant power in the Pacific Ocean. Our people . . . must . . . do the work of a great power."[13] But Jacob Gould Schurman, the first head of the Philippine Commission and a reluctant expansionist, informed his wife in 1899: "We must govern them [the Filipinos] in their own interests—not *ours*—as a trust of civilization."[14] But Schurman had a much more ambitious constitutional goal in mind: to make the Philippines a showcase of American constitutionalism and democracy for all the peoples of Asia to see. As he wrote in 1902,

> The destiny of the Philippine Islands is not to be a state or territory in the United States . . . but a daughter republic of ours—a new birth of liberty on the other side of the Pacific . . . a monument of progress and a beacon of hope to all the oppressed and benighted millions of the Asiatic continent.[15]

The controversy between imperialists and anti-imperialists raged on. Although the anti-imperialists lost the debate in Congress, the American public remained split. Annexation of the Philippines was so unpopular that the treaty with Spain covering the purchase of the islands was ratified in the Senate by a very close vote, which did not augur well for the future of American imperialism.

The struggle also played out in the courts, where the imperialists contended that acquisition did not automatically incorporate the new possessions into the United States and endow their inhabitants with all the constitutional privileges of American citizenship. The anti-imperialists argued that the Constitution "followed the flag." In other words, territorial acquisition made these dependencies an organic part of the United States and therefore entitled their inhabitants to all the constitutional guarantees of American citizens.

The constitutional status of the dependencies was presumably settled by the Supreme Court in the so-called Insular Cases heard between 1901 and 1922.[16] American possessions were judged to be either "incorporated" or "unincorporated." The question of what constituted an unincorporated territory depended on the *intent* of Congress as expressed in specific legislation. Thus, Alaska (which had been purchased from Russia in 1867) and Hawaii were declared by Congress to be "incorporated" in 1900 and 1905, respectively. The Philippines and Puerto Rico, however, were declared to be "unincorporated."[17]

The Court also made a crucial distinction between "fundamental rights" and "procedural rights" when it limited the powers of Congress over American possessions. Fundamental rights were extended to everyone who came under the sovereignty of the United States. By contrast, procedural rights, or "formal privileges" such as the right of trial by jury, were extended to unincorporated territories only if Congress so specified.

The Philippines

The annexation of the Philippines in 1899 proved highly significant for several reasons. It marked the entry of the United States into East Asia, a region where there had been little American constitutional presence previously. The islands as well brought Americans into contact with a foreign culture quite different from their own. For its part, the Philippines came under the influence of a Western power with a long-standing liberal tradition. This country became the only place outside the Western Hemisphere where the United States ruled an imperial possession through direct American constitutionalism. "With the possible exception of Cuba early in the twentieth century and the occupation of Japan after World War II, there is no other instance of America's exercising such power over people recognized to be permanently ineligible for American citizenship or out-side the protection of the Bill of Rights," wrote one scholar.[18]

While the war was in process, the Filipino patriot Emilio Aguinaldo was fighting for independence. On June 12, 1898, Filipino revolutionar-ies proclaimed their independence in a document patterned, in part, on the American Declaration. The Philippine declaration was historically sig-nificant not only because it was the first successful attempt by an Asian people to throw off colonialism but also because they did so by turning to a major document of American constitutionalism.[19] At Malalos, later in 1899, a Filipino congress met, drafted a constitution, and established the Philippine Republic. The Filipinos promptly requested recognition from the United States but were denied. The short-lived Malalos Constitution was not based on the U.S. Constitution; instead, it drew on the Spanish Constitution of 1869, several Latin American constitutions, and the char-ters of France and Belgium.[20]

The provisional Filipino government then plunged into a bloody war of independence against the United States. In the conflict, called "the Fili-pino-American War" in the Philippines and the "Philippine Insurrection" in the United States, atrocities were committed by both sides. Americans quickly realized that only by defusing the Filipino opposition could they hope to occupy the islands as a governable colony. Not only would the islands have to be conquered, but its inhabitants also would have to ac-cept American constitutionalism.[21] The result was a new policy, "imperial-ism by persuasion." William Howard Taft, architect of the policy, changed America's approach from military repression to pacification. As the first civilian governor, Taft slowly took over local governments, province by province, and eventually persuaded the Filipinos that it was in their best interest to cooperate rather than fight.[22]

This strategy was carried out by inviting Westernized Filipino elites to participate in local governments. The elites were then used to intro-duce America's policies to the rest of the Filipino people. "The Americans needed the elites to mediate with the mass of people; the elites needed the Americans to impose order and restore their leadership in society [against local guerrilla groups]."[23] Through this strategy of accommodation and collaboration, a more permissive constitutional policy was put into place.

The strategy worked because of the mutual interests of both groups. Americans inaugurated programs that were popular with the Filipinos: modernizing education, secularizing the state, eliminating diseases, build-ing roads, and granting preferential treatment of Filipino products in

American tariffs. The Filipino people, for their part, appreciated what was done, and America gained a governable colony. Calls for independence died down; from 1908 to 1946, only one revolutionary outbreak occurred, and it was aimed primarily at Filipino elites rather than at Americans.[24]

There was, however, a concealed cost in this strategy of suasion. The Filipino elites, who represented the upper classes, held all the important positions of authority. The Americans supported the elites and became collaborators in their policies. "While protecting and institutionalizing the power of the Filipino elite, Americans . . . allowed themselves to be used as an external device for deflecting criticism of . . . the regime."[25] The United States, in effect, surrendered its responsibility for governing the islands, but without ending its interference in the lives of ordinary Filipinos.

The formal experiment in American constitutionalism got under way in 1900 when President William McKinley instructed the Taft Commission to establish a government. He listed a series of rights called the "Magna Carta of the Philippines," consisting of a version of the American Bill of Rights, along with a number of important Civil War amendments. This list was destined to have a long life, as it was included in all subsequent Filipino constitutions and reflected an effort to pass on to the Filipinos some semblance of the American model.[26]

The government structure established in the Philippines in 1902 resembled in many ways that of the United States. It included the traditional tripartite division. Executive functions were carried out by an American-appointed governor-general. The Filipino legislature was made up of an elected lower house (the first popularly elected body in East Asia) and an American-appointed upper house. Although there was a judiciary, its cases were sometimes subject to review by the U.S. Supreme Court. By imposing American constitutionalism so strictly, however, the United States never allowed its colony to develop much self-rule, and over time, the Filipino government began to resemble the American constitutional system more and more.

The Jones Act of 1916, nevertheless, did confirm America's intention to grant self-rule to the Philippines as soon as conditions were appropriate, although progress toward that end turned out to be painfully slow. Plans for a transition to independence were not announced until the Tydings–McGuffie Act of 1934. A Filipino constitutional convention was to be called, a commonwealth established, and a republic declared. The constitution was to include a bill of rights and to establish a "republican form of government," which the Filipinos interpreted to mean an "American form of government."[27] Accordingly, the Filipinos included in their 1935 constitution all the main features of American constitutionalism except federalism. The constitution created a republican form of government, a bicameral legislature, and an executive headed by a strong president. There was a bill of rights, and the Filipino judiciary, already in existence, was continued. The Philippines was created as an autonomous commonwealth with a semisovereign status. Even though the United States maintained control over foreign affairs, defense, and finance, the Filipinos ran the day-to-day affairs of government.[28] The 1935 constitution also promised the Filipinos their independence within a decade.

When World War II intervened, the United States delayed its promise, but Filipino soldiers nonetheless fought side by side with Americans. On the Fourth of July, 1946, the Stars and Stripes were lowered, and the flag of the new Republic of the Philippines was raised. After a period of tutelage of more than a half century, the United States at last had fulfilled its pledge. The significance of this occasion was not lost on other Asians, and a surge of hope rippled through the colonial Far East from India to Indo-China and from Burma to Indonesia. The Philippines was the first major colony of any Western power to reclaim part of its sovereignty. Schurman's dream of making the Philippines a showcase of democracy seemed about to be realized.

What can be said about America's stewardship of the Philippines as a colony? The results were mixed, some good and some bad. Deadly diseases like malaria, cholera, and beriberi were eradicated, and life expectancy shot up from fourteen years in 1900 to forty by 1940. Literacy rates increased dramatically and in 1946 stood at almost 60 percent, one of the highest in the region. The infrastructure of roads, canals, and bridges was transformed, and some land reform was achieved.[29] More significant were the American constitutional principles grafted onto existing Filipino traditions. While not always practiced, these concepts exerted an important influence: adherence to the rule of law, representative government, observance of civil liberties, respect for the court system, and establishment of a civil service system based on merit. These ideas and attitudes radically transformed Filipino society.[30]

But there were signs also that all was not well. The American idea of a strong presidency, for example, created problems. The first president of the commonwealth, Manuel Quezon, was reported as saying that "under our Constitution, what is paramount is not individuals, it is the good of the state, not the good of the individual that must prevail."[31] Such sentiments were hardly in keeping with the principles of American constitutionalism and did not augur well for the future.

Although the Filipino people had succeeded in gaining some control over their affairs, they realized they were being manipulated by Filipino elites. Quezon had said in 1924 that he preferred "a government run like hell to one like heaven by the Americans." He was aware of the pitfalls of premature independence, however, and even helped sabotage a bill in the American Congress in 1924 that would have granted Filipino independence earlier.[32] "The trouble with Americans," he was rumored to have said, "is that they do not oppress us nearly enough."[33]

Puerto Rico: Commonwealth Experiment

Puerto Rico also was occupied by American troops during the Spanish-American War, but a newly independent Puerto Rico assembly had convened on July 17, 1898, eight days before American troops actually invaded the island. By then, Puerto Ricans had seized control, dissolved the old Spanish government, and had set about creating a new one. The war that was started to end Spanish colonialism resulted only in ending Puerto Rico's brief period of self-rule.

America's Foraker Act of 1900 provided for a civil government and made Puerto Rico an unincorporated territory. Its inhabitants were denied American citizenship, and in the Insular Cases, the Supreme Court ruled that the Foraker Act was constitutional, thus confirming the denial of American citizenship. Accordingly, Puerto Ricans could not enjoy such fundamental guarantees as trial by jury, grand jury indictment, or equality in taxation.[34] The attorney general informed the Supreme Court that this ruling was necessary because another situation similar to this might set a precedent for other possessions. Given the rapidly rising American empire, the Constitution had to be interpreted in such a way as to accommodate the needs of the United States.[35] Puerto Ricans, having been denied American citizenship, began to demand this right.[36]

The Jones Act of 1917 not only made Puerto Rico an American territory but also conferred citizenship on all inhabitants and provided male suffrage. The act included as well a bill of rights that gave Puerto Ricans virtually all the civil rights prescribed in the U.S. Constitution (except trial by jury). Although Puerto Ricans were provided such benefits, tight controls were imposed on self-government. Legislative acts were subject to veto by the American president, and he could appoint the governor and members of the Supreme Court.

Puerto Rico's economy fared poorly under America's colonial administration. During the Great Depression, the island suffered terribly and was known as the "poorhouse" of the Caribbean. There were riots and demonstrations throughout the mid-1930s. In 1939, a legislative committee urged statehood, but efforts for more self-government were blocked by a hostile Congress. The island's economy improved somewhat in the 1940s, when Puerto Rico became a key American naval base during World War II.

Conditions improved even more when a talented leader, Luis Muñoz Marín, later launched a successful industrialization program called Operation Bootstrap. Muñoz also founded the Popular Democratic Party and dedicated himself to cultivating closer ties with the United States. He campaigned on a single theme, that Puerto Rico's constitutional status was much more important than its economic situation.

Unhappy with their treatment at the hands of the Americans, the Puerto Rican political parties began to focus on this issue. One group wanted statehood, but a larger group believed that statehood could not be achieved without losing certain favorable economic concessions. Within this larger group some desired outright independence, but only if the United States continued certain economic guarantees such as duty-free trade between the island and the United States. Still others wanted complete independence with no conditions. These issues divided Puerto Ricans, as they still do today.

Encouraged by the island's economic progress and influenced by the wave of anti-imperial sentiment following World War II, the United States took steps to eliminate certain vestiges of colonialism. In 1947 Congress amended the Jones Act, allowing Puerto Ricans to elect their own governor. The following year, Muñoz became the first native Puerto Rican to be elected to the position. Under his leadership, the Popular Democratic Party began to transform the constitutional relationship between the colony and mother country. In 1950, Congress passed Public Law 600 which required a referendum by which Puerto Ricans could choose between continuing the status quo or creating a new self-governing commonwealth. As the charismatic Muñoz remarked at one time, "To govern is to invent."[37]

What the Puerto Ricans invented was a constitutional status never tried before. It was a solution that transcended the traditional idea of a federal union. Puerto Rico evolved from being an unincorporated territory to become an "associated" commonwealth of the United States. The idea of a free commonwealth voluntarily becoming an associated member of a federal union was different from any known constitutional arrangement.

Puerto Rico's newfound status became effective in mid-1953. "Nothing like it was envisaged by the fathers of the American Constitution," wrote Carl J. Friedrich.[38] The founding fathers ordinarily thought in terms of a single territorial entity, one composed solely of states and territories. But American federalism, Friedrich pointed out, could be interpreted more broadly as a *process* of federalizing existing composite communities. That is exactly what the Puerto Ricans chose. They provided a constitutional model for liberating a colonial people who did not wish, or were unable, to be absorbed into a fully integrated union like the United States.[39] The device of a freely associated commonwealth, Friedrich surmised, had worldwide ramifications. The "associating" of Britain and other European powers with the Coal and Steel Community as well as the Common Market Community at a later date, for example, was an arrangement somewhat similar to that of Puerto Rico.[40]

The steps by which Puerto Rico's historic transformation took place carefully followed the principles of American constitutionalism. First, Congress passed Public Law 600 which provided for consultation with the Puerto Rican people as to whether they wished to go forward to self-government and to elect a constituent assembly. Second, a referendum was held in June 1951, which resulted in an affirmative answer. Third, a constituent assembly was elected in August 1951. During the winter of 1951/1952, the electoral convention drafted a constitution which was approved by almost 50 percent of the electorate.[41] The draft constitution was then submitted to President Harry Truman and Congress and, after approval, was presented to the Puerto Rican legislature for final acceptance.[42] Governor Muñoz finally proclaimed the Commonwealth of Puerto Rico in 1953.

The Puerto Rican Constitution followed the U.S. Constitution in many particulars. It provided for a governor to be popularly elected every four years (though unlimited reelection was allowed). It provided for a bicameral legislature in which the representation of minority parties was guaranteed. Judicial power was vested in a supreme court and lower courts, but appeals to the federal court system were possible as well.

Despite popular support for the commonwealth, many people remained dissatisfied and wanted complete independence. Alaska and Hawaii had been granted statehood in 1959, which contributed to many Puerto Ricans' growing sentiment for the same status. A plebiscite held in July

1967, however, showed that more than 60 percent of the electorate still approved retaining the commonwealth status. Moreover, when President Lyndon B. Johnson wrote to the Puerto Rican governor later, expressing readiness to appoint an ad hoc committee to review the situation, he did not receive a response. Elections on this issue during the 1970s and 1980s showed the Puerto Ricans to be almost evenly divided, but a plebiscite in 1993 clearly favored the commonwealth status. In Puerto Rico, the unique accommodation of American constitutionalism appeared to have satisfied a majority of the population.[43]

The Northern Mariana Islands

The self-governing commonwealth arrangement was eventually extended in 1986 to the Northern Mariana Islands. Located fifteen hundred miles east of the Philippines, the fourteen islands, which include Saipan and Tinian, had been the scene of heavy fighting in World War II because of their strategic importance. After the war, the United States took over their administration under a United Nations mandate approved in 1947 and pledged to "promote development toward self-government or independence." In 1975, residents voted three to one in favor of becoming a self-governing commonwealth in union with the United States. The islands were formally given commonwealth status, and its residents became American citizens.

Aside from the Philippines and Puerto Rico, other unincorporated territories included Guam,[44] Wake Island,[45] Samoa,[46] and the Virgin Islands[47] were added mainly for reasons of national security. They were "unincorporated" because originally not all the provisions of the U.S. Constitution applied to them, and they were given less self-government than incorporated territories had. Over time, however, they too were granted greater authority over their own affairs.

Unincorporated Territories That Became States: Alaska and Hawaii

Alaska and Hawaii, two territories outside the contiguous United States, not only desired the benefits of American constitutionalism but also sought full incorporation as states in the Union. Their juridical status, however, remained in doubt for more than six decades, demonstrating how reluctant the country was to extend statehood.

Alaska, purchased from Russia in 1867, became America's first noncontiguous territory, and its governance remained rather limited for the next seventeen years. Jurisdiction passed successively to different government agencies, the army, treasury, and navy. In 1884 Congress passed the First Organic Act, making Alaska a civil and judicial district. The only offices for which the act provided were an appointed governor and a district court, but no legislature or any other form of self-government.

The gold rush of 1892 brought great changes. Alaska's population doubled, and in 1906 Congress responded by authorizing an elected Alaskan delegate to Congress.[48] The Second Organic Act of 1912 made Alaska a full-fledged territory and established a bicameral legislature. Because the United States maintained tight control, the powers of the territorial legislature remained quite restricted, constitutionally speaking. Alaska could not amend, modify, or repeal laws related to "customs, internal revenue, postal, or other general laws of the United States and specifically to any American laws related to fur-bearing animals."[49]

From 1912 until statehood was granted, Alaska was governed under the Second Organic Act.[50] When World War II demonstrated its strategic importance, statehood became a crucial issue. In Congress, however, there was a major political obstacle: southern senators feared that their two votes would jeopardize their position on states' rights and other matters.[51] In 1954 Alaska's fortunes became linked to those of Hawaii, which also was demanding statehood. At that time, since Alaska traditionally voted Democratic and Hawaii Republican, the chances of statehood improved dramatically. In January 1959, a political compromise resulted in Alaska's being admitted as the forty-ninth state.

Hawaii's constitutional history differed substantially from that of Alaska. The fervor created by the Spanish-American War, as discussed earlier, was primarily responsible for its annexation. Once the U.S. Navy was committed to fighting two-ocean wars, the islands' strategic importance became obvious.

America's interest in the Hawaiian Islands stretched back to the 1840s when the first generation of settlers, Christian missionaries, were followed by a second generation made up of their sons, more interested in business profits than in preaching. Although a lease was signed in 1887 with the kingdom of Hawaii to build a naval station at Pearl Harbor, the American government was reluctant to annex the islands. But international rivalry soon prompted a change of mind when the expansion of Britain, France,

Germany and Japan into the region raised the possibility that Hawaii could be seized.

Those Americans who had settled originally in Hawaii and now owned huge sugar and pineapple plantations strongly favored annexation to the United States.[52] They realized that the native population was in no position to resist if one of the great powers decided to invade. Opposition to their plans, however, came from the local ruler, Queen Liliuokalani, who wished to curb Hawaii's Americanization and Westernization. Her efforts to restrict the local legislature resulted in a coup in 1893, one openly supported by the U.S. Navy. Once in control, American residents set up a provisional government, proclaimed the Republic of Hawaii, and wrote a constitution.

Hawaii's constitution deliberately borrowed many American antecedents. Designed to appeal to the republican sentiments prevailing on the mainland, its lofty language reflected the Declaration of Independence and the U.S. Constitution. The Hawaiian Constitution declared that "God hath endowed all men with certain inalienable rights . . . Life, Liberty, and the Right . . . of pursuing and obtaining Happiness; . . . the Government [was to be] conducted for the common good, and not for the profit, honor, or private interest of any one man, family, or class of men." The document contained also a bill of rights similar to that of the United States, calling for freedom of religion, speech, press, meeting, and petition.[53] By following the principles of American constitutionalism, the founders hoped to persuade Congress to grant the islands statehood.

The provisional government created the Republic of Hawaii on July 4, 1894, an obviously symbolic date. Its president, Sanford Dole, the son of an American missionary and one of Hawaii's largest landholders, represented the local leaders. The government followed the American pattern, with one important exception. Requirements for citizenship were manipulated to ensure that the American minority would maintain political control. The Native Hawaiians, even those who could meet the citizenship requirements, refused to vote or to participate in the government once it was established.[54]

Following the coup by American residents, President Grover Cleveland rejected annexation, but in 1898 President William McKinley agreed to it. A territorial government was organized in 1900 as an unincorporated territory until the Insular Cases changed that designation in 1903. The islands were viewed as stepping-stones to the great market presumed to exist in heavily populated China. Although the United States defined a territory as being in a form of "pupilage" for statehood, Hawaii's request was denied seven times. It was finally admitted as the fiftieth state in August 1959 and followed Alaska as the second noncontiguous state in the Union.

Protectorates

A protectorate represents a different kind of constitutional relationship, albeit one recognized in international law over the centuries. It acknowledges a connection between two states in which the stronger one guarantees to protect the weaker from external aggression or domestic disorder. In return, the weaker state relinquishes full or partial control over its foreign and domestic affairs.

Cuba, Nicaragua, Haiti, and the Dominican Republic all were designated as American protectorates. The Roosevelt Corollary provided the rationale for the protectorate policy, and thus the United States intervened numerous times. What was significant in regard to American constitutionalism was that the United States either wrote the constitutions of these protectorates, as in the case of Haiti and the Dominican Republic, or demanded participation in the constitutional arrangements, as in Cuba and Nicaragua.

Historians disagree about the motives behind America's military interventions. Some argue that the primary purpose was national security, such as the safety of the strategic Panama Canal. Others insist that the reasons were largely economic. Still others claim that the Roosevelt Corollary represented a retreat from the formal kind of European imperialism to a more informal system of protectorates. Whatever the reasons, it is clear that American imperialism was more pronounced and stronger in those regions closest to the mainland.[55]

Cuba

The new protectorate policy was inaugurated in Cuba in 1901 by President McKinley and his military commander on the island, General Leonard Wood. A constituent assembly had been convened in 1900, but Wood informed the delegates that even though they could write their own laws, there would be certain restrictions. Any proposed constitution would have to grant the United States the right to intervene to protect Cuba's independence. This requirement, known as the Platt Amendment, limited

Cuba's sovereignty. "There is, of course, little or no independence left in Cuba under the Platt Amendment," observed Wood.[56]

The first Cuban Constitution of 1901 revealed the new hegemonic role the United States hoped to play throughout the Caribbean basin. Some Americans wished to dominate the region by setting up a series of sister American republics. President Theodore Roosevelt confided to a colleague in 1906 his desire to establish "control of [the] . . . regions by self-governing northern democracies."[57]

The Platt Amendment soon created constitutional tensions. Americans argued that given the United States' support of Cuba during the struggle for independence, it had a legitimate right to play a role in Cuban affairs. Cuban nationalists, however, considered this intrusion a humiliating concession. Under the 1901 constitution, a series of regimes with little real power operated under the watchful eye of the United States.[58]

Cuba was occupied under the Platt Amendment from 1898 to 1902. After General Wood became military governor, an uneasy temporary truce prevailed among Cuba's warring political parties, but at the same time, the colonial administration introduced a number of reforms. Under Wood, who was a doctor, the deadly yellow fever was eliminated. A competent and politically astute administrator, Wood initiated other public enterprises, building schools, roads, and bridges. His reputation for fairness enabled him to bring some small measure of stability to Cuba, and certain principles of American constitutionalism began to be observed.

Following the departure of American troops and military government, however, Cuba could not remain stable for long. Graft, corruption, and fiscal irresponsibility led to a revolt against the Cuban government in 1906. Accordingly, under the terms of the Platt Amendment, the Americans again occupied the country from 1906 to 1909.[59]

A third American intervention occurred in 1912, this time in response to a civil war between the leading political parties.[60] The Cubans complained that the American government appeared only too willing to intervene whenever any opposition party asked for help, and, in fact, the United States intervened a fourth time in 1917.[61] The reasons given were to provide American security in wartime, to stabilize Cuba's political parties, and to protect American investments in Cuba's sugar plantations. This time the intervention was protracted and lasted until 1922.[62] Then, in 1935 when a pro-American dictator was finally driven from office, steps were taken to draft a new constitution.

Cuba's second constitution of 1940 took years to write and was the result of a joint American and Cuban effort. In 1934 the Platt Amendment had been abrogated in an attempt to accommodate Cuba's rising nationalism. Cuban revolutionaries in the 1930s had demanded "Cuba for Cubans," and the constitution of 1940 promised important reforms, such as the nationalization of certain large industries. But these reforms were never carried out, and Fidel Castro, who came to power in the 1959 Cuban revolution, skillfully exploited the disappointed hopes of the 1930s revolutionary generation to seize power.

The Cuban revolution led eventually to the constitution of 1976, which introduced a completely different constitutional system, one modeled on that of the Soviet Union. It replaced the previous civil-law constitution with "socialist" law, recognized Marxist–Leninism as the state ideology, and made the Communist Party the only legal party on the island.[63] Needless to say, the 1976 constitution was a polar opposite from American constitutionalism.

The Dominican Republic

From its independence in 1849 until 1992, the Dominican Republic had twenty-five different constitutions.[64] Generally speaking, "the Dominican constitutional tradition has long reflected the forms of the U.S. Constitution," concluded two scholars.[65] Each constitution guaranteed human rights, established a separation of powers, provided for popular sovereignty, and included other features of the American model. But despite such rhetoric, the gap between the written charters and social reality remained wide. "Although the nation's numerous constitutions have articulated lofty ideals and principles," one scholarly report maintained, "the fact remains that these precepts have been routinely neglected by national leaders."[66] Public policies in the Dominican Republic "were shaped not so much by formal constitutional arrangements as they were by the personal ideas of the individuals occupying the national palace."[67] A caricature of the American concept of presidentialism was practiced constantly.

The Dominican Republic, in fact, led to the announcement of the Roosevelt Corollary in 1904. When German influence began spreading from neighboring Haiti during World War I, President Woodrow Wilson in 1916 ordered the Dominican Republic occupied for security reasons, an occupation that lasted until 1924, long after World War I was over. Like all the constitutions in the Dominican Republic in the early twentieth century, the constitution of 1924 retained numerous features of the U.S. Constitution, although actual political practices left much to be desired.[68]

While stationed in the Dominican Republic, American Marines trained and equipped the Guardia, a national police force. The Guardia was eventually taken over by Generalissimo Rafael Trujillo, who mounted a revolution in 1930 and seized control. He ruled for thirty-one years and ran "one of the tightest dictatorships the world has ever seen."[69] One way Trujillo remained in power was by cultivating ties with the United States as a staunch anticommunist ally. His constitutions, moreover, followed the U.S. model in sham rhetoric while he continued to exercise despotic personal control.[70]

Because of its constant interventions and support of Trujillo, the United States was partly responsible for the failure of American constitutionalism to gain a foothold in the Dominican Republic. Whether the Dominican Republic might have developed a constitutional democracy resembling that of the United States remains unclear. Driven by its obsessive desire for national security, the United States was often the cause for the failure of democracy in the Dominican Republic.

After Trujillo was assassinated in 1961, a reformist regime under Juan Bosch wrote a quite different constitution two years later. When a coup against Bosch succeeded, a new junta took control. A civil war then broke out in 1965 when rebels sought to restore Bosch to power. President Lyndon B. Johnson, fearing the rebels might come under communist control, ordered American marines to the island to restore order and installed an interim government. When elections were held in 1966 under American supervision, ex-President Joaquin Balaguer Ricardo was elected. Balaguer remained president from 1966 to 1978 but then returned to power in 1986 and inaugurated a "period of relatively democratic government."[71]

Haiti

After more than one hundred years of precarious independence, Haiti abruptly lost its freedom when U.S. Marines seized its capital in July 1915. A number of reasons were given for the occupation: financial instability; the threat to American life and property; and the fear—while World War I was in progress—that Germany might try to seize an island located on the approach to the Panama Canal. The treaty signed in September 1916 made Haiti an American protectorate and stipulated that its public debt might not be increased or its tariff diminished without American consent.

Franklin Delano Roosevelt, then assistant secretary of the navy, claimed that he drafted the constitution of 1918. There is, indeed, considerable evidence to that effect. The document provided for some new and unaccustomed democratic rights: freedom of assembly, trial by jury in political cases, direct election of senators, submission of amendments to popular vote, and freedom of the press.[72] Its most debatable provision, however, gave foreigners the right to own land, thereby ending a long-term tradition in Haiti's previous constitutions. The proposed five-year residency requirement for alien landownership would have allowed German settlers a majority, since they were the main European group attracted to the island. Because of the wartime situation, the U.S. State Department insisted that the provision be dropped.[73]

Although the 1918 constitution contained democratic features drawn from the U.S. Constitution, the process of ratification was decidedly undemocratic. The United States had already forced the treaty on Haiti in 1915 under duress. Under its terms, a puppet pro-American president was elected. The 1917 National Assembly, however, refused to adopt an American-sponsored document and instead drafted a constitution of its own, which was anti-American. While the Assembly was debating the issues, the proceedings were dramatically interrupted by Major Smedley Butler of the U.S. Marines. He read a decree, signed by the Haitian president, dissolving the Assembly, and carried it out, as Butler wrote, "by genuinely Marine Corps methods."[74] Butler not only held a commission as major in the U.S. Marines but also headed the Haitian gendarmarie with the rank of major general.

Once the Americans had dissolved the Assembly, it was necessary to submit the constitution to some other body for ratification. A plebiscite was thereby conducted which was carried out in a farcical manner: orders were given to arrest any antigovernment opponents who publicly expressed displeasure![75] Less than 5 percent of the population participated, but those who did overwhelmingly voted in favor of the document. Years later, Josephus Daniels, a former secretary of the navy, wrote shamefacedly to Roosevelt: "I never did wholly approve of that Constitution . . . you had a hand in framing. I expect in the light of experience, we both regret the necessity of denying even a semblance of 'self-determination' in our control of Haiti."[76]

Having imposed the 1918 constitution, the United States continued to maintain tight control over Haiti. A series of puppet presidents were placed in office; an American customs receivership was imposed; and the country was ruled through an American military high commissioner. The American-sponsored constitution wounded Haitian pride and left a legacy of bitterness. The Haitians' hatred was fanned also by the racism of the American occupiers, as well as by the repeated postponements of promised presidential elections. Although American officials improved the infrastructure on the Haitian half of the island, relations did not improve until the Good Neighbor policy was implemented in 1934. After order had been restored and finances had been stabilized, American troops finally were withdrawn that year.

Constitutions in the postoccupation period were written by native Haitians. Some were framed by accomplished scholar-diplomats, like Dantès Bellegarde who provided for female suffrage. But in 1957 the tyrannical François Duvalier, known as "Papa Doc," was elected and introduced a reign of terror. In 1964 he wrote his third constitution, making himself president for life.[77]

"Papa Doc" was succeeded by his son, Jean Claude Duvalier, called "Baby Doc," who also was supposed to rule for life. In 1985, however, "Baby Doc" wrote his second constitution granting the legislature new powers, creating a position of prime minister, and permitting political parties to operate. This last measure was nothing more than a public relations response to pressure from the United States.[78] The document was eventually approved by a fraudulent referendum. After ruling for fourteen years, "Baby Doc" was finally forced into exile in 1986, leaving Haiti the poorest country in the Western Hemisphere.

After many years of American occupation and nearly thirty years of dictatorship and political manipulation, Haiti had no democratic tradition to fall back on. Progress toward establishing a democratic government began when the provisional military–civilian government sponsored the first post–Duvalier constitution in 1987. This liberal constitution restored the two-house legislature, reduced the powers of the president and prime minister, and guaranteed human rights. This document, containing many features of American constitutionalism, was approved by a referendum. Jean-Bertrand Aristide, an American-supported candidate, was elected in 1990. U.S. interference in Haiti's political affairs over the years, including violations of the principles of American constitutionalism, had done much more harm than good. Not only did uneasy relations continue between the two countries, but Haiti failed to establish stable governments of its own.

Nicaragua

Like the Dominican Republic and Haiti, Nicaragua endured American military occupations and eventually became an American protectorate. Its constitutional history differed from that of Haiti and the Dominican Republic, however, because it was exposed to the influence of the U.S. Constitution much earlier. Nicaragua had been part of the 1824 Central American Federation, whose constitution incorporated certain features of the American model. When Nicaragua left the federation in 1838 and struck off on its own, it promulgated its first constitution, whose ideas of liberty, popular sovereignty, and the tradition of individual rights were borrowed essentially from both the U.S. Constitution and the French Revolution.[79]

During the first three decades of the twentieth century, Nicaragua suffered several American military interventions, initially because the United States feared that another trans-isthmus canal might be built in the region, a scheme that at one time or another attracted the attention of the British, Germans, and Japanese. American intervention began in 1912 when the provisional president, Adolpho Diaz, asked the U.S. military to intervene to restore order in his country. Four years later, the United States agreed to pay $3 million for the right to build a canal across the isthmus. That aroused protests in several surrounding Central American countries and resulted in an anticanal guerrilla war in Nicaragua which lasted until 1925. In the meantime, the Panama Canal had been built and opened to traffic in 1914.

After several other U.S. interventions, the leader of the national party, Augusto Sandino, continued a guerrilla war against American forces for several years. When the American Marines were finally withdrawn in 1933, Anastasio Somoza, commander of the Nicaraguan National Guard, had Sandino killed. In 1937 Somoza was elected president, and for the next twenty years, either as president or behind puppet presidents, Somoza sustained the longest dynastic dictatorship in Latin American history.[80]

Somoza family rule continued after Anastasio Somoza was assassinated in 1956. Like his father, the younger son of the former dictator, Anastasio Somoza DeBayle, periodically relinquished the presidency but maintained power. When the city of Managua was leveled by a huge earthquake in 1972, martial law was declared, and in 1974 Somoza was formally reelected president.

In hindsight, the earthquake proved to be a turning point for the Somoza family dictatorship. The disaster reversed the relative prosperity that had been enjoyed by the middle class and revealed the brutality, corruption, and undemocratic character of the regime. Anti-Somoza forces that had been divided joined together in 1974, despite continuing disagreements. One of the main groups was called the Sandinistas (FSLN) in honor of the murdered Augusto Sandino. The second group, the Democratic Union of Liberation (UDEL) was not long in finding its martyr. He was Pedro Chamorro, editor of *La prensa*, Managua's leading newspaper. When he was assassinated, Somoza was accused of complicity in the act, and a virtual civil war ensued.

Seeking to prevent the rise of another communist regime in the region besides Cuba, the United States raised a counterrevolutionary army, the "Contras." Eventually the United States prevailed on Somoza to go into exile and accused Castro's Cuba and the Soviet Union of using the Sandinistas to spread communism throughout the Western Hemisphere. In 1984, Daniel Ortega Saavedra, the Sandinista leader, was elected president, but any hopes of constitutional reforms were dashed when he suspended civil rights for a year under a state of emergency. American military aid to the "Contras," meanwhile, also was suspended in 1986 when Congress discovered that they had benefited from funds diverted from secret arms sales to Iran in a covert fiasco.

In 1988 the Sandinistas and the Contras finally agreed to a temporary truce, followed by internationally supervised elections in 1990, in which Violetta Barrios de Chamorro, widow of the martyred Pedro Chamorro, was elected president. At the urging of former President Jimmy Carter, who served as an international observer, Ortega made a gracious concession speech. Chamorro then launched a program of national reconstruction, including both the Contras and the Sandinistas, and began restoring constitutional order.

Panama

Given the special status of the canal, the constitutional history of Panama was quite different from that of the other American protectorates. In 1903 Panama declared its independence from Colombia with the tacit approval of President Theodore Roosevelt. The Panamanian junta that had won independence conducted elections for a constitutional convention. The resulting 1904 constitution had some slight resemblance to provisions of the U.S. Constitution, and Panama presumably became a democracy with a popularly elected president.[81] The three branches of government operated on the principle of separation of powers, and the constitution was quite liberal in its written form.[82]

The most controversial proviso, however, gave the United States the right to intervene at any time to maintain peace.[83] This situation led to anti-American demonstrations when the Panamanians resented the humiliating blow to their national self-esteem. Panamanians had no desire to be occupied by Americans who did not speak Spanish, administered discriminatory justice, and cut their country in half with the Canal Zone.

In 1941 a new constitution was drafted by a select group of jurists and promulgated by President Arnulfo Arias. The constitution was both nationalistic and chauvinistic: it expanded the role of government in civil society, centralized the government, and imposed more rules and regulations than the relaxed Panamanians were used to. One of its most objectionable measures was directed against non-Panamanian immigrants—West Indians, Chinese, and Middle Easterners—who lost their right to naturalization and sometimes even their citizenship. The 1941 constitution was not abrogated until 1946, but it was clearly not in keeping with the spirit of American constitutionalism. Although Arias attempted to restore the 1941 constitution in 1951, he was removed from power before he could do so.

The new 1946 constitution proved to be a far more liberal document. It provided for a democracy, universal suffrage, and a separation of powers and reflected some American influence in its protection of civil liberties, a four-year presidential term, and universal suffrage. It remained in force until 1968 when a military coup brought to power Omar Torrijos Herrera.[84]

The Torrijos administration marked a turning point in Panama's constitutional history. The constitution of 1972 was written by representatives from local municipalities, but they were convened by order of the military government under Torrijos. He was appointed "maximum leader" for six years, given broad powers, and allowed to conduct foreign affairs. Armed with this dictatorial authority, in 1977 Torrijos proceeded to negotiate two new treaties with the United States. The first recognized Panama's sovereignty over the canal, created a system of bilateral management of the canal, and outlined America's rights once Panama assumed control in the year 2000. The second agreed that the United States could intervene to keep the canal open after the year 2000.[85] The two treaties marked a historic change between the two countries, even though President Ronald Reagan in his 1976 campaign had boasted to his jingoistic supporters: "We bought it, paid for it, its ours, and we're going to keep it."[86]

By the 1970s, however, America's attitude toward the canal had changed. Military experts noted that the strategic significance of the canal had declined, as the largest aircraft carriers could no longer fit through it. Observers generally agreed that the most likely threat to the canal would come from Panamanian insurgents frustrated by America's continued military domination rather than from any foreign foe.

Conclusion

Wherever practiced, American imperialism invariably resulted in a guardian–ward relationship that placed native peoples in a subordinate status, which they naturally resented. This resentment usually spurred a struggle for independence (as in the case of Cuba) or a freer constitutional arrangement (like Puerto Rico). In only a few instances (such as Hawaii) was the guardian–ward relationship welcomed, though even there the native population remained resentful.

American constitutionalism within an empire brings to mind Lord Acton's dictum that power corrupts. Despite the constitutional limitations imposed on colonial administrators by Congress, they invariably overstepped their bounds and abused the trust given to them. Although sometimes performing good deeds in their pursuit of humanitarian goals or in their desire to bring democracy, their tutelage too often resulted in resentment by those whom they tried to help.

All imperialisms are contradictory in nature and can make those practicing it appear hypocritical. "When Woodrow Wilson set out to make the world safe for democracy, he spoke for *Realpolitik* as well as for humanitarianism, for the kind of democracy for which he wished to make the world safe was American democracy."[87] In his pursuit of such democracy, Wilson abused the trust when he intervened militarily in Caribbean countries and placed U.S. interests ahead of those of the native peoples. Although the United States performed some good deeds in the Philippines, it also manipulated the local population in order to further its own self-interests. Those indulging in imperialism do so at some risk.

America appeared to learn some lessons from history as a result of its experiences with imperialism. The United States rejected the temptation to expand its empire *formally* after World War II. Emerging from the war as a superpower, the United States was clearly in a position to increase its territorial holdings. But it generally declined to do so, and American imperialism assumed a new shape. Without formal colonies, the United States remained a great imperialist power through its economic dominance, which it exercised through a neocolonialism based largely on American capitalism.

9

Fifth Echo
World War I to World War II, 1919–1945

The fifth "echo" occurred in the era after World War I when there was an outbreak of democracy in Europe. During this time when monarchies were transformed into republics, many resorted to using features of the American model, issuing declarations of independence, calling constitutional conventions, adopting written constitutions, and incorporating bills of rights in their charters. Besides the emergence of democracy, hopes ran high for peace in the coming new world order.

The Allied victory resulted in a burst of democracy not seen in Europe since 1848. Many conservative monarchies were swept away. Before World War I, there had been nineteen monarchies and three republics, but after 1922, there were fourteen republics, thirteen monarchies, and two regencies. As a leader in the drive for democracy, the United States was more popular than ever before, and the reputation of American constitutionalism soared.

With the rising tide of republics came the "second significant moment" in the number of declarations of independence outside the United States. With the breakup of the huge Austro-Hungarian, Russian, and Ottoman empires, newly independent states turned again to Jefferson's manifesto. Czechoslovakia was typical of the new states that imitated or cited the American Declaration in Europe, and after President Woodrow Wilson's statement regarding the "self-determination of nations," such declarations could be heard from "the Balkans to Korea."[1]

The bill of rights tradition that American constitutionalism had established along with Britain and France also made great strides. Germany's Weimar Constitution of 1919 led the way. During the decade after the end of the war, constitutions in Austria and Czechoslovakia in 1920, Poland in 1921, Greece in 1927, and Lithuania in 1928 all included a bill of rights in their charters.[2]

The rising tide of democracy was evidenced also in the spread of universal suffrage in the Western world, in the United States, Britain, Germany, and Russia, as well as in some smaller European states. One interesting development was that for the first time, the franchise was extended to women in some countries. Democracy, it seems, had suddenly become gender blind.

What started off propitiously as a drive for greater democracy, however, deteriorated within a decade. Many newborn nation-states emerging from the breakup of European empires discovered they were ill prepared to become democracies, and before long, the new totalitarian ideologies—communism, fascism, and Nazism—overwhelmed many of them. In addition, the Great Depression had a shattering effect on all constitutional movements. With these developments, American constitutional influence suffered a decline well before the beginning of World War II.

America and Europe: *The Immediate Post—World War I Years*

American constitutionalism became identified more closely with democracy as the war was coming to an end. Two important developments in 1917 determined its outcome: Russia withdrew from the war and America entered it. The Russian Revolution—a truly cataclysmic event—changed the nature of the war by making it an ideological as well as a military struggle. President Woodrow Wilson expressed his ideas about the new world order he envisioned in his speech before Congress declaring war against Germany. The conflict, he stated, was being waged to make the world "safe for democracy."

Despite Wilson's hopeful rhetoric that America might become the successful model for newly emerging nation-states on the basis of the people's self-determination, he was disappointed.[3] First, he failed to realize that the ethnic, religious, and economic divisions in these multiethnic empires prevented them from following America's example. Because the United States had had almost a century and a half to assimilate such minorities into its two-party system, there were no serious German parties, Catholic parties, or communist parties in America. Europe's populations, however, often formed parties in the newly independent states that represented separate ethnic, religious, or economic constituencies.

The dawn of democracy proved to be false for another reason. None of the new countries in Europe came into being as the result of a long and persistent revolutionary movement giving rise to a strong sense of identity. Instead, several nation-states had simply been created artificially after the recent breakup of old empires. Four of them were successor states from the Hapsburg empire: Austria, Hungary, Czechoslovakia, and Yugoslavia; and five were former members of the Russian empire: Poland, Finland, Estonia, Latvia, and Lithuania. Unable to maintain their independence, many disappeared quickly, and by 1938, only ten out of the twenty-seven countries in Europe could call themselves democracies.

Wilson's dream of a democratic world order was hampered also because it was the diametric opposite of Vladimir Lenin's vision of a socialist world order. Lenin and the Bolsheviks regarded the Russian Revolution as only the opening phase of an international socialist revolution. The collapse of the German, Austrian-Hungarian, and Ottoman empires had presented to them, they believed, a great opportunity to overthrow the world capitalist system and to replace it with a new economic order based on the "dictatorship of the proletariat."

One result was that the victorious Allies found their position reversed and were on the defensive. According to the famed world historian William H. McNeill,

> Fear of proletarian revolt soon became a major preoccupation among the victors, who found themselves supporting a variety of upstart regimes in eastern Europe whose claims to respectability rested, often, more on their anti-Bolshevism than on any authentically democratic support they commanded. The fact was that democratic self-determination was an unworkable ideal in most of central and eastern Europe under the chaotic conditions that prevailed in 1918–20.[4]

There were other reasons for the rapid collapse of democracy. Extremists on both the Left and the Right of the political spectrum refused to compromise, which made it difficult for democratic governments backing American constitutionalism to spread their ideas. Nationalist-minded minorities made intolerable demands that could not be met. Besides domestic causes, many democratic governments could not cope with the foreign crises that eventually led to World War II. The Great Depression, meanwhile, had a crushing effect on all governments.[5] Capitalism, with which American constitutionalism was so closely associated, seemed about to disappear during the worldwide economic crisis, and the American model suffered accordingly.

Germany

While World War I was still under way, Wilson threatened to interfere with Germany's existing constitutional arrangement, declaring he would not deal with "monarchical aristocrats" (meaning Kaiser Wilhelm II).[6] Once Wilhelm II abdicated, a search began for a "substitute kaiser." The solution was to be a monarch-like ruler who might function within a republican framework in those areas where monarchical sentiment was still strong.

The conditions in Germany under which the Weimar Constitution was written hardly seemed favorable. There had been a brief revolution; the German government had to operate under the onus of the "war guilt" clause; and the wartime devastation had left the country's economy in shambles. Nevertheless, the document was written within a year. The major figure behind its formulation was Hugo Preuss, a constitutional lawyer, distinguished professor of Prussian constitutional theory, and important politician. Indeed, he was a formidable political theorist as well as a practical politician, having served as minister of the interior. Preuss drafted and redrafted the document, submitted it to the National Assembly, and finally, in August 1919, urged that it be signed and promulgated.[7]

The Weimar Constitution proved to be the most "ultrademocratic" charter in Europe if not the whole world.[8] What it created, though, was a liberal constitutional democracy. The sovereignty of the people was proclaimed in the preamble, replacing the former autocratic system under the Bismarck Constitution of 1871. Having failed to keep pace with the democratic advances in the past in 1849, 1867, and 1871, German constitution makers were determined to make amends. For the first time in Germany, a national code of fundamental rights for citizens was included. "There was . . . no charter of rights wider in scope or more modern in design," according to one constitutional authority.[9] Seeking to achieve equality in voting, the Weimar Constitution required that the national and Länder elections be based on proportional representation. In a complicated scheme, the country was divided into thirty-five electoral districts, each one returning a member to the Reichstag for a given number of voters. In each district, a series of party lists, instead of individual candidates, were voted on. "This striving after perfect democratic equality (not only one man one vote and one woman one vote, but also for every 30,000 votes for a given party at least one representative . . .) was painfully carried out."[10]

The results were disastrous. As one political scientist noted, "The German parliament became one of the most multi-colored [i.e., politically varied] representative assemblies ever seen."[11] This effort to achieve greater fairness for minorities created multiple parties, which proved to be one main reason for the downfall of the republic. No single party was able to achieve a majority.[12] Two other devices of direct democracy, the popular referendum and initiative borrowed from Switzerland, were incorporated as well but were allowed only under special circumstances. No other country in the world had introduced these forms of direct democracy on a national level.[13]

While the German formula for voting was new, other sources provided ideas and inspiration for the Weimar Constitution. The document tried to answer almost every constitutional question raised in German history, and at the same time, it incorporated new features designed to handle future problems. Casting their net wide, the constitution makers borrowed features from the American, French, and Swiss constitutions. But how much of the Weimar Constitution could be attributed to American influence? Hajo Holborn, a well-known German historian, found evidence of such influence based largely on the thought of Max Weber, the famed sociologist serving as an unofficial consultant to the constitutionalists, who brought both his American experience and thoughtful analysis of Germany's political problems to the constitution-making process.[14] Preuss had also thoroughly studied the American system, making great use of *The Federalist* and calling it "the canonical book of American constitutionalism."[15]

Further evidence of the American model can be found in the provisions of the constitution itself. Its bill of rights included such familiar rights as freedom of person, speech, assembly, and religion.[16] The idea of amending the constitution likewise was borrowed from the United States. Amendments required a two-thirds majority of either house to be initiated, but it also was possible to amend the constitution by referendum, quite unlike the American practice.[17] Finally, although the Weimar Constitution did not explicitly establish judicial review, the principle was recognized. Its implementation, however, differed from that of the United States. Although the independence of the judiciary from the executive and legislative branches was guaranteed, the courts were subject to the codified laws of the Reich.[18]

Presidentialism offers another example of how the American model motivated changes suited to Germany's needs. Although an American-style presidency was not instituted, the idea of a strong executive was constantly discussed. "With the framing of those provisions of the constitution that referred to the executive," Hajo Holborn observed, "we find a marked influence of the American Constitution."[19] After the kaiser was overthrown, the framers tried to find a "functional equivalent," but because the Weimar Constitution had established a partly parliamentary system, a pure presidential system was out of the question.[20] What was instituted instead was a dualist system, semipresidential and semiparliamentarian. It was here that Max Weber's practical vision was used, for he saw a balance of powers as being essential to any successful system of government. Power was divided between a popularly elected president and a cabinet responsible to the parliament. Both the president and the Reichstag (parliament) held positions of equal importance, each acting as a counterpoise to the other. The president had authority to dismiss the parliament, and while the president was subject to recall by parliament, the decision was not conclusive until approved by popular referendum. Although the president was elected directly by the people, each of his acts had to be countersigned by a cabinet minister responsible to the parliament. In the end, the entire structure of balanced powers was threatened by the infamous article 48 (Notverordnung), which gave the president broad powers to suspend civil liberties by means of "emergency decrees."

The fight to introduce an American-style president was led by Weber and Preuss. Despite his strong reservations, Weber recommended the U.S. system. His major misgiving arose from the conventional European view that the spoils system had destroyed the effectiveness of American government. Although he believed that trained bureaucrats should run the government, Weber was critical of what he called America's rank "amateurs," that is, party bosses. He predicted that the bureaucratization of government would soon become a worldwide phenomenon, extending even to America. Operating on this premise, he advocated that the president be elected directly by the people.[21]

Preuss, in contrast, preferred the more traditional system of having parliament appoint the president, but he was persuaded by Weber to change his mind. Preuss also shared Weber's opinion that the American presidential system had been corrupted by the spoils system, and he was even more pessimistic than Weber that this flaw would eventually lead to America's undoing. Despite his doubts, Preuss succeeded in persuading the warring political parties to accept the American idea of an elected president.[22]

The issue of presidentialism was of the utmost historical significance because of the subsequent failure of the Weimar Constitution. Whether a different kind of presidential regime might have prevented the rise of Nazism will never be known, but the weaknesses of the Weimar government—cabinet crises, dissolutions of the Reichstag, and the use of emergency powers by President Paul Hindenburg—set the stage for Adolf Hitler's appointment as chancellor (premier) in 1933. Although Hitler failed in his bid for the presidency three times, he eventually was able to achieve his goal through legitimate means under the Weimar Constitution.[23]

Federalism in Germany had a long history stretching back to the Middle Ages, the Holy Roman Empire, America's influence in the stillborn 1848 constitution, and Bismarck's constitution of 1871. As Holborn noted, the concept of federalism in the past "had been originally molded with a view to the American example," and the deliberations of the Frankfurt constitutionalists undoubtedly were still remembered. In the making of the Weimar Constitution, however, a strict form of federalism and a parliamentary government with strong unitary tendencies were considered incompatible. To complicate matters, the relationship of the central government and the Länder had substantially weakened federalism. When the constituent assembly was called to discuss the constitution, the states had yet to be invited. The result was that the status of the Länder turned out to be subservient: their boundaries could be changed without their consent; their form of government was required by law to be republican; and their internal affairs could be regulated by the Reich in the interests of the common welfare.[24] Under the constitution, the Länder had the main responsibility for administering the laws and collecting the taxes of the central government. The conclusion of one scholar that the 1919 constitution weakened the federal elements of the German nation-state and strengthened "the Reich authorities at the expense of the . . . *Länder*" seems correct.[25] Compared with Bismarck's Reich made up of strong sovereign states, the quasi-federal form of government in 1919 was extremely unequal.

Despite Germany's attraction to American federalism, the Weimar Constitution tried to be both a federal and parliamentary document, combining both American and French sources. In the end, however, the document turned out to be neither truly federal nor fully parliamentarian.[26] As one scholar observed, the Weimar Republic was only "reluctantly federal."[27] This situation was made worse by the overwhelming presence of Prussia. A large state compared with the others, Prussia had sabotaged earlier attempts at federalism. What further limited federalism was the authority given to the executive under article 48, which enabled him to rule by decree during periods of emergency. Under such limitations, American-style federalism was hardly possible.

The adoption of judicial review added another significant new dimension to German constitutionalism. Judicial review implied a number of propositions quite novel in German history: that the constitution took precedence over all other laws; that judicial decisions on constitutional matters were sources of law having the same effect as general (statutory) law; and that judges should have the last word in interpreting the constitution.

In view of their traditional respect for legalistic forms in decision making, however, it was not surprising that the Germans failed to create a judicial organ analogous to the U.S. Supreme Court. Several factors prevented such a development. Some German lawyers and legal scholars adhering to the civil-law tradition believed such a court was unnecessary. A trained regular judiciary administering a skillfully created body of codified law, they argued, should be capable of settling conflicts. Others tended to deny that constitutional law had a special position, claiming that both the constitution and statutes were manifestations of the same legislative power. Finally, German democrats of the Weimar period tended to view the judiciary as a reactionary force, not only in their own country, but throughout the world. That impression was reinforced by the conservative decisions being rendered by the U.S. Supreme Court.[28]

The Weimar Constitution created a court called the Tribunal of State Justice. It had jurisdiction over constitutional disputes between two or more Länder or between the national government and a Land. But no judicial institution was given jurisdiction to decide on the compatibility of national laws and the Weimar Constitution. The tribunal was not empowered with traditional judicial review because that was seen as being undemocratic, since the judges were not elected by the people and might oppose the popular will expressed in laws passed by the national legislature.[29] Although one case in 1925 raised the question of the right of judicial review of German laws, the issue remained unclear because there was no clear-cut decision.[30] This situation was still unresolved in 1933 when Hitler came to power. No one tried, therefore, to invoke the doctrine of judicial review to protect individual rights of citizens when the Nazi atrocities began. The Nazi regime suspended human rights, abolished the independence of the judiciary, and proceeded to establish complete totalitarian rule.[31]

Why did the Weimar Republic fail, and to what degree was the constitution responsible? One thing is certain: the many American features of the constitution were not responsible for its demise. Rather, the Weimar Republic failed primarily because there were too few checks and balances to prevent concentrations of political power at the top. Other extraneous conditions contributed to the republic's failure: Germany's defeat in the war, the harsh peace imposed by the Allies, the economic crisis of the Great Depression, and the extremism of Germany's minority political parties. When private armed groups headed by reactionary agitators like Adolf Hitler took to the streets in the early 1930s, the democratic Weimar Republic, which allowed free speech and a free press, was vulnerable to attacks that proved fatal.

Austria

With the breakup of the Austrian-Hungarian Empire at the end of World War I, the dual monarchy was abolished, and Austria declared itself a republic in 1918. Austria was able to combine a parliamentary government with the concept of federalism, a match that traditionally had been thought contradictory.[32] But domestic disorder ensued because of the hostility between private left-wing and right-wing armies, and a succession of regimes were unable to quell the unrest. A movement for unification with Germany (Anschluss), although prohibited by the peace treaties, was revived, and the two countries proclaimed such an agreement for a customs union in 1931. But vigorous protests by the Allies forced them to renounce the idea.

The story of the Anschluss is not germane to this study, except to say that it ended any further attempts at a republic inspired by the American example. By 1936 with the formation of the Rome–Berlin axis, Austria's days were numbered. In 1938, the Anschluss was completed when Austria was declared part of Germany and Nazi troops occupied the country.

During these years, Austria was distinguished for its development of the centralized Kelsen model of judicial review. Although there is no evidence that Hans Kelsen (1881–1973), a distinguished jurist and philosopher, had the American system in mind when he formulated his own, it is generally conceded that the original concept of judicial review could be dated back to the American practice beginning early in the nineteenth century.[33]

Czechoslovakia

Czechoslovakia's story is more representative of the postwar states' interest in American constitutionalism. The creation of Czechoslovakia resulted from Wilson's dictum of self-determination. When the northern provinces of the old Austrian-Hungarian Empire broke away, they declared their independence. Czechoslovakia's founding fathers placed great emphasis on America's democratic ideals, and they even signed their declaration of independence on October 18, 1918, in Independence Hall, Philadelphia. "As the nation of Comenius," they wrote, "we cannot but accept the American Declaration of Independence, the principles of Lincoln, and the declaration of the rights of man and the citizen."[34]

Despite the absence of previous liberal institutions, the Czech Constitution of 1920 turned out to be a very democratic document, reflecting American influence in its preamble from both the U.S. Constitution and the Declaration.[35] The Czech structure of government, however, followed that of three different countries—the United States, France, and Britain—and incorporated features of both parliamentary and presidential systems.[36]

The 1920 Czech Constitution proved to be a remarkably revolutionary document, given the nation's prior history as a semifeudal region. Its first clause read, "The people is the sole source of all power in the Czechoslovak Republic." Privileges and titles were swept away. Reflecting the bill of rights tradition, liberty, equality, and security all were guaranteed in the new republic.[37] The protection of certain rights of citizens—the right of petition, freedom of the press, and freedom of assembly—also were promised in the constitution.[38]

There was, however, no mention of the rights of minorities in the 1920 constitution,[39] an omission that proved to be fatal because of the serious differences between the Czech majority and the Slovak minority. The Czechs had benefited from the Industrial Revolution, lived primarily under Hungarian rule, and were oriented more toward the West, whereas the Slovaks were predominantly an agricultural people, had lived under many different rulers, and looked more to the East. An even more dangerous situation was created when the German minority, living in Bohemia and Moravia, were denied certain political rights altogether.

Despite a series of coalition governments representing a multiplicity of political parties, Czechoslovakia managed to establish a surprisingly stable government between the two world wars. The person most responsible was Tomáš Masaryk, the first president of the Czech Republic. He resorted to the old Hapsburg practice of dealing with any political impasse by operating the government mostly through civil servants rather than political parties.[40] A professor-president like Wilson, Masaryk was also a shrewd diplomat. When he stepped down, Eduard Beneš became president, and danger appeared from a different quarter: Nazi Germany. Following the annexation of Austria in March 1938, Germans living in the Sudetenland demanded that they be allowed to have their own administrative agencies. Beneš resisted, pointing out that the constitution did not recognize minorities as separate groups. Czechoslovakia, he insisted, was a single nation-state, and members of minorities enjoyed full civil rights.[41]

Beneš refused also to capitulate to Nazi Germany's demands in 1938. When the Allies, who had signed a treaty to protect Czechoslovakia against invasion, failed to honor their obligations, the country's fate was sealed. In an effort to appease Hitler, the Allies surrendered the German-speaking part of Czechoslovakia to Germany. The following year, Hitler invaded the country and declared it a German protectorate.

Poland

Poland came into being largely as a result of Wilson's theory of self-determination. In his famous Fourteen Points, Wilson had insisted on the establishment of a free and independent Poland as part of any peace settlement. Given its importance, size, and location, the new Polish republic was, without doubt, the most spectacular American diplomatic achievement of the peace accords.

In principle, the Polish Constitution of 1919 proved to be one of the most democratic documents in all of Europe. Although in the distant past, Poland had had powerful indigenous constitutional traditions, the constitutionalists of 1919 and 1921 borrowed freely from the most liberal nations in the West, including the United States. Wishing to establish the sovereignty of the people, the Polish framers provided a "parliamentary" bias in their constitution. But they allowed the legislative branch to dominate the president and cabinet to such a degree that it hobbled the executive. Poland emerged, therefore, as "an almost decapitated state," with the president, ministers, senate, and courts all subjected to the will of the legislature, or Seijm.[42]

The 1921 constitution was modeled mainly on the French Third Republic but contained traces of the American Declaration of Independence and the U.S. Constitution.[43] The document guaranteed to all the people in Poland "absolute protection of life, liberty, and property."[44] Such protection was accorded to all inhabitants in Poland, irrespective of their origin, nationality, language, race, or religion. This proviso became important because when Poland expanded its borders in the Polish-Soviet War of 1920, only 70 percent of the people in the country were of Polish extraction.[45] Although powerful minorities clamored for a federation to gain more rights, the Poles wanted to erect a unitary, centralized state, fearing the partitions that had dogged their past.

Traditional liberal safeguards were incorporated into the 1921 document as well. All citizens were to be equal before the law, no matter what their language, creed, or national affiliation.[46] They were to have rights of freedom of speech, conscience, and belief. Freedom of petition and of the press were also guaranteed.[47] All these rights, of course, reflected the bill of rights tradition with which American constitutionalism was associated. But the Polish Constitution of 1921 had been written primarily to curb the ambitions of Marshall Josef Pilsudski, the man who helped win Poland's independence. Fearing that he might seize control of the government, the document severely restricted the powers of the president. Enraged by the move, Pilsudski sulked and retired temporarily from public life. He refused, for example, to run for the presidency and resigned his post as chief of the general staff in 1923.

From this point on, any traces of American constitutionalism disappeared. Political parties in the Seijm soon were splintered into so many factions that any effective government became impossible. Worried lest the country he had helped create might be destroyed, Pilsudski led a successful coup in 1926. Although he came to power, he never accepted the office of the president and served as premier instead, bringing into the government only cronies, military men whom he could trust. Despite refusing to hold a truly important position, Pilsudski nonetheless dominated Poland's political life over the next nine years. His regime could best be described as a personal military dictatorship coupled with a centralized authoritarian oligarchy.[48] Under Pilsudski's rule, civil rights in Poland turned out to be a mockery of the liberal 1921 constitution; political opponents were arrested, jailed, or otherwise purged.

A new constitution was produced that proved to be the very antithesis of its predecessor.[49] The 1935 constitution bluntly declared that the "functions of governing the State do not belong to the *Seijm*."⁵⁰ The Seijm and senate were thereby transformed into rubber-stamp institutions, and the egalitarianism characteristic of the American-influenced 1921 constitution was scrapped in favor of the elitism of Pilsudski and his cronies. The ultrapresidential provisions of the new constitution made it almost impossible to call free elections.⁵¹ Four months after the constitution was adopted, Pilsudski died, leaving the country with an authoritarian constitution, an ailing economy, and no successor to cope with problems of the coming war.

Hungary

Like so many other newly created states, Hungary began in 1918 as a republic. When the communist leader, Béla Kun, tried to establish a Hungarian Soviet Republic in 1919, however, it brought back counterrevolutionaries who restored the Hapsburg monarchy. But their restoration was in principle only, and international pressure prevented the king from being restored to his throne. Hungary therefore became a monarchy without a king. An authoritarian ruler, Admiral Miklós Horthy, who had served as commander in chief of the navy, came to power and exercised his authority as "regent of the kingdom of Hungary" until forced from power in 1944. Faced with an authoritarian regime, American constitutionalism made very little headway in Hungary.⁵²

Finland

After gaining its independence from the Soviet Union, Finland wrote its constitution in 1919. The document, declaring itself a republic, showed distinct traces of American constitutional influence. Finland had been exposed to liberal institutions in its previous history. While under the sovereignty of the Russian czars from 1809 to 1917, Finland had preserved its autonomous status and therefore was able to continue certain practices from the old Swedish system. For this reason, the country was better able to introduce democratic institutions when the Finnish parliament declared independence in 1917.

The 1919 Finnish Constitution resembled that of the United States in one important respect, the election of the president. Like the president of the United States, the Finnish president was indirectly but popularly elected by an assembly of electors chosen by all who could vote in ordinary elections, a procedure that somewhat resembled the American electoral college.[53] During the discussions about the election of the president, one expert even opposed the draft constitution on the grounds that it was "too American." Despite this and other protests regarding the shape of the executive, the indirect universal election of the president based on the American model was agreed upon, and a semipresidential and semi-parliamentarian system was eventually established.[54]

During the years between the two world wars, however, the political parties in Finland remained deeply divided between monarchists and republicans. But in 1939, these domestic differences were overshadowed when Soviet troops invaded Finland to begin what was called the "winter war." A temporary peace between the two countries was signed in 1940. Then when Germany invaded the Soviet Union in 1941, Finland declared itself neutral. During the war, however, Finland was forced to fight against both the Germans and Soviets, and another republican government disappeared.

Lithuania

The three Baltic countries that emerged from the old Russian empire after World War I—Lithuania, Latvia, and Estonia—had much in common. All three adopted liberal democratic constitutions, even though each one's legislative branch dominated the executive when unilateral parliaments were created. All three, moreover, lived in fear of too much executive power. Given the radical assembly structure and electoral rules, the governments soon faced instability, which led to the emergence of an authoritarian system in each country.[55]

Lithuania's appearance as a nation-state can be explained in many ways. One is that the Lithuanians, fighting off all enemies, established a new nation without any outside help. Another attributed its birth to a sinister design by various Western powers that created the nation-state for reasons of self-interest. No one explanation, however, can tell the whole story. Lithuania actually came into being as the result of several developments: the outcome of World War I, the Russian Revolution of 1917, and, as one scholar put it, a "reflection of the twentieth century *Zeitgeist* of democracy and national self-determination" growing out of America's constitutional influence.[56]

In keeping with that zeitgeist, Lithuania declared itself a democratic republic. The United States, a sister republic, however, refused to recognize Lithuania in 1920 out of "loyal friendship" to the Soviet Union, with which it had good relations at the time—an ironic move given future developments.[57]

Lithuania was reborn as a modern state on December 16, 1918.[58] After signing a peace treaty with the Soviet regime in 1920, the Lithuanians called an American-style constituent assembly to write a constitution. While still waging an undeclared war with Poland, Lithuania adopted its constitution of 1922, which contained democratic ideas dominant throughout much of the Western world. It provided for a predominant unicameral parliament elected on the basis of proportional representation. The president was elected by the Seimas, or parliament, and a prime minister was appointed by the president within a parliamentary democracy. Citizens' rights were defined in terms quite familiar in the American model: equality before the law, inviolability of persons and property, freedom of religion and conscience, and freedom of the press. One important provision granted minority groups cultural autonomy, while another declared universal suffrage for both men and women.[59]

The Seimas introduced a system of checks and balances, one that vaguely resembled that of the United States. One provision, for example, made it possible for the parliament to impeach the president, which reflected the fear among minority groups that the president might possess too much power. But resistance soon developed when the Socialist and Center parties claimed that the constitution still was not democratic enough to protect citizens' civil rights.[60]

What happened next followed a familiar pattern. The political parties splintered into many factions. When the Christian Democrats, who had won three previous elections, lost in 1926, there was a military coup. The new regime promptly shifted power from the legislature to the president, and the new leaders introduced an authoritarian government that banned all political parties, placed limitations on private organizations, and imposed censorship. Reflecting this shift in power, the constitution of 1922 was amended in 1928 and again in 1938. With each change, the Lithuanian constitutions moved further away from the liberalism characteristic of American constitutionalism.

Latvia

Latvia, like Lithuania, declared its independence in 1918, but it had to defend itself against enemy forces from both the east and the west. In the east, the Soviet army was still waging war, while in the west, German forces occupied what was called Latvian territory. It was not until 1920 that Latvian soldiers finally freed the country of foreign troops. Until then, the country was run by a provisional government in the form of an American-style constitutional convention that conducted government affairs from 1918 to 1920.

In 1922 Latvia adopted a constitution and, like Lithuania, declared itself a democratic republic. The constitution, containing some elements of American constitutionalism, had two parts, the first dealing with the structure of the government and the second with the rights and obligations of the citizens. Latvia, like Lithuania, established a one-house parliament, the Saeima, which was allowed to elect the president. In addition, a system of checks and balances somewhat similar to that of the United States was created to limit the power of the president, and impeachment of the president was permitted under certain circumstances.[61]

In the beginning, the Latvian parliament functioned effectively and passed some significant social and economic legislation. Latvia, like the United States, granted universal suffrage to both men and women. But the system of proportional representation soon led to a fragmentation of political power, and dozens of political parties appeared on the scene. Once again, too much democracy proved dangerous. This situation was exacerbated further by the polarization of Left and Right. Unable to achieve constitutional reform because of the political divisions, Premier Kārlis Ulmanis declared a state of emergency in 1924, dissolved the Saeima, and assumed power by decree. The pendulum pattern of democracy to authoritarianism was repeated again, and the few features of American constitutionalism in Latvia disappeared.

Estonia

Estonia proclaimed itself an independent republic in February 1918, but German troops soon occupied the country and remained until the armistice was signed on November 11, 1918. Two weeks later, the Russian army attacked Estonia, and the Estonian war for independence began. With some help from the Allies, the Estonian army eventually drove the Soviet forces from its soil, and in 1920 the Soviet government recognized the Republic of Estonia.

Like the other two Baltic countries, Estonia started out with an ultrademocratic constitution, but even more extreme. Under the constitution of 1920, the country functioned without a one-man chief executive; instead, it had a council of cabinet members whose leader was designated as prime minister. The constitution stated further that the Diet, or Riigikogu, could dissolve the government at will and the council could be dismissed in its entirety or any individual minister removed. The administration had no veto power over legislation that the Diet passed, nor could it dissolve that body.[62] The executive was thus the servant of the Diet, and autonomous executive power was impossible.

The assembly system of government was made even stronger by the unicameral Diet. In its constitutional form, the Estonian regime represented a version of French parliamentarianism, but something new had been added: the Swiss-inspired institutions of direct democracy. The initiative, referendum, and popular veto all were introduced to reduce the power of the Diet even further. Thus, the Diet, albeit the sole master of the government, was subject to the direct control of the people, who held a popular veto. To say that the constitution operated with difficulty is an understatement: all the mechanisms based on the people were exercised frequently and with great vigor.[63] With so much direct democracy, the 1920 constitution failed to reflect much in the way of American constitutionalism.

The effects of the Great Depression, coupled with the failure of repeated attempts at constitutional reform, finally resulted in a new constitution in 1934. Under this document, the largely leaderless country was to have a president who resembled the American executive but only vaguely. He was to be elected by the people, was given broad powers, and was to serve for five years. When the newly approved constitution went into effect on January 1, 1934, Konstantin Päts became acting president. But a month before the election, Päts invoked the emergency powers given him by the new constitution and moved toward a dictatorship. When Päts prorogued the Diet, the takeover became complete.

Päts continued to operate as prime minister and to "act" as president. The new system was designed as a compromise between the presidentless republic of 1920 and the presidential republic called for in the 1934 constitution.[64] Leftist forces that had opposed all constitutional reforms finally acquiesced in the takeover because they saw Päts as the lesser of two evils.[65]

The proposal for a third constitution was eventually endorsed by popular referendum in 1936. Despite the fears of many that a corporate state might be established, Estonia proclaimed a democratic constitution in 1938 that reflected certain features of American constitutionalism. Like the United States, it provided for a bicameral legislature with a popular and freely elected lower house, but the president was elected directly by the people.[66] Within a short time, however, the issue of the Estonian Constitution of

1938 became moot. In 1939 the Soviet government imposed a treaty of mutual assistance that allowed Soviet military bases on Estonian soil. A year later, Soviet forces formally occupied the entire country.

False Dawn of Democracy

The post–World War I period in Europe represented a false dawn for democracy and the cause of American constitutionalism. Europe's new democracies were unprepared for the idea of limited government inherent in America's representative democracy. They were unable to reach or accept majority verdicts and then to compromise and reconcile conflicting interests without wholly satisfying or dismissing the other side. In their governments, moreover, they did not insist on the checks and balance mechanisms characteristic of American constitutionalism. Political parties on both the Left and Right resorted to extremism that proved destructive. Ethnic, religious, and cultural constituencies pursued their goals without any thought of the general welfare, and the same was true of powerful economic interests. The result was that countries were torn apart by political wrangling, making it possible for authoritarian rulers to take over with promises of restoring order.

During this period, many of the new democratic nations discovered the dark side of democracy. As Tocqueville had warned, too much democracy can prove fatal. The tyranny of the majority became evident as sizable majorities oppressed minorities. In sum, too much democracy often brought a swing in the opposite direction, to authoritarianism. Political parties allowed to express themselves through democratic devices— the referendum, initiative, and recall—and resort to proportional representation caused factions and splinter parties to form, resulting in chaos. This pattern of excessive democracy inevitably led to the appearance of authoritarian rulers, and many of the new nations arising during the period "died of democracy."

Waves of Democracy

The pattern of democratization swinging pendulumlike to excess and then provoking a counterreaction to authoritarianism was not confined to the post–World War I era in Europe. In his remarkable book *The Third Wave* (1991), Samuel P. Huntington traced this pattern in the context of global history. He identified three recurrent waves of democracy in world history over the past two centuries. During the first, a "long wave" (1828 to 1926), some thirty countries achieved democracy with their national institutions. The second (1943 to 1962), resulting from the decolonization movement during and after World War II, accounted for a total of thirty-six democratic regimes. The third wave, beginning in 1974, brought about fifty-nine democracies by 1989, when this book ends.[67] The first two waves ended with the appearance of "reverse waves," in which the number of countries making transitions to democracy was greater than that of regimes moving in the opposite direction to a nondemocratic status. The first reverse wave lasted from 1922 to 1942, and the second, from 1961 to 1974.[68] This "two steps forward and one step back" process was characteristic of the transitions to democracy after the 1920s.

Huntington connected the "first wave" with the democratic institutions that appeared during the Jacksonian era in the late 1820s. He argued that these institutions had originated in America after the country met two criteria: first, that 50 percent of adult white males were eligible to vote and, second, that elections would be free and open. The first wave met these criteria and lasted until the mid-1920s when the first reverse wave set in. Applying the same criteria to European countries, Huntington observed that they too had achieved these democratic goals over a similar period of time. They expanded their suffrage, introduced the secret ballot, and, in free and open elections, elected executives (prime ministers and cabinets) responsible to parliaments. As in America, this trend toward democratization continued until the mid-1920s.

The first "reverse wave" in Europe began in the 1920s (with some overlap) when Benito Mussolini marched on Rome in 1922, ending Italy's fragile democracy. This was followed by a dominant nondemocratic trend leading to authoritarian rule from roughly 1922 to 1942. These two decades were identified by the nondemocratic forces appearing in Italy, Germany, and other totalitarian European countries as well as in parts of Latin America, and Asia. By this time, many of the fledgling democracies that had arisen in Europe after World War I had disappeared.

Huntington's second wave of democracy refers to the decolonization movement beginning about 1943 and ending in 1961. Most of the countries gaining their independence in this way became democracies and accounted for the sharp rise in democracies following the decline during the first reverse wave. This democratic trend was countered in 1962 by a second reverse wave which lasted until 1974. The third wave of democracy began in 1974 and is described in the following chapters.

The regime changes reflected in the nondemocratic governments created in the first reverse wave had a great effect on Europe between the two world wars. Britain, France, and other Western democracies were threatened by the domestic nondemocratic forces alienated from their home governments and also by the Great Depression. "The war that had been fought to make the world safe for democracy had instead unleashed movements from both the Right and the Left that were intent on destroying it," concluded Huntington.[69]

Latin America: World War I to World War II

Some of the democratic and nondemocratic trends affecting Europe between the two world wars were evident as well in the Western Hemisphere. But the history of Latin America does not reveal any clear-cut linear progression from authoritarian regimes to democratic ones. Instead, individual countries took different paths through the period. The following is a brief history of some of the more important countries and certain developments affecting them.

One major event that touched all Latin American countries was the onset of the Great Depression of the 1930s. It devastated the economies of all countries, resulting in enormous constitutional changes. Government after government fell as the world economy collapsed and prices for the region's raw materials plummeted. One result was a decisive setback to the influence of North American constitutionalism because it was tied so closely to capitalism. When Latin Americans lost faith in capitalism, the appeal of the North American model suffered accordingly.

The 1930s witnessed another new phenomenon, the appearance of foreign constitutional ideologies. Europe's swing to the right resulted in fascist movements in the region patterned on Mussolini's blackshirts in Italy and Hitler's brownshirts in Germany. Although neither movement succeeded in winning control of the entire continent, both made serious inroads in the right-wing parties of Brazil, Argentina, Mexico, and Chile. Their greatest effect was to alert the United States to a possible threat from its Latin American flank. The threat never materialized, however, because during World War II most Latin American countries supported the United States or remained neutral. After the Allied victory had discredited these movements in Germany and Italy, the danger from them largely disappeared.

Mexico

Another important development in the hemisphere was the promulgation of the Mexican Constitution of 1917, which threatened the dominance of the North American model. The Mexican Constitution preceded the Soviet Constitution of 1918 by one year and represented the most radical constitution of its kind on the globe at the time. Its revolutionary role was distinctive because of its heavy emphasis on the "social and economic rights" of individual citizens.[70] But many of these rights were aspirational only because the Mexican government was unable to provide for their implementation. As one scholar commented, "Like most [Latin American] constitutions, it was more a blueprint for the future than a reflection of actual fact."[71] Despite its shortcomings, the constitution had considerable appeal in Latin America, especially in Guatemala and Chile, where it challenged the North American model.[72]

The document is recognized to this day as "the model of a radical, but not Marxist, constitution."[73] It guaranteed an eight-hour workday, minimum wages, equal pay without regard to sex or nationality, and the right to strike. Many of these features were ahead of their time, and some appeared only a generation later in the United States under the New Deal. At the same time, however, many features of this hybrid constitution were derived from the U.S. Constitution.[74]

Despite its rhetoric, the 1917 Mexican Constitution failed to create a truly democratic nation-state, and the country's political system failed to function as a constitutional democracy. Although elections were held periodically, they were neither honest nor open, and undemocratic methods were employed to keep the majority party in power. Human and financial resources were made available only to the ruling party, the PRI (Partido revolucionario institucional), which retained control for decades.[75]

Characteristic of the contradictory attitudes found in Mexican constitutionalism, however, was Mexican scholars' high praise of *The Federalist*, even though little interest was shown in applying its principles. As early as 1901, José María Gambosa referred to the essays as a "monumental work, which can without exaggeration be called a great monument for the defense of liberty."[76] In 1919 Emilio Rabasa called it a work deserving a worldwide reputation,[77] even though many of Mexico's political practices violated what *The Federalist* preached.

The most flagrant violation was the attitude toward human rights. Practices typical in many Latin American countries—arbitrary arrests, detention without cause, outright torture, assassination, and "disappear-ance" of persons—were in evidence in Mexico. Due process of law was often disregarded, and constitutional rights to protest against the govern-ment were habitually ignored.[78] As a result, most scholars did not recog-nize Mexico as a constitutional democracy.[79]

Argentina

Argentina, the country most strongly influenced by North American con-stitutionalism in the nineteenth century, entered the twentieth with high hopes of continuing its political stability and economic prosperity, but those hopes were dashed on both counts. For the first three decades of the twentieth century, Argentina was held up as an exemplar in Latin America. It had succeeded in making a transition to democracy because it followed the North American model closely and because it established universal manhood suffrage after 1912. In 1916 this last move made possible the elec-tion of the first popularly chosen chief executive in all of Latin America.[80]

But the 1930s turned out to be what political commentators referred to as the "infamous decade." A military coup took place in Argentina in 1930, the first successful one in more than a century, and caused the col-lapse of the government based on the North American model. The coup introduced an era of widespread electoral fraud. At the same time, the Great Depression struck the Argentine economy particularly hard, and prosperity disappeared. These developments set the stage for the dictator-ship of Juan Peron, to be discussed later.

Chile

Chile underwent a fundamental constitutional change in 1924 when the military suddenly entered political affairs, overthrew the civilian presi-dent, and established a junta of high-ranking officers. The constitution of 1925 promulgated the next year showed only slight traces of North Ameri-can constitutionalism. It restored the presidential form of government, and with the legislature's approval, the cabinet served at the president's pleasure, as in the United States.

But the Great Depression undermined Chile's constitutional, political, and economic structure, and the country lost both its markets and access to foreign capital.[81] During the 1940s, a strange malaise gripped Chile's social order as the country followed these events without much change.[82]

The malaise was attributable in part to delusions of national pride. Many upper-class Chileans encouraged the myth that the country was unique among the Latin American republics because its democratic constitutional institutions had been created by the largely white population. Other republics, some Chileans asserted, were racially inferior, an attitude resented by the other Latin American countries.[83]

Venezuela

Venezuela continued to experience the most chaotic constitutional history of all the Latin American countries, partly because of its efforts to follow closely the North American model of federalism. Venezuela had eight constitutions between 1830 and 1900, but under the dictatorship of General Juan Vicente Gómez, the country had seven constitutions between 1908 and 1935.

The reasons for such constitutional discontinuity are not hard to find. Owing to the chronic political instability, nearly every new regime insisted on writing a new constitution to declare its independence from the preceding one. Unlike the tradition in most of Latin America, where constitutional changes were made by amendments, Venezuelans wrote completely new constitutions.

Throughout the nineteenth century, two issues caused the writing of new constitutions in Venezuela. The first was the continuous debate over federalism versus centralism as the solution to the country's problems. Because of Venezuela's fascination with the North American idea of federalism, throughout the first three-quarters of the twentieth century, the country continued to pay lip service to federalism while nonetheless remaining a centralized republic most of the time.[84] The second issue was the expansion and contraction of the suffrage over time. One feature that remained constant, however, was that the government remained steadfastly presidential, following the practice of North American constitutionalism.[85]

Brazil

After gaining its independence, Brazil had either seven or eight constitutions, according to the particular record consulted.[86] This figure ranked well below the average of almost thirteen in other countries. The North

American–influenced constitution of 1891 which established the first Brazilian republic, however, failed to serve the country well.

Political problems resulted from two groups that resented the continued dominance of the coffee elites, who kept imposing "coffee presidents" on the country. One was the growing urban middle class which began to exploit its rising political prominence. The other was the restless and dissatisfied military. Although the two groups united in an attempt to win the election of 1922, they failed. The result unleashed eight years of political unrest, a period that came to be called the Old Republic.

The military "revolt" of 1930 proved to be a watershed in Brazil's constitutional history. It brought to power Getúlio Vargas, a master politician who introduced revolutionary changes and moved Brazil to the forefront of Latin American nations. At the head of the army-backed coup, Vargas ruled by decree as provisional president until 1934 when a new constitution was written that reflected the eclectic view of Brazil's constitution makers. Instead of the North American model featured in the 1891 constitution, the 1934 document followed the Weimar Constitution of 1919 and Spanish Constitution of 1931. The diminution of North American influence was caused by both Vargas's changes and the onset of the Great Depression.

Although two major features representing North American constitutionalism, federalism and the separation of powers, were retained, they underwent significant changes. The power of the federal government was enhanced at the expense of the states. Legislative power in the congress was controlled by the Chamber of Deputies. As a result, the Senate assumed the position of a fourth branch of government, and executive power began to be exercised by the president and his cabinet. There being no vice president, Vargas as president became the supreme authority.

In 1937, Brazil entered a critical period in its constitutional history as a result of Vargas's populist dictatorship. On the pretext of putting down a presumed communist plot, Vargas staged a self-generated coup and proclaimed an *estado novo* (new state) with himself as dictator. He replaced the 1934 charter with the 1937 charter, which was nothing but a shadow constitution allowing him to exercise dictatorial power.[87] Throughout the life of the 1937 constitution, individual rights were suspended, and the totalitarian nature of the Vargas regime soon caused great discontent among the people. Although Vargas tried to play down the contrast between the defeat of fascism abroad and the continued authoritarianism at home, he failed.[88] Following a military coup d'état in October 1945, he was forced to resign and go into exile.

The new 1946 constitution represented a reaction against the Vargas dictatorship. Like the 1891 constitution, it was considerably influenced by the U.S. Constitution. The judiciary recovered its autonomy as well as the power of judicial review, and it soon became one of the most independent institutions of its kind in Latin America.[89] The constitution likewise restored individual rights, including freedom from censorship.[90] Indeed, many features of the North American model that had lain dormant were revived.

Although Vargas had been out of office for five years, he was reelected in 1950. This time he began with a more modest and moderate program but was soon forced to make hard economic choices. This shift enabled his enemies on both the Right and Left to attack him, and by 1954, his austerity measures aimed at curbing inflation had aroused great opposition. Charges of corruption were levied, and when an assassination attempt on his life failed, the military accused him of being implicated and demanded his resignation. Leaving behind a bitter suicide note, the weary president shot himself on August 24, 1954.

Vargas remains the most important political leader in Brazil's modern history. He presided over an important shift in power from the states to the central government, a move in keeping with North American constitutionalism. Another move in that direction was the expansion of suffrage as political power was transferred from large landowners to the middle class. Vargas also allowed the central government to compete with private capital, permitted labor to organize, and stimulated the modernization of industry in what had been essentially a rural country. Although attacked from both the Right and the Left, he adopted a changing populist stance that enabled him to remain in power a long time and to bring Brazil closer to modernity.

Conclusion

The fifth "echo" of American constitutional influence during the period between the world wars was affected by several important developments. The first was the growing influence of American constitutionalism, as the six seminal documents were used extensively in writing the constitutions in Europe immediately after World War I. The second development was the democratization that occurred at the same time as many monarchies were transformed into republics and made the transition to democracy. The third was the expansion of suffrage in the early part of this period. But all this progress in the fifth echo was shattered by the onset of the Great Depression. When the economic situation deteriorated, the promise of American constitutionalism and democracy declined accordingly.

A new countertrend to democratization set in, exemplified by Huntington's first "reverse" wave that ran through the late 1920s and 1930s. In Italy, the fascist Mussolini ousted the elected government and declared himself dictator. In Germany, Hitler came to power in 1933 ending the days of the democratic Weimar Republic. In Russia, the new temporary republican regime with its democratically elected Duma was overthrown by the radical leftist Bolsheviks.

By 1939 and the outbreak of World War II, nearly every country in central and eastern Europe was under the control of a nondemocratic regime of either the Right or the Left. In southern Europe, the same pattern prevailed in Portugal and Spain.

The nondemocratic trend became worldwide and also affected the Western Hemisphere. In Latin America in the 1930s, almost every country that had installed a civilian government or attempted a limited democratic regime witnessed a change to military rule. It was almost a half century before Latin America recovered and installed democratic regimes again throughout the continent.

By the beginning of World War II, the influence of American constitutionalism worldwide had diminished markedly. The American model that had contributed so much in the 1920s had been driven from the scene by the late 1930s. The democracies in Europe numbered fewer than a dozen, and those in Latin America had all but disappeared. Autocracy, not democracy, seemed to hold the key to the future of the world.

10

Sixth Echo

American Crescendo, 1945–1974

Speaking before a hushed House of Commons on the eve of the Battle of Britain, Churchill described in apocalyptic terms the stakes involved in World War II:

> The Battle of Britain is about to begin. Upon this battle depends the survival of Christian civilization. Upon it depends our own British life, and the long continuity of our institutions. The whole fury and might of the enemy must very soon be turned on us. Hitler knows that he will have to break us in this Island or lose the war. If we stand up to him, all Europe may be free and the life of the world may move forward into broad, sunlit uplands. But if we fail, then the whole world, including the United States, including all that we have known and cared for, will sink into the abyss of a new Dark Age.[1]

World War II ranks as the most momentous event in modern world history. Had the Allies been defeated, Western constitutionalism might have disappeared or else emerged badly deformed. With it might have gone America's ideas about democracy, the rule of law, and limited government. To indulge in such speculation only underscores the great significance of American constitutionalism.

America came out of the war instead a superpower, its constitutionalism intact, when the sixth "echo" produced a crescendo. The three decades from 1945 to 1974 represent the highest peak of American constitutionalism abroad to that date. It was spurred by the decolonization movement giving rise at the same time to many of the constitutions of emerging new nations.

The American Declaration of Independence experienced a new lease on life with the decolonization movement after 1950. This "third historical moment" was distinguished from the earlier two because the countries involved alluded less directly to Jefferson's masterpiece, being more distant in time and often turning to intermediate models but making clear that the American Declaration was the ultimate source of their inspiration. "Some seventy new states were created from the wreckage of the British, French, and Portuguese empires, mostly in Africa and Asia. Declarations of Independence joined other instruments of independence devised for extinguishing empires."[2]

The bill of rights tradition was another indication of the great spread of American constitutionalism. The Holocaust, the slaughter of innocent victims, and the oppression of minorities by abusive majorities forced government leaders to recognize that the protection of individual liberties could no longer be left in the hands of executive and legislative branches of national governments. This situation became clearer when totalitarian leaders like Hitler began using legislative majorities to persecute minorities like the Jews. To protect minorities, a broader approach to the bill of rights tradition was needed. One result was that almost every constitution written in the postwar period included a bill of rights, whether or not such rights were enforced.

The expansion of the bill of rights tradition also began to develop along two quite different lines. One was the traditional way, a bill of rights embedded in a national constitution. The second approach differed when the tradition became "internationalized." Rights began to be protected by other written instruments, such as international treaties, covenants, and transnational agreements.[3] After the Holocaust, world leaders reconsidered the traditional notion of national sovereignty holding that a nation's government should be the ultimate authority on human rights. During the Nuremberg trials in 1945, Allied victors charged Nazi leaders with war crimes, crimes against humanity, and other massive human rights violations. In the course of the trials, a new notion was introduced, that international standards of conduct should sometimes outweigh national sovereignty when human rights were violated on a huge scale. The result was that the bill of rights tradition began to be articulated through international agreements like the 1948 Universal Declaration of Human Rights.

The expanded influence of American constitutionalism was evident as well in the changing relationship of the United States within Western constitutionalism itself. Whereas America emerged from the war a superpower, there was a concomitant decline in the status of the two former great powers, Britain and France. Devastation during the war left the economies of the two nations in chaos, and the loss of their colonies reduced their power further. The United States, by contrast, emerged with fewer casualties, its homeland unscathed, and its postwar economy more powerful than ever. No longer considered a junior partner, America emerged as the leader of Western constitutionalism.

With that position came the responsibility of being the leader of the free world as ideological tensions between constitutional democracy and Marxist–Leninist communism came to a head in the cold war. With the Soviet Union emerging as a competing superpower, the ideological clash of interests dating back to the Russian Revolution broke out anew. The two superpowers struggled to see whose constitutional ideology would prevail. Rivalry was intense, and both sides often felt they were just short of open or direct military hostilities. What made the cold war particularly frightening was that both countries possessed nuclear weapons which, if unleashed, could destroy all life on earth in a modern Armageddon.

From America's perspective, the Soviet Union seemed to be involved in a vast imperial expansion to occupy the countries conquered during the war or to be bent on a crusade to spread communism throughout the globe. The Soviets appeared determined to undermine America's capitalistic system. Many Americans tended to blame all global unrest on Moscow and to believe that the real aim of Soviet leaders was to destroy the free world. The mercurial Soviet premier Nikita Khrushchev, in fact, once pledged that the Soviets would "bury" the West.

From the Soviet perspective, which will not be clear until their archives are examined thoroughly, the Russians were disturbed lest America encircle their country with hostile capitalistic allies. The Soviets interpreted the Truman Doctrine as part of a long-range policy aimed at isolating Russia from the rest of the world and bringing down communist regimes wherever they existed.

Faced with these two contestants locked in deadly struggle (like a scorpion and a tarantula in a bottle, according to one description), some countries felt compelled to choose between the competing constitutional ideologies. Many nations allied themselves with the United States, became sympathetic to the aims of American constitutionalism, and began emulating its model. Others sided with the Soviet Union and its messianic appeal. Still others joined a nonaligned group of neutral nations seeking to stay above the fray altogether.

When dealing constitutionally with the defeated Axis foes—Germany, Italy, and Japan—the United States adopted a surprisingly liberal policy.

Given America's military power, the country could have been far more aggressive in pressing for the adoption of its constitutional model. Since the Soviet Union was superimposing its model on Czechoslovakia and East Germany, America would have been justified in taking similar action. But it did not and remained remarkably restrained. In West Germany, for example, America intervened only to insist on federalism simply to prevent any excessive concentration of power at the top. In Italy, America's interference was minimal. In Japan, as will be shown, America did not arbitrarily "impose" its constitutionalism, as was commonly supposed.[4] "When viewed in the light of the emerging rivalry with the Soviet model . . . the Americans showed themselves . . . to be the most liberal victors of modern times," concluded one scholar. "In no single country was the American model adopted *en bloc*. The process of adoption was limited to individual institutions."[5]

West Germany

For the first five years after World War II, America's constitutional influence abroad expanded mostly into the former Axis countries, especially with the democratization of Germany and Japan. Given the weakness of the democratic tradition in both countries, such an outcome hardly seemed possible. In retrospect, one scholar observed, "Today we see more clearly than before that the Second World War marked the defeat of fascism as a viable form of political organization; it . . . opened the possibility of fostering democracy in Germany and Japan."[6]

One myth to be dismissed was the charge raised by a few German politicians that the occupying powers had "imposed" their model on West Germany, the part of Germany that they controlled; the Soviet Union occupied East Germany.[7] Such remarks were made for political purposes and had little basis in fact. America insisted on federalism, to be sure, but that feature was one with which Germans were familiar. As one German scholar concluded, "Important borrowings on the American model in areas such as federalism . . . were not mere *Diktats*, but had local roots."[8]

Carl J. Friedrich, an important adviser to American military government authorities, agreed but on a different basis: "The compromise [of the Basic Law of 1949] is the result of constitutional ideas, partly German, partly French, partly English, and partly American." What made his remark more convincing was that Friedrich was the scholar most critical of America's supposed "interference" in the constitution-making process.[9]

The Germans refused to use the word *constitution* in the 1949 document, taking the position that in the German tradition, Verfassung (constitution) could be used only to designate the fundamental law of a "sovereign" nation. The Germans insisted that their country was not sovereign because it was still under military occupation. They agreed that the document instead be called the "Basic Law," that is, a "provisional constitution."[10]

When writing their Basic Law, the Germans received very general instructions. The guidelines provided by the Allied occupying powers called only for a "democratic constitution," one with a federal structure, bicameral legislature, and judicial review. Germany's response to these instructions remains obscure because of the lack of documentation. The specific American influence also remains uncertain because other Allied powers were involved.[11] But given what we do know, it is clear that America did not aggressively push its own model. In fact, the United States consistently urged the Germans to write their own constitutions on both the state and national levels.

Work on rebuilding the German government began on the local level in 1946 as the federal structure was erected from the ground up. In their zone, the Americans encouraged the Land (state) governments to hold local elections and to form constituent assemblies for the three Land governments in 1946. General Lucius Clay, the military governor of the American zone, kept insisting the Germans frame their own constitutions.[12] The Land charters, one scholar concluded, "became the model for the French and British zones and to some extent for the Basic Law."[13]

Encouraged by the occupying powers, the Germans called an American-style constitutional convention representing the ten Länder, which met in Bonn in 1948/1949. This body produced the Basic Law establishing the Federal Republic of Germany. The Soviets took steps in their zone to set up communist-dominated governments, and the result was the emergence of two separate countries, West Germany and East Germany.

The Basic Law should be viewed as an attempt to correct the excesses of both the Nazi regime and the old Weimar Constitution. When one liberal member of the convention proposed the American presidential system, he was accused of "crying after the Führer."[14] Although the Basic Law founded a parliamentary government along French lines, it introduced a significant modification derived from the British tradition. The chancellor (prime minister) had the right to propose to the president the dissolution of the representative assembly, an arrangement signaling a distinct change from the dangerous dualism existing under the Weimar Constitution. Power then had been divided between a popularly elected president and a chancellor and cabinet responsible to the parliament.[15] The new watered-down solution was balanced, however, by restrictions placed on the parliament's power to dissolve the government.

Other corrective measures were taken. Although the pattern of federalism was somewhat similar to that of the Weimar Constitution, it had two significant changes. First, Prussia, the most powerful state, disappeared when it became a part of East Germany, and the newly delineated states in West Germany were more equal in size and population. Second, the Bund and Länder now were recognized as autonomous within their own spheres, thus placing them on a more equal footing.[16] The occupying powers encouraged the federal arrangement as a way of fragmenting political power and preventing any recurrence of the disastrous centralization experienced under Hitler. Federalism, in other words, was a way to support democracy. The Germans, on their part, had had experience with the federal principle as far back as the Holy Roman Empire and, as one authority put it, did not have "to look to the occupying powers for the cue to return to their federalist tradition."[17]

Friedrich, serving as American adviser, confirmed that both the major political parties willingly accepted the federal principle partly as a result of America's influence. The impact of American ideas, he wrote, "occurred spontaneously through informal channels, as indeed most of them had become embodied in the German tradition since 1848."[18]

To enhance the protection of civil liberties (which had not been observed under either the Weimar Republic or the Nazi regime), such rights were expressed in more precise language. Their importance was emphasized by listing them in the preamble. To provide institutional safeguards, a constitutional court was established. In the Weimar Constitution, rights and liberties had been among the most democratic in the world and were made even more so in the Basic Law. A number of striking innovations were introduced, including rights regarding freedom of expression in speech, writing, and printing, many of which were drawn from American constitutionalism.[19]

Sensitive to what had happened under the Nazis when civil rights were abused, German constitution makers introduced certain unusual measures. Totalitarian movements had taken advantage of civil liberties, especially freedom of speech, of the press, and of assembly, to sabotage the Weimar regime. The German framers decreed, therefore, that these "unalienable" rights might be suspended if any person abused them for purposes of undermining the government.[20]

America's direct influence focused most on federalism, for which Germany already had its own tradition. Germany created a nation-state about as "federal" in its form as the United States and Switzerland. The Basic Law stated that Germany had been founded on the basis of a "federally united people." "The German people are united, but are composed of the people of the several states . . . as enumerated in the preamble."[21]

One way the Basic Law was made more "federal" and closer to the American model was by changing the method of taxation. German tradition had allowed the Länder considerable fiscal autonomy. But in the 1949 document, federal and state taxes were collected separately under a complicated formula, a change accepted only after a bitter debate between the "centralists" and the "federalists."[22]

The other prominent feature attributed largely to American influence was judicial review, which appeared first in the Land constitutions to solidify the trend toward democracy. Friedrich, who was involved in the process, observed:

> This policy bore fruit in the *Land* constitutions in the American zone, discussed and adopted in 1946 on American initiative. They could and did serve as models for the Basic Law. . . . [There were] marked differences between the American Supreme Court and the Federal German Constitutional Court. What matters [most] is that the latter, like the former, has acted as a guardian of the constitution, has gradually enhanced respect for it, and has brought home to Germans at large that they have a "basic law."[23]

Although there were German precedents for such an institution and the system did not operate in quite the same way as in the United States, evidence of considerable borrowing from the American model was obvious. "There is no doubt the [American] Supreme Court jurisprudence has had significant impact on the German Constitutional Court," concluded one authority.[24] American cases, in fact, were sometimes cited in West German decisions, indicating that German judges on the Constitutional Court were quite familiar with the workings of the American system.[25]

For constitutional jurisdiction, the Germans resorted to the centralized Austrian model. They were influenced most by Hans Nawiasky, the framer of the Bavarian Constitution who had studied under Hans Kelsen.

Donald Kommers, a leading scholar of the German constitutional court, reported that the Germans took it upon themselves to set up a specialized constitutional court "with power not only to decide intergovernmental disputes, but also to review the constitutionality of laws and other governmental actions, relying principally on German traditions."[26]

By creating democratic constitutions at the Land and federal level, the Germans learned to cope with the processes of democracy. Friedrich's conclusion regarding the course of events rings true: "Probably the most positive legacy, politically, of the occupation of Germany by the Western Allies is the conversion of a majority of Germans to a democratic constitutionalism. [And] the lion's share of the credit for bringing about this change falls to the United States."[27]

Japan

Japan remains the most striking example of American constitutional influence on any nation on earth. "Not even Napoleon, who reformed the [Old Regime] systems of conquered Europe could dream of such a thoroughgoing remaking of a society as that attempted and largely accomplished by the United States in postwar Japan," concluded one scholar.[28] The changes affected every facet of Japanese life: government, law, military defense, technology, public health, diet, dress, and even the value system of every Japanese citizen.[29] Indeed, America's role in reconstituting Japanese society ranks with the Marshall Plan in Europe.

Although Japan had previously been exposed to American ideas when writing the Meiji Constitution of 1889, the country had been influenced much more by German (Prussian) thought. During the Meiji era, constitutional rights had been riddled with qualifications.[30] Given that the democratic tradition in Japan was weak before World War II, the country's transformation is even more remarkable.[31] Indeed, democratization remains America's most enduring contribution to Japan.

Equally important was the role of the Japanese people, who were prepared to accept change. The idea of democratic governance reigned supreme throughout the Western world at the end of World War II, and the blending of democracy and constitutionalism seemed natural. "The revolutionary changes . . . and the coming into effect of the Constitution of Japan . . . were momentous and the attendant processes unique, when the concept was extended into the Eastern Hemisphere."[32] The Japanese people, nevertheless, were ready to embrace the change.

Unlike occupied Germany, Japan was not divided into zones, and the United States, rejecting Soviet demands to share in the occupation, had a freer hand. With the approval of the British and French, General Douglas MacArthur, supreme commander of the Allied Powers (known by the acronym SCAP), assumed authority for constitutional matters. Knowing that the Far Eastern Commission (FEC), which would include the Soviet Union and Australia, was being formed, MacArthur pressed forward as quickly as possible to forestall involvement by the FEC, with its possible Soviet veto. Washington's preoccupation with Europe gave him the opportunity to act.

The Framing of the Japanese Constitution

Although MacArthur raised the issue of revising the Meiji Constitution in the fall of 1945 with Prince Konoe, the former prime minister, the government was mainly occupied with other matters because the country was in such chaos. MacArthur was eager to accommodate the Japanese desire to revise the constitution themselves, but Konoe's superficial revisions were repudiated by the Americans on November 1, 1945. MacArthur therefore promptly discredited Konoe and undertook what he later called the "single most important accomplishment of the occupation," the replacement of the Meiji Constitution with a new national charter.[33] The cabinet of Prime Minister Shidehara Kijūrō appointed a committee headed by Minister Matsumoto Jōji to suggest new revisions, but MacArthur again found them cursory and unacceptable. This second submission came more than five months after MacArthur had informed the Japanese that a revision of the Meiji Constitution was imperative. Moreover, it took place only after a newspaper leak forced the issue.[34]

MacArthur, with the support of his aide, General Courtney Whitney, decided that he had sufficient authority to embark on constitutional reform himself.[35] The important turning point came on February 3, 1946, when MacArthur informed Whitney that three principles should govern any constitutional reform. First, the emperor was to be the head of the state, his succession dynastic, his powers exercised in accordance with the constitution, and his responsibility to the will of the people. Second, war as a sovereign right of the Japanese nation was to be abolished. Japan was to renounce war for settling international disputes, even in order to preserve its own security. Third, the feudal system in Japan should cease to exist. No rights of peerage, except those of the imperial family, were to

extend beyond those already in existence. To a considerable degree, Mac-
Arthur's principles became the major guidelines for the American draft of
the 1946 Japanese Constitution.[36]

Whitney then organized the Government Section of his staff into what
was jokingly called a "constitutional convention." The Occupation authorities, with a steering committee headed by Colonel Charles Kades, hastily
produced a draft in a single week and presented it to the Japanese. At first,
the two draft constitutions were far apart.[37] Japan's draft had been written by conservative elites, politicians, and lawyers in the government, who
paid little attention to others submitting drafts and ideas. The American
draft was produced by SCAP's Government Section, most of whose members had no expertise in constitutional law and instead had been trained
in military government during the war. But they were more inclined to
listen to ideas proposed by private individuals, ad hoc citizens' groups,
and opposition political parties.[38] Being more eclectic, they also consulted
foreign constitutions, international agreements, and the United Nations
Charter.[39]

MacArthur insisted on prompt action, and the speed with which the
negotiations were carried out led to the charge later that SCAP had "imposed" the constitution on the Japanese. This impression was heightened
because Matsumoto, the principal negotiator, a man enamored of the emperor system, abruptly left the bargaining sessions.[40] Unable to face the
reality of Japan's unconditional surrender and stubbornly refusing any advice from the Americans, Matsumoto kept trying to retain as much of the
old Meiji Constitution as possible. Like many conservatives, he was fearful that any reformation of Japanese society would upset the status quo
and open the door to communist influence. Once Matsumoto was gone,
the American team was able to deal with men more amenable to compromise. Although it took marathon sessions—one in which the Americans
forcibly insisted on all-night attendance—to produce an acceptable draft,
the compromise document was the basis for what came to be called the
"MacArthur Constitution."[41]

The context in which the constitution was written must also be kept in
mind. Despite being under military occupation, the Japanese people were
eager to accept what the Americans offered. In the words of John Dower,
the preeminent historian of the occupation of Japan, the Japanese people
"embraced" defeat. So great was their disillusionment with the wartime regime that for the most part, they willingly agreed to the proposed draft.[42]
The fact that the constitution has continued essentially unchanged (except

for interpretations of some of its articles) for almost a half century speaks for itself.

The readiness of the Japanese people to accept the new order was all the greater because of a decision that MacArthur made even before Japan's surrender: that the emperor and his throne should be preserved as the heart of Japanese identity.[43] It was a bold move in the face of Allied calls for the emperor's indictment as a war criminal, but it indicated an understanding of the Japanese culture crucial to the success of the country's postwar transformation. The role of the emperor, however, was radically transformed. Under the Meiji Constitution, he had been considered "sacred and inviolable," claimed to rule by divine right, and was invested with the power of sovereignty. In theory, all popular rights had been circumscribed because it was the people's duty to obey the emperor, and his power was considered absolute. It is important to note that the emperor's position in the American draft was quite different: the document proclaimed the people to be sovereign. The emperor was to be "the symbol of the State, and of unity of the people," and his position was derived "from the will of the people with whom resides sovereign power."[44] If the people were sovereign, what then was the emperor's role? He was to serve as the symbolic center of the new constitutional system.

On New Year's Day, 1946, the emperor renounced his claim to divinity and denied that he was a god in human form.[45] But the question of where sovereignty was located remained unclear. Although the sovereignty of the people was declared, the issue remained unresolved largely because of the emperor's actions. Even though he declared himself a human being, the emperor cleverly presented the new constitution as though it were his gift to the people as a revision of the Meiji Constitution. His grandfather had presented that charter to the country many years earlier, and the date of promulgation of the new constitution was set symbolically on his grandfather's birthday. For this reason, historian John Dower labeled the new system an "imperial democracy."[46] The emperor's move proved to be a classic case of "Japanizing" the constitution. His symbolic role thus became far more important than the Americans had intended.

When the draft constitution was submitted to the Japanese Diet (legislature) for consideration, it was presented by the emperor as an "amendment" to the Meiji Constitution. Dower commented on the implications of this move:

To both MacArthur and the Japanese royalists, this was fortuitous: constitution making and emperor saving became part and parcel of the same undertaking. Consequently, the emperor was involved at every stage in the process. Although the new constitution stipulated that sovereignty resided with the people, it was intimated that this sovereignty came from the emperor himself. "Revolution from above" and "imperial democracy" were fused in the most ceremonial manner conceivable.[47]

Transformation of the Constitution: Transformation of Society

A comparison of Japan's postwar constitution with the Meiji Constitution reveals what changes were made. Both documents had provisions for a bicameral legislature, a cabinet, national elections, and the emperor. But the power relationships among these components had shifted dramatically. The divine-right rule by the emperor was ended; he became a symbolic figure only. The cabinet answered to the Diet rather than to the emperor. Sovereignty was transferred from the emperor to the people, and national elections were based on popular sovereignty. A parliamentary form of government was established; suffrage was extended; and women given the right to vote. Both houses of the legislature were popularly elected, instead of only the lower house, as under the Meiji Constitution. Local self-government, moreover, was encouraged to make the society more democratic.

The occupation of Japan had two major objectives as far as the Americans were concerned: demilitarization and democratization. Demilitarization called for disbanding Japan's armed forces and dismantling the country's war machine. To make certain that Japanese militarism would not rise again to threaten neighbors or undermine America's interests in the Pacific, article 9 of the new constitution renounced Japan's sovereign right to wage war in settling international disputes. This article thus provided the basis for Japan's pacifism in any dispute with other countries. It read in part: "The Japanese people forever renounce war as a sovereign right of the nation and the threat or use of force as a means of settling international disputes." Japan was prohibited furthermore from maintaining any military forces. Although other constitutions had forbidden "aggressive" wars, the Japanese charter actually outlawed war itself. According to the prime minister at the time, the constitution outlawed all wars, whether defensive or aggressive, making it unique among the world's charters.[48]

Since a large military establishment was ruled out, expenditures for military purposes were plowed instead into Japan's industrial development. The principle of pacifism nonetheless aroused great controversy. The outbreak of the Korean War, tensions with the Soviet Union, and the civil war in China finally motivated the United States to pressure Japan into establishing a modest military force, and demilitarization as a major goal underwent some changes.

Democratization, the second aim, was designed to transform Japan's authoritarian form of government. Drawing on the seminal documents of American constitutionalism, the constitutionalists incorporated five features to achieve the goal of democratization: the principle of popular sovereignty, the idea of judicial review, the incorporation of a bill of rights, and the recourse that both the American Occupation authorities and the Japanese framers had to the theories of government in *The Federalist*. As Itō Masami, retired justice of the Supreme Court of Japan and professor emeritus of Anglo-American law at the University of Tokyo, attested: "The political theory behind the U.S. Declaration of Independence, the Preamble to the United States Constitution, the Federalist Papers . . . [and] the modern theory of natural law and the theory of democracy based on the idea of social contract—[were] alive throughout the whole draft" submitted by the American SCAP lawyers.[49]

Popular sovereignty was achieved by making all three branches of government subject to control by the people, either directly or indirectly. At the same time, the people were accorded certain fundamental rights reflecting the bill of rights tradition. These included the right of the people to elect and dismiss public officials, of peaceful petition, and of the secret ballot. Popular control was ensured also by recognizing the Diet as the "highest organ of state power."[50] Suffrage was broadened at the same time: the vote was extended to women in 1945, and the voting age was lowered to twenty.[51]

The American idea of judicial review was introduced as well, transforming Japan's judicial system. Before World War II, Japan had operated under three different legal traditions: the civil-law tradition, the Meiji Constitution, and an indigenous legal tradition based on local customs.[52] For the first time in Japanese history, the judiciary was established as a separate branch and guaranteed independence from the executive.[53] Judicial power was granted to the Japanese Supreme Court as well as to inferior courts created by law. The courts were empowered to determine the constitutionality of any law, and their power of review was extended even to cases involving an administrative arm of the government.[54]

The introduction of judicial review into a parliamentary country whose representative assembly was, by definition, dominant over the judiciary made Japan an anomaly. The government system as whole was committed to parliamentary supremacy, yet at the same time judicial review was introduced. Clearly the two were contradictory.[55] Despite the power given to it, the supreme court was reluctant to resort to judicial review because of the Japanese ethos against confrontation and in favor of cooperation.[56] The court also was not very willing to find laws of the Diet unconstitutional. During the first twenty years after the 1946 constitution went into effect, only two statutes were declared unconstitutional.[57] Another factor hindering the exercise of American-style judicial review was the difference in the public attitude toward litigation. The Japanese tradition of mediation and arbitration was ingrained in the national ethos.

The establishment of the court system, whatever its indigenous differences in practice from the American, had a profound effect when it became intertwined with the guarantee of personal freedoms included in chapter 3, the heart of the 1946 constitution.[58] A veritable revolution changed the lives of Japanese citizens once the idea of human rights was introduced. Although Japan had experienced a limited degree of democracy during the Taishō era that preceded the militarism of the 1930s, the Meiji Constitution stressed duty to the state over rights of the individual. In the words of one informed scholar,

> [For a] closed, repressed, ultranationalist and militaristic society just devastated by war, these new provisions and attendant reforms of law and institution, ushered in a dramatic increase in freedom, openness, and tolerance. . . . [T]he constructive consequences altered the context of all human rights in Japan, and began the long process of gradually opening a closed society.[59]

With the new constitution, Japan's previously restrictive society underwent a dramatic transformation. The Japanese bill of rights reflected in its language the ideals and traditions of the United States much more than those of Japan. The "Rights and Duties of the People" in chapter 3 of the constitution provides a good example. Its forty articles included, on the one hand, the usual American guarantees of criminal justice, universal suffrage, equality, separation of church and state, and freedom of thought. On the other hand, some rights guaranteed in the articles are not to be found in the U.S. Constitution. One example is the explicit statement of gender equality regarding the rights of women. Certain other "social and economic rights" pertaining to labor and livelihood also are not included in the American charter. Some of the bill of rights features were clearly aimed at meeting MacArthur's third principle: abolishing feudalism in Japan.

The human rights provisions in the 1946 constitution reflected the interpretation of these rights in America as they existed right after the New Deal and its social welfare legislation. Generally speaking, the rights of Japanese citizens were listed as being "eternal and inviolate," and "life, liberty, and the pursuit of happiness" were to be "the supreme consideration in legislation and in other governmental affairs." One provision recognized a right defensible in court "to maintain the minimum standards of wholesome and cultured living . . . social welfare and security." All citizens were to have a constitutional right to a free education. Workers were to have rights "to organize and bargain and act collectively" and to reasonable standards for "wages, hours, rest, and other working conditions."[60] Charles Kades, the able American lawyer who helped draft the constitution, was thoroughly conversant with the New Deal aspect of such legislation because of his background in the United States.[61]

Any comparison of prewar Japan human rights with those in America is complicated by two overriding considerations. The first was the group-oriented lifestyle of the Japanese compared with the individualism of the Americans. Although this cultural difference has sometimes been over-emphasized to the point of caricature, it represented in reality an enormous difference between the two societies. The second was Japan's status as a civil-law country compared with America's common-law tradition. Civil-law countries, as noted earlier, limit the role of the judiciary, making it difficult to exercise judicially enforceable rights as practiced in the United States.

It was one thing to introduce these major features into the constitution but quite another to implement them. There was a gap between the theory of American-style popular sovereignty and the way that the new government actually operated in practice. In addition to the ambiguous position of the emperor, another barrier was the formidable presence of the Japanese bureaucracy. Although the Diet was acknowledged to be Japan's highest government arm, the existing giant bureaucracy actually carried out governmental policies. That bureaucracy lay beyond the reach of the people and was not accountable to citizens. It had far-reaching controls over numerous administrative rules and regulations and certain civil codes that governed the daily lives of the Japanese. Undemocratic by tradition, it contravened the principle of popular sovereignty and made it impossible to carry out some of the intended American reforms.

A profound transformation occurred, nevertheless, in Japan's civil liberties. Freedom of speech, prohibition of censorship, freedom of assembly and association, and freedom of religion—all features of American constitutionalism—were introduced to a surprising degree. Decisions in the Japanese Supreme Court followed guidelines laid down by the new constitution to protect such freedoms. The underlying philosophy was pointedly expressed by justices who declared that the guarantee of freedom of assembly was "the most important feature that distinguishes democracy from totalitarianism."[62] Freedom of religion, which had been severely restricted under the Meiji Constitution, was broadened considerably. Among the six different kinds of religious rights enumerated was the statement that "the State cannot establish a state church or make adherence to any religion compulsory."[63] Although separation of church and state was too complex as far as the Shinto religion was concerned, the tendency toward greater religious freedom was clearly evident.[64]

In addition, civil liberties regarding free speech and other human rights were now protected by a special group of lay people, namely, volunteers called "civil liberties commissioners" and "local administrative counselors." Rights generally are accompanied in societies by remedies to vindicate or protect them, and such remedies normally include a wide variety of sociolegal mechanisms. Since the formal courts of law were costly, cumbersome, and intimidating, the Japanese usually resorted to a system of "conciliable rights," in which rights disputes were heard by either the commissioners or the counselors. Such a system differs substantially from the "judicially enforceable rights" practiced in America's formal courts.[65] The general framework for Japan's new civil rights, nevertheless, was essentially derived from American constitutionalism.

Was the Japanese Constitution "Imposed"?

The promulgation of the 1946 constitution resulted in a historiographical controversy that involved American scholars and Japanese politicians. Right after the war, two American scholars, Robert E. Ward and Ray A. Moore, protested that the constitution had been "imposed" arbitrarily on the Japanese by American Occupation authorities using methods contrary to American constitutionalism. Conservative Japanese politicians later made similar charges.

The constitution, particularly the question of whether it had been "imposed," did not become a heated political issue until five years after the document was promulgated. In the interim, several important developments had taken place. The outbreak of the Korean War in 1950 brought hostilities to Japan's doorstep, and the constitution was suddenly viewed in a different light. The question was raised of whether Japan could rearm, given the implications of article 9, which had renounced war "forever" and outlawed Japan's use of force. In 1951, moreover, Japan and the United States had signed peace and security treaties, which brought the Japanese much closer to the position of the West. The Japanese people also learned about the charge that the constitution had been "imposed" on them for the first time in the early 1950s. The drafting process in 1946 had been conducted in secret, but the publication of a private document in 1951 revealed details unknown until that time.[66]

Robert E. Ward published an article in 1956 insisting the constitution had been arbitrarily "imposed" on Japan and was totally unsuited to the needs of the Japanese people. "The ideals and experiences of vast majority of the population, [and] the long term interests of democracy may have been ill-served." Ward then delivered a damning indictment: "Instead of a system of government based upon and geared to the social, economic, and political realities of Japanese society, a hollow but elaborate facade modeled after an idealized version of Anglo-American political institutions was hastily patched together."[67]

Ray A. Moore, another American critic, charged in a 1979 article that the constitution reflected the biases of America's occupying authorities. In framing the constitution, Moore concluded, MacArthur and his staff had resorted to coercion and undemocratic methods.[68] The writings of these two scholars formed the basis of what for decades became the accepted interpretation in American academic circles.[69]

In fairness, it should be noted that Moore changed his mind almost a quarter of a century later, in 2002. His revised position was that Japan and America had been "partners for democracy" because they had cooperated in framing the constitution jointly.[70] His counterargument against the charge that the constitution had been "imposed" was supported by evidence he discovered of collusion between SCAP and the Japanese cabinet members. Throughout the negotiating procedure, the Shidehara and Yoshida cabinet members and SCAP worked together secretly to have the process of constitutional revision kept free from any interference by Washington, the Allies, and the Japanese public. The often unacknowledged communication between the conqueror and the conquered resulted in obvious collusion and thus weakened the charge of "imposition."[71]

Koseki Shōichi, a Japanese constitutional scholar who wrote the most authoritative study on framing the constitution, pointed out, moreover, how the charter had been "Japanized." One important development had been the input from Japanese citizens and laymen without any legal training. Ad hoc citizens' groups had written proposals that decidedly influenced the American draft. "No single Diet member or constitutional scholar came close to exercising the influence of those few laymen," Koseki concluded.[72]

Writing the constitution in the vernacular provided another example of "Japanizing." The Meiji Constitution had been phrased in archaic literary language almost unintelligible to laymen. So when the SCAP draft was made public in 1946, representatives from a private citizens' group requested that the document be rewritten in language understandable to the common people. When this was done, Koseki said, it contributed to "fostering a sense of individual rights and nurturing the development of postwar democracy."[73]

Another instance of "Japanizing" the constitution concerned the rights of foreigners living in Japan. During the early weeks of the Occupation, SCAP issued specific instructions regarding the protection of fundamental rights of ethnic minorities such as Korean, Taiwanese, and Chinese. A SCAP directive in October 1945 ordered the Japanese government to "abolish discrimination on grounds of race, nationality, creed or political opinion."[74] The Japanese draft constitution of February 1946 accordingly incorporated two articles guaranteeing that "all natural persons are equal before law" and that "aliens should be entitled to the equal protection of law."[75] In early March, however, the Japanese government submitted revisions changing these definitions in the final draft. The phrase "all natural persons" was changed to "all the people," and "caste or national origin" became "family origin."[76] These changes had the effect of excluding persons of foreign ancestry from constitutional rights and protections in subsequent legislation. Hundreds of thousands of persons of Korean, Chinese, and Taiwanese ancestry were thereby stripped of their constitutional rights when the Japanese peace treaty went into effect in 1952. This change was a deliberate maneuver by Japanese politicians and bureaucrats to maintain ethnic homogeneity, since they based their idea of nationality on patrilinear consanguinity derived from the jurisprudence of the Meiji Constitution.[77]

Numerous other instances of "Japanizing" the constitution indicate that the charge of "imposing" goes too far. MacArthur, for example, had made many important concessions when framing the constitution. The Japanese, on their part, accommodated or deflected many of the changes that SCAP and his staff wished to make. Both sides collaborated to keep the process of constitutional revision in their hands and free from much interference by outsiders. The result was a constitution that may be called a "hybrid Japanese-American" document rather than one arbitrarily "imposed."[78]

Japanese and German Constitution Writing Compared

The framing of the two postwar charters in Germany and Japan provides an excellent opportunity to compare the role that American constitutionalism played in each. The comparison yields as many insights into the United States—its national values, ethnocentrism, and foreign policy goals—as about its former enemies.

Japan and Germany were viewed quite differently by Americans in terms of their race, culture, and society. Japan represented "an exotic, alien society to its conquerors," according to Dower. It was

> non-white, non-Western, [and] non-Christian. Yellow Asian, pagan Japan, supine and vulnerable, provoked an ethnocentric missionary zeal inconceivable vis-à-vis Germany. Where Nazism was perceived as a cancer in a fundamentally mature "Western" society, Japanese militarism and ultranationalism were construed as reflecting the essence of a feudalistic, Oriental culture that was cancerous in and of itself.[79]

MacArthur himself reflected many of these views, but in a sophisticated way. He still bore the stamp of that colonial conceit known as "the white man's burden" and believed that Americans were engaged in a Christian mission to exert control over Japan's so-called pagan society.[80] He viewed democracy in universal terms, believing American democracy was destined to spread throughout the world in general and in Japan in particular. Under his guidance, Japan's 1946 constitution reflected many of these values either directly or indirectly.

MacArthur's view of Japan also revealed a Western, Anglo-Saxon eth-nocentrism that presumably compared Japan with Germany in an unfa-vorable light. He once said,

> If the Anglo-Saxon was say 45 years of age in his development, in the sciences, the arts, divinity, culture, the Germans were quite mature. The Japanese, however, in spite of their antiquity measured by time were in a very tuitionary condition. Measured by the standards of modern civiliza-tion, they would be like a boy of twelve as compared with our develop-ment of 45 years.[81]

Dower's interpretation places this quotation in the larger context of Mac-Arthur's political philosophy and concludes it was more subtle than mature Anglo-Saxons being compared with immature Japanese. What MacArthur meant was that in terms of modern development, the Japanese were con-sidered childlike compared with adult Germans, a more untrustworthy people than the Japanese, who had been responsive and impressionable during the Occupation. Dower's comment seems to be on the mark.[82]

Moreover, MacArthur, acting as a kind of proconsul, had a freer hand in carrying out the "revolution from above." As an indisputable overlord, he was in a better position to introduce far-reaching constitutional re-forms than was General Clay in Germany. Nothing of the sort was pos-sible in postwar Germany, especially because America had to share the occupation of Germany. Plans for a formal military government in Japan were soon dropped, whereas Germany was subjected to a much more rigid occupying regime. But when it came to a timetable for drafting con-stitutions, the schedule for both countries was about the same: the proc-esses were hurried in order to present the Soviets with a fait accompli.[83] One thing is certain, however, in any comparison: the constitution of 1946 exercised a much greater influence on the lives of the Japanese people than did the Basic Law of 1949 on the Germans.

Italy

Italy, the third member of the Axis, escaped the fate of Germany and Japan by getting out of the war early. In 1943, Italy signed an armistice, joined the Allies, and became an honorary member of the winning side. As a result, its constitutional evolution differed from the other two. But as in the case of all the defeated Axis powers, the United States made no aggressive move to impose its constitutional system on the country.

In June 1946 Italy voted to abolish the Savoy monarchy and to establish a republic. Bitter political strife followed as parties from the Left, Center, and Right fought for control, and the country teetered on the brink of civil war. A constitutional assembly along American lines was elected in 1947 and produced a new constitution effective January 1, 1948. It established a parliamentary system with a ceremonial presidency, cabinet government, and legislative supremacy. Proportional representation enabled equitable representation for all political parties.

During the proceedings of the 1947 constitutional convention, a concerted attempt was made to install the American presidential system. Piero Calamandrei, a great constitutional scholar, was the foremost advocate of the idea. He countered the argument that the institution might lead to another dictatorship like Mussolini's by pointing out that the fascist dictator had in fact emerged from a parliamentary system. But the Italian Left, which traditionally voted against the presidential idea, succeeded in squashing Calamandrei's proposal. The vote was extremely one-sided, and with such a resounding defeat, it was not possible even in the plenary session of the constituent assembly to reverse the decision.[84]

The American principle of judicial review was introduced, and a new institution, a constitutional court, was created.[85] Although Italy experimented briefly from 1948 to 1956 with the decentralized American system of judicial review, in a few years the country adopted Kelsen's centralized model, following the general European trend.[86] The fact remains, however, that the original impetus for judicial review in Italy can be traced back to American constitutional influence.[87]

The Federalist also reached its peak of popularity in Italy during this period. In 1954 Aldo Garosci produced a major study of the work praising *The Federalist* as a "book of great political value" and concluded that few political treatises in the world had shown "such lucidity."[88] The first Italian translation of *The Federalist* appeared about the same time, and Gaspare Ambrosini, who had published widely on constitutional subjects, wrote the introduction. In it he described *The Federalist* as "a profound and suggestive commentary on the Constitution and a great treatise of political science."[89] Although it is not possible to trace direct American influence through *The Federalist* to specific provisions in Italy's 1948 constitution, there is no doubt that in that country, as in others, the ideas of Publius had some indirect influence by being part of the democratic zeitgeist of the time.

Austria

Although Austria, annexed by Germany in 1938, fought on the side of the Axis, in 1943 the Allies signed an agreement proclaiming an independent Austria as one of their major war aims. When the conflict ended, Austria was divided into four zones of occupation, with the Americans holding the northern and western parts of the country. Austria, as was true of the other Axis powers, was not coerced into adopting the U.S. model of government.

A provisional government was formed in 1945 with permission of the occupying powers. The 1918 Constitution of the First Republic, modified in 1929, was reintroduced as the governing charter.[90] The most significant event in the postwar era was the restoration of Austria's sovereignty in 1955 with the establishment of the Second Republic. A peace treaty signed earlier that year pledged Austria to guarantee free elections and fundamental human rights comparable to the principles of American constitutionalism.

In regard to other features of American constitutionalism, judicial review figured most in Austria. Kelsen's centralized system, which had been established in 1920 and had operated until it was suppressed by the Nazis in 1939, was reestablished in the constitutional law system in 1945.[91] While the point has frequently been made that it was Kelsen's rather than the American system that prevailed not only in Austria but in most of Europe, the principle of judicial review can be traced back to American constitutionalism. In Austria, American military power helped restore the institution of judicial review, even though it did not follow the American style.[92]

France

American constitutionalism in France played a less significant role than in the defeated powers of Germany and Japan. As one of the Allies, France obviously remained in control of its own constitutional destiny. In the case of two institutions, presidentialism and judicial review, the United States appears to have exercised some slight influence, but little consideration was given to federalism, as had been the case in France's past all along.

After World War II, the political instability of France's Fourth Republic was demonstrated by the twenty-five cabinets it had from 1946 to 1958. Communist influence in the country was extensive and divisive. But the Fourth Republic did not differ much from the Third. The presidency was ceremonial, and the premier and cabinet remained responsible to the powerful National Assembly. General Charles DeGaulle, who was in office briefly, disliked the idea of an all-purpose legislature that interfered with his grand vision of restoring a strong France.

Then in the 1950s the colonial wars in French Indochina and Algeria brought France to the brink of civil war. The country turned again to De-Gaulle as the one person capable of saving France. In mid-1958, the National Assembly invested him as premier, granted him emergency powers for six months, and gave him the authority to prepare a new constitution. France, always the most monarchical of the democratic great powers, continued in that tradition.

The Fifth Republic established a semipresidential, semiparliamentary system.[93] Although there were many advocates for an American-type presidency, the charged political climate of the time rendered any foreign influences suspect. The move was quelled also by fears of DeGaulle's ambition for too much power. His ideas, submitted to the convention in May 1958, supported a decidedly dualist system.

Born in the 1958 constitution, the Fifth Republic produced the kind of presidency for which DeGaulle had long called. Following his election, he was granted supreme authority in foreign affairs and national defense. He could name the prime minister (as the premier was called), dissolve the National Assembly, assume emergency powers, and submit important questions to popular referenda. Political instability abated as a result, and the Fifth Republic had only three cabinets in its first eleven years. With the older political parties subdued and impotent, DeGaulle ran what was in effect a plebiscitory democracy. On difficult issues, he went over the heads of politicians and appealed directly to the people through referenda. Serving as a kind of uncrowned republican monarch, DeGaulle presided as an arbiter of French affairs.

Concerning the idea of America's pure presidentialism, Friedrich once remarked it might have inspired the 1958 French presidential system. The constitution, he argued, had been "tailored" to fit DeGaulle as president.[94] It is difficult to determine just how much influence the United States had because deliberations of the constitution framers were not made a matter of public record. The best we can do is to point to DeGaulle's previous views on the presidency, which showed that he did not favor the American model, and Michel Debré, the intellectual father of the 1958 constitution, did not either.

It is clear from the writings of Debré and other French constitutionalists that they did not understand the American presidential system very well. The French presidential system bore little resemblance to the American model because of how the American president fits into the federal system with its checks and balances. The French tended to overlook the fact that American presidentialism operates in accordance with a separation of powers, a principle that makes it difficult to convert the office into a dictatorship. In France's highly centralized system, the American idea of pure presidentialism thus would have encountered insuperable problems.[95]

After the constitution of 1958 was amended in 1962 to allow the direct election of the president, several proposals were made to introduce a system more closely resembling that of the United States. Such proposals met with severe criticism, however, and were given little consideration. As one critic noted, the entire American political system was so unusual that it could hardly be imitated anywhere else.[96]

Regarding the issue of judicial review, the American model did not influence France very much. It is true that the constitution of 1958 established the Conseil constitutionnel and invested it with very limited powers of judicial review, but most scholars point out that the Conseil was not modeled on the American Supreme Court. In fact, Friedrich called the Conseil "essentially a political body" rather than a judicial one.[97] When the Conseil assumed a more judicial role in 1971, most scholars did not assume that American jurisprudence was involved. Although the powers of the Conseil were expanded, they pertained less to the constitutionality of provisions regarding the separation of powers and more to cases guaranteeing individual rights.[98]

Ireland

Despite the revolutionary nature of its break with Britain in 1922, Ireland (Eire) did not get around to drafting its constitution until 1937, and it was not until 1949 that Ireland formally proclaimed itself a republic. A common-law country, Ireland had a detailed bill of rights, but its government was not federal in form. Thus it did not have one of the two requisites for the best performance of judicial review. The preamble, furthermore, was written in scholastic language and also recognized the special position in its society of the Roman Catholic Church.[99] In short, Ireland was too different from the United States to allow much American influence.

Eamon De Valera, the principal draftsman of the constitution, declared that he did not want the Irish Supreme Court to possess great power.[100] But the supreme court took a different view, expressing its philosophy in a 1947 case in no uncertain terms:

Constitutions frequently embody, within their framework, important principles of polity expressed in general language. In some Constitutions, it is left to the legislature to interpret the meaning of these principles, but in other types of institutions, of which ours is one, an authority is chosen with the power and burdened with the duty of seeing that the Legislature shall not transgress the limits set on its powers.[101]

Despite the strong language, the Irish Supreme Court proved less than daring. One reason was that the court was a private-law court as well as a constitutional court of review, and most cases were nonconstitutional in nature. This situation, along with other considerations, produced a narrow and inflexible approach in any constitutional interpretations.[102] The court was reluctant, for example, to override executive decisions made for reasons of national security, especially in cases involving terrorist activities in Northern Ireland.[103] Thus, while Irish courts could exercise judicial review and employed the American decentralized system, Ireland's supreme court operated on a very narrow basis.

The Philippines

Once the Philippines had gained their independence, resentment against the United States escalated. The economy had deteriorated to the point that the islands resembled a third world country.[104] America's reliance on Filipino elites backfired because they had veto power over reforms and refused to pursue them unless they fit elite interests. The "mutual free trade" policy distorted the Philippine economy and stunted industrial growth. In addition, the presence of American military bases became a major source of irritation because they violated Filipino sovereignty.

The deteriorating situation worsened with the appearance of Ferdinand Marcos on the scene. When first elected president in 1965, he earned a reputation as a reformer. In his first term, he became popular because "miracle rice" was developed as the result of a scientific breakthrough. Roads, bridges, and schools were built, and there was even a temporary restoration of a land reform program. As a result, Marcos was the first Filipino to be reelected president.

But his second term was a disaster. Civil unrest erupted with the rise of two insurgent groups, communists in Luzon and Muslims in Mindinao. The $1 billion that Marcos spent on his first reelection campaign caused currency devaluation and angered the common people who allied themselves with young student protestors. Marcos was accused also of neocolonialism when he sent a small military force to Vietnam to support the U.S. Army. Attacked in the press, Marcos called for a constitutional convention to establish a parliamentary system. In that way, he could continue to hold power as prime minister and get around the 1935 constitutional limitation of the presidency to two terms.

Marcos, meanwhile, kept expanding his power. After a political rally in 1971 in which some opposition candidates were injured, Marcos took advantage of the incident to suspend *habeas corpus* and sent alleged left-wing candidates to detention camps. In 1972, he declared martial law, which enabled him to manipulate the sitting constitutional convention and to propose a new constitution. This document permitted him to stay in power under its transitory provisions without any interference from "the legislature, the courts, the press, or the necessity of election."[105]

Marcos's control over the country grew even stronger. Under the newly approved but suspended constitution of 1973, Marcos was made prime minister. At the same time he continued to rule by decree under the transitory provisions of the suspended charter. The constitution was supposed to be ratified by the congress, but Marcos created instead local citizens' assemblies which approved the document by a show of hands under military supervision.[106] Marcos was obviously heading for a showdown.

The Marcos dictatorship made it clear that the American experiment to export democracy to the Philippines had failed for the time being. There were numerous reasons for the failure: the prevailing anti-Americanism among Filipinos, the rising tide of Filipino nationalism, the excessive centralization on the national level at the expense of local governments, and the neocolonialism involved in controlling commerce. Given the fact that the Philippines had been meant to serve as a showcase of American constitutionalism, the results did not bode well for exporting democracy to other American possessions.[107]

South Korea

South Korea, like Japan and the Philippines, also was exposed to American constitutional influence when that country was occupied by the United States after World War II. When the peninsula was divided with the Soviet Union, the American military government began administering the southern half of the Korean peninsula in 1945. The United States moved quickly to establish a democratic government to offset any possible

Soviet challenge. In the constitution of 1948 and the other five charters that appeared until 1989, some influence of American constitutionalism was evident, but there was steady deterioration and sometimes that influence disappeared completely.[108]

The American military government authorities ruling South Korea from 1945 to 1948 slowly began introducing American constitutional ideas to the nation-building process. The original basis of Korean law was related to two other very different legal traditions. One was Japanese law, since the peninsula had once been a Japanese colony. The other was the civil-law tradition borrowed from European legal sources.

The first American step was to repeal the notorious laws imposed by the Japanese which had stripped the Korean people of their political freedom and civil rights. In 1948, U.S. military government passed an ordinance consisting of twelve articles that guaranteed certain freedoms: religion, assembly, the right to trial, and equal protection under the law. The ordinance also prohibited the deprivation of any property without due process of law. These principles of American constitutionalism had considerable influence on Korea's political leaders when they began to write their first charter.[109]

The precise role of the U.S. military government in writing the 1948 constitution for the First Republic remains largely unknown. Many key documents are still missing and not available for research.[110] Ironically, the leader of the constitution drafting committee was Chin-O Yu, a noted scholar educated at a Japanese imperial university. Although he looked more to Europe for constitutional precedents than to the United States, he found the ordinance passed by the U.S. military government of great value when drafting the section on civil rights. American influence was limited, however, for two reasons: the absence of any preexisting self-government and the Americans' insistence that the Koreans be responsible for their own constitution.[111]

The 1948 constitution originally called for a combination of the presidential and parliamentary systems of government, with a president elected by a bicameral legislature. A supreme court was to be established with power of judicial review. Neither bicameralism nor judicial review, however, appeared in the 1948 document.[112]

Syngman Rhee, Korea's first president, drastically changed the original intent of the constitution. Educated in the United States, Rhee was familiar with American constitutional law through his doctorate from Princeton in political science.[113] He insisted on direct election of the president by the

people and, because of his long devotion to the cause of Korean independence, was swept into office. To guard against any abuse of power by the
president, the legislature originally had provided certain safeguards. But
when President Rhee founded his own political party and gained control
of the National Assembly, the legislature lost its power to serve as a check
on the executive.[114]

During the Korean War, Rhee further strengthened his position as president. The United States, needing him as an ally in the cold war, increasingly
supported him, and America's national interests once again contravened
the principles of American constitutionalism. But Rhee's authoritarianism
slowly lost him public support. He kept rigging elections, disregarding the
legislature, and refusing to abide by the constitutional prohibitions to his
reelection. In 1960, he was finally driven from power.[115]

Constitutional changes in 1960 led to the creation of the Second Republic, a government controlled by Rhee's opponents. Experience with the
Rhee presidency had led to disenchantment with the idea of presidentialism, so the 1960 constitution turned to the parliamentary system. Some
constitutional provisions for political and civil rights based on American
precedents continued, nevertheless, although abuses were evident everywhere. The Second Republic lasted less than a year, when military leaders
took over to establish the Third Republic in 1962.[116]

The 1962 constitution showed more of an "American flavor" than its
predecessors. It adopted the presidential system of government, although
the American occupiers were unhappy when a military regime was established. The constitution of the Third Republic also "imported" the idea
of judicial review.[117] This move represented a remarkable change in the
country's legal tradition, because it had followed the civil-law tradition
since the nineteenth century. Precisely where the power of judicial review should be located became a hotly contested issue during the drafting process.[118] Constitutional law professors wanted to establish a special
tribunal along the lines of West Germany's Federal Constitutional Court.
Judges and practicing lawyers maintained that constitutional adjudication
was only one aspect of litigation and that declaring legislative acts void
should be a normal part of the judicial function.[119]

The law professors on the drafting committee stubbornly held out for a
constitutional court. Developments in the United States, meanwhile, indirectly played a role in the eventual outcome. Since the United States was
experiencing a wave of judicial activism under Chief Justice Earl Warren,
it was no surprise that Korean judges pressed for judicial review.[120]

The judges won, but it proved to be a pyrrhic victory. Once the constitution of 1962 was promulgated, the constitutionality of several statutes was immediately challenged in the courts.[121] The Korean Supreme Court, as was the case in Japan, was reluctant to find legislation of the National Assembly unconstitutional.[122] When the supreme court finally did manage to rule a law unconstitutional, the results were disastrous and gave the authoritarian President Chung-hee Park an opportunity to scrap the whole constitution.

General Chung-hee Park had come to power after a military coup in 1961 and was elected president in 1963. He proceeded to write a new constitution for the Third Republic calling for a strong executive and a highly centralized government. The president was given the power to appoint and dismiss the prime minister and cabinet without the consent of the legislature. The Assembly, a weak unicameral body, was reduced in size and stature and did not even have the power to change legislation that the military junta passed in secret. By 1970, the Constitution of the Third Republic was more authoritarian than ever, and American constitutional influence was at a low ebb.[123]

India

India was the Asian country that the United States influenced most once it gained independence from Britain in 1947. Its 1950 constitution borrowed heavily, of course, from Britain's Westminster parliamentary model, but India turned also to the U.S. Constitution for guidance.[124] Given the enormous cultural differences between the two countries, the copying that took place was a rare phenomenon. "It is one of the few cases of massive borrowing by a country with a vastly different tradition that has had lasting effects on the legal and political culture of the borrowing country, yet without American control or pressure," concluded one scholar.[125] "Of all the Commonwealth countries, there can be no doubt that India has been more receptive to American constitutional concepts than any other," observed another.[126] India represents a classic case of the older American tradition of volition at work.

The main reason for India's receptivity to American ideas was obvious: both countries harked back to the same common-law tradition. India's constitution makers, moreover, took time to consult American presidents, jurists, and scholars and borrowed such features of American constitutionalism as federalism, judicial review, and the bill of rights tradition.[127]

The official adviser to the constituent assembly, Sri B. N. Rau, made a special trip to the United States to confer with President Harry Truman and other officials regarding federalism. Rau was advised, however, *not* to follow the American style of federalism. Given the religious differences between Hindus and Muslims, it was expected the proposed Indian nation-state would be split in two, with Muslim Pakistan striking off on its own. It was suggested that India instead set up a strong central government, and this advice was followed.[128]

There were both positive and negative consequences from this American suggestion. The Indian states were given limited powers compared with those of the American states. A distinction was made between states and provinces so that the state rulers were free *not* to join the federal system, whereas the provinces were obliged to do so. Hence the Indian union in which residual powers were vested expressly with the central government, and territories and other centrally administered areas were granted no states' rights, hardly resembled the American federal system.[129] The constitutional division of powers between the two sets of authorities—the central government and the states—in other instances generally followed the American model.[130] A paradox remained, nevertheless, because, as one Indian author remarked, "The constitutional system of India is basically federal, . . . with striking unitary features."[131]

The same ambiguity can be found in the due process clause in the Indian Constitution. Originally, the drafters had intended to model that clause after the Fifth Amendment in the U.S. Constitution. They were aware, however, that this clause had caused considerable difficulties in America, so they sought to limit the Indian version by changing its wording. They decided to eliminate the phrase "without due process" altogether and to replace it with "except according to procedure established by law." This phrase was borrowed from the Japanese Constitution of 1946.[132] Since that constitution had been written jointly by the American Occupation authorities and the Japanese, the American influence, thrown out the front door, returned through the back.[133]

Judicial review in India also was incorporated into the constitution of 1950 largely through the efforts of Rau, who had interviewed several American Supreme Court justices.[134] As a result, this document contained explicit provisions making the Indian Supreme Court the guardian and interpreter of the constitution from the beginning.[135] Besides these provisions, an early Indian Supreme Court decision had already cited *Marbury v. Madison* to uphold the right of judicial review.[136]

One reason that India embraced judicial review was that its society represented one of the most diverse populations in the world. The sheer multiplicity of ethnic, racial, religious, and linguistic groups had produced a multitude of minorities, each fearing oppression lest some majority become dominant. Hence, the Indian framers believed that judicial review would help protect the freedom and rights of minorities.[137] It was a classic case of majority rule versus minority rights, a situation increasingly evident throughout the world in the twentieth century, and one reason why the American idea of judicial review spread so quickly.

Judicial review, like federalism, worked out quite differently in India, for two reasons. First was the Indian tradition of treating groups rather than the individual as the social unit. Second was the Indian practice of giving states the right to employ a quota system when hiring public servants and to exercise what was called "compensatory discrimination." Such discrimination was established to favor members of specifically listed groups in the caste system known as the "backward classes." The constitution also makes special provisions along similar lines for women (article 16) and "socially and educationally backward classes" (article 15). No comparison will be made here of the vast constitutional differences between the two countries, except to acknowledge that given India's caste system, the dissimilarities between the two societies were great indeed.[138]

The bill of rights tradition also played a large part in India's 1950 constitution. The fundamental rights listed were enforceable in the courts and followed the American rather than the British model. As one scholar of Indian constitutionalism put it, "Almost every important fundamental right which was included in these drafts . . . had its counterpart in the United States Bill of Rights."[139]

Once again, specific rights were so close to American precedents as to make any detailed listing a tedious exercise. The Indian text was changed in many instances, however, to accommodate indigenous conditions. The guarantee of free speech is one example. Using the Indian languages to follow the express wording found in the American text would have created great difficulty in India's multilingual and multiethnic society.[140] A number of changes therefore had to be made to accommodate linguistic differences. In other cases, the wording was altered, as in the case of freedom of religion, to accommodate the multiplicity of religious practices.[141]

The same was true of the Thirteenth Amendment, which contained provisions against slavery and involuntary servitude. In America, Congress is empowered to take action in such matters, but in India the problem of "untouchability" presents a different issue. Untouchability and involuntary servitude in India raised a whole host of problems for which the language of the Thirteenth Amendment was inappropriate, so it was dropped.

There were other great differences between American constitutionalism and the features adopted in India's 1950 constitution, a problem compounded because what was transplanted was often transformed. Nevertheless, the interchange between the two countries remains one of the most astonishing examples of constitutional borrowing existing in the modern world.

Indonesia

Indonesia had a long history of being influenced by different American constitutional documents even while the region was still a Dutch colony. When the Indonesian Nationalist Party was formed on July 4, 1927, the date consciously commemorated the American Declaration. Decades before independence, phrases from the Declaration, Lincoln's Gettysburg Address, and other key documents kept circulating to support the nationalist cause.[142]

Once Indonesia gained its independence, American founding documents influenced the framers of the 1945 Indonesian Constitution even more. As one framer commented, "Before me is the structure of the Republic of the United States of America [which] contains three elements: (1) the Declaration of Rights in the city of Philadelphia (1774); (2) the Declaration of Independence . . . ; [and] finally the Constitution of the United States."[143] In the preamble to the 1945 constitution, the Declaration of Independence was quoted at great length. It is questionable, however, to what degree the move was idealistic or designed to suit General Sukarno's propaganda purposes.[144] The preamble also proclaimed an indigenous philosophy, called Pancasila, or "Five Principles," which proved to be more important than any American text.[145]

The 1945 constitution provided for a strong executive, which may have been modeled on American presidentialism. It established a nonparliamentary presidential cabinet system under which the president was both chief executive and head of state, as in the United States.[146] Under this constitution, President Sukarno eventually assumed power in what came to be called the "Old Regime." Indonesia's 1948 constitution showed additional traces of American influence. But the leaders of the new republic created a unitary rather than a federal state.[147] Even so, the document followed America's concept of natural rights, noting that independence was "the natural right of every nation."[148]

Once Indonesia finally gained its independence in 1949, a provisional constitution for the "United States of Indonesia" was written. The country experimented with a federal system similar in certain respects to that of the United States. But it proved to be ill suited to the fourteen-thousand-island archipelago with the largest Islamic population in the world. The federal constitution of 1949 thus remained in effect only briefly and was succeeded by the Provisional Constitution of 1950, which established a parliamentary system of government in which American constitutionalism had a very small part.[149]

President Sukarno called for overhauling the political party system in 1956 and replaced the existing liberal democracy with what he called "Guided Democracy." The new system gave him wider authority, and he soon seized political control, dissolved the constitutional assembly, and insisted on being reelected president for life. By this time, of course, traces of American constitutionalism had disappeared completely.

China

The People's Republic of China (PRC) and Republic of China (ROC), though disagreeing on most constitutional issues, agreed on one: the historical significance of Sun Yat-sen. Both viewed him as the source of their political legitimacy. In the Communist PRC he was hailed as the "pioneer of the revolution," and in the ROC, as the "father of the republic."

Born in China in 1860, Sun trained as a physician but soon abandoned medicine to start a career as revolutionary against the Manchu rulers. The new constitutional ideas he had learned in the United States and England enabled him to lead a movement that eventually brought about the downfall of the old regime. Although elected provisional president of the newly formed Republic of China in 1912, Sun held office only briefly.

Sun propounded his famous Three Principles of the People—nationalism, democracy, and livelihood—as early as 1905. These principles called for the unification of China under a democratic national government and, at the same time, a revolt against the West. Sun wanted a more equitable distribution of wealth, a gradual end to poverty, and a revolution against unjust economic exploitation.

When explaining his Three Principles, Sun was inspired by Lincoln's constitutional phrase: "a government of the people, by the people, and for the people." What Sun meant was that since the people were sovereign, they should be able to exercise their sovereign powers to govern. Although Lincoln's words provided evidence of American influence, Sun and his fellow constitutionalists were eclectic and borrowed from other foreign sources as well. In applying his Three Principles, moreover, Sun tended to interpret them in the context of Chinese history, customs, and traditions.[150] Any resemblance to American constitutionalism consisted merely of certain parallels.

The Provisional Constitution of 1912 marked the first attempt to implement republican ideals in China. Democracy and individual civil rights were emphasized in this American-influenced charter. First, a bicameral congress was adopted, consisting of a senate and a house of representatives. This basic governmental system was repeated in the constitutional drafts of 1919, 1923, and 1924, but these charters were soon either aborted or changed. The Provisional Constitution of 1912, for example, was "too often honored in the breach," according to two American scholars.[151]

Sun continued his efforts to unify China despite many setbacks. He helped form the Kuomintang (KMT), a major political party, and reorganized it in 1914 in order to place it under his control. When he tried to establish a new regime, however, local warlords prevented him from unifying the country. In 1924, he formed an alliance of the KMT with the Chinese communists. The result was the restructuring of the KMT and the creation of a party-directed army. After Sun died in 1925, Chiang Kai-shek took over, claiming to be his heir.

The next important constitutional development occurred when the May Fifth Draft Constitution of 1936 was written, a document that continued many of Sun's theories of the Three Principles. The governmental structure was made up of a popularly elected National Assembly, which could elect and recall the president and vice president of the republic. But the president had strong powers, many of which had parallels to those of the American president. Although work on the draft constitution had begun much earlier, its promulgation was delayed for more than five years.

Before the constitution could be implemented, its formation was interrupted by the Sino-Japanese War, which broke out in 1937 and continued for eight long years. At the same time, a vicious civil war erupted between the KMT and the Chinese communists, resulting in the emergence of two separate polities. One remnant of the KMT under Chiang Kai-shek was driven off the mainland to Taiwan in 1949. So there now were two Chinas: the People's Republic of China on the mainland, and the Republic of China on Taiwan, whose sovereignty remained moot.

The Republic of China

Before leaving the mainland, the KMT leaders headed by Chiang-Kai-shek met, and without the communists present, adopted a new constitution. This document, promulgated in 1946, presumably guaranteed political equality and civil rights to all citizens and vested supreme authority in the National Assembly. Its government structure was to consist of a legislative *yuan* (parliament) and an executive *yuah* (cabinet).

American influence in the 1946 constitution was evident in the formal wording of article 1: "The Republic of China, founded on the Three Principles of the People, shall be a democratic republic of the people, to be governed by the people and for the people."[152] Lincoln's words, echoed by Sun Yat-sen, had found their way into the Chinese document.

The 1946 constitution reflected the American influence in other ways. The executive branch resembled a combination of the American presidential system and the British cabinet system. The American idea of judicial review also had its counterpart in the 1946 document, despite significant differences in the way the principle operated. Under the chapter on the Rights and Duties of the People, for example, several provisions corresponded closely to the American bill of rights tradition. The wording of article 8 of the 1946 constitution, which dealt with the writ of *habeas corpus*, was obviously drawn from article 1, section 9, of the U.S. Constitution. The major laws of the Republic of China were eclectic, however, and contained provisions drawn from European models as well, especially those of the Germans and Swiss.[153]

Despite traces of American-inspired liberal provisions in the 1946 constitution, there was little democracy in evidence in Taiwan. Chiang-Kai-shek became a dictator and imposed military rule throughout much of the post–World War II period. Civil rights and liberties for the native Taiwanese were notoriously absent.

Resentment of the native Taiwanese majority against the Chinese minority from the mainland diminished somewhat with the appearance of the "economic miracle." Beginning in the 1950s, the Taiwanese economy shifted from a predominantly agricultural to a high-tech, export-oriented basis. The results were spectacular, and this economic development, along with the eventual disappearance of the Chiang Kai-shek family from political rule, brought remarkable changes on the island in the 1980s. But the problem of the "two Chinas" remained unresolved and the question of Taiwan's sovereignty, unchanged.

The People's Republic of China

The constitutions of the People's Republic of China, meantime, went off in a completely different direction. Communist leaders like Mao Zedong paid lip service to Sun's Three Principles and never repudiated them. They believed, however, that Sun's ideas had little relevance to modernizing the Chinese mainland. Initially, the Communist Chinese government was committed to Marxist–Leninist ideas.[154] The different constitutions written in Communist China meant very little, however. As in most communist countries, the totalitarian government was run according to the policies of the ruling party rather than by the constitutions. Existing constitutions were employed to symbolize the political and ideological changes in China on the way to an idealized socialist state. There was, of course, no influence of American constitutionalism.[155]

Latin America and the Caribbean, 1945–1974

During the three decades following the end of World War II, Latin America continued its chaotic constitutional history much the same as during the first half of the twentieth century. The continent was filled with insecure constitutional governments, repressive regimes, and military dictatorships. The cycle of alternating regimes of reform and repression continued in some countries, particularly in Argentina and Chile. Central America experienced even greater volatility in El Salvador, Nicaragua, and Honduras, where the situation intensified as a result of the cold war and clashes between North American–backed anticommunist forces and leftist elements supported by the Soviet Union. In the Caribbean, there also was great instability as the United States grew more concerned about its national security lest Cuba, a Soviet ally, were to expand its influence to the mainland. Because of the proximity of the Caribbean region to the U.S. homeland, American imperialism was more frequently in evidence.

Argentina

During World War II, Argentina suffered a serious military coup when a charismatic colonel, Juan Domingo Perón, came to prominence as head of a military junta in 1943. Twice elected president, Perón had a greater impact on Argentina's history in the twentieth century than did any other ruler. As the founder of the Peronista movement, he along with his two wives, Eva and Isabel, dominated the political scene for more than three decades, from 1943 to 1974.[156]

The civil rights provisions based on the North American–influenced constitution of 1853 were suspended during World War II, and democracy all but disappeared. Normal political activities resumed briefly in the postwar period until a new political group called the Peronistas appeared. First organized as the Labor Party, with Perón as its presidential candidate, the Peronistas found their main following among the dispossessed in the agricultural and industrial working classes. They campaigned with promises of more land, higher wages, and social welfare measures. Elected president in 1946, Perón brutally suppressed the opposition, which proved to be a sign of things to come. Severe restrictions were soon imposed on all anti-Peronista parties, while the United States kept denouncing Perón's antidemocratic moves.

In 1945 Perón married his mistress, Maria Eva Duarte, known as Evita. As first lady, she managed the labor relations and social services of her husband's government until her death in 1952. Through Evita's efforts, women were given the right to vote and became eligible for prominent political offices. In 1949, Perón ordered a new constitution that would permit the president to succeed himself. This constitution consolidated a number of corporative policies drawn partly from Europe.[157] Although reelected in 1951 and again in 1955, Perón gradually lost the support of the working class, the military, and the Catholic Church. A revolt by the army and navy led by democratically minded officers and some civilians finally forced Perón to resign in 1955 and go into exile for eighteen years.

The 1949 constitution was abrogated, and the liberal charter of 1853 reflecting North American constitutional principles was reinstated. In 1973, however, Perón returned from exile and was reelected, with his second wife, Isabel, as vice president. When he died suddenly in office in 1974, she succeeded him, becoming the first female chief executive in the Americas.

Perón was a man of great ambition both for himself and his country and tried to find a middle ground between capitalism and communism. His version of "national socialism," borrowed partly from Benito Mussolini, represented a variation of a mixed economy and a welfare state in which unions played an important role. His approach, therefore, was not completely totalitarian. He preached the virtues of an "organized community," and the basis of his socialism was Christian and not Marxist. *Justicialismo*, as he called his program, aimed at establishing a just social order but also maintained more centralizing power in the hands of the state. North American constitutionalism played no role whatsoever in Perón's vision.[158]

In the end, Perón proved to be a tragic figure and failed to attain the position in history to which he aspired. According to his biographer, Perón did not realize his greatest dream:

Instead of a country with a prosperous and expanding economy, he left one in the grip of an unprecedented crisis. Instead of a strong and stable government, he passed on a weak one, wracked in violence and virtually without leadership. Rather than a people full of confidence in themselves, and in their future, Perón left one torn by self-doubt, pessimism, and frustration. Instead of a nation of great prestige, with a voice listened to in world councils, Perón's legacy was a country with less influence than it had at any time before in the twentieth century.[159]

Chile

Chile's postwar years were tumultuous, as the country was caught in the drama of the cold war struggle between the United States and the Soviet Union. When Cuba became an ally of the Soviet Union, the United States worried about communist expansion in the hemisphere. Accordingly, Washington helped destabilize or overthrow possible Leftist regimes in Guatemala in 1954, Brazil in 1964, and Uruguay and Chile in 1973. Chile thus became part of the broad pattern of the U.S. containment policy to deter any Soviet influence south of its borders.

By intervening in the Chilean election of 1970 with covert CIA funds, the United States believed that a victory for a mildly reformist government and its supporters would not only deal a blow to the growing Left but would also make the country a showcase of constitutional democracy on the continent, countering Cuba's revolutionary example.[160] When Salvador Allende, a strong candidate of the Left, won the election instead, the United States faced a quandary. Its solution was to topple the Allende government in 1973 with a military coup.

The coup brought to power Auguste Pinochet Ugarte, a military commander. It had been a long time since Chile's army had intervened in civil affairs. By 1974, however, Pinochet had emerged as head of state and installed a dictatorship that became known for its brutality and viciousness yet was supported by the United States because of Pinochet's anticommunist stand in foreign affairs.

Venezuela

In the immediate post–World War II period, Venezuela made marked strides toward democracy. Its 1947 constitution proved to be liberal and showed evidence of North American influence. In fact, it was the most liberal charter in the country's history to that time. It provided for the direct election of the president, used the secret ballot, and explicitly guaranteed the individual rights of workers and peasants.[161]

Venezuela's 1961 constitution continued the practice of proclaiming the country a federal republic, while in reality it operated with a centralized system in which the president appointed the governors of the states.[162] When a liberal candidate won the election of 1968, Venezuela seemed on its way to making a transition to democracy and following the principles of North American constitutionalism. In fact, this was the first time that an incumbent government had peacefully surrendered power to an opponent. As matters turned out, Venezuela lost its way in making the transition and increasingly strayed from the North American model.

Venezuela's move was symptomatic of the state of Latin American constitutionalism as a whole before the 1970s. The American model and democracy on the continent were far from robust. The situation described by a scholar in the late 1960s could be applied to the period ending in the mid-1970s:

The evidence indicates that theory of Latin American constitutions and the facts of politics are far apart. Thus, more often than not, the student can find the following contradictions: instead of popular sovereignty, self-perpetuating oligarchy; instead of limited government, unlimited government; instead of federalism, centralization; instead of separation of powers and checks and balances, executive dictatorship; instead of protection of individual rights and guarantees, governmental violation of such rights; instead of peaceful democratic procedures, violent and anti-democratic procedures; instead of administrative responsibility and probity, administrative irresponsibility and irregularities; instead of social and economic benefits, the unavailability of funds to provide most of such benefits.[163]

Violations of American Constitutional Tenets during the Cold War

The rise of American constitutional influence elsewhere was spectacular during the cold war, particularly in countries like Germany, Italy, and Japan. But at the same time the United States, deeply involved in a global ideological conflict, countered the rising communist threat with a containment policy that sometimes turned out to be anticonstitutional, antidemocratic, and antithetical to its own constitutional ideals. America's containment policy sometimes even led the United States to overthrow governments that were leftist or were perceived to be communist in their orientation but were not so in fact. The CIA, established originally to operate within the United States, resorted to covert military operations abroad to undermine governments considered hostile or dangerous to America's national interest.

After his election in 1952, President Dwight Eisenhower authorized the CIA to destabilize two such regimes, in Iran and Guatemala. In Iran in 1951, Premier Mohammed Mossadeq, a fervent nationalist, believed that his country could better maintain its sovereignty by minimizing all foreign influences, Soviet, British, and American. He was reluctant, therefore, to seek American aid when attempting to establish Iran's control over the Anglo-Iranian Oil Company in 1953.[164] Mossadeq was forced to change his policy, however, when President Eisenhower applied pressure on international oil companies to prevent Iranian oil from reaching world markets.[165]

When Mossadeq called for a public referendum to approve his policy, he suspended the secret ballot and secured an almost unanimous vote in his favor. Eisenhower became suspicious that such actions smacked of communist tactics, in part because Washington policymakers were convinced that "the ultimate objective of Soviet-directed world Communism is the domination of the world."[166] After Mossadeq rejected an Anglo-American offer to settle the crisis in March 1953, the shah, Mohammed Reza Pahlavi, with whom the premier was battling for power, temporarily left the country. At this point, the United States agreed to a British plan to help overthrow the Iranian government. The CIA put into operation a scheme to destabilize the Iranian government. Anti-Mossadeq elements in the military were bribed; massive public demonstrations were backed in Tehran; and other hostile actions were taken. Mossadeq was arrested. The shah returned to claim his throne, and American companies were granted a share of Iran's oil by the British.[167]

The head of the CIA declared triumphantly that Iran had been rescued from the clutches of a communist-dominated regime. While it is true that the left-leaning Tudeh Party in Iran exercised considerable influence and the Soviets threatened the northern dominions of the country, the conclusion of historian Mark Lytle (whose study is one of the best on the episode) arrived at a different interpretation. He called America's move "interventionism of the worst kind" and concluded that the possibility that the Tudeh Party was capitalizing on Mossadeq's downfall was quite remote. In fact, rightist rather than leftist forces were in a stronger position to replace Mossadeq. Instead of overreacting and displacing a revered nationalist leader who was presumed to be a communist, the United States might have achieved the same outcome by "doing nothing," according to Lytle.[168] Eisenhower's intervention obviously contradicted the traditions of American constitutionalism.

The situation in Guatemala in 1954 was somewhat similar when the CIA overturned another nationalist regime in the name of anticommunism. The popularly elected government of Jacobo Arbenz Guzmán had inaugurated a land reform program in 1951 aimed at achieving a more equitable distribution of the country's lands to landless workers. The American-owned United Fruit Company, the largest landowner in the country, lost much of its acreage through the Arbenz program and therefore conspired to have the government overthrown. The Eisenhower administration had grown increasingly concerned about reports that communist influence was spreading throughout Guatemala. Although the country's Communist Party had grown slightly in popularity, only four communists held seats in the fifty-six-member congress. Arbenz and his top advisers, moreover, were not communists, nor for that matter were the country's two most powerful institutions, the Catholic Church and the army.

John Foster Dulles, the zealous American secretary of state, nevertheless, secured approval at an important inter-American conference in March 1954 to condemn "international Communism." When Dulles later sought assistance from the Organization of American States to take action against Guatemala, most Latin American countries refused. Dulles finally was forced to confess that it was "impossible to produce evidence tying the Guatemalan Government to Moscow."[169]

The United States decided, however, to go ahead with its plans for overthrowing the Arbenz regime. On June 18, 1954, a so-called liberation army of political exiles clandestinely trained by the CIA invaded Guatemala from Honduras and drove Arbenz from power. "The overthrow of Dr. Mossadegh . . . and President Arbenz . . . served as models of successful United States intervention," noted one American scholar. "Repeated over and over again, the events that occurred in Iran and Guatemala during 1953 and 1954 globalized that aspect of United States foreign policy known as gunboat diplomacy."[170] By destabilizing these regimes, the United States undermined its own principles of American constitutionalism instead of spreading democracy and ended by damaging its international reputation.

The 1965 intervention in the Dominican Republic was another case in which the United States, in the name of protecting democracy, used its power to violate its own constitutional ideals. All the early-twentieth-century constitutions of the Dominican Republic had been influenced either directly or indirectly by the principles reflected in the U.S. Constitution, although adherence to the spirit of those constitutions was often more in evidence in the breach than in the observance.[171] After almost a century of repeated military interventions in the Caribbean, President Franklin D. Roosevelt inaugurated his Good Neighbor policy in the 1930s, and the United States refrained from using military force in the region for many years.

There was a dramatic change in April 1965 when a revolt erupted in the Dominican Republic. Worried that the Dominican rebels might be led by communists, President Lyndon B. Johnson sent an incredible total of twenty-two thousand troops. He did so without the formality of consulting the Organization of American States or even securing congressional authorization. His move was motivated by the American worry of a potential "second Cuba" after Fidel Castro had announced his intention of extending his revolution to the island republic. To prevent what was presumed to be an imminent communist "takeover," President Johnson's overreaction became an embarrassment and demonstrated how weak the United States' commitment was to its pledges of nonintervention and to the use of the multilateral machinery of the Organization of American States. Although the brief intervention was praised and supported in the United States, it was condemned in Latin America.[172]

The Dominican Constitution, written in 1966, like most of the country's charters, contained many ideas derived from the U.S. Constitution. In its rhetoric, it guaranteed human rights, proclaimed the separation of powers, and provided for popular sovereignty. In reality, though, there was a great gap between the constitutionalism proclaimed and the policies put into practice.[173]

In all these interventions, misguided by exaggerated fears or distorted information, the U.S. government might have been better advised to heed the words of John Quincy Adams when, as secretary of state in 1821, he reminded the House of Representatives: "America . . . has, in the lapse of nearly half a century, without a single exception, respected the independence of other nations while asserting and maintaining her own. But she goes not abroad, in search of monsters to destroy."[174]

Conclusion

The years immediately following the end of World War II offered the United States an excellent opportunity to observe the practice abroad of many of the first principles of American constitutionalism: popular sovereignty, rule of law, limited government, and the protection of individual rights. These principles by now had become Western and international norms. As the United States encouraged conquered countries to frame their own postwar constitutions, American constitutionalism expanded as never before, and its standing in the family of nations rose to its highest level ever.

During the cold war that followed, however, the confrontation between the two superpowers resulted in an uneasy coexistence. Although the U.S. policy of containing Soviet power ultimately prevailed, as a superpower the United States faced the question of what moral standards should guide that containment policy. How far should the country defend itself against a mortal threat without compromising the constitutional values on which it was founded?[175] "Morality [in foreign policy]," Arthur Schlesinger Jr. once observed, "is basically a matter of keeping faith with a nation's own best ideals. A democracy is in bad shape when it keeps two sets of books—when it keeps one scale of values for its internal policy and uses another in foreign affairs."[176]

John Gaddis, a diplomatic historian, raised three questions in replying to Schlesinger's commentary:

To what extent was the United States obliged, in the course of ensuring its own safety, to adopt the strategies and tactics of those who threatened it?

To what extent could the nation act in a manner consistent with its moral standards when the other side did not share those standards?

To what extent, in short, was it necessary to sacrifice what one was attempting to defend, in the course of defending it?[177]

These queries, moral in nature, framed the dilemma in which the United States found itself after first becoming a superpower. They became even more pertinent when America eventually emerged as the world's sole superpower. To many other nations, American foreign policy all too often appeared to be based on an illusion of moral superiority and on faith in American exceptionalism, rather than a recognition that in human affairs moral choices are rarely, if ever, clear-cut. This propensity often permitted America's leaders to pursue policies clearly opposed to its own constitutional ideals. Whenever it violated those ideals, the United States not only compromised its own integrity but also damaged its image as a constitutional democracy worthy of emulation.

11

Seventh Echo
American Constitutionalism and Democratization, 1974–1989

The seventh and last "echo" was distinguished by four major developments. The first was the remarkable surge of democracy that started sweeping the globe. Thirty countries changed from nondemocratic to democratic regimes from 1974 to 1989, doubling the number of democracies to almost sixty.[1] The second was the important role of American constitutionalism in that surge. Although American influence was usually more indirect than direct, the United States as a model was of the utmost significance. The third development was that the increase in the number of democracies tipped the balance so that the forces of democracy exceeded those of autocracy around the globe for the first time in world history.[2] Finally, the collapse of the Soviet empire in 1989 signaled the end of the cold war, leaving the United States as the world's sole superpower.

The start of the seventh echo of American constitutionalism coincided with the beginning of Huntington's "third wave" of democratization, which he called "perhaps the most important . . . global political development in the late twentieth century."[3] Two other scholars agreed, "When historians look back at the twentieth century, they may well judge its last quarter as the greatest period of democratic ferment in the history of modern civilization."[4] Although the third wave continued long after 1989, this chapter concludes on that date when both the seventh echo and this book end.

Because the beginning of the seventh echo and the start of the third wave coincide, the geographic pattern of the third wave provides a useful way to organize the spread of American constitutional influence during the period. Calling attention to the coincidence does not mean to suggest that the two terms *constitutionalism* and *democracy* are synonymous, for they are not, as previously noted.[5] Rather, it simply demonstrates that

American constitutionalism and democracy overlapped and expanded side by side during this era.

By this time, the American model had spread worldwide, and many of its features had become international norms. America's Declaration of Independence, as David Armitage points out, had become the generic form for more than one hundred similar "declarations" of all sorts written since 1776. They were issued at all levels of government, national, regional, and even small localities. The declarations appeared in four distinct "moments" in history, with the fourth resulting largely from the breakup of the Soviet empire. "Between 1990 and 1993, more than thirty states became independent or regained independence." Averaging ten declarations a year, they constituted the most prolific period to that date.[6]

Other features of the American model—the four "inventions" of the first American state constitutions—had become international norms as well. By 1989 the idea of a constitution as a written document was nearly universal, and constitutional conventions were used quite often. Provisions for ratifying constitutions and procedures for amending them frequently followed the American pattern, though often with variations.

Foreign constitutionalists continued to be influenced heavily also by the three main institutions of the U.S. Constitution: presidentialism, federalism, and judicial review. American-style presidentialism continued to be adopted less often than the other two features. But it was followed in Korea, the Philippines, the former Soviet Union, and a few of the twenty-five new democracies in eastern and central Europe. Without a separation of powers and robust judicial review, however, it was believed that presidentialism would degenerate into dictatorship. More constitutions consequently adopted a hybrid semipresidential and semiparliamentary system, and in this way, American constitutionalism had indirect influence.

American-style federalism had been very influential during the nineteenth century and had been the major inspiration for federations in Switzerland, Germany, Canada, Venezuela, Brazil, and Argentina. But by the time of the seventh echo, it had given way to a variety of "federal arrangements," many of which reflected David Elazar's principle of "self-rule plus shared rule."[7] After the end of World War II, variations of American federalism had either directly or indirectly become standard in countries like Austria, Burma, Yugoslavia, India, Malaysia, Nigeria, Tanzania, and the Arab Emirates.[8]

Judicial review, however, was the fastest-growing American institution abroad. The constitutionality of legislative or executive acts usually was reviewed by one of two court systems, as noted earlier. The American model incorporated judicial review into the ordinary judicial hierarchy, culminating in a supreme court. In the nineteenth century it had influenced almost all the countries in Latin America as well as Canada, making it a common practice throughout the Western Hemisphere. In the twentieth century, common-law countries formerly in the British Empire—India, Pakistan, Bangladesh, Malaysia, and Singapore—followed the American model of judicial review in some form.[9] The same was true at some time or other of Greece, Italy, Switzerland, Norway, Denmark, Sweden, Japan, the Philippines, and South Korea, as will be noted.

The second model used special constitutional courts to review the constitutionality of executive and legislative acts based on Kelsen's Austrian system, and the trend among democratizing countries in the twentieth century increasingly favored the Kelsen model. One reason that this model had become so popular was that it was "easy to create a single constitutional court and to graft it onto existing institutions." A comparative study conducted shortly after the seventh echo ended indicated that the Austrian system had become the leading model around the world.[10]

Soon after the seventh echo ended, more than three-fourths of the countries of the world were using some kind of judicial review, broadly defined, according to one scholar.[11] But this figure must be qualified because it included nondemocratic regimes in which the effectiveness of judicial review would have been doubtful. Ratification of a 1989 United Nations human rights treaty required a UN committee to monitor actions of signatory states.[12] Therefore, numerous nondemocratic states made commitments to human rights, even though they habitually violated them, because it enhanced the legitimacy of their regime in the eyes of the international community. "In short, [human] rights consciousness and [human] rights enumeration along with judicial review [became] part of the democratic package," noted Donald Horowitz, an American legal scholar.[13]

What about *The Federalist* and its role in shaping American constitutional influence abroad during this period? The document was still being consulted by foreign constitutionalists. In Nigeria in 1978, for example, constitutionalists studied the text when that country returned to civilian rule. In fact, the constitutional assembly debated issues at great length with copies of *The Federalist* provided by the American embassy in Lagos. Nigerian delegates were particularly persuaded by the arguments regarding the separation of powers and finally decided to adopt a presidential regime, even though they knew from prior experience that if one of the three major tribes were to gain control of the Parliament, it would dominate and overwhelm the others.[14]

Horowitz pointed out, however, that "measuring the ultimate influence of *The Federalist* is difficult."[15] He speculated that one reason why *The Federalist* may have declined as a source of inspiration was because as time went on, the message of the Federalist founders had lost out to that of the Anti-federalists. The Anti-federalists had championed the bill of rights tradition at the founding, and this feature had increasingly taken center stage in the late twentieth century. "If rights have trumped structures in the incidence of their adoption, [this may be the] . . . overarching reason for the advantage [currently] enjoyed by the Anti-Federalist message."[16]

By 1989, the bill of rights tradition also had shown surprising influence not only in the world at large but also in some of the new republics of Central and Eastern Europe. As one scholar remarked, "An American who reads the draft of a bill of rights in constitutions for one of the fledgling democracies will find much that is familiar." Specifically, he noted, "Every draft bill of rights contains in some form or another assurances of free speech, freedom of conscience, and the right to form political parties." He went on to say, however, that "one should not be surprised that Central and East Europeans will draft documents that . . . bear more resemblance to fundamental laws in Western Europe than to American documents."[17]

From this general overview, it is obvious that many features of the American model were exercising considerable direct and indirect influence on foreign constitution makers during the seventh echo. What follows is a survey of countries democratized from 1974 to 1989 to show with some specificity how American constitutionalism influenced them. The geographical pattern of the third wave itself proved highly idiosyncratic. It began in Portugal and Spain, "swept through six South American and three Central American countries, moved on to the Philippines, doubled back to Mexico and Chile, and then burst through in the two . . . countries of Eastern Europe, Poland and Hungary."[18] Eight major regions were involved: southern Europe, Central and Eastern Europe, the Soviet Union, Latin America, Central America and the Caribbean, Asia, Africa, and the Middle East.

Southern Europe

Five countries in southern Europe—Portugal, Greece, Spain, Turkey, and Albania—had previously experienced regime instability, socioeconomic backwardness, and other problems that had hampered their transition to constitutional democracy. By 1989, however, each sufficiently resembled the existing Western democracies in Europe to be declared "democratized." All showed either direct or indirect evidence of some American constitutional influence.[19]

Democracy arrived in these countries in different ways. In Portugal in 1974, it came after the military (probably with the help of American funds) drove the dictator, Antonio de Oliveira Salazar, from power following his forty-two-year rule.[20] In Greece, it was aided by the ouster in 1975 of the military junta that had ruled there since 1967. Franco's death that same year opened the way to democracy in Spain after nearly four decades of dictatorship.[21] In Turkey, a military coup made possible the new constitution that provided not only some political stability but also the "standard rights of a modern and democratic welfare state."[22] Albania, last of the five, began taking small steps in the direction of democracy in 1990.[23]

With democracy came new constitutions incorporating elements of Western constitutionalism that included American features. The gap between the constitution as written and the constitution as practiced in these countries, however, was very wide. Their charters often incorporated aspirational provisions the countries hoped to achieve, rather than a statement of existing constitutional realities.

Portugal, where the third wave began in 1974, wrote a syncretic constitution in 1976 that drew on many European sources, including West Germany's Basic Law. That law, of course, had been framed under the auspices of American Occupation authorities, and American constitutionalism thus provided indirect influence. In its 1986 constitutional revision, moreover, Portugal adopted a presidential/parliamentary system, and the American model again had indirect influence.[24]

Greece's 1975 constitution likewise drew inspiration from the West German Basic Law,[25] and America's direct influence was evident also in its "fundamental laws."[26] Many had been expressed or implied earlier in America's Declaration of Independence, Constitution of 1787, and Bill of Rights. Civil rights were declared "unalienable," and article 4 stated: "All Greeks are equal before the law." Article 11 protected the right of Greeks "to assemble peacefully and without arms as the law provides," and article

13 declared that "freedom of religious conscience is inviolable."[27] Such guarantees, according to one scholar, "went further than any twentieth-century predecessor in protecting civil liberties and providing for equality before the law."[28]

Spain's 1978 constitution also drew on West Germany's Basic Law and thus was indirectly influenced by American constitutionalism.[29] The language of its list of "inherent rights" showed clear evidence of American precedents as well. Article 20 guaranteed freedom of expression, especially freedom from prior censorship. Article 22 guaranteed freedom of association, and article 16 recognized freedom of religion and conscience.[30]

Turkey's constitution of 1982 likewise revealed the indirect influence of American constitutionalism by listing its fundamental rights as "unalienable." Its use of that term indicated familiarity with the American Declaration of Independence. The charter guaranteed freedom of the press and prohibited censorship,[31] and these and other freedoms were listed in article 40: "Everyone whose constitutional rights and freedoms are violated has the right to demand prompt access to competent authorities."[32] Despite such lofty rhetoric, however, Turkey's record in respecting individual rights was so abysmal that the country's entry to the European Union was denied in 1997.

Albania, saddled by a Communist regime since the end of World War II, was the last country in southern Europe to overthrow its dictatorship. Albania then drafted an interim constitution in 1990 which introduced a parliamentary democracy with an elected president. But aside from an elected president, the constitution shows relatively little influence of American constitutionalism.[33]

More direct influence of the American model in these countries was visible in other ways. All five resorted to written constitutions. In four of five cases, the constitutions included a bill of rights that protected individual rights. Although we must not take hortatory statements too literally, the charters articulated democratic principles and practices that had not been observed under previous nondemocratic regimes.

The Revolution of 1989

The "revolution of 1989" marked the unexpected collapse of communist governments in East Germany, Czechoslovakia, Bulgaria, and Romania. In East Germany, Erich Honecker, in power since 1961, had built the Berlin Wall as a barrier to block the flight of East Germans to the West. But when Hungary suddenly opened its borders with Austria in September 1989, thousands came streaming out of Honecker's repressive regime. Then in November, the wall was torn down by joyous crowds, marking the climax of a nonviolent revolution in East Germany. When the entire Communist Party structure crashed, some reformers thought about creating a new socialist state. But most people insisted instead on reunification with West Germany. With the blessing of the four occupying Allied powers, the two German states were formally united in October 1990. Once the reunification had been completed, Germany's Basic Law was applied to the former East German Democratic Republic, and the American-influenced charter now applied to all the German people.

The people of Czechoslovakia watched the disintegration of communist power in East Germany in disbelief. When the communist regime imprisoned dissident leaders like Vaclav Havel in the autumn of 1989, many expected a repeat of the repressive "Prague spring" of 1968. Yet when many others joined in the increasingly large demonstrations, the party leaders suddenly resigned. Havel was freed and was elected the provisional president of the new Czech state in the Velvet Revolution, so-called because of the absence of widespread violence. Havel later acknowledged in his speech to the U.S. Congress that the real heroes of the "revolution of 1989" were the great mass of Czech citizens who had maintained their faith in American constitutional ideals through the long dark days of Soviet repression.

Czechoslovakia, the nation with the strongest democratic tradition in the region, moved quickly to establish a pluralist democracy. Indirect American influence was evident in the language of the Charter of Fundamental Rights and Freedoms written in Philadelphia for the Czech and Slovak Federal Republic of 1991.[34] Although the country split in two in 1993 when Slovak leaders insisted on establishing an independent state, the constitutions and bills of rights in both countries reflected the rule of law characteristic of the American model. The provisional 1992 Constitution of the Czech Republic declared that "all State power derives from the people," that "fundamental rights and freedoms enjoy the protection of the judiciary," and that the "Constitution may be amended or altered solely by constitutional laws."[35] The provisional Constitution of the Slovak Republic similarly proclaimed that the "power of the State comes from the people who exercise it either through their representatives or directly." It declared further that "the basic rights of the people are inalienable, imprescriptible, and irreversible" and that "the exercise of basic rights and freedoms must not be detrimental to the rights of any person who exercises them."[36]

In Bulgaria, the decades-long rule of Communist dictator Todor-Zhivkov was brought down by mass demonstrations in Sofia in 1989. After free parliamentarian elections in 1990, the Bulgarian Constitution of 1991 echoed sentiments indirectly reflecting American constitutionalism. It stated that "the entire power of the State shall derive from the people. . . . No part of the people, no political party nor any other organization, State institution or individual, shall usurp the expression of the popular sovereignty."[37] These statements were made even though the country had had no prior history of democratic constitutionalism.

Romania's 1989 uprising, unlike Czechoslovakia's and Bulgaria's, resulted in considerable bloodshed. Nicolae Ceausescu had ruled with an iron fist and protected himself with a personal security force instead of units from the regular national army. Consequently, when the upheavals in Central and Eastern Europe took place, he disregarded them, to his peril. But in an uprising in one of the provincial capitals, the army refused to fire on demonstrators, and soon battles broke out between Ceausescu's personal security forces and the regular army. Supporting the revolutionaries, the army emerged victorious, and Ceausescu and his wife were executed by a firing squad. Although former Romanian Communists dominated the new regime, the 1991 constitution declared that "pluralism in the . . . society is a condition and guarantee of constitutional democracy" and that "citizens are equal before the law and public authorities, without any privilege or discrimination." Thus, Romanian rulers indirectly acknowledged certain principles familiar in American constitutionalism.[38]

Two countries in Eastern Europe, Poland and Hungary, demonstrated considerable resistance to the American model. These two old nations liberated from the yoke of Soviet imperialism were presumably free to make a transition to American constitutionalism. Or were they? Not according to Stanley Katz, leading legal and constitutional scholar who predicted that attempts to universalize the American constitutional experience in Central and Eastern Europe were bound to fail. Long-standing indigenous influences—local traditions, ancient customary laws, and unique historical experiences—he predicted, would prevent American constitutional democracy from gaining a greater foothold. Katz's hypothesis, however, rejects the definition of "constitutionalism" used in the West, based on Enlightenment thought and ideas that have little meaning in non-Western cultures. His hypothesis would, therefore, overthrow all existing Western scholarship on the subject.[39]

In Poland's constitutional tradition, for example, rights had always been viewed as grants of privilege from rulers rather than social contracts with the people. In the Polish tradition, strong leaders granted favors to the people rather than acknowledging that the people already possessed unalienable rights.[40] This tradition included the expectation that the state would provide enhanced social and economic rights to citizens, contrary to the idea that individuals should be responsible for achieving them on their own. The tradition of granting substantial social and economic rights was continued in the draft Polish Constitution of 1992. "Such provisions are unique in the Central and Eastern European constitutions," noted one scholar. "They indicate how strongly Socialist ideology, although theoretically dismissed, in practice, continues to influence the process of constitution-making."[41]

Polish constitution makers had to contend with other long-term indigenous traditions if they were to adopt the American model. First, given Poland's history of constant partitions by foreign powers calling for a strong central government, the country lacked a tradition of limited government. Second, the country did not have "the traditions and mechanisms of submitting parliamentary acts to constitutional review."[42] Both factors blocked efforts to extend much American constitutionalism in the country.

Nonetheless after overcoming General Wojciech Jaruzelski's dictatorship in the free elections of 1989, under the leadership of Lech Walesa and his trade union Solidarity, some evidence of American constitutional influence was evident in Poland's Constitutional Act of 1992. The act guaranteed "freedom of speech, of the Press, and assembly," as well as freedom of conscience and religion,[43] and Poland's new leaders looked to the United States also for models of judicial enforcement for certain constitutional norms.[44] The special constitutional tribunal set up under the 1992 constitution, however, was quite different from the type of judicial review practiced in the United States.[45]

Hungary's constitutional history presented different barriers to any wholesale acceptance of the American model. The constitutional order had been regulated by ancient customary laws, some dating back as far as the thirteenth century. The great Golden Bull of 1222—the "Magna Carta" of Hungary that had protected the rights of nobles to resist the king—represented the most famous of these customary laws. Except for isolated instances of reformist influences, such as the 1848 revolution, Hungary rarely introduced major constitutional changes. The first written constitution, for example, was not forthcoming until 1949 when, as a Soviet satellite state, Hungary adopted a communist charter. After the country was freed from Soviet domination in 1989, "the constitutional revision . . . and the further amendments made in 1990 created a constitutional system without adopting a completely new single charter."[46] With these changes, nevertheless, Hungary became a free republic.[47] The Hungarian Constitution reflected mostly the influence of European national constitutions such as those of Spain, Portugal, Germany, and Italy.[48] But one statement had a familiar ring to American ears: "In the Republic of Hungary all power belongs to the people. The people exercise their sovereignty through elected representatives or directly."[49]

The Soviet Union

Three events opened the way to liberalization and constitutional changes in the Soviet Union: the new era of openness (*glasnost*) and the restructuring of the economy (*perestroika*) initiated by Mikhail Gorbachev in the mid-1980s; the loosening of the Soviet grip over its satellites near the end of the decade; and the dissolution of the Soviet Union itself in 1991.

Seeking to reform the Soviet Union rather than dismantle it, Gorbachev initiated a number of startling changes: the creation of a new national legislature, multiparty elections, and multicandidate contests. By 1990, these reforms introduced more freely contested elections and other liberalized political practices. Some slight trace of influence from the American model was evident in 1990 when the Congress of the People's Deputies created the first presidency. The Soviets also resorted to broad executive powers that followed somewhat the American and French example.[50] Once Gorbachev was elected president, he introduced a series of momentous constitutional changes unprecedented since the Russian Revolution.

After a coup against Gorbachev failed, Boris Yeltsin, president of the constituent Republic of Russia led a drive to formally dissolve the Soviet Union itself. In December 1991 the other constituent republics agreed: the Soviet Union suddenly no longer existed. The major successor state that emerged was called the Russian Federation, which accounted for 70 percent of the former Soviet territory, as well as 50 percent of the population. In December 1993, the draft Constitution of the Russian Federation was approved by 50 percent of the voters.

The new constitution reflected some indirect influence of the American model. Human rights and freedoms were declared "unalienable," and the constitution guaranteed freedom of speech, association and worship, and other freedoms familiar in America's six documents. It also borrowed certain features of American-style presidentialism. Like the American executive, the federation president had to be a citizen of the federation and be at least thirty-five years of age. He was to be elected by secret ballot for a term of four years and for not more than two consecutive terms.[51]

The drive for secession from the former Soviet Union was most pronounced, perhaps, in the three Baltic republics of Latvia, Lithuania, and Estonia. Recalling their twenty years of freedom, their occupation by Soviet forces, and the horrendous loss of lives and property to the Red Army, they demanded independence. After achieving it, they turned to the language commonly employed in the American model in creating their charters. Consequently, the Latvian Constitution of 1992 declared that "all citizens shall be equal before the law and the courts of justice." Lithuania's constitution, written in the same year, stated that "the rights and freedoms of individuals shall be inborn" and the "right to life of individuals shall be protected by law." The Estonian Constitution of 1992, meanwhile, stated that "all persons shall be equal before the law."[52]

The disintegration of the Soviet Union marked the second stunning development following the revolution of 1989. There was no Russian Revolution as in 1917; instead, it was an implosion. When the Soviet Union imploded into Russia and its component republics, communist rule in the region came to an end. Although some slight traces of the American model were evident, the Russian adoption of any constitutional democracy was quite tentative, and liberalization in the political system, limited.

Latin America

The resurgence of democracy sweeping through Europe also reached the southern half of the Western Hemisphere. Eight Latin American countries were affected: Argentina, Brazil, Chile, Uruguay, Ecuador, Peru, Bolivia, and Colombia. Given the large number of countries involved, the differences in their histories, cultures, ethnic makeup, and their varied relationships with the United States, any generalizations are difficult to make. Most countries, nevertheless, had one thing in common: their transitions to constitutional democracy took place within a single decade: the 1980s.[53] Transitions in many countries, however, really amounted to a process of "redemocratization" because their constitutions had been influenced earlier by North American, British, and French republican principles.

After the Great Depression, Latin Americans held North American constitutionalism in disrepute. They became disillusioned with democracy and cynical about "Yankee liberalism" and allowed democratic institutions to wither and die. Social groups on both the Right and Left expressed disdain for the North American model, especially when the capitalist system seemed about to go under as prices for Latin American products plummeted on the world market. Some Latin American leaders, like Perón, turned to the corporative constitutionalism derived from European countries such as Spain, Italy, and Portugal while others experimented with different foreign models, like those of Maoist China. This situation continued well beyond the end of World War II. By 1970, more than half the Latin American countries were operating under military regimes, some supported, aided, or tolerated by the United States.[54]

Beginning in the early 1980s, however, this hostile attitude toward North American constitutionalism changed suddenly. A broad spectrum of citizens in Latin American society—military officers, former guerrilla fighters, intellectuals from both the Right and Left, executives of large corporations, small businessmen, and secular and religious leaders—recognized anew the merits of democratic ideals. "In 1974 eight out of ten South American countries had nondemocratic governments, . . . [but] in 1990 nine had democratically chosen governments."[55] Country after country wrote liberal constitutions, abandoned military regimes, and drove dictators out. "The Western hemisphere . . . was on the verge of becoming fully democratic for the first time in its history," concluded two scholars in the early 1990s, "with only Castro's Cuba . . . standing in the way."[56]

Two developments were behind this sudden change in attitude. One was that the American model became more appealing after the collapse of communism in Europe and the discrediting of the Marxist–Leninist model. The other was the emergence of human rights as a prominent part of American foreign policy, particularly during the administration of President Jimmy Carter in the late 1970s.[57] Carter's policy on human rights was especially popular in Latin America because it helped keep alive democratic movements in some nondemocratic states.

Brazil made the greatest strides in responding to the North American model. Its 1988 constitution almost adopted the important due process clause of the Fifth and Fifteenth Amendments of the U.S. Constitution.[58] Indeed, the 1988 charter provided so many new freedoms that it was referred to as the "Brazilian Magna Carta."[59] The legal instrument for a general defense of human rights, the *mandato de seguranca*, was restored.[60] U.S. Supreme Court decisions, moreover, began to be cited far more frequently once the new constitutional provisions were reinvigorated.[61]

Brazil's constitution was extremely important for another reason: it contained provisions for replacing itself within five years. A plebiscite mandated for 1993 was to decide two key questions: Should Brazil adopt a parliamentary form of government, and should the country change to a constitutional monarchy or remain a republic? Brazilians voted for both republicanism and presidentialism. In effect, they confirmed two basic tenets of North American constitutionalism.[62]

But evidence that democracy was not faring well elsewhere on the continent and that the protection of human rights proposed by the United States was being violated could be seen in the brutal repression occurring elsewhere. In Argentina and Chile in the 1980s, the rulers killed or imprisoned political opponents without any regard to the law. Most notably after the Falkland Islands clash with Britain, the Argentine junta waged its "dirty war" that killed more than thirty thousand citizens between 1976 and 1983. In Chile, thousands of leftists "disappeared" under mysterious circumstances or were jailed under the military regime of General Augusto Pinochet Ugarte. Too often in these countries and elsewhere, the United States supported military dictatorships and conservative civilian oligarchs who persecuted human rights activists, labor leaders, and other reformers, all in the name of containing worldwide communism.

In the 1980s, the cycle of reform and repression represented by Brazil, on the one hand, and Argentina and Chile, on the other, typified the chaotic situation on the southern continent. Despite the tremendous progress made in the resurgence of democracy and the spread of American constitutional influence, the state of constitutional democracy throughout Latin America as a whole was far from robust.[63]

Central American and Caribbean Countries

American constitutional influence in Central America and the Caribbean also was affected by cold war concerns. American imperialism has always been practiced more strictly in regions closer to the homeland than in distant places like Asia. The 1959 Cuban revolution aroused suspicions among American policymakers that communism might spread to the mainland, and when Cuba allied itself with the Soviet Union, those fears were heightened. And after the Cuban missile crisis of 1962 demonstrated the vulnerability of most American cities to nuclear missiles, Cuba assumed an even greater importance.

Ronald Reagan, running as the Republican presidential candidate in 1980, revived cold war fears in his speeches regarding Central America: "The Soviet Union underlies all the unrest that is going on [in the region]."[64] The Republican Party platform deplored "the Marxist Sandinista takeover of Nicaragua and Marxist attempts to destabilize El Salvador, Guatemala, and Honduras."[65] Once Reagan was elected, such charges escalated to a fever pitch. In a joint session of Congress on April 17, 1983, the president declared:

> If Central America was to fall, what would be the consequences for our position in Asia and Europe and our alliances such as NATO? . . . The national security of all the Americas is at stake in Central America. If we cannot defend ourselves there, we cannot expect to prevail elsewhere. Our credibility would collapse, our alliances would crumble.

Reagan's "domino theory" led to covert military operations by the United States in Nicaragua to counter the leftist government established there.

Reagan accused the Soviets of using Castro's Cuba and leftist Sandinista forces in Nicaragua as proxies to spread communism throughout the Western Hemisphere. The United States promptly armed proxies of its own, called "Contras," in Nicaragua, Honduras, and neighboring states. Fighting soon broke out between the two forces in Nicaragua, with devastating results: 40,000 people killed and at least 250,000 displaced before peace talks began in 1988.

Reagan's foreign policy continued to support authoritarian regimes in the region as long as they maintained a strong anticommunist stance. His policy was based on the theory that one day such governments might be liberalized. This so-called Reagan Doctrine called for supporting indigenous anticommunist forces whenever possible to counter the Brezhnev Doctrine of 1956, which proclaimed the Soviet right to intervene in the name of proletarian internationalism in any communist country to prevent the restoration of capitalist regimes. It was a clash of two diametrically opposed constitutional systems.[66]

During the 1980s, the United States intervened twice with military force in the region, in Grenada and then in Panama. Both invasions unseated governments that had been popularly elected (though sometimes by dubious means) and that contradicted the tenets of North American constitutionalism. But Realpolitik asserted itself. Following the invasion of Grenada in 1983 for presumed reasons of national security, the United

States was criticized by the United Nations for violating international law.[67] But when documents were discovered indicating a connection between communist countries and Grenada, the criticism subsided.[68]

Panamanians remained anti-American even though treaties had been signed in 1977 to turn over the Panama Canal to them. In 1981 the death of the dictator Torrijos brought to power Antonio Noriega Moreno, the former head of the Panamanian secret police. Noriega once had been an agent for the CIA, but by the mid-1970s he had begun operating as a double agent, passing confidential information to Fidel Castro. Using funds from these activities, Noriega further expanded his personal power through the profitable drug trade.[69] But Noriega finally overreached himself when in December 1989, a resolution by the Noriega-led assembly declared war on the United States. Retaliation by the United States was swift and decisive as American forces invaded Panamanian territory on December 20. President George H. W. Bush announced that the invasion had three aims: to restore the constitutional liberties of the Panamanian people, to protect American lives, and to seize Noriega and force him to face charges. Noriega was captured, brought to the United States, tried, and sentenced to prison.

Following Noriega's removal, the new president, Guillermo Endara, declared that his government would be democratic, dedicated to reconstruction, and committed to a policy of reconciliation with the United States. After twenty-one years of military rule, the process of redemocratization in Panama got under way, and when some features of North American constitutionalism were restored, the prospects for peace in Panama improved.[70]

Asia

The course of American constitutionalism in Asia during the seventh echo was complicated by three major developments. The first was the declining influence of American constitutionalism in Japan and the Philippines, where its impact previously had been deep-rooted. The second was in South Korea where American influence had been established in 1948 by military occupation after the Korean War. U.S. influence, quite strong at first, went into a decline but eventually was restored by the end of the seventh echo. The third development was the continued spread of the American model into some newly independent countries that had been former colonies in the British Empire. Because of their similar common-law tradition, these countries proved to be more receptive to American constitutional ideals and ideas.

Japan

Japan proved to be the country most affected by American constitutionalism after World War II. But during the seventh echo, America's constitutional influence in Japan began to wane, suggesting to some scholars
that the influence had been more shallow than previously believed. When
SCAP archives were opened, historians discovered that the break between
Japan's prewar period and the presumed postwar transformation had not
been as decisive as thought. First, in subtle ways the Japanese had succeeded in reviving many old Meiji institutions without overtly changing
the 1946 constitution. Second, the emperor system, supported by SCAP
as a symbol of Japanese national unity, turned out to be a more powerful
link of continuity than the American occupiers had intended. Finally, the
dominant rule of the Liberal Democratic Party for more than forty years
frustrated the hopes of the U.S. occupying authorities to create a more
openly contested democracy.

Scholars concluded that despite the revolutionary constitutional
changes made during the Occupation, many conditions had remained the
same; that is, conservative elites still dominated the political system, the
inevitable result of the U.S. Occupation's decision to work covertly hand
in hand with Japanese negotiators to establish the new regime.[71] In particular, they preserved the powerful government bureaucracy that was
beyond the reach of the public and controlled many day-to-day affairs of
ordinary citizens. The bureaucracy was unelected, independent, and self-
perpetuating and blocked many intended American reforms.

Greater economic democracy had been one of the major reforms the
Occupation sought when introducing American constitutionalism. This
reform was related to the New Deal ideology held by some of the American occupiers.[72] Articles 25, 27, and 28 of Japan's constitution guaranteed
workers the right of collective bargaining, in hopes of promoting a strong
trade union movement to achieve a fair and equitable society. In reality,
however, 40 percent of the workforce was organized in labor unions in
1946, a figure that remained largely unchanged for the next thirty years.
Labor unions thus remained an "articulate but subordinate and largely defensive force" in the postwar era.[73] The national ethos for cooperation and
conciliation frustrated the growth of a strong labor movement.

Another reform related to American constitutionalism was the role
of the giant cartels, the *zaibatsu*. American Occupation authorities had
planned to break up these huge conglomerates which had contributed so

much to Japan's undemocratic, hierarchical pattern of privilege. Until 1949, however, the U.S. Occupation remained indecisive about what course to take. On one hand, they wanted to recoup reparations and require the cartels to produce a profit to pay off the punitive war debt imposed on Japan. But on the other hand, Japan's economic structure had to be decentralized to achieve the desired equality of economic opportunity. Then, with the outbreak of the Korean War, the American military, seeking supplies, encouraged the continuation of the cartels rather than demanding their dissolution.[74] This so-called reverse course helped reestablish Japan's economic power and paved the way for its "economic miracle," but it hindered the hopes for American constitutional reform of the *zaibatsu*.

Demilitarization was another key feature of the 1946 constitution. After the war, steps were taken to reduce the power of the military in Japanese society. Although article 65 stipulated that members of the armed forces were prohibited from occupying important positions in the government, these restrictions were relaxed as time went on and posts continued to be filled by former military men. Even more surprising was the fate of the pronounced pacifism of article 9 itself. It stated: "In order to accomplish the aim of [forever renouncing war as a sovereign right of the nation] land, sea, and air forces . . . will never be maintained." When the Korean conflict erupted, the United States resorted to another "reverse course." American policy planners favored the remilitarization of Japan as an ally against the Soviet Union. Accordingly, contrary to the wishes of the people who remembered the horrors of the war, Japanese leaders proceeded to build up Japan's "Self-Defense Forces" (SDF). Although the SDF's constitutionality was challenged, Japanese courts consistently affirmed their legality, and American authorities supported them. By the end of 1990, Japan had one of the world's largest military forces and the world's third highest defense budget.[75]

The Occupation of Japan, therefore, left an ambiguous legacy under the 1946 constitution. On one hand, Japanese society underwent tremendous constitutional changes: "Postwar Japan was a vastly freer and more egalitarian nation than imperial Japan had been."[76] This democratic transformation was the result of America's constitutional influence. On the other hand, American Occupation officials, with the support of Japanese politicians, conservative forces, and the government bureaucracy, sometimes resorted to undemocratic methods to frustrate and undermine intended American reforms. The result was that the hybrid nature of the 1946 constitution actually strengthened the authoritarian nature of Japan's bureaucracy and ruling political party, which left the country far less changed by the influence of American constitutionalism than it might otherwise have been.[77]

One clue to the waning of American influence was Japan's changed attitude toward the Declaration of Independence. Tadashi Aruga, a longtime scholar of comparative American and Japanese legal history, commented on this shift:

> Once the principle of democratic government enunciated in the Declaration had been transplanted to the Japanese Constitution and once that Constitution had begun to take root, the American document tended to lose its role as a source of inspiration to the Japanese people. The Declaration is very inspiring in a society where there is much discontent, but not in a complacent society.[78]

The Philippines

The Philippines, second only to Japan as the strongest example of the influence of the American model abroad, witnessed a similar decline during the dictatorship of Ferdinand Marcos. The 1973 constitution, as previously noted, had introduced a parliamentary system that never really went into effect as long as Marcos continued his dictatorial rule.[79] The constitution itself, however, represented a break from the American model that the Filipinos had closely followed since the Spanish-American War.

Although Marcos lifted martial law in 1981, the constitution allowed him to detain any citizen on suspicion. Moreover, he sponsored constitutional amendments that provided for an even stronger president, thereby relegating the prime minister to handling daily affairs. Because his opponents boycotted the election, Marcos was returned as president for a six-year term with a right to reelection.

Opposition to Marcos's rule kept rising. His principal opponent, Benigno Aquino, went into exile and, upon his return in 1983, was killed under mysterious circumstances. Demonstrators filled the streets demanding Marcos's resignation, but an investigating commission failed to implicate him. As tensions mounted, the U.S. government tried to stabilize the political situation by persuading Marcos to hold an early election in hopes of making his rule more secure. His opponent, Corazon Aquino, widow of the murdered Benigno, appeared to defeat Marcos in the 1986 election, but the Assembly declared him the winner, and he was inaugurated in a private ceremony. The popular uprising that followed, however, finally forced Marcos into exile, and with his fall, a dismal chapter in Philippine history came to a close.[80]

Corazon Aquino soon restored democratic government by helping write the constitution of 1987, which greatly changed Filipino constitutionalism.[81] First, the Filipinos relied less on American constitutionalism than ever before and instead reverted to their indigenous traditions. Although they did retain certain features of the U.S. Constitution, the new document relied more on the original Malalos Constitution of 1899. Second, the Filipinos returned to their Asian heritage and Catholic culture. Finally, the 1987 constitution placed less emphasis on the capitalist free-enterprise system and more on the socioeconomic rights of the individual under a strong welfare state system.[82] Three major principles of American constitutionalism thus survived: the separation of powers, the bill of rights tradition, and judicial review. The trend, nevertheless, toward de-emphasizing the American model was unmistakable.[83]

What conclusions can we make about the nearly century-long experiment in constitutional tutelage in the Philippines? One scholar believes that the experiment was "unsuccessful." "The cloning of America did not effectively protect the Philippines from a dictatorship, and even the best commentators could not see why the result was not what America intended." The reasons given for the failure were many: excessive centralization, lack of attention to local government, too much dependence on the United States, and an "overly mechanistic transplantation of the American model."[84] There was, in addition, the American policy of relying on Filipino elites to conduct government affairs, and their interests were often at odds with the principles of a constitutional democracy. Marcos's self-aggrandizement was, in that sense, only an exaggeration of the widespread tendency to value aristocratic privilege at the expense of the common people.

A caveat is in order. In a more balanced view of the entire history of Philippine independence, the nineteen years preceding Marcos's rise to power and the first years of his presidency seemed to have been periods when features of American constitutionalism served the Filipino people well. Some land reform was carried out; the rebellion by Huk insurgents was put down; and prosperity flourished for a time. The Marcos dictatorship unfortunately overshadowed these years of constitutional legitimacy, and America's support of Marcos squandered the goodwill the Filipinos had once held toward the United States. In 1981,

Filipinos became incredulous when Vice President George H. W. Bush toasted Marcos, "We love your adherence to democratic principles and to democratic practices."[85] After watching Marcos gun down political opponents and suspend civil liberties, with America continuing its support of the dictator, Filipinos were disillusioned with American constitutional ideals, as the perceived security needs of the United States seemed more important than any consideration of its constitutional principles.

One scholar aptly characterized the weaknesses of the Filipino–American constitutional relationship: "Surveying the wreckage of democratic political institutions, the mass poverty and gross inequities of Philippine life, and the growing alienation of many Filipinos from the United States, one can at least say that eight decades of collaboration [had] been tried and found wanting."[86]

South Korea

The experience of South Korea, the third country in the region most directly influenced by American constitutionalism, was different from that of Japan and the Philippines. Recall that General Park came to power through a military coup in 1961, dashing hopes of Korea's becoming a constitutional democracy. The alternating swings between democracy and military dictatorships plagued the country for the next two decades.

The Korean Constitution of 1972 had been written to perpetuate Park's lifelong tenure as president. Under his rule, Korea reverted to the old-style politics characteristic of the time when the country had been a Japanese colony: strict authoritarianism, political repression, and constant surveillance of citizens. Until Park's regime, Korean constitutions had retained certain traces of American constitutionalism, such as a presidential government, separation of powers, and a court system with some powers of judicial review. But with the 1972 charter, any vestiges of American constitutionalism disappeared.[87] Although the constitution gave the constitutional committee the power of judicial review, President Park was given the authority to renominate all judges and promptly dropped from the court all those justices who had voted against him. Even before this, the presence of American military authorities and the ongoing cold war prevented the legislature from implementing any meaningful separation of powers to free the legislative branch from subordination to a powerful executive.

At the same time, however, Park instituted Korea's "economic miracle" by opening the country to Japanese investors, supplying America's needs for the Vietnam War, and exposing Korea to other Western influences. Even though he succeeded in turning the country into one of the world's most modernized nations,[88] Park's popularity declined. In 1973, he forced through the legislature a constitutional amendment allowing him to rule by emergency decree. Repressive Yushin restrictions were applied with increasing force, and public unrest soon reached an all-time high. When Park was assassinated in 1979, it finally brought to an end one of the most authoritarian regimes in Asia.

His successor, General Doo Hwan Chun, staged a military coup to become the country's next strong man in 1980. Although the public reluctantly accepted his rule, there were signs the people desired more democracy.[89] The Chun Constitution of 1980 only mildly corrected the worst excesses of the Yushin Constitution.[90] As opposition to the constitution continued, Chun's enemies demanded that the charter be amended to permit the next president to be elected by popular vote instead of by the government-controlled electoral college. The result was a constitutional crisis in 1987. Faced with mounting unrest, President Chun made a fatal mistake. In April, he called for the debate on constitutional reform to be postponed until after the Summer Olympics in Seoul. With the eyes of the world on South Korea, violent demonstrations erupted, and with the world press looking on, Chun was forced to abstain from any repressive measures. He finally backed down and recommended that a presidential candidate be nominated from the opposing party.

That candidate, retired General Roh Tae Woo, took matters into his own hands. On June 29, 1987, he went on television to announce the abolition of the electoral college, thereby permitting direct popular election of the president. Roh's announcement proved to be a turning point in South Korea's constitutional history. The Sixth Korean Republic, created under the new 1987 constitution, made other democratic political changes. Roh's own election as president, moreover, made constitutional history, as it represented the first peaceful transition of political power in South Korea since World War II.

The 1987 constitution marked also a return to many features of American constitutionalism. It stripped the president of the power to dissolve the Assembly or to issue emergency decrees. It banned press censorship as well as all arrests without a court warrant, and it restored the right of judicial review, requiring the chief justice of the supreme court to be appointed by the president for a nonrenewable term of six years.[91] The preamble to the constitution, moreover, called on the military to "observe neutrality in political affairs."[92] The political pendulum that had been swinging between authoritarianism and constitutional democracy since 1948 finally came to rest. Constitutional democracy returned to Korea after an absence of almost forty years, and the American model, whose constitutional influence had all but disappeared, was restored to a considerable degree.

Former British Commonwealth Countries in Asia

The third major development in Asia was in new nation-states that had been members of the British Empire before the decolonization movement. They adopted certain features identified with the common-law tradition that they shared with the United States. In casting about for constitutional models to follow after gaining their independence, they looked to the American system for guidance.[93]

The Indian Constitution of 1950 represented one of the most striking cases of borrowing from American constitutionalism by any nation with a completely different political culture. During its early years, the new Indian constitutional system underwent surprisingly little change, but that shifted dramatically once Indira Gandhi became prime minister in 1966. Her overwhelming success in the 1971 election, India's victory in the war with Pakistan, and the country's temporary prosperity allowed her power to peak. Nonetheless, Gandhi's rapid rise in popularity was soon followed by a sharp decline, and severe domestic problems finally led her to declare a state of emergency in 1975. In doing so, she turned her back on many principles of American constitutionalism, particularly those regarding individual rights.

The nation with the second largest population in the world suddenly plunged from a constitutional democracy to a dictatorship. During the nineteen months of the emergency, the government arrested people without a warrant, suspended civil rights, and imposed censorship.[94] In 1977, however, Gandhi felt secure enough to end the emergency. She called for a general election, ordered political prisoners released, and lifted censorship. Although repudiated at the polls, she was returned as prime minister in 1980. Nine years later, however, she was assassinated.

The pattern of interrupted democracy during Gandhi's tenure demonstrated once again that a democratic regime once established could not always be taken for granted. Rahjiv Gandhi, who became prime minister after his mother's death, also encountered pressing problems, and in the midst of a national election campaign, he too was assassinated in 1991. Although America's constitutional influence continued to be direct and extensive, it had been exposed to serious challenges.[95] Despite these setbacks, India eventually returned to democratic ways and represents one of the most striking examples of the widespread acceptance of the American model in the world.

Pakistan likewise followed the common-law tradition after gaining independence from Britain with India in 1947 and then breaking with India to gain self-rule. Pakistan generally followed the British traditions inherited from the Government of India Act of 1935. But after gaining independence, the country borrowed the American idea of judicial review. When Pakistan's supreme court was established, it served as a watchdog on major constitutional questions somewhat along the lines practiced in the United States.[96] Pakistan's judiciary was made superior to all other institutions in regard to interpretation of law. The supreme court was granted the power to declare void any laws inconsistent with fundamental rights.[97] Yet every attempt to create a viable constitution after 1956—in 1963, 1969, 1973, and 1985—ran into the same problem: a power struggle among Muslim groups over which ethnic and religious laws should be observed.[98]

When the drift toward a military–theocratic state began, the power of the judiciary was crippled by two important measures passed between 1979 and 1981. The first took away the power of judicial review to judge the constitutionality of executive decisions. The second deprived the judiciary of the authority to protect individual rights. Matters grew worse when the constitution of 1979 established a system of military courts for trying certain offenses under martial law.[99] American constitutional influence suffered a drastic decline.

An even more severe measure was passed in March 1980 with the Provisional Constitution Order, which ended any judicial oversight of politically important executive actions. It also declared null and void any court decisions regarding the legality of martial law. Finally, judicial protection for citizens was eliminated when the right of prisoners to *habeas corpus* was taken away for the first time in Pakistan history.

In the meantime, as the struggle for power continued, Zulkifar Ali Bhutto served as prime minister from 1974 to 1977, but in 1977, General Zia-ul Haq seized control, executed Bhutto, and established a military regime. After Zia was killed in a plane crash, a caretaker military government assumed control, and Benazir Bhutto, the daughter of Zulki-far Ali Bhutto, became Pakistan's prime minister in 1988. She was the first woman to head a modern Islamic state but was dismissed in August 1990 on charges of corruption and abuse of power. Parliamentary elections brought victory to the opposing party headed by Nawaz Sharif, who had had close ties with the Zia administration. Legislation passed in 1991 made the Shari'a (Islamic law) the law of the land, and any remaining American constitutional influence disappeared.

Bangladesh, formerly East Pakistan, emerged as an independent repub-lic in 1971 after a bitter civil war with Pakistan. The country, which previ-ously had been part of India, derived some American constitutional influ-ence indirectly through Indian constitutionalism. In 1972, a parliamentary constitution was adopted, and Abu Sayeed Chowdhury, the first president, consulted American scholars before drafting the document.[100] When writ-ing about individual rights, Chowdhury observed that in addition to Brit-ish documents, he had consulted the U.S. Constitution. The "full benefit of the written Constitution of the United States was taken as a model," Chowdhury wrote, "and . . . the courts of Bangladesh [felt free to] refer to the judicial pronouncements of the Supreme Courts of Britain, America, and the Commonwealth countries."[101]

The most important of the enumerated rights in Bangladesh's 1972 con-stitution was article 27, which reads, "All citizens are equal before the law and entitled to the equal protection of the law." This article confers, for example, "the right to equality as visualized in the Fourteenth Amend-ment to the U.S. Constitution."[102] After listing many other articles provid-ing for freedom of thought and of religion, Chowdhury concluded, "A study of the Amendments to the U.S. Constitution would show that these cherished principles were incorporated therein."[103]

The 1972 constitution provided for an independent judiciary in keeping with the American model, stipulating that the chief justice of the Bangla-desh Supreme Court and other judges "shall be independent in the ex-ercise of judicial functions." This document not only provided explicitly for judicial review but also guaranteed constitutional remedies for the en-forcement of certain fundamental rights.[104]

Despite these constitutional provisions, there was a sharp lessening of American constitutional influence in 1974 when General Mujibur Rahman assumed the presidency, declared a state of emergency, and limited the in-dependence of the judiciary.[105] After a military coup in 1975, a presidential form of government was established, but the amended 1972 constitution was suspended again in 1982 after another coup d'état. Although the constitution was reinstated in 1986, American constitutional influence in Bangladesh was markedly diminished.

Sri Lanka, meantime, presented a curious case of both the negative and positive influence of American constitutionalism. Under British rule, Sri Lanka specifically rejected the idea of an American-style bill of rights in its 1940 constitution. This step was deliberate: Britain had no bill of rights at the time, and Sri Lanka wanted to follow the mother country.[106] After Sri Lanka gained its independence in 1948, however, its judges, without any provisions for individual rights, began to rely more on the law and judicial precedents to affirm the protection of rights. In doing so, they drew on precedents from both the Indian and American courts. When the Sri Lankans wrote their constitutions of 1972 and 1978, therefore, they specifically included a bill of rights derived from many sources, including that of the United States. These inherent rights were "reminiscent of the Constitutions of the United States, . . . India, and of certain countries in Europe."[107]

An indirect American constitutional influence on judicial review and individual rights was evident also in the 1959 constitution of Malaysia, another former British colony. The Malaysian constitution was modeled to a great degree on the Indian constitution of 1950. The basic idea of a written constitution guaranteeing the rights of the people, however, was "adopted in Malaysia from the U.S.A.," according to experts. The institution of judicial review to safeguard and protect these rights was likewise "borrowed from the U.S. Constitution." Indeed, "most of the rights guaranteed in the U.S. would seem to be guaranteed in Malaysia as well," declared a knowledgeable scholar.[108]

In Asia, only Malaysia and India followed the form of federalism practiced in the United States. The 1956 and 1963 Malaysian constitutions emulated the U.S. Constitution in granting powers to the central government, while the Indian constitution adopted the American practice with respect to concurrent powers and powers accorded to the states.[109] The 1963 Malaysian Constitution followed the American federal principle in making citizens subject to both the general and regional governments.[110] Writing about the constitutional borrowing from the United States, Tun Mohamed Suffian bim Hashim, a Malaysian scholar, declared:

> I should . . . frankly admit that the Malaysian Constitution has been little influenced by the U.S. Constitution at least directly, except for the incorporation of concepts that are universal and are found in the constitution,

the rule of law, the independence of the judiciary and of the bar, the out-lawing of discrimination, the guarantee of fundamental liberties, and the like.[111]

It hardly needs saying that many of these so-called universal concepts had been initially drawn from the original six documents of American constitutionalism.

Singapore, another British colony, withdrew from the Federation of Malaysia in 1965 and proclaimed itself a republic. The self-styled "framers" of the Constitution of the Republic of Singapore were influenced most directly by the British and Malaysian constitutions.[112] There were, nevertheless, at least two instances of indirect American influence on the Singapore Constitution. The first was the "supremacy clause," which provided that courts should declare void any statutes inconsistent with the provisions of the constitution. The second was the Report of the 1966 Constitutional Commission which discussed the questions of fundamental liberties. One provision recommended that "no person shall be subjected to torture or inhumane or degrading punishment or other treatment," language that clearly paralleled the Eighth Amendment of the U.S. Constitution.[113]

Although the constitutional practices of many of these former British colonies had been drawn primarily from British and Indian traditions while they were colonies, traces of American constitutional influence were evident everywhere. In some cases, as noted, some American influence passed through the Indian filter first. India, in turn, borrowed many of its constitutional practices from the American model, providing an excellent illustration of world constitutional syncretisms at work.

Africa and the Middle East

American constitutionalism had little influence on the African continent in the nineteenth century because the United States had not created a huge empire there, as had many European powers. Only two countries, Liberia and the Orange Free State, showed evidence of American constitutional influence in the nineteenth century. In both instances, America's constitutional documents were used in ironic ways.

Although treated here out of chronological sequence, Liberia belongs in the same category as the colonies of European powers. Its status was unique, however, because of its close association with the United States. Liberia owed its establishment to the American Colonization Society founded in 1836 to repatriate freed black American slaves to Africa. The movement, supported by the U.S. government, had the backing of prominent American leaders, including Abraham Lincoln, who viewed the experiment as one way of resolving the race problem in America.

Despite its promising start, "the tree of liberty [bore] bitter fruit," as one scholar put it.[114] Faced with growing indifference by the American government, suffering from lack of funds, and under assault by extremists in the North and South, the society declined rapidly after 1840. Liberia, virtually an overseas branch of the society up to that time, declared its independence in 1847.[115]

America's constitutional influence was evident when descendants of the freed slaves, called Americo-Liberians, became the ruling group over native tribes and helped frame the Liberian Constitution of 1847. Given the earlier connection, the new republic relied on the American model. Referring to themselves as "originally . . . inhabitants of the United States," the Americo-Liberians proceeded to emulate the American experience. They declared independence, called a constitutional convention, and wrote a constitution.[116] Despite similarities in form and language, however, Liberia's constitutional documents were not simple imitations. The Liberian Declaration of Independence, for example, repeated many phrases word for word from the American document, but its intent was totally different and deliberately ironic. Although the Liberian document declared that all men had "certain natural and inalienable rights: among these [being] life, liberty, and the right to . . . possess . . . property," it went on to state that while living in the United States, African Americans had been denied such rights.[117] It noted the hardships that blacks had endured as a result of racism: they had been excluded from participation in government, shut out of civil service positions, taxed without their consent, and compelled to contribute to the resources of a country that had given them little protection.[118]

Several provisions in the Liberian Constitution were directly copied from another of America's six documents, the Massachusetts Constitution of 1780. These included sections providing for natural and unalienable rights for all men, forbidding taxation without representation, and requiring term limits for elected officials.[119]

The document that had the greatest influence, however, was the U.S. Constitution.[120] The Liberian government followed America's tripartite system consisting of an executive, legislature, and court system. The president and vice president were to be elected on the same ticket. The bicameral legislature was made up of a senate with two members from each county, a house of representatives with seats based on population, and an independent judiciary. Liberian courts, moreover, declared themselves competent to judge the constitutionality of both legislative and executive acts.[121] The American Bill of Rights is another document that the Liberians followed closely, sometimes repeating verbatim the language of the first ten amendments. Article 1, sections 1 through 20, in the Liberian Constitution, called the "Declaration of Rights," contains phrases drawn from the American document. But Liberia was well ahead of the United States in one important regard: slavery. Article 1, section 4, forbids slavery in Liberia, and in that respect, the stepchild has progressed further than the parent.

The subsequent constitutional history of Liberia was troubled, however. Although the Liberian Constitution contained much of the rhetoric of the U.S. Constitution, it failed to follow its spirit. Provisions upholding the independence of the judiciary were constantly violated because whenever the law and interests of the ruling elite (the Americo-Liberians) were in conflict, the law lost.[122] As the citizens of Liberia grew more distant from their American past, moreover, the attempt to transplant American constitutionalism in a culture as different as Africa's failed in the face of civil wars, corruption, and coups. By the time of the seventh echo, the Liberian government's 1983 revision of its constitution, though still modeled on that of the United States, could not prevent it from straying so far from democracy as to draw international economic sanctions against it.[123]

The other case of American constitutional influence in Africa during the nineteenth century pertains to the Orange Free State. That influence, however, was largely indirect. Originally the area had been settled in the 1820s and 1830s by the Boers, dissatisfied Dutch pioneers who had emigrated in the "great trek" from the British Cape Colony to establish their own settlement. The Constitution of the Orange Free State, written in 1854, was modeled quite closely on the U.S. Constitution. In fact, many of its provisions were copied almost verbatim, after being translated into Dutch. The provisions regarding freedoms and liberties, however, specifically applied only to whites. Ironically, the language of freedom in the American Declaration was distorted in a perverse way to deny liberty to the blacks in the Orange "Free" State.[124] A few years later, however, the *Dred Scott* decision confirmed in the United States what the Boers had earlier done more explicitly.[125]

Although the first half of the twentieth century was a dark period for constitutional democracy in Africa, massive decolonization brought some remarkable transformations after World War II. Those European powers that had built enormous empires—notably Britain, France, Portugal, and Belgium—either granted their former colonies independence or lost them after protracted wars trying to hold them. By the close of the 1970s, almost all of Africa was made up of independent nation-states.

The United States had a mixed record in regard to the support of decolonization. Sometimes, as in the case of President Franklin Delano Roosevelt, it supported such movements. Then the civil rights movement in the United States later in the 1960s contributed even more to changing the attitude of many Americans toward race relations and decolonization. At other times, however, there was considerable opposition to decolonization from certain American interests.

In sub-Sahara Africa, the region where the United States had the most influence, an ideological controversy broke out regarding the transferability to Africa of Western constitutional democracy. Some so-called conservatives argued the case for "African exceptionalism," claiming that democracy was an "alien concept" whose introduction would contradict indigenous elements in the African cultures. Liberals asserted, however, that such an argument was "premised on a misconception that democracy is solely a Western creation [and] stems from a confusion between the principles of democracy and their institutional manifestation." The controversy continues in some form to this day and affects the role American constitutionalism continues to play in the region.[126]

A case study of the Union of South Africa is instructive. When the Union of South Africa Act of 1909, which created the white-controlled Union of South Africa, was proposed, it seemed to have a great deal in common with the U.S. Constitution. One contemporary observed that the two documents appeared similar on the surface: both provided for bicameral legislatures, supreme courts, and some version of federalism. But as he concluded quite rightly, "In spirit the difference is profound."[127] The differences between the two documents became clear when the 1909 act was implemented, and both American-style federalism and a supreme court were missing. In American federalism, the states retain many rights and privileges, but a strong states' rights component was anathema to South African whites. Surrounded by a huge black population, they wanted a strong centralized government. Many white South Africans believed, in fact, that federalism had been the cause of the American

Civil War. Having recently emerged from their own bitter civil conflict, the Boer War, they were unwilling to grant much in the way of states' rights.[128]

South African framers worried also about the possible effects of a political-minded supreme court. Through its power of judicial review, the American Supreme Court could compel a reconciliation between legislative acts and constitutional principles. Such a supreme court in South Africa, it was feared, might indeed operate in the same way. The *Dred Scott* and *Plessy v. Ferguson* decisions notwithstanding, the American experience was used as an argument to deny judicial review in the South African Constitution. The 1909 act, therefore, hardly resembled the U.S. Constitution.[129]

When the Union of South Africa was finally freed from subordination to the British Parliament under the Statute of Westminster in 1931, the racial situation remained unchanged. South African whites supported the Westminster-type of government because parliamentary sovereignty would continue the racial status quo. By the end of World War II, however, world opinion on race relations had changed radically. The suppression of human rights and individual liberties was no longer considered the exclusive domain of domestic governments. South Africa's oppressive racial policies with regard to blacks and Asians were increasingly challenged in the United Nations and by liberals the world over.

The predominantly white National Party responded by creating a constitutional crisis. In 1948, it *officially* implemented the doctrine of apartheid, which was already widely practiced. A series of inhumane laws banned interracial marriages and sexual relations between members of different races and imposed strict racial segregation in public places. America responded to these changes with two contradictory policies. The U.S. government, on the one hand, supported and even sponsored certain international human rights policies that attacked apartheid.[130] On the other hand, many American businessmen were reluctant to support international proposals for economic boycotts against the South African regime.

American constitutionalism indirectly influenced South Africa also through the 1954 Supreme Court decision *Brown v. Board of Education*. That ruling greatly affected South African blacks, who until that time saw the United States in quite contradictory terms, applauding its anticolonial stance but deploring its Jim Crow practices. After the *Brown* decision, however, they viewed the American model more favorably.[131]

Two groups held opposing views and argued about what kind of solution some future regime might propose. Most whites supported the idea of the British parliamentary system because it would continue white supremacy. After *Brown*, most blacks advocated the idea of American judicial review, hoping to provide a bill of rights under which rights and liberties could be extended to the entire population, blacks and whites alike.

Following the Sharpsville Massacre in 1960, the black reform movement, which had practiced the philosophy of nonviolent resistance, changed tactics and became confrontational. By the mid-1980s, the South African government was facing a constitutional crisis of unprecedented proportions. The white-controlled 1984 constitution still denied blacks any role in the political process except in the homelands, but a new escalation of violence erupted in the late 1980s. Advocates for political change were urged on by the African National Congress (ANC). Nelson Mandela, who had been imprisoned for twenty-seven years by the white regime, emerged eventually as the leader of the black opposition. In 1990, President F. W. de Klerk, anxious to defuse the explosive situation, released Mandela and lifted the official ban imposed on the ANC. These moves accelerated the reform effort and opened the way for talks between the two sides. The following year the government repealed all apartheid laws, thus ending a half century of enforced legal separation. In 1992 the white electorate voted to end white minority rule, and as Mandela observed, the "countdown to democracy" had begun.

American constitutionalism indirectly influenced the 1996 South African Constitution, which contained one of the broadest bills of rights in the world. "The state must respect, protect, promote, and fulfill the rights in the Bill of Rights," it declared, and this applied "to all laws, and binds the legislature, the executive, the judiciary, and all organs of state." Besides a bill of rights, the charter included a constitutional court with broad powers. The principle of the separation of powers was likewise incorporated, leaving no doubt that American constitutionalism had profoundly influenced South Africa's 1996 charter both directly and indirectly.

Of all the African countries that came into being after World War II, Nigeria also was a nation directly influenced by American constitutionalism.[132] Nigerian constitutions were mainly affected by the three most prominent features of the U.S. Constitution: presidentialism, federalism, and judicial review. The context in which these features operated, however, was quite different from that in the United States because Nigeria operated under military rule most of the time, and whenever the military took over, American constitutionalism had only marginal influence or no impact at all.[133]

America's influence on presidentialism in Nigeria was most marked between 1979 and 1983. Civilian government was temporarily restored under Shehu Shagari, who tried to approximate the "American experience." The constitution of 1979 established a presidential system with directly elected state legislatures and executives. But in 1983, a military coup overthrew the government, and this feature of American constitutionalism disappeared.[134]

Federalism was a longer-lasting American influence in Nigeria. The concept of federalism had already been introduced in the colonial era as a means of coping with ethnic and geographical differences within the country. The constitution of 1950 had created a federal system of shared power between the central authority and three regional legislatures representing the main tribal groups. After Nigeria declared its independence in 1960, the federal structure was continued under the constitutions of 1960, 1963, and 1979 in an attempt to restrain the country's rampant pluralism. One scholarly work on the 1979 constitution declared that Nigerian federalism had been directly influenced by the American model.[135] But from 1965 to 1979 Nigeria operated under a federal structure controlled by the military. American-style federalism under military rule, as has been pointed out, is an oxymoron. The form of Nigerian federalism, therefore, though imitating the American model, was no longer functioning along American lines.[136] But when the 1979 constitution operated under civilian rule, Nigerian federalism again showed direct influence of the American model.

Direct American influence was also in evidence with respect to judicial review, which was guaranteed by the 1963 constitution.[137] This guarantee, however, did not mean much. "The record of African states in assuring the fulfillment of positive rights," according to one scholar in 1993, "has been abysmal and will remain so for the foreseeable future."[138] As another constitutional scholar observed, despite the presence of the American model, Nigeria's party politics made it difficult for democratic institutions to operate:

> The main cause of Nigeria's difficulties is clear. In terms of a Western system of government, institutions have been warped because politics count for too much. There are not as yet sufficient groups unaffected by changes

in party fortunes, to provide the background necessary if western institutions are to operate in a normal way.[139]

During the seventh echo, America's constitutional influence in sub-Sahara Africa generally was mostly indirect, except for South Africa and Nigeria and the unique case of Liberia. Although African countries experimented with different forms of government after gaining independence, most adopted the parliamentary system, which left little room for introducing American constitutionalism. But by 1994 the picture had changed, with eighteen electoral democracies, up from only three in 1988, marking the beginning of a "second liberation" on the African continent and introducing a new period of American constitutional influence.[140]

Israel: A Special Case

Israel represents a special case in the history of American constitutionalism. It is the only country in the Middle East directly influenced by the United States. At the same time, Israel is also one of the few countries in the world not to have a written constitution. Although Israel's founders believed that every modern state should have a written charter, they failed to frame one after gaining independence in 1948. Deep divisions among Israel's political parties regarding the role of Jewish religious law in the new state frustrated such efforts. One powerful minority wanted Israel to become a theocratic state, and a much larger majority wanted the state to be secular. On specific issues, the undecided center swung the country one way or the other. The absence of a written constitution, however, was continued for another important reason. Since its founding, Israel has faced a permanent state of emergency, being constantly threatened by surrounding hostile Arab governments and subjected to terrorist attacks.

Israeli leaders decided, therefore, to postpone the immediate preparation of a written constitution and to work on it only piecemeal.[141] Israel emerged as a unitary republic with a theoretically supreme parliament (the Knesset) whose government was run by a powerful cabinet, a largely ceremonial president, and an independent judiciary. The Knesset created the government, oversaw government activities, and passed necessary legislation. Like the British Parliament, it enjoyed constitutional supremacy and could alter its laws at will.

The transplantation of American constitutionalism to Israel was limited further by other differences explored in Gary Jacobsohn's insightful study of comparative constitutionalism.[142] Jacobsohn pointed out first the differences between the two Declarations of Independence. Although they used similar language, they projected two very different visions. The American Declaration used the language of universal principles and natural rights, while the Israeli Declaration opened with a statement of national and historical identity. The contrast highlighted the predominantly individualistic political culture in America and the highly communitarian one in Israel.[143] This contrast underscored other distinctions between the two political systems that made it difficult to transplant American constitutional principles. The notion of group rights, for example, has never been really accepted in America. In Israel, that concept was the constitutional norm. Israel not only recognized group rights but also supported them vigorously.[144]

Because of these and other differences, America's direct constitutional influence was restricted mainly to the Israeli judiciary. But even there, the influence was limited by four factors: British traditions inherited from laws under the colonial mandate; the influence of other legal traditions derived from the region's past history; the limited power of judicial review over legislation in Israel because the Knesset could override ordinary laws; and the absence of any formal bill of rights. As a result, American influence was primarily outside judicial review proper and was located instead in American constitutional jurisprudence which the Israeli judiciary often consulted. More often than not, such influence came through borrowings by the Israeli Supreme Court from its American counterpart in areas such as free speech, equality, and freedom of religion.[145]

The transplantation of American jurisprudence was especially evident in the subject of free speech. In the celebrated case of *Kol Ha'am* in 1953, Justice Simon Agranat declared that the right of free speech represented the very cornerstone of democracy. He went on to insist that it had been abridged when an earlier suspension order by the minister of the interior tried to shut down a communist newspaper. The minister suggested that America's "clear and present danger" doctrine might be interpreted to apply to the situation. In the landmark *Kol Ha'am* ruling, however, Justice Agranat restricted the discretion of the minister. Agranat's opinion recognized the right of freedom of speech and freedom of the press in Israel's legal system along American lines.[146] But as the political pendulum swung from liberal to conservative over the years, the Israeli Supreme Court took a different approach and began to suppress Arab terrorists.

Israeli courts, nevertheless, continued to be influenced by American judicial practices on other occasions.[147] Given the similarities in rhetoric of human rights and freedoms between the two countries, the practice of citing American cases in Israeli courts may continue for some time to come.[148] As long as there was no peace between the Israelis and their enemies, however, the country's security concerns would continue to limit the individual rights of citizens, and American constitutional influence would be problematical.[149]

Conclusion

What was the status of American constitutionalism throughout the globe when the seventh echo ended in 1989? The United States had become a more vigorous promoter of the American model and constitutional democracy. American policymakers had concluded that democracies were better barriers against communism than were the authoritarian regimes they had long supported. They looked on while democratic movements swept the earth motivated by the U.S. example. As Huntington reported:

> In the 1980s movements for democracy throughout the world were inspired by and borrowed from the American example. In Rangoon supporters of democracy carried the American flag; in Johannesburg they reprinted *The Federalist*; in Prague they sang "We Shall Overcome"; in Warsaw they read Lincoln and quoted Jefferson; in Beijing they erected the Goddess of Democracy; in Moscow John Sununu advised Mikhail Gorbachev on how to organize a presidency.[150]

The identification of the United States with constitutional democracy was complete. Caught up in the spirit of the times, a "remarkable consensus" emerged around the globe concerning the minimal conditions required for a country to "qualify as a democracy."[151] By 1989, many countries in Latin America, the Caribbean, Europe, and parts of East Asia had met that test, and by the mid-1990s "more countries were democratic than ever before in history, with the percentage of all democratic forms of government also the highest in history."[152] The wave of democratic revolution had transformed the constitutional universe.

The end of the cold war in 1989 thus gave rise to an astonishing euphoria which some triumphalist scholars called the "democratic moment."[153] The most famous scenario along these lines was by Francis Fukuyama, an

American political scientist, who wrote in 1989 that the end of the cold war marked the end of any significant ideological global conflict, and the emergence of a one world order free of previous determinisms. To Fukuyama, the collapse of communist regimes in the revolution of 1989 had affected more than Europe: it signaled the universalization of Western constitutionalism for the foreseeable future. In the new unipolar post–cold war world in which the United States was the sole superpower, humankind would have arrived at "Western liberal democracy as the final form of human government."[154] "There are no serious ideological competitors to liberal democracy," he noted several years later.[155]

Ideas about the "democratic moment" were shared by many foreign political and intellectual leaders. Speculation about a possible new international harmony was rampant. It was assumed the United Nations would become a more effective governing body; former cold war rivals would cooperate; and successful economic globalization would replace competition among the traditional great powers.[156]

But a more realistic appraisal of the world situation would have shown that the triumphalist expectations for democratic constitutionalism were an illusion. Far from being universal, American influence had not affected vast regions in Asia, Africa, and the Middle East that had resisted, to one degree or another, constitutional democracy, the American model, and modern Western ideas. In 1990, there were still seventy-one nondemocratic nation-states, and some of them, such as Confucian China and Islamic Iran, had autocratic regimes that were deeply hostile to American constitutionalism.[157] Other countries in central and eastern Europe, moreover, had shown that traditional indigenous values and practices often blocked any complete absorption of American constitutionalism. History has recorded too many fluctuating patterns of liberal constitutional advance and then decline to permit anyone to make confident predictions about the ultimate triumph of constitutional democracy. The end of the cold war failed to produce the overwhelming victory that the triumphalists had predicted. Their "moment" proved a mirage, despite the surprising progress made by the American model and constitutional democracy during the seventh echo.

Finally, the end of the cold war left unanswered the all-important question about what role the United States might play in the unipolar world in which it was the world's most militarily powerful nation. Huntington referred to the situation as a "uni-multipolar system with one superpower and several major powers" because he expected it to be a brief transition to genuine multipolarity.[158] It might be wise at this point to recall the prediction of George Kennan in 1999: "I can say without hesitation that this planet is never going to be ruled by any single political center, whatever its military power."[159] It might be even more advisable to note that even were such complete military power attainable, it would not necessarily lead to the spread of liberal constitutionalism or democracy in the world. As this book has shown, that spread has far more to do with the appeal of American constitutional ideas than with the force of American arms.

12

Global Consciousness
Then and Now

When formulating the principles of American constitutionalism and creating institutions to realize them, the founding fathers were
well aware of their role as innovators. Their goal was to originate for their
compatriots a workable and lasting system of republican government. But
did they intend something more? Did they claim that they were writing
for the world at large as well as for their fellow Americans? Did they invent ideas and institutions that they considered to be of universal importance for future ages as well as for their own time? Surely, many did.

Madison, seeking to rally support for the new constitution, noted that
the framers had produced what he called "innovations." They had rejected
timeworn solutions of government and the

> blind veneration for antiquity, for custom, or for [great] names that might
> override their good sense. . . . Happily for America, happily we trust for
> the whole human race . . . they accomplished a revolution which has no
> parallel in the annals of human society: They reared the fabrics of gov-
> ernments which have no model on the face of the globe.[1]

Madison was hardly alone among the delegates in the convention to
assert the importance of the Philadelphia undertaking to the world. What
they did there, he reminded his listeners, would "decide forever the fate
of Republican Government."[2] Elbridge Gerry, urging support for what became the Connecticut Compromise, similarly warned the convention that
if it failed to reach agreement, "we shall not only disappoint America, but
the rest of the world."[3]

Jefferson had addressed the Declaration to "a candid world." Later, as
president, writing about the "interesting experiment in self-government"
to the former British, and now American, intellectual Joseph Priestley,

he commented on both the new nation's burdens and its blessings: "We feel that we are acting under obligations not confined to the limits of our own society. . . . It is impossible not to be sensible that we are acting for all mankind." That other people still lived without liberty "imposes on us the duty of proving the degree of freedom and self-government" a society might leave to its members.[4] Years later in a letter to his old friend and fellow revolutionary, John Adams, Jefferson wrote, "The flames kindled on the fourth of July, 1776 have spread over too much of the globe to be extinguished by the feeble engines of despotism."[5]

Adams, of course, did not need a refresher course on the subject. Even before the new constitution had been drafted, he had written about his high hopes for expanding American constitutionalism: "Thirteen governments, thus founded on the natural authority of the people alone, . . . [are] destined to spread over the northern part of that whole quarter of the globe, [and] are a great point gained in favor of the rights of mankind."[6]

Washington expressed his sentiments in his famous 1790 letter assuring the Jewish congregation of Newport, Rhode Island, of his administration's respect for the principles of religious toleration. He universalized his message by congratulating his countrymen for "having given to mankind examples of an enlarged and liberal [religious] policy," one "worthy of imitation."[7]

As might be expected of one who believed in America's bright future, Thomas Paine wrote admiringly in 1792 in his *Rights of Man* about the government created by the constitution:

> The government of America is wholly on the system of representation . . . the only real republic in character and practice, that now exists. Its government has no other object than the public business of the nation; and therefore it is properly a republic . . . establishing government on the system of representation only.[8]

None of the founding generation was more certain of the universal implications of America's emerging constitutionalism, however, than the Scottish-born jurist from Philadelphia, James Wilson. In a speech at the Pennsylvania ratifying convention, Wilson argued that the U.S. Constitution represented the best form of government yet offered to the world.[9] He pointed out in another speech that America had a global mission as well as a national one. By erecting a new system of government under the proposed constitution, the United States would provide leadership to liberty-loving individuals everywhere:

> By adopting this system, we shall probably lay a foundation for erecting temples of liberty in every part of the earth. It has been thought by many that on the success of this struggle America has made for freedom will depend the exertions of the brave and enlightened of other nations. The advantages resulting from this system will not be confined to the United States; it will draw from Europe many worthy characters who pant for the enjoyment of freedom.[10]

The American example would do even more; it would compel monarchical rulers throughout the earth to surrender some of their power over their subjects:

> It will induce princes, in order to preserve their subjects, to restore to them a portion of that liberty of which they have for many ages been deprived. It will be subservient to the great designs of Providence with regard to this globe; the multiplication of mankind, their improvement of knowledge, and their achievement of happiness.[11]

Finally, Wilson predicted that as a result of America's political "inventions," the country would become a world leader: "The great improvements [the United States] has made and will make in the science of government will induce the patriots and literati of every nation to read and understand our writings on that subject, and hence it is not improbable that [this country] will take the lead in political knowledge."[12]

No one put the issue more boldly and baldly than Gouverneur Morris in the Constitutional Convention. He had come to the proceedings as a "Representative of America," to be sure, but as something more. "He came here to some degree as a Representative of the whole human race; for the whole human race will be affected by the proceedings of this Convention."[13]

That Americans thought that what they did mattered to the rest of the world and could influence the course of history should not be surprising, for most people who made revolutions in nations of consequence felt the same. Certainly the French did in 1789, and the Russians did in 1917, and with much justification. The fact that Americans in the 1770s and 1780s also did so was remarkable only because they believed that their new country of fewer than four million was already a nation of such consequence.

How shall we judge these confident expectations of the founders? At the outset we must acknowledge that the influence of American constitutionalism, while extremely important for the next two centuries, was not accepted universally. Most of the constitutions throughout the world from 1776 to 1989 were invariably affected by other considerations as well. One reason was the serious competition from other constitutional traditions. Of the three that comprised Western constitutionalism, the British had the greatest influence by far. "Seen against the lasting effect of the Westminster model, either in Europe or in the Commonwealth countries, or even the rest of the developing world, the influence of the American form of government pales by comparison," one scholar concluded rightly.[14] Even after decolonization, British constitutionalism continued to leave its imprint on numerous former colonies, although American constitutionalism also often influenced these fellow common-law countries.

French constitutionalism was followed most in the former parts of the French empire: Algeria, Senegal, Dahoney, and Chad in Africa; Vietnam, Cambodia, and Laos in Asia; and French Guiana in South America. All looked to the Declaration of the Rights of Man and the Citizen for inspiration and emulation. These Francophile regimes were therefore only indirectly affected by American constitutionalism. Each of the great European powers that had colonies in Asia and Africa transmitted to them its constitutional forms and practices.

Some other influential constitutions also competed successfully with the American model. The great Cadiz Constitution of 1812 drew the interest of constitution makers in both Europe and Latin America; the Belgian Constitution of 1831 had a profound influence throughout Europe in the nineteenth century; and in Latin America some countries followed tenets of the Mexican Constitution of 1917.

The rise of Marxism and Socialism in the nineteenth and twentieth centuries, moreover, threw up barriers that blocked the spread of American constitutionalism. Intellectuals of these two ideologies claimed that American constitutionalism was hardly worth heeding, as it was associated with capitalism. Communism, indeed, posed the greatest single obstacle to the spreading influence of America's founding principles after the Russian Revolution. Immediately after World War II, countries in Central and Eastern Europe, in particular, were nearly impervious to the influence of American constitutionalism because of Soviet control. As Stanley N. Katz pointed out, the persistence of "indigenization" coupled with the continuing legacy of the Soviet model prevented any wholesale adoption of the American model.

In many other countries, moreover, American constitutionalism played a reduced role for other reasons, even after the United States attained superpower status. By 1990, about half the countries of the world with a population greater than one million still had nondemocratic regimes.[15] Most were located in regions that fell broadly into three categories: (1) countries in East and Southeast Asia, such as Burma, China, Vietnam, and North Korea, which were still identified with communist systems, personal dictatorships, or both; (2) Islamic countries stretching in a huge arc from North Africa to Southeast Asia and living under dictatorships, monarchies, or mostly theocratic regimes; and (3) African countries operating under personal dictatorships, military regimes, single-party systems, or some combination of all three.

Scholars like Huntington now theorize that *culture*, not ideology, was the most important variable differentiating these nondemocratic countries, that is, "the rest from the West." Their belief systems and lifestyles were generally unsuitable to constitutional democracy because cultural loyalties, blood ties, and common traditions tightly bound them together in the constitutions they wrote.[16] Confucianism and Islam, two of the world's greatest cultures, played the most important roles. Confucianism, for example, affected not only China but also, in its different variations, Korea, Vietnam, Singapore, and Taiwan. Generally, Confucian societies emphasized the group over the individual, authority over liberty, hierarchy over equality, and kinship responsibilities over rights. Such values were at odds with practices generally associated with Western democratic constitutionalism.

Based on these cultural values, many Asian and Middle Eastern countries developed competing constitutionalisms antithetical to American constitutionalism.[17] One was the "East Asia model" which emphasized that a free-market economy should be introduced first, before any transition to Western democratic constitutionalism was attempted. Analysts of this model, like the author Fareed Zakaria, suggest that such a two-stage sequence would prevent the negative effects of introducing too much democracy too fast. This model was adopted by South Korea, Taiwan, Singapore, Malaysia, Thailand, and Indonesia.[18] Its success was so striking that it even attracted the attention of some former Soviet republics.[19]

In the 1980s, mainland China strengthened the appeal of the East Asia model by abandoning its Marxist approach in favor of a limited market economy while still operating within an authoritarian system. Called the *new authoritarianism*, this Chinese model sometimes borrowed elements from the East Asian model based on the experiences of Taiwan, Singapore, and South Korea. The Chinese claimed that at their stage of economic development, they still needed authoritarian rulers to reach a balanced economic growth and contain the restless consequences of such development. This was also the reason the Chinese leaders gave for suppressing the democratic movement in Tiananmen Square in 1989.[20]

In contrast, Islam contained some features generally compatible with democracy in theory but in practice they rarely were allowed free play. Insistence by Islamic fundamentalists that political rulers be practicing Muslims, that the religious and political community be one, and that legitimacy of government institutions be based on religious grounds all departed from the democratic, secular values of the West.

Demographically, Islam presented the greatest challenge to the West. In 1900 more than 40 percent of the world's population had been under control of the West during the era of European imperialism, a figure that fell to 15 percent by 1990, largely as the result of decolonization. Conversely, by 1990 the percentage of countries with mostly Islamic populations had risen from 4 to 14 percent.[21] On the whole, Islamic nations historically have been the most hostile to and constitutionally the furthest from democracy. Freedom House's annual surveys between the early 1980s and 1990 listed as free only two of the world's thirty-seven countries with Muslim majorities.[22] Although Turkey and Indonesia had established democratic systems by 1990, even these two countries raised questions about how Islamic principles were put into practice. History records that Islam and American constitutional ideals do not coexist easily, and the gap separating them continues to be very wide.[23]

The cultural-political picture in Africa was even more mixed. Many countries on the continent began their "second liberation" in 1990, reaching different stages of development in their transitions to democracy. By 1993 there were "25 countries in Africa, or approximately half of the states, on the continent . . . [that] could be classified as either democratic or strongly committed to democratic change."[24] Although the number of nondemocratic African countries continued to shrink, the pace of change remained uncertain. Some countries paused, tried democracy, became disillusioned, and slipped back into authoritarian regimes.[25] Others pressed on. Established democracies in the region by the early 1990s included Botswana, Gambia, Mauritius, Namibia, and Senegal.[26] Despite these democratic advances, however, American constitutionalism played only a modest role, except, as noted, in the case of the Union of South Africa and Nigeria.

Three other variables limited the spread of democracy and, implicitly, American constitutionalism, in all these non-Western regions. One was the economic status of countries seeking to make a transition. "Poverty is a principal and probably *the* principal obstacle to democratic development," Huntington concluded.[27] Only when countries achieved a sufficient economic level was a transition to democracy possible. Fareed Zakaria estimated that level as a per capita GDP (gross domestic product) of between $3,000 and $6,000 (in 2003 U.S. dollars), and many poor countries simply did not qualify.[28]

A second significant variable was the lack of political leadership. American constitutional influence and democracy can take hold only when political elites believe them to be the most suitable form of government for themselves and their societies. Skilled political leadership was necessary to overcome radical political opportunists, on the one hand, and determined authoritarians, on the other. But such leadership was often absent in nondemocratic regimes.[29]

A third variable seems to be prior exposure to democracy. Nondemocratic countries that had never had any contact with democracy were less likely to make a successful transition. Although it was by no means automatic, some earlier exposure to democracy usually facilitated a transition to American constitutionalism.

Given the limitations on the spread of American constitutionalism, one scholar of comparative constitutionalism, Andrzej Rapaczynski, stated in 1990: "In the long run, American influences turned out to be shallow and unstable," and this judgment became the conventional wisdom among scholars. The U.S. Constitution, Rapaczynski acknowledged, had influenced developments, but its influence had been limited to presidentialism, federalism, and judicial review. "Each of these ideas found its imitators around the world," Rapaczynski pointed out, "but hardly ever was the transplant received in soil sufficiently like American soil to produce an approximation of the original."[30]

What should we make of this judgment? One cannot take issue with Rapaczynski's observations regarding the limited influence of American presidentialism. As this book has shown, the countries that tried the purely presidential system were few in number: Latin America and Liberia in the nineteenth century and the Philippines, Indonesia, South Korea, and Nigeria in the twentieth. Latin American experiments with presidentialism all too often degenerated into the rise of *caudillos*, and these failures discouraged other countries from experimenting with this feature. At the same time, however, it is clear that some foreign constitutionalists saw in the American model one way of redressing the balance when it tipped too far in the direction of parliamentarianism. They adopted hybrid constitutions, therefore, that embraced some combination of semipresidential/semiparliamentarian systems.[31] Despite such hybrids, by the end of the seventh echo the parliamentary system remained twice as popular as presidentialism throughout the world.[32]

On federalism, Rapaczynski, while correct in narrow terms, missed the larger point. Although federalism had a history stretching back centuries, "it is still correct to say," another scholar maintained, "that the modern idea of federalism has been determined by the United States and that, of all the institutions within the American constitutional structure, it is federalism that has had the greatest influence in the world."[33] The adoption of certain principles by the founders had given the concept of American-style federalism a new lease on life with its innovative notions: the idea of dual sovereignty, the division of federal and state power, the participation of states in the decision-making process, and the constitutional review of state decisions. Most important, the federal system was made more effective because individual citizens became subject to the jurisdiction of both the national and state governments.

It is certainly true, as this book has shown, that most countries failed to follow the American federal idea as set forth in *The Federalist*. They used the concept instead in various ways to fulfill a number of different purposes. Some federations had as their primary aim the protection of the rights of minority groups within society—whether ethnic, geographic, religious, economic, or linguistic—against a central government that might threaten them. One thinks in this regard of the French-speaking population in Canada, the Tamils in Sri Lanka, and the Chinese in Malaya. Other federations were formed to cope with problems created by vast geographical distances that made it impossible for the central government to communicate with its distant citizens—as in the case of Latin America. American-style federalism, therefore, had been very influential in the nineteenth century, and this despite the midcentury collapse into the American Civil War. That the concept continued to hold sway throughout the world in the twentieth century can hardly be denied. Indeed, in the second half of the twentieth century, there was an enormous proliferation of different kinds of federations throughout the globe, many of them inspired either directly or indirectly by the American model.[34]

Rapaczynski does not deal extensively with the American idea of judicial review abroad, which one scholar referred to as "America's most important export."[35] It is true that for the first 150 years after its American invention, the concept had little impact in Europe for two reasons: the French doctrine that the "general will" of the people was sovereign, and the British theory of the sovereignty of Parliament. Other reasons included the presence of the centralized constitutional courts in Europe after 1920, the different role of judges in civil as opposed to common-law countries, the fact that the constitution in many countries did not function as the supreme law of the land, and the European view of the American Supreme Court before the New Deal as being a conservative institution.

After the harrowing experience of the Holocaust and other forms of discrimination in World War II, however, the feeling grew gradually throughout much of the world that a new theory of judicial review was needed. The test of a government's legitimacy, it was said, should not be whether its institutions complied with the "will of the people," as implied previously, but whether a government's aim was to protect the civil liberties of unpopular minorities against oppressive legislative majorities.

Judicial review became more relevant than ever before as a result of this new attitude. It gave "effect to a consensus that began to emerge in the late 1930s and that since then has become widely shared by Americans and most of the other people of the world: a consensus that racial, religious, and comparable forms of discrimination are profoundly evil and unjust."[36] Within the United States, for example, this new theory found its expression in cases like *Brown v. Board of Education*, which signaled the end of state-sanctioned racial discrimination. In Europe and throughout much of the rest of the world, some special constitutional courts began emulating the Supreme Court's decisions that declared acts of the legislative branch invalid in civil rights cases that infringed on individual rights.

Even so, the American practice of life tenure for appointed judges was not widely adopted. Many countries resisted that practice, and thus judges were subjected to intense pressure from the executive and legislative branches. Legislatures in other countries, moreover, could circumvent the

American model simply by making the constitutional amendment process more flexible. Furthermore, federalism and the separation of powers—constitutional features that made the American model work effectively—were not always the practice in foreign countries.

Despite these limitations, the American model of judicial review began to enjoy its greatest success abroad in the post–World War II years from 1945 to 1989. At no other time in U.S. history was the American idea more popular abroad. Despite the growing popularity of American-style judicial review, however, it never outnumbered the European constitutional court system based on the Kelsenian model.

The judicial review principle has been applied not only to nation-states but also, by analogy, to international organizations. America's successful experiment with the doctrine was applied to achieve stability among organizations operating on a transnational level during the period after World War II. When the Court of Europe in 1953 adopted the European Convention for the Protection of Human Rights and Fundamental Freedoms, the European Court of Human Rights was established with powers of review. The same was true when the Treaty of Rome created the European Economic Community (EEC) in 1967, which was empowered to determine whether the actions of member states were consistent with the community's charter.[37]

Rapaczynski's larger conclusion regarding the alleged shallowness and instability of American constitutional influence in the world was based on his equating American constitutionalism solely with the U.S. Constitution. As this book has argued, however, American constitutionalism was composed of five other seminal documents as well. The Declaration affected numerous countries from 1776 to 1989 and beyond, experiencing its greatest revival after Western constitutionalism underwent its transition with the collapse of the Soviet empire. Although the effect of the first state constitutions was limited in terms of time and space to the early years of the republic and confined primarily to Europe and Latin America, their influence was extended by virtue of the four "inventions" that generally became the norms for Western constitutionalism as it spread throughout the world for more than two hundred years. The Articles of Confederation, it is true, proved much more limited in influence, but large sections were embedded in the Constitution and thus indirectly continued their impact. *The Federalist* still remains underappreciated as an interpretive constitutional document, but its influence on Tocqueville's thought and that of other leading foreign constitutionalists has been profound and long lasting. Finally, the American bill of rights tradition played an important role in the formulation and continuation of Western constitutionalism and served as the basis for the sweeping human rights revolution around the globe during the latter half of the twentieth century.

Rapaczynski's critique aside, one needs to recognize the role of another critically important element in American constitutionalism: republicanism. The American version of republicanism flowered during the debates over the ratification of the Constitution when the Federalists advanced the idea that sovereignty resided in the people rather than in any single branch of government. All branches, they said, represented the people. This theory marked the end of the classical conception of politics that had been practiced previously. According to Gordon Wood, it resulted in the creation of a new governmental system that was "more modern and with a more realistic sense of political behavior in society."[38] The outcome was astonishing. Within a half century, "Americans had become . . . the most liberal, the most democratic, the most commercially minded, and the most modern people in the world."[39]

American republicanism abroad yielded equally surprising results. It helped put an end to certain absolutist monarchies by its example and transformed them into constitutional monarchies, a more democratic form of government. In some European countries, American republicanism resulted in demands for elected officials or for new constitutions. Kings and queens either granted such charters or were forced to limit their powers while they broadened those of the people. This was especially true after the American-influenced Belgian Constitution of 1831 served as a model for limited monarchy throughout Europe. Today monarchies in Europe and other parts of the world are much fewer in number, and those that survive sometimes do so largely as symbols of national unity (though kingships are still found in Asia, Africa, and the Middle East). American republicanism scored its greatest triumph, of course, in the numerous republics scattered throughout the world that followed its example.

That the United States was a world leader in developing another powerful historical force—democracy—is incontestable. The right of almost all adult white males to vote had already been achieved in America by the 1820s when, as Huntington has shown, the first of three great waves of global democratization began. As early as 1835, Tocqueville, now back in France and observing changes in European society, wrote: "A great revolution is taking place in our midst. . . . I admit that I saw in America more than America; it was the shape of democracy itself."[40]

To European liberals like Tocqueville, this new shape of democracy had an enormous effect on the way they viewed the United States. Before the 1820s, they had considered America a republic: a significant advance over the monarchical and aristocratic models that then dominated Europe. Now, however, they saw America as leading the way toward popular self-government, a representative democracy with significant limits on control of the government by the people. "The liberal groups, which increased their influence in France after 1830, were now . . . ready to accept some of the American institutions and the liberalism behind them," wrote one scholar.[41]

The image of the United States as the world's leading representative democracy was enhanced further by steps taken later in America on the state level to broaden the right to vote by removing virtually all property qualifications before the Civil War. The right of adult white males to vote became nearly universal throughout the United States. Compared with Britain, America was far ahead. After the Reform Bill of 1832, only 1.8 percent of Britain's population could vote, and even after the 1884 reform measure, this figure was only 12.1 percent.[42] The Southern states' thwarting of the Fourteenth and Fifteenth Amendments over the next century became a huge obstacle, to be sure, but even in the face of this failure, the United States continued to be regarded as the world's leading democratic society. During the subsequent civil rights movement in the 1950s and 1960s, America finally moved to even greater racial equality when the federal government took steps in the Civil Rights Act of 1964 to check state legislation that had flagrantly violated the constitutional right of African Americans to vote.

Similarly, the United States was well ahead of much of the rest of the world in attacking the idea of discrimination against women. Women's suffrage, which in America began in the 1890s in a handful of western states, was made nationwide by constitutional amendment in 1920, when only New Zealand, Australia, Finland, and Norway had given women the vote. In 1970, the U.S. Supreme Court applied the equal protection clause to override any state action that resulted in unequal treatment of women. To be sure, for many reasons, gender equality remained incomplete, but as an ideal it continued to spur change. America's leadership in this reform movement was followed with great interest by other democratic countries and served as a catalyst to bring about advances in women's suffrage as well as other manifestations of equality on a global scale.

This trend toward greater equality could be seen also in the veritable revolution that expanded the protection of rights of citizens in Supreme Court decisions of the 1960s and 1970s, such as the *Miranda* ruling. Such decisions helped establish a social and intellectual ethos that affected other democratic countries involved in similar reform movements. Many were already committed to the idea of greater individual freedoms because of the terrible experiences endured during World War II and the Holocaust, but in writing their constitutions, they were motivated also by American court rulings.

Democracy, Winston Churchill once observed, was the worst form of government—except for all others. But it is a prize worth fighting for. This was made evident in the work of the Nobel laureate economist Amartya Sen, who insisted in his *Development as Freedom* (1999) that constitutional democracy remains critical to the material fate of millions of people in developing nations throughout the world. Although countries may vary and adapt forms of democracy in different ways, without it the ruling elites have no incentive to distribute the pains and gains of economic development in fair and equitable ways. Without the apparatus of democracy—a political bargaining system of some sort, independent judiciaries, a free press, and a competitive party system—inequality will go unchecked, even to the point of allowing famine, as in North Korea. Lacking democracy with its guaranteed rights to argue and bargain, most people will be ill served by their governments. There is no unfree short cut to economic development, Sen concluded. Democracy counts![43]

This book ends in 1989 because the end of a half century of conflict between constitutional democracy and Marxist–Leninism marked the close of the cold war. The bipolarity that had provided a certain sense of coherence in international politics came to an end, and the world entered a new era in which the future of constitutional democracy could not be foretold. Indeed, powerful forces still threatened the very existence of constitutional democracy in many instances. The growth of "malignant nationalism" was one such factor, especially in the "balkanization" of Eastern Europe. A second was "religious intolerance" and "theocratic aspirations," as evidenced in Islamic fundamentalist movements. A third was terrorism, which threatened not so much in conquest per se as in driving democratic governments to adopt undemocratic means to counter it. Finally, there were general threats to human welfare arising from overpopulation, diminishing natural resources, environmental catastrophes such as global warming, and the increasing concentration of wealth in the hands of a privileged few. In creating misery, such forces provided opportunities for antidemocratic movements to gain acceptance by promising easy solutions.[44]

Three representative scholars offered possible scenarios about what the future of democratic constitutionalism, faced with such threats, might be. The first, George Kennan, the diplomat-turned-historian, fell back on the thesis of Western exceptionalism. Only Western cultures, he argued in the 1970s, provided a suitable setting for developing democracy, because they presumably possessed a particular genius for establishing democratic institutions.

[Democracy] evolved in the eighteenth and nineteenth centuries in northwestern Europe, primarily among those countries which border on the English Channel and the North Sea (but with a certain extension into Central Europe), and which they carried into other parts of the world, including North America, where people from that northwestern European area appeared as original settlers, or as colonialists, and laid down the prevailing patterns of civil government.

[Hence, democracy had] a relatively narrow base both in time and space; and the evidence has yet to be produced that it is the natural form of rule for peoples outside those narrow perimeters.[45]

Kennan's interpretation was actually a variation of the old thesis of Anglo-Saxon superiority: that the race had achieved worldwide influence because of its unique and innate ability to create and perpetuate democratic institutions. Because democracy did not seem suited to non-Western cultures, Kennan was pessimistic about its future expansion.

Francis Fukuyama's 1989 essay "The End of History?" took an opposite view. Representing the triumphalist school of historians, he was highly optimistic about the future of democracy. His assumption was that the 1989 collapse of communism marked the end of all forms of government other than that of Western constitutional democracy. Caught up in the euphoria and democratic zeitgeist of the moment, he envisaged a new world order. "We may be witnessing," he wrote, "the end of history as such: that is the end point of mankind's ideological evolution and the universalization of Western liberal democracy as the final form of human government."[46]

Samuel P. Huntington, in contrast, was ambivalent about democracy's future. In *The Third Wave*, published in 1991, he wondered what would happen if America "no longer embodied strength and success, no longer seemed to be the winning model." By the end of the 1980s, many scholars were arguing that America's decline had already begun. "If this happened, the perceived failures of the United States would inevitably be seen as the failures of democracy. The worldwide appeal of democracy would be significantly diminished."[47] In short, constitutional democracy and American power seemed inextricably linked, and the failure of the latter would be viewed as the failure of the former.

Whether Kennan's pessimism, Fukuyama's optimism, or Huntington's ambivalence will ultimately prove to be most trustworthy in predicting the future of constitutional democracy cannot be known. Instead, we are left to ponder the prophecy of America's founders, who claimed that their work would exert an influence beyond America's shores for years to come and that they had created a "New Order for the Ages." To a remarkable extent, they have been proved right! Within the framework of Western constitutionalism, American constitutionalism was, as this book has demonstrated, heard round the world for more than two centuries. For Europeans chafing under monarchies and aristocracies, it provided a catalyst for change, a model to follow, and a source of inspiration. For Latin Americans and, later, Asians and Africans throwing off colonial rule, it offered paradigms for new structures of government and a more persuasive definition of the just relationship between governors and the governed. From the American Revolution to the European Revolution of 1989, the American model powerfully, if sometimes unevenly, supported constitutional government, greater democracy, and expanded human rights. For those two hundred years, no matter what the future might hold, the United States merited Abraham Lincoln's praise as "the last, best hope on earth."

Appendix

*A Note on the Historiography of the
Influence of American Constitutionalism
Abroad: 1776–1989*

The historiography on the influence of American constitutionalism abroad from the American Revolution to the breakup of the Soviet empire in 1989 reveals a serious gap in the literature published in the United States. No single historical narrative synthesizes the worldwide influence of American constitutionalism abroad between these two cataclysmic events. Books and articles abound, however, reflecting different disciplines—history, political science, comparative constitutional law, and philosophy of law—covering different perspectives on the subject. This abbreviated account of the historiography focuses on the literature published in this country and makes no attempt to include the voluminous literature in transnational history.

The modern historiographical record began in Europe around the turn of the twentieth century with a controversy between two scholars, Georg Jellinek and Emile Doumergue, who debated the origins of the bill of rights tradition. Jellinek, a German jurist, argued in his book *Die Erklärung der Menschen und Bürgerrechte* in 1895 that the French Declaration of the Rights of Man and Citizen of 1789 was derived from American bills of rights. An authorized translation by Max Farrand was published as *The Declaration of the Rights of Man and of Citizens: A Contribution to Modern Constitutional History* (New York: Henry Holt, 1901). In his 1904 essay *Les origines historique de la Déclaration des Droits de l'Homme et du Citoyen* (Paris: V. Giard & E. Brière, 1905), Doumergue drew a line of descent of these rights from European sources running from Calvin to the French Revolution.

A half century later in America during the sesquicentennial of the U.S. Constitution, Conyers Read edited a book of essays by distinguished scholars entitled *The Constitution Reconsidered* (New York: Columbia University Press, 1938), with selections indicating the influence of the U.S. Constitution on Canada, South Africa, Latin America, and federal systems in the British Empire.

About the same time, an English scholar, John A. Hawgood, published *Modern Constitutions since 1787* (London: Macmillan, 1939). Hawgood did not focus on the U.S. Constitution but summarized instead the constitutions of almost every major political power. Written on the eve of World War II, the book was a treatise defending the democratic way of life against fascism and communism.

Carl J. Friedrich, a Harvard professor and German émigré, produced a pioneering textbook on comparative government entitled *Constitutional Government and Politics: Nature and Development* (New York: Harper, 1937), which used a functional and topical analysis of the constitutional form of government rather than a country-by-country approach. Thirty years later, in 1967, Friedrich published *The Impact of American Constitutionalism Abroad* (Boston: Boston University Press, 1967), using the same technique. This is a work that, despite its brevity, remains one of the major landmarks in the field.

The second major landmark in the post-World War II era was Robert R. Palmer's magisterial two-volume work *The Age of the Democratic Revolution* (Princeton, NJ: Princeton University Press, 1959 and 1964). Although it covers more than comparative constitutional history, his synthesis, arguing that the whole of Western civilization was swept up in a single revolutionary movement stretching from the 1770s to the 1840s, incorporated major constitutional reforms. Palmer's work focused on the revolutionary nature of the American Revolution and the novel constitutional features emerging from it, like the idea of a constituent constitutional convention, which had worldwide ramifications. Palmer's book remains one of the most brilliant studies on the subject. His work, however, was confined primarily to Europe and North America when tracing constitutional influence abroad and concentrates on the later eighteenth and early nineteenth century. Although it has been subjected to attack, the sweep of Palmer's synthesis and his thoughtful analysis of constitutional ideas and institutions make it the best place to begin any study of the subject.

The third landmark study by a single author was Richard B. Morris's *The Emerging Nations and the American Revolution* (New York: Harper & Row, 1970). Morris was concerned with the influence of the American

Revolution on the world and its constitutional repercussions. He was interested in the new nation-states emerging from World War II after decolonization and how the American constitutional model affected them. Professor Morris was my mentor at Columbia University, and his work motivated me to undertake two studies on the subject. When following Professor Morris's lead, however, I was guilty of the tendency to overemphasize nationalism in the volume of collected essays I edited, *American Constitutionalism Abroad: Selected Essays in Comparative Constitutional History* (Westport, CT: Greenwood Press, 1990). The current study, therefore, represents a revision of my earlier approach.

Several different kinds of studies have appeared in more recent years. The most important was a collection of essays entitled *Constitutionalism and Democracy: Transitions in the Contemporary World* (New York: Oxford University Press, 1993). Edited by Douglas Greenberg, Stanley N. Katz, Melanie Beth Oliviero, and Steven C. Wheatley, the essays were originally written for presentation and discussion by foreign and American scholars at a series of international conferences held in different countries over a period of five years. The project, organized by the American Council of Learned Societies under the leadership of Stanley N. Katz, included pieces that were comparative in nature across disciplines, cultures, and regimes as well as through time.

A second general scholarly enterprise was incorporated in a book of collected essays edited by Louis Henkin and Albert J. Rosenthal entitled *Constitutionalism and Rights: The Influence of the United States Constitution Abroad* (New York: Columbia University Press, 1990), which grew out of papers given at a conference to honor the Constitution bicentennial. The "Bibliographical Essay," by Andrzej Rapaczynski included in that study calls for special commendation. His precise analyses and comparisons from original documents in many languages make his work a model of comparative history, and my own book is indebted to his study at many points. But my work disagrees with some of his conclusions because like all previous scholars, he focused solely on the U.S. Constitution when dealing with American constitutionalism abroad. I maintain that five other revolutionary republican documents, like the Declaration of Independence, should be included in the definition.

The brief but penetrating and learned book by Klaus von Beyme entitled *America as a Model: The Impact of American Democracy in the World* (New York: St. Martin's Press, 1987), sought to advance Carl J. Friedrich's approach by updating and expanding certain themes from a political science point of view. But the book was published before the fall of the Soviet Union, a key date for any study of the subject.

Two other kinds of studies need to be mentioned. The first were those on a given region, like Lawrence W. Beer's edited collection of essays by specialists in Asia, *Constitutionalism in Asia: Asian Views of the American Influence* (Berkeley: University of California Press, 1979); and his *Constitutional Systems in Late Twentieth Century Asia* (Seattle: University of Washington Press, 1992). The second category concentrates on specific features of the Constitution, such as Mauro Cappelletti's *Judicial Review in the Contemporary World* (Indianapolis: Bobbs-Merrill, 1971) and David Armitage, *The Declaration of Independence: A Global History* (Cambridge, MA: Harvard University Press, 2007).

The best treatment of the historiography of American constitutionalism abroad from the broadest possible perspective—multidisciplinary, comparative history, legal theory, and political science—is in the footnotes of Walter Murphy's *Constitutional Democracy: Creating and Maintaining a Just Political Order* (Baltimore: Johns Hopkins University Press, 2007).

Finally, any account of the history of American constitutionalism abroad must take note of the massive international constitution project undertaken by Professor Horst Dippel of the University of Kassel in Germany, "The Rise of Modern Constitutionalism, 1776–1849." Its aim is to produce edited volumes of primary sources under the general title *Constitutions of the World from the Late Eighteenth Century to the Middle of the Nineteenth Century*. Their publication is continuous, both in electronic format and as printed volumes by K. G. Saur Verlag. Begun in 2001 with an international group of more than fifty editors, the date of completion is projected for mid-2008, with some two thousand constitutional documents from Europe, the Americas, Liberia, and the Hawaiian Islands. A second project already well under way ranges from 1850 to the present and includes Asia and Africa as well as Australia. This invaluable resource came to my attention when my own research, which synthesizes findings based largely on secondary sources, was substantially completed. With the availability of scholarly editions of these primary constitutional documents, more analytical research can be conducted in comparative constitutional history from a global perspective. For that reason, my book should be considered mainly as a pioneering effort.

Notes

1. For an account of the studies on the subject to date, see the appendix, "A Note on the Historiography of the Influence of American Constitutionalism Abroad: 1776–1989."

2. Andrzej Rapaczynski, "Bibliographical Essay: The Influence of U.S. Constitutionalism Abroad," in *Constitutionalism and Rights: The Influence of the United States Constitution Abroad*, ed. Louis Henkin and Albert J. Rosenthal (New York: Columbia University Press, 1990), 460.

3. Carl J. Friedrich, *The Impact of American Constitutionalism Abroad* (Boston: Boston University Press, 1967), 11 (italics in original).

4. I refer in particular to my overly nationalistic approach in the earlier book of collected essays I edited, *American Constitutionalism Abroad: Selected Essays in Comparative Constitutional History* (Westport, CT: Greenwood Press, 1990). David Armitage's brilliant book, *The Declaration of Independence: A Global History* (Cambridge, MA: Harvard University Press, 2007), represents a historiographical breakthrough, as he placed his study of the document in the context of global history rather than in the framework of American national history. See also Armitage's article "The Declaration of Independence and International Law," *William and Mary Quarterly*, 3rd ser., 59 (2002):39–64.

For other scholars seeking to escape the overreliance on a nationalistic approach in writing American history, see Thomas Bender, ed., *Rethinking American History in a Global Age* (Berkeley: University of California Press, 2002); and his *Nation among Nations: America's Place in World History* (New York: Hill & Wang, 2006); Eric Foner, "American Freedom in a Global Age," *American Historical Review* 106 (2002):1–16; and C. A. Bayly, *The Birth of the Modern World: Global Connections and Comparisons, 1780–1914* (Malden, MA: Blackwell, 2004).

5. William H. McNeill, *The Great Frontier: Freedom and Hierarchy in Modern Times* (Princeton, NJ: Princeton University Press, 1983), 8. For the dangers connected with excessive emphasis on American exceptionalism, see Rheinhold Niebuhr, *The Irony of American History* (1952; repr., Chicago: University of Chicago Press, 2008), esp. the introduction by Andrew J. Bacevich.

6. The phrase was used in the title of the book by John M. Headley, *The Europe-anization of the World: On the Origins of Human Rights and Democracy* (Princton, NJ: Princeton University Press, 2007). Headley posits Western civilization as distinctive, based on two traditions traceable to the Renaissance and Reformation. The first–the idea of a common humanity–was derived from ancient times, developed later through natural law, and resulted in the modern concept of universal human rights. The second—the idea of tolerating political dissent—was a notion postulated first in the Protestant Reformation and eventually culminating in the practices associated with the British political system of constitutional democracy. These two Western traditions are unique, Headley argues, and need to be reaffirmed in view of the challenges presented by other civilizations and cultures in the modern world. Headley's approach is far different from mine, which focuses primarily on American constitutionalism and its spread throughout the globe under the rubric of the expansion of Europe.

7. Three other caveats are in order regarding the focus of my study. It is not a comparative constitutional history, which would be much more comprehensive in its approach. Rather, the primary emphasis is on the American dimension of Western constitutionalism. It also does not deal directly with the internal domestic politics of the various governments involved. Finally, the story of the major common-law countries—the advanced societies in the English-speaking world that share the same tradition, namely, Britain, Canada, and Australia—will be published in a separate volume.

CHAPTER 1

1. Esther B. Fein, "Clamor in the East; Unshackled Czech Workers Declare Their Independence," *New York Times*, November 28, 1989.

2. David Armitage, *The Declaration of Independence: A Global History* (Cambridge, MA: Harvard University Press, 2007), 3.
For Armitage's interpretation of the Declaration in the context of the discourse on "the law of nature and of nations" that was emerging but not yet established and called "international law," see his article "The Declaration of Independence and International Law," *William and Mary Quarterly*, 3rd ser., 59 (2002):39–64. Armitage interprets the Declaration within the two existing conceptions of international law and claims that its role in these conceptions partly accounts for both its form and ready reception. It was not until later—generally around the turn of the nineteenth century—that there was "the shift from the natural-jurisprudential foundations of the law of nations toward a conception of positive international law became generally observable" (57). For the total number of declarations of independence since 1776, see *Declaration of Independence*, 20.

3. R. R. Palmer, *The Age of the Democratic Revolution: A Political History of Europe and America, 1760–1800*, 2 vols. (Princeton, NJ: Princeton University Press, 1959 and 1964), 1:282.

4. Henry St. John, Viscount Bolingbroke, "Dissertation on Parties," Letter X in *Works*, 5 vols. (London: C. Mallet, 1754), 2:130. Note, however, that in its inclusiveness, Bolingbroke's definition is far closer to the British concept than to the later innovative American concept.

5. Louis Henkin, introduction to *Constitutionalism and Rights: The Influence of the United States Constitution Abroad*, ed. Louis Henkin and Albert J. Rosenthal (New York: Columbia University Press, 1990), 1.

6. Louis Henkin, *The Rights of Man Today* (Boulder, CO: Westview Press, 1978), 33.

7. Gisbert H. Flanz, *Comparative Study of Constitutions and Constitutionalism*, transcription of a lecture given by Flanz in Seoul, Korea, at the College of Law, Seoul National University (Seoul, 1963 [?]), 2. Flanz was coeditor with Albert P. Blaustein of *Constitutions of the Countries of the World*, 20 vols. loose-leaf (Dobbs Ferry, NY: Oceana Publications, 1971–1991).

8. Don E. Fehrenbacher, *Constitutions and Constitutionalism in the Slaveholding South* (Athens: University of Georgia Press, 1989), 1.

9. See, for example, some of the essays in J. G. A. Pocock, ed., *Three British Revolutions: 1641, 1688, 1776* (Princeton, NJ: Princeton University Press, 1980), esp. that by John Murrin, "The Great Inversion, or Court vs. Country: A Comparison of the Revolutionary Settlement in England (1688–1721) and America (1776–1816)," 319–453.

10. Walter Hamilton, "Constitutionalism," in *Encyclopaedia of the Social Sciences*, ed. Edwin R. A. Seligman and Alvin Johnson, 15 vols. (New York: Macmillan, 1930), 4:255.

The literature on the subject of modern constitutionalism is overwhelming. Charles H. McIlwain's classic, *Constitutionalism, Ancient and Modern*, rev. ed. (Indianapolis: Liberty Fund, 2007) is dated but still helpful. Bruce Ackerman's essay "The Rise of World Constitutionalism," *Virginia Law Review*, 83 (1997):771–79, is sketchy and not very convincing. Between the old works and the new, despite the enormous amount of writing, Horst Dippel may be right that while we acknowledge the global acceptance of a political principle referred to as modern constitutionalism, "we uneasily have to admit that . . . we definitely do not know how all this came about." See Horst Dippel, "Modern Constitutionalism, an Introduction to a History in the Need of Writing," *Legal History Review* 73, nos. 1-2 (2005):153.

The massive project in which Professor Dippel is engaged has two parts, *Constitutions of the World from the Late Eighteenth Century to the Middle of the Nineteenth Century* (Munich: K. G. Saur, 2006–), and its continuation from 1850 to the present, which may help scholars finally begin to grapple with the problem more definitively. But the issue is not lacking materials as much as agreeing on precise definitions, overcoming linguistic problems, and dealing with different cultural particularisms.

11. "The Virginia Declaration of Rights and Constitution," commentary by Donald S. Lutz, in *Roots of the Republic: American Founding Documents Interpreted*, ed. Stephen L. Schechter, Richard B. Bernstein, and Donald S. Lutz (Madison, WI: Madison House, 1990), 154.

12. Dippel, "Modern Constitutionalism," 157.

13. Ibid.

14. Ibid.

15. Although my definition follows to some extent that of Walter F. Murphy in his 1999/2000 Eckstein Lecture at the Center for the Study of Democracy, "Constitutional Interpretation as Constitutional Creation," University of California at Irvine, November 1, 2000, it seeks to escape what he calls "constitutionism": mistaking a thing (the constitution) for a process (constitutionalism). By positing six documents rather than the U.S. Constitution as the expression of the underlying principles of American constitutional values in my definition, a more dynamic interaction is recognized within a more complex whole. Furthermore, the processive development of American constitutionalism through time demonstrates that while it may be considered a "thing" as textual, it *also* is a process.

See also Murphy's penetrating essay, "Constitutions, Constitutionalism, and Democracy," in *Constitutionalism and Democracy: Transitions in the Contemporary World*, ed. Douglas Greenberg, Stanley N. Katz, Melanie Beth Oliviero, and Steven C. Wheatley (New York: Oxford University Press, 1993), 3–25. Murphy's more recent book, *Constitutional Democracy: Creating and Maintaining a Just Political Order* (Baltimore: Johns Hopkins University Press, 2007), which addresses the tensions inherent in the relationship between constitutionalism and democracy, is an unparalleled masterpiece.

16. The alternative "approximate" definition of constitutionalism arrived at by the international group of scholars convened by Stanley N. Katz emphasizes that in light of the cultural differences represented in the contemporary world, constitutionalism is best defined in functional terms as a dynamic, ongoing process rather than as reified in a single document or underlying theory. It encompasses "a commitment to limitations on ordinary political power; it revolves around a political process, one that overlaps with democracy in seeking to balance state power and individual and collective rights; it draws on particular cultural and historical contexts from which it emanates; and it resides in public consciousness." See introduction to Greenberg et al., *Constitutionalism and Democracy*, xxi.

This definition is original, cogent in its inclusiveness, and highly relevant to many contemporary situations. If successful in supplanting the traditional concept derived from the European Enlightenment, it would overturn the existing scholarship in the field. It is, of course, contrary to the documentary approach taken in this book, which originates in the context of America's founding years when constitutional thought was grounded in compact theory and wedded to the written word.

17. See Donald S. Lutz, *The Origins of American Constitutionalism* (Baton Rouge: Louisiana State University Press, 1988), passim.

18. All the spelling in the Declaration is based on the engrossed manuscript copy in the National Archives, which is reprinted in *The Documentary History of the Ratification of the Constitution*, ed. Merrill Jensen, John P. Kaminski, and Gaspare J. Saladino, et al., 22 vols. to date (Madison: State Historical Society of Wisconsin, 1976–), 1:73–76.

19. Klaus von Beyme, *America as a Model: The Impact of American Democracy in the World* (New York: St. Martin's Press, 1987), 1.

20. Palmer, *Age of the Democratic Revolution*, vol. 1, app. IV, 518–21.

It bears mentioning, however, that as a methodology for tracing the spread of American constitutionalism abroad, the documentary approach makes it possible to reduce some of the problematic aspects inherent in the project. Despite the difficulty of definitively asserting influence, it enables scholars to trace textual parallels and appropriations more easily and to make more solid empirical claims regarding possible "influence." For foreign constitutionalists, it enables them to grasp the larger contours of the American model and to understand better the significant content immanent in the documents themselves.

21. The phrase is used by Kim Lane Scheppele in "Aspirational and Aversive Constitutionalism: The Case for Studying Cross-Constitutional Influence through Negative Models," *International Journal of Constitutional Law* 1, no. 2 (2003):313–20 and passim.

22. The writing on the "originalists" controversy is enormous. See, for example, Jack N. Rakove, *Original Meanings: Politics and Ideas in the Making of the Constitution* (New York: Knopf, 1996); Ronald Dworkin, *Taking Rights Seriously* (Cambridge, MA: Harvard University Press,1977); Robert H. Bork, *The Tempting of America: The Political Seduction of the Law* (New York: Free Press, 1990); and Edwin Meese, "The Supreme Court of the United States: Bulwark of a Limited Constitution," *South Texas Law Review* 26 (1986):458–66.

23. In 1998 two historians, David Thelen and Willi Paul Adams, called together scholars from different countries to explore the international history of foreign translations of the Declaration of Independence. For the published report, see "Interpreting the Declaration of Independence by Translation: A Round Table," *Journal of American History* 85, no. 4 (March 1999):1280–1460. What they discovered was that translators from different countries changed the meaning of the document when they attempted to convey its message through the filter of their respective cultures. Sometimes the translators found they could not convey certain concepts with any degree of accuracy, and at other times their translations led to misconceptions and misunderstandings. There were definite limits to translatability, and what was true about translating the Declaration applies equally to the other five seminal documents.

24. Gordon S. Wood, *The Radicalism of the American Revolution* (New York: Vintage Books, 1993), 95.

25. Samuel P. Huntington, *The Third Wave: Democratization in the Late Twentieth Century* (Norman: University of Oklahoma Press, 1991), 26.

CHAPTER 2

1. Thomas Jefferson to Roger O. Weightman, June 24, 1826, in *The Life and Selected Writings of Thomas Jefferson*, ed. Adrienne Koch and William Peden (New York: Modern Library, 1944), 729.

2. Carl J. Friedrich, *The Impact of American Constitutionalism Abroad* (Boston: Boston University Press, 1967), 6.

3. Jefferson to Roger O. Weightman, June 24, 1826, in Koch and Peden, eds., *The Life and Selected Writings of Thomas Jefferson*, 729.

4. For legal realists, who take the position that the Declaration is not a constitutional document, see John Phillip Reid, "The Irrelevance of the Declaration," in *Law in the American Revolution and the Revolution in Law: A Collection of Review Essays on American Legal History*, ed. Hendrik Hartog (New York: New York University Press, 1981), 46–89. Recall the statement of Professor Benno Schmidt, former dean of Columbia Law School and former president of Yale University: "American constitutional law is positive law, and the Declaration of Independence has no standing in constitutional interpretation whatsoever," in *Original Intent and the Framers of the Constitution: A Disputed Question*, ed. Harry V. Jaffa, Bruce Ledewitz, Robert L. Stone, and George Anastaplo (Washington, DC: Regnery Gateway, 1994), 5. For David Armitage, the Declaration is "neither a statute nor a constitution." See "The Declaration of Independence and International Law," *William and Mary Quarterly*, 3rd ser., 59 (2002):39. Despite some differences regarding the status of the Declaration as a near-constitutional document, Armitage's work and mine are complementary. Both view the document from a global perspective, consider its importance as a model for other declarations worldwide, and acknowledge its significance in regard to the lawful rights of states (though Armitage stresses the latter much more than I do). See his *The Declaration of Independence: A Global History* (Cambridge, MA: Harvard University Press, 2007).

The more general literature on the Declaration is, of course, voluminous. Some key works include the following: Carl L. Becker's classic *Declaration of Independence: A Study in the History of Political Ideas* (1922; repr., Birmingham, AL: Palladium Press, 2002); Julian Boyd, *The Declaration of Independence: The Evolution of the Text*, ed. Gerard W. Gawalt, rev. ed. (Washington, DC: Library of Congress, 1999); Scott Douglas Gerber, ed., *The Declaration of Independence: Origins and Impact* (Washington, DC: CQ Press, 2002); Morton White, *The Philosophy of the American Revolution* (New York: Oxford University Press, 1978); Garry Wills,

Inventing America: Jefferson's Declaration of Independence (Boston: Houghton Mifflin, 2002); and I. Bernard Cohen, *Science and the Founding Fathers: Science in the Political Thought of Jefferson, Franklin, Adams, and Madison* (New York: Norton, 1995). Pauline Maier's *American Scripture: Making the Declaration of Independence* (New York: Knopf, 1997) represents a remarkable scholarly achievement. It not only traces the antecedents of the document, presents an original interpretation, and dismisses many mythologies, but also deals with the afterlife of the Declaration to show how by sacralizing the text the American people have undermined the moral standard that the founders sought to establish.

5. Emer de Vattel, *The Law of Nations, or, Principles of the Law of Nature, Applied to the Conduct and Affairs of Nations and Sovereigns*, ed. Bela Kapossy and Richard Whatmore and trans. Thomas Nugent (1758; repr., Indianapolis: Liberty Fund, 2008). The first English translation from the original French *Le droit de gens* appeared in 1759 in numerous reprints and editions.

6. Armitage, *Declaration of Independence*, 38–44.

7. Ibid., 103. See also the enlightening critiques in the "Critical Forum" (a kind of "book review by committee") in which Lynn Hunt, Robert A. Ferguson, Laurent Dubois, and Daniel J. Hulsebach, as well as Armitage himself, analyze key concepts and contexts. *William and Mary Quarterly* 65, no. 2 (2008):347–69.

8. Armitage, *Declaration of Independence*, 16. Armitage made another breakthrough when he observed that in its day, the Declaration was aimed at several audiences: fellow lawyers, the Continental Congress, the divided thirteen colonies, and the world at large. To appeal to these various groups, the document had to be what Armitage called "jurisprudentially eclectic." It was partly grounded in natural-law theory (which was beginning to wane) and partly on positive law (which lay more in the future). Armitage noted:

> It was . . . somewhat ironic that the language of individual natural rights—which in its modern form had sprung from this [older] tradition—should become so prominent during the era of the American and French Revolution: only as the philosophical underpinnings that had made sense of it gave way did that language gain a temporary, though far from permanent, hegemony over [the] political discourse [of the day]. (89–90)

9. Armitage, *Declaration of Independence*, 16.

10. Maier, *American Scripture*, 48.

11. John Hancock to the New Jersey Convention, July 5, 1776, in *Letters of Delegates to Congress, 1774–1789*, ed. Paul H. Smith, Gerard W. Gawalt, Rosemary Fry Plakas, and Eugene Sheridan, 26 vols. (Washington, DC: Library of Congress, 1976–2000), 4:392. The added emphasis is mine to stress the idea that both "the People" and the states were addressed in the letter of transmittal, making them party to a constituent act.

For another essay stressing a point of view somewhat different from that held in this book, see Dennis J. Mahoney, "The Declaration as a Constitutional Document," in *The Framing and Ratification of the Constitution*, ed. Leonard W. Levy and Dennis J. Mahoney (New York: Macmillan, 1987), 54–68.

12. For an account of numerous disadvantaged groups who later sought to publish their grievances using the language of the Declaration, see Philip S. Foner, ed., *We the Other People: Alternative Declarations of Independence by Labor Groups, Farmers, Woman's Rights Advocates, Socialists, and Blacks, 1829–1975* (Urbana: University of Illinois Press, 1976).

13. James H. Kettner, *The Development of American Citizenship, 1608–1870* (Chapel Hill: University of North Carolina Press, 1978), 175.

14. Maier, *American Scripture*, 49.

15. *Pennsylvania Evening Post*, August 15, 1776, cited in Armitage, *Declaration of Independence*, 17–18 and n. 30.

16. Thad Tate, "The Social Contract in America, 1774–1787: Revolutionary Theory as a Conservative Instrument," *William and Mary Quarterly*, 3rd ser., 22 (1965):375–91.

17. In view of the importance of Armitage's work on the Declaration, one must address his assertion that the claim of rights of the individual in the second paragraph was "strictly subordinate" to the rights of states and that not until the global human rights movement in the second half of the twentieth century did the rights of individuals emerge as such an important part of the Declaration. See Armitage, *Declaration of Independence*, 17–18. Although I find Armitage's work admirable for its originality, historical accuracy, and breadth of vision, my interpretation differs from his in this instance. In my view, the rights of states and those of individuals were somewhat more balanced from the perspective of the Declaration's important contributions to modern world constitutionalism—a subject on which I had been working for many years before the publication of Armitage's book.

18. New York State Constitution (Fishkill, NY, 1777).

19. The dominance of Locke's thought in the ideology of both Britain and America has been challenged by recent revisionists. But even though counter-revisionists granted that his role in the early eighteenth century may have been overemphasized, they stress the centrality of his ideas after 1760 and the onset of the ensuing constitution crisis. See Isaac Kramnick, "Republican Revisionism Revisited," in *John Locke's Two Treatises of Government*, ed. Peter Laslett, rev. ed. (New York: New American Library, 1965), 637.
Among the best books explaining the Lockeian tradition in America and linking it to the Constitution in terms of political philosophy is Scott Douglas Gerber's multidisciplinary study, *To Secure These Rights: The Declaration of Independence and Constitutional Interpretation* (New York: New York University Press, 1995).

20. Bernard Bailyn, *The Ideological Origins of the American Revolution* (Cambridge, MA: Harvard University Press, 1967), 27.

21. Garrett Sheldon, "The Political Theory of the Declaration of Independence," in Gerber, ed., *The Declaration of Independence*, 16–28.

We owe the discovery of the strain of classical republican tradition primarily to Bailyn in his path-breaking *Ideological Origins of the American Revolution*. He uncovered a theory of politics at the heart of America's revolutionary ideology which could be traced to the anti-authoritarian tradition of seventeenth-century England. It gave rise to a conspiracy theory which postulated that power-seeking British ministers were bent on destroying liberty in both England and America. Gordon S. Wood, in *The Creation of the American Republic, 1776–1787* (Chapel Hill: University of North Carolina Press, 1969), elaborated on this theme, showing how the anti-authoritarian tradition was transformed after independence into a distinctive republican ideology. The paradigm of what came to be called the "republican synthesis" was completed by J. G. A. Pocock's *The Machiavellian Moment: Florentine Political Thought and the Atlantic Republican Tradition* (Princeton, NJ: Princeton University Press, 1975), which traced the republican tradition from ancient times to the Renaissance, thence to Cromwell's Commonwealthmen and to Harrington's philosophy in the seventeenth century. Wood in his preface to the 1998 edition of his *Creation* reinforced the republican synthesis by enlarging on the ramifications of republicanism, showing that it existed in both monarchical and republican governments. A wide-ranging symposium of scholars engaged in the "republican synthesis" controversy can be found in *The Republican Synthesis Revisited: Essays in Honor of George Athan Billias*, ed. by Milton M. Klein, Richard D. Brown, and John B. Hench (Worcester, MA: American Antiquarian Society, 1992).

For an older work tracing the antiauthoritarian tradition in England, see Caroline Robbins, *The Eighteenth-Century Commonwealthman: Studies in the Transmission, Development, and Circumstance of English Liberal Thought from the Restoration of Charles II until the War with the Thirteen Colonies* (Cambridge, MA: Harvard University Press, 1959).

22. Jefferson to Henry Lee, May 8, 1825, in *Thomas Jefferson: Writings*, ed. Merrill D. Peterson, Library of America, vol. 17 (New York: Viking Press, 1984), 1500–1.

23. The Declaration was responsible for the first important human rights proclamation in history. The notion of individual rights is usually grounded on three propositions: the equality of all humankind, the inherent rights of people, and the duty of government to protect such rights. "Human rights require three interlocking qualities," according to Lynn Hunt, a leading scholar on the subject. "Rights must be *natural* (inherent in human beings); *equal* (the same for everyone); and *universal* (applicable everywhere)." Such universalism has never been achieved, of course. But what began as a simple proposition

in America in 1776 turned into a sweeping global rights movement in the late twentieth century. See Lynn Hunt, *Inventing Human Rights* (New York: Norton, 2007), 20.

24. Maier, *American Scripture*, 213–14. One reason why Maier's book is so insightful in this regard is its Namierist approach. Namier's conception stressed interests more than ideas—and political interests at that. Maier confessed she was more at home and "more comfortable in the grubby world of eighteenth century politics" than in the transatlantic world of ideas. Her approach enabled her, therefore, to correct much of the received mythology on the Declaration. For Maier's Namierist approach, see Richard B. Bernstein, review of *American Scripture: Making the Declaration of Independence*, by Pauline Maier, H-Law, H-Net Reviews, September, 1997. Available at http://www.h-net.org/reviews/showrev.cgi?path=16070878688644.

25. For this information, I am indebted to John Phillip Reid, New York University School of Law, and to Stanley I. Kutler, University of Wisconsin, who supplied manuscript lists of relevant cases citing the Declaration. See also the published list in Gerber, ed., *The Declaration of Independence*, 303–14.

26. Richard B. Morris, *The Emerging Nations and the American Revolution* (New York: Harper & Row, 1970), xi.

27. Benjamin Fletcher Wright, *Consensus and Continuity, 1776–1787* (Westport, CT: Greenwood Press, 1984), 20.

28. Robert R. Palmer, "The Impact of the American Revolution Abroad," in *The Impact of the American Revolution Abroad: Papers Presented at the Fourth Symposium, 1975*, Library of Congress Symposia on the American Revolution (Washington, DC: Library of Congress, 1976), 13. The work of Willi Paul Adams, *The First American Constitutions: Republican Ideology and the Making of the State Constitutions in the Revolutionary Era,* trans. Rita Kimber and Robert Kimber, expanded ed. (Lanham, MD: Rowman & Littlefield, 2001), first helped correct the disregard of these documents that Palmer complained about in his essay.

29. Donald S. Lutz, *The Origins of American Constitutionalism* (Baton Rouge: Louisiana State University Press, 1988), 30-32; and Joseph Ellis's review of the Lutz book, *American Historical Review*, 91 (1990):902-3.

30. Robert B. Strassler, ed., and Richard Crawley, trans., *The Landmark Thucydides: A Comprehensive Guide to the Peloponnesian War* (New York: Free Press, 1996), 112.

For the controversy between those who believe American constitutional ideals were the same as British constitutional ideals and those who do not, see John Phillip Reid, *Constitutional History of the American Revolution*, vol. 1, *The Authority of Rights*, 4 vols. (Madison: University of Wisconsin Press, 1986), 1:50-51; and Shannon C. Stimson, *The American Revolution in the Law: Anglo-American Jurisprudence before John Marshall* (Princeton, NJ: Princeton University Press, 1990). See also the important article by Jack P. Greene, "From the Perspective of

the Law: Context and Legitimacy in the Origins of the American Revolution,"
Southern Quarterly 85 (1986):56-77.

The literature on the background of American constitutionalism in world history is voluminous. Besides the works of Bailyn and Wood and Pocock already mentioned, see the following selective works from an extensive bibliography: Charles H. McIlwain, *Constitutionalism, Ancient and Modern* (Indianapolis: Liberty Fund, 2007); Andrew C. McLaughlin, *The Confederation and the Constitution, 1783-1789* (1905; repr., New York: Collier Books, 1962); Andrew C. McLaughlin, *The Foundations of American Constitutionalism* (Gloucester, MA: P. Smith, 1972); and Forrest McDonald, *Novus Ordo Seclorum: The Intellectual Origins of the Constitution* (Lawrence: University Press of Kansas, 1985). For the Enlightenment, see Peter Gay, *The Enlightenment: An Interpretation*, 2 vols. (New York: Norton, 1977); Ernst Cassirer, *Philosophy of the Enlightenment*, trans. Fritz C. A. Koelin and James P. Pettegrove (1951; repr., Princeton, NJ: Princeton University Press, 1979); Paul Hazard, *European Thought in the Eighteenth Century: From Montesquieu to Lessing*, trans. J. Lewis May (1952; repr., Cleveland: World, 1963); Henry Steele Commager, *The Empire of Reason: How Europe Imagined and America Realized the Enlightenment* (Garden City, NY: Doubleday, 1977); and Henry F. May, *The Enlightenment in America* (New York: Oxford University Press, 1976). Absolutely crucial is Jack N. Rakove's brilliant book *Original Meanings: Politics and Ideas in the Making of the Constitution* (New York: Knopf, 1996).

31. R. R. Palmer, *The Age of the Democratic Revolution: A Political History of Europe and America, 1760–1800*, 2 vols. (Princeton, NJ: Princeton University Press, 1959 and 1964), 1:215.

32. The idea of recognizing that legislatures were not competent bodies on which to rest a constitution and that it should rest on the people goes back to John Lilburne, the English leader of the Levellers. Lilburne wanted to distinguish between "the people" and their "mere representatives." Hence he proposed in 1649 that an "Agreement of the people," or constitution, be signed by every person in voting to give a representative the powers defined in it. Others also proposed that a special convention, as distinct from Parliament, might be a device employed to frame "fundamental constitutions." But the idea made little headway in England. In 1688 such a convention in effect accused King James II of violating the social contract, deposed him, and wrote the Declaration of Right to limit the power of his successors. But then that body turned itself into a regular Parliament, thus transforming the declaration into a statute. As a result, it became like any other statute: it could be repealed or changed in the same way as any ordinary legislation. Therefore, England's "last and only constitutional convention failed to establish a constitution." The idea then was first implemented in Massachusetts. See Edmund S. Morgan, review of *We the People*, by Bruce Ackerman (Cambridge, MA: Harvard University Press, 1991), in *New York Review of Books*, April 23, 1992; and Leonard W. Levy, "Constitutional Convention,"

in *Encyclopedia of the American Constitution*, ed. Leonard W. Levy, Kenneth L. Karst, and Dennis J. Mahoney, 4 vols. (New York: Macmillan,1986), 1:359.

33. See Marc W. Kruman, *Between Authority and Liberty: State Constitution Making in Revolutionary America* (Chapel Hill: University of North Carolina Press, 1997), ix; and Edward McWhinney, *Constitution-Making: Principles, Process, Practice* (Toronto: University of Toronto Press, 1981), 36.

34. The idea of a constituent constitutional convention never caught on to become a universal method for framing constitutions throughout the world, however. Those attending constitutional conventions in other countries often did not reflect all the constituents, and the charters were framed by various groups usually made up of local elites or notables.

35. Palmer, *The Age of the Democratic Revolution*, 1:266.

36. Howard McBain, "Constitutions," in *Encyclopaedia of the Social Sciences*, ed. Edwin R. A. Seligman and Alvin Johnson, 15 vols. (New York: Macmillan, 1937), 4:261.

37. Richard D. Brown, "The Ideal of the Written Constitution: A Political Legacy of the Revolution," in *Legacies of the American Revolution*, ed. Larry R. Gerlach, James A. Dolph, and Michael Nicholls (Logan: Utah State University Press, 1978), 85–101, is the key article on this perspective of the first state constitutions.

38. Gordon S. Wood, "The American Revolution and Constitutional Theory," in *Encyclopedia of the American Constitution, Supplement 1*, ed. Leonard W. Levy, Kenneth L. Karst, and John G. West Jr. (New York: Macmillan, 1992), 17–18.

39. Wood, "The American Revolution and Constitutional Theory"; and Gordon S. Wood, *The American Revolution: A History* (New York: Modern Library, 2002), 66.

40. McIlwain, *Constitutionalism: Ancient and Modern*, 14.

41. Palmer, *The Age of the Democratic Revolution*, 1:501 and 2:110.

42. Willi Paul Adams, *The First American Constitutions* (1980 ed.), 140.

43. Since Rhode Island and Connecticut were already republics in fact, all they had to do was eliminate any mention of royal authority contained in their charters.

44. Gordon S. Wood, *The Radicalism of the American Revolution* (New York: Vintage Books, 1993), 229.

45. "Virginia Bill of Rights, June 12, 1776," in *Documents of American History*, ed. Henry Steele Commager and Milton Cantor, 2 vols., 10th ed. (Englewood Cliffs, NJ: Prentice-Hall, 1988), 1:103.

46. Lutz, *The Origins of American Constitutionalism*, 10.

47. Kruman, *Between Liberty and Authority*, 155.

48. Ibid., 85.

49. Merrill Jensen, *The Articles of Confederation: An Interpretation of the Social-Constitutional History of the American Revolution, 1774-1781* (1940; repr.; Madison: University of Wisconsin Press, 1970), took a different view. Jensen's

thesis was that the Articles might have provided a viable system of government with a few minor adjustments. This point of view was countered by Jack N. Rakove's *The Beginnings of National Politics: An Interpretive History of the Continental Congress* (Baltimore: Johns Hopkins University Press, 1982), 111-359; and Forrest McDonald, *Novus Ordo Seclorum*, 143–53, which are more convincing.

50. *The Records of the Federal Convention of 1787*, ed. Max Farrand, 4 vols., rev. ed. (New Haven, CT: Yale University Press, 1966), 1:166–67.

51. "Articles of Confederation," in Commager and Cantor, eds., *Documents of American History*, 1:111.

52. Wood, *Creation of the American Republic, 1776-1787*, 359.

53. Wood, *Radicalism of the American Revolution*, 179.

54. "Articles of Confederation," in Commager and Cantor, eds., *Documents of American History*, 1:112.

55. Wood, *Radicalism of the American Revolution*, 8.

56. Donald S. Lutz, "The Articles of Confederation," in *Roots of the Republic: American Founding Documents Interpreted*, ed. Stephen L. Schechter, Richard B. Bernstein, and Donald S. Lutz (Madison, WI: Madison House, 1990), 229.

57. Henry J. Bourguignon, *The First Federal Court: The Federal Appellate Prize Court of the American Revolution, 1775–1787* (Philadelphia: American Philosophical Society, 1977), 330–43.

58. Merrill Jensen, *The American Revolution within America* (New York: New York University Press, 1974), 140.

59. Richard P. McCormick Sr., "Ambiguous Authority: The Ordinances of the Confederation Congress, 1781-1789," *American Journal of Legal History* 41 (1997):421.

60. Peter S. Onuf, *The Origins of the Federal Republic: Jurisdictional Controversies in the United States, 1775-1787* (Philadelphia: University of Pennsylvania Press, 1983), 3–145. In a sophisticated conceptual analysis, Onuf indicates that the states were willing to expand the power of the Confederation government while at the same time they reinforced the idea of their own state sovereignty.

61. Peter S. Onuf, *Statehood and Union: A History of the Northwest Ordinance* (Bloomington: Indiana University Press, 1987).

62. Quoted in Peter S. Onuf, "The First Federal Constitution: The Articles of Confederation," in Levy and Mahoney, eds., *Framing and Ratification of the Constitution*, 82.

63. Friedrich, *Impact of American Constitutionalism Abroad*, 45.

64. Michael Kammen, "'The Most Wonderful Instrument Ever Drawn by the Hand of Man': Changing American Perceptions of Their Constitution," in *The United States Constitution: Its Birth, Growth, and Influence in Asia*, ed. J. Barton Starr (Hong Kong: Hong Kong University Press, 1989), 3. See also the thoughtful discussion by Walter F. Murphy, "Constitutions, Constitutionalism, and Democracy," in *Constitutionalism and Democracy: Transitions in the Contemporary*

World, ed. Douglas Greenberg, Stanley N. Katz, Melanie Beth Oliviero, and Steven C. Wheatley (New York: Oxford University Press, 1993), 3-15.

Recent writing on the Constitution is voluminous, but the best work on the Philadelphia Convention is still the old study by Max Farrand, *The Framing of the Constitution of the United States* (1913; repr., Buffalo, NY: W. S. Hein, 2000). Charles A. Beard's *An Economic Interpretation of the Constitution of the United States* (New York: Macmillan, 1913) has been pretty much discredited and succeeded by Forrest McDonald's *We the People: The Economic Origins of the Constitution* (New Brunswick, NJ: Transaction Publishers, 1992); and Forrest McDonald, *E Pluribus Unum: The Formation of the American Republic, 1776-1790*, 2nd ed. (Indianapolis: Liberty Press, 1979). Wood's *Creation of the American Republic, 1776-1787* and Rakove's *Original Meanings* cast the writing of the Constitution in a new context. Merrill Jensen provided a different approach in *The New Nation: A History of the United States during the Confederation, 1781-1789*, Northeastern Classics ed. (Boston: Northeastern University Press, 1981), as does E. James Ferguson's *The Power of the Purse: A History of American Public Finance, 1776-1790* (Chapel Hill: University of North Carolina Press, 1961). A recent work, Akhil Reed Amar, *America's Constitution: A Biography* (New York: Random House, 2005), focuses on the domestic history of the document.

65. *McCulloch v. Maryland*, in Commager and Cantor, eds., *Documents of American History*, 1:217.

66. John A. Hawgood, *Modern Constitutions since 1787* (London: Macmillan, 1939), 18.

67. Oscar Handlin and Mary Handlin, *The Dimensions of Liberty* (Cambridge, MA: Harvard University Press, 1961), 55.

68. The American experiences they drew on included, of course, the colonial charters in addition to the documents discussed in this chapter.

69. For an excellent treatment of the creation of the presidency in the Constitutional Convention, see Rakove, *Original Meanings*, 244–87; and also Wood, *Creation of the American Republic, 1776-1787*, 132–50.

70. Patrick Henry's speech of June 5, 1787, most memorably voiced this attitude toward the powers granted to the president: "It squints toward monarchy. Your president may easily become a king. I would rather . . . have a king, lords, and commons than a government replete with such insupportable evils." Quoted in Norine Dickson Campbell, *Patrick Henry: Patriot and Statesman* (New York: Devin-Adair, 1969), 345.

71. Farrand, ed., *Records of the Federal Convention of 1787*, 2:523.

72. Ibid., 1:65.

73. For the manner of indirect election of the president, see Shlomo Slonim, "The Electoral College at Philadelphia: The Evolution of an *Ad Hoc* Congress for the Selection of a President," *Journal of American History* 73 (1973):35-58. Slonim rejects the views of Progressive historians like Beard and the antideterminist

interpretation of scholars like John Roche and suggests instead that the electoral college with its indirect election was a practical solution to a practical problem: to protect the president from "gusts of popular passion." In his view, it represented a compromise to resolve, in part, the central dispute in the convention: the large state / small state controversy. See Slonim's book, *Framers' Construction / Beardian Deconstruction: Essays on the Constitutional Design of 1787* (New York: Peter Lang, 2001), whose argument has considerable merit.

74. Seymour Lipset, *The First New Nation: The United States in Historical and Comparative Perspective* (1963; repr., New Brunswick, NJ: Transaction Books, 2003), 17.

75. Madison, *Federalist 51*, in *The Federalist*, ed. Jacob E. Cooke (Middletown, CT: Wesleyan University Press, 1961), 350.

76. So great was the increase in the twentieth century of the presidential power that Arthur M. Schlesinger Jr. wrote a book on the subject entitled *The Imperial Presidency* (1973; repr., Boston: Houghton Mifflin, 1989), esp. ix–x.

77. Carl J. Friedrich, *Man and His Government: An Empirical Theory of Politics* (New York: McGraw-Hill, 1963), 188 ff.

The term *presidential government* with which presidentialism is associated is of later vintage. The term *parliamentary system* to describe Britain's government first came into being in the 1830s and 1840s. *Presidential system* was not used to refer to the United States, however, because it was considered misleading. Congress and the president were seen as equal and independent institutions, each one vying for supremacy. Not until 1860 did Robert von Mohl, a German constitutionalist, first coin the term *presidential government*. See Klaus von Beyme, *America as a Model: The Impact of American Democracy in the World* (New York: St. Martin's Press, 1987), 34.

78. Friedrich, *Impact of American Constitutionalism Abroad*, 27.

79. Ibid., 26; and Beyme, *America as a Model*, 34.

80. In Daniel J. Elazar's apt phrase, federalism can be simply defined as "self-rule plus shared rule," which applies equally to a central government and the constituent states. See his *Exploring Federalism*, (Tuscaloosa: University of Alabama Press, 1987), 612.

81. Carl J. Friedrich, "Origin and Development of the Concept [of Federalism]," in Friedrich, *Trends of Federalism in Theory and Practice* (New York: Praeger, 1968), 11-29. The precise meaning of the term *federalism* at the time of the founding is still a matter of debate among scholars. See Martin Diamond, "The *Federalist*, 1787-1788," in *History of Political Philosophy*, ed. Leo Strauss and Joseph Cropsey (Chicago: University of Chicago Press, 1981), 631–51. Three essays that debate Diamond's definition are to be found in *Publius* 15 (1985): Vincent Ostrom, "The Meaning of Federalism in *The Federalist*: A Critical Examination of the Diamond Theses," 1–21; Paul Peterson, "Federalism at the American Founding: In Defense of the Diamond Theses," 23–30; and Jean Yarborough,

"Rethinking *The Federalist*'s View of Federalism," 31–53. See also Daniel Walker Howe, "The Political Psychology of *The Federalist*," *William and Mary Quarterly*, 3rd ser., 44 (1987):485–509.

82. For Althusius, see Friedrich, *Impact of American Constitutionalism Abroad*, 44. Although there were earlier theories of federalism as a confederation of sovereign states, the American framers devised a pragmatic system that added the unique feature of establishing a relationship between the central government and individual citizens. See Friedrich, *Trends of Federalism in Theory and Practice*, esp. 13–14, 17, and 20–21. In 1932 the Harvard Political Classics Series published a Latin edition of Johannes Althusius's *Politica Methodice Digesta* for which Friedrich wrote the introduction.

83. McLaughlin, *Foundations of American Constitutionalism*, passim; and Daniel J. Elazar, *The American Constitutional Tradition* (Lincoln: University of Nebraska Press, 1988), 16-17.

For an older definition of American federalism, see Andrew McLaughlin, "The Background of American Federalism," *American Political Science Review* 12 (1918):215 ff. Also giving an older formulation of the theory of federalism is Kenneth Wheare in *Federal Government*, 4th ed. (New York: Oxford University Press, 1964), and *Modern Constitutions*, 2nd ed. (Oxford: Oxford University Press, 1966). Recent political scientists have generally abandoned Wheare's formulation, in part because he himself distinguished between "true federal" and "quasi-federal" based on his conviction that particular federal experiences and the "federal principle" as he defined it deviated from each other. Wheare then went on to contrast "federal government" (i.e., practice) and "federal constitution" (i.e., law or principle). Scholars have expressed skepticism about the usefulness of Wheare's "quasi-federal" concept or whether it describes any real phenomenon at all.

For another perspective on the problem of federalism regarding its location, see Jack P. Greene, *Peripheries and Center: Constitutional Development in the Extended Politics of the British Empire and the United States, 1607–1788* (Athens: University of Georgia Press, 1986).

84. John M. Murrin, "The Invention of American Federalism," in *Essays on Liberty and Federalism: The Shaping of the United States Constitution*, ed. John M. Murrin, David E. Navett, and Joyce S. Goldberg, Walter Prescott Web Memorial Lectures, University of Texas at Arlington (College Station: Texas A&M University Press, 1988), 21-47. See also Peter Onuf's introduction to the same volume, 9-10.

85. Friedrich, *Impact of American Constitutionalism Abroad*, 47.

86. Article 4, section 4, U.S. Constitution.

87. Wood, *The American Revolution*, 161.

88. At the risk of oversimplification, it may be said there are three classic models of democratic federalism in the world today: the American system, the Swiss system, and the Canadian system, which are discussed in later chapters.

The three definitions are from Elazar, *Exploring Federalism*, 612. There were, of course, models of federated states common to certain communist countries during the cold war, including the former Soviet Union, but they were nondemocratic in nature, so the federalism consequently was suspect regarding the distribution of powers.

The relationship of the federalizing process to the functioning of democracy is important. If no degree of democracy exists, as in a totalitarian regime or an absolute monarchy, shared government is impossible, and federalism has no basis for existence. However, as Friedrich noted, unlimited democracy likewise negates any basis for federalism. "If democracy is understood in terms of the absolute and unrestrained rule of the majority of members of a given political community, then an unresolved conflict between federalism and democracy must be recognized. Absolute democracy is incompatible with federalism because it [does not] permit an effective division of power." See Carl J. Friedrich, *Limited Government: A Comparison* (Englewood Cliffs, NJ: Prentice-Hall, 1974), 54. See also Morris, *Emerging Nations and the American Revolution*, 20. For a recent work that stresses the dangers of too much democracy, see Fareed Zakaria, *The Future of Freedom: Illiberal Democracy at Home and Abroad* (New York: Norton, 2004). For a discussion of the changes in the federal–state relationship over time, see Daniel J. Elazar, *American Federalism: A View from the States*, 2nd ed. (New York: Crowell, 1972).

89. Elazar, *The American Constitutional Tradition*, 13-14.

90. Karl Loewenstein, *Beiträge zu Staatssoziologie* (Tübingen: Mohr, 1961), 332, quoted in Beyme, *America as a Model*, 85.

The literature on judicial review is enormous. The following selected works were important to my research for this chapter: Bailyn, *Ideological Origins of the American Revolution*; Wood, *Creation of the American Republic, 1776-1787*; Reid, *Constitutional History of the American Revolution*; Alexander M. Bickel, *The Least Dangerous Branch: The Supreme Court at the Bar of Politics*, 2nd ed. (New Haven, CT: Yale University Press, 1986); William Blackstone, *Commentaries on the Laws of England*, facs. of 1st ed. of 1765–1769, 4 vols. (Chicago: University of Chicago Press, 2002); Charles McIlwain, *The High Court of Parliament and Its Supremacy: An Historical Essay on the Boundaries between Legislation and Adjudication in England* (1910; repr., New York: Arno Press, 1979); Oscar Handlin and Mary Handlin, eds., *Popular Sources of Political Authority: Documents on the Massachusetts Constitution of 1780* (Cambridge, MA: Harvard University Press, 1966); William E. Nelson, *Americanization of the Common Law: The Impact of Legal Change on Massachusetts Society, 1760-1830* (Cambridge, MA: Harvard University Press, 1975); William E. Nelson, *Roots of American Bureaucracy, 1830-1900* (Cambridge, MA: Harvard University Press, 1992); William E. Leuchtenburg, *The Supreme Court Reborn: The Constitutional Revolution in the Age of Roosevelt* (New York: Oxford University Press, 1995); Charles F. Hobson, *The Great Chief*

Justice: John Marshall and the Rule of Law (Lawrence: University Press of Kansas, 1996); George Lee Haskins and Herbert A. Johnson, *Foundations of Power: John Marshall, 1801-15* (New York: Macmillan, 1981); Rakove, *Beginnings of National Politics*; Rakove, *Original Meanings*; Maeva Marcus, ed., *Origins of the Federal Judiciary: Essays on the Judiciary Act of 1789* (New York: Oxford University Press, 1992); and R. Kent Newmyer, *Supreme Court Justice Joseph Story: Statesman of the Old Republic* (Chapel Hill: University of North Carolina Press, 1985).

Works focusing on the *Marbury v. Madison* decision and its implications include William E. Nelson, *Marbury v. Madison: The Origins and Legacy of Judicial Review* (Lawrence: University Press of Kansas, 2000); Robert Lowry Clinton, *Marbury v. Madison and Judicial Review* (Lawrence: University Press of Kansas, 1989); Scott Douglas Gerber, ed., *Seriatim: The Supreme Court before John Marshall* (New York: New York University Press, 1998); Jack M. Sosin, *The Aristocracy of the Long Robe: The Origins of Judicial Review in America* (Westport, CT: Greenwood Press, 1989); Jean Edward Smith, *John Marshall: Definer of the Nation* (New York: Henry Holt, 1996); Silvia Snowiss, *Judicial Review and the Law of the Constitution* (New Haven, CT: Yale University Press, 1990); Herbert A. Johnson, *The Chief Justiceship of John Marshall, 1801-1835* (Columbia: University of South Carolina Press, 1997); Christopher Wolfe, *The Rise of Modern Judicial Review: From Constitutional Interpretation to Judge-Made Law*, rev. ed. (Lanham, MD: Rowman & Littlefield, 1994); Gordon S. Wood, "The Origins of Judicial Review Revisited, or How the Marshall Court Made More Out of Less," *Washington and Lee Law Review* 56 (1999):787–817; Gordon S. Wood, "The Origins of Judicial Review," *Suffolk University Law Review* 22 (1988):1293–1307; Jack Rakove, "The Origins of Judicial Review: A Plea for New Contexts," *Stanford Law Review* 49 (1997):1031–65. Philip Hamburger, *Law and Judicial Duty* (Cambridge, MA: Harvard University Press, 2008). Scott Douglas Gerber has a forthcoming study on the origins of an independent judiciary which examines the practices of the original thirteen states and their colonial antecedents.

91. The American pattern of judicial review is quite different, of course, from that of the United Kingdom, which is distinguished precisely by the lack of judicial review of parliamentary statutes. The unique feature of the British constitution—the principle of the sovereignty of Parliament—makes the American system inapplicable.

> It implies that, even if it is true that British courts are the ultimate guarantors of the rule of law, they are bound to apply an Act of Parliament irrespective of the view the judges take of its morality or justice, or of its effects on important individual liberties or human rights.

See Allan R. Brewer-Carias, *Judicial Review in Comparative Law* (Cambridge: Cambridge University Press, 1989), 2. There are indications that Britain is undergoing a change with respect to the sovereignty of Parliament because of the Human Rights Act of 1998.

Note that Kenneth Wheare points out that the courts in unitary countries have the power, unless it is expressly denied to them, to indicate whether a government institution is acting within the limits of its power. See *Federal Government* (1947 ed.), 49.

92. The two cases were *Trevett v. Weeden* in 1786, the Rhode Island case in which technically the superior court did not throw out the law but just refused to entertain an action for damages under the paper money force act because it said the act was "internally repugnant" and denied a right to a jury "according to the law of the land." In *Bayard v. Singleton* in 1781 in North Carolina, the U.S. Supreme Court ruled that an act of the North Carolina legislature was unconstitutional. The two cases established clear precedents for judicial review on the state level.

93. Thomas Jefferson, *Notes on the State of Virginia, 1787*, in Peterson, ed., *Thomas Jefferson: Writings*, 245.

94. Alexander Hamilton, *Federalist 78*, in Cooke, ed., *The Federalist*, 521–30.

95. *Marbury v. Madison* is commonly accepted as the case that established the principle of judicial review, though some legal historians challenge that assumption as incorrect.

96. George Washington to Alexander Hamilton, August 28, 1788, in *Writings of George Washington: From the Original Manuscript Sources, 1745-1799*, ed. John C. Fitzpatrick, 39 vols. (Washington, DC: U.S. Government Printing Office, 1931–1944), 30:66.

97. Roy P. Fairfield, *Federalist Papers: A Collection of Essays Written in Support of the Constitution of the United States*, 2nd ed. (Baltimore: Johns Hopkins Press, 1981), has compiled the foreign editions of the work published up to 1981. See his bibliographical appendices, 308-11 and 321.

98. Douglass Adair, "*The Federalist Papers*: A Review Article," *William and Mary Quarterly*, 3rd ser., 22 (1965), 133, writes that "it was a world classic, a searching analysis . . . of the enduring universal problems of every democratic state."

99. W. R. Brock, introduction to *The Federalist* (London: Dutton, 1961), quoted in Adair, "*The Federalist Papers*," 133.

100. Bernard Bailyn, *To Begin the World Anew: The Genius and Ambiguities of the American Founders* (New York: Knopf, 2003), 107.

101. Viewing *The Federalist* from a worldwide perspective rather than the domestic view of American history represented a major shift in American historiography. Before the 1930s, the treatise had been seen within a narrowly nationalistic framework. After that time, however, scholars entered a new age of Publius scholarship, one that evaluated the work from the broad perspective of world history.

The literature on *The Federalist* is voluminous, and the interpretations of the work vary widely. The list given here proved most useful to me, including the recent papers editions of the works of Alexander Hamilton, James Madison, and John Jay. One issue on which scholars disagree is the influence of Lockeian liberalism on the treatise. In *Explaining America: The Federalist* (Garden City, NY: Doubleday, 1981), Garry Wills argues (mistakenly, in my view) that the Scottish Enlightenment thinkers, not Locke, were the main source for Publius's ideas. At the opposite end of the spectrum, Martin Diamond and Thomas Pangle maintain that Locke had the greatest influence. See Martin Diamond, "Democracy and *The Federalist*," in *As Far as Republican Principles Will Admit: Essays by Martin Diamond*, ed. William A. Schambra (Washington, DC: AEI Press, 1992), 27–30; and Thomas Pangle, *The Spirit of Modern Republicanism: The Moral Vision of the American Founders and the Philosophy of Locke* (Chicago: University of Chicago Press, 1988), passim. David F. Epstein, in *The Political Theory of The Federalist* (Chicago: University of Chicago Press, 1984), claims that the literary antecedents of the work were Locke, Hume, and Montesquieu; and in *Philosophy, The Federalist and the Constitution* (New York: Oxford University Press, 1987), Morton White states the treatise was a combination of Locke's political philosophy and Hume's political science. For a recent commentary on the presumed lessening influence of *The Federalist*, see also Donald L. Horowitz, "*The Federalist* Abroad in the World," Duke Law School Legal Studies Research Papers no. 194, March 2008.

In the meantime, the writing on the Anti-federalists exploded. The most trenchant of the early analyses is Cecelia Kenyon's "Men of Little Faith: The Anti-federalists on the Nature of Representative Government," *William and Mary Quarterly*, 3rd ser., 12 (1955):3–46. This work was updated in Stanley Elkins, Eric McKitrick, and Leo Weinstein, eds., *Men of Little Faith: Selected Writings of Cecelia Kenyon*, with an insightful introduction emphasizing the originality of Kenyon's thought at the time her essays were first published (Amherst: University of Massachusetts Press, 2002). Herbert J. Storing, ed., *The Complete Anti-Federalist*, 7 vols. (Chicago: University of Chicago Press, 1981), contains much material, but it is not "complete" and must be supplemented by the Merrill Jensen project: *The Documentary History of the Ratification of the Constitution*, ed. John P. Kaminski, Gaspar J. Saladino, Richard Leffler, Charles H. Schoenleber, and Margaret A. Hogan; Bernard Bailyn, comp. and ed., *The Debate on the Constitution: Federalist and Antifederalist Speeches, Articles, and Letters during the Struggle for Ratification*, Library of America, 2 vols. (New York: Viking Press, 1993); Saul Cornell, *The Other Founders: Anti-Federalism and the Dissenting Tradition in America, 1788–1828* (Chapel Hill: University of North Carolina Press, 1999); Harry N. Scheiber, "Federalism and Constitutional Order," in *American Law and the Constitutional Order: Historical Perspectives*, ed. Lawrence M. Friedman and Harry N. Scheiber (Cambridge, MA: Harvard University Press, 1978), 85–98; and David Waldstreicher, *In the Midst of Perpetual Fetes: The Making of American*

Nationalism, 1776–1820 (Chapel Hill: University of North Carolina Press,1997). See also Murray Dry, "The Debate over Ratification of the Constitution," in *The Blackwell Encyclopedia of the American Revolution*, ed. Jack P. Greene and J. R. Pole (Cambridge, MA: Blackwell Reference, 1991), 471–85; Herbert Storing, *What the Anti-Federalists Were For*, with editorial assistance by Murray Dry (Chicago: University of Chicago Press, 1981); Wood, *The Creation of the American Republic, 1776-1787*; Bernard Bailyn, *Faces of Revolution: Personalities and Themes in the Struggle for American Independence* (New York: Knopf, 1990); Jackson Turner Main, *The Anti-federalists: Critics of the Constitution, 1781-1788* (1961; repr., Chapel Hill: University of North Carolina Press, 2004); Richard C. Sinopoli, *The Foundations of American Citizenship: Liberalism, the Constitution, and Civic Virtue* (New York: Oxford University Press, 1992); selected essays in Richard Beeman, Stephen Botein, and Edward C. Carter, eds., *Beyond Confederation: Origins of the Constitution and American National Identity* (Chapel Hill: University of North Carolina Press, 1987); and Michael Lienisch, "In Defense of the Anti-federalists," *History of Political Thought* 4 (1983):65–87.

102. Other ways of looking at *The Federalist* have been examined by three revisionist historians on that subject. In his 1969 *Creation of the American Republic, 1776-1787*, Gordon S. Wood pictured the Anti-federalist leaders in terms of their notions of populist democracy. They opposed the new national government for the same reasons the Federalists favored it. That is, its structure and distance from the people would preclude actual and local interest representation and would prevent "those who were not rich, well-born or prominent from exercising political power" (516). The Federalists, in contrast, introduced institutional devices in the Constitution to contain popular control with their "new science of politics" expressed in *The Federalist*: "Thus, the Federalists did not reject democratic politics in order to control and mitigate its effects. In short, they offered the country an elitist theory of democracy" (517).

Herbert Storing edited the writings of the Anti-federalists in the 1980s in *The Complete Anti-Federalist* and *What the Anti-Federalists Were For*. He described them as thoughtful politicians who critiqued the solutions for the national government set forth in *The Federalist*.

In *The Other Founders*, Saul Cornell took a broader view and examined the followership as well as the elite leaders of the Anti-federalists and discovered a wider diversity of ideas and rhetorical strategies among them. Cornell sought to extend the influence of their ideas into the Jeffersonian and Jacksonian eras but, in my view, does not make his case.

103. Gerry spoke more than 153 times during the convention and ranks as the sixth most talkative delegate. See George Athan Billias, *Elbridge Gerry, Founding Father and Republican Statesman* (New York: McGraw-Hill, 1976), 158.

104. Madison Notes, September 15, 1787, in Farrand, ed., *Records of the Federal Convention of 1787*, 2:633.

105. Elbridge Gerry, "Hon. Mr. Gerry's Objections," *Massachusetts Sentinel*, November 3, 1787, in *The Documentary History of the Ratification of the Constitution*, ed. Kaminski et al., 13:549. Gerry's essay was reprinted forty-six times, more than any other Anti-Federalist piece. Cornell, *The Other Founders*, 28.

106. Kaminski et al., eds., *The Documentary History*, 13:549.

107. Billias, *Elbridge Gerry*, 197–98.

108. George Mason, "Objections to the Constitution of Government Formed by the Convention (1787)," in Storing, ed., *The Complete Anti-Federalist*, 2:13.

109. Farrand, ed., *Records of the Federal Convention of 1787*, 1:66.

110. Ibid., 2:632.

111. Bailyn, *To Begin the World Anew*, 108–9.

112. Billias, *Elbridge Gerry*, 154.

113. *Federalist* 10, in Cooke, ed., *The Federalist*, 64–65.

114. *Federalist* 15, in Cooke, ed., *The Federalist*, 93.

115. *Federalist* 16, in Cooke, ed., *The Federalist*, 101 and 103.

116. *Federalist* 25, in Cooke, ed., *The Federalist*, 162–63.

117. *Federalist* 30, in Cooke, ed., *The Federalist*, 189 and 191.

118. *Federalist* 39, in Cooke, ed., *The Federalist*, 257 and 256.

119. *Federalist* 51, in Cooke, ed., *The Federalist*, 352.

120. *Federalist* 67–71, in Cooke, ed., *The Federalist*, 452–86.

121. *Federalist* 78, in Cooke, ed., *The Federalist*, 526.

122. John Jay, *Federalist* 4, in Cooke, ed., *The Federalist*, 21.

123. *Federalist* 51, in Cooke, ed., *The Federalist*, 348.

124. Wood, *The American Revolution*, 159. In this discussion of the change in thinking regarding divided sovereignty, I have leaned heavily on Wood.

125. Wood, *The American Revolution*, 161.

126. Bernard Schwartz, "Magna Carta, 1215," "Petition of Right, 1628," and "Bill of Rights, 1689," in *The Bill of Rights: A Documentary History*, comp. Bernard Schwartz, 2 vols. (New York: Chelsea House, 1971), 1:12, 19–21, and 41–46.

The literature on the Bill of Rights, as might be expected, is extensive. A good place to start is with the documentary histories and sources. Jensen et al., eds., *Documentary History of the Ratification of the Constitution; Documentary History of the First Federal Congress of the United States of America, March 4, 1789–March 3, 1791*, ed. Linda Grant DePauw, Charlene Bangs Bickford, Lavonne Siegel Hauptman, Helen E. Veit, Kenneth R. Bowling, and William Charles DiGiacomantonio, 17 vols. to date (Baltimore: Johns Hopkins University Press, 1972–); Gales, comp. and ed., *The Debates and Proceedings in the Congress of the United States*.

The following books address the Bill of Rights either directly or in a peripheral way: Louis Henkin, *The Age of Rights* (New York: Columbia University Press, 1990); Robert Allen Rutland, *The Birth of the Bill of Rights, 1776–1791*, bicentennial ed. (Boston: Northeastern University Press, 1991); Robert Allen Rutland, *The Ordeal of the Constitution: The Anti-federalists and the Ratification Struggle of 1787–1788* (1966; repr., Boston: Northeastern University Press, 1983); Michael J. Lacey and Knud Haakonssen, eds., *A Culture of Rights: The Bill of Rights in Philosophy, Politics, and Law, 1791 and 1991* (Cambridge: Cambridge University Press, 1991); Bailyn, *The Debate on the Constitution*; Wood, *Creation of the American Republic*; Wood, *Radicalism of the American Revolution*; Patrick T. Conley and John P. Kaminski, eds., *The Constitution and the States: The Role of the Original Thirteen in the Framing and Adoption of the Federal Constitution* (Madison, WI: Madison House, 1988); Ronald Dworkin, *Taking Rights Seriously* (Cambridge, MA: Harvard University Press, 1977); Leonard W. Levy, *Original Intent and the Framers' Constitution* (New York: Macmillan, 1988); Terrence Ball, James Farr, and Russell L. Hanson, eds., *Political Innovation and Conceptual Change* (Cambridge: Cambridge University Press, 1989); Rakove, *Original Meanings*; and Donald Hoffman and Peter J. Albert, eds., *The Bill of Rights: Government Proscribed* (Charlottesville: University Press of Virginia, 1997). Gordon S. Wood has written two important articles with the same title: "The Origins of the American Bill of Rights." The first appeared in the *Proceedings of the American Antiquarian Society* 101 (1991):255–74. The second, which is cast in the context of world rather than American history and is therefore more pertinent to this study, appeared in *La revue Tocqueville* 14 (1993):33–47.

For the fight of the Federalists and Anti-federalists over the Bill of Rights, see, for the Federalists, Lance Banning, *The Sacred Fire of Liberty: James Madison and the Founding of the Federal Republic* (Ithaca, NY: Cornell University Press, 1995); Jack Rakove, "The Madisonian Moment," *University of Chicago Law Review* 55 (1998):473–505; McDonald, *Novus Ordo Seclorum*; and Epstein, *The Political Theory of the Federalist*. For the Anti-federalists, see Cornell, *The Other Founders*; Storing, *What the Anti-Federalists Were For*; Steven R. Boyd, *The Politics of Opposition: Anti-federalists and the Acceptance of the Constitution* (Millwood, NY: KTO Press, 1979); Billias, *Elbridge Gerry*; Ralph L. Ketcham, ed., *The Anti-Federalist Papers; and, The constitutional convention debates* (New York: Signet Classics, 2003); Main, *The Antifederalists*; and Michael Allen Gillespie and Michael Lienisch, eds., *Ratifying the Constitution* (Lawrence: University Press of Kansas, 1989).

For a review of the historiography, see James Hutson, "The Birth of the Bill of Rights: The State of Current Scholarship," *Prologue* 20 (1988):143–61; and Gaspar Saladino, "The Bill of Rights: A Bibliographic Essay," in *Contexts of the Bill of Rights*, ed. Stephen L. Schechter and Richard B. Bernstein (Albany: New York State Commission on the Bicentennial of the United States Constitution, 1990), 65–109. The best historiographical essay on the Anti-federalists is Saul Cornell's "The Changing Historical Fortunes of the Anti-Federalists," *Northwestern University Law Review* 84 (1989):39–74, which needs updating.

127. Logan quoted in Wood, "The Origins of the American Bill of Rights," *La revue Tocqueville*, 38.

128. James Wilson in the Pennsylvania Convention, November 28, 1787, in Jensen et al., eds., *The Documentary History of the Ratification of the Constitution*, 2:388–89.

129. Hamilton, *Federalist* 84, in Cooke, ed., *The Federalist*, 378.

130. Madison to Jefferson, October 18, 1788, in *Papers of James Madison*, ed. William T. Hutchinson and William M. E. Rachal, 17 vols. (Chicago: University of Chicago Press, 1962–), vols. 11–17, ed. Robert Allen Rutland et al. (Charlottesville: University Press of Virginia, 1977–), vol. 11, 297–98.

131. Jefferson to William Stephens Smith, February 2, 1788, in *Papers of Thomas Jefferson*, ed. Julian P. Boyd, Lyman H. Butterfield, Charles T. Cullen, John Catanzarini, Barbara B. Oberg, et al., 33 vols. (Princeton, NJ: Princeton University Press, 1950–), 12:558.

132. Rutland, *The Birth of the Bill of Rights*, 129-30.

133. Rutland, ed., *Papers of James Madison*, 12:197-210.

134. *Independent Chronicle*, January 22, 1789.

135. Helen Hill Miller, *George Mason, Gentleman Revolutionary* (Chapel Hill: University of North Carolina Press, 1975), 321-22.

136. Storing, *What the Anti-Federalists Were For*, 65. For a more thorough account, see also Storing's *The Complete Anti-Federalist*.

CHAPTER 3

1. Durand Echeverria, *Mirage in the West: A History of the French Image of American Society to 1815* (Princeton, NJ: Princeton University Press, 1957), 39.

2. For a statement of "Atlantic history" as a grand design, see Bernard Bailyn, *Atlantic History: Concepts and Contours* (Cambridge, MA: Harvard University Press, 2005) and his earlier essay, "The Idea of Atlantic History," *Itinerario* 20 (1996): 1- 27. Bailyn's work represented an attempt to break from the narrow approach of viewing history from the national perspective of a single state to a more pan-Atlantic treatment in keeping with the new age of globalism. See David Armitage and Michael J. Braddick, eds., *The British Atlantic World, 1500-1800*, (New York: Palgrave Macmillan, 2000), 11 and 235.

3. My citing Palmer does not mean that I subscribe wholeheartedly to the Palmer-Godechot hypothesis. See R. R. Palmer, *The Age of the Democratic Revolution: A Political History of Europe and America, 1760-1800*, 2 vols. (Princeton, NJ: Princeton University Press, 1959 and 1964), and Jacques Godechot, *France and the Atlantic Revolution of the Eighteenth Century, 1770-1790*, trans. by Herbert H. Rowen (New York: Free Press, 1965).

Palmer's synthetic study claimed the "Atlantic world" was affected by a single wave of revolutions in which aristocratic and oligarchical "constituted bodies" were challenged by hitherto excluded groups. Palmer's interpretation may have gone too far. His argument linking the American and French revolutions to each other and to the upheavals in other parts of Europe–Switzerland, the Netherlands, Belgium, Poland, and Ireland–has been criticized by scholars who did not find the similarities in these events that he did. For example, a case study by T. C. W. Blanning, *The French Revolution in Germany: Occupation and Resistance in the Rhineland, 1792-1802* (New York: Oxford University Press, 1983), shows that the Palmer hypothesis cannot be applied to the Rhineland during the period under consideration.

But far more such case studies would have to be done before the Palmer-Godechot hypothesis could be considered discredited. Palmer's great insight regarding the constituent power of the people at work and its recognition as America's greatest contribution to world constitutionalism remains the best single explanation for the growth of democracy in the Atlantic basin. Despite the criticisms, Palmer's seminal work is still the best place to start for studies in constitutional history in the region because it places the American Revolution and its aftermath in a global perspective and comparative Atlantic history.

4. Carl J. Friedrich, *The Impact of American Constitutionalism Abroad* (Boston: Boston University Press, 1967), 12.

5. The concept is developed by Geoffrey Bruun in "The Constitutional Cult in the Early Nineteenth Century," in *The Constitution Reconsidered*, ed. Conyers Read (New York: Columbia University Press, 1938), 261–69, and my discussion closely follows his essay.

6. Quoted in Bruun, "The Constitutional Cult," 262.

7. Quoted in ibid., 263.

8. Ibid., 267.

9. Howard Mumford Jones, *O Strange New World: American Culture: The Formative Years* (1964; repr., Westport, CT: Greenwood Press, 1982), viii.

10. Echeverria, *Mirage in the West*.

11. Although not one of the six seminal documents, Thomas Paine's *Common Sense: Addressed to the Inhabitants of America* (Philadelphia: R. Bell, 1776) is included here because of its extraordinary constitutional significance, and the same applies to Paine himself.

12. See Thomas J. Schlereth, *The Cosmopolitan Ideal in Enlightenment Thought: Its Form and Function in the Ideas of Franklin, Hume, and Voltaire, 1694-1790* (South Bend, IN: Notre Dame University Press, 1977).

13. See Eric Foner, *Tom Paine and Revolutionary America*, updated ed. (New York: Oxford University Press, 2008), passim.

The literature on Paine is immense, but the following works were especially helpful in this study: Alfred Owen Aldridge, *Man of Reason: The Life of Thomas Paine* (Philadelphia: Lippincott, 1959); David Freeman Hawke, *Paine* (New York: Harper & Row, 1974); Foner, *Tom Paine and Revolutionary America*; Jack

Fruchtman Jr., *Thomas Paine and the Religion of Nature* (Baltimore: Johns Hopkins University Press, 1993); John Keane, *Tom Paine: A Political Life* (Boston: Little, Brown, 1995); Marilyn Butler, ed., *Burke, Paine, Godwin and the Revolutionary Controversy* (Cambridge: Cambridge University Press, 1984); David A. Wilson, *Paine and Cobbett: The Transatlantic Connection* (Kingston, ON: McGill–Queens University Press, 1988); Bernard Bailyn, "Common Sense," *Fundamental Testaments of the American Revolution*, Library of Congress Symposia on the American Revolution (Washington, DC: Library of Congress, 1973); Colin Bonwick, *English Radicals and the American Revolution* (Chapel Hill: University of North Carolina Press, 1977); J. G. A. Pocock, ed., *Three British Revolutions, 1641, 1688, 1776* (Princeton, NJ: Princeton University Press, 1980); and Moncure Daniel Conway, ed., *The Writings of Thomas Paine*, 4 vols. (1894–1896; repr., New York: AMS Press, 1967).

14. William R. Everdell, *The End of Kings: A History of Republics and Republicans* (New York: Free Press, 1983), 160.

15. Conway, ed., *Writings of Thomas Paine*, 1:99.

16. Ibid., 1:72–84 and 99.

17. Ibid., 1:99 (italics added).

18. Cecilia Kenyon, "Where Paine Went Wrong," *American Political Science Review* 45 (1951):1087; and Conway, ed., *Writings of Thomas Paine*, 1:69–72.

19. Conway, ed., *Writings of Thomas Paine*, 1:98.

20. Ibid.

21. Kenyon, "Where Paine Went Wrong," 1092.

22. Conway, ed., *Writings of Thomas Paine*, 1:61.

23. Ibid., 1:54.

24. Wilson, *Paine and Cobbett*, 4; and John Adams, *Diary and Autobiography of John Adams*, ed. L. H. Butterfield, Leonard C. Faber, and Wendell D. Garrett, 4 vols. (Cambridge, MA: Harvard University Press, 1961), 3:333. For one interpretation of the ideas current at the time and focusing on the recovery of languages available to a writer in a given period, see J. G. A. Pocock, *Politics, Language, and Time: Essays on Political Thought and History* (New York: Atheneum, 1971).

25. Paine, "*Common Sense*," app., in *Collected Writings*, ed. Eric Foner, Library of America (New York: Penguin Books, 1995), 52–53.

26. Foner, *Tom Paine and Revolutionary America*, xi.

27. Solomon Lutnick, *The American Revolution and the British Press, 1775–1783* (Columbia: University of Missouri Press, 1967), 45–49.

28. Richard Price, *Discourse on the Love of Our Country, Delivered on Nov. 4, 1789* (London: T. Cadell, 1789).

29. Edmund Burke, *Reflections on the Revolution in France, and on the Proceedings in Certain Societies in London Relative to That Event* (London: J. Dodsley, 1790).

30. Conway, ed., *Writings of Thomas Paine*, 1:118–19.

31. Peter J. Stanlis, "Edmund Burke in the Twentieth Century," in *The Relevance of Edmund Burke*, ed. Peter J. Stanlis (New York: P. J. Kenedy, 1964), 26.

32. Paine, "Rights of Man," part 1, in Conway, ed., *Writings of Thomas Paine*, 2:309–10 (italics in original). Paine was not always ahistorical in his views. He sometimes echoed strains drawn from the seventeenth-century theory of the Norman Yoke, the myth that the free constitution of Anglo-Saxon England had been extinguished by the Norman conquerors of the eleventh century. See James A. Epstein, *Radical Expression: Political Language, Ritual, and Symbol in England, 1790–1850* (New York: Oxford University Press, 1994), 5.

33. George Spater, "American Revolutionary, 1774–89," in *Citizen of the World: Essays on Thomas Paine*, ed. Ian Dyck (London: Christopher Helm, 1987), 47.

34. Paine, "Rights of Man," part 2, in Conway, ed., *Writings of Thomas Paine*, 2:424.

35. Ibid., 429.

36. See Michael Durey, *Transatlantic Radicals and the Early American Republic* (Lawrence: University Press of Kansas, 1997).

37. Hawke, *Paine*, 184.

38. Carl L. Becker, "Thomas Paine," in *Dictionary of American Biography*, ed. Allen Johnson and Dumas Malone, 22 vols. (New York: Scribner, 1928–1958), 14:165.

39. See Foner, *Tom Paine and Revolutionary America* (1st ed.), 269–70; and John Belchem, "Republicanism, Popular Constitutionalism, and the Radical Platform in Early Nineteenth Century England," *Social History* 6 (1981):passim.

40. Louis Henkin, *The Rights of Man Today* (Boulder, CO: Westview Press, 1978), 135.

41. John A. Hawgood, *Modern Constitutions since 1787* (London: Macmillan, 1939), 44.

42. Palmer, *Age of the Democratic Revolution*, 1:265 and 352–53. See also Thomas Gorman, *America and Belgium: A Study of the Influence of the United States upon the Belgian Revolution of 1789–1790* (London: T. F. Unwin, 1925), vii; Richard B. Morris, *The Emerging Nations and the American Revolution* (New York: Harper & Row, 1970), 91; and E. H. Kossmann, *The Low Countries, 1780–1940* (Oxford: Clarendon Press, 1978), 60.

43. Wiktor Osiatyński, "Constitutionalism and Rights in the History of Poland," in *Constitutionalism and Rights: The Influence of the United States Constitution Abroad*, ed. Louis Henkin and Albert J. Rosenthal (New York: Columbia University Press, 1990), 285 and 310, nn. 5 and 6.

44. David Thelen, "Reception of the Declaration of Independence," in *The Declaration of Independence: Origins and Impact*, ed. Scott Douglas Gerber (Washington, DC: CQ Press, 2002), 194–95. Newspapers carried copies of the Declaration to major cities: London in mid-August; Edinburgh, August 20; Dublin, August 24; London, August 30; Copenhagen, September 2; Florence, mid-

September; and a German translation in Basel in October. See David Armitage, "The Declaration of Independence and International Law," *William and Mary Quarterly*, 3rd ser., 59 (2002):nn. 48–54.

45. Gordon S. Wood, *The Radicalism of the American Revolution* (New York: Vintage Books, 1993), 96.

46. Committee of Secret Correspondence to Silas Deane, July 8, 1776, in *Letters of Delegates to Congress, 1774–1789*, ed. Paul H. Smith, Gerard W. Gawalt, Rosemary Fry Plakas, and Eugene R. Sheridan, 26 vols. (Washington, DC: Library of Congress, 1976–2000), 4:405.

47. Silas Deane to Gentlemen [of the Continental Congress], November 28, 1776, in *Pennsylvania Magazine of History and Biography* 11 (1887):199–200.

48. Palmer, *Age of the Democratic Revolution*, 1:249. For a full account of the publication of the Declaration in the French press, see Durand Echeverria, "French Publications of the Declaration of Independence and the American Constitutions, 1776–1783," *Papers of the Bibliographical Society of America* 47 (1953):313–38.

49. Bailyn, *To Begin the World Anew*, 134.

50. Echeverria, "French Publications of the Declaration of Independence and the American Constitutions," 322–23; and Elise Marienstras and Naomi Wulf, "French Translations and Reception of the Declaration of Independence," *Journal of American History* 85 (March 1999):1304–5.

51. *Constitutions des treize États-Unis de L'Amérique*, trans. Louis Alexandre, duc de La Rochefoucauld-d'Enville (Paris: P. D. Pierres, Pissot, 1783); see Marienstras and Wulf, "French Translations and Reception of the Declaration of Independence," 1305.

52. [Honoré-Gabriel Riqueti, comte de Mirabeau], *Des lettres de cachet et des prisons d'état*, 2 vols. (Hamburg, 1782), 1:284. This work, which was composed in 1778 and published posthumously, has sometimes been attributed to Étienne Claviere. A translation was published in 1787 in both London and Dublin (Dublin: Mess. Whitestone, 1787).

53. Carl L. Becker, *The Declaration of Independence: A Study in the History of Political Ideas* (New York: Vintage Books, 1958), 231.

54. Echeverria, "French Publications of the Declaration of Independence and the American Constitutions," 316. For the best recent accounts of the complicated history of the publication of the Declaration, see Bailyn, *To Begin the World Anew*, 134–35; Armitage, "The Declaration of Independence and International Law," 50 ff.; and David Armitage, *The Declaration of Independence: A Global History* (Cambridge, MA: Harvard University Press, 2007), esp. chap. 2.

55. David Thelen and Willi Paul Adams, "Previews," in "Interpreting the Declaration of Independence by Translation," *Journal of American History* 85 (March 1999):1276.

56. Marienstras and Wulf, "French Translations and Reception of the Declaration of Independence," 1282 (italics in original).

57. Ibid., 1309.

58. Echeverria, "French Publications of the Declaration of Independence and the American Constitutions," 313–38; and Robert R. Palmer, "The Impact of the American Revolution Abroad," in *The Impact of the American Revolution Abroad, 1975,* Library of Congress Symposia on the American Revolution (Washington, DC: Library of Congress, 1976), 12.

59. Quotation from the dedication page of *Recuiel,* cited in Bailyn, *To Begin the World Anew,* 135.

60. Echeverria, "French Publications of the Declaration of Independence and American Constitutions," 316, 319–20, and passim.

61. According to Palmer in "The Impact of the American Revolution Abroad," 13, the first state constitutions "clarified and formulated the very thoughts that the French themselves had already entertained."

62. Franklin to Samuel Cooper, May 1, 1777, in *Papers of Benjamin Franklin,* ed. Leonard W. Labaree et al., vols. 1–38 to date (New Haven, CT: Yale University Press, 1959–), 24:6.

63. Echeverria, "French Publications of the Declaration and the American Constitutions," 323–25.

64. Quoted in Gottfried Dietze, *The Federalist: A Classic on Federalism and Free Government* (Baltimore: Johns Hopkins University Press,1960), 10.

65. Roy Fairfield, *The Federalist Papers: A Collection of Essays Written in Support of the Constitution of the United States,* 2nd ed. (Garden City, NY: Doubleday, 1966), 308.

66. *Le fédéraliste: Commentaire de la constitution des États-Unis,* trans. and ed. Gaston Jèze (Paris: V. Giard & Briere, 1902), xxxiv.

67. Dietze, *The Federalist,* 10.

68. Ibid.

69. I have not gone through the public debates published in the *Archives parlementaires,* however, which would indicate the depth and extent of the influence in the French legislatures of the American and British constitutions.

For further exploration of the constitutional thought of Charles de Secondat, baron de Montesquieu, see his *De l'esprit des lois* (Geneva: Barrillot & fils, 1748), esp. book 11, chap. 6, book 8, chap. 16, and the analytical discussion of political and civil liberty in books 11 and 12. See also Bernard Manin, "Montesquieu," in *A Critical Dictionary of the French Revolution,* ed. François Furet and Mona Ozouf and trans. Arthur Goldhammer (Cambridge, MA: Harvard University Press, 1989), 728–41. M. J. C. Vile's *Constitutionalism and the Separation of Powers* (Oxford: Clarendon Press, 1967), demonstrates that Montesquieu's doctrine of separation of powers lost much of its dogmatic purity as it was applied in different eras and countries. For a brilliant discussion of the doctrine, see Carl J. Friedrich, *Constitutional Government and Democracy: Theory and Practice in Europe and America,* 4th ed. (Waltham, MA: Blaisdell, 1968), chap. X. Paul

Spurlin's *Montesquieu in America, 1760–1801* (Baton Rouge: Louisiana State University Press, 1940), is a distinct disappointment in treating this doctrine and other ideas of Montesquieu. Montesquieu's doctrine of the necessity of virtue in a republic is ably treated in Paul A. Rahe's *Republics Ancient and Modern: Classical Republicanism and the American Revolution* (Chapel Hill: University of North Carolina Press, 1992), 38–39, 58–59, and 136. This majestic and learned book emphasizes the idea of the republic in ancient and medieval times, which my study does not. On Madison's correction of Montesquieu's argument regarding the limited size of republics, see especially *Federalist* 10 and the insightful discussion in Lance Banning, *Sacred Fire of Liberty: James Madison and the Founding of the Federal Republic* (Ithaca, NY: Cornell University Press, 1995), 216–17 and 467–68.

Both Jefferson, who cited Montesquieu twenty-seven times in his commonplace book, and John Adams, who wrote his *A Defence of the Constitutions of Government of the United States of America*, vols. 4, 5, 6, *Works of John Adams, Second President of the United States (1787)*, ed. Charles Francis Adams, 10 vols. (Boston: Little, Brown, 1850–1856) in part to refute Montesquieu as well as Turgot, grew disenchanted with the Frenchman's ideas. See Lawrence S. Kaplan, *Jefferson and France: An Essay on Politics and Political Ideas* (New Haven, CT: Yale University Press, 1967), esp. 3; and Spurlin, *Montesquieu in America*, 190–92.

The literature on Rousseau is equally abundant, but his influence on the American founders was far less than that of Montesquieu. A ready source is Paul Spurlin's *Rousseau in America, 1760–1809* (Tuscaloosa: University of Alabama Press, 1969).

70. Emile Boutmy, *Études de droit constitutionnel, France—Angleterre—États-Unis* (Paris: E. Plon, Nourrit, 1885), trans. Edward M. Dicey from 2nd French ed. as *Studies in Constitutional Law: France—England—United States* (London: Macmillan, 1891), 58. This misconception might have resulted because such French authors were still reading Turgot's old work, written before the U.S. Constitution was promulgated.

71. Boutmy, *Studies in Constitutional Law*, 61–68.

72. René Rémond, *Les États-Unis devant l'opinion française 1815–1852*, 2 vols. (Paris: A. Colin, 1962), 2:617.

73. Lloyd S. Kramer, *Lafayette in Two Worlds: Public Cultures and Personal Identities in an Age of Revolutions* (Chapel Hill: University of North Carolina Press, 1996), 21–22.

74. Stanley J. Idzerda, Roger E. Smith, Linda J. Pike, and Mary Ann Quinn, eds., *Lafayette in the Age of the American Revolution: Selected Letters and Papers, 1776–1790*, 5 vols. (Ithaca, NY: Cornell University Press, 1977–1983), 1:58–59. Louis Reichenthal Gottschalk takes a negative view despite Lafayette's protestations to the contrary. He attributes Lafayette's motivation solely to self-centeredness and to his youthful naïveté; see his *Lafayette between the American and the French Revolution (1783–1789)* (Chicago: University of Chicago Press, 1950), 428.

75. Stanley J. Idzerda, "Lafayette," in *Encyclopedia Americana*, 30 vols. (Danbury, CT: Grollier, 1992), 16:660.

76. Lafayette to Washington, February 4, 1788, in *The Letters of Lafayette to Washington, 1777–1799*, ed. Louis Reichenthal Gottschalk and Shirley A. Bill, 2nd rev. ed. (Philadelphia: American Philosophical Society, 1976), 338.

77. Kramer, *Lafayette in Two Worlds*, 34. Kramer's biography provides a cultural approach that tries to restore Lafayette's reputation among historians who have disagreed about him since the romantic age of the nineteenth century. Critics on the Right and Left have held opposing views regarding his role in the French Revolution and as an advocate of natural rights. The royalist critics on the Right denounced Lafayette's self-proclaimed identity as a unifier and mediator in France when he was commander of the National Guard. They claim that his actions subverted his advocacy of natural rights and that he tolerated popular movements that hastened the disintegration of French society. The Republican critics on the Left argued that his revolutionary role in America was undermined by his determination in France to put down popular disturbances and to support the king. Lafayette symbolizes the continuing controversy in France over their revolution.

78. As Dumas Malone, Jefferson's biographer, commented, the Virginian's contribution was even greater perhaps than can be proven by documentary evidence, since the two men were talking daily. See Dumas Malone, *Jefferson and the Rights of Man* (Boston: Little, Brown, 1959), 224–25. See also Julian Boyd, "Proposed Declaration of Rights by Marquis de Lafayette and Dr. Richard Gem," in *Papers of Thomas Jefferson*, ed. Julian Boyd, Lyman H. Butterfield, et al., 21 vols. (Princeton, NJ: Princeton University Press, 1950–2000), 14:438–40.

79. Becker, *Declaration of Independence*, 231–32.

80. Malone, *Jefferson and the Rights of Man*, 229.

81. Jefferson to Madison, August 29, 1789, in *The Works of Thomas Jefferson*, ed. Paul Leicester Ford, 12 vols. (New York: Putnam, 1904–05), 5:140.

82. Lloyd Kramer, "The French Revolution and the Creation of American Political Culture," in *The Global Ramifications of the French Revolution*, ed. Joseph Klaits and Michael H. Haltzel (Cambridge: Cambridge University Press, 1994), 28.

83. John Simpson Penman, *Lafayette and Three Revolutions* (Boston: Stratford, 1929), 123.

84. Lafayette to Washington, August 23, 1789, in Gottschalk and Bill, eds., *Letters of Lafayette to Washington*, 350.

85. Lafayette to Washington, March 7, 1791, in ibid., 213.

86. Lafayette to Washington, January 1792, in ibid., 358 (italics added).

87. Lafayette to the Assembly, June 16, 1792, in Gilbert du Motier marquis de Lafayette, *Mémoires, Correspondance, et Manuscrits*, 6 vols. (Paris: H. Fournier, 1837–38), 3:329.

88. Patrice Gueniffey, "Lafayette," in *Critical Dictionary of the French Revolution*, 232.

89. Richard Price, *Observations on the Importance of the American Revolution, and the Means of Making It a Benefit to the World* (Boston: Powars and Willis, 1784). The letter to Price from Anne-Robert-Jacques Turgot appears on 71–87.

90. W. Walker Stephens, ed., *The Life and Writings of Turgot: Comptroller General of France, 1774–76* (1895; repr., New York: Burt Franklin, 1971), 299.

91. Stephens, ed., *The Life and Writings of Turgot*; and Edward Handler, *America and Europe in the Political Thought of John Adams* (Cambridge, MA: Harvard University Press,1964), 40.

92. Stephens, ed., *The Life and Writings of Turgot*, 300.

93. Ibid., 299.

94. Palmer, *The Age of the Democratic Revolution*, 1:271.

95. Adams, ed., *Works of John Adams*, vols. 4, 5, and 6.

96. Ibid., 4:292–93.

97. Gordon S. Wood, *The Creation of the American Republic, 1776–1787* (Chapel Hill: University of North Carolina Press, 1969), 567.

98. Adams, ed., *Works of John Adams*, 4:298. There is a disagreement between Robert R. Palmer and Joyce Appleby on this point. In *The Age of the Democratic Revolution*, 1:273–74, Palmer stresses Adams's anti-aristocratic emphasis; whereas Appleby emphasizes more the balance among the three orders and would appear to be more accurate. See Joyce Appleby, "The Jefferson–Adams Rupture and the First French Translation of John Adams' *Defence*," *American Historical Review*, 73 (1968):1088.

99. See C. Bradley Thompson, "John Adams' Machiavellian Moment," *Review of Politics* 57 (1995):389–417. Thompson argues that the *Defence* reads more clearly from the perspective of the inductive method of fact and experience rather than the usual deductive method of hypothesis and systems building. But in a celebrated chapter, "The Relevance and Irrelevance of John Adams," Wood finds the work "bulky, disorganized, [a] conglomeration of political glosses on a single theme" because Adams continued to cling to the older theory of balanced government in the face of changing times. See Wood, *Creation of the American Republic*, 568.

100. Wood, *Creation of the American Republic*, 579.

101. Turgot to Richard Price, May 22, 1778, in Stephens, ed., *Life and Writings of Turgot*, 300–301.

102. Zoltán Haraszti, *John Adams & the Prophets of Progress* (Cambridge, MA: Harvard University Press, 1952), 148.

103. Ibid., passim.

104. Palmer, *Age of the Democratic Revolution*, 1:268–69 and 405–53.

105. Condorcet, "The Influence of the American Revolution on Europe," trans. and ed. Durand Echeverria, *William and Mary Quarterly*, 3rd ser., 25 (1968):91.

106. Quoted in J. Salwyn Schapiro, *Condorcet and the Rise of Liberalism* (New York: Harcourt Brace, 1934), 222–23; Jean-Antoine-Nicolas de Caritat, Marquis

de Condorcet, *Lettres d'un citoyen des États-Unis à un français, sur les affaires presentes,* in *Oeuvres complètes de Condorcet,* ed. M. L. S. Caritat, marchioness de Condorcet, A. A. Barbier, P. J. G. Cabanis, and Count D. J. Garat, 21 vols. (Paris: Chez Henrichs, Fuchs, Koenig, Levrault, Shoeli et Coie, 1804), 12:175; and Condorcet, *Essai sur la constitution et les fonctions des assemblées provinciales,* in *Oeuvres complètes de Condorcet,* 13:158.

107. Quoted in Schapiro, *Condorcet and the Rise of Liberalism,* 226.

108. Horst Dippel, "Popular Sovereignty and the Separation of Powers in American and French Revolutionary Constitutionalism," in *European and American Constitutionalism in the Eighteenth Century,* ed. Michal Rozbicki (Warsaw: Warsaw University, 1990), 22.

109. Condorcet, *The Influence of the American Revolution on Europe,* 91.

110. Ibid., 105. As Henry F. May noted in *The Enlightenment in America* (New York: Oxford University Press, 1976), the Enlightenment was more moderate in this regard in America and did not carry the harsh anti-Christian tone so characteristic of France in this period.

111. Condorcet, *The Influence of the American Revolution on Europe,* 93–94.

112. Ibid., 99; and Schapiro, *Condorcet and the Rise of Liberalism,* 229.

113. Condorcet, *The Influence of the American Revolution on Europe,* 100.

114. Ibid., 93–94.

115. Schapiro, *Condorcet and the Rise of Liberalism,* 229.

116. Condorcet to Franklin, July 8, 1788, in *The Works of Benjamin Franklin: Containing Several Political and Historical Tracts,* ed. Jared Sparks, 10 vols. (Boston: Tappan and Whittemore, 1836–1840), 10:353.

117. Condorcet, *Projet de constitution,* in *Oeuvres complètes,* 11:370.

118. Condorcet, quoted in Schapiro, *Condorcet and the Rise of Liberalism,* 225.

119. Ibid.

120. Condorcet, *Projet de constitution,* in *Oeuvres complètes,* 11:373–74 and 389–90.

121. Ibid., 378–79.

122. Ibid., 373–74 and 381.

123. Condorcet, *Lettres d'un bourgeois de New-Haven à un citoyen de Virginia,* in *Oeuvres complètes,* 12:3–60; see also Alexandre Koyre, "Condorcet," *Journal of the History of Ideas* 10 (1948):147; and Victor Rosenblum, "Condorcet as a Constitutional Draftsman: Dimensions of a Substantive Commitment and Procedural Implementation," in *Condorcet Studies,* ed. Leonard Rosenfield (Atlantic Highlands, NJ: Humanities Press, 1984), 1:191. (This last is an excellent detailed article on comparative constitutional law, comparing that of the United States and France.)

124. Schapiro, *Condorcet and the Rise of Liberalism,* 225.

125. John Stevens, *Examen du gouvernement d'Angleterre, comparé aux constitutions des États-Unis* (Paris: Chez Froullé, 1789), Massachusetts Historical Society.

For the background of this episode, see Appleby, "The Jefferson–Adams Rupture," 1084–91.

126. François Furet, *In the Workshop of History*, trans. Jonathan Mandelbaum (Chicago: University of Chicago Press, 1984), 160.

127. Condorcet, *Plan de constitution: Présenté à la convention nationale (1793), Oeuvres complètes*, 12:153–90; Condorcet, *Esquisse d'un tableau historique de progrès de l'esprit humain* (Paris: Agasse, 1795).

128. Haraszti, *John Adams and the Prophets of Progress*, 252–53.

129. Eloise Ellery, *Brissot de Warville: A Study in the History of the French Revolution* (Boston: Houghton Mifflin, 1915), 49; see Étienne Claviére and Jacques-Pierre Brissot de Warville, *De la France et des États-Unis; ou de l'importance de la revolution de l'Amerique pour le bonheur de la France* (London [s.n.], 1787), passim; and Leonard Loft, "Brissot: Revolutionary Disciple of the *Philosophes*" (PhD diss., Columbia University, 1971).

130. Quotation from Palmer, *Age of the Democratic Revolution*, 1:262.

131. *La patriote française*, August 1, 1789.

132. Ellery, *Brissot de Warville*, 49.

133. For a shift in argument of the *Américanistes* on the issue of a unicameral legislature after copies of the American Constitution reached France in 1787, see Joyce Appleby, "America as a Model for the Radical French Reformers of 1789," *William and Mary Quarterly*, 3rd ser., 28 (1971):275–80.

134. Brissot de Warville, *Nouveau voyage dans les États-Unis de l'Amérique septentrionale, fait en 1788*, 3 vols. (Paris: Buisson, 1791).

135. Ellery, *Brissot de Warville*, 50 and 83–84.

136. Ibid., 84.

137. Echeverria, *Mirage in the West*, 268.

138. Pierre-Samuel Du Pont de Nemours to Thomas Jefferson, November 9, 1787, in Boyd, ed., *Papers of Thomas Jefferson*, 12:325–26.

139. Friedrich calls the time after the adoption of the U.S. Constitution "a period of general enthusiasm for the American model in France," *The Impact of American Constitutionalism Abroad*, 4.

140. Furet, *In the Workshop of History*, 158.

141. A. E. Dick Howard, "State Constitutions," in *Encyclopedia of the American Constitution, Supplement* 1, ed. Leonard W. Levy, Kenneth L. Karst, and John G. West Jr. (New York: Macmillan, 1992), 512 and 514.

142. Keith Michael Baker, "Constitution," in *Critical Dictionary of the French Revolution*, 479–493. See also William Doyle, *The Oxford History of the French Revolution* (New York: Oxford University Press, 1989), 149–420; and *The French Revolution and the Creation of Modern Political Culture*, ed. Keith Michael Baker, 4 vols.(New York: Pergamon Press, 1987-1994), 4:39–54.

143. Although Ozouf's article is on the nature of the American and French revolutions, by implication it applies to the nature of constitutions as well. See Mona

Ozouf, "Revolution," in *Critical Dictionary of the French Revolution*, 806–17. In fact, in the article (809) she quotes a speech by Jean-Joseph Mounier referring to the model of the English Constitution.

144. Quoted in Ozouf, "Revolution," 809.

145. Lafayette's ideas at this stage were expressed in his *Mémoires*, written sometime between 1795 and 1799. See Louis Gottschalk and Margaret Maddox, *Lafayette in the French Revolution; from the October Days through the Federation* (Chicago: University of Chicago Press, 1973), 117.

146. Crane Brinton, *A Decade of Revolution, 1789–1799* (New York: Harper Bros., 1934), 42.

147. Baker, "Constitution," 492. The historiography of the French Revolution is voluminous, complicated, and contentious. Certain contemporary historians like François Furet rejected the Marxist interpretation of a violent revolution based on class considerations and substituted a revolution characterized more by a sense of renovation and rejuvenation that began in the last decades of the *ancien régime*. Furet, following Tocqueville, argued that the twin concepts of national sovereignty and legislative supremacy reestablished royal absolutism in a new guise and provided the government under the constitution of 1791 with practically unlimited powers. The revolutionaries abused those powers, according to Furet, when they encountered resistance in pursuit of their utopian goals. In this interpretation, the Terror was attributable to both the heritage of absolutist monarchy and the failure to solve the problem of national sovereignty in the absence of an absolute monarch. The problem of "ending the revolution" remained unresolved under successive regimes—the Jacobins, the Thermidoreans, and the Directory—until Napoleon provided a solution by sacrificing political liberty while achieving civil equality in the form of the Napoleonic Code, which modernized the French state. See François Furet, *Revolutionary France, 1770–1880*, trans. Antonia Nevill (Cambridge, MA: Blackwell, 1992); and his entries in *Critical Dictionary of the French Revolution*, as well as Elizabeth Eisenstein's review of Furet's *Revolutionary France*, *American Historical Review* 99 (1994):1323–24.

In contrast, Keith Michael Baker located, several generations before the Revolution, a break in the political culture in the state, church, and other institutions. See his "On the Problem of the Ideological Origins of the French Revolution," in *Modern European Intellectual History: Reappraisals and New Perspectives*, ed. Dominic LaCapra and Stephen Kaplan (Ithaca, NY: Cornell University Press, 1982), 197–217; Keith Michael Baker, *Inventing the French Revolution: Essays on French Political Culture in the Eighteenth Century* (Cambridge: Cambridge University Press, 1990), 12–27; and Baker, introduction to *The French Revolution and the Creation of Modern Political Culture*, xiii–xxvii.

148. Chilton Williamson, *American Suffrage from Property to Democracy, 1760–1860* (Princeton, NJ: Princeton University Press, 1960).

149. Patrice Gueniffey, "Suffrage," in *Critical Dictionary of the French Revolution*, 578.

150. Georg Jellinik, *Die Erklärung der Menschen- und Bürgerrechte: Ein Beitrag zur modernen Verfassungsgeschichte* (Leipzig: Duncker & Humblot, 1895), and Max Farrand's authorized translation, *The Declaration of the Rights of Man and of Citizens: A Contribution to Modern Constitutional History by Georg Jellinek* (1901; repr., Westport, CT: Hyperion Press, 1979).

151. Emile Doumergue, "Les origines historique de la Déclaration des Droits de l'Homme et du Citoyen," *Revue du droit public et de la science politique en France et à l'étranger* 21 (1904):673–733. See David G. Ritchie, *Natural Rights: A Criticism of Some Political and Ethical Conceptions* (New York: Macmillan, 1903). For an earlier important statement on this issue see Boutmy, *Études de droit constitutionnel* (1885). For a fuller bibliographical entry on this controversy over time, see Roland Bainton, "The Appeal to Reason," in *The Constitution Reconsidered*, ed. Richard B. Morris, rev. ed. (New York: Harper & Row, 1968), 126–27.

152. Morris, *Emerging Nations and the American Revolution*, 56.

153. Palmer, *Age of the Democratic Revolution*, 1:487. In an appendix, Palmer compares the two documents side by side (518–21).

154. The term *citizen* had a different meaning, moreover, when it came to American and British usage. The person that Americans called *citizen* continued in England to be considered a "subject"—one, in other words, who was involved in a special subject–king relationship. See James H. Kettner, *The Development of American Citizenship, 1608–1870* (Chapel Hill: University of North Carolina Press, 1978); and Richard D. Brown, *The Strength of a People: The Idea of an Informed Citizenry in America, 1650–1870* (Chapel Hill: University of North Carolina Press, 1996). Kettner treats the American antecedents of citizenship in Britain, the American colonies, and into the Revolutionary era and beyond. See also Palmer's fruitful discussion of the term *citizen* as used in France, in Robert R. Palmer, *Some Centennials of the American Constitution and Others* (Ann Arbor, MI: William L. Clements Library, 1987), 8–10.

155. Jacques Godechot, "L'influence des États-Unis sur les constitutions françaises de l'époque," n.p., unpublished and undated paper provided by the late Prof. Albert Blaustein of Rutgers University. The Blaustein Papers are in the archives of Rutgers University.

156. Godechot, "L'influence des États-Unis," n.p.; see also Godechot, *France and the Atlantic Revolution*, 96 and 98.

157. Hawgood, *Modern Constitutions since 1787*, 36.

158. Furet, *Revolutionary France*, 163.

159. Quoted in Godechot, *France and the Atlantic Revolution*, 96.

160. Marcel Gauchet, "Rights of Man," in *Critical Dictionary of the French Revolution*, 820.

161. Gilbert Chinard, *Thomas Jefferson: The Apostle of Americanism* (Boston: Little, Brown, 1929), 232–33; and Boyd, ed., *Papers of Thomas Jefferson*, 15:387.

162. Gordon S. Wood, "The Origins of the American Bill of Rights," *La revue Tocqueville* 14 (1993):34.

163. Ibid.

164. Jefferson to John Jay, with enclosure, May 23, 1788, in Boyd, ed., *Papers of Thomas Jefferson*, 13:193.

165. Kramer, *Lafayette in Two Worlds*, 35.

166. Lafayette to Washington, October 14, 1777, in Idzerda et al., eds., *Lafayette in the Age of the American Revolution*, 2:121.

167. Jefferson to James Madison, December 20, 1787, in Boyd, ed., *Papers of Thomas Jefferson*, 12:440; and Wood, "The Origins of the American Bill of Rights," *La revue Tocqueville*, 41.

168. Wood, "The Origins of the American Bill of Rights," *La revue Tocqueville*, 41.

169. Godechot, "L'influence des États-Unis sur les constitutions françaises de l'époque," n.p. For an example of the Jefferson–Lafayette collaboration, see Lafayette to Jefferson, July 9, 1789, in Boyd., ed., *Papers of Thomas Jefferson*, 15:255.

170. Echeverria, *Mirage in the West*, 194.

171. Ibid., 192.

172. John Emerich Edward Dalberg-Acton, First Baron Acton, *Lectures on the French Revolution*, ed. John Neville Figgis and Reginald Vere Laurence (London: Macmillan, 1910), 107.

173. Hawgood, *Modern Constitutions since 1787*, 142.

174. Cited in Morris, *Emerging Nations and the American Revolution*, 102, in *Complete Works of A. N. Radishchev*, ed. Alexandr K. Borozdin et al., 2 vols. (St. Petersburg: M. I. Akenfieva, 1907), 1:318–30.

175. Aleksandr Nikolaevich Radishchev, *A Journey from St. Petersburg to Moscow*, trans. Leo Wiener and notes by Roderick Page Thaler (Cambridge, MA: Harvard University Press, 1958), 184–86.

176. Simon Schama, *Patriots and Liberators: Revolution in the Netherlands, 1780–1813* (New York: Knopf, 1977), 60–61; and Jan Willem Schulte Nordholt, "The Impact of the American Revolution on the Dutch Republic," *Impact of the American Revolution Abroad, Papers Presented at the Fourth Symposium, 1975, Library of Congress Symposia on the American Revolution*, 52. The complicated history of the United Netherlands and its relation to the American Revolution antedated 1776. The United Netherlands provided another example of the two-way flow of exchanges across the Atlantic. When the American colonies had become involved in the French and Indian War in the 1750s, they had cast about for models of a confederation that might help them counter the French threat. The 170-year-old Union of Utrecht which had held the United Provinces of the

Netherlands intact seemed to fit the purpose. Benjamin Franklin may have had that confederation in mind when he proposed his "Short Hints" which eventually led to the Albany Plan of Union in 1754.

Franklin's plan proposed a form of union for some of the colonies, but his design never anticipated American independence nor was it ever implemented. For that matter, neither the Union of Utrecht nor the Albany Plan was ever conceived as a constitution. Nevertheless, there is little doubt that the Albany Plan was in certain ways a predecessor of the Articles of Confederation. Franklin, in fact, never lost sight of the Dutch example and in 1778 compared the Articles with the Union of Utrecht quite favorably. See "Proceedings of the Congress at Albany, a.d. 1754," in Labaree, ed., *Papers of Benjamin Franklin*, 5:346–54. Bruce E. Johansen, *Forgotten Founders: Benjamin Franklin, the Iroquois, and the Rationale for the American Revolution* (Ipswich, MA: Gambit, 1982), makes the argument that the Iroquois Confederation served as a model for Franklin's plan. See also Benjamin Franklin to Charles W. F. Dumas, April 10, 1778, in *The Writings of Benjamin Franklin*, ed. Albert Henry Smyth, 10 vols. (New York: Macmillan, 1907), 7:139; James R. Tanis, "The Dutch-American Connection: The Impact of 'The Dutch Example' on Our Constitutional Beginnings," in *New York Notes*, New York State Commission on the Bicentennial of the United States Constitution (Albany, n.d.).

For the best discussion of the Albany Plan, see Timothy J. Shannon, *Indians and Colonists at the Crossroads of Empire: The Albany Congress of 1754* (Ithaca, NY: Cornell University Press, 2000). Shannon points out that the Albany Plan did not look forward to independence. Taken on its own terms, though it did not look to the Revolution, the plan broke new ground, constitutionally speaking, by conceiving of the colonies as a single unit within a greater body politic. "The Albany Plan placed a new level of constitutional authority between the Crown and the colonies that would reduce the singularity [of each colony] . . . and incorporate them as a whole more effectively into the empire" (196–97). Concerning the thesis regarding the Iroquois influence on the making of the U.S. Constitution, Shannon takes a different view, with which I agree (7–8).

177. J. W. Schulte Nordholt, *The Dutch Republic and American Independence*, trans. Herbert H. Rowen (Chapel Hill: University of North Carolina Press, 1982), 123.

178. Ibid.; Pieter Paulus, *Verklaring der Unie van Utrecht*, 4 vols. (Utrecht: J. van Shoorhoven, 1775–1778).

179. Schulte Nordholt, *The Dutch Republic and American Independence*, 11-12 and 265–66.

180. J. W. Schulte Nordholt, "The Paradox of Example: Contemporary European Perceptions of the American Constitution," in *The Early Republic: The Making of a Nation, the Making of a Culture*, ed. Steve Ickringill, Zoltan Abádi-Nagy, and Aladár Sarbu (Amsterdam: Free University Press, 1988), 151 and 154.

181. Quoted in Schulte Nordholt, "The Paradox of Example," 157.

182. Ibid.

183. Ibid., 153; Gerhard Dumbar, *De oude en nieuwe Constitutie der Vereenigde Staten van Amerika, uit de beste schriften in haare gronden ontvouwd*, 3 vols. (Amsterdam: J. A. Crajenschot, 1793–1796).

184. Schulte Nordholdt, *The Dutch Republic and American Independence*, 161–62. R. J.Schimmelpenninck, the leader of the Moderates who had cited the Massachusetts Constitution of 1780 in his doctoral dissertation at the University of Leiden, warned that American examples were not applicable to the Dutch situation:

> Don't present me with the example of North America and don't point out to me the happiness and the astonishing prosperity which are enjoyed in these provinces thanks to a Constitution built on the federal principle. Who doesn't get lost in the enormous differences in territory between these two countries? Who compares these Netherlands of ours, this little dot of ours on the globe, with a country where a single province, Georgia, is larger than the entire country of France? (quoted in Schulte Nordholdt, *The Dutch Republic and American Independence*, 287)

185. Schulte Nordholdt, *The Dutch Republic and American Independence*, 162.

186. *Papers of James Madison*, ed. William T. Hutchinson and William M. E. Rachal, 17 vols. (Chicago: University of Chicago Press, 1962–), 9:9; and James H. Hutson, *The Sister Republics: Switzerland and the United States from 1776 to the Present* (Washington, DC: Library of Congress,1991), 27.

187. Hutchinson and Rachal, eds., *Papers of James Madison*, 9:10–11.

188. Max Farrand, ed., *Records of the Federal Convention of 1787*, 4 vols., rev. ed. (1937; New Haven, CT: Yale University Press, 1966), 1:285–86.

189. Ibid., 1:317.

190. Ibid., 1:454.

191. Ibid., 1:296, 303, 307, 317, 319, 326, 330, 343, 348, 350, 354; and 3:105,153, 184.

192. Hutson, *The Sister Republics*, 33.

193. Quoted in Horst Dippel, *Germany and the American Revolution, 1770–1800: A Sociohistorical Investigation of Late Eighteenth-Century Political Thinking*, trans. Bernhard Uhlendorf (Chapel Hill: University of North Carolina Press,1977), ix.

194. Ibid., passim.

195. Ibid., 276–78.

196. Quoted in Schulte Nordholt, "The Paradox of Example," 155–56. Ernst Fraenkel claimed that Forster was the first European to emphasize the conservative element in the U.S. Constitution. See his *Amerika im Spiegel des deutschen politischen Denkens: Äusserungen deutscher Staatsmänner und Staatsdenker über Staat und Gesellschaft in den Vereinigten Staaten von Amerika* (Cologne: Westdeutscher Verlag, 1959), 72.

197. Friedrich von Gentz, *The Origin and Principles of the American Revolution, Compared with the Origin and Principles of the French Revolution*, trans. John Quincy Adams (Philadelphia: Asbury Dickins, 1800) from "Der Ursprung und die Grundsätze der Amerikanischen Revolution, verglichen mit dem Ursprunge und den Grundsätzen der Französischen," *Historisches Journal* 2 (Berlin, 1800):1010–28; reprinted in *Three Revolutions: The French and American Revolutions Compared* (Chicago: Regnery, 1959), passim. See Wood, *Radicalism of the American Revolution*, 231; and Palmer, *Age of the Democratic Revolution*, 1:188. To show that the social upheaval of the American Revolution was underestimated, Palmer argues that in per capita terms, more people emigrated from America during the Revolution and more property was confiscated than in France.

198. Abbé Guillaume-Thomas-François Raynal, *Storia dell'America settentrionale*, 3 vols. (Venice: Antonio Zatta, 1778–1780); See Emiliana P. Noether, "The Constitution in Action: The Young Republic in the Observations of Early Italian Commentators (1770s–1830s)," in *The American Constitution as a Symbol and Reality for Italy*, ed. Emiliana P. Noether (Lewiston, NY: Mellen Press, 1989), 82 and 93. The work of Prof. Noether on Italian–American contacts during this period has been indispensable to the Italian segment of this study.

199. Noether, "The Constitution in Action," 82.

200. Edoardo Tortarolo, "Philip Mazzei and the Liberty of the New Nation," in Noether, ed., *The American Constitution as a Symbol and Reality for Italy*, 57.

201. Tortarolo, "Philip Mazzei and the Liberty of the New Nation," 57.

202. Ibid., 58–59.

203. The American state constitutions compiled by Franklin and translated by Rochefoucauld as *Constitutions des treize États-Unis de l'Amérique* in 1783 were circulated in Italy, and three prominent Italian journals reported on the book in 1784. See Emiliana Noether, "As Others Saw Us: Italian Views on the United States during the Nineteenth Century," *Transactions, Connecticut Academy of Arts and Sciences* 50 (1990):127.

204. Philip Mazzei, *Recherches historiques et politiques sur les États-Unis de l'Amérique septentrionale: Où l'on traite des établissements des treize colonies, de leurs rapports & de leurs dissentions avec la Grand-Bretagne*, 4 vols. (Paris: Chez Froullé, 1788).

205. Quoted in Tortarolo, "Philip Mazzei and the Liberty of the New Nation," 63.

206. Mazzei, *Recherches historique et politique sur les États-Unis de l'Amérique septentrionale*, 1:168, 216–17.

207. Mazzei may have been responsible for the suggestion that the Virginia Constitution of 1776 be considered as a model of government for a single Italian

state, Tuscany. Mazzei sent a copy to Prince Leopold. See Howard R. Marraro, "Mazzei's Correspondence with the Grand Duke of Tuscany during His American Mission," *William and Mary Quarterly*, 2nd ser., 22 (July and October 1942). There is, however, some dispute about which state constitution was Leopold's model: Virginia's or Pennsylvania's early state constitution. See Palmer, *Age of the Democratic Revolution,* 1:386, which claims that Virginia's constitution was the Grand Duke's model. In "As Others Saw Us," 129, Noether supports the same conclusion. She cites Joachim Zimmerman, *Das Verfassungsprojeht des Grossherzogs Peter Leopold von Tuscana* (Heidelberg, 1901), which identifies passages in Italian that were practically literal translations from the Virginia text. But Ulrich Schuener, in "Constitutional Traditions in the United States and Germany," in *Deutsch-Amerikanisches Verfassungsrechtssymposium 1976: Pressefreiheit; Finanzverfassung im Bundesstaat,* ed. Wilhelm A. Kewenig (Berlin: Duncker und Humblot, 1978), 25, indicates that the Pennsylvania document provided the inspiration to the duke. Both Paula Fichtner, "Viennese Perspectives on the American War of Independence," in *East Central European Perceptions of Early America,* ed. Béla Király and George Barany, Brooklyn College Studies on Society in Change (Lisse: Peter de Ridder Press, 1977), 20–21; and Gerald Davis, "Observations of Leopold of Hapsburg on the Pennsylvania Constitution of 1776," *Pennsylvania History* 29 (1962), support Schuener. On the basis of the translation, my position here is that of Palmer and Noether.

208. Madison to Mazzei, October 8, 1788, in Hutchinson and Rachal, eds., *Papers of James Madison,* 2:278–79 (2nd italics added).

209. A Milanese botanist, Luigi Castiglioni, published *Viaggo negli Stati Uniti dell'America settentrionale, fatto negli anni 1785, 1786 e 1787,* 2 vols. (Milan: Stamperia di G. Marelli, 1790) after a two-year stay in America. He included the first full-scale Italian translation of the U.S. Constitution and summarized all the first state constitutions, explaining how each functioned. For the English edition, see *Luigi Castiglioni's Viaggio = Travels in the United States of North America, 1785–87,* ed. and trans. Antonio Pace (Syracuse, NY: Syracuse University Press, 1983). See also Alexander Grab, "The Italian Enlightenment and the American Revolution," in Noether, ed., *The American Constitution as a Symbol and Reality in Italy,* 41–42; and Noether, "The Constitution in Action," 83–85.

210. Richard B. Bernstein, "Afterword," in *Roots of the Republic: American Founding Documents Interpreted,* ed. Stephen L. Schechter, Richard B. Bernstein, and Donald S. Lutz (Madison, WI: Madison House, 1990), 440–48.

211. Thomas Jefferson to Roger O. Weightman, June 24, 1826. "The text of this letter is taken from the Jefferson Papers in the Library of Congress. The first letter in every sentence is capitalized, which Jefferson usually did not do" (Bernstein, "Afterword," 444–45).

212. Bernstein, "Afterword," 446.

CHAPTER 4

1. Robert Kolesar, paraphrasing novelist Isabel Allende's *The House of Spirits*, trans. Magda Bogin (London: Jonathan Cape, 1985): "North American Constitutionalism and Spanish America: A Special Lock Ordered by Catalogue, Which Arrived with the Wrong Instructions and No Keys," in *American Constitutionalism Abroad: Selected Essays in Comparative Constitutional History*, ed. George Athan Billias (Westport, CT: Greenwood Press, 1990), 41–43. I have relied on Kolesar's essay at various points in this chapter.

2. Andrzej Rapaczinski, "Bibliographic Essay: The Influence of U.S. Constitutionalism Abroad," in *Constitutionalism and Rights: The Influence of the United States Constitution Abroad*, ed. Louis Henkin and Albert J. Rosenthal (New York: Columbia University Press, 1990), 411–12.

3. Atilio Borón, "Latin America: Constitutionalism and the Political Traditions of Liberalism and Socialism," in *Constitutionalism and Democracy: Transitions in the Contemporary World*, ed. Douglas Greenberg, Stanley N. Katz, Melanie Beth Oliviero, and Steven C. Wheatley (New York: Oxford University Press, 1993), 339.

4. The best recent comparative study is that by Keith S. Rosenn: "The Success of Constitutionalism in the United States and Its Failure in Latin America," in *The U.S. Constitution and the Constitutions of Latin America*, ed. Kenneth W. Thompson (Lanham, MD: University Press of America, 1991), 53–96. Rosenn wrote two articles on the same subject, the preceding one, which is cited most, and an earlier one with the same title in the *University of Miami Inter-American Law Review* 22 (1990):1–39. The two articles differ in some details and will therefore be cited separately.

Throughout this chapter I have used the term *North American constitutionalism* instead of *American constitutionalism* in order to distinguish it from Latin American constitutionalism. Also in this chapter, Latin America is defined as embracing only the countries on the mainland, that is, continental Spanish America and Portuguese Brazil. The islands in the Caribbean archipelago remained mostly European colonies until 1900 or thereafter and are treated later.

If the influence of North American constitutionalism seems exaggerated, remember that this study is focused on telling the U.S. side of the story. It does not purport to present a complete history of comparative constitutionalism in the region. Such an approach would deal with indigenous and constitutional developments in the colonial period, the continuing influence of Spanish constitutionalism, as well as the enormous contributions from French and British constitutionalism in the region.

5. Karl Loewenstein, "The Presidency outside the United States: A Study in Comparative Institutions," *Journal of Politics* 11 (1949):447 and 452.

6. William Sylvane Stokes, *Latin American Politics* (New York: Crowell, 1959), 474.

7. Kolesar, "North American Constitutionalism and Spanish America," 40 and 45. The Enlightenment in Latin America has not received the treatment it deserves. See, however, the essays in *Latin America and the Enlightenment: Essays by Arthur P. Whitaker [and others]*, ed. Arthur Preston Whitaker, 2nd ed. (Ithaca, NY: Great Seal Books, 1961); Tulio Halperin-Donghi, *Tradición política español e ideología revolucionario de mayo* (Buenos Aires: Editorial Universitaria de Buenos Aires, 1961); and especially Kenneth Maxwell, "The Influence of the U.S. Constitution and Latin America," in Thompson, ed., *The U.S. Constitution and the Constitutions of Latin America*, 3–31. Maxwell's distinction between a Catholic enlightenment in southern and central Europe and the more traditional view of the Enlightenment elsewhere is significant. In the northern climes— North America, Britain, and France—the Enlightenment helped develop political systems that controlled the state, which was viewed as an enemy and therefore was not granted absolute power. Hence there arose such features of enlightened constitutionalism as separation of powers, declarations of rights of citizens, and defense of the press. To the south—southern Europe, Spanish America, and Brazil—there emerged an enlightened absolutism that viewed the state as a guarantor of a more modern developed society quite unlike that of North America. Spanish America was influenced more by the Bourbon reforms in Spain, and Brazil, by the Portuguese reforms of the marquis de Pombal, and were classic cases of enlightened despotism, according to Maxwell.

8. Santos Amadeo, *Argentine Constitutional Law: The Judicial Function in the Maintenance of the Federal System and the Preservation of Individual Rights* (New York: Columbia University Press, 1943), 11–12 and 15–20. Charles A. Hale, *Mexican Liberalism in the Age of Mora, 1821–1853* (New Haven, CT: Yale University Press,1968), 94; Victor Andrés Belaúnde, *Bolívar and the Political Thought of the Spanish American Revolution* (Baltimore: Johns Hopkins University Press, 1938), 151; and Simon Collier, *Ideas and Politics of Chilean Independence, 1808–1833* (Cambridge: Cambridge University Press, 1968), 152, 176.

No single work on the constitutional history of all the Latin American constitutions exists. But the ongoing debate is whether Latin American constitutions failed primarily because they did not reflect indigenous conditions or because foreign adoptions and adaptations proved counterproductive. See Russell Fitzgibbon, "Development in Latin America: A Synthesis," *American Political Science Review* 39 (1945):511–22; and J. Lloyd Mecham, "Latin American Constitutions: Nominal and Real," *Journal of Politics* 21 (1959):258–75. Claudio Véliz, *The Centralist Tradition of Latin America* (Princeton, NJ: Princeton University Press, 1980), has a different thesis: that Latin America had an enduring centralist tradition and that attempts at other forms of constitutionalism were destined to fail in the face of it because the region lacked the experience of feudalism and nonconformity of countries like England and the Netherlands. In a more recent work, *The New World of the Gothic Fox: Culture and Economy in English and Spanish America* (Berkeley: University of California Press,1994), Véliz continues his theme that Hispanic America was essentially Spanish, as distinct from European, because it represented the supreme expression of the Spanish Counter-Reformation. For a strong statement about the persistence of a single Spanish American tradition that did not aspire to achieve liberal constitutionalism and gain democratic goals, see Glen Caudill Dealy, "Prolegomena on the Spanish American Political Tradition," *Hispanic American Historical Review* 48 (1968):37–58.

9. Frank Safford, "Politics, Ideology and Society in Post-Independence Spanish America," in *The Cambridge History of Latin America*, ed. Leslie Bethell, 11 vols. (Cambridge: Cambridge University Press, 1984–1995) 3:384; and quotation from Collier, *Ideas and Politics of Chilean Independence*, 302 (caps in original).

10. Miranda to Gual, December 31, 1799, *Archivo del General Miranda*, ed. Vicente Dávila, 24 vols. (Caracas: Editorial Sur-América, 1929–1950), 15:404. For the best overview of the revolutions in Spanish America, see John Lynch, *The Spanish-American Revolutions: 1808–1826*, 2nd ed. (New York: Norton, 1986).

11. Loewenstein, "The Presidency outside the United States," 452. Although Loewenstein claims the Latin American countries "adopted the 'presidential pattern' of the United States constitution," one must consider the pattern of degeneration into *caudillismo* discussed later.

Latin American countries also experimented with parliamentarianism, but the attempts were mostly short lived and ended in failure. Brazil lived under a parliamentary government while under monarchical rule until 1891 when it adopted the U.S. model of presidential government until 1961, after which it tried parliamentarianism but then reverted again to the North American model. Two other countries experimented with parliamentarian government: Bolivia in the 1930s and Venezuela in the 1940s. The longest and most successful parliamentary regime was that of Chile from 1891 to 1925. See Jacques Lambert, *Latin America: Social Structure and Political Institutions*, trans. Helen Katel (Berkeley: University of California Press, 1967), 270.

12. Hugh M. Hamill, introduction to *Caudillos: Dictators in Spanish America*, ed. Hugh M. Hamill (Norman: University of Oklahoma Press, 1992); and Hugh M. Hamill, "Caudillismo, Caudillo," in *Encyclopedia of Latin American History and Culture*, ed. Barbara A. Tenenbaum, Georgette Magassy Dorn, et al., 5 vols. (New York: Scribner, 1996), 2:38–40.

13. Lambert, *Latin America: Social Structure and Political Institutions*, 335–37.

14. Claudio Grossman, "States of Emergency: Latin America and the United States," in Henkin and Rosenthal, eds., *Constitutionalism and Rights*, 188.

15. Alexander T. Edelmann, *Latin American Government and Politics: The Dynamics of a Revolutionary Society*, rev. ed. (Homewood, IL: Dorsey Press, 1969), 392–93.

16. The best single essay on the subject of federalism in Latin America is Keith S. Rosenn's "Federalism in the Americas in Comparative Perspective," *University of Miami Inter-American Law Review* 26 (1994):1–50.
Three other countries or groups of countries experimented with federalism—Honduras (1824–1831), United Provinces of Central America (1829–1838), and Colombia (1853–1856)—but their experiences were relatively short lived.

17. Lambert, *Latin America: Social Structures and Political Institutions*, 300.

18. Edelmann, *Latin American Politics and Government*, 395.

19. Daniel J. Elazar, *Exploring Federalism* (Tuscaloosa: University of Alabama Press, 1987), 10. Elazar, moreover, places great emphasis on the Protestant theological roots of American federalism, particularly on the covenant tradition within Calvinism, a tradition not available to largely Catholic Latin American countries.

20. Rosenn, "The Success of Constitutionalism in the United States and Its Failure in Latin America," *Inter-American Law Review*,30.

21. W. J. Wagner, *The Federal States and Their Judiciary: A Comparative Study in Constitutional Law and Organization of Courts in Federal States* ('s-Gravenhage: Mouton, 1959), 119.

22. Lambert, *Latin America: Social Structure and Political Institutions*, 287–96; and Rosenn, "The Success of Constitutionalism in the United States and Its Failure in Latin America," *Inter-American Law Review*, 27. See also Keith S. Rosenn's authoritative article, "The Protection of Judicial Independence in Latin America," *University of Miami Inter-American Law Review* 19 (1987):7–35.

23. Rosenn, "The Success of Constitutionalism in the United States and Its Failure in Latin America," *Inter-American Law Review*, 25–26.

24. Ibid., 26.

25. The total number of 253 constitutions, which includes some of the Caribbean countries as well, is as follows: Argentina 6, Bolivia 15, Brazil 8, Chile 9, Colombia 12, Costa Rica 9, Cuba 7, Dominican Republic 32, Ecuador 19, El Salvador 14, Guatemala 9, Haiti 24, Honduras 14, Mexico 8, Nicaragua 14, Panama 4, Paraguay 5, Peru 12, Uruguay 7, and Venezuela 25. See Rosenn, "The Success of Constitutionalism in the United States and Its Failure in Latin America," in Thompson, ed., *The U.S. Constitution*, app. A, 87–96.

26. Rosenn, "The Success of Constitutionalism in the United States and Its Failure in Latin America," *Inter-American Law Review*, 21. For a recent, particularly good book on nineteenth-century liberalism, see Carlos A. Forment, *Democracy in Latin America 1760–1900*, vol. 1, *Civic Selfhood and Public Life in Mexico and Peru* (Chicago: University of Chicago Press, 2003–).

27. Rosenn, "The Success of Constitutionalism in the United States and Its Failure in Latin America," *Inter-American Law Review*, 1–30. The discussion that follows relies heavily on Rosenn's analysis.

28. Gordon S. Wood, *The Radicalism of the American Revolution* (New York: Vintage Books, 1993), 3–8.

29. George Blanksten, "Revolutions," in *Government and Politics in Latin America*, ed. Harold Eugene Davis (New York: Ronald Press, 1958), 141.

30. Thomas E. Skidmore and Peter H. Smith, *Modern Latin America*, 3rd ed. (New York: Oxford University Press, 1992), 33 (italics in original). The successive editions of this work contain important insights into the constitutional history of Latin America as well as the influence of North American constitutionalism throughout the region. See also Stanley J. Stein and Barbara H. Stein, *The Colonial Heritage of Latin America: Essays on Economic Dependence in Perspective* (New York: Oxford University Press, 1970), 133–38. Peggy K. Liss, *Atlantic Empires: The Network of Trade and Revolution, 1713–1826* (Baltimore: Johns Hopkins University Press,1983), traces the connection between the revolutionary political theory in Latin America and its position in rising world trade in the Atlantic network from 1713 to 1826.

31. Rosenn, "The Success of Constitutionalism in the United States and Its Failure in Latin America," in Thompson, ed., *The U.S. Constitution*, 69–70. For Bolívar's quotation, see R. A. Humphreys, "The Fall of the Spanish American Empire," in *Tradition and Revolt in Latin America and Other Essays*, ed. R. A. Humphreys (New York: Columbia University Press, 1969), 83.

32. Skidmore and Smith, *Latin America*, 3d ed., 18.

33. Rosenn, "The Success of Constitutionalism in the United States and Its Failure in Latin America," in Thompson, ed., *The U.S. Constitution*, 70–71. See also Russell H. Fitzgibbon, *Latin America: A Panorama of Contemporary Politics* (New York: Appleton-Century-Crofts, 1971), 15.

34. John J. Johnson, *The Military and Society in Latin America* (Stanford, CA: Stanford University Press, 1964), 33.

35. Ibid., 38.

36. Rosenn, "The Success of Constitutionalism in the United States and Its Failure in Latin America," *Inter-American Law Review*, 30.

37. Rosenn, "The Success of Constitutionalism in the United States and Its Failure in Latin America," in Thompson, ed., *The U.S. Constitution*, 73.

38. Arthur Preston Whitaker, *The Western Hemisphere Idea: Its Rise and Decline* (Ithaca, NY: Cornell University Press,1954), 41–52.

39. Stein and Stein, *Colonial Heritage of Latin America*, 138.

40. Skidmore and Smith, *Modern Latin America*, 3rd ed., 42.

41. Rosenn, "The Success of Constitutionalism in the United States and Its Failure in Latin America," in Thompson, ed., *The U.S. Constitution*, 69, 74–76.

42. Simón Bolívar, *Selected Writings*, comp. Vincente Lecuna, ed. Harold A. Bierck, and trans. Lewis Bertrand, 2 vols. (New York: Colonial Press, 1951), 1:307.

43. E. Bradford Burns, *Latin America: A Concise Interpretive History* (Englewood Cliffs, NJ: Prentice-Hall, 1972), 69; and William Spence Robertson, *Hispanic-American Relations with the United States,* ed. David Kinley (New York: Oxford University Press, 1923), 64.

44. Manuel Garcia de Sena, *La independencia de la costa firma* (Philadelphia: T. & J. Palmer, 1811); *Gazeta de Caracas,* January 14 and 17, 1812; Robertson, *Hispanic-American Relations with the United States,* 70–71; José Luis Romero, "La independencia de Hispano América y el modelo político Norteamericano," *Inter-American Review of Bibliography* 26 (1976):452; and Collier, *Ideas and Politics of Chilean Independence,* 174.

45. Robertson, *Hispanic-American Relations with the United States,* 76–77. Three writers on constitutional matters who had actually lived in the United States and praised its political system in their writings were Vicente Rocafuerte, an Ecuadorian; Manuel Lorenzo Viduarre, a Peruvian; and Manuel Dorrego, exiled for a time from Argentina. See Robertson, *Hispanic-American Relations with the United States,* 64–65; Belaúnde, *Bolívar and the Political Thought of the Spanish American Revolution,* 29–31; and John Lynch, "The River Plate Republics from Independence to the Paraguayan War," in Bethell, ed., *The Cambridge History of Latin America,* 3:632–33.

46. Francisco de Miranda, *The New Democracy in America, Travels of Francisco de Miranda in the United States, 1783–84,* trans. Judson P. Wood and ed. John S. Ezell (Norman: University of Oklahoma Press, 1963), 163.

47. Robertson, *Hispanic-American Relations with the United States,* 83. Moreno also published a modified version of the U.S. Constitution; see Kolesar, "North American Constitutionalism and Spanish America," 61.

48. Quoted in Robertson, *Hispanic-American Relations with the United States,* 81.

49. *La aurora de Chile,* June 4, November 12, December 10, and December 17, 1812.

50. Gene Brack, *Mexico Views Manifest Destiny, 1821–1846: An Essay on the Origins of the Mexican War* (Albuquerque: University of New Mexico Press, 1975), 24.

51. Ibid.

52. Ibid., 24–25. The Massachusetts State Constitution of 1780 was described in detail in *El aquila mexicana,* May 21 and 22, 1823.

53. Safford, "Politics, Ideology and Society in Post-Independence Spanish America," 106.

54. Ibid., 44.

55. Burns, *Latin America,* 26.

56. Antonio Pina and Gloria Moran, "Spanish Constitution of 1812," in *Constitutions That Made History,* ed. Albert P. Blaustein and Jay A. Sigler (New York: Paragon House, 1988), 114–16.

57. Richard J. Cleveland, *Voyages and Commercial Enterprises of the Sons of New England* (1855; repr., New York: B. Franklin, 1968), 174 and 194; and Roy Nichols, "William Shaler, New England Apostle for Rational Liberty," *New England Quarterly* 9 (1936):73.

58. Nichols, "William Shaler, New England Apostle for Rational Liberty," 73.

59. J. Fred Rippy, *Joel R. Poinsett, Versatile American* (Durham, NC: Duke University Press, 1935), vii.

60. Ibid., 44.

61. Ibid., 106; Collier, *Ideas and Politics of Chilean Independence*, 97–98 and 112; and Kolesar, "North American Constitutionalism and Spanish America," 46.

62. Brack, *Mexico Views Manifest Destiny*, 36 and 44. For a full description of Poinsett's activities, see 28–38; and Rippy, *Joel R. Poinsett*, chaps. 4 and 5.

63. W. G. D. Worthington to Bernardo O'Higgins, May 5, 1818, in *Diplomatic Correspondence of the United States Concerning the Independence of Latin American Nations*, ed. William R. Manning, 3 vols. (New York: Oxford University Press, 1925–1926), 2:923–24. See also 1029–30.

64. Ibid. 1:188.

65. Ibid. 1:655.

66. The first Latin American edition of *The Federalist*, however, may have been published in Portuguese, not Spanish. In 1840, a Portuguese translation appeared in Rio de Janeiro. Although this work was cited frequently in Spanish-speaking Latin America, no other edition seems to have been published before this one. See Roy P. Fairfield, *The Federalist Papers: A Collection of Essays Written in Support of the Constitution of the United States*, 2nd ed. (Baltimore: Johns Hopkins University Press, 1981), 309. Copies of the Brazilian edition were reported circulating in Argentina as late as the 1880s. See Gottfried Dietze, *The Federalist: A Classic on Federalism and Free Government* (Baltimore: Johns Hopkins University Press, 1960), 8.

67. Dietze, *The Federalist*, 8. Dietze apparently confuses Henry M. Brackenridge, a lawyer and journalist, who wrote this account, with his father, Hugh Henry Brackenridge, a jurist and writer. The report that Manuel Garcia de Sena published a book in 1811 containing a Spanish translation of the work has been discredited (7–8).

68. [No author] *Cartas de un americano sobre las ventajas de los gobiernos republicanos federativos* (London: M. Calero, 1826). The work was a response to Juan Egaña, *Memorias políticas obre la federaciones y legislaturas en general y con relacion a Chile* (Santiago: Impr. de la Independencia, 1825). See Dietze, *The Federalist*, 7–8.

69. Herman G. James, *The Constitutional System of Brazil* (Washington, DC: Carnegie Institute, 1923), 6–7; and Peter Flynn, *Brazil: A Political Analysis* (London: E. Benn, 1978), 11.

70. Amadeo, *Argentine Constitutional Law*, 29–30. See Juan Bautista Alberdi, *Bases y puntos de partida para la organización política de la República Arjentina: Derivados de la lei que preside al desarrollo de la civilización en la América del Sud*, 2nd ed. (Valparaiso: Impr. del Mercurio, 1852).

71. David Bushnell and Neill Macaulay, *The Emergence of Latin America in the Nineteenth Century* (New York: Oxford University Press, 1988), 27.

72. Safford, "Politics, Ideology, and Society in Post-Independence Spanish America," 3:357–58; and Charles McIlwain, "Bills of Rights," in *Encyclopaedia of the Social Sciences*, ed. Edwin R. A. Seligman and Alvin Johnson, 15 vols. (New York: Macmillan, 1937), 2:545.

73. Carmen Ramos-Escandon, "Constitution of 1857," in *Encyclopedia of Latin American History and Culture*, 4:25.

74. Fitzgibbon, *Latin America: A Panorama of Contemporary Politics*, 61–62. See also Richard D. Baker, *Judicial Review in Mexico: A Study of the Amparo Suit* (Austin: University of Texas Press, 1971); Rosenn, "Federalism in the Americas in Comparative Perspective," 26; and Vicki C. Jackson and Mark Tushnet, *Comparative Constitutional Law*, University Casebook Series (New York: Foundation Press, 1999), 472.

75. The single exception was Brazil, where Prince Dom Pedro proclaimed independence orally; see Richard B. Morris, *The Emerging Nations and the American Revolution* (New York: Harper & Row, 1970), 141. But there is no evidence of his declaration being influenced by Jefferson's manifesto. See David Armitage, *The Declaration of Independence: A Global History* (Cambridge, MA: Harvard University Press, 2007), 117. For the Declaration affecting Spanish America in its first wave outside the United States (1790–1848), see 108, and for the heavy emphasis of the document during the decades of the 1810s and 1820s, see 118.

76. *La constitución federal de Venezuela de 1811 y documento afinos* (Caracas: Academia nacional de la historia, 1959), 94–95.

77. William Spence Robertson, *Rise of the Spanish-American Republics as Told in the Lives of Their Liberators* (New York: D. Appleton, 1918), 63. For a different account, see Armitage, *The Declaration of Independence*, 119.

78. Robertson, *Rise of the Spanish-American Republics*, 224. See Armitage, *The Declaration of Independence*, 120.

79. D. A. Brading, *The First America: The Spanish Monarchy, Creole Patriots, and the Liberal State, 1492–1867* (Cambridge: Cambridge University Press, 1991), 5.

80. Pauline Maier, *American Scripture: The Making of the Declaration of Independence* (New York: Knopf, 1997), 280, n. 67.

81. Robertson, *Rise of the Spanish-American Republics*, 118.

82. Robertson, *Hispanic-American Relations with the United States*, 87.

83. Robertson, *Rise of the Spanish-American Republics*, 197–98.

84. Joedd Price, "Images and Influences: the Legacy of the Founding Fathers and Federal System in Ecuador," *Latin America Research Review* 10 (1975):128.

85. In the traditional approach to the historiography of Spanish American independence, the dominant view was that the early juntas of 1810 and the revolutionary movements that developed out of them were associated with the same revolutionary process that produced the American Revolution of 1776 and the French Revolution of 1789. Coupled with Enlightenment ideas, it was thought that these were the main root causes of the early Spanish American revolutionary movements. But this interpretation has been challenged on two counts. First was the Hispanic influence of the thought of Francisco Suárez, a Spanish thinker (1548–1617), who rejected the idea of the divine right of kings and held as his thesis that civil power is derived from God by way of the people. Thus, the idea of the natural right of the people in Latin America to set up governments in response to the Spanish monarchy crisis could well have been derived from Suárez rather than men like Jefferson and Rousseau. Second, the role of political ideology as a cause of the revolutionary movements has been deemphasized recently, as pragmatic and material considerations such as Creole-peninsula rivalry and internal and external economic pressures have loomed larger. See Bethell, ed., *The Cambridge History of Latin America*, 2:106–7. See also Josefina Zoraida Vázquez, "The Mexican Declaration of Independence," *Journal of American History* 85 (March 1999):1369.

86. Vázquez, "The Mexican Declaration of Independence," 1369.

87. Armitage, *The Declaration of Independence*, 121–22.

88. Kolesar, "North American Constitutionalism and Spanish America," 47.

89. Ibid.

90. *La verdad*, March 5, 1833.

91. Alberdi, *Bases y puntos de partida para la organización política de la República Argentina*, in *Obras completas de J. B. Alberdi*, 3 vols. (Buenos Aires: Imp de "La tribuna nacional," 1886–1887), 3:509, 510.

92. Ibid., 3:556.

93. Robertson, *Hispanic-American Relations with the United States*, 85.

94. The Virginia State Constitution of 1776 seemed of special interest to the conspirators, since they had carefully annotated their copy. See Kenneth Maxwell, "The Influence of the U.S. Constitution and Latin America," 11–12.

95. Charles Francis Adams, ed., *Works of John Adams, Second President of the United States (1787)*, 10 vols. (Boston: Little, Brown, 1850–1856), 10:145; and Jefferson to John Adams, January 21, 1821, in *The Adams-Jefferson Letters: The Complete Correspondence between Thomas Jefferson and Abigail and John Adams*, ed. Lester J. Cappon, 2 vols. (Chapel Hill: University of North Carolina Press, 1959), 2:370. There is a wealth of information regarding attitudes of North Americans toward Latin America in Lars Schoultz, *Beneath the United States: A History of U.S. Policy toward Latin America* (Cambridge, MA: Harvard University Press, 1998).

96. Hale, *Mexican Liberalism in the Age of Mora*, 194; Brack, *Mexico Views Manifest Destiny*, 45; and Kolesar, "North American Constitutionalism and Spanish America," 46–47.

97. Leo Lott, "Venezuelan Federalism," *American Political Science Review* 50 (1956):21. See also the eminent Venezuelan constitutionalist, Ernesto Wolf, *Tratado de derecho constitucional venezolano*, 2 vols. (Caracas: Tipografía americana, 1945).

98. Leo Lott, "Venezuelan Federalism: A Case of Frustration" (PhD diss., University of Wisconsin, 1954), 22; and Robertson, *Hispanic-American Relations with the United States*, 73. There were, of course, other foreign influences on the 1811 Venezuelan Constitution, but the focus here, as in all constitutions to be discussed, is solely on the U.S. influence.

99. Robertson, *Hispanic-American Relations with the United States*, 72.

100. Bolívar, *Selected Writings*, 1:180 and xx.

101. Ibid., 1:21.

102. Ibid., 45; and Kolesar, "North American Constitutionalism and Spanish America," 49.

103. Bolívar, *Selected Writings*, 1:179–80.

104. Ibid., 2:599.

105. Ibid., 2:541.

106. Belaúnde, *Bolívar and the Political Thought of the Spanish American Revolution*, 76 and 86.

107. Robertson, *Rise of Spanish-American Republics*, 34.

108. Rosenn, "The Success of Constitutionalism in the United States and Its Failure in Latin America," in Thompson, ed., *The U.S. Constitution*, 94. This figure includes the constitutions when Venezuela was part of the Republic of Colombia and the Republic of Gran Colombia.

109. Winfield Burggraff, "Venezuela, Constitutions," *Encyclopedia of Latin American History and Culture*, 5:394.

110. Paul Vanorden Shaw, *The Early Constitutions of Chile, 1810–1833* (New York: Chile Publishing Company, 1931), 67–68; Collier, *Ideas and Politics of Chilean Independence*, 307; and, for the quotation, article 8 of the draft constitution.

111. *Sesiones de los cuerpos lejislativos de la República de Chile 1811–1845*, comp. Valentín Letelier, 37 vols. (Santiago: Cervantes, 1887–1908), 12:56 and 102. For an excellent account of the years 1810 to 1833, see the work of the leading scholar, Luis Galdames, *Historia de Chile, la evolución constitucional* (Santiago: Balcells, 1925). The sixteenth edition of the work was published in 1996 under the imprint "Editorial universitaria."

112. Domingo Santa-Maria Gonzalez, *Vida de don José Miguel Infante* (1853; repr., Santiago: G. Miranda, 1902), 104.

113. Kolesar, "North American Constitutionalism and Spanish America," 50; and Collier, *Ideas and Politics of Chilean Independence*, 359.

114. David Pantoja Morán and Jorge Mario García Laguardia, *Tres documentos constitucionales en la América española preindependiente* (Mexico City: UNAM, Instituto de investigaciones jurídicas, 1975), 11.

115. Ibid., 12.

116. Virginia Guedea, "Chilpancingo, Congress of," in *Encyclopedia of Latin American History and Culture*, 2:138.

117. Robertson, *Hispanic-American Relations with the United States*, 65; and Eugene C. Barker, *The Life of Stephen Austin, Founder of Texas, 1793–1836: A Chapter in the Westward Movement of the Anglo-American People*, 2nd ed. (Nashville: Cokesbury Press, 1925), 75–76. Barker agrees that Austin's draft was "thoroughly assimilated and coordinated" with Arispe's document.

118. Hale, *Mexican Liberalism in the Age of Mora*, 195; José María Luis Mora, *México y sus revoluciones*, 3 vols. (Mexico City: Porrua, 1965), 1:256; and H. G. Ward, *Mexico in 1827*, 2 vols. (London: H. Colburn, 1828), 1:iii.

119. *Coleccion de ordenes y decretos de la soberana junta provisional gubernativa y soberanos congresos generales de la nacion Mexicana*, 4 vols. (Mexico City: M. Arévalo, 1829–1840), 3:18–105.

120. Hale, *Mexican Liberalism in the Age of Mora*, 193–95; and Lynch, *The Spanish American Revolutions*, 325. In the English version of *La diputación provincial y el federalismo Mexicano: The Provincial Deputation in Mexico: Harbinger of Provincial Autonomy, Independence, and Federalism* (Austin: University of Texas Press, 1992), Nettie Lee Benson claims that Mexican federalism owed little to the United States and more to the Spanish Cortes of 1812 which authorized provincial deputations evolving from that time to 1824, passim.

121. Kolesar, "North American Constitutionalism and Spanish America," 43.

122. *American Constitutions: A Compilation of the Political Constitutions of the Independent Nations of the New World*, comp. and trans. José Ignacio Rodríguez, 2 vols. (Washington, DC: U.S. Government Printing Office, 1906–1907), 1:39-96; and Robertson, *Hispanic-American Relations with the United States*, 65.

123. Mexico, Constitution of 1857, article 101.

124. The power of the state courts is reduced, however, since questions about interpretation of state laws are routinely referred to federal courts. See Rosenn, "Federalism in the Americas in Comparative Perspective," 26.

125. Julie A. Erfani, *The Paradox of the Mexican State: Rereading Sovereignty from Independence to NAFTA* (Boulder, CO: Lynne Rienner Publisher, 1995), 1–7.

126. Amadeo, *Argentine Constitutional Law*, 16–18. The influence of the U.S. Constitution was evident also in four drafts of earlier constitutions that were either not submitted or not approved (12).

127. Ibid., 18–20.

128. Carl J. Friedrich, *The Impact of American Constitutionalism Abroad* (Boston: Boston University Press, 1967), 8, argues that Brazil's Constitution of 1891 was perhaps the closest case to the U.S. Constitution. But Rosenn and I agree

that Argentina's constitution of 1853 was more closely modeled after that of the United States than Brazil's. See Rosenn, "The Success of Constitutionalism in the United States and Its Failure in Latin America," *Inter-American Law Review*, 24.

129. Robertson, *Hispanic-American Relations with the United States*, 89–90.

130. Amadeo, *Argentine Constitutional Law*, 31.

131. Juan José Díaz Arana, *Influencia de Alberdi en la constitución nacional, juicio ante una controversia* (Buenos Aires: V. Abeledo, 1947), sums up the controversy and establishes Alberdi's contribution.

132. Amadeo, *Argentine Constitutional Law*, 29.

133. *Asambleas constituyentes argentinas, seguidas de los textos constitucionales, legislativos y pactos interprovinciales que organizaron políticament la nación . . . ,* ed. Emilio Ravignani, 7 vols. (Buenos Aires: Casa Jacobo Peuser, 1937–1939), 4:468.

134. Ibid., 4:479.

135. Amadeo, *Argentine Constitutional Law*, 37–38.

136. In an old study, Paul Groussac, director of the national library in Argentina, estimated that sixty-three articles resembled corresponding provisions from the North American document. He argued that the striking resemblances resulted mainly from provisions in the 1819 and 1826 constitutions that had been influenced by the U.S. model and then transmitted to the 1853 constitution. Santiago Baqué, another scholar, differed with Groussac and made the exaggerated claim that the nucleus of that document, the constitutions of 1819 and 1826, and the Alberdi project all were dependent on material drawn "for about two-thirds of the articles" from the U.S. Constitution. A subsequent study more realistically estimated that forty-four sections of the two constitutions were identical, twenty-two were similar, forty-eight were different, and sixty sections of the Argentine Constitution were not to be found in the U.S. Constitution at all. Robertson, *Hispanic-American Relations with the United States*, 92; and Linares Quintana, "Comparisons of United States and Argentine Constitutional Systems," *University of Pennsylvania Law Review* 97 (1948–1949):641–64.

137. Amadeo, *Argentine Constitutional Law*, 32.

138. Clarence Haring, "Federalism in Latin America," in *The Constitution Reconsidered*, ed. Richard B. Morris, rev. ed. (New York: Harper & Row, 1968), 344.

139. José Luis Romero, *A History of Argentine Political Thought* (Stanford, CA: Stanford University Press, 1963), 3-4; and Amadeo, *Argentine Constitutional Law*, 219. See also Morris, *Emerging Nations and the American Revolution*, 143.

140. Amadeo, *Argentine Constitutional Law*, 217.

141. Romero, *History of Argentine Political Thought*, 152; and Stokes, *Latin American Politics*, 463. See Jorge Reinaldo Vanossi, "La influencia de la Constitución de los Estados Unidos de Norteamérica en la Constitución de la República Argentina," *Separato de la revista de San Isidro*, December 1976, 95. In his important article, Vanossi stresses seventeen ways in which the two constitutions differ,

94–101. The essay is reprinted in *Visiones de una constitución* (Buenos Aires: Universidad de ciencias empresariales y sociales, 2004), 27–66.

142. Amadeo, *Argentine Constitutional Law,* 49.

143. Ibid., 63.

144. Ibid., 73–74.

145. Ibid., 74–77.

146. Skidmore and Smith, *Modern Latin America,* 5th ed. (2001), 140–41.

147. James, *Constitutional System of Brazil,* 3. Brazil's constitutional history is much more complicated than the account given here.

148. Morris, *Emerging Nations and the American Revolution,* 143; Robertson, *Hispanic-American Relations with the United States,* 97; and Burns, *Latin America,* 91.

149. Charles W. Turner, *Ruy Barbosa: Brazilian Crusader for the Essential Freedoms* (New York: Abingdon-Cokesbury Press, 1945), 109.

150. Ibid., 111. For the continuing influence of European ties, see Gilberto Freyre, *Order and Progress: Brazil from Monarchy to Republic,* ed. and trans. Rod W. Horton (New York: Knopf, 1970), 31.

151. Turner, *Ruy Barbosa,* 111.

152. Ibid., 110.

153. James, *Constitutional System of Brazil,* 10; and Robertson, *Hispanic-American Relations with the United States,* 98. There is a controversy regarding the degree to which Barbosa was the author of the draft constitution; see Felisbello Freire, *Historia constitucional da Republica dos Estados Unidos do Brasil,* 3 vols. (Rio de Janeiro: Typ. Aldina, 1894–1895), cited in James, *Constitutional System of Brazil,* 10. For a comparison article by article of the draft constitution with the finished document, see the work of the great Brazilian constitutional historian, João Barbalho, *Constituição federal brazileira; commentarios* (Rio de Janeiro: Sapopemba, 1902).

154. Fitzgibbon, *Latin America,* 262. See also James, *Constitutional System of Brazil,* 32–34 and 106–26.

155. Brazil, Constitution of 1891, article 59 (1), 60.

156. James, *Constitutional History of Brazil,* 106.

157. Rosenn, "Federalism in the Americas in Comparative Perspective," 42.

158. Friedrich, *The Impact of American Constitutionalism Abroad,* 56.

159. James, *Constitutional System of Brazil,* 221–36.

160. Ibid., 51.

161. Rosenn, "The Success of Constitutionalism in the United States and Its Failure in Latin America," *Inter-American Law Review,* 24–25.

162. Brian E. Loveman, "Military Constitutionalism," in *Encyclopedia of Democratic Thought,* ed. Paul Barry Clarke and Joe Foweraker (New York: Routledge, 2001), 437.

CHAPTER 5

1. John A. Hawgood, *Modern Constitutions since 1787* (London: Macmillan, 1939), 92.

2. Ibid., 104.

3. The concept of a "representative democracy" as distinctly different from a constitutional monarchy did not begin to emerge in Europe until after the 1830s. See Klaus von Beyme, *America as a Model: The Impact of American Democracy in the World* (New York: St. Martin's Press, 1987), 17.

4. Frede Castberg, *Norway and the Western Powers: A Study of Comparative Constitutional Law* (Oslo: Oslo University Press, 1957), 12.

5. Richard B. Morris, *The Emerging Nations and the American Revolution* (New York: Harper & Row, 1970), 95–96; Franklin D. Scott, *Scandinavia*, rev. and enlarged ed. (Cambridge, MA: Harvard University Press, 1975), 47; Stefan Björklund, comp., *Kring, 1809* (Stockholm: Wahlström & Widstrand, 1965), 114–19; and Castberg, *Norway and the Western Powers*, 5.

6. Franklin D. Scott, *The United States and Scandinavia* (Cambridge, MA: Harvard University Press, 1950), 66.

7. Morris, *Emerging Nations and the American Revolution*, 96; T. K. Derry, *A Short History of Norway*, 2nd ed. (London: Allen & Unwin, 1968), 134; and Castberg, *Norway and the Western Powers*, 13.

8. Lloyd Kramer, *Lafayette in Two Worlds: Public Cultures and Personal Identities in an Age of Revolution* (Chapel Hill: University of North Carolina Press, 1996), 65. Kramer, Lafayette's most recent biographer, goes out of his way to deemphasize the unfair label of "fool" fastened on Lafayette by Napoleon. Kramer emphasizes instead Lafayette's important intellectual activities during this period, and I am inclined to agree with him. See Kramer, *Lafayette in Two Worlds*, chap. 3. The article "Lafayette," by Patrice Gueniffey in *Critical Dictionary of the French Revolution*, ed. François Furet and Mona Ozouf and trans. Arthur Goldhammer (Cambridge, MA: Harvard University Press, 1989), 224–33, is much less favorable.

9. *New York Commercial Advertiser*, August 19, 1824; and Kramer, *Lafayette in Two Worlds*, 204.

10. *Cincinnati Advertiser*, May 25, 1825.

11. Auguste Levasseur, *Lafayette in America in 1824 and 1825: Or, Journal of a Voyage to the United States*, trans. J. D. Godman, MD, 2 vols. (Philadelphia: Carey & Lea, 1829), 2:253.

12. Kramer, *Lafayette in Two Worlds*, 246.

13. Quoted in John McBride, "America and the French Mind during the Bourbon Restoration" (PhD diss., Syracuse University, 1953), 268.

14. Emmet Kennedy, *A Philosophe in the Age of Revolution: Destutt de Tracy and the Origins of "Ideology"* (Philadelphia: American Philosophical Society,

1978), x–xi; and Lawrence S. Kaplan, *Jefferson and France: An Essay on Politics and Political Ideas* (New Haven, CT: Yale University Press, 1967), 92.

15. Kramer, *Lafayette in Two Worlds*, 56. *Ideologist* was the word coined by Tracy in 1802 to label the philosophical movement based mainly on the sensationalist theory of knowledge as a science of ideas. Although it was not intended to identify any group in particular, it affected many leaders involved in the French Revolution, except for followers of Rousseau and the Terrorists (91–93). See Cheryl Welch, *Liberty and Utility: The French Idéologues and the Transformation of Liberalism* (New York: Columbia University Press, 1984).

16. Destutt de Tracy, along with his fellow ideologists, criticized Rousseau for having led the French Revolution astray by encouraging its experiments with egalitarianism and authoritarian rule. See Bernard Manin, "Rousseau," in *Critical Dictionary of the French Revolution*, 830.

17. Kramer, *Lafayette in Two Worlds*, 57.

18. Jefferson to Destutt de Tracy, January 26, 1811; cited in Kennedy, *A Philosophe in the Age of Revolution*, 211.

19. Kennedy, *A Philosophe in the Age of Revolution*, 211.

20. Antoine Louis Claude, comte Destutt de Tracy, *Commentaire sur l'esprit de lois de Montesquieu* (Paris: Mme. Levi, 1828), 19–20 and 97–98. Tracy qualified his generalization about republicanism in small-sized countries by pointing out that the Roman Senate had successfully governed a large territory in the Roman Empire. Tracy's tract was published in English in Philadelphia by William Duane (1811). The edition cited here is that published in Paris in 1828.

21. Kramer, *Lafayette in Two Worlds*, 60.

22. Kennedy, *A Philosophe in the Age of Revolution*, 211.

23. Ibid., 212.

24. Jefferson to Francis Wayles Eppes, June 27, 1821, in *The Family Letters of Thomas Jefferson*, ed. Edwin Morris Betts and James Adam Bear Jr. (Columbia: University of Missouri Press, 1966), 439–40. Jefferson and Tracy also were in general agreement on economic matters, with Jefferson subscribing to the critique of Montesquieu found in Tracy's *A Treatise on Political Economy* (Washington, DC: J. Milligan, 1817); also see Drew R. McCoy, *The Elusive Republic: Political Economy in Jeffersonian America* (Chapel Hill: University of North Carolina Press, 1980), 253. For a more detailed analysis of Tracy's ideas, see David N. Mayer, *The Constitutional Thought of Thomas Jefferson* (Charlottesville: University Press of Virginia, 1994), 140.

25. Kennedy, *A Philosophe in the Age of Revolution*, 231–32.

26. See Alexis de Tocqueville, *Democracy in America*, ed. J. P. Mayer and trans. George Lawrence, 2 vols. in 1 (Garden City, NY: Doubleday, 1969); George Wilson Pierson, *Tocqueville and Beaumont in America* (New York: Oxford University Press, 1938); Jean-Claude Lamberti, *Tocqueville and the Two Democracies*, trans. Arthur Goldhammer (Cambridge, MA: Harvard University Press,

1989); J. P. Mayer, *Alexis de Tocqueville: A Biographical Study in Political Science*, 2nd ed. (Gloucester, MA: P. Smith, 1966); and James T. Schleifer, *The Making of Tocqueville's* Democracy in America (Chapel Hill: University of North Carolina Press, 1980), among many other works. There are, of course, many different ways of interpreting Tocqueville: see Robert Nisbet, "Many Tocquevilles," *American Scholar* 46 (1976/1977):59–75. Whether Tocqueville embodied the true liberal temper of his times has been debated endlessly.

27. Mayer, ed., *Democracy in America*, 165.

28. Ibid., 156.

29. Ibid., 157.

30. Ibid., 674–79.

31. Ibid., 373.

32. Ibid., 163–70.

33. Ibid., 58–98.

34. Schleifer, *The Making of Tocqueville's* Democracy, 9.

35. Mayer, ed., *Democracy in America*, 122–25.

36. Ibid., 125–26.

37. Ibid., 8, 104, and 101.

38. Ibid., 149. There is an important typographical error in the Mayer edition which reads "every" instead of "ever."

39. Mayer, ed., *Democracy in America*, 99. It is impossible to do justice here to the many perceptive insights of Tocqueville regarding the U.S. Constitution. My treatment is admittedly cursory.

40. Mayer, ed., *Democracy in America*,115.

41. James Schleifer identified the exact 1831 edition that Tocqueville used and showed that he borrowed heavily without attribution. See Schleifer, *The Making of Tocqueville's* Democracy, 88.

42. Quoted in Schleifer, *The Making of Tocqueville's* Democracy, 89 (italics in original).

43. Compare Madison's *Federalist* 39 in *The Federalist*, ed. Jacob E. Cooke (Middletown, CT: Wesleyan University Press, 1961), 257, with Mayer, ed., *Democracy in America*, 157.

44. See esp. Mayer, ed., *Democracy in America*, 262–76.

45. Ibid., 292.

46. Ibid., 180–88.

47. Ibid., 287–90.

48. Ibid., 520–24.

49. Ibid., 112–15 and 155–56.

50. Ibid., xiv.

51. Ibid.

52. See J. P. Mayer, *Political Thought in France from Sieyès to Sorel* (London: Faber & Faber, 1943); E. L. Woodward, *Three Studies in European Conservatism:*

Metternich, Guizot, the Catholic Church in the Nineteenth Century (London: F. Cass, 1963); and Gordon Wright, *France in Modern Times: From the Enlightenment to the Present*, 3rd ed. (New York: Norton, 1981).

53. Mcbride, *America in the French Mind during the Bourbon Restoration*, 104–5.

54. Louis-Philippe, comte de Ségur, *Memoires ou souvenirs et anecdotes*, 3 vols. (Paris: A. Eymery, 1825–1826), 1:423; Marquis de François Barbé-Marbois, *Complot d'Arnold et de Sir Henry Clinton contre les États-Unis d'Amérique et contre le Général Washington* (Paris: P. Didot, 1816), passim.

55. *Le Conservateur* 4 (1819):373–74.

56. Durand Echeverria, *Mirage in the West: A History of the French Image of American Society to 1815* (Princeton, NJ: Princeton University Press, 1957), 212; *Journal des débats*, July 5 and October 25, 1826. For the posthumous record, see François-René, vicomte de Chateaubriand, *Mémoires d'outre tombe*, 12 vols. (Paris: E. et V. Penaud frères, 1849–1850), discussed in McBride, *America in the French Mind during the Bourbon Restoration*, 187.

57. Hawgood, *Modern Constitutions since 1787*, 142–46.

58. Albert P. Blaustein and Jay A. Sigler, eds., *Constitutions That Made History* (New York: Paragon House, 1988), 182–83.

59. Hawgood, *Modern Constitutions since 1787*, 141 and 146; and F. Reyntjiens, "Belgian Constitution of 1831," in Blaustein and Sigler, eds., *Constitutions That Made History*, 131.

60. E. H. Kossman, *The Low Countries, 1780–1940* (Oxford: Clarendon Press, 1978), 157.

61. Reyntjiens, "Belgian Constitution of 1831," 131.

62. For Hamilton's use of the term, see Willi Paul Adams, *The First American Constitutions: Republican Ideology and the Making of the State Constitutions in the Revolutionary Era*, trans. Rita Kimber and Robert Kimber, expanded ed. (Lanham, MD: Rowman & Littlefield, 2001), 289.

63. Beyme, *America as a Model*, 17.

64. Ibid.

65. Among the first to contribute to this better understanding was the historian Christophe Ebeling. His massive seven-volume work on the history and geography of America published between 1793 and 1816 was a tremendous success, representing the most thorough work on the United States done by anyone, European or American, to that time. A professor at Hamburg Gymnasium, Ebeling taught a course on the history of free states. As he wrote to a friend with regard to America, he hoped to paint a "faithful picture of a truly free republic." See Christophe Daniel Ebeling, *Erdbeschreibung und Geschichte von Amerika, Die Vereinten Staaten von Nord-amerika*, 7 vols. (Hamburg: C. E. Bohn, 1794–1816); Michael Kraus and Davis D. Joyce, *The Writing of American History*, rev. ed. (Norman: University of Oklahoma Press, 1985), 87; and Christophe Ebeling to

William Bentley, June 25, 1805, in "Letters of Christophe Daniel Ebeling," ed. William C. Lane, *Proceedings of the American Antiquarian Society* 35 (1925):371. In his first volume, Ebeling declared, "The new constitution and the development of its consequences for the happiness of the people . . . is far too noteworthy to enable one to be satisfied with a brief presentation" (Ebeling, *Erdbeschreibung*, 1:viii).

66. Erich Angermann, "Early German Constitutionalism and the American Model," in *Reports, XIV International Congress of Historical Sciences*, 3 vols. (New York: Arno Press, 1977), 3:1499–1516.

67. Gottfried Dietze, "Robert von Mohl, Germany's de Tocqueville," in *Essays on the American Constitution* ed. Gottfried Dietze (Englewood Cliffs, NJ: Prentice-Hall, 1964), 187–212.

68. Robert von Mohl, *Das Bundes-staatsrecht der Vereinigten Staaten von Nord-Amerika* (Tübingen: J. G. Cotta, 1824), 192.

69. Robert von Mohl, "German Criticism of Mr. Justice Story's Commentaries on the Constitution of the United States," *American Jurist* 15 (1837):3–6.

70. Mohl, *Das Bundes-staatsrecht der Vereinigten Staaten von Nord-Amerika*, vii–viii and 121–24. The language here closely follows Dietze, "Robert von Mohl, Germany's de Tocqueville," 193–94.

71. Dietze, "Robert von Mohl, Germany's de Tocqueville," 203–7. Mohl's reviews of Tocqueville's work were published in 1836 and 1844: "Amerikanisches Staatsrecht," *Kritische Zeitschrift* 8 (1836):359; and "Entwicklung der Demokratie in Nordamerika und in der Schweiz," *Kritische Zeitschrift* 16 (1844):275. The reports on the constitutional conventions appeared in Mohl's *Staatsrecht, Völkerrecht und Politik: Monographien* (Tübingen: H. Laupp'schen, 1860), but Mohl's ideas about American constitutionalism remained remarkably consistent over time.

72. Dietze, "Robert von Mohl, Germany's de Tocqueville," 203.

73. Ibid., 204.

74. Ibid., 205.

75. Ibid., 204.

76. Ibid., 206.

77. Ibid., 199 and 212.

78. Ibid. 200.

79. Mohl, *Das Bundes-staatsrecht der Vereinigten Staaten von Nord-Amerika*, 377–78.

80. Ibid., 532–33.

81. Quoted in Gottfried Dietze, *The Federalist: A Classic on Federalism and Free Government* (Baltimore: Johns Hopkins University Press, 1960), 13.

82. Ibid.

83. Dietze, "Robert von Mohl, Germany's de Tocqueville," 204.

84. Quoted in Dietze, "Robert von Mohl, Germany's de Tocqueville," 210–11.

85. But see also Richard Marsh, "The American Influence in German Liberalism before 1848" (PhD diss., University of Minnesota, 1957), 213.

86. Quoted in Margaret E. Hirst, *Life of Friedrich List, and Selections from His Writings* (London: Smith, Elder, 1909), xix.

87. William Rappard, "Pennsylvania and Switzerland: The American Origins of the Swiss Constitution," in *Studies in Political Science and Sociology*, University of Pennsylvania Bicentennial Conference, ed. Hu Shih, Newton Edwards, Mark A. May, et al. (Philadelphia: University of Pennsylvania Press, 1941), 51. See also two other major works devoted to similarities between the constitutions of the two countries: Johann Jakob Rüttimann's monumental *Das nordamerikanische bundesstaatsrecht verglichen mit den politischen einrichtungen der Schweiz*, 3 vols. (Zurich: Orell Fussli, 1867–1876); and Myron Luehrs Tripp, *The Swiss and United States Federal Constitutional Systems: A Comparative Study* (Paris: Libr. sociale et économique, 1940).

88. James H. Hutson, *The Sister Republics: Switzerland and the United States from 1776 to the Present* (Washington, DC: Library of Congress, 1991), 36.

89. Heinrich Zschokke, *Ausgewählte Schriften*, 16 vols. (Aarau: H. R. Sauerländer, 1830), 10:322; cited in Rappard, "Pennsylvania and Switzerland," 69.

90. Heinrich Zschokke, [*Das verhältniss der Helvetischen gesellschaft zum zeitalter*] *Rede an die Helvetische gessellschaft zu Shinznach* (Aarau: Sauerländer, 1829), 42.

91. Rappard, "Pennsylvania and Switzerland," 91.

92. Ignaz Paul Troxler, *Die Verfassung der Vereinigten Staaten Nordamerika's als Musterbild der schweizerischen Bundesreform* (Schaffhausen: Brodtmann, 1847), cited in Rappard, "Pennsylvania and Switzerland," 93–95.

93. Cited in Rappard, "Pennsylvania and Switzerland," 96.

94. Ibid., 97.

95. Ibid., 101–2; quotation cited on 102.

96. Ibid., 102–3; and Sigmund Skard, *The American Myth and the European Mind* (Philadelphia: University of Pennsylvania Press, 1961), 31.

97. Tripp, *The Swiss and United States Federal Constitutional Systems*, 28–30. See also Rappard, "Pennsylvania and Switzerland," 105.

98. Georges Sauser-Hall, *The Political Institutions of Switzerland*, trans. Hugh Felkin (Zurich: Swiss National Tourist Office, 1946), 200.

99. In Charles Francis Adams, ed., *Works of John Adams, Second President of the United States (1787)*, 10 vols. (Boston: Little, Brown, 1850-1856), 4:374.

100. James Hutson, "The Partition Treaty and the Declaration of Independence," *American Historical Review* 58 (1972):892. Others expressing similar fears at the time of partition and later were Thomas Jefferson, John Adams, and Thomas Paine (894–96).

101. Piotr Wandycz, "The American Revolution and the Partitions of Poland," in *The American and European Revolutions 1776–1848: Sociopolitical and Ideological Aspects*, ed. Jaroslaw Pelenski (Iowa City: University of Iowa Press, 1980), 106.

102. Stephan Kieniewicz, "The Revolutionary Nobleman: An East European Variant of the Liberation Struggle in the Revolutionary Era," in Pelenski, ed., *The American and European Revolutions*, 272.

103. Ibid., 279–80.

104. Ibid., 279; Marc Raeff, *The Decembrist Movement* (Englewood Cliffs, NJ: Prentice-Hall, 1966), 100–18; and David Hecht, *Russian Radicals Look to America, 1825–1894* (Cambridge, MA: Harvard University Press, 1947), 17–19.

105. George Barany, *Stephen Széchenyi and the Awakening of Hungarian Nationalism, 1791–1841* (Princeton, NJ: Princeton University Press, 1968), 3. This first-rate biography portrays incisively the intellectual history of Hungary at the time.

106. Barany, *Stephen Széchenyi and the Awakening of Hungarian Nationalism*, 86.

107. Ibid.

108. Ibid., 176.

109. Ibid., 176–77.

110. Sándor Bölöni Farkas, *Journey in North America, 1831*, ed. and trans. Arpad Kadarkay (Santa Barbara, CA: ABC-Clio, 1978), 5–6.

111. Arpad Kadarkay, introduction to *Journey in North America, 1831*, by Sándor Bölöni Farkas, 71; Farkas, *Journey in North America*, 112–13, 132–33, and 190–91.

112. Farkas, *Journey in North America*, 112; Kadarkay, introduction, 50–51.

113. Farkas, *Journey in North America*, 112–13.

114. Ibid., 190–91.

115. Kadarkay, introduction, 71.

116. Ibid., 37.

117. See Béla Király and George Barany, eds., *East Central European Perceptions of Early America*, Brooklyn College Studies on Society in Change (Lisse: Peter de Ridder Press, 1977), 111–12.

118. Raymond Grew, "One Nation Barely Visible: The United States as Seen by Nineteenth-Century Italy's Liberal Leaders," in *The American Constitution as a Symbol and Reality for Italy*, ed. Emiliana P. Noether (Lewiston, NY: Mellen Press, 1989), 120. I disagree with the fundamental premise of the Grew article, which tends to deemphasize the influence of American constitutionalism in Italy.

119. Carlo Botta, *Storia della guerra dell'independenza degli Stati Uniti d'America*, 4 vols. (Paris: D. Colas, 1809). Michael Kammen, *A Season of Youth: The American Revolution and the Historical Imagination* (New York: Knopf, 1978), 282, reports that in the spring of 1839 Jared Sparks gave the first course of lectures on the American Revolution and used Botta's *History* as the assigned text; see Herbert B. Adams, *The Life and Writings of Jared Sparks, Comprising Selections from His Journals and Correspondence*, 2 vols. (Boston: Houghton Mifflin, 1893) 2:375. See also Giuseppe Buttà, "Carlo Botta's *History of the War of Independence of the United States of America*," in *The American Constitution as a Symbol and Reality for Italy*, ed. Emiliana P. Noether (Lewiston, NY: Mellen Press, 1989), 69–79.

120. Carlo Botta, *History of the War of Independence of the United States of America*, trans. George Alexander Otis, 2 vols., 6th ed. rev. (New Haven, CT: N. Whiting, 1834), 1:263–64, 344, and 355.

121. Carlo Giuseppe Londonio, *Storia delle colonie inglesi in America dalla loro fondazione, fino allo stabilimento della loro indipendenza*, 3 vols. (Milan: G. G. Destefanis, 1812–1813); and Emiliana P. Noether, "As Others Saw Us: Italian Views on the United States during the Nineteenth Century," *Transactions, Connecticut Academy of Arts and Sciences* 50(1990):133–34.

122. [Giuseppe Compagnoni], *Storia dell'America in continuazione del compendio della storia universale del sign. Conte di Segur*, 2 vols. (Milan: Stella, 1820–1822), quoted in Noether, "As Others Saw Us," 134–35. Compagnoni's work was printed anonymously under Segur's name as part of his twenty-eight-volume universal history, but Compagnoni is listed in the index as the author of these two volumes.

123. Giovanni Antonio Grassi, *Notizie varie sullo stato presente della Repubblica degli Stati Uniti dell'America settentrionale* (Rome: L. P. Salvioni, 1818).

124. Ibid., 43–44.

125. Emiliana P. Noether, "Giuseppe Cerrachi," in *Biographical Dictionary of Modern European Radicals and Socialists*, vol. 1, ed. David Nicholls and Peter E. Marsh (New York: St. Martin's Press, 1988), 50–51.

126. Nicholas Kaltchas, *Introduction to the Constitutional History of Modern Greece* (New York: Columbia University Press, 1940), 16. See also Paschalis M. Kitromilides, "Tradition, Enlightenment, and Revolution: Ideological Change in Eighteenth and Nineteenth Century Greece" (PhD diss., Harvard University, 1979).

127. Paul Constantine Pappas, *The United States and the Greek War for Independence, 1821–1828* (New York: Columbia University Press, 1985), 28.

128. Ibid., xvi, 15, and 26. Stephen A. Larrabee, *Hellas Observed: The American Experience of Greece, 1775–1865* (New York: New York University Press, 1957), chap. 3; Pappas, *The United States and the Greek War for Independence*, chap. 3; and Edward Earle, "American Interest in the Greek Cause," *American Historical Review* 58 (1972):44–63.

129. Pappas, *The United States and the Greek War for Independence*, 27–28.

130. Thomas Jefferson to A. Coray [Adamantios Korais], October 23, 1823, in *The Writings of Thomas Jefferson*, ed. Andrew A. Lipscomb and Albert Ellery Bergh, 20 vols. (Washington, DC: Thomas Jefferson Memorial Association of the United States, 1903–1905), 15:480–94; and Kaltchas, *Introduction to the Constitutional History of Modern Greece*, 16–17.

131. Kaltchas, *Introduction to the Constitutional History of Modern Greece*, 16–17.

132. Ibid., 52–57.

133. Beyme, *America as a Model*, 14.

134. Thomas J. Archdeacon, *Becoming American: An Ethnic History* (New York: Free Press, 1983), 42.

CHAPTER 6

1. George Bancroft to Edward Everett, March 10, 1848, in *The Life and Letters of George Bancroft*, ed. M. A. DeWolfe Howe, 2 vols. (New York: Scribner, 1908), 2:31.

2. George Bancroft to James Buchanan, March 24, 1848, in Howe, ed., *The Life and Letters of George Bancroft*, 2:33.

3. Klaus von Beyme, *America as a Model: The Impact of American Democracy in the World* (New York: St. Martin's Press, 1987), 18–19.

4. Peter N. Stearns, "Revolutions of 1848," in *Encyclopedia Americana*, 30 vols. (Danbury, CT: Grolier, 1995), 23:455–56. The best treatment of the revolutions from the point of view of this study is Peter N. Stearns's *1848: The Revolutionary Tide in Europe* (New York: Norton, 1974). See also Roger Price, *The French Second Republic: A Social History* (Ithaca, NY: Cornell University Press, 1972); Maurice Agulhon, *The Republican Experiment, 1848–1852*, trans. Janet Lloyd (Cambridge: Cambridge University Press, 1983); and Priscilla Smith Robertson, *Revolutions of 1848: A Social History* (Princeton, NJ: Princeton University Press, 1952).

5. George Bancroft, Despatch no. 65, March 10, 1848, from the London Legation, quoted in Emiliana P. Noether, "The American Response to the 1848 Revolutions in Rome and Budapest," in *The Consortium on Revolutionary Europe, 1750–1850: Proceedings, 1985*, ed. Warren Spencer (Athens, GA: The Consortium, 1985), 379.

6. Beyme, *America as a Model*, 16 and 41.

7. Carl Schurz, *The Reminiscences of Carl Schurz*, 3 vols. (New York: McClure, 1907), 1:29.

8. Speech by Tocqueville, quoted in Odilon Barrot, *Mémoires posthumes*, 4 vols. (Paris: Charpentier et cie, 1875–1876), 1:478.

9. François Furet, *Revolutionary France, 1770–1880*, trans. Antonia Nevill (Cambridge, MA: Blackwell, 1992), 413.

10. See Eugene N. Curtis, *The French Assembly of 1848 and American Constitutional Doctrines* (1918; repr., New York: Octagon Books, 1980), 152, 160. Although an older work and dated in many respects, this study as updated remains extremely useful.

11. Curtis, *The French Assembly of 1848*, 154.

12. Ibid., 155.

13. Ibid., 325. Even in this instance, however, American influence was limited in part by insufficient or mistaken information about the American institution, in spite of Tocqueville's informed suggestions. See J. P. Mayer, ed., and Alexander Teixeira de Mattos, trans., *The Recollections of Alexis de Tocqueville* (London: Harville Press, 1948), 213–14.

14. Andrzej Rapaczynski, "Bibliographic Essay: The Influence of U.S. Constitutionalism Abroad," in *Constitutionalism and Rights: The Influence of the United*

States Constitution Abroad, ed. Louis Henkin and Albert J. Rosenthal (New York: Columbia University Press, 1990), 416–17.

15. Curtis, *The French Assembly of 1848*, 325; and Beyme, *America as a Model*, 35.

16. Curtis, *The French Assembly of 1848*, 160–61.

17. Mayer and Mattos, *The Recollections of Alexis de Tocqueville*, 213–14.

18. Beyme, *America as a Model*, 43.

19. Mayer and Mattos, *The Recollections of Alexis de Tocqueville*, 213–14.

20. Curtis, *The French Assembly of 1848*, 194.

21. Rapaczinski, "Biographical Essay," 417.

22. Ibid.

23. Beyme, *America as a Model*, 41.

24. Ibid., 42.

25. Curtis, *The French Assembly of 1848*, 324 and 267.

26. Ibid., 324.

27. Ibid., 167, although not a complete coverage. See also André Hauriou and Jean Gicquel, with Patrice Gélard, *Droit constitutionnel et institutions politiques*, 7th ed. (Paris: Montchrestien, 1980), 813–14; and Jean Petot, *Les grandes étaps du régime républicain français, 1792–1969: Études d'histoire politique et constitutionnelle* (Paris: Éditions Cajas, 1970), 276–77.

28. Henry Blumenthal, *A Reappraisal of Franco-American Relations, 1830–1871* (Chapel Hill: University of North Carolina Press, 1959), 12.

29. Beyme, *America as a Model*, 20.

30. George Bancroft to Elizabeth Bancroft, April 23, 1848, in Howe, ed., *The Life and Letters of George Bancroft*, 2:91.

31. Andrew Donelson to James Buchanan, Secretary of State, March 23, 1848, in *American Historical Review* 23 (1918):368 (italics in original); and Merle Eugene Curti, *Austria and the United States, 1848–1852: A Study in Diplomatic Relations*, Smith College Studies in History 11, no. 3 (Northampton, MA: Smith College, 1926), 143. Curti's study, though older, is excellent and still of great use.

32. Maximillian Schele DeVere to R. M. Hunter, June 23, 1848, in *Annual Report of the American Historical Association*, ed. Charles H. Ambler (1916), 1:93.

33. John L. Snell, *The Democratic Movement in Germany, 1789–1914*, ed. and completed by Hans A. Schmitt (Chapel Hill: University of North Carolina Press, 1976), 59.

34. Merle Curti, "Calhoun and the Unification of Hungary," *American Historical Review* 40 (1934–1935):476–78.

35. Anton Scholl, *Einfluss der nordamerikanischen Unionsverfassung auf die Verfassung des Deutschen Reiches vom 28. März 1849* (Borna-Leipzig: R. Noske, 1913), 47.

36. J. A. S. Grenville, *Europe Reshaped, 1848–1878* (Hassocks: Harvester Press, 1976), 140.

37. Hajo Holborn, *A History of Modern Germany, 1840–1945*, 3 vols. (New York: Knopf, 1959–1969), 3:86.

38. See the debates in the Assembly in the multivolume edition, *Stenographis-cher Bericht über die Verhandlungen der deutschen constituirenden Nationalver-sammlung zu Frankfurt am Main*, ed. Franz Wigard, 9 vols. (Leipzig: Breitkopf und Hartel, 1848–1849), passim. See also the committee debates in Johann Gustav Droysen, *Die Verhandlungen des Verfassungs-Ausschusses der deutschen Nationalsversammlung* (1849; repr., Vaduz: Topos-Verlag, 1986). The quotation about resemblances is from Robert C. Binkley, "The Holy Roman Empire versus the United States: Patterns for Constitution-Making in Central Europe," in *The Constitution Reconsidered*, ed. Richard B. Morris, rev. ed. (New York: Harper & Row, 1968), 278. See also the insightful remarks about the 1848 revolution in James J. Sheehan, *German History, 1770–1866* (Oxford: Clarendon Press, 1989), 710.
The conclusion that the U.S. Constitution was probably more influential than either the British or French models is also stated in Eckhart Franz's *Das Amerik-abild der deutschen Revolution von 1848/49: zum Problem der Übertragung gewa-chsener Verfassungsformen* (Heidelberg: C. Winter, 1958), 134.

39. Erich Angermann, "Early German Constitutionalism and the American Model," in *Reports, XIV International Congress of Historical Sciences*, 3 vols. (New York: Arno Press, 1977), 3:1499. See also Scholl, *Einfluss der nordamerikanischen Unionsverfassung*; Franz, *Das Amerikabild der deutschen Revolution*; and Thomas Ellwein, "Der Einfluss des nordmerikanischen Bundesverfassungsrechtes auf die Verhandlungen der Frankfurter Nationalversammlung im Jahre 1848/49" (mas-ter's thesis, University of Erlangen, 1950), cited in Beyme, *America as a Model*, 68, n. 34. All the essays in *Deutsch-Americanisches Verfassungsrechtssymposium 1976: Pressefreiheit; Finanzverfassung im Bundesstaat*, ed. Wilhelm A. Kewenig (Berlin: Duncker und Humblot, 1978) are useful. See also Hermann Wellen-reuther, Claudia Schnurmann, and Thomas Krueger, eds., *German and American Constitutional Thought: Contexts, Interaction, and Historical Realities* (New York: St. Martin's Press, 1990), esp. the essays by Peter S. Onuf and Hans Boldt.

40. Robert von Mohl, *Das Bundes-staatsrecht der Vereinigten Staaten von Nord-Amerika* (Tübingen: J. G. Cotta, 1824), vii–viii and 121–24.

41. Angermann, "Early German Constitutionalism and the American Model," 1503.

42. Robert von Mohl, "German Criticism of Mr. Justice Story's Commentaries on the Constitution of the United States," *American Jurist* 15 (1837):3–6.

43. Angermann, "Early German Constitutionalism and the American Model," 1503–4; and Snell, *Democratic Movement in Germany*, 58.

44. Carl von Rotteck and Karl Theodor Welcker, *Staats-Lexikon oder Encyk-lopädie der Staatswissenschaften / in Verbindung mit vielen der angesehensten Publicisten Deutschlands*, 15 vols. (Altona: Hammerich, 1834–1843).

45. Hans Zehnther, *Das Staatslexikon von Rotteck und Welcker: Eine Studie zur Geschichte des deutschen Frühliberalismus* (Jena: G. Fischer, 1929); and Angermann, "Early German Constitutionalism and the American Model," 1503–4.

46. Friedrich von Raumer, *Die Vereinigten Staaten von Nordamerika*, 2 vols. (Leipzig: F. A. Brockhaus, 1845), 1:vi, viii, xiv, 217–78, and 2:268–339. See also John L. Snell, "The World of German Democracy, 1789–1914," *The Historian* 31 (1969): 530–31.

47. Both quotations are from John A. Hawgood, *Modern Constitutions since 1787* (London: Macmillan, 1939), 204–5.

48. Angermann, "Early German Constitutionalism and the American Model," 1503.

49. Holborn, *History of Modern Germany*, 3:56–57.

50. Beyme, *America as a Model*, 43.

51. Wigard, ed., *Stenographische Bericht*, 8:6065; and Franz, *Das Amerikabild der deutschen Revolution*, 134.

52. Quotations are from Carl J. Friedrich, *The Impact of American Constitutionalism Abroad* (Boston: Boston University Press, 1967), 53.

53. Ibid., 53–54.

54. Wigard, ed., *Stenographischer Bericht*, 4:2742–43.

55. See Daniel J. Elazar, *Exploring Federalism* (Tuscaloosa: University of Alabama Press, 1987), 612; and Beyme, *America as a Model*, 74.

56. Beyme, *America as a Model*, 88, cites Hans Joachim Faller, "Die Verfassungsgerichtsbarkeit in der Frankfurter Reichsverfassung vom 28. März 1849," in *Menschenwürde und Freiheitliche Rechtsordnung: Festschrift für Willi Geiger*, ed. Gerhard Leibholz, Hans Joachim Faller, Paul Mikat, and Hans Reis (Tübingen: J. C. B. Mohr, 1974), 827–55.

57. Quoted in Friedrich, *The Impact of American Constitutionalism Abroad*, 81–82; and Beyme, *America as a Model*, 89–90.

58. Quoted in Beyme, *America as a Model*, 90, from Faller, but the report is given earlier in Rudolph Hübner, "Der Verfassungsentwurf der siebzehn Vertrauensmänner," in *Festschrift für Eduard Rosenthal zum Siebzigsten Geburtstag, Juristischen Fakultät der Universität Jena* (Jena: Gustav Fischer, 1923), 163.

59. Binkley, "The Holy Roman Empire versus the United States," 278.

60. Holborn, *History of Modern Germany*, 3:59–60.

61. Hawgood, *Modern Constitutions since 1787*, 198.

62. Holborn, *History of Modern Germany*, 3:64–65.

63. Hawgood, *Modern Constitutions since 1787*, 184.

64. Eduard His, "Americanische Einflusse im schweizerischen Verfassungsrecht," in *Festgabe der Basler Juristenfakultät und des Basler Juristenvereins zum schweizerischen Juristentag* (Basel: Helbing & Lichtenhahn, 1920), 82, cited in Beyme, *America as a Model*, 72.

65. Thomas Fleiner-Gerster, "Federalism, Decentralization, and Rights," in Henkin and Rosenthal, eds., *Constitutionalism and Rights*, 27.

66. William Rappard, *La constitution fédéral de la Suisse, ses origines, son élaboration, son évolution, 1848–1948* (Boudry: La Baconnière, 1948), 143–44, cited in Friedrich, *The Impact of American Constitutionalism Abroad*, 52.

67. Hawgood, *Modern Constitutions since 1787*, 188–89.

68. William Rappard, "Pennsylvania and Switzerland: The American Origins of the Swiss Constitution," in *Studies in Political Science and Sociology*, University of Pennsylvania Bicentennial Conference, ed. Hu Shih, Newton Edwards, Mark A. May, et al. (Philadelphia: University of Pennsylvania Press, 1941), 115.

69. Ibid., 49–121; and Myron Luehrs Tripp, *The Swiss and United States Federal Constitutional Systems: A Comparative Study* (Paris: Libr. sociale et économique, 1940), passim.

70. Rappard, "Pennsylvania and Switzerland," 112–15.

71. Tripp, *The Swiss and the United States Federal Constitutional Systems*, 34–35.

72. Rappard, "Pennsylvania and Switzerland," 119–20.

73. Rappard, *La constitution fédérale de la Suisse*, 48.

74. James H. Hutson, *The Sister Republics: Switzerland and the United States from 1776 to the Present* (Washington, DC: Library of Congress, 1991), 58–65.

75. István Deák, *The Lawful Revolution: Louis Kossuth and the Hungarians, 1848–1849* (New York: Columbia University Press, 1979), 261–62.

76. *Annual Register for 1849* (London, 1850), 332–33.

77. Richard B. Morris, *The Emerging Nations and the American Revolution* (New York: Harper & Row, 1970), 114–15.

78. F. W. Newman, ed., *Select Speeches of Kossuth* (London: Trübner, 1853), 149.

79. Ibid.

80. Ibid., 279.

81. Curti, "Austria and the United States," 169–201.

82. Deák, *The Lawful Revolution*, xvi.

83. Merle Curti, "Young America," *American Historical Review* 32 (1927):34–55.

84. Charles McCurdy to Daniel Webster August 28, 1851; quoted in Curti, "Austria and the United States," 204.

85. The quotations and substance of this paragraph are drawn from Noether, "The American Response to the 1848 Revolutions in Rome and Budapest," 390.

86. *Papers of Daniel Webster*, Series 3: Diplomatic Papers, ed. Kenneth E. Shewmaker, Kenneth R. Stevens, Alan Berolzheimer, and Daniel Webster, 2 vols. (Hanover, NH: University Press of New England, pub. for Dartmouth College, 1983–1987), 2:32.

87. Daniel Webster to Johann Georg Hulsemann, December 21, 1850, in *Papers of Daniel Webster*, 52.

88. Ibid., 53.

89. A Czech deputy in the imperial parliament in Vienna wrote a bill of rights at the time based on the Texas State Constitution, among other sources. See George Barany, "The Appeal and the Echo," in *East Central European Perceptions of Early America*, ed. Béla Király and George Barany, Brooklyn College Studies on Society in Change (Lisse: Peter de Ridder Press, 1977), 128–29.

90. Stanley Z. Pech, *The Czech Revolution of 1848* (Chapel Hill: University of North Carolina Press, 1969), 65–67.

91. E. E. Y. Hales, *Mazzini and the Secret Societies: The Making of a Myth* (New York: P. J. Kenedy, 1956).

92. For Mazzini's thought, see Gaetano Salvemini, *Mazzini*, trans. I. M. Rawson (Stanford, CA: Stanford University Press, 1957).

93. Stearns, *1848: The Revolutionary Tide in Europe*, 209–10.

94. Emiliana P. Noether, "American Federalism and Republicanism: Constitutional Models for Italian Nationalists in the XIXth Century," 14; manuscript of a lecture at the Boston Public Library, November 12, 1987, kindly provided to me by Prof. Noether.

95. Seamus Heaney, "Chorus," *The Cure at Troy: A Version of Sophocles' Philoctetes* (New York: Farrar, Straus & Giroux, 1961), 77.

96. Gordon S. Wood, "The American Revolution and the World," in *Liberty's Impact: The World Views 1776*, ed. Donald K. Moore (Providence, RI: Brown University Press, 1976), n.p.

CHAPTER 7

1. David Armitage pointed out that nationalism was a "force for consolidation and integration during the second half of the nineteenth century" but that it was also the "zenith of extra-European imperialism," which was characterized by contradictory tendencies of "fragmentation and separation." Since American constitutionalism did not play a major role in European imperialism at this stage, the focus of this chapter is primarily on nationalism. See David Armitage, *The Declaration of Independence: A Global History* (Cambridge, MA: Harvard University Press, 2007), 130.

2. Gordon S. Wood, "The American Revolution and the World," in *Liberty's Impact: The World Views 1776*, ed. Donald K. Moore (Providence, RI: Brown University Press, 1976), n.p.

3. Serge Gavronsky, *The French Liberal Opposition and the American Civil War* (New York: Humanities Press, 1968), 245.

4. John A. Hawgood, *Modern Constitutions since 1787* (London: Macmillan, 1939), 218.

5. Ibid.

6. Quoted in Rembert W. Patrick, *Jefferson Davis and His Cabinet* (Baton Rouge: Louisiana State University Press, 1944), 14.

7. Alexander Stephens, quoted in George C. Rable, *The Confederate Republic: A Revolution against Politics* (Chapel Hill: University of North Carolina Press, 1994), 59.

8. Alexander H. Stephens, *A Constitutional View of the Late War between the States: Its Causes, Character, Conduct and Results*, 2 vols. (1868; repr., New York: Kraus, 1970), 1:7–170.

9. Charles Robert Lee, *The Confederate Constitutions* (Westport, CT: Greenwood Press, 1974), 82–140.

10. Hawgood, *Modern Constitutions since 1787*, 219–29, gives a perceptive summary of the Confederate Constitution, which I follow in this discussion.

11. See Don E. Fehrenbacher, *Constitutions and Constitutionalism in the Slaveholding South* (Athens: University of Georgia Press, 1989), passim. This is, in my judgment, the most penetrating work on the Confederate Constitution.

12. Walter Bagehot, *The English Constitution* (1867; repr., Ithaca, NY: Cornell University Press, 1966), 81.

13. Donald G. Nieman, "Republicanism, the Confederate Constitution, and the American Constitutional Tradition," in *An Uncertain Tradition: Constitutionalism and the History of the South*, ed. Kermit L. Hall and James W. Ely Jr. (Athens: University of Georgia Press, 1989), 213–15.

14. Clement Eaton, *A History of the Southern Confederacy* (New York: Macmillan, 1954), 382–83.

15. Nieman, "Republicanism, the Confederate Constitution, and the American Constitutional Tradition," 208. Nieman points out that Richard Hofstadter, in his *The Idea of A Party System: The Rise of Legitimate Opposition in the United States, 1780–1840* (Berkeley: University of California Press, 1969); and Ralph L. Ketcham, in his *Presidents above Party: The First American Presidency, 1789–1829* (Chapel Hill: University of North Carolina Press, 1984); also dealt with this theme of a patriot president.

16. Charles A. Beard and Mary R. Beard, *The Rise of American Civilization*, 2 vols. (New York: Macmillan, 1930), 2:100.

17. Klaus von Beyme, *America as a Model: The Impact of American Democracy in the World* (New York: St. Martin's Press, 1987), 24.

18. *Journal des débats*, July 20, 1861; W. Reed West, *Contemporary French Opinion on the American Civil War* (Baltimore: Johns Hopkins Press, 1924), 25.

19. *Constitutionnel*, May 16, 1861.

20. Andrew J. Torrielli, *Italian Opinion of America: As Revealed by Italian Travelers, 1850–1900* (Cambridge, MA: Harvard University Press, 1941), 8.

21. Giuseppe Mazzini, quoted in Donaldson Jordan and Edwin J. Pratt, *Europe and the American Civil War* (New York: Houghton Mifflin, 1931), 266.

22. Emiliana Noether, "As Others Saw Us: Italian Views on the United States during the Nineteenth Century," *Transactions, Connecticut Academy of Arts and Sciences* 50(1990):141–42.

23. Torrielli, *Italian Opinion of America*, 57–59.

24. Ibid., 60–61.

25. Ibid., 70–71.

26. *Moniteur belge*, December 22, 1861, quoted in Torrielli, *Italian Opinion of America*, 97.

27. King Leopold to Queen Victoria, October 17, 1861; and *L'independence belge*, January 10, 1861, both quoted in Torrielli, *Italian Opinion of America*, 98 and 28.

28. *El pensamiento español*, September, 1862, quoted in Jordan and Pratt, *Europe and the American Civil War*, 251–52.

29. René Rémond, *Les États-Unis devant l'opinion française, 1815–1852*, 2 vols. (Paris: A. Colin, 1962), 2:851. There is no adequate biography of Laboulaye. Emile Boutmy, Laboulaye's pupil who dealt with the constitutional controversy over the relationship between the American Declaration of Independence and the French Declaration of the Rights of Man, wrote about his mentor in *Taine, Scherer, Laboulaye* (Paris: A. Colin, 1901). John Bigelow's *Some Recollections of the Late Edouard Laboulaye* (New York: Putnam, 1889?) is brief and disappointing. Ainé Alkan, *Un fondeur en caractères, membre de l'Institut* (Paris: Bureau de la typologie-Tucker, 1886) is more anecdotal. But Jean de Soto's "Édouard Laboulaye," in *Revue internationale d'histoire politique et constitutionelle* 5 (1955):114–50, is substantial and presents a scholarly analysis of his political thought. The most recent biography, Walter D. Gray's *Interpreting American Democracy in France: The Career of Edouard Laboulaye, 1811–1883* (Newark: University of Delaware Press, 1994), is good as far as it goes but is far too brief. Gray's biography contributed to the recent renewed interest in nineteenth-century French liberalism. See André Jardin, *Histoire du libéralisme politique: De la crise de l'absolutisme à la constitution de 1875* (Paris: Hachette littérature, 1985); and Louis Girard, *Les libéraux française, 1814–1875* (Paris: Aubier, 1985). Both these works, though beginning at different starting points, see the struggle of liberal thinkers as culminating in the triumph of liberalism with the 1875 constitution. See also Alan B. Spitzer's splendid *The French Generation of 1820* (Princeton, NJ: Princeton University Press, 1987), which, although covering an earlier period, serves as a superb introduction.

30. Laboulaye, *Histoire des États-Unis*, 3 vols., 6th ed. (Paris: Charpentier, 1877), 1:ii and xiii. Hereafter, the second edition of this work, published in 1867, will be cited.

31. Charles Hale, "The Revival of Political History and the French Revolution in Mexico," in *The Global Ramifications of the French Revolution*, ed. Joseph Klaits and Michael H. Haltzel (Cambridge: Cambridge University Press, 1994), 169.

32. Walter Gray, "Edouard Laboulaye and His Circle," in *Liberty/liberté: The American and French Experiences*, ed. Joseph Klaits and Michael H. Haltzel (Washington, DC: Woodrow Wilson Center Press, 1991), 76.

33. Gray, *Interpreting American Democracy in France*, 15 and 64.

34. Édouard Laboulaye to General Cavaignac, July n.d., 1848; reproduced in *Histoire des États-Unis*, 1:iii–iv.

35. Édouard Laboulaye, "De la constitution américaine et de l'utilité de son étude" (Paris: Hennuyer, 1850).

36. Gray, *Interpreting American Democracy in France*, 61.

37. Laboulaye, *Histoire des États-Unis*, 1:23.

38. Ibid., 1:2–3 and 20.

39. Rémond, *Les États-Unis devant l'opinion française*, 1:349.

40. The identity of Laboulaye the Americanist and Laboulaye the follower of Savigny remains a puzzle. The influence of the historical school of jurisprudence appears to have been strongest in his earlier works before the 1840s. Savigny's subsequent influence seems to have been more of method than of content. Laboulaye followed Savigny in his emphasis on history as one foundation for the establishment of politics. But at the same time he hoped, like the men of the Enlightenment, that the new science would discover universally valid institutions. See H. S. Jones, review of Gray's *Interpreting American Democracy in France*, *French History* 9 (1995):380.

41. Laboulaye, *Histoire des États-Unis*, 1:35.

42. Gray, *Interpreting American Democracy in France*, 60.

43. Laboulaye, *Histoire des États-Unis*, 1:214–15.

44. Ibid., 1:256.

45. Alan B. Spitzer, "La république souterraine," in *Le siècle de l'avènement républicain*, ed. François Furet and Mona Ozouf (Paris: Gallimard, 1993), 354.

46. Laboulaye, *Histoire des États-Unis*, 3:370.

47. Ibid., 3:371–72.

48. Ibid., 3:466.

49. Ibid., 3:368.

50. Ibid., 3:224 and 227; and Gottfried Dietze, *The Federalist: A Classic on Federalism and Free Government* (1960; repr., Westport, CT: Greenwood Press, 1977), 11. Guizot's praise of the American document gains added weight in the light of his impressive scholarship, particularly the early two-volume series of lectures on representative government (1821–1822) published later as *Histoire des origines du gouvernement représentatif en Europe* (Paris: Didier, 1851).

51. Laboulaye, *Histoire des États-Unis*, 3:372.

52. Ibid., 106–17.

53. Ibid., 119.

54. Ibid. Laboulaye claimed that the president in the French system was being given more power than the president of the United States had, but his argument was absurd. See D. W. Brogan, *The Development of Modern France, 1870–1939*, rev. ed. (Gloucester, MA: Peter Smith, 1970), 111.

55. Giacomo Grasso was another Italian constitutionalist, though somewhat later in the century, who expressed great enthusiasm for the American system

with particular emphasis on *The Federalist*, which he called the best commentary on the U.S. Constitution to date. See Giacomo Grasso, *La constituzione degli Stati Uniti dell'America settentrionale* (Florence: G. Barbèra, 1894), cited in Dietze, *The Federalist*, 20–21.

56. Emiliana Noether, "American Federalism and Republicanism: Constitutional Models for Italian Nationalists in the XIXth Century," 9, manuscript of a lecture at the Boston Public Library, November 12, 1987.

57. Howard Marraro, "Mazzini on American Intervention in European Affairs," *Journal of Modern History* 21 (1949):111.

58. Ibid. See also Denis Mack Smith, *Mazzini* (New Haven, CT: Yale University Press, 1994), 167.

59. Noether, "American Federalism and Republicanism," 11.

60. Noether, "As Others Saw Us," 138.

61. Ibid., 139. My interpretation differs from Noether's, who feels Mazzini was ambivalent toward the United States because of his criticism of federalism, slavery, and America's emphasis on individualism and materialism. The objections on the grounds of slavery disappeared after the Civil War, and Mazzini's rejection of federalism for Italy made good sense. But in view of his glowing remarks about America's worldwide mission to extend republicanism, it is difficult to see how his attitude could be described as "ambivalent."

62. Rudolph Ullner, *Die Idee des Föderalismus im Jahrzehnt der deutschen Einigungskriege*, Historische Studien 393 (Lubeck: Mathiesen, 1965): passim; cited in Andrzej Rapaczynski, "Bibliographical Essay: The Influence of U.S. Constitutionalism Abroad," in *Constitutionalism and Rights: The Influence of the United States Constitution Abroad*, ed. Louis Henkin and Albert J. Rosenthal (New York: Columbia University Press, 1990). Rapaczynski calls Ullner's the most important study of the influence of American federalism on German unification (423).

63. As Gottfried Dietze pointed out, Georg Waitz's early work was not widely known until nearly a decade later when it was republished in his *Grundzüge der Politik: Nebst einselnen Ausführungen* (Kiel: E. Homann, 1862). See Dietze, *The Federalist*, 13, n. 52.

64. Dietze, *The Federalist*, 14.

65. Edward Crankshaw, *Bismarck* (New York: Viking Press, 1981), 232–33. See also Otto Pflanze, *Bismarck and the Development of Germany*, 3 vols., 2nd ed. (Princeton, NJ: Princeton University Press,1990), 1:341–63.

66. Hawgood, *Modern Constitutions since 1787*, 219 and 240–41. Hawgood further calls attention to the influence of the bill of rights tradition in the Austrian Constitution of 1867, which was prefaced by a declaration of fundamental rights (259).

67. Ulrich Scheuner, "Constitutional Traditions in the United States and in Germany," in *Deutsch-Americanisches Verfassungsymposium 1976: PressFreiheit, Finanzverfassung im Bundestaat*, ed. Wilhelm A. Kewenig (Berlin: Duncker und

Humblot, 1978), 27. See also Hans Boldt, "Federalism as an Issue in the German Constitutions of 1849 and 1871," in *German and American Constitutional Thought: Contexts, Interaction, and Historical Realities*, ed. Hermann Wellenreuther, Claudia Schnurman, and Thomas Krueger (New York: St. Martin's Press, 1990), 259–92, which shows how some of the American influence on the 1849 German Constitution indirectly influenced the 1871 constitution.

68. Hajo Holborn, "The Influence of the American Constitution on the Weimar Constitution," in *The Constitution Reconsidered*, ed. Conyers Read (New York: Columbia University Press, 1938), 285.

69. Ibid. See also Beyme, *America as a Model*, who compared the draft constitution of the German empire with the American and claimed, "The effects of the American model were considerable, especially as regards the allocation of powers in the federal state and its financial constitution" (75).

70. Hawgood, *Modern Constitutionalism since 1787*, 219.

71. Larry Diamond, "Democracy, future of," in *Encyclopedia of Democratic Thought*, ed. Paul Barry Clarke and Joe Foweraker (New York: Routledge, 2001), 154–55 (caps in original).

72. Despite Diamond's conclusion regarding the astonishing progress of democracy, he remained one of the sharpest critics of the claims made for democratization, which he considered largely "illusory." Diamond considered it necessary for "electoral democracies" to consolidate into "liberal democracies" before democracy could realistically claim the advances that presumably had been made. See Larry Diamond, introduction to *Consolidating the Third Wave Democracies*, ed. Larry Diamond, Marc F. Plattner, Yon-hon Chu, and Hung-Mao Tren (Baltimore: Johns Hopkins University Press, 1997), xv–xxi.

CHAPTER 8

1. Walter LaFeber, *The American Age: United States Foreign Policy at Home and Abroad since 1750* (New York: Norton, 1989), 181.

2. There is a dispute among scholars on this score. In *The New Empire*, Walter LaFeber claimed that there was continuity in the American outlook and policies from the Civil War to 1898 and that America's global presence did not suddenly begin with the Spanish-American War. But Ernest R. May concluded that this presence began closer to 1898. See Walter LaFeber, *The New Empire: An Interpretation of American Expansion, 1860–1898*, 35th anniversary ed. (Ithaca, NY: Cornell University Press, 1998), xvii; and Ernest R. May, *Imperial Democracy: The Emergence of America as a Great Power*, new ed. (Chicago: Imprint Publications, 1991). My study falls more in the LaFeber camp. For a long history of American imperialism dating back to the antebellum period, see Thomas Bender, *A Nation among Nations: America's Place in World History* (New York: Hill & Wang, 2006), 192–206.

3. Thomas J. Archdeacon, *Becoming American: An Ethnic History* (New York: Free Press, 1983), 62.

4. The writing on imperialism is voluminous, but see the old classic by John Hobson, *Imperialism: A Study*, rev. ed. (Ann Arbor: University of Michigan Press, 1965), which refers to the "economic taproot of imperialism." For a revisionist work stressing the humanitarian aspects, see James C. Thomson Jr., Peter W. Stanley, and John Curtis Perry, *Sentimental Imperialists: The American Experience in East Asia* (New York: Harper & Row, 1981).

A number of studies on American imperialism stress the connections among the Spanish-American War, America's Open Door policy, and intervention in the Far East and the Caribbean: May, *Imperial Democracy*, 243–62; Charles S. Campbell Jr., *Special Business Interests and the Open Door Policy* (1951; repr., Hamden, CT: Archon Books, 1968); and Dana Gardner Munro, *Intervention and Dollar Diplomacy in the Caribbean, 1900–1921* (1964; repr., Westport, CT: Greenwood Press, 1980). William Appleman Williams, *The Tragedy of American Diplomacy*, 2nd rev. and enlarged ed. (New York: Dell, 1972), popularized the "Open Door" thesis, which held that the domestic economic drive of American capitalism was behind the formation of America's foreign policy at the turn of the century. Walter LaFeber's *The American Age* is particularly good in linking America's foreign policy to domestic concerns during this period. A good comparative study of different European imperialisms is D. K. Fieldhouse's *The Colonial Empires: A Comparative Survey from the Eighteenth Century*, 2nd ed. (London: Macmillan, 1982).

5. For a discussion of some of these considerations in a comparative context, see Robin Winks, "Imperialism," in *The Comparative Approach to American History*, ed. C. Vann Woodward (New York: Oxford University Press, 1997), 253–68.

6. Fieldhouse, *The Colonial Empires*, 341–42.

7. LaFeber, *The American Age*, 232.

8. For an incisive and critical overview of the imperial policies of the United States in Central America, see Walter LaFeber, *Inevitable Revolutions: The United States in Central America*, 2nd ed. (New York: Norton, 1993).

9. Winks, "Imperialism," 259.

10. David K. Fieldhouse, quoted in Winks, "Imperialism," 264.

11. For arguments with the two opposing views, see David Healy, *US Expansionism: The Imperialist Urge in the 1890s* (Madison: University of Wisconsin Press, 1970); and E. Berkeley Tompkins, *Anti-Imperialism in the United States: The Great Debate, 1890–1920* (Philadelphia: University of Pennsylvania Press, 1970).

12. Stanley Karnow, *In Our Image: America's Empire in the Philippines* (New York: Random House, 1989), 137.

13. Quoted in Howard K. Beale, *Theodore Roosevelt and the Rise of America to World Power* (Baltimore: Johns Hopkins University Press, 1956), 54.

14. Quoted in Alejandro M. Fernandez, *The Philippines and the United States: The Forging of New Relations* (Quezon City: NSDP-UP Integrated Research Program, 1977), 114 (italics in original).

15. Quoted in Garel A. Grunder and William E. Livezey, *The Philippines and the United States* (Norman: University of Oklahoma Press, 1951), 2.

16. See Bartholomew H. Sparrow, *The Insular Cases and the Emergence of an American Empire* (Lawrence: University Press of Kansas, 2006), in which the author shows that the constitution followed the flag but only selectively. The guiding principle emerged eventually in the well-known case *Rasmussen v. United States*, 1905. Sparrow shows that long before Congress had exercised authority over the extracontinental territories for the purposes of temporary government, this arrangement had been taken for granted in the Northwest Ordinance (15 and passim).

17. Note that the language used to establish constitutional relations with the Native Americans in *Worcester v. Georgia* (1832) was the same language as that used in the Insular Cases, in which Native American tribes also were referred to as "domestic dependent nations." This seems to indicate that the transition from volition to imposition was not as abrupt or as late in U.S. history as the end of the nineteenth century.

18. Thomson et al., *Sentimental Imperialists*, 197.

19. Renato Constantino, with the collaboration of Letizia R. Constantino, *A History of the Philippines: From the Spanish Colonization to the Second World War* (New York: Monthly Review Press, 1975), 205.

20. Ibid., 214. The Malalos Constitution is reproduced in Diosdado Macapagal, *A New Constitution for the Philippines* (Quezon City: Mac Pub. House, 1970). For its background, see Cesar Adib Majul, *The Political and Constitutional Ideas of the Philippine Revolution*, rev. ed. (New York: Oriole Editions, 1974).

21. Thomson et al., *Sentimental Imperialists*, 115–16.

22. William Howard Taft, "Special Report to the President on the Philippines" (Washington, DC: U.S. Government Printing Office, 1908).

23. Thomson et al., *Sentimental Imperialists*, 117.

24. Ibid., 118.

25. Ibid., 119.

26. Andrzej Rapaczynski, "Bibliographical Essay: The Influence of U.S. Constitutionalism Abroad," in *Constitutionalism and Rights: The Influence of the United States Constitution Abroad*, ed. Louis Henkin and Albert J. Rosenthal (New York: Columbia University Press, 1990), 440.

27. Ibid.

28. Fernandez, *The Philippines and the United States*, 169–70.

29. See Robert Aura Smith, *Philippine Freedom, 1946–1958* (New York: Columbia University Press, 1958), 54–62.

30. Salvador P. Lopez, "The Colonial Relationship," in *The United States and the Philippines*, ed. Frank H. Golay (Englewood Cliffs, NJ: Prentice-Hall, 1966), 19 and 24.

31. George Edward Taylor, *The Philippines and the United States: Problems of Partnership* (New York: Praeger, 1964), 70.

32. Lopez, "The Colonial Relationship," 17.

33. Russell H. Fifield, *Americans in Southeast Asia: The Roots of Commitment* (New York: Crowell, 1973), 3.

34. The relevant cases were *Downes v. Bidwell* and *DeLima v. Bidwell* in 1901.

35. LaFeber, *The American Age*, 199; and Louis Henkin, *Foreign Affairs and the Constitution* (Mineola, NY: Foundation Press, 1972), 208 and 330. In subsequent Insular Cases, however, legal justification was provided for ruling Guam and other Pacific possessions.

36. Raymond Carr, *Puerto Rico: A Colonial Experiment* (New York: New York University Press, 1984), 30.

37. Carl J. Friedrich, *Puerto Rico: Middle Road to Freedom* (New York: Rinehart, 1959), 16.

38. Ibid.

39. Ibid.

40. Ibid. Note, however, that Friedrich later changed his mind and desired greater autonomy for Puerto Rico in the commonwealth relationship. See Carr, *Puerto Rico*, 82.

41. Those opposed to the draft constitution pointed out that less than a majority of the electorate had voted affirmatively in the referendum.

42. Friedrich, *Puerto Rico: Middle Road to Freedom*, 32.

43. See the thoughtful essays in Christina Duffy Burnett and Burke Marshall, eds., *Foreign in a Domestic Sense: Puerto Rico, American Expansion, and the Constitution* (Durham, NC: Duke University Press, 2001), which provide a completely different view of the Insular Cases: the constitutional status of Puerto Rico is described as "foreign in a domestic sense."

44. Guam, the largest of the Mariana Islands, had been ceded to the United States at the end of the Spanish-American War. Lying some fourteen hundred miles east of the Philippines, the island soon became an important military base in the Pacific. From 1899 until the Japanese occupied the island during World War II, the governor of the island was a naval officer appointed by the president. After the war, the Organic Act of Guam in 1950 made the island an unincorporated territory, and it was placed under a civilian administrator responsible to the U.S. Department of the Interior. The Organic Act made all residents citizens, though they could not vote in national elections and were not represented in Congress. The act, amended in 1968, gave the islanders more self-rule. A popularly elected governor and lieutenant governor were allowed four-year terms. A unicameral legislature became primarily responsible for local matters, but the

conduct of foreign affairs was left to the United States. Guam had no constitution other than the Organic Act, but in 1982, seeking to improve their constitutional status, the Guamanians voted to pursue commonwealth status. A draft commonwealth act was approved by the people in 1987. See Timothy P. Maga, *Defending Paradise: The United States and Guam, 1898–1950* (New York: Garland, 1988), 208 and passim.

45. Wake Island was claimed by the United States in 1899 at the end of the Spanish-American War. It was used as the site for a cable station and lay astride the route from the United States to the Hawaiian Islands and the Philippines. In 1939, the navy, under whose jurisdiction Wake was placed in 1934, began building an air and submarine base on the tiny atoll. As a result, it was attacked by the Japanese in 1941. After the island was returned to the United States in 1945, American presidents placed it under the jurisdiction of different government departments.

46. American Samoa was awarded to the United States in the 1900 convention after a great international rivalry developed in the region. An agreement was signed by the United States, Britain, and Germany, by which America was ceded the Samoan Islands in the east and Germany, those to the west. Congress did not see fit, however, to formally accept the deed of cession until 1929. From 1900 to 1951, the navy administered American Samoa and maintained a naval base at Pago Pago. When the U.S. Department of the Interior took charge in 1951, it appointed a governor with full powers of administration, including the authority to appoint political advisers and senior civil servants from the United States to assist him. As a result, the islanders kept agitating for greater control of their own affairs, and the first territorial constitution was approved by the people in 1960, with a revised charter adopted in 1967. The governor was still appointed by the Department of the Interior, however, until 1976 when, as the result of a referendum, that post was filled by popular election, and the first Samoan became governor in 1977. Samoa's lawmaking body is the Fono, a bicameral legislature, but its actions are subject to the governor's approval. Samoans are U.S. nationals, able to move freely between the island and the mainland. In 1981, the first official delegate was elected to the U.S. Congress.

47. A fourth unincorporated territory was located in the Caribbean, the American Virgin Islands, composed of St. Croix, St. John, and St. Thomas. They share with the British Virgin Islands an archipelago of more than one hundred islets, which were purchased from Denmark in 1917 when the opening of the Panama Canal prompted the move. Placed under jurisdiction of the U.S. Navy at the outset, they were transferred in 1931 to the U.S. Department of the Interior. In 1954 Congress passed the Organic Act of the Virgin Islands, by which a governor was to be appointed, and the first black governor took office in 1968. In 1970, election of the governor by the islanders was granted. The Virgin Islanders were American citizens but could not vote in presidential elections. Since 1972, however, they

have been represented by an elected delegate to the U.S. House. Given the right to draft a constitution, the islanders completed a document in 1978, but it was rejected in a referendum in 1979 and, after revisions, again in 1981. There was little demand for autonomy for fear of disrupting the lucrative tourist trade. The Virgin Islands are an anomaly because most of the other unincorporated territories had demanded more self-government and the benefits of American constitutionalism. See Darwin D. Creque, *The U.S. Virgin Islands and the Eastern Caribbean* (Philadelphia: Whitmore, 1968); and James E. Moore, *Everybody's Virgin Islands* (New York: Lippincott, 1979).

48. In *Rasmussen v. United States* in 1905, the Supreme Court declared Alaska an incorporated territory. See Leonard W. Levy, Kenneth L. Karst, and Dennis J. Mahoney, eds., *Encyclopedia of the American Constitution*, 4 vols. (New York: Macmillan, 1986), 2:987.

49. Raymond Cravens, "The Constitutional and Political Status of the Non-Contiguous Areas of the United States" (PhD diss., University of Kentucky, 1958), 55.

50. George Washington Spicer, *The Constitutional Status and Government of Alaska*, Johns Hopkins University Studies in Historical and Political Science, 45th ser., no. 4 (Baltimore: Johns Hopkins University Press, 1927), 113, noted the territory was "almost without law of any kind."

51. Cravens, "The Constitutional and Political Status of the Non-Contiguous Areas of the United States," 58.

52. For a sympathetic view of American interests on the island, see the old account by Ethel Moseley Damon, *Sanford Ballard Dole and His Hawaii* (Palo Alto, CA: Pacific Books, 1957).

53. William Adam Russ, *The Hawaiian Republic (1894–98): And Its Struggle to Win Annexation* (London: Associated University Presses, 1992), 32.

54. Ibid., 32–33.

55. Beyme, *America as a Model*, 118.

56. Quoted in LaFeber, *The American Age*, 197.

57. Robert Freeman Smith, "Latin America, the United States, and the European Powers," in *The Cambridge History of Latin America*, ed. Leslie Bethell, 11 vols. (Cambridge: Cambridge University Press, 1984–1995), 4:96 and 102.

58. Barbara A. Tenenbaum, Georgette Magassy Dorn, et al., eds., *Encyclopedia of Latin American History and Culture*, 5 vols. (New York: Scribner, 1996), 2:317.

59. Jorge I. Domínguez, *Cuba: Order and Revolution* (Cambridge, MA: Harvard University Press, 1978), 15–16.

60. Louis A. Pérez, *Cuba: Between Reform and Revolution* (New York: Oxford University Press, 1988), 273.

61. Domínguez, *Cuba: Order and Revolution*, 16.

62. Ibid., 16–17.

63. Tenenbaum et al., eds., *Encyclopedia of Latin American History and Culture*, 2:318.

64. Richard S. Hillman and Thomas J. D'Agostino, *Distant Neighbors in the Caribbean: The Dominican Republic and Jamaica in Comparative Perspective* (New York: Praeger, 1992), 82.

65. Howard J. Wiarda and Michael J. Kryzanek, *The Dominican Republic: A Caribbean Crucible*, 2nd ed. (Boulder, CO: Westview Press, 1992), 109. The constitutional situation is complicated by the fact that the Dominican Republic had adopted the Napoleonic Code in 1844.

66. Hillman and D'Agostino, *Distant Neighbors in the Caribbean*, 82.

67. Ibid.

68. Winfield Burggraff, "Dominican Republic Constitutions," in Tenenbaum et al., eds., *Encyclopedia of Latin American History and Culture*, 2:398.

69. Wiarda and Kryzanek, *Dominican Republic*, 37.

70. Burggraff, "Dominican Republic Constitutions," 398.

71. Joshua Muravchik, *Exporting Democracy: Fulfilling America's Destiny* (Washington, DC: AEI Press, 1991), 160.

72. *New York Times*, August 19, 1920; and James G. Leyburn, *The Haitian People* (New Haven, CT: Yale University Press, 1941), 240.

73. Hans Schmidt, *The United States Occupation of Haiti, 1915–1934* (New Brunswick, NJ: Rutgers University Press, 1971), 97.

74. Ibid.

75. Ibid., 99.

76. Ibid. The undemocratic methods used by the Americans in Marine-controlled elections are documented in *Inquiry into Occupation and Administration of Haiti and Santo Domingo, Hearing before a Select Committee on Haiti and Santo Domingo*, U.S. Congress, Senate, part I, August 5, 1921 (Washington, DC: U.S. Government Printing Office).

77. James Ferguson, *Papa Doc, Baby Doc: Haiti and the Duvaliers* (New York: Blackwell, 1987), 49.

78. Ibid., 83–84.

79. Tenenbaum et al., eds., *Encyclopedia of Latin American History and Culture*, 4:188.

80. Thomas W. Walker, introduction to *Nicaragua without Illusions: Regime Transition and Structural Adjustment in the 1990s*, ed. Thomas W. Walker (Wilmington, DE: SR Books, 1997), 3. See also Knut Walter, *The Regime of Anastasio Somoza, 1936–1956* (Chapel Hill: University of North Carolina Press,1993), xiii, xix, and 288–305.

81. Jiri Valenta and Esperanzo Durán, eds., *Conflict in Nicaragua: A Multidimensional Perspective* (Boston: Allen & Unwin, 1987), 199; and see 386 for American efforts to influence the constitution-writing process.

82. Tenenbaum et al., eds., *Encyclopedia of Latin American History and Culture*, 4:279.

83. Michael L. Conniff, *Panama and the United States: The Forced Alliance* (Athens: University of Georgia Press, 1992), 72.

84. Tenenbaum et al., eds., *Encyclopedia of Latin American History and Culture*, 4:279.

85. The Senate rewrote a reservation stating that the United States could intervene to keep the canal open but did not have the right of intervention. For this curious use of wording, see J. Michael Hogan, *The Panama Canal in American Politics: Domestic Advocacy and the Evolution of Policy* (Carbondale: Southern Illinois University Press, 1986), 6–7 and 194–95.

86. Ronnie Dugger, *On Reagan: The Man and His Presidency* (New York: McGraw-Hill, 1983), 362.

87. Winks, "Imperialism," 267.

CHAPTER 9

1. David Armitage, *The Declaration of Independence: A Global History* (Cambridge, MA: Harvard University Press, 2007), 109.

2. John A. Hawgood, *Modern Constitutions since 1787* (London: Macmillan, 1939), 240–41. The state of Bavaria also came up with a bill of rights in 1919.

3. While the fighting was still going on, President Woodrow Wilson called for any peace plan to be based on two broad principles with democratic implications from a constitutional point of view. One was the right of the self-determination of peoples. The other was the establishment of an international society in which all peoples, weak or strong, would be entitled equally to exercise a right to self-determination. Although the Russian Bolsheviks were the first to call for a peace plan based on self-determination (the statement did not appear in Wilson's famed Fourteen Points), the American president had made the term his own through his speeches by the time of the armistice. His high-flown rhetoric led militant nationalist leaders in the non-Western world—Egypt, India, China, and Korea—to hope that Wilson would champion their cause at the Paris Peace Conference. But he was forced to back down in the face of opposition from his imperialist Western Allies. Despite the outcome, in the popular mind Wilson remained a hero in the eyes of millions in the East as well as the West. See the stimulating study by Erez Manela, *The Wilsonian Moment: Self-Determination and the International Origins of Anticolonial Nationalism* (New York: Oxford University Press, 2007), 8–9, 40–41, and 60–61.

4. William H. McNeill, *A World History*, 3rd ed. (New York: Oxford University Press, 1979), 497.

5. Arno J. Mayer, *Politics and Diplomacy of Peacemaking: Containment and Counterrevolution at Versailles, 1918–1919* (New York: Knopf, 1967), passim, but esp. 875–93.

6. John Wheeler-Bennett, *Nemesis of Power: The German Army in Politics, 1918–1945* (New York: St. Martin's Press, 1954), 17.

7. For Preuss's role in drafting the constitution, see Hans Mommsen, *The Rise and Fall of Weimar Democracy*, trans. Elborg Forster and Larry Eugene Jones (Chapel Hill: University of North Carolina Press, 1996), 52–56.

8. Herman Finer, *Governments of Greater European Powers: A Comparative Study of the Governments and Political Culture of Great Britain, France, Germany, and the Soviet Union* (New York: Holt, 1956), 615. Klaus von Beyme points out that the document, although democratic in outlook, was also aimed at accommodating the strong monarchist feelings that still prevailed among the people. See his *America as a Model: The Impact of American Democracy in the World* (New York: St. Martin's Press, 1987), 45.

9. Finer, *Governments of Greater European Powers*, 621.

10. Hawgood, *Modern Constitutions since 1787*, 353.

11. Carl J. Friedrich, *Constitutional Government and Democracy: Theory and Practice in Europe and America*, 4th ed. (Waltham, MA: Blaisdell, 1968), 288.

12. Robert G. Neumann, *European and Comparative Government*, 3rd ed. (New York: McGraw-Hill, 1960), 385.

13. Ibid., 354.

14. Hajo Holborn presents a broad historical survey, with emphasis on Weber's participation, in his essay, "The Influence of the American Constitution on the Weimar Constitution," in *The American Constitution Reconsidered*, ed. Conyers Read (New York: Columbia University Press,1938), 285–95. Holborn's account is particularly valuable because of his unique access to German archives in the years 1929 to 1932. In his "Bibliographical Essay: The Influence of U.S. Constitutionalism Abroad," in *Constitutionalism and Rights: The Influence of the U.S. Constitution Abroad*, ed. Louis Henkin and Albert J. Rosenthal (New York: Columbia University Press, 1990), Andrzej Rapaczynski sums up Holborn's conclusion as showing only "diffuse" American influence with "no measurable impact" (424). I argue, however, that if one interprets "influence" to include the discussion of the ideals and ideas of the seminal documents as well as institutional solutions by the German constitution makers, American influence was definitely present.

15. Quoted in Gottfried Dietze, *The Federalist: A Classic on Federalism and Free Government* (1960; repr., Westport, CT: Greenwood Press, 1977), 15.

16. See Louise W. Holborn, Gwendolen M. Carter, and John H. Herz, eds., *German Constitutional Documents since 1871: Selected Texts and Commentary* (New York: Praeger, 1970), 137–66.

17. Finer, *Governments of Greater European Powers*, 627.

18. John R. P. McKenzie, *Weimar Germany, 1918–1933* (London: Blanford Press, 1971), 80.

19. Holborn, "The Influence of the American Constitution on the Weimar Constitution," 288.

20. Beyme, *America as a Model*, 45–47.

21. Peter Lassman and Ronald Speirs, eds., *Weber: Political Writings* (Cambridge: Cambridge University Press, 1994), 276–79, 345, and 347; and Beyme, *America as a Model*, 46.

22. Beyme, *America as a Model*, 47.

23. Ibid. See also Martin Cyril Needler, "The Theory of the Weimar Presidency," *Review of Politics* 21 (1959):692–98; and Martin Cyril Needler, "The Concept of the Presidency in the Weimar Constitution" (PhD diss., Harvard University, 1960).

24. Hawgood, *Modern Constitutions since 1787*, 363–64.

25. Nevil Johnson, "Territory and Power: Some Historical Determinants of the Constitutional Structure of the Federal Republic of Germany," in *German Federalism Today*, ed. Charlie Jeffery and Peter Savigear (New York: St. Martin's Press, 1991), 13.

26. Beyme, *America as a Model*, 76.

27. Daniel J. Elazar, *Exploring Federalism* (Tuscaloosa: University of Alabama Press, 1987), 132.

28. Finer, *Governments of Greater European Powers*, 267.

29. William E. Nelson, *Marbury v. Madison: The Origins and Legacy of Judicial Review* (Lawrence: University Press of Kansas, 2000), 105; and Dieter Grimm, "Human Rights and Judicial Review in Germany," in *Human Rights and Judicial Review: A Comparative Perspective*, ed. David M. Beatty (Dordrecht: M. Nijhoff, 1994), 269.

30. Nelson, *Marbury v. Madison*, 106.

31. Grimm, "Human Rights and Judicial Review in Germany," 269.

32. Beyme, *America as a Model*, 76.

33. Ibid., 91.

34. R. W. Seton-Watson, *A History of the Czechs and Slovaks* (Hamden, CT: Archon Books, 1965), 316.

35. Malbone W. Graham, "Constitutionalism and Political Structure," in *Czechoslovakia*, ed. Robert J. Kerner (Berkeley: University of California Press, 1945), 15.

36. H. Gordon Skilling, *Czechoslovakia's Interrupted Revolution* (Princeton, NJ: Princeton University Press,1976), 11 and n. 12. On this last point, there is disagreement among scholars. Some find traces of an American pattern of government, while others deny this is the case. See Edward Taborsky, *Czechoslovak Democracy at Work* (London: Allen & Unwin, 1945), 14.

37. Elizabeth Wiskemann, *Czechs and Germans: A Study of the Struggle in the Historic Provinces of Bohemia and Moravia* (New York: Oxford University Press, 1938), 119.

38. Graham, "Constitutionalism and Political Structure," 130–33.

39. Zbyněk Zeman and Antonín Klimek, *The Life of Eduard Beneš, 1884–1948: Czechoslovakia in Peace and War* (Oxford: Clarendon Press, 1997), 50.

40. Zbyněk Zeman, *The Masaryks: The Making of Czechoslovakia* (London: Weidenfield & Nicolson, 1976), 135.

41. Zeman and Klimek, *Life of Eduard Beneš*, 123.

42. Hawgood, *Modern Constitutions since 1787*, 336.

43. Antony Polonsky, *Politics in Independent Poland, 1921–1939: The Crisis of Constitutional Government* (New York: Oxford University Press, 1972), 45; and William John Rose, *The Rise of Polish Democracy* (London: Bell & Sons, 1944), 161–62.

44. Joseph C. Gidyński, "Constitutional Development in Poland," in *Poland*, ed. Bernadotte E. Schmitt (Berkeley: University of California Press,1945), 95.

45. Robert Machray, *The Poland of Pilsudski: Incorporating Poland, 1914–1933 . . . and Carrying on the History of Poland until mid-July, 1936* (New York: Dutton, 1937), 134.

46. Rose, *Rise of Polish Democracy*, 162.

47. Polonsky, *Politics in Independent Poland*, 49.

48. Edward D. Wynot Jr., *Polish Politics in Transition: The Camp of National Unity and the Struggle for Power, 1935–1939* (Athens: University of Georgia Press, 1974), 22.

49. Ibid., 23.

50. Quoted in ibid., 24.

51. Józef Garliński, *Poland in the Second World War* (New York: Macmillan, 1985), xx.

52. R. R. Palmer, Joel Colton, and Lloyd Kramer, *A History of the Modern World*, 9th ed. (Boston: McGraw-Hill, 2002), 745–46.

53. Hawgood, *Modern Constitutions since 1787*, 342.

54. Beyme, *America as a Model*, 48.

55. Romuald J. Misiunas and Rein Taagepera, *The Baltic States: Years of Dependence, 1940–1980* (Berkeley: University of California Press, 1983), 10–11.

56. Alfred Erich Senn, *The Emergence of Modern Lithuania* (New York: Columbia University Press, 1959), 221.

57. Ibid., 217.

58. There is a dispute about this date, but the one used here seems to be the most widely accepted. See Alfred Erich Senn, *Lithuania Awakening* (Berkeley: University of California Press, 1990), 265.

59. Albertas Gerutis, "Independent Lithuania," in *Lithuania: 700 Years*, ed. Albertas Gerutis and trans. Algirdas Budreckis, 2nd rev. ed. (New York: Manyland Books, 1969), 145 ff.

60. Ibid.

61. Clarence Augustus Manning, *The Forgotten Republics* (New York: Philosophical Library, 1952), 64.

62. Bronis J. Kaslas, *The Baltic Nations: The Quest for Regional Integration and Political Liberty: Estonia, Latvia, Lithuania, Finland, Poland* (Pittson, PA: Euramerica Press, 1976), 104.

63. Ibid., 104–5.

64. Hawgood, *Modern Constitutions since 1787*, 333.

65. V. Stanley Vardys and Romuald J. Misiunas, eds., *The Baltic States in Peace and War, 1917–1945* (University Park: Pennsylvania State University Press, 1978), 74.

66. Hawgood, *Modern Constitutions since 1787*, 333–34.

67. Samuel P. Huntington, *The Third Wave: Democratizaion in the Late Twentieth Century* (Norman: University of Oklahoma Press, 1991), 16–17, 18–19, 21–25.

68. Ibid., 16.

69. Ibid., 18.

70. Thomas E. Skidmore and Peter H. Smith, *Modern Latin America*, 3rd ed. (New York: Oxford University Press, 1992), 231.

71. Carmen Ramos-Escandón, "Constitution of 1917," in *Encyclopedia of Latin American History and Culture* ed. Barbara A. Tenenbaum, Georgette Magassy Dorn, et al., 5 vols. (New York: Scribner, 1996), 4:25–26.

72. Thomas E. Skidmore and Peter H. Smith, *Modern Latin America*, 5th ed. (New York: Oxford University Press, 2001), 348.

73. Robert Payne, "Mexican Constitution of 1917," in *Constitutions That Made History*, ed. Albert P. Blaustein and Jay A. Sigler (New York: Paragon House, 1988), 283.

74. Ibid., 285.

75. Jorge G. Castañeda, *Perpetuating Power: How Mexican Presidents Were Chosen*, trans. Padraic Arthur Smithies (New York: New Press, 2000), xii.

76. José María Gamboa, *Leyes constitucionalis de México durante el siglo XIX* (Mexico City: Secreteriá de fomento, 1901), 5.

77. Emilio Rabasa, *El juicio constitucional, orígines, teoría y extensión* (Paris: Ch. Bouret, 1919), 54.

78. Castañeda, *Perpetuating Power*, xiii. The list of repressive incidents is long: the labor union coups of 1948; the government actions in the Nueva Rosita miners' strike in 1992; the terrible repression of the railroad workers' and teachers' strikes in 1958/1959; the assassination of the peasant leader Ruben Jaramillo in 1962; the "dirty" counterinsurgency wars in the early 1970s with their retinue of disappeared or tortured youth; the Salinas years of harassment, intimidation, and occasional violence; and the brutal excesses and use of force against the Chiapas in the 1990s.

79. Mexico failed to fit any traditional classification of existing political regimes. As one scholar observed: "It was not a classical one-party regime under Maurice Duverger's classification. . . . It did not really correspond to Guillermo O'Donnell's much later category of 'bureaucratic authoritarianism'; but it certainly did not fulfill the requirements for democracy under the Lipset, Dahl, and Huntington taxonomies of the fifties and sixties" (xiv).

80. Mark Falcoff, "Argentina, The Twentieth Century," in Tenenbaum et al., eds., *Encyclopedia of Latin American History and Culture*, 1:154.

81. Frederick B. Pike, *Spanish America, 1900 to 1970: Tradition and Social Innovation* (New York: Norton, 1973), 95.

82. Ibid., 98.

83. Ibid.

84. Ibid., 394.

85. Winfield Burggraff, "Venezuela: Constitutions," in Tenenbaum et al., eds., *Encyclopedia of Latin American History and Culture*, 5:394–95.

86. Keith Rosenn, "The Constitution of Brazil," unpublished paper kindly sent to me by the author, n.d., first page. The number depends on whether or not the 1969 constitution should be counted as a new constitution or a constitutional amendment.

87. Skidmore and Smith, *Modern Latin America* (5th ed.), 157.

88. Ibid., 160.

89. Robert G. Wesson and David V. Fleisher, *Brazil in Transition* (New York: Praeger, 1983), 15.

90. Ibid., 13.

CHAPTER 10

1. Speech in the House of Commons, June 18, 1940, in *Winston S. Churchill: His Complete Speeches, 1897–1963*, ed. Robert Rhodes James, 8 vols. (London: Chelsea House, 1974), 6:6238.

2. David Armitage, *The Declaration of Independence: A Global History* (Cambridge, MA: Harvard University Press, 2007), 111.

3. Jack Donnelly, *Universal Rights in Theory and Practice* (Ithaca, NY: Cornell University Press, 1989), 205–28.

4. Klaus von Beyme, *America as a Model: The Impact of American Democracy in the World* (New York: St. Martin's Press, 1987), 75.

5. Ibid., 28.

6. Tony Smith, *America's Mission: The United States and the Worldwide Struggle for Democracy in the Twentieth Century* (Princeton, NJ: Princeton University Press, 1994), 146–47.

7. For the term *imposed*, see Carl J. Friedrich, introduction to *The Origin of the West German Republic*, by Peter H. Merkl (New York: Oxford University Press, 1963), xvii. Carlo Schmid, a German politician, once claimed that some passages in the Basic Law had been "foisted on us." See the quotation in Beyme, *America as a Model*, 27. But Beyme dismisses the charge and gives the Schmid quotation a different interpretation. Beyme also quotes a left-wing scholar who made the same charge and gives him short shrift (25).

8. Beyme, *America as a Model*, 25. See also Carl J. Friedrich et al., *American Experiences in Military Government in World War II* (New York: Rinehart, 1948).

9. Carl J. Friedrich, "Rebuilding the German Constitution, Pt. 1," *American Political Science Quarterly* 43 (June 1949):481. Friedrich tried to impress the advantages of the American presidential system on German politicians, but it was to no avail. See Beyme, *America as a Model*, 51.

10. See the discussion in Friedrich, "Rebuilding the German Constitution, Pt. 1," 477.

11. Andrzej Rapaczinski, "Bibliographical Essay: The Influence of U.S. Constitutionalism Abroad," in *Constitutionalism and Rights: The Influence of the United States Constitution Abroad*, ed. Louis Henkin and Albert J. Rosenthal (New York: Columbia University Press, 1990), 436-437; and "Military Governors' *Aide Mémoire* . . . ," in *The Founding of the Federal Republic of Germany*, by John Ford Golay (Chicago: University of Chicago Press, 1958), app. B, 263–64.

12. It is true, however, that some of Clay's advisers urged unsuccessfully that the Germans consider the American presidential system. Friedrich, introduction to Merkl, *The Origin of the West German Republic*, xvii. Friedrich, who was an adviser to Clay notes that the "origin" of the moves cannot be clarified because of the absence of key documents. The missing documents in this case, as in that of South Korea's first constitution, raise some troubling questions. Future historians should pursue research for the unexplained missing documents.

13. Merkl, *The Origin of the West German Republic*, 9.

14. Beyme, *America as a Model*, 50.

15. Carl J. Friedrich, "Rebuilding the German Constitution, Pt. 2," *American Political Science Quarterly* 43 (August 1949):707.

16. Ibid., 711.

17. Merkl, *The Origin of the West German Republic*, 28.

18. Carl J. Friedrich, *The Impact of American Constitutionalism Abroad* (Boston: Boston University Press, 1967), 68.

19. Friedrich, "Rebuilding the German Constitution, Pt. 2," 709.

20. Ibid.

21. Ibid. See also the important essay by Carl J. Friedrich and Herbert Shapiro, "The Constitution of the German Republic," in *Governing Postwar Germany*, ed. Edward Harold Litchfield (Ithaca, NY: Cornell University Press, 1953), 117–51.

22. Friedrich, "Rebuilding the German Constitution, Pt. 2," 718.

23. Carl J. Friedrich, "The Legacies of the Occupation of Germany," *Public Policy* 17 (1968):14–15.

24. Rapaczynski, "Bibliographical Essay," 438.

25. Ibid.

26. Donald Kommers, cited in "Structure, Composition, Appointment and Jurisdiction of Constitutional Courts," in *Comparative Constitutional Law*, by Vicki

Jackson and Mark Tushnet, University Casebook Series (New York: Foundation Press, 1999), 519.

27. Quoted in Joshua Muravchik, *Exporting Democracy: Fulfilling America's Destiny* (Washington, DC: AEI Press, 1991), 112.

28. Rapaczynski, "Bibliographical Essay," 429.

29. The literature on the 1946 constitution is voluminous, particularly on the key issue of "imposing" the document and the various attempts to revise it. The majority of works, however, are descriptive rather than analytical. Most miss the mark by not dealing with the "constitutional consciousness of the people," which was absolutely crucial to answering the question of whether or not the document was "imposed." The following works are useful for pursuing research on the subject: John McGilvrey Maki, ed. and trans., *Japan's Commission on the Constitution: The Final Report* (Seattle: University of Washington Press, 1980); Dan Fenno Henderson, ed., *The Constitution of Japan: Its First Twenty Years, 1947–1967* (Seattle: University of Washington Press, 1968); Lawrence Ward Beer, *Freedom of Expression in Japan: A Study in Comparative Law, Politics, and Society* (Tokyo: Kodansha International, 1984); Robert E. Ward, "Origins of the Present Japanese Constitution," *American Political Science Review* 50 (1956):980–1010; Robert E. Ward, "The Commission on the Constitution and Prospects for Constitutional Change in Japan," *Journal of Asian Studies* 24 (1965):401–29; Ray A. Moore, "Reflections on the Occupation of Japan," *Journal of Asian Studies* 38 (1979):721–34; Theodore McNelly, *The Origins of Japan's Democratic Constitution* (Lanham, MD: University Press of America, 2000); Charles L. Kades, "The American Role in Revising Japan's Imperial Constitution," *Political Science Quarterly* 104 (1989):215–47; Kenzō Takayanagi, "Some Reminiscences of Japan's Commission on the Constitution," *Washington Law Review* 43 (1968):961–78. In his "Bibliographical Essay," 429, Andzrej Rapaczynski called the 1946 constitution "American-imposed," but since the Kades article was published the year before, he undoubtedly had had no opportunity to see it. One of the most important studies of the issue is John W. Dower's brilliant study, *Embracing Defeat: Japan in the Wake of World War II* (New York: Norton, 1999). Koseki Shōichi's *The Birth of Japan's Postwar Constitution*, ed. and trans. Ray A. Moore (Boulder, CO: Westview Press, 1989), is one of the best studies on the subject of imposition. Richard B. Finn, *Winners in Peace: MacArthur, Yoshida, and Postwar Japan* (Berkeley: University of California Press, 1992), provides important insights on MacArthur and the Japanese prime minister, Yoshida Shigeru. Dale M. Hellegers, *We the Japanese People: World War II and the Origins of the Japanese Constitution*, 2 vols. (Stanford, CA: Stanford University Press, 2001), is an exhaustive examination of the framing of the 1946 constitution as seen from the point of view of Washington and Tokyo. Ray A. Moore and Donald L. Robinson, *Partners for Democracy: Crafting the New Japanese State under MacArthur* (New York: Oxford University Press, 2002), provides the most insightful treatment of the subject.

30. Moore and Robinson, *Partners for Democracy*, 216.

31. John McGilvrey Maki, *Government and Politics in Japan: The Road to Democracy* (New York: Praeger, 1962), passim; see also Moore and Robinson, *Partners for Democracy*, esp. 13–20.

32. Lawrence Ward Beer, "The Present Constitutional System of Japan," in *Constitutional Systems in Late Twentieth Century Asia*, ed. Lawrence Ward Beer (Seattle: University of Washington Press,1992), 175–76.

33. Douglas MacArthur, *Reminiscences* (New York: McGraw-Hill, 1964), 392.

34. Koseki, *Birth of Japan's Postwar Constitution*, 60–65.

35. The idea of drafting a model constitution was probably MacArthur's, but its origins are obscure. Charles Kades, a learned American lawyer who participated in writing the draft, reported that the principles listed for the draft constitution had been handwritten in pencil and then typed. "Although Whitney did not say so, I assumed the note had been written by MacArthur personally or dictated by MacArthur to Whitney," wrote Kades in "The American Role in Revising Japan's Imperial Constitution," 221. Kades confirmed this point when I personally interviewed him in 1986.

36. Koseki, *The Birth of Japan's Postwar Constitution*, 79.

37. Hellegers, *We the Japanese People*, 2:518.

38. Koseki, *The Birth of Japan's Postwar Constitution*, 5.

39. Ibid., 84.

40. Hellegers, *We the Japanese People*, 2:465–68, 527, 530–31, 540–43. For the background of the historiographical controversy that the constitution had been "imposed" on Japan during the drafting process, as well as on the issue of "Japanizing" the constitution, see Koseki, *The Birth of Japan's Postwar Constitution*, x–xii and 1–6, and "Japanizing the Constitution," *Japan Quarterly* 35 (July–September 1988):234–40.

41. Hellegers, *We the Japanese People*, 2:541.

42. Dower, *Embracing Defeat*, passim.

43. Ibid., 279.

44. Article 1, Constitution of Japan, 1947.

45. Glenn D. Hook and Gavan McCormack, *Japan's Contested Constitution: Documents and Analysis* (London: Routledge, 2001), 5. For a different interpretation of what is known in Japanese as the Declaration of Humanity, see Lawrence W. Beer and John M. Maki, *From Imperial Myth to Democracy: Japan's Two Constitutions 1889–2002* (Boulder: University Press of Colorado, 2002), 68–72.

46. Dower, *Embracing Defeat*, 305–18.

47. Ibid., 388.

48. Hook and MacCormack, "Parchment and Politics," in *Japan's Contested Constitution*, 8.

49. Masami Itō, "The Modern Development of Law and Constitution in Japan," in Beer, ed., *Constitutional Systems in Late Twentieth Century Asia*, 142.

50. Hook and MacCormack, *Japan's Contested Constitution*, 78–79.

51. Beer, "The Present Constitutional System of Japan," in Beer, ed., *Constitutional Systems in Late Twentieth Century Asia*, 178.

52. Itō, "The Modern Development of Law and Constitution in Japan," 130–31.

53. Takeo Hayakawa and John R. Schmidhauser, "A Comparative Analysis of the Internal Procedures and Customs of the Supreme Courts of Japan and the United States," in *Comparative Judicial Systems: Challenging Frontiers in Conceptual and Empirical Analysis*, ed. John R. Schmidhauser (London: Butterworth, 1987), 203.

54. The literature on America's influence on judicial review in the Japanese Constitution of 1946 is voluminous. Besides the Itō section (129–74) of the article jointly written by him and Lawrence Beer entitled "The United States Constitution and Japan's Constitutional Law," in Beer, ed., *Constitutional Systems in Late Twentieth Century Asia*, the following works were especially helpful on judicial review: Nobushige Ukai, "The Significance of American Constitutional Institutions and Ideas in Japan," in *Constitutionalism in Asia: Asian Views of the American Influence*, ed. Lawrence Ward Beer (Berkeley: University of California Press, 1979), 111–27; Lawrence Ward Beer, "The Influence of American Constitutionalism in Asia," in *American Constitutionalism Abroad: Selected Essays in Comparative Constitutional History*, ed. George Athan Billias (Westport, CT: Greenwood Press, 1990), 121 and 133–35; Mauro Cappelletti, *Judicial Review in the Contemporary World* (Indianapolis: Bobbs-Merrill, 1971), 49, 51, 61, 64, 69, 86; and Henderson, ed., *The Constitution of Japan*, 125, 145, 165.

55. Moore and Robinson, *Partners in Democracy*, 323.

56. Percy R. Luney, "The Judiciary: Its Organization and Status in the Parliamentary System," *Law and Contemporary Problems* 53 (1990):135.

57. Cappelletti, *Judicial Review in the Contemporary World*, 64.

58. Itō, "The Modern Development of Law and Constitution in Japan," 154.

59. Lawrence W. Beer, "Constitutionalism and Rights in Japan and Korea," in Henkin and Rosenthal, eds., *Constitutionalism and Rights*, 238.

60. Beer, "The Influence of American Constitutionalism in Asia," 133–34.

61. Itō, "The Modern Development of Law and Constitution in Japan," 154–55; and Beer's section of the joint article, "The Present Constitutional System of Japan," 181.

62. Dower, *Embracing Defeat*, 79–80. For other forms of expression and assembly, see also Beer, "Present Constitutional System of Japan," 194–95.

63. Peter J. Herzog [Hoshii Iwao], *Japan's Pseudo-Democracy* (New York: New York University Press, 1993), 99–100.

64. Beer, "Present Constitutional System of Japan," 195–96.

65. Lawrence W. Beer, "Law and Liberty," in *Democracy in Japan*, ed. Takeshi Ishida and Ellis S. Krauss (Pittsburgh: University of Pittsburgh Press, 1989), 78. The commissioners and counselors were unpaid men and women carefully

selected for their integrity and commitment to the ideals of human rights. They helped also in transforming the arrogant functionaries of the prewar period into postwar officials who were viewed instead as "servants" of the people (78–79).

66. Mark Gayn, *Japan Diary* (New York: Sloan Associates, 1948), cited in Koseki, *Birth of Japan's Postwar Constitution*, xi and 1.

67. Ward, "Origins of the Present Japanese Constitution," 1010.

68. Moore, "Reflections on the Occupation of Japan," 721–26.

69. Moore and Robinson, *Partners for Democracy*, 339.

70. Ibid., passim.

71. Ibid., 4, 91–92, and 141.

72. Koseki, *The Birth of Japan's Postwar Constitution*, 5.

73. Koseki, "Japanizing the Constitution," 239–40.

74. Ibid., 235.

75. Quoted in ibid.

76. Quoted in ibid.

77. Ibid.

78. "Paradoxically, . . . mutual misunderstandings probably made it possible for the two sides to 'agree' on the final version of the Constitution" was the conjecture of a Japanese scholar who conducted a linguistic and cultural study of the document. See Kyoko Inoue, *MacArthur's Japanese Constitution: A Linguistic and Cultural Study of Its Making* (Chicago: University of Chicago Press, 1991), 5.

79. Dower, *Embracing Defeat*, 79–80.

80. Ibid., 23.

81. Ibid., 550.

82. Ibid., 550–52.

83. Beyme, *America as a Model*, 27.

84. Ibid., 49–50.

85. Norman Kogan, *A Political History of Postwar Italy* (New York: Praeger, 1966), 117.

86. Cappelletti, *Judicial Review in the Contemporary World*, 49–50.

87. Nevil Johnson, "Constitutionalism in Europe since 1945: Reconstruction and Reappraisal," in *Constitutionalism and Democracy: Transitions in the Contemporary World*, ed. Douglas Greenberg, Stanley N. Katz, Melanie Beth Oliviero, and Steven C. Wheatley (New York: Oxford University Press, 1993), 54.

88. Aldo Garosci, *Il pensiero politico degli autori del "Federalist"* (Milan: Edizioni di comunità, 1954), ix.

89. See the translation by Bianca Maria Tedeschini Lalli, published as *Il federalista; commento alla constituzione degli Stati Uniti* (Pisa: Nistri-Lischi, 1955), xi; another source gives Bologna 1950 as the first publication of Tedeschini Lalli's translation, but this has not been verified.

90. Gerhard Botz, "Janus-Headed Austria: Transition from Nazism as Restoration, Continuity, and Learning Process," in *Modern Europe after Fascism,*

1943–1980s, ed. Stein Ugelvik Larsen, with Bernt Hagtvet, 2 vols. (New York: Columbia University Press, 1998), 1:370.

91. Jackson and Tushnet, *Comparative Constitutional Law*, 469.

92. See the discussion in Beyme about the competition between the American and Austrian model of judicial review concerning the establishment of an American-style supreme court in 1949 in the Federal Republic of Germany. The United States was always wary of special courts because of the history of Star Chambers in England.

93. Friedrich, *The Impact of American Constitutionalism Abroad*, 24–25. The preceding account necessarily simplifies a complicated history. See Francis Goquel, "The Evolution of the French Presidency, 1954–1981," in *Constitutional Democracy: Essays in Comparative Politics*, ed. Fred Eidlin (Boulder, CO: Westview Press, 1983), 48–61. For a comparative constitutional approach that shows how the features of semipresidentialism and semiparliamentarianism were combined in a somewhat similar way earlier in the Weimar Republic, see Cindy Skach, *Borrowing Constitutional Designs: Constitutional Law in Weimar Germany and the Fifth French Republic* (Princeton, NJ: Princeton University Press, 2005).

94. Carl J. Friedrich, "The New French Constitution in Political and Historical Perspective," *Harvard Law Review* 72 (1959):802–3.

95. Ibid., 25.

96. Rapaczynski, "Bibliographical Essay," 419–20.

97. Friedrich, "The New French Constitution in Political and Historical Perspective," 826.

98. Rapaczinski, "Bibliographical Essay," 420.

99. Edward McWhinney, *Judicial Review*, 4th ed. (Toronto: University of Toronto Press, 1969), 156–57.

100. Quoted in Richard H. Grimes and Patrick T. Horgan, *Introduction to Law in the Republic of Ireland: Its History, Principles, Administration, & Substance* (Dublin: Wolfhound Press, 1981), 171.

101. Ibid.

102. Ibid.

103. Gerard W. Hogan and Clive Walker, *Political Violence and the Law in Ireland* (New York: St. Martin's Press, 1989), 185.

104. James C. Thomson Jr., Peter W. Stanley, and John Curtis Perry, *Sentimental Imperialists: The American Experience in East Asia* (New York: Harper & Row, 1981), 169; and James Magavern, "Editorial Note," in Beer, ed., *Constitutionalism in Asia*, 141–42.

105. Magavern, "Editorial Note," 142.

106. Ibid.

107. Rapaczynski, "Bibliographical Essay," 441–42.

108. Contacts between the United States and Korea existed long before World War II. Before then, Korea's movement for independence often combined

nationalist preoccupations with American notions of constitutionalism, Christianity, and human rights. Responding to Woodrow Wilson's call for self-determination of all peoples, the Koreans launched their March First Movement in 1919, which was a prolonged series of massive peaceful nationwide demonstrations for independence. The eloquent Korean Declaration of Independence called for freedom and equality, echoing the American Declaration. Christian political leaders such as Syngman Rhee were educated in schools founded by American missionaries who also established churches and public health facilities. South Korea's liberation did not come, however, until the 1945 defeat of Japan.

For a study focusing on colonial nationalist leaders in Egypt, India, and China as well as Korea, who used Wilson's rhetoric regarding the self-determination of peoples to advance their anticolonial nationalism, see Erez Manela, *The Wilsonian Moment: Self-determination and the International Origins of Anticolonial Nationalism* (New York: Oxford University Press, 2007).

For the historical background of these and other constitutional matters, see Chong-sik Lee, *The Politics of Korean Nationalism* (Berkeley: University of California Press, 1965), 167, 277–78, and passim; Gregory Henderson, *Korea: The Politics of the Vortex* (Cambridge, MA: Harvard University Press, 1968), 80–86; Bruce Cumings, *The Two Koreas*, Headline Series no. 269 (New York: Foreign Policy Association, 1984); Bruce Cumings, *Korea's Place in the Sun: A Modern History*, updated ed. (New York: Norton, 2005); and Pyŏng-ho Pak et al., *Modernization and Its Impact upon Korean Law* (Berkeley: University of California Center for Korean Studies, 1981). For the texts of South Korean constitutions, see Se-Jin Kim and Chang-Hyun Cho, *Government and Politics of Korea* (Silver Springs, MD: Research Institute on Korean Affairs, 1972), 275 ff.; *Journal of Korean Affairs*, April 1973, 39, the Yushin Constitution; and *Korea Times*, September 30, 1980. See also Bruce Cumings, ed., *Child of Conflict: The Korean-American Relationship, 1943–1953* (Seattle: University of Washington Press, 1983). This history is instructive in showing how the United States served as an inspiration for Korean independence.

109. Tscholsu Kim and Sang Don Lee, "The Influence of U.S. Constitutional Law Doctrines in Korea," in Beer, ed., *Constitutional Systems in Late Twentieth Century Asia*, 304–5.

110. Although Colonel Emery J. Woodall, a U.S. military legal officer, prepared a draft constitution and gave it to members of the Korean drafting committee, there is no evidence that it played a significant part in the final version. See Kim and Lee, "The Influence of U.S. Constitutional Law Doctrines in Korea," 305 and 309.

111. Beer, "The Influence of American Constitutionalism in Asia," 128–29.

112. Kim and Lee, "The Influence of U.S. Constitutional Law Doctrines in Korea," 305.

113. Robert T. Oliver, *Syngman Rhee and American Involvement in Korea: A Personal Narrative, 1942–1960* (Seoul: Panmun Book, 1978), 4.

114. Kim and Lee, "The Influence of U.S. Constitutional Law Doctrines in Korea," 307.

115. Ibid., 310.

116. Ibid., 311.

117. Ibid., 313.

118. Ibid.

119. Ibid.

120. Ibid.

121. Ibid.

122. Ibid., 314.

123. Gregory Henderson, "Constitutional Changes from the First to the Sixth Republics, 1948–1987," in *Political Change in South Korea,* ed. Ilpyŏng J. Kim and Young Whan Kihl (New York: Paragon House, 1988), 32.

124. In this regard, India deliberately rejected the American presidential system in a move that was clearly a case of negative influence. See Rapaczynski, "Bibliographical Essay," 449.

125. Ibid., 447.

126. David Williams, "Constitutional Law—Reception and Impact," in *The Impact of American Law on English and Commonwealth Law: A Book of Essays,* ed. Jerome B. Elkind (St. Paul: West, 1978), 26.

127. Besides British and American influences, the Indians studied and drew on other foreign constitutions.

128. Rapaczynski, "Bibliographical Essay," 449.

129. P. K. Tripathi, "Perspectives on American Constitutional Influence on the Constitution of India," in Beer, ed., *Constitutionalism in Asia,* 64–71. The complexity of the federal–state relationship in India, however, as well as the one-sided powers conferred on the central government, raised questions by some scholars as to whether India could even be called a federal state. See P. K. Tripathi, "Federalism: Reality and Myth," *Journal of the Bar Council of India* 3 (1974):251–77.

The subject of India's federal system has produced a voluminous literature, but the following books proved especially helpful: Durga Das Basu, *Commentary on the Constitution of India: Being a Comparative Treatise on the Universal Principles of Justice and Constitutional Government . . . ,* 7th ed., 4 vols. (Calcutta: S. C. Sarkar, 1993), vol. A; P. K. Tripathi, "Perspectives on the American Constitutional Influence on the Constitution of India," in *The Framing of India's Constitution,* ed. B. Shiva Rao et al., 5 vols. (New Delhi: Institute of Public Administration, 1966–1968); M. V. Pylee, *Constitutional Government in India,* 3rd rev. ed. (London: Asia Publishing House, 1977); Asok Kumar Chanda, *Federalism in India* (London: Allen & Unwin, 1965); Ramesh Thakur, *The Government and Politics of India* (New York: St. Martin's Press, 1995), 68–120; and Rajeev Dhavan, "Republic of India," in Beer, ed., *Constitutional Systems in Late Twentieth Century Asia,* 373, 407–12.

130. Thakur, *Government and Politics of India*, 71–72.

131. Basu, *Commentary on the Constitution of India*, 36.

132. Rapaczynski, "Bibliographical Essay," 449–50.

133. Ibid., 450–51.

134. Tripathi, "Perspectives on American Constitutional Influence on the Constitution of India," 68–71.

135. S. C. Dash, *The Constitution of India: A Comparative Study*, 2nd ed. (Allahabad: Chaitanya Publishing, 1968), 403–28.

136. Elkind, ed., *Impact of American Law on English and Commonwealth Law*, 22.

137. Nelson, *Marbury v. Madison*, 108.

138. On the preferential policies erected by the Indian higher judiciary to bring about "compensatory discrimination," see the superb study by Marc Galanter, *Competing Equalities: Law and the Backward Classes in India* (Berkeley: University of California Press, 1984).

139. Tripathi, "Perspectives on the American Constitutional Influence on the Constitution of India," 80.

140. Ibid.

141. Ibid., 81.

142. Adam Malik, *In the Service of the Republic* (Singapore: Gunung Agung, 1980), 8–9, 129.

143. Mr. Muhammad Yamin, quoted in Oemar Seno Adji, "An Indonesian Perspective on American Constitutional Influence," in Beer, ed., *Constitutionalism in Asia*, 104.

144. Adji, "An Indonesian Perspective on American Constitutional Influence," 104.

145. Briefly, the ideology of Pancasila had five elements: belief in one god, nationalism, democracy, social justice, and a just and civilized humanitarianism. The Pancasila seems to have originated in a speech by President Sukarno in June 1945 during discussions to prepare for independence as the Japanese occupation drew to a close at the end of the war.

146. Adji, "An Indonesian Perspective on American Constitutional Influence," 102–3.

147. A. Arthur Schiller, *The Formation of Federal Indonesia, 1945–1949* (The Hague: W. Van Hoeve, 1955), 4.

148. *The Constitution of the Republic of Indonesia* and "Elucidation of the Constitution (1945 and 1959), provided by the *Pancasila* Council," (Jakarta: Department of Information, 1984); Charles Wolf, *The Indonesian Story: The Birth, Growth, and Structure of the Indonesian Republic* (New York: J. Day, 1984); and Adji, "An Indonesian Perspective on American Constitutional Influence," 103–4.

149. Adji, "An Indonesian Perspective on American Constitutional Influence," 102.

150. Herbert Han-pao Ma, "American Influence on the Formation of the Constitution and Constitutional Law of the Republic of China: Past History and Future Prospects," in Beer, ed., *Constitutionalism in Asia*, 43. There is considerable controversy about the Sun "myth." For an example of an uncritical and overly sympathetic approach, see Sidney H. (Hsu-Hsin) Chang and Leonard H. D. Gordon, *All under Heaven: Sun Yat-sen and His Revolutionary Thought* (Stanford, CA: Hoover Institution Press, 1991).

151. Albert P. Blaustein and Jay A. Sigler, eds., *Constitutions That Made History* (New York: Paragon House, 1988), 276.

152. Quoted in Ma, "American Influence on the Formation of the Constitution and Constitutional Law of the Republic of China," 45.

153. Ibid., 46–48, 52, and 55.

154. Julie Lee Wei, Ramon H. Myers, and Donald G. Gillin, eds., and Julie Lee Wei, E-su Zen, and Linda Chao, trans., *Prescriptions for Saving China: Selected Writings of Sun Yat-sen* (Stanford, CA: Hoover Institution Press, 1994), xxiii.

155. William Jones, "People's Republic of China," in Beer, ed., *Constitutional Systems in Late Twentieth Century Asia*, 74.

156. The best biography of Perón is Robert J. Alexander's *Juan Domingo Perón: A History* (Boulder, CO: Westview Press, 1979), which, although lacking footnotes, is Alexander's second biography of Perón. There is a flood of literature on Perón, the Perónist movement, and his wives. Among the most interesting are Joseph A. Page, *Perón: A Biography* (New York: Random House, 1983); Nicholas Fraser and Marysa Navarro, *Eva Perón* (New York: Norton, 1981); John Barnes, *Evita: First Lady: A Biography of Eva Perón* (New York: Grove Press, 1978); Robert A. Potash, *The Army and Politics in Argentina, 1928–1945*, 3 vols. (Stanford, CA: Stanford University Press, 1969–1996); Samuel L. Bailey, *Labor, Nationalism, and Politics in Argentina* (New Brunswick, NJ: Rutgers University Press, 1967); David Rock, *Argentina, 1567–1987: From Spanish Colonization to Alfonsin* (Berkeley: University of California Press, 1987); Juan E. Corradi, *The Fitful Republic: Economy, Society, and Politics in Argentina* (Boulder, CO: Westview Press, 1985); James P. Brennan, ed., *Peronism and Argentina* (Wilmington, DE: SR Books, 1998); Michael L. Conniff, ed., *Latin American Populism in Comparative Perspective* (Albuquerque: University of New Mexico Press, 1982); and Frederick C. Turner and José Enrique Miguens, eds., *Juan Perón and the Reshaping of Argentina* (Pittsburgh: University of Pittsburgh Press, 1983).

157. Corradi, *The Fitful Republic*, 68.

158. Christian Buchruker, "Interpretations of Peronism: Old Frameworks and New Perspectives," in Brennan, ed., *Peronism and Argentina*, 10–11.

159. Alexander, *Juan Domingo Perón*, 152. Tulio Halperin Donghi's *The Peronist Revolution and Its Ambiguous Legacy* (London: Institute of Latin American Studies, 1998) is crucial to any evaluation of Peronism.

160. Heraldo Muñoz, "Chile: The Limits of 'Success,'" in *Exporting Democracy: The United States and Latin America*, ed. Abraham F. Lowenthal (Baltimore: Johns Hopkins University Press, 1991), 41.

161. Leo Lott, "Executive Power in Venezuela," *American Political Science Review* 50 (1956):394.

162. Ibid.

163. William Sylvane Stokes, *Latin American Politics* (New York: Crowell, 1959), 458–59.

164. For the orientalist views of Eisenhower and American diplomats stationed in the Middle East, see Douglas Little, *American Orientalism: The United States and the Middle East since 1945* (Chapel Hill: University of North Carolina Press, 2002), 28 and 57.

165. Mark H. Lytle, *The Origins of the Iranian-American Alliance, 1941–1953* (New York: Holmes & Meier, 1987), xvii; and Walter LaFeber, *The American Age: United States Foreign Policy at Home and Abroad since 1750* (New York: Norton, 1989), 517–18.

166. The quotation is from the famous memorandum NSC-7 of 1948.

167. LaFeber, *The American Age*, 548.

168. Lytle, *Origins of the Iranian-American Alliance*, 208. For a different version of this episode see Little, *American Orientalism*, 216–17; and for a remarkably candid account of the CIA activities in the first unsanitized edition of the book, see Kermit Roosevelt, *Countercoup: The Struggle for the Control of Iran* (New York: McGraw-Hill, 1979).

169. Blanche Wiesen Cook, *The Declassified Eisenhower: A Divided Legacy* (Garden City, NY: Doubleday, 1981), 269.

170. Ibid., 218.

171. Winfield Burggraff, "Dominican Republic: Constitutions," in *Encyclopedia of Latin American History and Culture*, ed. Barbara A. Tenenbaum, Georgette Magassy Dorn, et al., 5 vols. (New York: Scribner, 1996), 2:398.

172. Abraham F. Lowenthal, *The Dominican Intervention* (Cambridge, MA: Harvard University Press, 1972), 30–31.

173. Richard S. Hillman and Thomas J. D'Agostino, *Distant Neighbors in the Caribbean: The Dominican Republic and Jamaica in Comparative Perspective* (New York: Praeger, 1992), 82.

174. John Quincy Adams, Secretary of State, speech delivered to the House of Representatives on July 4, 1821.

175. This question was posed in John Lewis Gaddis's essay "Morality and the American Experience in the Cold War," in John Lewis Gaddis, *The United States and the End of the Cold War: Implications, Reconsiderations, Provocations* (New York: Oxford University Press, 1992), 47.

176. Quoted in ibid.

177. Ibid., 48.

CHAPTER 11

1. Samuel P. Huntington, "Democracy's Third Wave," in *The Global Resurgence of Democracy*, ed. Larry Diamond and Marc F. Plattner (Baltimore: Johns Hopkins University Press, 1993), 3. Huntington's number is actually about thirty countries from 1974 to 1990. On the number of constitutions in the world at the time, there is also some discrepancy between Huntington and Lawrence Ward Beer, introduction to *Constitutional Systems in Late Twentieth Century Asia*, ed. Lawrence Ward Beer (Seattle: University of Washington Press, 1992), 4. Huntington's figure is only 130 as of 1990 because he excludes those countries with a population of less than one million people. See Samuel P. Huntington, *The Third Wave: Democratization in the Late Twentieth Century* (Norman: University of Oklahoma Press, 1991), 26. Beer lists 167 single-document constitutions as of 1991. The avalanche of constitution writing in the seventh echo was extraordinary. There were more than one hundred written constitutions in 1991, for example, but only twenty were dated earlier than 1950. See Beer, ed., *Constitutional Systems in Late Twentieth Century Asia*, 4. The seventh echo represents the greatest period of constitution writing in human history.

Huntington's *The Third Wave* gave rise to a host of studies supporting or attacking his thesis or providing alternative explanations for the surge of global democracy. See Nancy Bermeo, ed., *Liberalization and Democratization: Change in the Soviet Union and Eastern Europe* (Baltimore: Johns Hopkins University Press, 1992); Frederick Weil, Jeffrey Huffman, and Mary Gautier, eds., *Democratization in Eastern and Western Europe* (Greenwich, CT: JAI Press,1993); Adam Przeworski, *Democracy and the Market: Political and Economic Reforms in Eastern Europe and Latin America* (Cambridge: Cambridge University Press, 1991); Giuseppe Di Palma, *To Craft Democracies: An Essay on Democratic Transitions* (Berkeley: University of California Press, 1990); Larry Diamond, Juan J. Linz and Seymour Martin Lipset, eds., *Politics in Developing Countries: Comparing Experiences with Democracy*, 2nd ed. (Boulder, CO: Lynne Rienner, 1995); David Beetham, ed., *Defining and Measuring Democracy* (London: Sage, 1994); and Georg Sørenson, *Democracy and Democratization: Processes and Prospects in a Changing World*, 3rd ed. (Boulder, CO: Westview Press, 2008).

The great surge of democracy in the "third wave" from 1974 to 1989 might have been even higher than Huntington's estimate of sixty. According to the annual survey by Freedom House, the most widely accepted organization for gauging democracy, almost seventy-five countries were judged to be politically "free" by the end of 1991. The annual survey in 1992, applying a more generous definition, counted eighty-nine democracies, roughly one-half the independent countries in the world and twice the number of twenty years earlier. See Diamond and Plattner, eds., *The Global Resurgence of Democracy*, ix.

2. K. Jaggers and T. Gunn, "Tracking Democracy's Third Wave with the Polity Data," *Journal of Peace Research* 32, no. 4 (1995):76.

3. Huntington, *The Third Wave*, xiii.

4. Diamond and Plattner, eds., *The Global Resurgence of Democracy*, ix.

5. While it is true that historically, the principles of American constitutionalism gave rise to democracy, one must recognize the distinction between the two. Democracy emphasizes individualism and political rights, whereas constitutionalism emphasizes political order and the need for societal control. Democracy, in theory, is the antithesis of constitutional government and has little sympathy for the rule of law or property rights as such. Constitutionalism, in contrast, supports property rights, rights of minorities, and the rule of law. When they blend in American constitutional democracy, the tension between them creates an unstable, ongoing compromise, even when, as in the seventh echo, they expand side by side.

6. David Armitage, *The Declaration of Independence: A Global History* (Cambridge, MA: Harvard University Press, 2007), 20–21, 104, 107–12. The one hundred "declarations" cover from 1776 to 2007.
Sometimes the language of the Declaration was deliberately distorted for propaganda purposes. The most famous, perhaps, is the well-known case in 1945 when Ho Chi Minh patterned Vietnam's Declaration of Independence after the American one and referred specifically to the second paragraph regarding the natural rights of men. He listed grievances against French colonial rulers as Americans had against British rule in order to appeal to the anticolonial sentiments of Americans and to remind them that they had been in a similar situation. See Bernard B. Fall, *The Viet-Minh Regime: Government and Administration in the Democratic Republic of Vietnam,* rev. and enlarged ed. (Westport, CT: Greenwood Press, 1975), 4. Armitage also makes reference to this declaration in his *Declaration of Independence*, 134–35.

7. Daniel J. Elazar, *Exploring Federalism* (Tuscaloosa: University of Alabama Press, 1987).

8. Thomas Fleiner-Gerster, "Federalism, Decentralization, and Rights," in *Constitutionalism and Rights: The Influence of the United States Constitution Abroad*, ed. Louis Henkin and Albert J. Rosenthal (New York: Columbia University Press, 1990), 19–36. Donald Horowitz's comment on the decline of federalism takes into account only the specific model following *The Federalist* and not other forms of federation. See Donald Horowitz, *"The Federalist* Abroad in the World," Duke Law School Legal Studies Research Papers no. 194 (March 2008):22–26.

9. Donald Horowitz, "Constitutional Courts: A Primer for Decision Makers," *Journal of Democracy* 17, no. 4 (2006):127. See also David Robertson, "Judicial Review," in *Encyclopedia of Democratic Thought*, ed. Paul Barry Clarke and Joe Foweraker (New York: Routledge, 2001), 380–82.

10. Horowitz, "Constitutional Courts," 125. By 2005, 44 percent preferred the separate constitutional court system, compared with 32 percent that resorted to a supreme court or other ordinary court.

11. Horowitz, "Constitutional Courts," 125. There is a wealth of valuable data in the Ginsberg–Elkins Comparative Constitutions Project at the University of Illinois cited by Horowitz.

12. This treaty was Optional Protocol Number 1 to the International Covenant on Civil and Political Rights. See Horowitz, "*The Federalist* Abroad in the World," 20.

13. Ibid., 19–20.

14. Ibid., 9.

15. Ibid., 2.

16. Ibid.

17. A. E. Dick Howard, ed., *Constitution Making in Eastern Europe* (Washington, DC: Woodrow Wilson Center Press, 1993), 14 and 16.

18. Huntington, "Democracy's Third Wave," 4.

19. There is some justification for considering the countries of Southern Europe as a unit when making a transition to democracy by 1990, in what was called the Mediterranean model of liberal democracy. See Geoffrey Pridham, "Abstracts," in *The New Mediterranean Democracies: Regime Transition in Spain, Greece, and Portugal*, ed. Geoffrey Pridham (London: Frank Cass, 1984), 188. Although the stress is mainly on these three countries, the other two also were included in the literature.

20. The CIA probably sent millions of dollars to the Socialist Party in Portugal in 1975 to help solidify the new regime. See Huntington, *The Third Wave*, 94.

21. Geoffrey Pridham, "Comparative Perspectives on the New Mediterranean Democracies: A Model or Regime Transitions?" in Pridham, ed., *The New Mediterranean Democracies*, 2. For an early statement of the theory of transition to democracy in the new Mediterranean democracies, see Dankwart Rustow, "Transitions to Democracy: Towards a Dynamic Model," in *Comparative Politics*, April 1970, 347.
The great differences among the five countries, however, may make the Mediterranean subarea concept somewhat suspect. The unique historical development of each nation, different customs and institutions, and differing rates of economic development make any sweeping generalizations difficult. Regionalism in Spain resulting from the rebellious Basque minority, for example, differed from that of the Kurds in Turkey. There were, nevertheless, enough parallelisms to entertain the idea of a Mediterranean Europe. See Pridham, ed., "Comparative Perspectives on the New Mediterranean Democracies," 2–16.

22. Frank Tachau, *Turkey: The Politics of Authority, Democracy, and Development* (New York: Praeger, 1984), 44.

23. For Portugal, see Kenneth Maxwell, *The Making of Portuguese Democracy* (Cambridge: Cambridge University Press, 1995), a brilliant analysis, superior to other accounts. See also Kenneth Maxwell and Michael H. Haltzel, eds., *Portugal: Ancient Country, Young Democracy* (Washington, DC: Wilson Center Press, 1990), esp. the preface, xi.

Greece, bearing the burden of a bitter civil war from 1946 to 1948, was slower in achieving political stability following the strong-men rule of authoritarian colonels until 1974. After the colonels were overthrown, more democratic rule was established. The 1975 Greek Constitution achieved a degree of stability and showed some direct influence of American constitutionalism in protecting certain civil liberties. See John O. Iatrides, "Perceptions of Soviet Involvement in the Greek Civil War, 1945–1949," in *Studies in the History of the Greek Civil War, 1945–1949*, ed. Lars Baerentzen, John O. Iatrides, and Ole L. Smith (Copenhagen: Museum Tuscalanum Press, 1987); Stylianes Itajiyannis, "Democratization and the Greek State," in *Transitions from Dictatorship to Democracy: Comparative Studies of Spain, Portugal, and Greece*, ed. Ronald H. Chilicote (New York: Crane Russak, 1990); P. Nikiforos Dramandouros, "Transition to, and Consolidation of Democratic Politics in Greece, 1974–1983: A Tentative Assessment," in Pridham, ed., *New Mediterranean Democracies*; and C. Tebbs et al., eds., *Global Constitutional Law Collection*, 3 vols. (Nijmegen: Global Law Association, 1996–).

The Spanish dictator Francisco Franco remained in control from 1939 to 1975, an unconscionably long time. The transition to democracy, however, proved difficult. There was no direct American influence in the Spanish Constitution of 1978, although the list of "inherent rights" emphasized values expressed or implied in the Declaration of Independence, U.S. Constitution, and the federal Bill of Rights. See E. Ramon Arango, "Excerpts from the Constitution," in *Spain: From Repression to Renewal*, ed. E. Ramon Arango (Boulder, CO: Westview Press, 1985). For the question whether the transition to democracy was orderly or disorderly, see Arango, ed., *Spain: From Repression to Renewal*, 93; and Robert Graham, *Spain: A Nation Comes of Age* (New York: St. Martin's Press, 1984), 277.

For Turkey's long constitutional struggle to achieve more democracy, see the following: C. H. Dodd, *The Crisis of Turkish Democracy* (Northgate: Eothen Press, 1983); Dankwart Rustow, "Ataturk as an Institution-Builder," in *Ataturk: Founder of a Modern State*, ed. Ali Kazancigil and Ergun Ozbudun (Hamden, CT: Archon Books, 1981); Enver Ziya Karal, "Principles of Kemalism," in Kazancigil and Ozbudun, eds., *Ataturk*; Richard D. Robinson, *The First Turkish Republic: A Case Study in National Development* (Cambridge, MA: Harvard University Press, 1963); Dodd, "Extracts of the Constitution of the Republic of Turkey," in Dodd, *The Crisis of Turkish Democracy*, 96–102; and Heinz Kramer, *A Changing Turkey: Challenges to Europe and the United States* (Washington, DC: Brookings Institution Press, 2000).

For Albania, see Raymond Zickel and Walter R. Iwaskiw, eds., *Albania: A Country Study*, 2nd ed. (Washington, DC: Library of Congress, 1994); and Miranda Vickers, *The Albanians: A Modern History*, rev. ed. (London: I. B. Tauris, 1999).

24. Jordi Sole Tura, "Iberian Case Study: The Constitutionalism of Democratization," in *Constitutionalism and Democracy: Transitions in the Contemporary World*, ed. Douglas Greenberg, Stanley N. Katz, Melanie Beth Oliviero, and Steven C. Wheatley (New York: Oxford University Press, 1993), 296.

25. Dramandouros, "Transition to and Consolidation of Democratic Politics in Greece," 65; and Pridham, "Comparative Perspectives on the New Mediterranean Democracies," 9.

26. Although the language of the "fundamental laws" differed in the Greek context, the democratizing intent was clear, and the same was true in the case of the other countries treated later.

27. "Constitution of Greece," in C. Tebbs et al., eds., *Global Constitutional Law Collection*, 2:173, 175, 176.

28. David H. Close, "The Legacy," in *The Greek Civil War: Studies of Polarization*, ed. David H. Close (London: Routledge, 1993), 226. I am indebted to Niki Kaltsoya of Panteion University of Athens, who called my attention to the article by Prof. Alexander Svolos, "The First Greek Constitutions and the Influence of the French Revolution," *Ephimeris ton Ellinon Nomikon*, October 1935, 737–47.

29. Arango, ed., *Spain: From Repression to Renewal*, 110.

30. "Excerpts from the Constitution," in Arango, ed., *Spain: From Repression to Renewal*, 118.

31. "Extracts of the Constitution of the Republic of Turkey, 1982," in Dodd, *The Crisis of Turkish Democracy*, 96–102.

32. Ibid., 104.

33. Zickel and Iwaskiw, eds., *Albania*, 185–89.

34. Howard, ed., *Constitution Making in Eastern Europe*, 16–17. The charter contained the language of the American Bill of Rights, though in many instances it made more explicit rights that were only implicit in American constitutionalism.

35. "The Constitution of the Czech Republic," in *The Constitutions of New Democracies in Europe*, ed. Peter K. Raina (Braunton: Merlin, 1995), 30–31.

36. "The Constitution of the Slovak Republic," in Raina, ed., *The Constitutions of New Democracies in Europe*, 288–89.

37. "The Constitution of Bulgaria," in Raina, ed., *The Constitutions of New Democracies in Europe*, 2.

38. "The Constitution of Romania," in Raina, ed., *The Constitutions of New Democracies in Europe*, 218–19. For additional information on Romania's transition, see the essays in Daniel N. Nelson, ed., *Romania in the 1980s* (Boulder, CO:

Westview Press, 1981), esp. the one by Mary Ellen Fischer, "Idol or Leader? The Origins and Future of the Ceausescu Cult," 117–41.

39. Stanley N. Katz, *Constitutionalism in East Central Europe: Some Negative Lessons from the American Experience*, German Historical Institute Lectures no. 7 (Providence, RI: Berghahn Books, 1994), 9 and 15; Greenberg, Katz, et al., eds., *Constitutionalism and Democracy*, xvii; and Katz's Jefferson Lecture at University of California, Berkeley, April 25, 2000, kindly provided by the author.

When president of the American Council of Learned Societies, Katz headed a study of comparative constitutionalism along with American and foreign scholars for five years beginning in 1987. The lecture cited here was an outgrowth of the study whose findings were published in *Constitutionalism and Democracy*. Katz's critique of the "negative lessons" was, however, but the tip of the iceberg of a much more ambitious project: his hypothesis for rejecting the definition of "constitutionalism" used by most current scholars in the West, including that employed in this book. Katz argues that the conventional definition implied that "all constitutions must be written, legitimized by bodies other than ordinary legislatures, based on individual rights, and conducted by rigorous, formal limitations on the power of government" (*Constitutionalism in East Central Europe*, 9). Derived from Enlightenment idealism and based on Lockeian individualism, this Western idea of liberal democratic constitutionalism cannot be applied universally to socialist regimes, non-Western cultures, or certain other forms of government. Katz suggests a more realistic and functional definition that rejects the idea of universalism. It is based on indigenous traditions, autochthonous elements, and local historical experiences rooted in a given society that establish the basis for any prevailing constitutionalism. Katz held that the traditional definition led "toward a highly formalistic view that relied principally on the structural features of constitutional documents." Katz's definition regarded the constitutionalism of a particular society as a dynamic process, rooted in underlying indigenous social realities (Greenberg et al., eds., *Constitutionalism and Democracy*, xvii). Katz's hypothesis threatens to overturn all the conventional scholarship in the field on this issue but would have to be substantiated by additional research.

40. Wiktor Osiatyński, "Perspectives on the Current Constitutional Situation in Poland," in Greenberg et al., eds., *Constitutionalism and Democracy*, 313–14.

41. Joanna Regulska, "Self-Governance or Central Control? Rewriting Constitutions in Central and Eastern Europe," in Howard, ed., *Constitution Making in Eastern Europe*, 147.

42. Osiatyński, "Perspectives on the Current Constitutional Situation in Poland," 313.

43. "The Constitution of Poland, October 17, 1992," in Raina, ed., *The Constitutions of New Democracies in Europe*, 213.

44. Andrzej Rapaczynski, "Constitutional Politics in Poland: A Report on the Constitutional Committee of the Polish Parliament," in Howard, ed., *Constitution Making in Eastern Europe*, 105.

45. "The Constitution of Poland," in Raina, ed., *The Constitutions of New Democracies in Europe*, 205 and 216.

46. Howard, ed., *Constitution Making in Eastern Europe*, 48.

47. "The Constitution of Hungary," in Raina, ed., *The Constitutions of New Democracies in Europe*, 94.

48. Peter Paczolay, "The New Hungarian Constitutional State: Challenges and Perspectives," in Howard, ed., *Constitution Making in Eastern Europe*, 36.

49. "The Constitution of Hungary," in Raina, ed., *The Constitutions of New Democracies in Europe*, 94.

50. R. R. Palmer, Joel Colton, and Lloyd Kramer, *A History of the Modern World*, 9th ed. (Boston: McGraw-Hill, 2002), 980.

51. Martin McCauley, "From Perestroika Towards a New Order, 1885–1995," in *Russia: A History*, ed. Gregory L. Freeze (New York: Oxford University Press, 1997), 271.

52. "The Constitution of Latvia," "The Constitution of Lithuania," and "The Constitution of Estonia," in Raina, ed., *The Constitutions of New Democracies in Europe*, 127, 144, and 150.

53. Peter Hakim and Abraham Lowenthal, "Latin America's Fragile Democracies," in Diamond and Plattner, eds., *Global Resurgence of Democracy*, 294–95; Huntington, *The Third Wave*, 275, 24, and 98; Bruce Winick, "Comparison of the Protection of Individual Rights in the New Constitutions of Colombia and Brazil," *University of Miami Inter-American Law Review* 23 (1992):660–91.

54. Kenneth Maxwell, "The Influence of the U.S. Constitution on Latin America," in *The U.S. Constitution and the Constitutions of Latin America*, ed. Kenneth W. Thompson (Lanham, MD: University Press of America, 1991), 21.

55. Huntington, *The Third Wave*, 25.

56. Hakim and Lowenthal, "Latin America's Fragile Democracies," 293.

57. Jack Donnelly, *International Human Rights*, 2nd ed. (Boulder, CO: Westview Press, 1998), 86.

58. Winick, "Comparison of the Protection of Individual Rights in the New Constitutions of Colombia and Brazil," 660.

59. Joseph A. Page, *The Brazilians* (Reading, MA: Addison-Wesley, 1995), 23.

60. Hugo Frühling, "Human Rights in Constitutional Order and Political Practice in Latin America," in Greenberg et al., eds., *Constitutionalism and Democracy*, 95. The *mandado de seguranca*, as noted, is a procedure that combines aspects of Anglo-American writs of *mandamus*, injunction, and *quo warranto* and is a unique Brazilian institution. See Keith S. Rosenn, "Annotated English Translation" of the "1988 Constitution of the Federative Republic of Brazil," in

A Panorama of Brazilian Law, ed. Jacob Dolinger and Keith S. Rosenn (Coral Gables, FL: North–South Center, 1992), 389.

61. Keith S. Rosenn, "Brazil's New Constitution: An Exercise in Transient Constitutionalism for a Transitional Society," *American Journal of Comparative Law* 38 (1990):193.

62. Despite this reliance on the North American model, the 1988 constitution was likewise influenced by the charter of the former mother country: Portugal. The Portuguese Constitution has been described, however, as "a hodge-podge of progressive, conservative, liberal, radical, and moderate provisions" (Rosenn, "Brazil's New Constitution," 779–80).

63. Hakim and Lowenthal, "Latin America's Fragile Democracies," 293, 306.

64. *New York Times*, October 20, 1980.

65. *New York Times*, July 13, 1980.

66. Walter LaFeber, *The American Age: United States Foreign Policy at Home and Abroad since 1750* (New York: Norton, 1989), 677.

67. Kai P. Schoenhals and Richard A. Melanson, *Revolution and Intervention in Grenada: The New Jewel Movement, the United States and the Caribbean* (Boulder, CO: Westview Press, 1985), 162.

68. Laurence Whitehead, "The Imposition of Democracy," in *Exporting Democracy: The United States and Latin America*, ed. Abraham F. Lowenthal (Baltimore: Johns Hopkins University Press, 1991), 255.

69. Walter LaFeber, *Panama Canal: The Crisis in Historical Perspective*, updated ed. (New York: Oxford University Press, 1989), 195.

70. Margaret E. Scranton, *The Noriega Years: U.S.–Panamanian Relations, 1981–1990* (Boulder, CO: Lynne Rienner, 1991).

71. Ray A. Moore and Donald L. Robinson, *Partners for Democracy: Crafting the New Japanese State under MacArthur* (New York: Oxford University Press, 2002), 331–32. The authors argue that MacArthur and the Japanese collaborated behind the scenes to get the constitution accepted.

72. Moore and Robinson, *Partners for Democracy*, 7.

73. Christena Turner, "Democratic Consciousness in Japanese Labor Unions," in *Democracy in Japan*, ed. Takeshi Ishida and Ellis S. Krauss (Pittsburgh: University of Pittsburgh Press, 1989), 300.

74. John W. Dower, "Reform and Reconsolidation," in *Japan Examined: Perspectives on Modern Japanese History*, ed. Harry Wray and Hilary Conroy (Honolulu: University of Hawai'i Press, 1983), 348.

75. Jeff Kingston, *Japan in Transformation, 1952–2000* (New York: Longman, 2001), 12.

76. John W. Dower, *Embracing Defeat: Japan in the Wake of World War II* (New York: Norton, 1999), 561.

77. Ibid., 560.

78. Tadashi Aruga, "The Declaration in Japan: Translation and Transplantation, 1854–1997," *Journal of American History* 85 (March 1999):1428–29.

79. Andrzej Rapaczynski, "Bibliographical Essay: The Influence of U.S. Constitutionalism Abroad," in *Constitutionalism and Rights: The Influence of the United States Constitution Abroad*, ed. Louis Henkin and Albert J. Rosenthal (New York: Columbia University Press, 1990), 440–41.

80. Leonard Casper, "The Philippines," *The Encyclopedia Americana*, 30 vols. (Danbury, CT: Grolier, 1997), 21:919.

81. Enrique Fernando and Emma Quisumbing-Fernando, "Republic of the Philippines: The 1987 Constitution of the Philippines: The Impact of American Constitutionalism Revisited," in Beer, ed., *Constitutional Systems in Late Twentieth Century Asia*, 574.

82. Ibid., 571, 594.

83. Ibid., 581.

84. Rapaczynski, "Bibliographical Essay," 441.

85. LaFeber, *The American Age*, 680.

86. James C. Thomson, Peter W. Stanley, and John Curtis Perry, *Sentimental Imperialists: The American Experience in East Asia* (New York: Harper & Row, 1981), 275.

87. Tscholsu Kim and Sang Don Lee, "The Influence of U.S. Constitutional Law Doctrines in Korea," in Beer, ed., *Constitutional Systems in Late Twentieth Century Asia*, 317.

88. Chung Lim Kim, "Potential for Democratic Change in a Divided Nation," in *Political Change in South Korea*, ed. Ilpyŏng J. Kim and Young Whan Kihl (New York: Paragon House, 1988), 53.

89. Gregory Henderson, "Constitutional Changes from the First to the Sixth Republics, 1948–1987," in Kim and Kihl, eds., *Political Change in South Korea*, 35–36.

90. Ibid., 39.

91. Kim and Lee, "The Influence of U.S. Constitutional Law Doctrines in Korea," 326.

92. Henderson, "Constitutional Changes from the First to the Sixth Republics," 40.

93. Three major countries that also followed the common-law tradition—Britain, Canada, and Australia—and showed evidence of the influence of American constitutionalism will be published elsewhere, as noted earlier.

94. Pupul Jayakar, *Indira Gandhi: An Intimate Biography* (New York: Pantheon Books, 1992), 208.

95. Rapaczinski, "Bibliographical Essay," 411.

96. Edward McWhinney, *Judicial Review*, 4th ed. (Toronto: University of Toronto Press, 1992), 153.

97. M. K. U. Molla, "The Influence of the U.S. Constitution on the Indian Sub-Continent: Pakistan, India, and Bangladesh," in *The United States Constitution: Its Birth, Growth, and Influence in Asia*, ed. J. Barton Starr (Hong Kong: Hong Kong University Press, 1989), 167.

98. Ashok Kapur, *Pakistan in Crisis* (London: Routledge, 1991), 53.

99. Omar Noman, *Pakistan: A Political and Economic History since 1947* rev. and updated ed. (New York: Kegan Paul, 1990), 123.

100. Beer, ed., introduction to *Constitutional Systems in Late Twentieth Century Asia*, 37.

101. Abu Said Chowdhury, "The Bangladesh Constitution in American Perspective," in *Constitutionalism in Asia: Asian Views of the American Influence*, ed. Lawrence W. Beer (Berkeley: University of California Press, 1979), 30.

102. Ibid.

103. Ibid.

104. Molla, "The Influence of the U.S. Constitution on the Indian Sub-Continent," 165.

105. Craig Baxter, *Bangladesh: A New Nation in an Old Setting* (Boulder, CO: Westview Press, 1984), 57.

106. Beer, ed., introduction to *Constitutional Systems in Late Twentieth Century Asia*, 37.

107. Ibid.

108. M. P. Jain, "Malaysia: The Constitution of Malaysia and the American Constitutional Influence," in Beer, ed., *Constitutional Systems in Late Twentieth Century Asia*, 528.

109. Tun Mohammed Suffian bin Hashim, "The Malaysian Constitution and the United States Constitution," quoted in Beer, ed., *Constitutionalism in Asia*, 120.

110. Ahmad Ibrahim, "The Constitution of Malaysia and the American Constitutional Influence," in Beer, *Constitutional Systems in Late Twentieth Century Asia*, 516.

111. Suffian, "The Malaysian Constitution and the United States Constitution," in Beer, ed., *Constitutionalism in Asia*, 131.

112. The Constitution of Singapore occupies a unique place in the annals of constitutional history. Since the Singapore government was wary of drafting its own new constitution, it was permitted to depend on the provisions of the 1963 Constitution of Malaysia. Thus it operated in terms of the constitution of another country! In 1979 a constitutional amendment was passed authorizing the Singaporean attorney general to publish a "reprint" of the Constitution of Singapore which amalgamated those provisions of the Malaysian Constitution of 1963 that were applicable to Singapore. The resulting charter then began serving as Singapore's constitution. See Valentine S. Winslow, "Republic of Singapore," in Beer, ed., *Constitutional Systems in Late Twentieth Century Asia*, 629.

113. S. Jayakumar, "The Singapore Constitution and the United States Constitution," in Beer, ed., *Constitutionalism in Asia*, 184–85.

114. J. Gus Liebenow, *Liberia: The Evolution of Privilege* (Ithaca, NY: Cornell University Press, 1969), 1.

115. Ibid., v. The constitutional relationship between Liberia and the American Colonization Society regarding whether the society had sovereignty over Liberia was long and tortured. See the classic work by Charles Henry Huberich, *The Political and Legislative History of Liberia: A Documentary History of the Constitutions, Laws, and Treaties*, 2 vols. (New York: Central Book, 1947), 1:259–65.

116. For a copy of the Liberian Constitution of 1847, see Huberich, *Political and Legislative History of Liberia*, 1:827–32.

117. Huberich, *Political and Legislative History of Liberia*, 1:829.

118. Ibid. Huberich argued that the Liberian Declaration was not modeled on the American Declaration and had nothing in common with it except the name. He rightly declared that the document was a "political manifesto" designed to arouse the conscience of the world to the evils of racism but then, ignoring the verbal links with the American document, went on to state that the Liberian Declaration was a synthesis of British, French, and American sources. He pushed his thesis too far, however, missing the deliberate, and very effective, irony achieved by imitation of Jefferson's language to turn it against itself as a condemnation of the harsh treatment of blacks in America (1:833–34).

119. Ibid., 2:891, 991, 997, 1006.

120. There is some controversy regarding the authorship of the 1847 charter. Huberich claimed it was written by Simon Greenleaf, Royall Professor of Law in the Harvard Law School. Given Greenleaf's impressive legal background, training in constitutional law, and the fact that he was contacted in 1846 by a member of the Massachusetts Colonization Society to make suggestions for the document, Greenleaf's credentials for authorship appeared impeccable. But Huberich's interpretation gives too much credit to Greenleaf, whose draft was meant to serve only as a basis for deliberations by members of the Liberian constitutional convention. Subsequent research has shown that the constitution was the result of joint efforts by Liberian delegates and Greenleaf. See Robert Brown, "Simon Greenleaf and the Liberian Constitution," *Liberian Studies Journal* 9 (1980–1981):52–53. See also James Wesley Smith, *Sojourners in Search of Freedom: The Settlement of Liberia by Black Americans* (Lanham, MD: University Press of America, 1987), 197–98.

A letter written by Liberian delegate Samuel Benedict (later candidate for presidency) to the Harvard professor in 1848 tells the story: "We endeavored to use as much of this [document] as suited our circumstances. Several words, or parts of sections in our constitution, both myself and a few others would prefer to have been left out and others inserted but the majority in convention—you know, will govern" (Samuel Benedict to Simon Greenleaf, April 4, 1848; Simon Greenleaf Papers, Harvard University Law Library).

121. Huberich, *Political and Legislative History of Liberia*, 2:869.

122. Martin Lowenkopf, *Politics in Liberia: The Conservative Road to Development* (Stanford, CA: Hoover Institution Press,1976), 109.

123. Claude Ake, "Rethinking African Democracy," in Diamond and Plattner, eds., *Global Resurgence of Democracy*, 72.

124. John Dugard, "Toward Racial Justice in South Africa," in Henkin and Rosenthal, eds., *Constitutionalism and Rights*, 351.

125. Another example of distorting the language of the American Declaration in Africa came more than a century later when the Unilateral Declaration of Independence (UDI) was issued by the white minority government in Southern Rhodesia in 1965. That declaration patterned its language on the American document but deliberately excluded blacks from any reference to human equality. Once again, the Declaration's message was distorted to serve an ulterior motive. The Rhodesian document ranks among the most cynical uses to which Jefferson's manifesto was ever put. See Robert R. Palmer, "The Revolution," in *The Comparative Approach to American History*, ed. C. Vann Woodward (1968; repr., New York: Oxford University Press, 1997), 56. See also Armitage, *Declaration of Independence*, 135–36.

126. Ake, "Rethinking African Democracy," 72.

127. Hon. Robert Henry Brand, *Union of South Africa* (Oxford: Clarendon Press, 1909), 43.

128. Dugard, "Toward Racial Justice in South Africa," 355.

129. Ibid.

130. William A. Hance, ed., with Leo Kuper, Vernon McKay, and Edwin S. Munger, *Southern Africa and the United States* (New York: Columbia University Press, 1968), 19.

131. See Ali Mazuri, "The American Constitution and Liberal Option in Africa: Myth and Reality," in *The U.S. Constitution and Constitutionalism in Africa*, ed. Kenneth W. Thompson (Lanham, MD: University Press of America, 1990), 5–6.

132. Ibid., 14.

133. Eboe Hutchful, "Reconstructing Political Space: Militarism and Constitutionalism in Africa," in Greenberg et al., eds., *Constitutionalism and Democracy*, 222.

134. For the quotation, see Mazuri, "The American Constitution and Liberal Option in Africa," 14. See also J. S. Read, "The New Constitution of Nigeria: The Washington Model?" *Journal of African Law* 23 (1979):131.

135. B. O. Nwabueze, *Federalism in Nigeria under the Presidential Constitution* (London: Sweet and Maxwell, 1983), passim.

136. Sam Egite Oyovbaire, *Federalism in Nigeria: A Study in the Development of the Nigerian State* (New York: St. Martin's Press, 1984), 274.

137. S. A. deSmith, *The New Commonwealth and Its Constitution* (London: Stevens, 1964), 177–93.

138. Hutchful, "Reconstructing Political Space," 231.

139. Daniel P. Franklin and Michael J. Baum, eds., *Political Culture and Constitutionalism: A Comparative Approach* (Armonk, NY: Sharpe, 1995), 203.

140. Larry Diamond, Mark Plattner, Yon-hon Chu, and Hung-Mao Tren, eds., *Consolidating the Third Wave Democracies* (Baltimore: Johns Hopkins University Press, 1997), xvi and 4.

141. Interview with Zerah Warhaftig, May 1994. Warhaftig, one of the original signers of Israel's declaration of independence in May 1948, recounted his own visits to America to consult with political leaders, professors, and jurists in preparation for the writing of a constitution and bemoaned the fact that circumstances delayed that process indefinitely.

142. Gary J. Jacobsohn, *Apple of Gold: Constitutionalism in Israel and the United States* (Princeton, NJ: Princeton University Press, 1993). Jacobsohn's title refers to Lincoln's speech of January 1861 when he used a metaphor to express the relationship between the Declaration (the apple of gold) and the Constitution (the picture of silver). Jacobsohn implies that they were related in terms of their natural-law ideals and attempts at universal principles.

143. Jacobsohn, *Apple of Gold*, 7.

144. Ibid., 9, 18, 54, and 35–52.

145. Rapaczinski, "Bibliographical Essay," 456. The Israeli judicial system was based mainly on the British system but included religious courts operating on the basis of different traditions. These were the Jewish, Muslim, Christian, and Druze courts which have authority over marriages, divorces, burials, and wills. Different also from the British system was the existence of a supreme court, which served as the highest court of appeal and acted also as a high court to hear charges of arbitrary or illegal action by public authorities. The literature on such issues is extensive.

146. See also Pnina Lahav, *Judgement in Jerusalem: Chief Justice Agranat and the Zionist Century* (Berkeley: University of California Press, 1997), 79–112.

147. Pnina Lahav, "American Influence on Israel's Jurisprudence of Free Speech," *Hastings Constitutional Law Quarterly* 9 (1981):23–108, esp. 27–37 and 63–69. I am indebted to Prof. Lahav for her comments on this section. See Pnina Lahav, "Rights and Democracy: The Court's Performance," in *Israeli Democracy under Stress*, ed. Ehud Sprinzak and Larry Diamond (Boulder, CO: Lynne Rienner, 1993), chap. 7. For example, in the case of *Ha'aretz v. Electric Company*, the Israeli Supreme Court explicitly rejected the American approach to the issue of free press employed in *New York Times v. Sullivan* (ibid., 140).

The American doctrine of justiciability, however, has had an influence in Israel. The Israeli court, for example, found a presidential decision concerning the appointment of a prime minister to be nonreviewable. A similar situation occurred in the case of a military decision concerning the resettlement of a Bedouin sheik. See Rapaczynski, "Bibliographical Essay," 458.

The Israeli Court generally has not had a good record in defending the rights of the Arab minority, and in the West Bank and Gaza Strip the record has been very bad. See Lahav, "Rights and Democracy: The Court's Performance," 145; and also Marina Lowy, "Restructuring a Democracy: An Analysis of the New Proposed Constitution for Israel," *Cornell International Law Journal* 22 (1989):115–46.

148. See the article written in Hebrew on an American-style judicial review by Pnina Lahav and D. Kretzmer, "Bill of Human Rights in Israel: A Step Forward?" *Mishpatim* 7 (1976):154, cited in Rapaczinski, "Bibliographical Essay," 460.

149. See Aharon Barak, "Foreword: A Judge on Judging: The Role of a Supreme Court in a Democracy," *Harvard Law Review* 116 (2002):19–162.

150. Huntington, *The Third Wave*, 286.

151. Phillipe C. Schmitter and Terry Lynn Karl, "What Democracy Is and Is Not," in Diamond and Plattner, eds., *The Global Surge of Democracy*, 39.

152. Indeed, the third wave continued beyond 1989, and by the year 2000 Freedom House counted 120 electoral democracies as "free," amounting to 63 percent of all the states on earth. See Larry Diamond, "Democracy, Future of," in Clarke and Foweraker, eds., *Encyclopedia of Democratic Thought*, 154.

However, other scholars, led by Diamond, began to challenge the measure of success used in assessing democratization during the third wave. They claimed that the progress made was "illusory" because the bar for identifying countries as "electoral democracies" had been set so low. Countries listed as "free" by Freedom House qualified simply by holding free and fair elections on a regular basis. Such a definition left out important dimensions of democracy like the protection of individual freedoms, the rule of law supported by an impartial judiciary, and the role of party politics. Diamond, a well-known constitutional scholar, considered it necessary for countries to evolve and become "liberal democracies" instead, which would include these additional dimensions in any definition: "Democracy may be the most common form of government in the world, but outside of the wealthy and industrialized nations it tends to be shallow, illiberal, and poorly institutionalized." Many "electoral democracies" were, in fact, illiberal in their policies because they were corrupt, irresponsible, and dominated by special interests. See Larry Diamond, introduction to Diamond et al., eds., *Consolidating the Third Wave Democracies*, xv–xxi.

153. Marc Plattner, "The Democratic Moment," in Diamond and Plattner, eds., *The Global Resurgence of Democracy*, 20.

154. Francis Fukuyama, "The End of History?" *The National Interest*, summer 1989, 4.

155. Francis Fukuyama, *The End of History and the Last Man* (New York: Free Press, 1992), 211.

156. Huntington, *The Clash of Civilizations and the Remaking of the World Order* (New York: Simon & Schuster Paperbacks, 1991), 31.

157. For the number of nondemocratic states with populations of more than one million in 1990, see Huntington, *The Third Wave*, 26, table 1.1.

158. Samuel P. Huntington, "The Lonely Superpower," *Foreign Affairs* 78, no. 2 (1999):36.

159. "The US and the World: An Interview with George Kennan," *New York Times*, August 12, 1999.

CHAPTER 12

1. *Federalist* 14, in *The Federalist*, ed. Jacob E. Cooke (Middletown, CT: Wesleyan University Press, 1961), 88–89.

2. Max Farrand, ed., *The Records of the Federal Convention of 1787*, 4 vols., rev. ed. (New Haven, CT: Yale University Press, 1966), 1:423.

3. George Athan Billias, *Elbridge Gerry: Founding Father and Republican Statesman* (New York: McGraw-Hill, 1976), 176.

4. Jefferson to Priestley, June 19, 1802, in *Works of Thomas Jefferson*, ed. Paul Leicester Ford, 12 vols. (New York: Putnam, 1904–1905), 8:158–59.

5. Jefferson to John Adams, September 12, 1821, in *The Adams–Jefferson Letters: The Complete Correspondence between Thomas Jefferson and Abigail and John Adams*, ed. Lester J. Cappon, 2 vols. (Chapel Hill: University of North Carolina Press, 1959), 2:52.

6. Charles Francis Adams, ed., *The Works of John Adams, Second President of the United States*, 10 vols. (Boston: Little, Brown, 1850–1856), 9:292–93.

7. Washington to Jewish Congregation of Newport, Rhode Island [August 18, 1790] in *Papers of George Washington, Presidential Series*, vol. 6 ed. Mark A. Mastromarino in 1996 (13 vols. to date) (Charlottesville: University Press of Virginia, 1987–), 6:284–85.

8. *The Complete Writings of Thomas Paine*, ed. Philip S. Foner, 2 vols. (1945; repr., New York: Citadel Press, 1969), 1:370.

9. Speech by James Wilson, October 6, 1787, in *The Documentary History of the Ratification of the Constitution*, ed. Merrill Jensen, John P. Kaminski, Gaspar Saladino, Richard Leffler, Charles H. Schoenleber, and Margaret A. Hogan, 22 vols. to date (Madison: State Historical Society of Wisconsin, 1976–), 2:172.

10. Speech by James Wilson, December 7, 1787, in ibid., 2:584.

11. Ibid.

12. Ibid.

13. Madison's Notes, July 5, 1787, in Farrand, ed., *Records of the Federal Convention of 1787*, 1:529.

14. Andrzej Rapaczynski, "Bibliographical Essay: The Influence of U.S. Constitutionalism Abroad," in *Constitutionalism and Rights: The Influence of the United States Constitution Abroad*, ed. Louis Henkin and Albert J. Rosenthal (New York: Columbia University Press, 1990), 460–61.

15. Samuel P. Huntington, *The Third Wave: Democratization in the Late Twentieth Century* (Norman: University of Oklahoma Press, 1991), 26.

16. Huntington notes carefully that any blanket statement regarding democratic values in Islamic and Confucian cultures need to be qualified (*The Third Wave*, 298–315). In his *Clash of Civilizations and the Remaking of the World Order* (New York: Simon & Schuster, 1996), Huntington postulates a future conflict of world civilizations on these grounds but subsequently qualified his hypothesis.

17. For the discussion of non-Western cultures, I have relied heavily on Huntington, *The Third Wave*, 15–25.

18. Fareed Zakaria, *The Future of Freedom: Illiberal Democracy at Home and Abroad* (New York: Norton, 2004), 55–58.

19. Samuel P. Huntington, "Democracy for the Long Haul," in *Consolidating the Third Wave Democracies*, ed. Larry Diamond, Marc F. Plattner, Yon-hon Chu, and Hung-Mao Tren (Baltimore: Johns Hopkins University Press, 1997), 11.

20. Huntington, "Democracy's Third Wave," in *The Global Resurgence of Democracy*, ed. Larry Diamond and Marc F. Plattner (Baltimore: Johns Hopkins University Press, 1993), 15–16.

21. Fouad Ajami, "The Clash," *New York Times*, January 6, 2008.

22. Huntington, "Democracy's Third Wave," 308.

23. But see Robert W. Hefner, *Civil Islam: Muslims and Democratization* (Princeton, NJ: Princeton University Press, 2000), which shows that Muslim democrats in Indonesia

> tend to be more civil democratic or Tocquevillian than they are (Atlantic) liberal in spirit. They deny the need for an Islamic state. But they insist that society involves more than autonomous individuals and democracy involves more than markets and the state. Democracy requires a noncoercive culture that encourages citizens to respect the rights of others as well as to cherish their own. Such a public culture depends on mediating institutions in which citizens develop habits of free speech, participation, and toleration. (13)

Turkey, also an Islamic culture, perhaps represents another exception to the generalization.

24. Richard Joseph, "Africa: The Rebirth of Political Freedom," in Diamond and Plattner, eds., *The Global Resurgence of Democracy*, 307.

25. See Claude Ake, "Rethinking African Democracy," in Diamond and Plattner, eds., *The Global Resurgence of Democracy*, 70–82; and Joseph, "Africa: The Rebirth of Political Freedom," 307–20. See also H. W. O. Okoth-Ogendo, "Constitutions without Constitutionalism: Reflections on an African Paradox," in *Constitutionalism and Democracy*, ed. Douglas Greenberg, Stanley N. Katz, Melanie Beth Oliviero, and Steven C. Wheatley (New York: Oxford University Press), 65–82.

26. Joseph, "Africa: the Rebirth of Democracy," 308.

27. Huntington, *The Third Wave*, 311.

28. Zakaria, *The Future of Freedom*, 70.

29. Huntington, *The Third Wave*, 316.

30. Rapaczynski, "Bibliographical Essay," 460.

31. Alfred Stephen and Cindy Skach, "Democratic Frameworks and Democratic Consolidation: Parliamentarianism *versus* Presidentialism," *World Politics* 46 (1993):1–22.

32. Donald Horowitz, "*The Federalist* Abroad in the World," Duke Law School Legal Studies Research Papers no. 194, March 2008, 22.

33. Klaus von Beyme, *America as a Model: The Impact of American Democracy in the World* (New York: St. Martin's Press, 1987), 71.

34. Thomas Fleiner-Gerster, "Federalism, Decentralization, and Rights," in Henkin and Rosenthal, eds., *Constitutionalism and Rights*, 19–36.

35. Beyme, *America as a Model*, 85.

36. William E. Nelson, *Marbury v. Madison: The Origins and Legacy of Judicial Review* (Lawrence: University Press of Kansas, 2000), 119.

37. Ibid., 111.

38. Gordon S. Wood, *Creation of the American Republic, 1776–1787* (1969; repr., Chapel Hill: University of North Carolina Press, 1998), 606.

39. Gordon S.Wood, *The Radicalism of the American Revolution* (New York: Vintage Books, 1993), 7.

40. Alexis de Tocqueville, *Democracy in America*, ed. J. P. Mayer and trans. George Lawrence, 2 vols. in 1 (Garden City, NY: Doubleday, 1969), 1:9 and 19.

41. Beyme, *America as a Model*, 17.

42. Zakaria, *Future of Freedom*, 50.

43. Amartya Kumar Sen, *Development as Freedom* (New York: Knopf, 1999).

44. Leszek Kolakowski, "The Uncertainties of a Democratic Age," in Diamond and Plattner, eds., *The Global Resurgence of Democracy*, 321–24. See also the introduction, xxv–xxvi.

45. George F. Kennan, *The Cloud of Danger: Current Realities of American Foreign Policy* (Boston: Little, Brown, 1971), 41–43.

46. Francis Fukuyama, "The End of History?" *The National Interest* 16 (summer 1989): 4.

47. Huntington, *The Third Wave*, 287.

Index

abolitionism, 85

Acton, Lord, 93, 248

Adams, Charles Francis, 166

Adams, John: British constitutionalism, 77; Condorcet, marquis de, 76; constitutional monarchy, 77; *Defence of the Constitutions of Government of the United States*, 76–77, 79, 408n99; *Esquisse* by Condorcet, 84; first American state constitutions, 76–77; in France, 71; Jefferson, Thomas, 358; Lafayette, marquis de, 72, 145; Luzac, Johan, 94; Miranda, Francisco de, 124; natural-law theory, 5; in Netherlands, 94; republicanism, 71, 77; Turgot, Anne-Robert-Jacques, 76–78

Adams, John Quincy, 146, 318

Adams, Samuel, 116

Adams, Willi Paul, 381n23

Affaires de l'Angleterre et de l'Amérique (journal), 67, 69

Africa: 1974-1989 (*see* Africa from 1974 to 1989); democratization, 362–363; French constitutionalism, 360; influence of American constitutionalism on, 355, 363; nondemocratic regimes, 361; "second liberation," 362

Africa from 1974 to 1989, 345–352; "African exceptionalism," 348; American influence on, 355; decolonization movement, 348; federalism, 321, 348–349, 350–351; influence of American Bill of Rights on, 347; influence of American constitutionalism on, 345, 349–352; influence of Declaration of Independence on, 346; influence of *The Federalist* on, 322–323; influence of U.S. Constitution on, 346–347; judicial review, 350–351; Liberia, 345–347; Nigeria, 321, 322–323, 350–352; presidentialism, 322–323, 350–351; separation of powers, 322–323; South Africa, 347–350; sub-Saharan Africa, 352; Tanzania, 321

African National Congress (ANC), 350

African slave trade, 85

Age of Reason (Paine), 63

"age of the democratic revolution," 53

Agranat, Simon, 353

agriculture: American imperialism, 225; *encomienda* system, 114; land reform in Philippines, 338; "miracle rice" in Philippines, 300; Slovakia, 259; Taiwanese shift away from, 310

Aguinaldo, Emilio, 230

Alaska, 229, 235, 236–237, 454n48

Albania, 324, 325

Albany Plan of Union (1754), 27, 36, 413n176

Albemarle County Instructions Concerning the Virginia Constitution (Mazzei), 101

Alberdi, Juan Bautista, 119, 123, 133–134

Christianity, influence on Declaration
of Independence, 20
Chun, Doo Hwan, 340
Churchill, Winston, 276, 369
CIA, 313, 315–317, 334, 475n20
Cicero, 6
citizen (the term), 412n154
citizenship: American Samoa, 453n46;
dual citizenship (nation and state),
37; Fourteenth Amendment, 207;
Guam, 452n44; Hawaii, 238; Paine,
Thomas, 64; Puerto Rico, 233
civil law, judiciary and, 257, 259
civil liberties, 281–282, 291
civil rights: antebellum South, 209;
Argentine Constitution (1853),
312; Belgian Constitution (1831),
156; Brazil, 140; *Brown v. Board
of Education*, 365; Czechoslovakia,
259; Declaration of the Rights of
Man and the Citizen (1789), 91;
Europe from 1776 to 1800, 59–60;
Europe in 1848, 176; *Federalist 10*,
45; France, 90; German Basic Law
(1949), 281–282; Greek Constitution
(1975), 324–325; individual rights,
365; Japan, 291; Korean Constitution (1960), 303; Latin America
from 1945 to 1974, 312; Lithuanian
Constitution (1922), 264; minorities, 365; natural rights philosophy
distinguished from, 59–60; Poland,
261; South Africa, 348–349; South
Korea, 302
Civil Rights Act (1964), 368
civil society, 59, 153
Clay, Lucius, 280, 295
Cleveland, Grover, 238
Cleveland, Richard, 117–118
"Code of Conduct" (Széchenyi), 169
Cold War from 1945 to 1976, 276–
319; Africa (*see* Africa from 1974 to
1989); American constitutionalism

subordinated to America's national
interests, 303, 315; American
imperialism, 313–314; American
support for dictatorships, 314; Asia
(*see* Asia from 1945 to 1974); bill
of rights tradition, 277; CIA, 313,
315–317, 475n20; containment
policy, 315; Cuba, 311, 317; Dominican Republic, 317–318; effect
on American constitutionalism,
317, 318–319; Europe (*see* Europe
from 1945 to 1974); federalism,
321; federated states, 392n88; freedom of expression, 281; Guatemala,
316–317; gunboat diplomacy, 317;
Honduras, 311, 317; influence of
American constitutionalism during, 276; interventions overseas,
313, 316–317; Iran, 315–316; Latin
America (*see* Latin America from
1945 to 1974); Soviet Union, 278;
Truman Doctrine, 278; violations
of American constitutional tenets,
315–318
Cold War from 1974 to 1989, 320–
356; Africa (*see* Africa from 1974 to
1989); American support for dicta-
torships/authoritarian regimes, 332,
333; Asia (*see* Asia from 1974 to
1989); bill of rights tradition, 323;
CIA, 334; close of, 369; declarations
of independence per year, 321;
"democratic moment," 354–355;
Europe (*see* Europe from 1974 to
1989); Guatemala, 333; Honduras,
333; human rights, 322; influence
of American constitutionalism on
democratization, 320–323; interventions overseas, 333–334; judicial
review, 321–322; Latin America
(*see* Latin America from 1974 to
1989); nondemocratic regimes,
322; presidentialism, 321; Reagan

166–167; bill of rights tradition, 250, 261; civil rights, 261; Constitution (1791), 66, 166–167; Constitution (1919), 260; Constitution (1921), 261; Constitution (1935), 261–262; Constitution (1992), 328; equality before the law, 261; influence of American constitutionalism on, 66, 166–167, 327–328; influence of British constitutionalism on, 66; influence of French constitutionalism on, 66, 261; influence of U.S. Constitution on, 261; influence on Declaration of Independence, 166; property rights, 261; rights, traditional view of, 327–328; Sejm, 260, 261; Socialism, 328; written constitutions, 166
political order, 474n5
political rights, 474n5
Polk, James K., 35, 183
Pomba, Miguel de, 115–116
popular sovereignty: American Revolution, 26; Asia from 1945 to 1974, 287, 288, 290–291; Europe from 1800 to 1848, 159, 174; Europe from 1919 to 1945, 253; federalism, 38; *The Federalist*, 46; Federalists, 46; first American state constitutions, 22; France, 86; Germany, 253; Greece, 174; Japan, 287, 288, 290–291; Mohl, Robert Von, 159; Paine, Thomas, 60; ratification of constitutions, 25; Virginia Declaration of Rights (1776), 26; Weimar Constitution (1919), 253; Wood, Gordon, 38
Portugal, 113, 324, 475n20
positive law, 16, 383n8
poverty, democratization and, 363
presidential government (the term), 391n77
presidential system (the term), 391n77

presidentialism: Africa from 1974 to 1989, 322–323, 350–351; Anti-federalists, 43, 45–46; Asia from 1945 to 1974, 302–303; Asia from 1974 to 1989, 321, 343–344; Bangladesh, 343–344; Brazil, 139, 332, 420n11; Cold War from 1974 to 1989, 321; Condorcet, marquis de, 82; Confederate States of America Constitution (1861), 205, 206; Europe from 1776 to 1800, 82, 102; Europe from 1800 to 1848, 151; Europe from 1919 to 1945, 254–255, 262–263; Europe from 1945 to 1974, 296, 298; Europe in 1848, 181, 182, 188–189; *The Federalist*, 45–46; Federalists, 45–46; Finland, 262–263; France, 181, 298; Germany, 188–189, 254–255; Hamilton, Alexander, 45–46; Henry, Patrick, 390n70; Indonesia, 364; Italy, 296; Latin America, 420n11; Latin America from 1811 to 1900, 106, 108–109, 110, 130, 139, 364; Latin America from 1974 to 1989, 332; Liberia, 364; Mazzei, Philip, 102; Mexico, 130; Montesquieu, Baron de, 34; Nigeria, 322–323, 350–351, 364; Philippines, 232–233, 321, 364; powers, 34–35; "pure presidentialism," 35; pure presidentialism, countries with, 363–364; Rapaczynski, Andrzej, 363–364; separation of powers, 299; South Korea, 302–303, 321, 364; Soviet Union, 321; Tocqueville, Alexis de, 151, 182; U.S. Constitution, xiii, 34–36; Venezuela, 108; Weimar Constitution (1919), 254–255; Wilson, James, 34
presidentialism (the term), 35
Preuss, Hugo, 253, 254, 255
Price, Richard, 62, 75
Priestley, Joseph, 357–358
private property. *See* property rights

About the Author

GEORGE ATHAN BILLIAS is the Jacob and Frances Hiatt Professor of History, emeritus, at Clark University. He is the author, editor, and coeditor of a number of books, including *The Massachusetts Land Bankers of 1740*; *General John Glover and His Marblehead Mariners*; *Elbridge Gerry: Founding Father and Republican Statesman*; and *American Constitutionalism Abroad: Selected Essays in Comparative Constitutional History.*